MW00780137

AMERICA'S CIVIL WAR

ALSO BY BRIAN HOLDEN REID

J. F. C. Fuller: Military Thinker (1987)

The Origins of the American Civil War (1996)

Studies in British Military Thought (1998)

The American Civil War and the Wars of the Industrial Revolution (1999)

Robert E. Lee: Icon for a Nation (2005)

EDITED BY BRIAN HOLDEN REID

Americana: Essays in Memory of Marcus Cunliffe
(with John White, 1991, 1998)

The American Civil War: Explorations and Reconsiderations
(with Susan-Mary Grant, 2000)

BRIAN HOLDEN REID

AMERICA'S CIVIL WAR
The Operational Battlefield
1861–1863

Prometheus Books

59 John Glenn Drive
Amherst, New York 14228–2119

Published 2008 by Prometheus Books

Inquiries should be addressed to
Prometheus Books
59 John Glenn Drive
Amherst, New York 14228–2119
VOICE: 716–691–0133, ext. 210
FAX: 716–691–0137
WWW.PROMETHEUSBOOKS.COM

12 11 10 09 08   5 4 3 2 1

Library of Congress Cataloging-in-Publication Data

Reid, Brian Holden.
    America's Civil War : the operational battlefield / Brian Holden Reid.
        p. cm.
    Includes bibliographical references and index.
    ISBN 978–1–59102–605–1
    1. United States—History—Civil War, 1861–1865—Campaigns. I. Title.

E470.R45 2008
973.7—dc22

                                                                    2007051811

To My Mother

CONTENTS

8 CONTENTS

PREFACE

America's Civil War seeks to explore the military nature of an event of the first historical magnitude. The United States is a vast country and the crisis of 1861 detonated a vast conflict, the greatest ever waged in the Western Hemisphere. The immensity of a historical event can often be gauged by its impact on small communities. For about half a century the American branch of my family, the Reids, have lived in Bedford, Ohio, founded in 1837. This small town was (and is) typical of so many throughout the northern United States. Located fifteen miles from Cleveland, Ohio, Bedford developed as the first stagecoach stop on the route from Cleveland to Cincinnati and thence to Pittsburgh, Pennsylvania. Located in the Western Reserve, this part of Ohio evinced strong antislavery views and powerful loyalty to the Republican Party. Abraham Lincoln passed through Bedford on his way to his inauguration (he stopped but did not speak); Civil War general and future president James A. Garfield spoke there often.

With the outbreak of war in April 1861 some 202 men, a quarter of Bedford's population of 859, volunteered for military service. They served in the

9

103rd Ohio Volunteer Infantry, in the volunteer artillery, and took part in some of the war's greatest general actions—including Antietam and Vicksburg—and participated in the Stones River (Murfreesboro) campaign. Some 40 percent of these men became casualties, including not just those killed or wounded but also the many who succumbed to disease. Such proportionate losses were not uncommon in small Civil War–era communities, North and South. The Civil War monument at Bedford Commons looms over the town in the way that similar memorials to the Great War of 1914–1918 lay at the heart of virtually all British towns of similar size. This parallel can often be invoked, and the human cost of war cannot fail to impress, but we must be guarded in assuming that such a cost has necessarily been made in vain.

My book focuses in various ways on this problem and warns against the undiscriminating application of what has been called the "Vietnam Syndrome" to this conflict. I have no consistent policy on using Northern or Southern names for the great battles and, having no sectional ax to grind, used them interchangeably as the fancy has taken me. This volume is the first of two parts that attempts to reassess some of the fundamental problems of the Civil War and mass involvement. The concluding part will examine the great campaigns of 1864–65 and discuss the nature of the forces on which the eventual Northern strategy of attrition rested.

During the process of writing, the book subtly changed. As Rudyard Kipling once explained, "Like Topsey 'it growed' while I write." During the interval that resulted, I benefited from the stream of literature published on various aspects of the war. The current book is thus a work of synthesis. I have not sought refuge in the detail of minor tactics, but have kept the broad contours of the war firmly in view.

In my efforts I have been assisted by a number of people and it is appropriate that they receive due thanks. I owe a particular debt of gratitude to my friend Professor Joseph G. Dawson III of Texas A&M University, for taking on the onerous task of reading all my draft chapters as they were written. Professor Dawson discharged this undertaking happily, even though he had many other duties to perform, greatly to my benefit.

I am also deeply indebted to Professor Sir Michael Howard OM CH, and Professor Richard H. Kohn for their lively interest in my work, and also to Professor Robert Cook, Professor Susan-Mary Grant, Professor Gary W. Gallagher, Dr. Andrew Haughton, Professor Gary L. McDowell, Professor George Rable, and Keith Simpson, a member of Parliament, for help on specific points.

Also important have been my numerous trips to Civil War battlefields.

Often these have been undertaken with serving soldiers who have taught me so much about the art of war. I can single out for mention a series of memorable visits to Manassas and Fredericksburg in 1990 with (as he is now) Lieutenant General Sir Alistair Irwin KCB, CBE; in 1996 to Gettysburg with the Henderson Society of the former Staff College, Camberley; and to Chickamauga and Chattanooga with the newly constituted Joint Services Command and Staff College the following year. As it was, the sight of a large group of British Army officers, suitably turned out in flat caps and barbour jackets, brandishing maps and binoculars, provoked a lot of interest on their first visit and, in 1999, a slightly bemused article in the *Chattanooga Times Free Press*. I am deeply grateful to Professor Charles M. Hubbard of Lincoln Memorial University for his kindness for giving me a personal tour of Tennessee battlefields. But such visits serve to remind Americans of the wide interest in their Civil War outside North America. One of my more memorable encounters at a visitors' center in Winchester, Virginia, elicited the admission that I was "not from around here."

Finally, both Mrs. Pam Bendall and Simon Blundell, librarian of the Reform Club, have gone to extraordinary lengths to search out obscure books and check references, and have saved me much labor. My sense of obligation to my former secretaries, Mrs. Penny Eldridge and Mrs. Gill Woods, is very heavy. Both have exhibited what Ernest Hemingway called "grace under pressure" as they have coped with great patience with innumerable drafts, redrafts, and amendments over long periods of time, and as their own duties changed and became more demanding. I also want to acknowledge the very positive contribution of Jacinta Meyers, my copy editor at Prometheus, in improving the text and saving me from a number of errors as it was seen through the press. Of this host of debts, by far the greatest is to Mother, who has created just the right conditions that have enabled me at long last to finish this book; she more than anybody else deserves this dedication. As for the author, who has received so much help from both sides of the Atlantic Ocean, he must bear the responsibility for the faults that still linger undetected.

Brian Holden Reid
King's College, London

INTRODUCTION

This book on the first two and a half years of the American Civil War is the successor volume to my *Origins of the American Civil War* (1996). Another work covering the final eighteen months of the conflict will follow. These two books are efforts at a military history informed by knowledge of political and social forces. The book on the origins of the war was a political and social history informed by an understanding of war. A grasp of the forces that brought about the eruption of war has proved useful in understanding the form that the first phase of the war assumed and why it proved so difficult to bring this phase to a victorious conclusion.

I hope to complete the series eventually with a book on the legacy of the Civil War. This will be a study of the "impacts of war," to borrow from the title of a book by John Terraine.[1] It will survey the effects of the war on political debate, the United States Army itself, and on American social thought and mythology. Such a book would be a social history rather than the conventional military or political history. It would take an approach to American history pioneered by the late Marcus Cunliffe, though I could not do it half as well as he might have done.

Writing two further books about the Civil War raises a number of questions. This is one of the most written-about wars in world history, and is certainly the most written-about war in American history. The flood of books shows no sign of receding: indeed, often the more obscure and neglected the subject, the larger the book written on it that eventually appears. Popular interest has also been stimulated by several television series, notably that by Ken Burns. The Burns series was screened just before the opening of the land war in the Persian Gulf in 1991. It touched a poignant national sensibility. A visit that I made to the Gettysburg battlefield in 1996, I recall, coincided with a national holiday, and I was amazed to see literally thousands of enthusiastic visitors flooding onto the field—a sight that would be inconceivable in Great Britain.

With such a huge outpouring of books and essays, and a wide popular interest, what, therefore, is my own contribution? How and why do I think another military history of the Civil War is justified? It is true that many previous studies have appeared, but very few make sense of the war as a whole and analyze its general features. Much recent writing seems to delight in piling up huge quantities of factual detail, so great indeed that its overall significance is apt to be missed. Amassing detail for its own sake has occurred before in Civil War historiography, for example, in the years before the First World War. The American Civil War was closely studied by the British Army, especially at the Staff College, Camberley (and this tradition has continued in various guises). At the completion of their studies, however, officers could not see the war's overall significance or outline. As Sir Basil Liddell Hart remarked rather scornfully in 1927, they could merely "enumerate the blades of grass in the Shenandoah Valley."[2]

As long ago as 1956 T. Harry Williams wrote, "Now the time has undoubtedly come to stop and take stock, to evaluate what we have, to rethink the meaning of the vast knowledge we possess." After the passage of half a century we need to undertake this task afresh. There have been several general surveys of the Civil War over the last thirty years. Some of these assess the military significance of the Civil War and analyze it within the general context of developments in the art of war. Like them, the focus of this book is on operational military history. Generalship, command decisions, strategy, and tactics have been given an extended treatment. Attention has also been accorded to the experience of ordinary soldiers in the conflict in line with the pioneering work of Sir John Keegan's *The Face of Battle* (1976). Considerable care has been given to relate this to important political and social developments during the war itself, as the views of ordinary soldiers at the front were an important catalyst in the hardening of attitudes toward the South and unleashing greater levels of force against it until the Confederacy was subdued. It is important to resist the temptation to believe (all too common in our own time) that once started war has no logic, order, or sense whatsoever, that it is mere catalogs of chaos and appalling suffering sustained by nothing more than what appears to be willful perversity.

Judging the utility of any war by such standards can be dangerous and misleading. In reconsidering the general meaning of the Civil War it soon became apparent that this book would have to challenge a number of assumptions about warfare in general that have permeated writings about the war; they have become so widespread as to be accepted as received wisdom. Without doubt these assumptions reflect the dominance for a long period of the Vietnam Syndrome in American life. It has certainly had a distorting influence on the writing of military commentary and scholarship. The Vietnam Syndrome underwrites the presumed "futility" of war: the notion that war can *never* succeed in its aims, never produce a positive outcome, and is thus destined to fail even before its initial operations are launched.

The Civil War raises several significant problems for those who adhere to such beliefs. It *did* have a positive outcome in two important respects: first, the survival of the United States as a unitary, continental republic, and second, the destruction of slavery. However, the discussion of the human cost over the last thirty years has excited more soul searching than at any time since the war itself, and has led instead to the acceptance of a number of contentious arguments about the "futility" of offensive military operations. If the outcome of the war itself cannot be challenged, then the wisdom of the way it was attained could certainly be questioned.[3]

But first, a definition of the Vietnam Syndrome is required. It is first and foremost an emotional reaction to the American defeat in the Vietnam War. Commentators have assumed that as the implications of the defeat sunk into public consciousness, American public opinion would be hostile to any participation in further foreign conflicts and appalled by any casualties sustained in such reckless adventures. In medical terms, a syndrome is a cluster of symptoms that characterize a disease. It is important to establish the precise nature of these symptoms and demonstrate how they have affected our interpretation of this "vast struggle" that determined the course of American history.[4]

Perhaps the most striking feature of the Vietnam Syndrome as it has influenced Civil War history is the ease with which so many historians deprecate "risk." Caution, especially in the attack, is praised. The prime assumption underlying such an approach is that defensive-minded measures are inherently more economical in lives. One is tempted to conclude that such an outlook is founded on the idea that the object of military operations is not to gain victory over the enemy but to economize on the loss of human life. It is underpinned, too, by another argument—namely, that no cause warrants great loss of human life. An American desire to minimize casualty levels has been read back in time as a major priority. Those generals who seemed to ignore this imperative have been at the receiving end of a lot of criticism. Robert E. Lee, as the defeated general in chief, has been the butt for severe denunciation rather than Ulysses S. Grant.[5]

The Vietnam Syndrome has thus had its greatest influence on Civil War strategy and operations rather than on its political dimensions and outcome. A defensive caste of mind has been imposed on the analysis of Civil War campaigns. It is a commonplace assumption that Civil War armies were "invulnerable" once they had taken up a strong position.

It follows that campaigns could not be won by battles, but by maneuvers or "raids." The "relative insignificance of battle," claim Herman Hattaway and Archer Jones in their seminal work, *How the North Won* (1984), "is simply another way of perceiving the primacy of the defensive when well articulated . . . units of rifle-armed infantry dominated the battlefield."[6] The logical conclusion of such an interpretation is that the attritional deadlock that ensues from 1864 onward is marked by a certain Tolstoyan inevitability that the human agency is powerless to alter.[7]

While attempts are made to explain the process of victory and defeat, those historians influenced by the Vietnam Syndrome have curiously switched attention to the *defeated* side, to the Confederacy. They have unwittingly sustained a pro-Confederate bias in studies of the Civil War. This is not to suggest bias in the sense of expressing sympathy for the Southern side, but rather in giving it an undue significance in the explanatory model, or discussing issues predominately from an angle that gives greater priority to their impact on the South. Consequently, historians have tended to focus on the reasons for the Southern defeat, rather than the Northern victory. Hattaway and Jones, plus Richard E. Beringer and William N. Still Jr., developed a thesis that the Confederacy failed because it was imbued with a faltering and shallow sense of national feeling, and consequently, lacked the will and determination to win. Such a conclusion chimed with disillusionment about war that prevailed in the 1980s despite all the bold talk of spokesmen of the Reagan administration.[8]

The atmosphere of darkness, a hellish vision of the war, has been extended from Vietnam to the Civil War. This has taken its cue from the incredibly influential motion picture *Apocalypse Now* (1970), which is full of brooding and disconcerting images derived from Joseph Conrad's novella set in Africa, *Heart of*

Darkness (1902). In 2000 Russell F. Weigley produced a curiously ambivalent history that tended to accept the "failure of will" thesis. He concludes gloomily that it was "tragic" that so many lives were lost "around a flag [the Stars and Stripes] whose opponents [Confederates] did not really want to pull it down." David J. Eicher the following year offered a new history, *The Longest Night*, a book suffused with the imagery of darkness inherited from *Apocalypse Now*.[9]

This book rejects the assumptions, taken as a package, inherent in the Vietnam Syndrome as an explanation for the course of the Civil War. Similar sorts of arguments have been advanced in Britain to explain the futility of Britain's part in the First World War. These have been revised significantly over the last fifteen years by a new generation of military historians. The approach adopted here does not accept the notion that the defensive is an inherently superior form of war. Still, it cannot shy away from explaining the prevalence of tactical deadlock and the failure to secure a decisive conclusion by the autumn of 1862, when the year started off so well for the North. It does this by emphasizing contingency rather than inevitability, and stresses the importance of command and the manifest failure of so many entrusted with it to fulfill their obligations. Tactical failure on so many Civil War battlefields had just as much to do with command inexperience and the failure to exploit offensive opportunities as it did with the power of the defensive, the rifled musket, and the breastworks, as the second in any case did not become prevalent until 1863.[10]

So what analytical tools does this book employ? They are rooted in a contemporary understanding of modern war and are not fundamentally different from those employed by Hattaway and Jones, although this work arrives at conclusions radically different from theirs. The most important device is one that has been used before, but which I have made a modest contribution to propagate in Britain—namely, the operational level of war. This is the area of military activity that links strategy and tactics, that conceives of campaigns as comprising distinct but linked phases of effort that can be conceived as a coherent whole. Without an understanding of the operational level, a tactical success— and tactics constitute the art of fighting—cannot lead to the successful conclusion that strategy has laid down. The events of a campaign, therefore, should not be regarded as a miscellaneous string of engagements that lack any relationship with one another or are bereft of any order and beyond the control of rigorous mental effort. On the contrary, all engagements must enjoy a logical connection. The operational level fulfills strategic objectives "through the conception, planning and execution of major operations and campaigns."[11]

The use of such terms raises the rather vexed question of the relationship between military thought and practice. Of course, in the 1861–65 United States and Confederate States, generals had no idea such a theorem existed. Many on both sides were not well versed in the military theory of their own day. So how then can we apply this sort of thinking to their plans and actions? This book is dedicated to the belief that if a commander has any ability he will draw up plans that are not dependent on or attempting to emulate the ideas of any theorist; only generals who lack ability, experience, or confidence as field commanders seek to copy theoretical prescriptions. When I was a young and overly enthusiastic postgraduate student of British military thought, I once asked the victor of Beda Fomm in the Cyrenaica campaign of 1940–41, General Sir Richard O'Connor, if he had been influenced by the writings of Major General J. F. C. Fuller. His reply rather startled me, as I expected him to have read as much British military theoretical writing as I had. No, he said, Fuller "did not influence me. I have only glanced through one [book], but that was quite good."

A contemporary of O'Connor's, General Sir James Marshall-Cornwall, suggests that no great soldier has ever invented a new system of warfare. Napoleon, for instance, "was the supreme craftsman of his trade"; successful commanders make "the most effective use of the tools" at their disposal. Their skill in the execution, in short, represents the last word on the relationship of theory and practice in the art of war.[12] That is to say, instinct rather than imitation underlines the approach of successful commanders. Historians of the Civil War have a habit of trying to locate military styles of the war in either a work of military theory or in European models (especially the Napoleonic Wars) when sometimes they have scant connection with both. Military theory is useful as a tool of retrospective analysis, and it is in this spirit that it is used in this work; it is very rare for a military plan to bounce unmodified from the pages of a book. This approach also governs the treatment of generalship in this book. Robert E. Lee and Ulysses S. Grant *instinctively* acted at the operational level, and that is one of the reasons why they were so successful. Tools of analysis drawn from our own time can, in other words, illuminate the methods used in a nineteenth-century war. If comparisons are made here between Civil War generals and those of an earlier period, like Napoleon or Wellington, they have been made because the technique that has emerged out of a complex process demonstrates enduring parallels; there can be no *assumption* of conscious emulation.

One of the reasons why such an approach is valuable in enhancing our understanding is that the operational level of war is founded on timeless concepts that were rationalized and expounded by the Prussian military thinker Carl von Clausewitz (1780–1831) and also the Swiss theorist Baron Jomini

(1779–1869). Among the concepts they employed was the idea of the *decisive point*. This was defined by Jomini in two ways: "as those points that are capable of exercising a marked influence either upon the result of the campaign or upon a single enterprise." He further cautioned that "all decisive points cannot be at the same time the objective of operations."[13] There is, in other words, a measure of judgment in seeking these out and this is a matter of choice. Jomini counsels that a flank, the side of an army, is often the decisive point because it is the shortest and easiest route to the enemy's rear. Such thought processes led to a British concept, namely, the *point of main effort*—the concentration of sufficient resources to ensure that the level of military success is commensurate with the effort made either to frustrate designs of one side or enhance those of the other. It has been defined as "a location in time and space at which or from which the enemy's center of gravity can be most gravely threatened."[14] Clausewitz described the crucial concept of the *center of gravity* as "the hub of all power and movement, on which everything depends. That is the point against which all our energies should be directed." Finally, *the culminating point*, which Clausewitz believes to be "that point when the force of an attack gradually diminishes"; once it is passed, the "remaining strength is just enough to maintain a defense. . . . Beyond that point the scale turns and the reaction follows with a force that is usually much stronger than that of the original attack."[15] Central to any discussion of these concepts is the theory and practice of command. The personality of the commanding general is a crucial component in the choices he makes. Command is first and foremost about choices.[16]

The study of the techniques and styles of command has been strangely neglected by historians. Command is fundamentally a managerial function and is related to leadership, but the talents it demands are not managerial in inspiration; furthermore, although some good leaders make bad generals, a good general is rarely a bad leader. The ideal commander is a compound of all these elements. For, as T. Harry Williams reminds us, "In modern war, which is total and all-embracing, the factor of command is of overriding importance." The commander never enjoys anything like complete knowledge of his enemy; he must employ intellectual power to assess what he has, must rely on his instincts and insight into human nature; he must inspire trust, for without this, however much he inspires fear among his subordinates and soldiers, they will not sacrifice themselves for him; and he must *decide*; generals who dodge making decisions do not prosper. The compounds formed by human chemistry are mixed and uncertain, and their effects unpredictable.[17]

A tension existed in the Civil War between the general as commander and the general as leader because of the increasing range, accuracy, and lethality of rifled-musket fire. The kind of inspired, personal, tactical direction provided by the Duke of Wellington during the battle of Waterloo (1815) was becoming increasingly hazardous. The Confederacy's second most-senior general, Albert Sydney Johnston, was killed during his first great battle, Shiloh, doing what Wellington had done throughout his military career. Eventually, the commanding general was forced farther back from the front line or rationed his appearances there. The American Civil War, so it is often claimed in this regard as in so many others, foreshadowed developments that reached a supposed culmination on the western front in 1914–18, with aloof and isolated generals presiding over an ill thought-out war of attrition. This book will question some of these presumed links with the First and Second World Wars.[18]

It is often claimed, too, that the American Civil War was the "first of the modern wars." Although American historians have not been slow to endorse this idea, it was actually developed with no little originality by Major General J. F. C. Fuller and Captain Sir Basil Liddell Hart, two British writers who rank among the greatest Civil War historians. They both pointed to the economic and social sources that brought a Union victory in 1865, "the eventual attrition, physical, moral and economic of the entire Confederacy, a condition such as we do not meet with again until 1918."[19] Writers considering the general history of war after 1945 noticed striking parallels between operations of the American Civil War and the Second World War. R. E. Dupuy and T. N. Dupuy saw the operations of 1862 as a "stepping-stone to the lightning war—*blitzkrieg*—of 1939 to 1945."[20]

It would be foolish and misleading to deny that the Civil War does share a number of features with the two World Wars of the last century: in command, communications, logistics, strategy, and tactics, it certainly foreshadowed some of the features of these wars. It is more debatable though whether these deserve the designation "modern." There is a growing literature—and three writers are especially noteworthy: Evan Luard, Martin van Creveld, and K. J. Holsti— which argues that the structure of modern warfare is changing. It no longer has a clear-cut beginning and end, well-defined "fronts," or even armies. Wars at the beginning of the twenty-first century run on for decades and are fought primarily by guerrilla forces that are virtually untrained. They tend increasingly to be civil rather than international wars, and obviously their character will change our appreciation of the central features of the American Civil War. The use of untrained, rapidly raised volunteer forces in the Yugoslavian civil war in the 1990s altered my own perspective on the use of similar volunteers in 1861–65.

Union and Confederate volunteers seem much more akin to the "forces" raised in Bosnia than the American conscripts deployed in 1941–45. The latter were trained and equipped within a much more rigid, regular framework.[21]

If we accept the argument that the Civil War inaugurated a style of war based on technology and industrialization like the two World Wars, we must acknowledge that such wars seem a thing of the past. Since 1945 only 18 percent of all wars have fit the regular, defined pattern of the World Wars on a smaller scale. Civil wars were the predominant form of war in the second half of the twentieth century, but these wars for the most part (with the exception noted above) do not resemble the American Civil War. In 1865, moreover, Confederate leaders unanimously ruled out the possibility that the war should be continued by guerrilla action. It is therefore possible to argue that far from being modern, the American Civil War initiated a form of warmaking that has had its day. The term "modern" perhaps can no longer be applied to it.[22]

I am not unaware that the overall thrust of my interpretation—particularly the operational focus—harkens back in some ways to an earlier school of historiography. It was dominated by British writers C. C. Chesney, Colonel G. F. R. Henderson, and Brigadier General Sir James Edmonds. Yet there are two even more significant figures whose spirits waft over these pages, General Fuller and Captain Liddell Hart. I came to be interested in their work via their books on the Civil War, not through their works on military theory. So there is a pleasing symmetry in my returning to follow the paths that they laid down, even though my conclusions are quite different from theirs. Writers of their ability, discernment, and literary skill embellish and enlarge our understanding of a subject even when they are mistaken. In acknowledging this, perhaps it is a way of discharging the massive intellectual debt I owe to them both. The nature of that debt will become clear in the pages that follow.

NOTES AND REFERENCES

1. John Terraine, *Impacts of War* (1970; London: Leo Cooper, 1993).
2. Quoted by Brian Bond, *The Victorian Army and the Staff College, 1854–1914* (London: Eyre Methuen, 1972), p. 157.
3. For an earlier rejection of the "futility" approach from which I have learned much, see Brian Bond, *The Pursuit of Victory* (New York: Oxford University Press, 1996).
4. These arguments were first explored in Brian Holden Reid, "The Influence of the Vietnam Syndrome on the Writing of Civil War History" (inaugural lecture, King's

College, London, November 26, 2001); an amplified version appeared in *Royal United Services Institute (RUSI) Journal* 147 (February 2002): 44–52; Roger Spiller, *An Instinct for War* (Cambridge, MA: Belknap Press of Harvard University Press, 2005), p. 186.

5. Brian Holden Reid, "America and War," in *A New Introduction to American Studies,* ed. Howard Temperley and Christopher Bigsby (London: Pearson/Longman, 2005), pp. 315–17.

6. Herman Hattaway and Archer Jones, *How the North Won: A Military History of the Civil War* (Urbana: University of Illinois Press, 1984), pp. 230, 415, 420n91, 570, 701; Steven E. Woodworth, *Six Armies in Tennessee* (Lincoln: University of Nebraska Press, 1993), p. 9.

7. Leo Tolstoy, *War and Peace* (London: Macmillan; Oxford University Press, 1943), p. 824, praises the Russian commander at the battle of Borodino (1812), Prince Kutusov, for understanding "there is something stronger and more important than his own will—the inevitable course of events."

8. Holden Reid, "The Influence of the Vietnam Syndrome," *RUSI Journal*, p. 45.

9. Russell F. Weigley, *A Great Civil War: A Military and Political History* (Bloomington: Indiana University Press, 2000), pp. 85, 486; yet see his call (p. 452) for the "rethinking of the attitude . . . that it [war] is always futile."; David J. Eicher, *The Longest Night: A Military History of the Civil War* (New York: Simon and Schuster, 2001), pp. 15, 22, 42.

10. For a spirited survey of British literature with some American echoes, see Brian Bond, *The Unquiet Western Front* (Cambridge: Cambridge University Press, 2002); Paddy Griffith, *Rally Once Again: Battle Tactics of the American Civil War* (Ramsbury, UK: Crowood Press, 1987) is an important pioneering study.

11. J. P. Kiszely, "The British Army and Approaches to War since 1945," in *Military Power: Land Warfare in Theory and Practice,* ed. Brian Holden Reid (London: Frank Cass, 1997), pp. 179–206; see the definitions in *ATP(A)NATO Land Force Tactical Doctrine,* annex A, p. xxv.

12. James Marshall-Cornwall, *Napoleon as Military Commander* (London: Batsford, 1967), pp. 11–12, 24–25.

13. Antoine-Henri Baron Jomini, *The Art of War* (1862; London: Greenhill, 1992), p. 86.

14. *Design for Military Operations: The British Military Doctrine,* Army Code 71451 (1989), p. 84, quoted in A. S. H. Irwin, *The Levels of War: Operational Art and Campaign Planning* (SCSI Occasional Paper No. 5, 1993), p. 17.

15. Carl von Clausewitz, *On War* (Princeton, NJ: Princeton University Press, 1976), bk. 7, p. 528; bk. 8, pp. 595–96.

16. G. D. Sheffield, "Command, Leadership and the Anglo-American Military Experience," in idem., *Leadership and Command: The Anglo-American Experience since 1861* (London: Brassey's 1997, 2002), pp. 1–3.

17. T. Harry Williams, "Introduction," in *Rebel Brass: The Confederate Command System*, Frank E. Vandiver (Baton Rouge: Louisiana State University Press, 1956), p. xv.

18. John Keegan, *The Mask of Command* (London: Jonathan Cape, 1987), pp. 172, 210–12; Brian Holden Reid, *J. F. C. Fuller: Military Thinker* (1987; London: Macmillan, 1990), pp. 122–27; idem., "'A Signpost That Was Missed?' Reconsidering British Lessons from the American Civil War," *Journal of Military History* 70 (April 2006): 402– 406, 413–14.

19. J. F. C. Fuller, *War and Western Civilization, 1832–1932: A Study of War as a Political Instrument and the Expression of Mass Democracy* (London: Duckworth, 1932), p. 95, quoted in Holden Reid, "'A Signpost That Was Missed?'" pp. 388–89.

20. R. E. Dupuy and T. N. Dupuy, *A Compact History of the United States Army* (New York: Hawthorn Books, 1956).

21. Evan Luard, *The Broken Sword* (London: I. B. Tauris, 1988); Martin van Creveld, *The Transformation of War* (New York: Free Press, 1990); K. J. Holsti, *The State, War and the State of War* (Cambridge: Cambridge University Press, 1996),

22. Hidemi Suganami, *On the Causes of War* (Oxford: Clarendon Press, 1996), pp. 60–61; Holsti, *State of War*, pp. 25–27, 37.

Chapter One

WHY THE WAR CAME, HOW IT WAS FOUGHT

In world history the rise of the United States to major power status was the greatest development of the nineteenth century. For the first, and surely the last, time a country was allowed to develop its resources and economy, and extend an urban network of towns and cities connected by railroads over a continent that was virtually untouched by the processes of Western civilization. The other remarkable development was that this unremitting growth was, thanks to great geographical distance, hardly interfered with by other nations more powerful than the United States. There was an important ideological dimension to these developments. The United States was the first unfettered experiment in republican democracy and her system was underpinned by a respect for the rule of law; the courts played an important role in American politics. Americans ostentatiously set their face against the corrupt and tyrannical European balance-of-power system, with its over-mighty and capricious monarchs, its huge armies, and its wicked and never-ending wars.

For the most part, the United States was isolated from the dangers posed by these predatory European powers. Only in 1798 and 1812–15 was her security directly threatened by them; though for both France and Great Britain in these years, American conflicts were a tiresome diversion from more important wars. Moreover, the United States was fortunate in her neighbors. The British colony of the Canadian Confederation to the north was huge, underpopulated, and weak. To the south lay the equally overextended and brittle republic of Mexico. For most of the nineteenth century many Americans believed it was inevitable that Canada would be absorbed by the United States. Some believed that Mexico would be swallowed up too. The United States saw herself as Great Britain's legitimate heir to a dominant position in the Western Hemisphere, and a great *imbalance* of power existed in the Americas in her favor after 1783.[1]

In the very strength of this position lay weakness and tensions pregnant with civil disruption. The historical experience of the United States and her colonial heritage was considerably different from the other Latin American states that secured their independence by 1822. The former colonial territories of Spain and Portugal had been more centralized than Great Britain's, and their resources more systematically plundered. The resulting states were more patri- archal and hierarchical; they were also much more oligarchical, with patronage being dispersed among the family networks of huge landowners. The Roman Catholic Church was a most powerful institution there.

The United States had certainly inherited an ambivalent republican outlook and her early years were characterized by controversy over the relative merits of centralization versus decentralization. Yet she developed a cohesive ideology based on freedom under the law and democratic rights. The Anglo-Saxon republic did not have to overcome the vexed question of legitimacy that so crip- pled the early development of many Latin American states. This pervasive idea of freedom was based on property rights and the operation of the free market. The spread of white universal male suffrage and a strict regulatory system of elections legitimized the aspirations expressed in the United States Constitu- tion. In the years before 1840 the United States became more cohesive, while most Latin American states were on the verge of disintegration. Above all, the United States, because of its comparative stability, escaped the rule of the *caudillo*—the military dictator.[2]

Yet centrifugal forces were present in American society dating from inde- pendence. The American experiment in democracy was based on the assumption that the imbalance of power in North America should be maintained. For only by banishing all aspects of European colonialism from North America could the experiment be nurtured and secured. The removal of colonial influence demanded the expansion of the United States until it occupied territory of continental ocean-to-ocean dimensions. Under no circumstances could the United States tolerate European colonial expansion in North or Central America. Nor would she allow ambitious adventurers, such as Aaron Burr, to create a personal empire by detaching the western states from the Union with British support. If the great European powers expanded their Canadian foothold or regained new ones in North America, then the balance of power would return, American predominance would end, and the United States' security would be endangered. But the drive for expansion would open up a ferocious debate over the character and destiny of this great continental state.[3]

In a country as huge as the United States, localism was a significant political factor. During the War of 1812 the New England states had already suffered disproportionately from the trade embargo announced by President Thomas Jefferson in 1807 and they were less than enthusiastic about the war. In December 1814 a constitutional convention of many New England states met at Hartford, Connecticut. This was a prudent if not timorous gathering. All delegates recoiled at the idea of secession and stressed local grievances. Timely action by President James Madison's administration prevented the Hartford Convention from becoming more adventurous and radical. It lacked a burning issue around which discontent could fester; it lacked a network of sympathetic states to offer support (Vermont and New Hampshire refused to send delegates); and it lacked inspiring and courageous leaders.[4]

In short, in a country as comparatively stable as the United States, bereft of large armies and politically ambitious generals desiring to seize power by force, localism by itself was not as sufficient to provoke civil war as it was in Latin America.

There was one region in the United States that shared some of the characteristics of Latin America—the South. With the exception of John Adams, all American presidents before 1824 were from the South (indeed from Virginia). Before 1861 Southerners dominated American political institutions. The South was demarcated from other regions of the United States by its dependence on slave labor and its large population of black slaves. By 1819 there were already one and a half million slaves in the Southern states, worth more than $300 million, capital that could not be transferred into other investments. Between 1810 and 1860 the slave population increased by more than a factor of three, totaling 3,953,760. The future of the South was increasingly wrapped up in slavery. Slavery also appeared to be the most efficacious method of controlling race relations. Southern whites were terrified of the consequences of a slave rebellion—given point by the savage and successful Haitian slave rebellion in the 1790s. Yet the South set its face against the prevaling winds of Western liberal opinion, because by 1850 slavery only survived elsewhere in Brazil, Cuba, and Puerto Rico.[5]

Slavery was a regional issue around which discontent and anxiety could cluster. But to repeat: regionalism by itself need not be a cause of civil war. This was clear in the other crisis of the early republic—the nullification crisis (1831–33). South Carolina had the largest slave population of any state and her economy depended on the growing and export of cotton; her great planters resented deeply the tariff policy of the federal government that contributed to a rise in consumer prices, which kept their cotton prices expensive. White South Carolinians were also intensely sensitive at the slightest hint of "abolitionist" sentiment. Denmark Vesey's slave conspiracy had been discovered in 1822 in Charleston and in 1831 William Lloyd Garrison had begun his abolitionist newspaper, the *Liberator*, in Massachusetts. The nullification crisis acts as a kind of initial snapshot of crude Southern secessionism. A powerful motive behind appeals for nullification of the federal tariff was that it would serve as a check to abolitionist influence without requiring a wholesale examination of the slavery issue.[6]

The South Carolina Association argued that the national government's powers had been delegated by the states; the latter, preserving their sovereignty, retained reserve powers and thus could "nullify" any federal legislation that did not serve its interests. South Carolina's greatest son, John C. Calhoun, then vice president of the United States, wrote a book entitled *South Carolina Exposition and Protest* (1828) that had developed an intricate theory of the tyranny of the majority. Calhoun asserted that the states should be given a right of veto over central government—they were "distinct and independent communities." He acknowledged that a political defense would only delay the onset of some kind of conflict with the North. The main result of theories like Calhoun's could be anarchy—and this instability slaveowners needed to avoid like the plague. Here was a contradiction that secessionists never resolved.

Nevertheless, Calhoun's prolific writings served as a theoretical, constitutional interpretation of American politics and law that was employed to challenge the legitimacy of the federal government. This was a significant step toward civil war. It served as a cloak for secessionist ambitions. It also underlined an important rejection of Jacksonian democracy (this had a personal basis because Calhoun feuded with Andrew Jackson). Calhoun and his followers loathed the corruption of the "spoils system" (under which all federal appointments were filled by the president's supporters to whom he owed favors), and disapproved of the increasing egalitarian tone of American democracy by 1828. These political changes were repellent to Calhoun; they were an affront to his deep-seated oligarchic instincts.

"There is no instance on record," he lamented, "of so sudden a degeneracy of a people as that of ours within the last twelve years." He considered that presidential elections were the product of "a corrupt system" that was "founded on the abuse of the powers and patronage of the government." Given Southern dissatisfaction, contention was "inevitable . . . for the system of plunder such as it is now was the most despicable of all governments." The opinion became steadfast after 1830 that the South must maintain control of the federal government, despite her declining population and wealth vis-à-vis the North, or the result would be disastrous for Southern institutions, especially slavery. The South tolerated the distasteful business of "politics" so long as it served the interests of slavery. The clash over the tariff was a preliminary skirmish in this long battle.[7]

In November 1832 a South Carolina nullification convention decreed that the protective tariff would not be enforced in that state and threatened to secede should the federal government use force. Military measures were taken by President Andrew Jackson and Charleston Harbor was blockaded, but he lowered the tariff. On December 10 he issued his Nullification Proclamation. Five thousand stands of arms were dispatched to Unionist volunteers, his *posse comitatus*. Faced with Jackson's belligerent actions, no other Southern state did anything to help South Carolina; it was completely isolated. The nullifiers could either launch an attack on the federal forces or give way with as much grace as could be mustered. With more prudence than would be displayed in 1861 the latter course was chosen. In March 1833 the ordinance of nullification was repealed.

The main lessons of the controversy were that the federal government could effectively over-awe individual, isolated states. Those who favored states' rights believed that the Southern states should act in closer concert and, in Langdon Cheves's words, guarantee "a measure of strength, almost certain of success." Secessionist strength lay in numbers and cooperation. Civil war did not explode because the nullifiers were too weak, Jackson had kept them under unremitting pressure, and the nullifiers, for all their bluster, acted cautiously. South Carolina Unionism remained strong and vital.[8]

From about 1840 the Southern states began to develop a consistent proslavery ideology. This not only defended slavery, it argued that slavery was a positive good and provided a binding point of view around which the slave states could rally; but the South was not a monolithic unit. The strident, extreme defense of slavery and states' rights that is associated with "the South" was really the clarion call of the Deep South. Thus the development of a Southern self-conscious sectional identity was by no means akin to a straight line on a graph. Indeed, the notion of Southern "separateness" has been greatly exaggerated, and is largely a post-1865 phenomenon. In particular, the attempt by some historians to explain Southern identity by its supposed "Celtic" character is shallow and unconvincing. It is the institution of slavery that marks out the South from other regions of the United States. Other distinguishing features include attempts to control freedom of thought and speech within the slave states, and the movement of ideas and publications from without. Increasingly, the South became a "closed system," conservative and insular, passionately resisting the liberal currents of the age.[9]

As the South committed itself more fervently to slave agriculture, it raised the great question of the future character of the United States. The precise meaning conferred on the hallowed documents of the Founding Fathers, especially the Declaration of Independence and the Constitution, was open to differing interpretations. "Freedom" to Southern slaveholders meant the unrestricted right to take their property (including their slaves) where they saw fit. "Freedom" to Northerners, among other things, meant a free economy, free labor, and free soil—so that virgin territories could be exploited by all, not just by a small, slaveowning oligarchy. This divergence of opinion was accentuated by the huge bounty of territory that followed the crushing American victory in the Mexican War (1846–48). A previous addition of territory, the Louisiana Purchase (1803), had given slavery a major boost by allowing it to expand into the fertile territories of the Mississippi basin. With the Treaty of Guadalupe Hidalgo (1848), at a cost of $15 million, the United States acquired half of Mexico—more than half a million square miles. What political and social system would dominate the settlement of this vast area, slavery or free labor?[10]

Slavery had been prohibited north of the Ohio River by the Northwest Ordinance of 1787. The Wilmot Proviso of 1846 attempted to extend this prohibition by declaring that "neither slavery nor involuntary servitude" could exist in these new territories seized from Mexico. The Missouri Compromise (1820) had laid down a hypothetical line of expansion through the territories carved out of the Louisiana Purchase, allowing slavery to dominate below lat. 36°30', but free labor north of it. A further increase of territory offered a hypothetical expansion of slavery to the Pacific. The character of the new states being created was therefore a source of contention. The South demanded "compensation" for the entry in 1849 of California as a "free state." Some Southern extremists threatened secession. The strife was ended by the Compromise of 1850. The South was compensated for California statehood by the Fugitive Slave Act that permitted slaveowners to retrieve their runaway property with the full support of Northern federal and state authorities.[11]

Although sectional controversies abated for several years (and secessionist candidates were defeated in the elections even in South Carolina), the compromise only amounted to a truce. It represented more a patching up of differences among politicians, not an allay of quarrels between peoples. War had not come in 1850 because no means existed whereby an alliance, or confederation, of the slave states could be forged. A Southern convention met at Nashville but this achieved little. The Compromise of 1850 revealed that all such political compacts with the slave states were based on a series of assumptions that were fundamentally proslavery. Its success also depended on the good behavior of Northern politicians and electorates. If these acquiesced to Southern designs, all would be well. But this did not happen.

The mood in the North after 1852 became increasingly hostile to slavery, and antislavery politics became more influential. After 1852 the Republican Party gradually took the place of the Whig Party and rose as the main opposition to the proslavery Democrats. The rise of this party had as much to do with ethnic and cultural tensions in the North as with slavery.[12] It was a response to massive immigration to the Northern states that was having a significant influence on Northern behavior vis-à-vis the South and slavery. The two Democratic administrations of Franklin Pierce (1853–57) and James Buchanan (1857–61) followed a pro-Southern policy that attempted to defend the Compromise of 1850. But each legislative step that sought to eradicate the sectional issue once and for all only seemed to make it worse. The most significant step was the Kansas-Nebraska Act of 1854 opening the settlement of territories above the line 36°30'; but the sponsor of this act, Illinois Senator Stephen A. Douglas, did not believe that slavery would expand because of "popular sovereignty"—the settlers would decide for themselves their social order, and slaveowners would always be in a minority. Northern outrage followed, for it opened up the possibility that slavery could be introduced into the territories. The Republican candidate, John C. Frémont, did respectably during the 1856 presidential election. Further controversy followed with the Dred Scott Decision (1857), in that the Supreme Court ruled that Congress had no power to forbid slavery in the territories, and Buchanan's attempt to impose a proslavery constitution on Kansas in the same year. Violence broke out in Kansas, but its ferocity was greatly exaggerated in the press and public discourse.[13]

Then developments gave an impression of domestic crisis. The arbitrary and shocking use of the Fugitive Slave Act, with the connivance of federal authorities in a small number of highly publicized cases, seemed to lend credence to the notion of a creeping, insidious, and calculating "slave power" that was wriggling its tentacles around Northern liberties. It appeared likely that before too long the whole country would fall under the "slave power's" tyrannical sway. Abraham Lincoln gave voice to these fears in his "House Divided" speech of 1857 and in his famous debates with Stephen A. Douglas in the Illinois senatorial election of 1858. The response of the South to the rise of a Northern sectional party that was determined to *restrict* slavery to its present confines, and allow no expansion into the territories, was to make greater demands on the political system while abdicating a national perspective on its problems. Southern leaders believed, quite erroneously, that they were confronted by legions of "abolitionists." The tacit assumptions of the Compromise of 1850 had been abandoned by both sides.[14]

The result was the disintegration of the second party system (1828–60). During the presidential election of 1860 the Democratic Party, the last surviving national institution, split into two sectional halves. The Republican nominee, Abraham Lincoln, won both a plurality of the popular vote and a majority in the electoral college but took no states outside the North. The prime reason for the coming of the Civil War in 1861 was the Southern decision not to accept the majority verdict of the voters. The triumph of a Northern sectional party represented a major challenge to the proslavery consensus that had developed in the early 1850s; it also summoned up a specter of Republicanism actually organizing in the South, a threat to the "closed system" that quashed any criticism of slavery, however guarded. Where the two-party system had most completely collapsed, in the Deep South mainly, secessionist fervor advanced most rapidly. The secessionist crisis quickly followed. Separatism does not bring war but secession invariably does. The manner in which the crisis evolved also made war more than likely. There was no agreed Southern plan, policy, organization, or design. The disaffected states introduced an uncoordinated series of unilateral state ordinances of secession. Each greatly increased state armaments. The final crisis was detonated by the secession of South Carolina in December 1860, followed over the next two months by Alabama, Louisiana, Mississippi, Georgia, Florida, and Texas. Four other states, Virginia, North Carolina, Tennessee, and Arkansas, where some semblance of the two-party system survived and where Unionism persisted, held back. An important theme in secessionist controversy in all the future Confederate states was a rejection of "politics" and the consolidation of the power of the "best" elements in Southern political life, the planter oligarchy.[15]

Secession was based ultimately on *force*.[16] Force and secession march hand in hand in managing a highly successful and aggressive coup d'état. The South *was* the aggressor. The seceded states seized all federal military installations, except for forts Sumter and Moultrie (abandoned on December 26, 1860) in Charleston Harbor, and Fort Pickens in Pensacola, Florida. This aggression provided a classic confrontation between the two sides. The secessionist government of the seven seceded states then sat at Montgomery, Alabama, and elected Jefferson Davis as its provisional president on February 9, 1861. The fledgling Confederate government was determined to acquire the unseized forts at the earliest opportunity and had a remarkably casual attitude toward the use of force, compared with the agonized one currently prevailing in Washington, DC. In his inaugural address, Abraham Lincoln disavowed any aggressive acts. Lincoln sought to defuse the crisis by reprovisioning Fort Sumter and warning the Confederates beforehand that he was going to do so. Before the victuals arrived on April 12, 1861, President Davis ordered the bombardment of Fort Sumter. Perhaps Davis calculated that the North would be intimidated by this move; if so, he miscalculated gravely. The casus belli was an unprovoked attack on the fort itself, and *not* an attempt to repulse the forces seeking to relieve the beleaguered garrison.

The American Civil War shared with other nineteenth-century wars the feature that the actual conflict was ignited by the side standing on the *defensive*. Precise military calculations had no influence on the decision to go to war for the simple reason that President Lincoln had virtually no forces to command. The tiny regular army of about sixteen thousand men had to be supplemented by the state militias. On April 15 Lincoln issued a proclamation calling upon the state governors to provide the manpower necessary to restore the Union. The governors of Virginia, Tennessee, North Carolina, and Arkansas refused to be a party to the "coercion" of their sister slave states and approved secession ordinances; the first two thus placed themselves in the immediate firing line. Although it was a response to flagrant aggression, Lincoln's proclamation was the single act that triggered off a great conflict. Yet by its belligerent stance during the Sumter crisis, the Confederacy had guaranteed that Northern opinion would be galvanized to crush its attempt at independence.[17]

The political issues that gave rise to the war are important in understanding its scope and character. Although much predicted, the crisis that led to the outbreak of war dated only from November 1860. Two important features immediately presented themselves: Northern politicians had not believed Southern threats of secession and were unprepared for war. A high measure of improvisation was demanded. Indeed, the South had to start from scratch. All parties, moreover, believed that the war would be short. To a significant degree, some believed that "war" in any organized sense would be unnecessary to bring the conflict to an end. There was little appreciation of the strength of secessionist feeling. Many Northerners assumed that Unionism would reassert itself once Southerners realized the extremities of the dangers to which the Confederacy was exposing herself. The initial strategic problem with which the North had to come to terms was that its task was not just to arrest an unlawful combination of ranting politicians but to suppress a sullen and resentful people. This imperative was rather obscured when in May 1861 the Confederacy moved its capital to Richmond, Virginia. The Confederate Congress agreed to meet there on July 20. This was but a hundred miles from Washington and offered the opportunity for a rapid strike at the impertinent rebels by the federal army. Once Richmond was occupied and this rebellious body incarcerated, it was widely believed, the rebellion would be over.

There was an initial reluctance to accept that the conflict was broader than this simple formula. The South demanded nothing less than the recognition of its independence. The longer the Confederacy survived, the greater the likelihood that such an acceptance would be forthcoming. The North had to be persuaded that the immense effort required to subjugate the South was futile and debilitating. Foreign powers were to be encouraged to intervene and deliver the beleaguered Confederacy. The North, in turn, had realized before the firing on Fort Sumter that the easiest way to strike at the South was by a gigantic interdict: a naval blockade covering a coastline of 3,500 miles and demanding an expansion of the US Navy from 40 ships and 7,600 officers and men to 671 ships and 51,000 men. Such were the two halves of the strategic circle that grew out of the political issues that provoked the war and contributed to the deadlock and attrition that would shape it. The finely weighed calculations and optimistic hopes of politicians were shattered. Passions were heightened; for both sides could only justify the immense slaughter by bringing the war to a successful conclusion. Hence the desire to strike at the very foundations of Southern warmaking capacity; slowly the North committed itself to extirpating slavery and destroying the social cohesion of Southern plantation agriculture. As Ohio Senator John Sherman (Republican) assured his brother, William, "However, delay, defeat or a much longer continuance in the barbarity of rebel warfare will prepare the public mind in the North for a warfare that will not scruple to avail itself of every means of subjugation."[18]

There were a number of striking geographical factors that influenced grand strategy. The immensity of the theater of war was inescapable and could not be reduced by naval power, except down the Mississippi River and its tributaries. By European standards the communications available for coordinating forces over immense distances were primitive—there were few and inadequate roads and a paucity of canals. The telegraph was an important aid but had distinct limitations, not least that its lines could be cut. There was an abundance of low wooded country and the population was thinly diffused. All of these factors might have appeared to favor the spread of guerrilla warfare, though this brutal form of warfare never became crucial to either side. Railroads and railroad junctions, such as Manassas, Chattanooga, and Atlanta, were to acquire an immense strategic importance. Yet initially the focus was on the vicinity around Washington. Politicians are always inclined to view the world as revolving around their expostulations and institutions, and so it was in 1861. The geographic proximity of Washington and Richmond hypnotized decision makers. Strategic matters in the West were neglected unless they forced politicians to pay attention to them. The overriding preoccupation was with the security of Washington, DC.[19]

Historian Geoffrey Blainey has argued that a belief in a short war is a reflection of confidence in an overwhelming material superiority. In terms of material strength the North had a preponderant advantage. The total Northern population, including Kansas and the states on the Pacific shore, was 18,907,753 compared with that of 8,726,644 in the Confederate states. But this latter figure included over 3,900,000 slaves who in 1861–62 were not considered suitable material for soldiers. In the vital category of white men of military age (fifteen to forty years old) the North could draw upon a population of 4,000,000 while the South had only a quarter of that figure, 1,100,000. The margin of industrial production was even greater. The individual value of industrial goods produced by the states of Pennsylvania and New York was double the entire production of all the Confederate States. A striking indication of this is revealed by the number of locomotives built by the South in the year ending June 1, 1860: 19; the North: 451.[20] Predictions that a war is likely to be short are based on three main propositions. First, they rely heavily on faith in economic resources, especially financial prosperity. The South, despite the paucity of its resources, was buoyed up by the expectation that a Confederacy would inaugurate a new age of free trade with Europe, transforming Charleston into another New York. In the North financial strength conferred faith that the South could be defeated without much effort. The secretary of the treasury, Salmon P. Chase, took pleasure in informing Lincoln on April 2, 1861, that as bids for federal loans were oversubscribed four times, "All this shows decided improvement on finances and will gratify you."[21]

Second, both the North and the South believed they had right on their side.

One claimed they were defending the Union against the depredations of traitors; the other that they were the true heirs of George Washington and asserting just (and legal) Southern rights. A sense of moral ascendancy was important here. The *Times* correspondent William Howard Russell recorded a number of conversations with Southerners who asserted "that the white men in the slave States are physically superior to the men in the free States; and indulged in curious theories in morals and physics to which I was a stranger." He noted, moreover, a curious insistence that moral superiority in war was proven by instances of duels and personal confrontations with Northerners in Congress; the caning of Massachusetts Senator Charles Sumner by a South Carolina congressman in 1857 was an especially comforting example, "as the type of affairs of this kind between the two sides." Southerners assumed that their manliness and courage was greater than that of Northerners. Many Northerners agreed that this was so, believing that their martial prowess had been sapped by an undue preoccupation with business.[22]

Third, groups who are confident in their cause usually expect success to come rapidly. Both sides tended to assume that victory in battle and victory in war were synonymous. Here it might be pointed out with profit in contradistinction to the usual generalization that Americans are excessively passionate in the conduct of their wars and too prone to transform them into crusading ventures, that most Americans have entered them—especially in the nineteenth century—thinking they would be short. Their expansion into brutal, ideological wars to the finish, what Clausewitz called "absolute wars," was as much a product of disillusion with initial failures as from any inherent penchant for crusading. At the outset, most politicians were imbued with optimism. Edwin M. Stanton informed John A. Dix of his faith in early success. "Nor indeed do I think hostilities will be so great an evil as many apprehend. A round or two often serves to restore harmony; and the vast consumption required by a state of hostilities, will enrich rather than impoverish the North."[23]

Turning from strategy to operations, the main problem that both sides faced was coping with a war of mass involvement. As in the French Revolution and the Napoleonic Wars, the ranks were filled with enthusiastic amateurs who were prepared for action with the minimum of drill and training. This was consistent with the American military tradition that placed immense faith in the "natural genius" of the American people, and deprecated military discipline as "artificial" and detrimental to that genius and precious, democratic rights. President Lincoln is often criticized for asking for "only" seventy-five thousand men for three months in his Proclamation of April 15, 1861. But it is often forgotten that this was a huge number of men for the time and also that many Northern politicians believed that the Civil War would resemble the rebellions of the eighteenth century, like Shays's Rebellion in Massachusetts (1786) or the Whiskey Rebellion in Pennsylvania (1794).

Improvising an army would therefore be a short-term problem. The regular United States Army was tiny. In 1860 it consisted of 16,215 men (1,080 officers and 15,135 enlisted men). Of the officers, 313 resigned their commissions to go with the Southern states. The response to Lincoln's call was overwhelming. The summons had been governed by the Militia Act of 1792 that placed control of the militia in the hands of the states. The volunteers could be raised from out of the militia regiments but recruitment more often arose from spontaneous gatherings of those eager to serve, who elected their own officers and noncommissioned officers (NCOs). The raising of an army was inhibited by the fact that Congress was not sitting; thanks to the organized volunteer companies, they provided Lincoln with what Russell F. Weigley terms a "stop gap" army. These men certainly did not lack enthusiasm. Lincoln's April 15 proclamation raised 91,816 men. With further calls for volunteers on May 3 for 42,034 volunteers to serve for three years, by July 1, 1861, Lincoln's first secretary of war, Simon Cameron, was able to state that 310,000 men were in uniform in 208 regiments, of which 153 were in active service. The Union armies continued to grow. In his message to Congress on July 4 the president asked for four hundred thousand volunteers for three years, and Congress increased it to half a million. The day after the Union defeat at Manassas (Bull Run) in July 1861, a bill for a further five hundred thousand volunteers was hastily passed. Thus within three months of the firing on Fort Sumter, contrary to Southern allegations, the Union had shown admirable pertinacity and raised an army of a million men. By August 3 the US War Department could reveal that 485,640 three-year volunteers were in arms in 418 regiments of infantry, 31 of cavalry, and 10 of artillery.[24]

A growth of an army by twenty-seven times its original size invariably leads to severe administrative strains. Each state had to provide a certain quota of recruits, and often the first wave of enthusiasm wore off. Various payments, or bounties, were made to tempt the men to join. The states were ultimately responsible for recruiting and this was the province of the state governor. The federal government took over responsibility for clothing and equipping the men. At any rate, that was the theory. More often, the states, private individuals, and groupings, such as the Philadelphia Committee of Public Safety, paid for or purchased weapons. The North had 457,660 muskets and rifles available in 1861; 120,000 of these were appropriated by the South (which already had

300,000 firearms distributed among the militia). The federal arsenals at Spring-field and Harpers Ferry only produced 22,000 weapons a year. The deficit was made up by extensive purchasing abroad. The North bought 726,705 muskets and rifles by November 1862, mainly from Great Britain, on which it also relied for the import of saltpeter, crucial for the production of gunpowder. It also acquired 30,788 rifles, 31,210 carbines, and 86,607 pistols from American firms. The federal arsenals increased their levels of production by ten fold. Almost 1,700,000 weapons were produced by them before April 1865.

The South, too, was active in the purchasing market. She managed to buy 200,000 weapons in various European countries despite strenuous Northern efforts to stop her, and another 150,000 were captured in the field by her troops. It was in the organization of its manpower that the Confederacy showed itself superior. It was fighting to create a new nation and thus for its very existence; high stakes demanded drastic measures. In March 1861 the Confederate Congress voted for an army of 100,000 volunteers for one year. This was increased to 400,000 for three years in July. In April 1862 conscription was introduced for white men between eighteen and thirty-five years of age (although exceptions were introduced later). This legislation allowed the Confederacy to retain its original volunteers for the duration of the war. It was decisive in providing strong, enthusiastic armies in 1862 that were to attain those victories that permitted the Confederacy to survive the crisis of April–July 1862. The draft produced 300,000 soldiers, or one third of the Confederate total, a splendid achievement for a country of about 5.5 million whites. The argument, frequently reiterated, that the North was more efficient and more "modern" in its organization, is greatly overdone. As for the North, so confident was the new secretary of war, Edwin M. Stanton, that enough men had been raised to defeat the South, that on April 3, 1862, he closed the recruiting offices.[25]

The provision of heavy weapons was a greater problem. In 1861 there were only 163 cannons fit for service. Yet American industry, both Northern and Southern, rose to the challenge of equipping sizeable armies with the appropriate quantity of artillery. When Major General George B. McClellan set out on his Peninsular campaign in April 1861 the Army of the Potomac could field three guns per thousand men; in the Gettysburg campaign it rose to four guns per thousand men. In 1861–65 Northern foundries produced 7,892 field guns and howitzers. The Southern achievement, given its paucity of industrial resources, was even more impressive. In May 1861 the Confederate Congress voted $4,440,000 for ordnance, including sixteen batteries of six guns each. The

Confederacy's chief ordnance officer, a renegade Pennsylvanian named Josiah Gorgas, was an administrator of drive and foresight. Between October 1862 and November 1863 his bureau had fielded 677 guns. During the Gettysburg campaign, Robert E. Lee's Army of Northern Virginia was no whit inferior to the federal forces in artillery, enjoying 3.4 guns per thousand men. In 1864–65 the Army of Northern Virginia had 240 guns, with 5 guns per brigade, and 20 guns per division of cavalry. Gorgas also experimented with technical innovations, such as the Bormann fuse. This was bitterly criticized as overly elaborate, but the problem lay with inexperienced or poorly trained gunners, and the Confederate artillery returned to cruder but simpler fuses. Confederate gunpowder was subject to constant scrutiny and attempts at improvement.[26]

The result was that Union and Confederate armies enjoyed a provision of artillery comparable to European armies. French artillerists were of the opinion that two guns per thousand men was the bare minimum for a force of one hundred thousand men. Lee believed in 1864 that European armies fielded three guns per thousand men, and that therefore he should be sent 395 guns. Gorgas proposed that he should receive one gun per five hundred men. During the Franco–Prussian War the Prussians deployed 3.5 guns per thousand, which was comparable to Lee's provision in 1863, although this had declined by 1864. The major technical development was the rifled cannon, which improved range and effectiveness. The striking feature of the Civil War, despite its many sieges, was the complete absence of elaborate, scientific siegecraft. During the siege of Sebastopol in the Crimea (1855–56) the British artillery alone fired 252,640 heavy shells. No American bombardment in the Civil War compared with this. Furthermore, the lack of a siege train or many heavy weapons prevented the Confederacy from taking full advantage of its first victory at Manassas (Bull Run) in July 1861 and seizing Washington, DC. Thus although levels of improvisation were impressive, lack of preparation ensured that the rapid decisive victory that both sides expected to win was beyond the resources of both sides, especially the South.[27]

The overwhelming military reality was that the scale and intensity of the war took both North and South completely by surprise. Consequently, commanders on both sides were mentally and professionally unprepared for its demands. The major obstacle they had to overcome, in the first two years of the war at least, was to adjust their thoughts to the right level of military activity. A man who is an energetic and capable commander of a regiment may procrastinate and fumble in command of a corps. The Confederate corps commander, Lieutenant General Richard S. Ewell, declared that the United States Military

Academy at West Point taught officers of the "old army" everything they needed to know about commanding a company of fifty dragoons on the western plains against the Cheyenne Indians, but nothing else. For budding commanders, transcending this experience was a paramount need. Some, like Lee and Thomas J. Jackson, succeeded quickly. Ambrose E. Burnside, commanding a brigade at First Manassas, behaved like a regimental commander and was never at ease commanding armies, even though he was marginally more effective commanding a corps. It was hardly surprising that generals found this process arduous, as the prewar course at West Point on strategy and the art of war lasted no more than a week; the keen cadet could supplement this meager mental refreshment by joining informal gatherings like the Napoleon Club.[28]

The only soldier alive in America who had commanded forces of any size was Brevet Lieutenant General Winfield Scott. He had led fourteen thousand men from the port of Vera Cruz, fought a number of battles en route, and had taken Mexico City in 1847. Scott had thus waged a skillful campaign in the mountains, far distant from his base, relying heavily on maneuver. His favorite expedient was a turning movement that drove the Mexicans from their strong positions. Scott's aims were modest; it was not in his interest either to attempt to destroy the Mexican army or wreak havoc on the local population, which would thus stimulate passionate resistance, when his own small army (though by American standards it was large) was so precariously placed. In any case, such restrained, disciplined modes of attack were in line with his own personal preferences. Despite this, Scott's generalship had much more in common with the campaigns of British generals, like Sir Garnet Wolseley, who were skilled in "colonial" warfare than it did with the celebrated European generals that United States historians are wont to compare him. To describe him as "old-fashioned" is inaccurate. Scott's generalship was limited by the political imperatives that were so important in colonial warfare, and to which the successful commander must respond sensitively. He was not attempting to put into practice the academic precepts of a European theorist, like Jomini, who had studied the great campaigns of Turenne, Saxe, or Napoleon. In 1846–48, Scott was indifferently acquainted with these theories.[29]

It is a curious feature of Civil War historiography that historians assume it is axiomatic that the conduct of military operations in this war can and must be linked to a body of military thought. As American military theorists are conspicuous in their absence before Alfred Thayer Mahan, the prime candidates are Baron Jomini and Carl von Clausewitz, two of the greatest European theorists. Historians have attempted to make tenuous links between the generalship displayed in

1861–65 and these eminent writers, and such efforts have been misleading. Not only did historians of the post-1945 years show limited knowledge of their theories, they assumed that any link between military thought and practice was demonstrable and that when such links exist, they must have their source in some theoretical work. Given the massive need for improvisation in the Civil War, the greatly underdeveloped state of strategic studies in America before 1861, and the undereducated and inexperienced state of American higher commanders, a deep knowledge of European military thought was unlikely. Even where it did exist, it is doubtful whether theoretical considerations were more important than those relating to geography or the enemy's position. There is nothing more difficult in military history than to attempt to prove that military theory has influenced generalship. This has not discouraged Civil War historians who leap on any coincidence to demonstrate labels and false compartmentalization.[30]

The plain fact of the matter is that in war the number of solutions presented to any commander are not great. Armies are just crowds of men on which varying degrees of discipline are imposed. They attempt to block the passage of the enemy by maintaining a cohesive line supported by weaponpower that will either refuse to let the enemy pass, or force the enemy to give way so that their own objectives may be attained. Maintaining *organization* is integral to success in war because without it armies will dissolve, unable to maintain that cohesive front that makes the regulation of armed force possible. The means to destroy that organization in the enemy's ranks are sought by all generals, whatever expedients they adopt. It is usually found by getting behind the enemy where he is both physically unprotected and psychologically most vulnerable.[31] This has been realized since antiquity. Caesar wrote of the crisis at the height of the siege of Alesia in 52 BCE, that his men "were unnerved, too, by the shouts they could hear behind them as they fought, that indicated that their lives were not in their own hands, but depended on the bravery of others. It is nearly always invisible dangers that are most terrifying."[32]

At the operational level there are only two ways of achieving this, by *envelopment* or by *penetration*. Nineteenth-century warfare was two dimensional. Generals could only see what could be observed from the ground. Experiments with balloons in 1862 were not successful. Commanders tried to seize high ground or tall buildings from which they could observe the enemy. After Gettysburg the Union commander, George G. Meade, could not see the Confederate position because of heavy rain and a pall of smoke.[33] The enemy's army could be defeated by equating force with space in a given period of time; the latter is maximized by mobility. If the most force is placed on the enemy's side—his flanks—then he can be *enveloped*. This is either of a single flank or both—but Civil War armies were usually not large enough to effect a double envelopment. Ulysses S. Grant only attained a double envelopment of Lee's Army of Northern Virginia in the last week of the war, when it was on the verge of collapse.

The alternative is penetration. The enemy's front is broken by a direct frontal assault. His flanks are pinned by feints and the main strength is thrown at his center in the attempt to shatter it in the shortest period of time. This is the crudest and most direct method of assaulting the enemy, but it does have the advantage of allowing the greatest concentration of force at the enemy's decisive point; its corresponding disadvantage is that the enemy can concentrate his strongest force against the attacker, because the defender knows the direction of the attack. There is, of course, no artificial barrier between these two operational forms and most campaigns of the Civil War, like Lee's Pennsylvania campaign of 1863, are blends of both forms. Such important variables as logistics, weapon-power, and reconnaissance determine how the campaigns evolve. Detailed consideration will be given to how these factors influenced the war in the chapters that follow.

Winfield Scott's campaigns in Mexico in 1847 revealed some excellent examples of how envelopments could be organized under more difficult terrain than that faced by most Civil War commanders. Yet Civil War generals encountered problems he did not face. The first was control of large armies. The Army of the Potomac in the Virginia theater usually numbered in excess of one hundred thousand men, and the Army of the Tennessee in the Mississippi basin, usually more than eighty thousand men. Scott's army was only about a tenth of the size of the Army of the Potomac. The other army deployed in Mexico, that of Zachary Taylor in the north, was only half the size of Scott's. It was initially four to six thousand men strong, although by August–September 1846 it had been increased to almost fifteen thousand. But moving forces of this size was such a challenge to American generals and their staffs that Taylor adopted the expedient of breaking up his force into four columns, each separated by a day's march.[34] This is testimony to the intellectual and moral challenge faced by Civil War generals a generation later with forces ten and twenty times the size of the armies of 1846–47.

The second problem was defensive firepower. Mexican soldiers, though individually brave, were poorly motivated, had little sense of regimental cohesion, and were indifferently equipped. Even in the hardest fought battles, such as Zachary Taylor's victory at Buena Vista which took place over two days, February 22–23, 1847, US casualties were only 750. This kind of experience confirmed the antebellum idée fixe that warfare consisted of much picturesque movement and histrionic gesture in which the enemy did little but obligingly depart from his position at the earliest opportunity. War was seen as a chess match or a sport, a test to enhance personal and family reputation; soldiers were viewed as "warriors" rather than organizers and managers, a curious contradiction considering that organizational skills are one of the main American contributions to generalship. The challenge was thus twofold. When they discovered that war was more than just running about and that the enemy stayed in place, generals had to concentrate their thoughts on how to organize attacks in face of the rifled musket and rifle, and sustain their own morale when casualties by American standards were so unexpectedly high. Any risky operation, such as an envelopment, needed even more resolution than in Mexico in 1847 because of the obstinacy and defensive strength of the enemy. This made even greater moral demands on the commander. We should never forget the immense psychological strain on commanding generals, to which many in the Civil War succumbed. Furthermore, as Captain Cyril Falls reminds us, "military history affords more examples of failure through over-caution than of failure through excessive boldness." The Civil War certainly confirms the wisdom of this assertion.[35]

Speed of maneuver was (and remains) essential. Therefore at the operational level roads and road junctions were of supreme importance. This is especially true in warfare that, as in Virginia, was waged in woods and forests. The essence of a Napoleonic envelopment, the *maneuver à la derrière*, was to strike at the enemy's rear and force him to fight for his lines of communication and then to seize control of them. This would be achieved by fighting a decisive battle, or at any rate one of signal importance, with the main body of the enemy's forces. In 1861 virtually all consulted believed that the Civil War would be brought to an end by a single decisive battle. It has become a commonplace of Civil War historiography that a decisive battle was a chimera impossible to attain under Civil War conditions. It has been assumed, often rather casually, that because American generals failed to secure decisive military victories, they were impossible to attain. But failure is not a convincing guarantee that the original quest was misguided or insuperable.

Clearly the rise of levels of firepower complicated the operational level and tactics, but it did not render the decisive battle impossible to attain; because Civil War generals did not attain it until December 1864 at the earliest does not mean it was unattainable. Whether it would have had the political consequences attributed to it is, however, quite another matter. Yet as a test of technical, operational art it was by no means impossible. In the first instance levels of firepower, especially in 1862–63, were exaggerated. The attacker could be driven from the battlefield in panic with his cohesion and organization completely smashed, as at the two battles of Manassas (Bull Run). A decisive victory was possible but it demanded much of generalship. First, the general should control his subordinates and they must be imbued with his aim, which should be thoroughly understood; reserves should be distributed with the pursuit in mind; thought should be given to the pursuit before the battle began, and not as it ended; the troops should not be asked to do too much, otherwise they would be exhausted prematurely; the timing of the decisive strokes needed to be carefully managed; and the topography should have been carefully surveyed—for instance, the seizure of the bridge over the Bull Run should have been a prime objective. In the battles of the Civil War some of these factors were operative, but not all, and the reasons for this will be discussed below.[36]

Battles form a sequence in a campaign and campaigns fit into the strategic view. All of these elements must be integrated if the war is to have efficacy. Therefore, to conclude this chapter, the question must be posed: what military strategic alternatives presented themselves? Hans Delbrück, as interpreted by J. F. C. Fuller, argued that there are two strategic forms: the strategy of annihilation and the strategy of exhaustion or attrition. These two forms need to be carefully distinguished because they are derived from the two types of war, limited and unlimited. As Fuller reminds us, "in the first the aim is the decisive battle, in the second battle is but one of several means, such as maneuver, economic attack, political persuasion and propaganda, whereby the political end is attained."[37] In Civil War historiography these two forms have become confused and muddled up. The Union initially sought to deploy a strategy of annihilation but ended up, mainly because of frustration, failure, and the strength of Confederate resistance, to resorting to a strategy of exhaustion. Both means sought the complete defeat of the Confederacy, but the latter involved much more far-reaching social and political consequences.

It has been argued that the South should have resorted to a defensive strategy that would have made the most effective use of the Confederate assets of time and space, especially the latter, and exhausted the North's will to continue the war. Whether this was politically acceptable to the parts of the Confederacy about to be given up is less adequately explained away. The South certainly enjoyed the advantage of "interior lines," one of Jomini's favorite nostrums. This may be compared in operations to the inside, as opposed to the outside, lane of a running track. Those on the "inside" move greater distances in less time. Interior lines clearly accord an advantage, ruthlessly exploited by

Napoleon, when armies are dependent on long marches and therefore rely on muscle power. Yet, even in the first phase of any war, interior lines are not a universal panacea that guarantees success. Technological change, the strategic use of railroads, greatly reduced the interior lines' advantage in the American Civil War. Indeed, if anything, the possession of interior lines points to the fundamental problem faced by the Confederacy. Even if her armies won victories in the field how could these be transformed into strategic success and the war won? Captain Falls observes sensibly that "interior lines afford opportunities for defeating the enemy piece-meal with force of inferior strength; but, on the other hand, do not promise such decisive victory as operations on exterior lines when pushed home until the enemy is enveloped." This was the eventual fate of the Confederacy. So it is to the first phase of the war, and these intractable strategic dilemmas, that we must now turn.[38]

NOTES AND REFERENCES

1. Gordon Connell-Smith, *The United States and Latin America* (London: Heinemann, 1974), pp. 2–5, 38–39, 41–45.

2. Ibid., pp. 25–26; Edwin Williamson, *The Penguin History of Latin America* (Harmondsworth, UK: Penguin, 1992), pp. 146–47, 237–38, 240–41, 280, 342, 373–77.

3. Dumas Malone, *Jefferson the President: Second Term, 1805–1809* (Boston: Little, Brown, 1974), pp. 215–16.

4. J. C. A. Stagg, *Mr. Madison's War: Politics, Diplomacy, and the Early American Republic, 1783–1830* (Princeton, NJ: Princeton University Press, 1983), pp. 471–74, 477–83.

5. Charles M. Wiltse, *The New Nation, 1800–1845* (New York: Macmillan, 1965), p. 69; Peter Kolchin, *American Slavery, 1619–1877* (Harmondsworth, UK: Penguin, 1993, 1995), p. 93.

6. William W. Freehling, *Prelude to Civil War: The Nullification Controversy in South Carolina, 1816–1836* (New York: Oxford University Press, 1965, 1992), pp. 49–51, 60, 63, 85–86.

7. Irving H. Bartlett, *John C. Calhoun: A Biography* (New York: Norton, 1991), pp. 149–52, 162, 178, 234, 238, 240, 242, 286, 288–90, 301–302.

8. Brian Holden Reid, *The Origins of the American Civil War* (London: Longmans, 1996), pp. 61–63.

9. Ibid., ch. 2; see also Grady McWhiney, *Cracker Culture* (Tuscaloosa: University of Alabama Press, 1988); James M. McPherson, "Antebellum Southern Exceptionalism: A New Look at an Old Question," *Civil War History* 29 (1983): 230–44.

10. David Potter, *The Impending Crisis, 1848–1861* (New York: Harper and Row, 1976), pp. 1–6.

11. W. R. Brock, *Parties and Political Conscience: American Dilemmas, 1840–1850* (Millwood, NY: KTO Press, 1979), pp. 159–60.

12. William E. Gienapp, *The Rise of the Republican Party, 1852–1856* (New York: Oxford University Press, 1987).

13. Holden Reid, *Origins*, pp. 189–90.

14. Bruce Collins, "American Federation and the Sectional Crisis, 1844–1860," in *The Federal Idea*, ed. Andrea Bosco, pt. 1, 54–65 (London: Lothian Foundation, 1991); Bruce Levine, *Half Slave and Half Free: The Roots of Civil War* (New York: Hill and Wang, 1992), p. 189.

15. See Michael P. Johnson, *Toward a Patriarchal Republic: The Secession of Georgia* (Baton Rouge: Louisiana State University Press, 1977).

16. This is an important theme of my *Origins*, especially ch. 7.

17. Brian Holden Reid, "The Crisis at Fort Sumter in 1861 Reconsidered," *History* 77 (February 1992): 27–32.

18. John Sherman to William T. Sherman, May 19, 1862, *The Sherman Letters*, ed. Rachel Sherman Thorndyke (1894; New York: Da Capo, 1969), p. 151.

19. One of the best discussions of grand strategic realities in 1861 is still J. F. C. Fuller, *War and Western Civilization, 1832–1932: A Study of War as a Political Instrument and the Expression of Mass Democracy* (London: Duckworth, 1932), pp. 86–91. Also see W. R. Brock, *Conflict and Transformation: The United States, 1844–1877* (Harmondsworth: Penguin, 1973), pp. 259–61; Richard E. Beringer, Herman Hattaway, Archer Jones, and William N. Still Jr., *Why the South Lost the Civil War* (Athens: University of Georgia Press, 1986), pp. 51–52, 154, 192, 245, 339.

20. Peter J. Parish, *The American Civil War* (London: Eyre Methuen, 1975), pp. 107–10.

21. Geoffrey Blainey, *The Causes of War*, 3rd ed. (London: Macmillan, 1988), pp. 45, 56, 95, 208–209, 285, 293, 294; Salmon P. Chase to Lincoln, Mar. 16, Apr. 2, 1861, Robert Todd Lincoln Collection of the Papers of Abraham Lincoln, Library of Congress, Washington, DC.

22. W. H. Russell, *My Diary North and South*, ed. Eugene H. Berwanger (New York: Alfred A. Knopf, 1988), pp. 61–63, 89 (entries for Apr. 5, Apr. 17, 1861). Michael C. C. Adams, *Fighting for Defeat: Union Military Failure in the East, 1861–1865* (Lincoln: University of Nebraska Press reprint, 1992), pp. 56–57.

23. Benjamin P. Thomas and Harold M. Hyman, *Stanton: The Life and Times of Lincoln's Secretary of War* (New York: Alfred A. Knopf, 1962), p. 120.

24. Russell F. Weigley, *History of the United States Army* (London: Batsford, 1968), pp. 198–99, 200–201.

25. Ibid., pp. 202–206; Thomas and Hyman, *Stanton*, pp. 201–202, 206.

26. Weigley, *United States Army*, p. 203; Frank E. Vandiver, *Ploughshares into Swords: Josiah Gorgas and Confederate Ordnance* (College Station: Texas A&M University Press edition, 1994), pp. 65, 146, 204, 238.

27. Richard Holmes, *The Road to Sedan: The French Army, 1866–1870* (London: Royal Historical Society, 1984), p. 42; Weigley, *United States Army*, p. 203; Vandiver, *Gorgas*, p. 238; Hew Strachan, *From Waterloo to Balaclava* (Cambridge: Cambridge University Press, 1985), p. 134.

28. Stephen E. Ambrose, *Duty, Honor, Country: A History of West Point* (Baltimore: Johns Hopkins University Press, 1966), pp. 136–37; also see James L. Morrison Jr., *"The Best School in the World": West Point, the Pre-Civil War Years, 1833–66* (Kent, OH: Kent State University Press, 1986).

29. For an attempt to label Scott thus, see Russell F. Weigley, *The American Way of War* (Bloomington: Indiana University Press, 1973, 1977 reprint), pp. 71–76; James W. Pohl, "The Influence of Antoine Henri de Jomini on Winfield Scott's Campaign in the Mexican War," *Southwestern Historical Quarterly* 77 (July 1973): 85–110, actually offers no hard evidence of "influence."

30. See Thomas L. Connelly and Archer Jones, *The Politics of Command* (Baton Rouge: Louisiana State University Press, 1973), pp. 3–26 for an attempt to explain the influence of Jomini on Civil War generalship.

31. All of these are themes of Brian Holden Reid, *J. F. C. Fuller: Military Thinker* (London: Macmillan, 1987, 1990).

32. Julius Caesar, *The Conquest of Gaul* (Harmondsworth: Penguin, 1970), VII, 5.

33. Kent Masterson Brown, *Retreat from Gettysburg: Lee, Logistics and the Pennsylvania Campaign* (Chapel Hill: University of North Carolina Press, 2005), p. 164.

34. U. S. Grant, *Personal Memoirs*, vol. 1 (London: Sampson Low, 1886), p. 85.

35. Anne C. Rose, *Victorian America and the Civil War* (Cambridge, MA: Cambridge University Press, 1992), pp. 86, 97–98, 106; Cyril Falls, *The Nature of Modern Warfare* (London: Methuen, 1941), p. 84.

36. See pp. 180–84, for a more detailed discussion.

37. Maj. Gen. J. F. C. Fuller, *The Second World War* (London: Eyre and Spottiswoode, 1947), p. 32.

38. Falls, *Nature of Modern Warfare*, p. 82.

Chapter Two

THE FIRST PHASE
APRIL 1861 TO MARCH 1862

The questions demanding answers when civil war broke out were twofold. What was the war about? How could it be brought to an end? They were easy to ask, rather more difficult to answer. Many assumed that one strategic act would be sufficient to bring the war to an end. But the federal government was totally unprepared for the challenge. During the secession crisis Congress had passed provision for the construction of seven new sloops, which would attempt to collect customs dues at sea. There had been discussion of overhauling the Militia Act of 1795. Impassioned debate focused around its allusion to powers to "disperse hostile combinations" and whether this referred to the general suppression of rebellion. A bill designed to sweep away this ambiguity was debated on a number of occasions but never allowed by secessionist sympathizers to come to the vote. This was the full extent of mobilization before April 1861. The federal government could not deter war because it had no power to do so.[1]

Efforts to increase federal military power had been hamstrung by the need to avoid giving the impression that the North would "coerce" the seceded slave states. If this was done it might provoke the secession of the upper South, Virginia, North Carolina, Arkansas, and Tennessee. Perhaps the border states, Maryland, Delaware, Kentucky, and Missouri, would follow; if the first was lost, Washington, DC, would be rendered untenable. The firing on Fort Sumter and the issue of Lincoln's Proclamation of April 15 resulted in the loss of the upper South, which refused to provide troops and assist in the coercing of their sister slave states. The loss of Virginia and Tennessee was a blow to the Union and a corresponding gain for the Confederacy, adding greatly to its viability as an independent nation-state. But preparation for war was now possible without the earlier constraints.

The gravity of the crisis highlighted the issue of what the war was actually to be fought over. All except the abolitionists and radical Republicans believed that the war was first and foremost to restore the Union. The Confederate government was to be dismantled, its armies dispersed and the Southern states brought back into the Union without any change in the existing race relations. Military action had been resorted to because American political mechanisms had broken down. The president, Abraham Lincoln, admitted that he was "naturally anti-slavery" but he hurried to qualify his belief. "Yet," he continued, "I have never understood that the presidency conferred upon me an unrestricted right to act officially on this judgment and feeling." Although Senator Charles Sumner on the morning of April 15 urged Lincoln to abolish slavery through his war powers, in his proclamation the president did not mention it. He simply reassured Americans North and South that, in undertaking military operations, "the utmost care will be observed . . . to avoid any devastation, any destruction of or interference with, property or any disturbance of peaceful citizens in any part of the country." If the Lincoln administration indicated any desire to interfere with property rights in the states, the acquiescence of the border states in their allegiance to the Union—in Kentucky's case an ambiguous declaration of "neutrality"—could be hazarded.[2]

Strategy is framed by war aims. Yet stating overall aims did not lessen the problem of how the federal government was going to restore its writ in the Southern states. It had yet to take full advantage of the great wave of popular support and enthusiasm to organize its military power. On July 22, 1861, the House of Representatives passed a resolution supporting the president's position. The Senate, three days later, resolved that the war was "not for the purpose of overthrowing or interfering with the rights of established institutions of those [seceded] states" but to preserve the Union and its laws, and it affirmed, "as soon as these objects are accomplished the war ought to cease." These were the Crittenden-Johnson Resolutions. Their sponsors, one from Kentucky and the other from Tennessee, were the voices of moderate border state and upper South Unionism. The Crittenden-Johnson Resolutions were designed as a tactical ploy to support the administration and its view of war aims. But they were dependent on early success against the Southern Confederacy. If Northern arms faltered, then calls for more severe measures would become not just strident, but persuasive. Indeed, after the failures of the first six months of the war, the House of Representatives voted by a clear Republican majority not to reaffirm its support for the resolutions.[3]

These political moves underline Clausewitz's argument that a tendency toward greater and greater levels of violence in war is dependent on the duration of a conflict and the competition of various interest groups who have different ideas of what the war is about. The longer the Civil War lasted the stronger became the case of elements in the Republican Party—generically known as "radicals"—who demanded more ambitious war aims and harsher war measures. In any case, once federal armies moved onto Southern soil and encountered runaway slaves, and they realized the extent to which the Southern war economy was dependent on slavery-based plantation agriculture, the more difficult it became to maintain limited war aims which left slavery untouched.

Radical war aims were already having an effect within a month of the outbreak of the war. Major General Benjamin F. Butler at Fortress Monroe in Virginia declared all slaves who entered his lines as "contraband of war." He justified his action on military grounds. So did Major General John C. Frémont in Missouri, who emancipated all slaves in that state on August 30, 1861, as a way of striking back at Confederate irregular forces. Lincoln was angry with Frémont because his unilateral proclamation was an infringement of the president's war powers, and it was revoked. Yet the measure had gained a significant amount of approbation. George Templeton Strong for instance, who was hardly a radical, wrote in his diary, it "looks like war in earnest, at last," but his enthusiasm was premature. Lincoln's first strategic priority was maintaining the loyalty of the border states. "To lose Kentucky," he warned, "is nearly the same as to lose the whole game." Yet this whole episode illustrated how limited war aims could only be maintained if military success was complete and came quickly.[4]

All military campaigns are the product of the political environment that spawn them. It is natural for political pressures, constraints, and irritations to shape the plans, aspirations, and hopes of commanders in the field. In 1861 that political environment was riven by doubts and anxieties. All politicians agreed only on one thing: that the war should and could be brought to an end quickly. Most agreed that this should be achieved with a minimum of force and destruction. Others were more doubtful, but still thought that punitive and rapid action would crush the Confederacy quickly. But could rapid action and complete victory be reconciled with the use of minimum force? How much was "minimum"? The Confederacy was a huge area, was such a scheme practicable? There was a contradiction lying at the heart of these debates. Lincoln would soon learn after taking office that there was an abundance of advice and no shortage of men determined to thrust their views on him, but there was a great shortage of knowledge about war.

The result was that strategic debate, or what passed for strategic debate, took two directions simultaneously and this reflected political ambivalence. During the secession crisis the general-in-chief, Winfield Scott, wrote to the secretary of state, William H. Seward, that physical conquest of the Confederacy was possible but would require an army of "300,000 disciplined men," and this would need training. "The destruction of life would be frightful—however perfect the moral discipline of the invaders." The members of Lincoln's cabinet agreed with Scott's emphasis on "moral discipline," for this reinforced a view that a way could be found to wage war without actually engaging in any fighting. Conservatives like the attorney general, Edward Bates, agreed that Scott's approach gave "the least occasion for social and servile war, in the extreme southern states, and to disturb as little as possible the accustomed conditions of the people." Hence blockade was favored as "the easiest, cheapest, and most humane method of restoring those States and developing their Confederation." He doubted whether high-spirited and highly strung Southerners had either the patience or obstinacy to withstand "the steady and persistent pressure which we can easily impose and which they have no means to resist." Should more dramatic "bold and warlike" action be required, then Bates advocated seizing ports on the margins of the Confederacy, such as New Orleans.[5]

This attitude provided the political context for the composition of the Anaconda Plan in May 1861. This document, in so far as it exists as a cogent, integral statement, was an extended version of Scott's gloomy and pessimistic advice rendered during the secession crisis. The Anaconda Plan was an attempt to develop a strategy of exhaustion on a large scale. Scott aimed "to envelop the insurgent states and bring them to terms with less bloodshed than by any other plan." The plan itself was not a coherent, conceptual document but was developed in a series of letters exchanged with Major General George B. McClellan, then commander of the Department of Ohio. It was also a rejection of oversimplified, overly ambitious sweeps on the map with which officers of McClellan's generation, who had no experience of high command, were prone to indulge themselves, aping the Napoleonic manner (P. G. T. Beauregard was another) while ignoring logistics, training, and the ability of the troops to carry out their tasks. Scott enjoyed a great advantage over commanders such as these, who were still captains playing at being generals. To think and act like a general, not like a colonel, still less a subaltern or captain, was the principal challenge facing the commanders of the American Civil War at this stage of the conflict.

Whereas McClellan advocated surging drives up the Kanawha Valley to Richmond, Scott urged the necessity of water transport. Having launched an amphibious operation himself in 1847 with the object of seizing Vera Cruz during the Mexican War, Scott immediately grasped the signal advantage of Union naval power, allowing it a projection of military force down the Mississippi, "enveloping them all (nearly) at once by a cordon of ports on the Mississippi to its mouth from its junction with the Ohio, and by blockading ships of war on the seaboard." Scott urged that "the transportation of men and all supplies by water is about the fifth of the land cost, besides the immense savings in time." In this regard, McClellan would prove a keen and attentive pupil.[6]

Scott sought nothing less than the envelopment and the strangulation of the entire Confederacy with his strategy of exhaustion. Scott may have been consumed by pomposity, old, and infirm, but his intellect was still clear and perceptive. The most impressive part of his plan was the case he advanced for the use of waterborne transport to economize on manpower, allowing more men to be concentrated at the decisive point, and to speed up military strategic movement. Yet this was to implement operations that would have a slow grand strategic effect. Social dislocation and upheaval in race relations would be minimized. There was a contradiction here because the only way that a restricted strategy could be successful was by achieving swift and decisive success at the grand strategic level. Such contradictions lay at the heart of all the limited strategies advocated in 1861–62 and were never satisfactorily resolved. They ignored slavery as a cause of the war and as a prime stimulus to the Confederate war effort. Even news of Scott's limited and cautious military move was sufficient to provoke a conspiracy among slaves to rebel in Adams County, Mississippi.[7]

The details of the plan show a measure of prescience. Scott envisaged a dozen or a score of gunboats accompanied by forty river steamers carrying materiel sufficient for eighty thousand men. The force would be divided into two, the smaller contingent aboard the river steamers, the larger "to proceed as nearly abreast as practicable by land—of course without the benefit of rail transportation—and receiving at certain points on the river its heavier articles of consumption of the first column." The huge distances constituted "a great impediment to the movement." It would nonetheless be possible to reduce or outflank all Confederate forts and strongpoints on the Mississippi. But Scott realized that the time factor might not be on his side and feared, rightly as it turned out, "the impatience of our patriotic and loyal Union friends," that might overwhelm decision makers. Furthermore, he understood the importance of good relations with Kentucky, Tennessee, and Missouri for his long, tenuous advance into the Confederate heartland. His plan was the grandest and most cogent statement of the conservative view of Union war aims.[8]

Still, the plan's essential ambiguity was not a recommendation. The onus was placed on the Confederacy to block Union moves rather than on Union power to crush Confederate resistance. The Anaconda enshrined a fallacy shared by virtually all members of the United States government and its military advisers. They assumed that the war could be brought to an end by one strategic move. Critics of the slowness (and mildness) of the Anaconda believed that Confederate surrender would follow a great, decisive victory in northern Virginia that would culminate in the fall of Richmond. Such ideas were overly optimistic yet they exhibited one important insight. The general-in-chief, Scott, was advocating a strategy that would direct Union forces away from the political heart of the Confederacy. Secession had certainly gained its momentum from the Deep South, but the Mississippi basin did not constitute the political heart of the new republic. Union strategy could not ignore the two wealthiest and industrially most advanced states, Tennessee and Virginia. More than one strategic move would thus be required to bring the Confederacy to its knees.[9]

Scott had sought to isolate military operations from political and social pressures, but these kept breaking in. Popular pressure for a move on Richmond and the great battle that would end the war quickly could not be resisted. "The idea of waiting until frost had set in, and merely defending our capital was a preposterous one in a political point of view, and our struggle is not a purely military one," wrote newspaperman Joseph Medill to Senator Lyman Trumbull on July 13, 1861. Horace Greeley's New York *Tribune* coined the phrase "On to Richmond" and the clamor grew. Greeley advanced his case with a confidence not overswayed by military knowledge. For example, he confused "tactics" with "strategy," but this was not especially unusual in 1861. Certainly, the huge geographical barriers that seemed insurmountable in the west were absent in Virginia. An advance of a mere 110 miles to the Confederate capital would bring the rebellion to an end. It would cost much concentrated toil spread over four years, and many thousands of lives, before this deceptively simple objective was attained.[10]

On June 29 President Lincoln and his cabinet met. Lincoln himself preferred an offensive strategy, so the newspaper clamor suited his purposes. The cabinet agreed that they needed a strategy that secured greater results in a shorter period of time than the Anaconda could offer. It was agreed also that the Army of the Potomac, commanded by Brigadier General Irvin McDowell who attended the meeting with Scott, would launch an attack on the Confederate forces gathered around Manassas Junction. It would slowly emerge that forces in the Virginia and Mississippi basin theaters would be complementary rather than in competition, but this required mature consideration which was not a high priority in the summer of 1861 because so few people thought the war would last. After the June 29 meeting a reporter urged on Scott the opinion that the people wanted results. Scott retorted that this was true, "but they expected successful results. War, sir, requires money, men, time, and *patience*."[11]

The challenge to Confederate strategic thinking was less onerous because the South only had to defend its independence, not use force to overcome the enemy. This was probably just as well, for the Confederate forces in Virginia were not impressive and they were incapable of offensive movement. Brigadier General Joseph E. Johnston commanded eleven thousand men in the Shenandoah Valley and Brigadier General P. G. T. Beauregard commanded fifteen thousand before Manassas Junction. There was little order, no system, and inexperience prevailed. Johnston, for example, had only commanded once in battle, when he had led four companies of *voltigeurs* at the battle of Chapultepec in 1847.[12]

Yet these deficiencies should not be allowed to conceal the strength of the Confederate strategic position. It is always easier for the power standing on the defensive to muster, organize, and control forces because they need only withstand force, not attempt to exert it. Levels of training and preparation need not be so refined because the defender needs only to react to the attacker's designs. The Confederacy's defensive position was strong. In the east the river lines provided natural, though not necessarily very strong, defensive cordons. Water lines rarely provide uncrossable defensive positions, and throughout the Civil War their defensive potential was exaggerated. In the west the rivers provided avenues of penetration for Union armies, but these could still be caught unawares, overextended and far from their bases, and defeated. The blockade declared by President Lincoln was still weak and fractured, and Southern ports remained inviolate. A "neutral" Kentucky was more of an asset to the Confederacy than if she had joined it, because the Confederate heartland was protected at virtually no cost. Furthermore, the Virginia theater could bring great political pressure to bear on the federal capital and deeply embarrass the Lincoln administration. Over the next year all of these strategic advantages save the last would be frittered away.[13]

On May 30, 1861, Major General Robert E. Lee, recently appointed military "adviser" to President Jefferson Davis, an anomalous position with no clear-cut responsibilities or executive authority, predicted that when the federal forces began their advance on Richmond, they would advance on Manassas Junction. The planning for such a campaign in Washington, DC, ran in tandem with the discussion of the Anaconda alternative. Consequently, the Union was adopting strategies of exhaustion and annihilation simultaneously. On June 3 Scott anticipated the wishes of his political masters by ordering McDowell to plan an advance on Manassas Junction. McDowell was a solemn and humorless man prone to overeating, but a competent if inexperienced commander. The expectations loaded onto McDowell's ample shoulders grew heavier as the weeks passed. He drew up a respectable plan for an advance overland toward Richmond that he wished to commence on July 8 so that he could enjoy two weeks to win a victory before the expiration of the three-month enlistments called into service by President Lincoln after Fort Sumter's surrender. McDowell intended to outflank any Confederate forces he might encounter. Central to his plan was pinning down Johnston's Confederate Army of the Shenandoah in the Shenandoah Valley, a force of about eleven thousand men. This was an important element in the Confederate defense of Virginia because this crucial state could not be held without control of the Shenandoah Valley, and at its northern end lay the federal arsenal at Harpers Ferry (although this would prove indefensible). McDowell wished to avoid any concentration of Confederate forces before Richmond.

McDowell was harassed, careworn, and overworked. He lacked a chief of staff and did not use his small staff well. The command system was not well established, its workings were chaotic and geared at the wrong level. McDowell had nobody to help him plan or direct a battle, let alone a campaign. The result was that the commanding general wasted his energies on trivia. The *Times* war correspondent, William Howard Russell, met McDowell at Union Station in Washington, DC, upon his arrival there on July 16. Russell reported that an anxious McDowell asked whether Russell had seen two batteries of missing artillery. He records in his diary:

> I was surprised to find the General engaged in such duty, and took leave to say so. "Well it is quite true, Mr. Russell; but I am obliged to look after them myself, as I have so small a staff, and they are all engaged out with my headquarters. You are aware I have advanced? No! Well you have just come in time,

and I shall be happy, indeed, to take you with me. I have made arrangements for the correspondents of our papers to take the field under certain regulations, and I have suggested to them they should wear a white uniform, to indicate the purity of their character."[14]

The irony of this last remark passed McDowell by. Not many federal generals would be so sanguine about newspapermen after a year at war.

The Confederate command system was in a similar state of disarray. General Beaureguard, commanding the Confederate forces north of Richmond (confusingly also known as the Army of the Potomac) was formal, shrewd, and capable but inclined to flamboyant gesture, extreme defensiveness, and vanity. He was highly sensitive to criticism of any kind. This last was a debilitating feature of Confederate generalship and led to a number of crippling personal feuds. The reason for this sensitivity and reluctance to take responsibility for decisions (which was shared fully by Johnston) was the pressure felt by commanders to justify reputations they had either cultivated or been awarded by the newspapers on the basis of very slender experience. Observers were obsessed with "genius." The ghost of Napoleon wafted above their heads. Governor Francis W. Pickens of South Carolina thought Beauregard "too cautious, and his very science makes him hesitate to make a dash." Pickens shared the widespread fallacy that war constituted movement without organization. Yet he made the shrewd observation that, "His [Beauregard's] Reputation is so high that he fears to risk it," though Pickens goes on in the commonplace way, "and yet he wants the confidence of perfect genius."[15]

The first battle of Manassas (Bull Run), July 21, 1861, the greatest battle fought on American soil to that date, was a traumatic and salutary experience for its participants. It serves as a representative symbol of the prevailing illusions and miscalculation enshrined in the view of conflict and soldiering held before 1861, when compared with the harsh reality of war. Marcus Cunliffe judged it as "the epitome of the variegated confusion of a century and more of American warfare."[16] It also illustrated a striking characteristic of the war at this stage. Commanders could fashion impressive and shrewd designs for battle but could not carry them out once the troops had been brought to the battlefield. Movements before the battle were more impressive than those that took place once it was joined.

The commanders' performance on both sides revealed that they found thinking out military problems in the abstract easier than actually fulfilling them. McDowell was earnest and conscientious, but did not assert himself strongly enough. He deferred to Scott and their relations hint at one of the Civil

War's thorniest problems—the structural tension between the commanding general and the army commanders. More specifically, McDowell failed to provide his troops with uniform training. Throughout the campaign McDowell failed to realize, as Kenneth P. Williams notes shrewdly, "that he had stars on his shoulders and not only maple leaves"; having only been a major two months before, McDowell found the adjustment difficult.[17]

Beauregard by comparison, although more colorful, had difficulty restraining his tactical thoughts from soaring into the operational clouds. On June 10 he dispatched to Jefferson Davis a fanciful plan whereby, once combined with Johnston, his army could sweep forward and occupy Arlington Heights and Alexandria "if not too strongly fortified and garrisoned" and thus force a federal evacuation of Virginia in order to protect Washington, DC. If Johnston evacuated the Shenandoah Valley and joined Beauregard, then he hoped to dash between "the several columns of the enemy, which I have supposed would move on three or four different lines." He dreamed of emulating Napoleon in the 1814 campaign. With thirty-five thousand men he would "annihilate 50,000 of the enemy." Neither of his schemes were based on reliable information, just supposition. Davis's considered rejection of this derivative fantasy did not discourage Beauregard, who deployed forces on the right of his position behind the Bull Run in anticipation of launching an attack, and continued to draw up extravagant plans.[18]

McDowell deployed thirty thousand men; he put four divisions into the field and retained a fifth as a reserve; the largest division, under Brigadier General Daniel Tyler, consisted of four brigades and thirteen thousand men, more than Scott had commanded in Mexico. McDowell's biggest weakness lay in cavalry. He had but one battalion available, and he attached it to the second division and did not bother to give it a distinct mission. Even such a small force should have been placed under his personal command and used to gather intelligence.

Beauregard's command received the initial designation of the Army of the Potomac and fielded seven brigades of infantry, three regiments of cavalry, and twenty-nine cannon, a total of twenty-four thousand men. He failed to organize them into divisions, though he confusingly referred to such formations when the campaign opened; dealing with so many individual commanders would prove distracting, especially as his army was strung out along a front extending eight to ten miles.[19]

Beauregard's ambitious plans had referred frequently to Johnston's Army of the Shenandoah. This force amounted to just under eleven thousand men organized into four brigades and a cavalry regiment. McDowell intended to pin

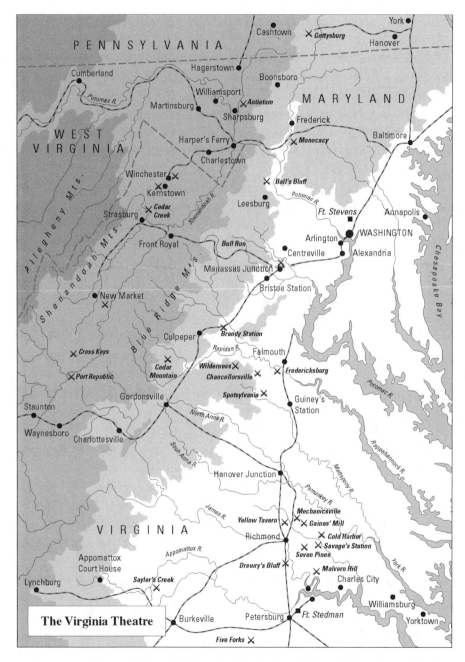

The Virginia Theatre

From Brian Holden Reid, *Robert E. Lee: Icon for a Nation*
(London: Weidenfeld & Nicolson, 2005). Map © Peter Harper.
Reprinted by permission of the Orion Publishing Group.

down Johnston's force in the Shenandoah Valley, a task entrusted to Brigadier General Robert Patterson, who was almost seventy years old, a veteran of the War of 1812, and Scott's former second-in-command in Mexico. Patterson has often been singled out as a scapegoat for federal failures in this campaign. His movements appear timorous and he consulted his subordinates too much. R. M. Johnston went so far as to declare that "A critique of Patterson's generalship belongs less to the domain of military art than to that of musical comedy." Yet many of his problems had been created by others. Blame for Patterson's caution could be laid at Scott's door because he demanded "demonstrations" while not permitting Patterson to attack. On June 16 he took away Patterson's best troops because of an undue preoccupation with the security of Washington. Patterson lacked cavalry, artillery, even a rudimentary line of supply, and had no telegraph to keep in contact with either Scott or McDowell. As he groped forward blindly, Patterson tended to exaggerate Johnston's strength. By June 28 Patterson had about fourteen thousand men available.[20]

McDowell's advance began nine days later on July 17 when three Union columns headed for Fairfax Courthouse. The progress of the march had been retarded by a fussy field order issued by McDowell the previous day that outlined no particular mission but warned against surprise attack. The troops were not used to even short marches and were soon worn out by the constant delays. On July 17 Beauregard responded to the Union action by asking Johnston to come and join him; once Johnston received orders from the Confederate war department, he prepared on the following day to move nine thousand men, shifting each regiment individually. He eventually decided to use the Manassas Gap Railroad, boarding the train at Piedmont, rather than marching, although the artillery and cavalry went by road. Colonel J. E. B. Stuart screened this move with his 1st Virginia Cavalry easily. The first units of the Army of the Shenandoah arrived at Manassas Junction at 7 AM on July 19, although most men had traveled painfully slow. Perhaps 4,500 of Johnston's troops arrived in time for the battle, sufficient to ward off disaster.[21]

Beauregard had failed to entrench along the line of the Bull Run because he persisted in thinking in terms of attack. When Johnston arrived on the morning of July 19 and conferred with Beauregard, he did not overrule the latter's vision of "a perfect Waterloo" with the two Confederate forces striking the Union flanks simultaneously. He acquiesced in this diffident course because he feared that Patterson would follow him to Manassas Junction. Confederate strength remained on the center and the right. An attack there would have been disastrous, for it would have exposed the Confederate rear just as McDowell put in a

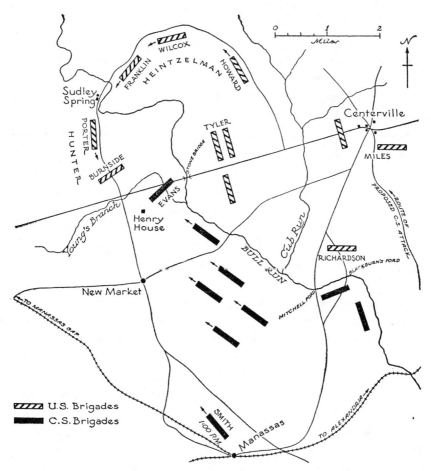

Reprinted with the permission of Scribner, an imprint of Simon &
Schuster Adult Publishing Group, from *Lincoln Finds a General:
A Military Study of the Civil War*, vol. 1, by Kenneth P. Williams.
Copyright © 1949 by Kenneth P. Williams. Copyright renewed
© 1976 by Evelyn W. Currie. All rights reserved.

strong attack on the weakly held left. Beauregard welcomed the arrival of Johnston's troops but not their commander, as the latter's seniority conferred on him command of the joint force. Beauregard's memoirs contain snide references to Johnston's low-key conduct. The chain of command was anomalous, as Johnston did not know the ground over which he was operating; but in the end, he made a respectable effort to make it work.[22]

McDowell had drawn up a good plan but it was ill served by a feeble and misleading reconnaissance carried out on July 19 by Major John G. Barnard of his staff. Barnard underestimated by two to three miles the distance to Sudley Ford, the spot Union troops needed to reach before they turned to envelop the Confederate left. He failed to find closer crossing points at Poplar Ford and at the Red House, which would have saved much time and marching. The Bull Run itself was hardly a formidable obstacle, but had steep banks covered with trees and bushes. Barnard failed to notice that the bridge over Cub Run, a tributary that flowed into Bull Run at right angles, was too narrow and weak to carry the artillery and trains. He decided against using the stone bridge that carried the Alexandria–Warrenton Turnpike from Centreville on the unverified grounds that it would be stoutly defended by the Confederates.[23]

McDowell accepted Barnard's recommendations and ordered two divisions, those of David Hunter and Samuel P. Heintzelman, to advance on the Confederate left via Sudley Ford. The troops had little sleep the previous night and thus resumed the march unrested in the summer heat. Their resources were overstrained but McDowell's plan relied on celerity, deception, surprise, and exact timing; the latter especially had been undercut by sloppy reconnaissance and a paucity of intelligence.[24]

The first battle of Manassas unfolded as a series of separate skirmishes. On both sides, the lack of any coherent tactical control of the battle tailored to any specific operational design is evident. Small units moved hither and thither and collided with one another, lacking the guidance of a directing brain. Consequently, the battle developed as a series of meeting engagements. Generals on both sides sought to win, but fumbled to do so.

McDowell intended to anchor his outflanking maneuver on his biggest division, Daniel Tyler's, which would cross the Bull Run, open an artillery bombardment, and fix the Confederates to their position. At the last minute, he held back the last of Heintzelman's brigades, that of Oliver O. Howard, keeping it in reserve in case Beauregard attacked his left flank. At about 10 AM Hunter's leading brigade, commanded by Ambrose E. Burnside, was engaged by the Confederate brigade of Nathan G. Evans. His 1,100 men and two guns were the only force covering the Confederate left; Evans had marched to engage Burnside's brigade on his own initiative. In the meantime a Confederate signal station sent an urgent message to Beauregard, "Look out for your left, you are turned."[25]

After a good start McDowell committed two errors. He spotted a cloud of dust and assumed that this force had been sent to delay Hunter and Heintzelman; he began to express doubts that the plan would work. His first mistake soon followed. He ordered Tyler to launch an attack but failed to make it clear that he should throw in his entire force. Tyler sent only two brigades forward and thus missed an opportunity to punch a hole in the Confederate line. Second, McDowell compounded the error by sending Oliver Howard's troops on a debilitating march to catch up with Heintzelman's other brigades, when they could have added considerably to Tyler's strength.

Indeed, three brigades of Johnston's troops had been sent to shore up the Confederate left. Johnston asserted himself increasingly by late morning. A good defensive fighter, at 11 AM, upon hearing a cascade of musketry from the direction of Matthews Hill on the left, he announced, "I am going there!" En route, Johnston ordered all Confederate artillery to the left. As more federal units arrived down the Sudley Springs Road, two Confederate brigades, those of Evans and Bernard Bee, were driven back to Henry House Hill.

As more federal units debouched from the Sudley Springs Road, Andrew Porter's brigade moved to the right of Burnside's spent brigade and William B. Franklin's brigade followed. Such an unintended dispersal occurred just at the time of a new Confederate concentration. At midday perhaps six thousand Confederate troops were in the vicinity of Henry House Hill; by 1:30 PM another eight thousand were en route. Johnston decided to return to his vantage point at Portici House to maintain overall control of the battlefield, and delegated tactical control of the left to Beauregard. The combination of the two commanders' staffs also gave the Confederates a slight edge over McDowell's small and overworked staff.[26]

Even so, McDowell still held several strong cards. He had four brigades on Matthews Hill by 1 PM and could, with luck, seize Manassas Junction by early evening. But the dispersal of his advancing units raised the imminent danger that the Union army might split into two wings with Confederates between them. Thus McDowell faced difficulties in bringing the climactic, crushing blow to bear, and a lot of time had already been frittered away. Tyler still could not get his guns across the Bull Run until a pontoon bridge had been completed. McDowell felt the strain of his predicament. Although he had gone to Sudley Springs, he was tired out as he had failed to get enough sleep, and he fell into a torpor, quite incapable of dynamic mental effort.[27]

The decision to attack Henry House Hill emerged almost casually. McDowell agreed with Heintzelman that it was the key to the Confederate position. He ordered two batteries to advance to the top of the hill to enfilade Confederate forces opposing Tyler and those advancing to the left. One of McDowell's staff, Lieutenant W. W. Averell urged on him the need for infantry support. "Go and give any orders you deem necessary Mr. Averell," groaned McDowell. As a result, 2,400 Union infantry and twelve guns were sent forward against four thousand Confederate infantrymen and thirteen guns. The advance was a product of no agreed plan, had not benefited from even rudimentary reconnaissance, and took a piecemeal form. The Union guns exchanged hands at least three times. Thomas J. Jackson's well-handled brigade employed enfilading fire against individual Union regiments and their fighting power was worn away, not least by a charge made by two of his regiments that unnerved Union troops. Sherman's brigade was brought up from Tyler's division, but each of his regiments went forward individually, and were all thrown back one after the other. This part of the battle lasted about two hours, but the Union repulse did not ensure a Confederate victory.[28]

McDowell had two divisions and thirty-three guns on the north side of the Bull Run. Tyler's division on the south side remained in good order with two brigades available, plus Sherman's that had not disintegrated thanks to outstanding leadership. At this juncture, Howard's brigade of Heintzelman's division caught up with their comrades. McDowell ordered him to take Chinn Ridge opposite Henry House Hill, turn the Confederate left, and roll up the entire front. Howard rushed forward, but McDowell's staff failed to arrange any support from Tyler's division. Howard was severely outnumbered (perhaps five to one) and provoked the first concentrated Confederate counterstroke of the day. Elements of the newly arrived brigades of Jubal A. Early and Kirby Smith rushed up from Manassas Junction and charged the exposed Union right. Howard's troops ran from the field.[29]

After a second repulse, a hapless McDowell announced ponderously, "Gentlemen, it seems evident that we must fall back to Centreville." Once Confederate cavalry came into action in the late afternoon, panic spread to some but by no means all of the withdrawing Union regiments. The Union high command gave the impression of being paralyzed by the reverse. It "never occurred" to Tyler to throw a screen around the stone bridge to protect the retreat. As for McDowell, when Tyler asked him what should be done, be replied frankly, "I don't know."[30]

The first battle of Manassas shattered many illusions. Not the least of these was that warfare consisted of display and heroic gesture and little else. This notion, of course, would persist. But never again would a battle be fought in an atmosphere of civilian naiveté in such a gorgeous variety of costumes. There was a strong element of fancy dress, with Zouaves on both sides, and individually attired formations such as the Confederate Black Horse Cavalry. It was almost a throwback to pre-mid-eighteenth century warfare, in which bodies of troops lacked uniformity of dress.

For the South this battle confirmed some illusions, especially the untested notion that Southerners were morally superior to their Northern kin. John S. Mosby was convinced that the federals "never once stood to a clash of the bayonet—always broke and ran." Union demoralization was almost complete. The Confederates captured twenty-eight field guns, thirty-seven caissons, and five hundred thousand rounds of ammunition. Federal casualties were 491 killed, 1,072 wounded, with about 1,460 prisoners taken. Confederate losses were in the region of two thousand (of which 387 were killed and 1,582 were wounded). The defeat at Manassas demonstrated that the war would not be won by a single, decisive battle. The North had been routed. Never again would a Northern army be so completely dislocated and driven from the battlefield after such comparatively light fighting. Yet an effective pursuit was beyond the resources of the Confederacy—the victors were as worn, confused, and ill organized as the vanquished. Tensions developed between Johnston and Beauregard as to who deserved the laurels of victory; Confederate generals were prone to such unseemly squabbling, and this would be a recurring feature of the war. In truth, the South had been lucky to win, and would have lost had it not been for the fortuitous movements of individual brigades.

As Northern confidence was uneven, oscillating between boastfulness and despair, the defeat along the Bull Run was followed by a search for scapegoats. George B. McClellan, who had occupied West Virginia in a campaign more closely resembling the prewar notions of war, with much dash and the issue of grandiloquent, Napoleonic pronouncements, was brought to Washington to retrain the army. After three months the federal government remained on the strategic defensive. The Lincoln administration wanted the battle, but its crude attempt to combine a strategy of annihilation and exhaustion had failed. Lincoln's dominance of his administration, and his success in resisting efforts to reconstruct it in favor of one pressure group or another, depended crucially on the progress of the campaign in Virginia.[31]

Another Union setback was endured in Missouri in August. This battle, Wilson's Creek, fought on August 10, resembled the defeat at Manassas. The

Union cause had prevailed in this border state. The prosperous northern and central regions, the Missouri River and the main towns (including the state capital), and railroads were all in Union hands. The Confederates had been pushed back into the poor and sparsely settled Ozark area. The great majority of Missouri citizens supported the Union or declined to support the Confederacy. Brigadier General Nathaniel Lyon, the Union commander, had moved with determination and dynamism and had not allowed the secessionist contagion to spread; the Confederate cause was a minority. Confederate sympathizers from Missouri had antagonized Jefferson Davis who considered them timorous and untrustworthy. But Lyon, like McDowell, was faced with the impending expiration of enlistments. When the Confederates undertook a desperate advance to improve their untenable logistical position, Lyon launched an impulsive attack with only four thousand men on a Confederate column three times the size. He took them completely by surprise cooking in their encampments. But an attempt to mount a flanking operation by Fritz Sigel on the Confederate left was repulsed—the first of Sigel's many defeats. Lyon's forces were driven back amid intense fighting. The ground was thick with trees and bushes and movements could be made within fifty yards of the enemy and remain invisible. Soldiers had to aim at powder clouds. A Confederate reserve of 2,700 cavalry and two thousand infantry remained intact and proved to be the vital margin for success in this battle of attrition. As at Manassas the Confederates enjoyed an advantage in numbers and this made the vital difference. Lyon was killed though his army managed to escape complete defeat. Western Missouri was open to Confederate invasion, and Union prestige received a further battering.[32]

The kind of audacious outflanking movements that Union commanders had attempted to mount in both of these battles demanded trained and experienced troops, and these had not been developed. Union leaders had discovered that however imaginative and audacious the strategy, that strategic designs and thus successful operations largely rest on efficacious tactics. And these demand, in turn, a practicable tactical plan, clear orders, a cooperation of all arms at the decisive point, and a firm operational grip and allocation of priorities; the coordination of troops on the battlefield also requires a high measure of staff training. Furthermore, in these early defeats the Confederate forces had enjoyed a numerical superiority and standing on the defensive—strategically at Manassas and tactically at Pea Ridge—the Confederate generals had not been tested in a skillful coordination of forces in the attack to anything like the same degree. The battles of Shiloh (April 1862) and Seven Pines (Fair Oaks, May 1862) would demonstrate that Southern skills were not superior in this department to their

Northern counterparts. The question of command and control was also complicated by the degree to which battles were fought in wooded areas, so that
Northern commanders at all levels could not see far and detect Southern countermoves. The pursuit, in any case, is one of the most difficult techniques to
master successfully, and Civil War generals had not yet consistently mastered
the art of maintaining a reserve.[33]

The Lincoln administration's failure to gain an early and rapid success by
launching strategies of annihilation and exhaustion simultaneously before it had
the resources to sustain them, resulted in a prolonged period of political controversy and fervent debate as to the future direction of military policy. Much of
the denunciation and complaint revolved around the failure to achieve a rapid
victory, which is the underlying idée fixe of this debate. Generals had to promise
an immediate victory to attain political support, and then were criticized when
they failed to win it. Given the fevered atmosphere of the time, the result of so
much "treachery" during the secession crisis and the last days of the Buchanan
administration, agitated minds found only one reason for Northern failures—
"treason." In July 1861 the Potter Committee began its investigation of treason
in the US government. This committee rode roughshod over the civil rights of
its witnesses. Republican Senator Benjamin F. Wade published a tract, *Traitors
and Their Sympathizers* (1861). Washington, DC, in the summer of 1861 hardly
provided a relaxed, detached atmosphere during which a calm reassessment of
Northern strategic priorities could be made, but then this was never likely.[34]

George B. McClellan was fêted because it was believed that he was the
"young Napoleon" who would deliver the great, cataclysmic and *decisive* victory
that would bring the war to an end. Yet there were elements in McClellan's
character that made this virtually impossible. He has become the most controversial of all federal generals. McClellan was young by prevailing standards,
thirty-four and a half years old in 1861 (though more than eight years older than
Napoleon when he was called to field command). He was a man of considerable
intellectual acumen, well read, and cultivated, but he was smug and conceited,
and could not throw off the conviction that he, and he alone, could save the
Union. McClellan recognized at once that if he won a "decisive battle" his political prospects were assured. Thoughts of the presidential nomination were never
far from his mind over the course of the next year. Apart from a few skirmishes
in West Virginia, the success of which he owed to his subordinates, McClellan
was completely inexperienced in field command. When tested, his character
revealed a number of grave flaws. These included a tendency to refuse to accept
responsibility and blame everybody (especially his political masters) except him-

self. He did not inspire trust and was incapable of dynamic effort even when all the cards were in his hand. More than anything else he was prone to self-serving delusion. "The inability to see things as they were," writes T. Harry Williams, "is the key to the whole McClellan problem."[35]

McClellan should not, however, be wrenched out of the context of his time. His caution and reluctance to unleash punitive war on the South was shared by many soldiers of the "old" army, who recoiled before the blood-tingling rhetoric of the radical Republicans. The beginning of the war exhibited a certain cleavage between some politicians who were determined to destroy the Confederacy (without a full understanding of the cost involved) and professional military men, who had a bare idea of the war's cost but who at this date had little stomach for the fight. Major General Ethan Allan Hitchcock, who was later to advise the secretary of war, Edwin M. Stanton, wrote, "Many friends urge my return to the Army. But I have no heart for engaging in a Civil War. . . . If fighting could preserve the Union (or restore it) I might consider what I could do to take part—but when did fighting make friends?" William T. Sherman remarked disapprovingly during the secession crisis that "Civilians are far more willing to start a war than military men and so it appears now." He later deplored calls to shoot the generals responsible for the defeat at Manassas.[36]

Although steadfastly in favor of restoring the Union, McClellan expressed similar hesitant views. But McClellan's first task lay not in the sphere of strategy but in training and organizing his army, a task that even his severest critics have agreed he was accomplished at. It was a pity that the chaotic system of command did not permit him to develop these skills rather than be tempted into field command for which he was temperamentally unsuited. With further training and experience, and an urgent recognition of the need for humility on his part, he would have made a fine chief of the general staff. However, no opportunities were possible for him to develop his potential as a staff officer at a high level. This was partly McClellan's own fault because of his tactless behavior, especially in consorting with critics of the Lincoln administration, but mainly because of the obsession of contemporaries with field command as the true province of a general's "genius." McClellan's critics insisted on judging him solely as commander of the Army of the Potomac. He was discredited in this role because of his caution, inactivity, and political obsession. In civilian eyes it was the army commander that counted; and most contemporaries failed to give him credit for his organizational achievements, and while he was general-in-chief, for successes on other fronts.[37]

It is, however, a valid criticism of McClellan that his views on field strategy— or what is now termed "military strategy," that is applicable to a particular theater of operations—only emerged obliquely. Again, this development was the result of a combination of McClellan's errors and institutional weaknesses. In November 1861, after an intrigue, McClellan succeeded in ousting the aged Scott as general-in-chief. The need for a fresh mind and youthful vigor was self-evident after the initial failures, but Scott did not go without a tussle. Scott preferred that he be succeeded by Major General Henry W. Halleck, who was currently commanding in the west. It would have been better to keep field and superior command separate, but McClellan felt that he could only achieve a rational control of operations in Virginia if he could control all other theaters as well. Lincoln thus nominated the ambitious general to the dual role of general-in-chief and commander of the Army of the Potomac. But the two were not synonymous. The respective roles of the two positions were not clearly delineated. Combining them only added to the muddle and failure to think through strategic priorities.[38]

The position was greatly complicated by a minor action fought in October south of Washington, DC, at Ball's Bluff, just before McClellan's elevation. A small Union force commanded by Colonel Edward D. Baker, a serving senator from Oregon and friend of the president, was defeated and driven from the field. Several hundred Union troops were in such a panic-stricken state that they drowned in the Potomac River. Baker himself was killed. He had already denounced the policy of inaction in the Senate and wished to see more vigor introduced into Union operations. He was the embodiment of pre-1861 illusions about war. T. Harry Williams writes of him: "He was a romantic character in the best nineteenth century tradition, capable of quoting poetry in the heat of battle and telling others to follow when they saw his plume shining. He knew almost nothing about how to direct men in battle." The defeat at Ball's Bluff began a prolonged political controversy in Washington with important strategic ramifications.[39]

The main source of the dissatisfaction provoked by Ball's Bluff was McClellan's sluggishness. He had done nothing since taking command in July except drill his troops, hold parades with sumptuous entertainments, and issue bulletins beginning "All Quiet on the Potomac." The Confederates held the hills just on the other side of the Potomac, which were clearly visible from Capitol Hill, and many senators considered this an affront to federal authority. "Champagne and oysters on the Potomac must stop," they intoned. McClellan claimed that Virginia roads were inadequate to sustain a major advance; skeptical critics replied that the weather was fine and the roads hard. Some kind of effort was required to drive the rebels from the capital's environs; Baker had tried and failed. The death of one of their own number agitated the imagination of those senators who believed that treason underlay the early Union failures.

The result was the formation in December 1861 of the Congressional Joint Committee on the Conduct of the War. This was designed as "the committee of inquiry into the general conduct of the war." Senator Henry Wilson went further and issued a warning that it "should teach men in civil and in military authority that the people expect they will not make mistakes, and that we shall not be easy with their errors." Its membership was drawn from both the Senate and House of Representatives and was chaired by Senator Benjamin F. Wade from Ohio. True to its word, Ball's Bluff was investigated and Wade identified the culprit for the defeat—Brigadier General Charles P. Stone, who was proslavery, had been rash enough to challenge Charles Sumner to a duel, and was a friend of McClellan. This "slimy traitor" was immediately imprisoned without trial at the behest of the secretary of war, Edwin M. Stanton, who had succeeded Simon Cameron in January 1862.[40]

The Joint Committee's main target in this draconian, much-criticized action was McClellan. (Although it is often overlooked how the committee was only acting on the precedents set by the Potter Committee.) Not only had McClellan made no move into Virginia, but the main outlines of his strategy were unclear. Shortly after arriving in Washington he had indeed composed an able memorandum surveying the war, emphasizing the importance of railways and amphibious operations, arguing that Virginia was the decisive theater, and that "overwhelming strength" should be concentrated to "crush the rebellion at one blow" and "terminate the war in one campaign." McClellan was clearly playing on the preconceptions of his political masters, including Lincoln. But the force he asked for was too large (273,000 men), and by December he still had produced no substantial, persuasive, reassuring strategic design.[41]

As presented in his posthumously published account, *McClellan's Own Story* (1887), the general appeared to be a rational, moderate patriot, with sensible, attainable objectives that were confounded by ignorant, hysterical, selfish, and demagogic politicians, including the president. McClellan appeared content to restrict the Confederacy to its present size of eleven states (thirteen if Missouri and Kentucky were included; Missouri and Kentucky were given seats in the Confederate Congress and stars on the Confederate flag, but Maryland had neither) and prove that it was not viable as a nation-state. But there were a number of weaknesses in his approach to his duties. On McClellan's taking overall command, Lincoln had advised him "to enlarge the sphere of his thoughts and feel the weight of the occasion." The confused command system made this difficult in any case, but the deficiency was aggravated by McClellan's faith that he could "do it all." McClellan could not, and he tried to do too much. Command was administratively overcentralized while remaining decentralized in the field because McClellan could not be everywhere. Thus he failed to advise and communicate; but above all, worn down by the burdens of administration, he failed to reassure.[42]

It was as well for McClellan that his critics had no practicable, alternative strategy. Their nostrums were a series of rationalized prejudices. They were essentially stirred by faith in the moral forces unleashed by war with armies "sweeping" this way and that, carrying out a "vigorous" policy. This romantic vision of Napoleonic marches with perpetual movement and cataclysmic action was a carryover from pre-1861 notions with one difference: the radical Republicans on the Joint Committee sought the utter extirpation of plantation slavery. Their military views were thus contradictory, demanding a punitive strategy but spurning industrialized, highly organized military methods. Democrat generals were automatically suspect in their eyes because they tended to promote cautious strategies. They placed great stress during the committee's hearings on "bases of operation," methodical sieges, "lines of communication," and even more suspect, "lines of retreat." As far as Wade and his colleagues were concerned, this was just arcane jargon designed to conceal sheer cowardice and worse, treachery. By January 1861 all committee members (including the Democrats) were convinced that McClellan was a traitorous dog who slipped over the Potomac at night to confer with Jefferson Davis.[43]

Such slanderous accusations were a measure of McClellan's enormous problems. Yet he conducted himself in such a way as to make them worse and undermine his credibility. His critics' only real proposal was that he should repeat the battle of Manassas, this time successfully, and make a strategic direct approach across northern Virginia taking Richmond, simultaneously covering Washington, DC, from attack. This was hardly a subtle or novel idea and it had failed before. Yet McClellan committed the elementary but astounding blunder of not ensuring that he kept a tight hold on the president's esteem. On the contrary, he refused to take him into his confidence on the most specious grounds. Exhausted by overwork, McClellan succumbed to typhoid over Christmas 1861 and was confined to bed for three weeks. Without the flywheel the whole engine ground to a halt. Lincoln, bereft of military advice, subject to the continual harassment from members of the Joint Committee (who fed him rumors about McClellan's disloyalty), was reduced to despair at his inability to make the military machine do anything. He turned to the quartermaster general, Major General Montgomery C. Meigs, and bewailed, "The bottom is out of the tub."[44]

At a loss, facing a hurricane of political dissatisfaction, Lincoln accepted

Meigs's suggestion and convened a "council of war" to give him advice. McClellan naturally judged this a slight on his conduct of affairs and struggled from his sickbed to attend. He still refused to reveal his plans on the grounds of operational secrecy, despite Meigs urging that he do something to propitiate his political masters. This did not prevent him later from giving a reporter of the Democrat *New York Herald* a full briefing. McClellan had conceded that an advance would be made in Kentucky as soon as possible. With this assurance the meeting broke up; but McClellan had done nothing to shore up his crumbling political position. The president was still inclined to give him the benefit of the doubt but the full force of the accusations made about McClellan, because of their remorseless repetition, could hardly leave him unscathed. "The war had dragged its slow length along under generals who never meant to *fight*," alleged Senator Zachariah Chandler of Michigan, another radical Republican member of the Joint Committee.[45]

It was only after his credibility had been impaired that McClellan turned to the urgent duty of codifying and expounding his strategic ideas. The president issued a series of war orders requiring an advance on certain dates. McClellan at least responded to War Order No. 1 of January 31. On February 3 he drew up a lengthy memorandum for Secretary Stanton showing how he intended to achieve "combined and decisive operations." McClellan's exposition elaborated a strategy of annihilation that would, curiously, avoid battle. He preferred to avoid the unnecessary casualties that would inevitably result from a drive across northern Virginia, and preferred to utilize seapower to the full by transferring the army across Chesapeake Bay to a new "base of operations," Urbana. This offered the shortest direct route to Richmond, up the Peninsula to the east of the city, "and strikes directly at the heart of the enemy's power in the East." McClellan's flanks would be protected by the sea and his lines of communication would be inviolate. McClellan intended to remain on the tactical defensive and force the Confederates to attack him. "We demoralize the enemy, by forcing him to abandon his prepared position for one we have chosen," he argued, "in which all is in our favor, where success must produce immense results." In short, during his strategic offensive, McClellan intended to seize centers of great value to the Confederates, fortify them, deploy heavy artillery, and let themselves batter their forces to destruction against his positions.[46]

McClellan had shown himself to be the one general that could think out a subtle plan that revealed a measure of insight and could find a military strategic means to implement it. Yet he had played his political cards badly. He did not inspire trust and it appeared less and less likely that his plan would be accepted, mainly because he advocated it. Such discussion would not be based primarily on the plan's military merits, which were numerous. Many historians have been impressed by McClellan's plan. It showed discernment and breadth of vision. If command of the sea gave Union armies a flexibility and mobility denied to the Confederates, attacks could be launched to control their lines of communication, notably on the railroads running east from the Mississippi valley—Memphis via Chattanooga to Knoxville, and from Vicksburg via Atlanta to Charleston—and the lines running along the east coast. When these arteries were cut Confederate armies could no longer be supplied and they would either disperse or launch suicidal attacks on federal positions. Rowena Reed praises this "comprehensive plan." It aimed to mount concentric, economical offensives against the Southern rimlands, the most important of which was the advance on Richmond. After the Confederate capital had fallen, "all Virginia would be in our power; and the enemy forced to abandon Tennessee and North Carolina."[47]

The president still preferred an overland advance toward Richmond. McClellan tried to appease him by calling a council of war of all the divisional commanders of the Army of the Potomac to discuss future strategy on March 8, 1862; the president agreed to this and then allowed the plan to proceed when the commanders voted eight to four in its favor. McClellan had shown some adroitness in turning the device of a conciliar meeting against the president (most of the divisional commanders were his protégés). The whole episode is redolent of their deteriorating relations. Indeed, the president had no viable alternative to offer as a substitute for McClellan's strategy. "We can't reject it [McClellan's plan]," he admitted to Stanton, "and adopt another without assuming all the responsibility in the case of the failure of the one we adopt." Yet Lincoln did not trust McClellan. He was called to the White House the following day to discuss an "ugly matter." Lincoln was fearful that McClellan's advance would expose Washington, DC, to a Confederate riposte. He had heard rumors that McClellan would deliberately expose the capital, and "that it did look to him much like treason." Lincoln withdrew the remark when McClellan demanded an apology. The true significance of this episode lay in indicating McClellan's weak political position. The general's Peninsular campaign was a great gamble; only a striking success would restore his prestige. Indicating the administration's loss of confidence in McClellan, before he set out on campaign Lincoln relieved him of the position of general-in-chief.[48]

As McClellan planned to embark his troops the war was almost a year old. McClellan believed that he was about to launch the campaign that would bring the war to an end. One great battle had been fought in the east, and a smaller one in Missouri, but the intensity of military operations had not yet been great. Strategically, the Lincoln administration had struggled to impose its will on the forces of time and space that had so far operated in the Confederacy's favor. The idée fixe that the war would be short and decisive also worked in favor of the South because it was easier for the power standing on the defensive to organize its forces to resist an incursion than it was for the attacker to mount one. This was especially so when the forces available were so inexperienced and untrained. Through a combination of political pressure and opportunism the Lincoln administration had simultaneously employed strategies of annihilation and exhaustion, and had failed at both. The result was an impassioned strategic debate which had generated rather more hysteria than understanding. Yet by the spring of 1862 Union fortunes were improving. Nonetheless it was as well for the Union that the Confederacy was no more agreed as to its strategic priorities than the North. It is the Union successes beyond Virginia that must now take center stage.

NOTES AND REFERENCES

1. Kenneth M. Stampp, *And the War Came: The North and the Secession Crisis, 1860–1861* (Baton Rouge: Louisiana State University Press, 1950), pp. 115–18.

2. Lincoln, "By the President of the United States, A Proclamation," Apr. 15, 1861, original draft, Robert Todd Lincoln Collection of the Papers of Abraham Lincoln, Library of Congress, Washington, DC; James M. McPherson, *Abraham Lincoln and the Second American Revolution* (New York: Oxford University Press, 1991), p. 128; David Donald, *Charles Sumner and the Coming of the Civil War* (New York: Alfred A. Knopf, 1965), p. 388.

3. Hans L. Trefousse, *Andrew Johnson: A Biography* (New York: Norton, 1989), p. 144; Peter J. Parish, *The American Civil War* (London: Eyre Methuen, 1975), p. 206.

4. B. F. Butler, *Butler's Book* (Boston: Thayer, 1892), p. 258; Butler's measures are discussed in more detail in the next chapter; Allan Nevins, *The War for the Union* (New York: Scribner's, 1959), vol. 1, p. 322; *The Diary of George Templeton Strong*, eds. Allan Nevins and Milton H. Thomas (New York: Macmillan, 1952), vol. 3, p. 178 (entry for Sep. 2, 1861); Stephen E. Woodworth, "'The Indeterminate Quantities': Jefferson Davis, Leonidas Polk, and the End of Kentucky Neutrality," *Civil War History* 38 (December 1992): 289.

5. Edward Bates, memo in cabinet, Apr. 15, 1861, Lincoln papers.

6. McClellan to Scott, Apr. 27, 1861, with an annotation by Scott, May 2, 1861, *War of the Rebellion: The Official Records of the Union and Confederate Armies* (Washington, DC: Government Printing Office, 1897) [hereafter *O.R.*], series 1, vol. 51, part 1, pp. 338–39.

7. Brian Holden Reid, "Rationality and Irrationality in Union Strategy, April 1861–March 1862," *War in History* 1 (March 1994): 26; Winthrop D. Jordan, *Tumult and Silence at Second Creek* (Baton Rouge: Louisiana State University Press, 1993), pp. 116, 217, 225, 234–35.

8. Brian Holden Reid, "The Grip of the Anaconda Plan," *British-American* 5 (Winter 1993): 16.

9. Holden Reid, "Rationality and Irrationality in Union Strategy," pp. 27–28.

10. T. Harry Williams, *Lincoln and the Radicals* (Madison: University of Wisconsin, 1941, 1965), p. 28; Glyndon G. Van Deusen, *Horace Greeley: Nineteenth Century Crusader* (Philadelphia: University of Pennsylvania Press, 1953), pp. 275–78.

11. David Detzer, *Donnybrook: The Battle of Bull Run, 1861* (Orlando, FL: Harcourt, 2004), pp. 67, 76–77.

12. Craig L. Symonds, *Joseph E. Johnston* (New York: Norton, 1992), p. 101.

13. R. M. Johnston, *Bull Run: Its Strategy and Tactics* (1913; Carlisle, PA: Kallmann, 1996), p. 12.

14. McDowell's operational staff (G3 in today's military usage) consisted of a chief of artillery and four aides-de-camp who served primarily as couriers. See Kenneth P. Williams, *Lincoln Finds a General* (New York: Macmillan 1949), vol. 1, p. 67; Detzer, *Donnybrook*, p. 74; W. H. Russell, *My Diary North and South*, ed. Eugene H. Berwanger (New York: Alfred A. Knopf, 1988), p. 250.

15. Symonds, *Johnston*, pp. 108–109, 127; Brian Holden Reid, "First Blood to the South: Bull Run, 1861," *History Today* 42 (March 1992): 22–23.

16. Marcus Cunliffe, *Soldiers and Civilians: The Martial Spirit in America, 1775–1865*, 3rd ed. with a new introduction by Brian Holden Reid (London: Gregg, 1993), pp. 3–27.

17. Detzer, *Donnybrook*, p. 75; Johnston, *Bull Run*, p. 62; Williams, *Lincoln Finds a General*, vol. 1, pp. 68–92.

18. Douglas Southall Freeman, *Lee's Lieutenants*, 3 vols. (New York: Scribner's, 1943), vol. 1, pp. 40–43.

19. Williams, *Lincoln Finds a General*, vol. 1, p. 86; Johnston, *Bull Run*, pp. 161, 163, 176.

20. Johnston's indictment is in *Bull Run*, p. 74; for a defense see Detzer, *Donnybrook*, pp. 57–58, 97, 101, 107, and Williams, *Lincoln Finds a General*, vol. 1, pp. 70, 74–75, 81–82.

21. William C. Davis, *Battle at Bull Run* (New York: Doubleday, 1977), pp. 132–39.

22. Detzer, *Donnybrook*, p. 216; Alfred Roman, *The Military Operations of General Beauregard*, 2 vols. (New York: Harper, 1884), vol. 1, p. 104, even claims disingenuously that Beauregard "had planned the battle" as well as enjoyed a knowledge of the ground.

23. Davis, *Battle at Bull Run*, p. 156; Detzer, *Donnybrook*, pp. 186–94; Williams, *Lincoln Finds a General*, vol. 1, p. 186; Johnston, *Bull Run*, p. 184.

24. Williams, *Lincoln Finds a General*, vol. 1, p. 165; Detzer, *Donnybrook*, p. 226.

25. Williams, *Lincoln Finds a General*, vol. 1, p. 93; Johnston, *Bull Run*, pp. 180–81, Detzer, *Donnybrook*, p. 243.

26. Johnston, *Bull Run*, pp. 178–79; Detzer, *Donnybrook*, pp. 327–28, 335.

27. Johnston, *Bull Run*, pp. 211–12.

28. Jackson's actions later acquired great symbolic importance in Confederate folklore and thus propaganda. On the acquisition of the "most famous nickname" in American history, see James I. Robertson Jr., *Stonewall Jackson: The Man, the Soldier, the Legend* (New York: Macmillan, 1997), pp. 264–68.

29. Colonel G. F. R. Henderson's account of the final stages of the battle still has much to commend it; see *Stonewall Jackson*, 2 vols. (London: Longmans Green, 1898), vol. 1, pp. 150–54.

30. Johnston, *Bull Run*, p. 234; Detzer, *Donnybrook*, pp. 388–89, 398–99, 406, 420–22.

31. Davis, *Battle at Bull Run*, pp. 236–42; for the aftermath see Holden Reid, "First Blood to the South," p. 26; Symonds, *Johnston*, pp. 123–24; T. Harry Williams, *P. G. T. Beauregard: Napoleon in Gray* (Baton Rouge: Louisiana State University Press, 1955, 1989), pp. 90–91; Johnston, *Bull Run*, pp. 254, 260.

32. Christopher Phillips, *Damned Yankee: The Life of General Nathaniel Lyon* (Columbia: University of Missouri Press, 1980); Albert Castel, *General Sterling Price and the Civil War in the West* (Baton Rouge: Louisiana State University Press, 1968, 1993), pp. 27, 31; the most detailed study is William Garrett Piston and Richard W. Hatcher III, *Wilson's Creek* (Chapel Hill: University of North Carolina Press, 2000).

33. P. Griffith, *Rally Once Again: Battle Tactics of the American Civil War* (Ramsbury, UK: Crowood Press, 1987), pp. 62–63, 70.

34. Hans L. Trefousse, *Benjamin Franklin Wade: Radical Republican from Ohio* (New York: Twayne, 1963), p. 186; Allan G. Bogue, *The Congressman's Civil War* (New York: Cambridge University Press, 1989), pp. 74–75.

35. Stephen Sears, *George B. McClellan: The Young Napoleon* (New York: Ticknor and Fields, 1988), pp. 90–93, 106–108; T. Harry Williams, *McClellan, Sherman, and Grant* (New Brunswick, NJ: Rutgers University, 1962), pp. 24–25; see also Thomas J. Rowland, "In the Shadows of Grant and Sherman: George B. McClellan Revisited," *Civil War History* 40 (September 1994): 202–25, and idem., *George B. McClellan and Civil War History* (Kent, OH: Kent State University Press, 1998), who scores some debating points but does not convince because Grant and Sherman overcame their psychological difficulties to score success in the field of a high order; this McClellan could not do.

36. E. A. Hitchcock, *Fifty Years in Camp and Field*, ed. W. A. Croffat (New York: Putnam's, 1909), p. 430; Lloyd Lewis, *Sherman: Fighting Prophet* (New York: Harcourt Brace, 1929, 1958), p. 142.

37. Williams, *McClellan, Sherman, and Grant*, p. 23; Brian Holden Reid, "General McClellan and the Politicians," *Parameters* 17 (September 1987): 108; Rowland, "McClellan Revisited," p. 214.

38. T. Harry Williams, *Lincoln and His Generals* (New York: Alfred A. Knopf, 1952), pp. 42–43.

39. Kim B. Holien, *Battle at Ball's Bluff: Leesburg, Virginia, October 21, 1861* (Mechanicsville, VA: Rapidan Press, 1985); T. Harry Williams, "Investigation: 1862," *American Heritage* 6, no. 6 (December 1954): 16–21; Philip S. Paludan, *The Presidency of Abraham Lincoln* (Lawrence: University Press of Kansas, 1994), p. 97. Lincoln's second son, Edward, was named after him.

40. Brian Holden Reid, "Historians and the Joint Committee on the Conduct of the War," *Civil War History* 38 (December 1992): 319–20; Richard B. Irwin, "Bull's Bluff and the Arrest of General Stone," *Battles and Leaders of the Civil War*, eds. Robert U. Johnson and Clarence C. Buel (New York: Century, 1884–88), vol. 2, pp. 131–35; Benjamin P. Thomas and Harold H. Hyman, *Stanton: The Life and Times of Lincoln's Secretary of War* (New York: Alfred A. Knopf, 1962), pp. 260–62; Bruce Tap, *Over Lincoln's Shoulder: The Committee on the Conduct of the War* (Lawrence: University Press of Kansas, 1998), pp. 21–24, 67–78.

41. See Holden Reid, "Historians and the Joint Committee on the Conduct of the War," p. 335; Tap, *Over Lincoln's Shoulder*, pp. 75–79, 106–109.

42. McClellan to Lincoln, Aug. 2, 1861, *The Civil War Papers of George B. McClellan; Selected Correspondence, 1860–1865*, ed. Stephen W. Sears, 71–75 (New York: Ticknor and Fields, 1989); Williams, *Lincoln and His Generals*, pp. 29–31.

43. George W. Julian, *Political Recollections, 1840–1872* (Chicago: Jansen McClurg, 1884), p. 205; Holden Reid, "General McClellan and the Politicians," p. 107. Democrat member Senator Andrew Johnson was keen to convince himself of McClellan's treachery because he and McClellan were rivals for the 1864 presidential nomination. Trefousse, *Andrew Johnson*, p. 149.

44. Sears, *McClellan*, pp. 136–37, 138–42; Williams, *Lincoln and His Generals*, pp. 53–55; Montgomery C. Meigs, "General M. C. Meigs on the Conduct of the Civil War," *American Historical Review* 26 (1921): 292–94.

45. Williams, *Lincoln and His Generals*, pp. 56–57; Sears, *McClellan*, pp. 138–43; Holden Reid, "McClellan and the Politicians," p. 106.

46. McClellan to Stanton, Feb. 3, 1862, in McClellan, *Civil War Papers*, pp. 163–65, 166–67.

47. Russell F. Weigley, *The American Way of War* (New York: Macmillan, 1973), pp. 133–35; Rowena Reed, *Combined Operations in the Civil War* (Lincoln: University of Nebraska Press, 1978, 1993 paperback), pp. 34–36, 38, 43. Reed exaggerates McClellan's consistency. See Holden Reid, "Rationality and Irrationality in Union Strategy," p. 35. Reed's arguments are dealt with in more detail in the next chapter.

48. Williams, *Lincoln and His Generals*, p. 67; Holden Reid, "McClellan and the Politicians," p. 107; for more detail on McClellan's weakening position, see idem., "Rationality and Irrationality in Union Strategy," pp. 35–37.

WAR ON THE MARGINS
SEPTEMBER 1861 TO JUNE 1862

T he first battle of Manassas had permitted the Confederacy to survive but its existence remained precarious. The choking embrace of Union power could never be pushed away from its throat. The Confederacy's greatest ally during the war's first year could be found not among European powers, but in the extent of its sprawling geography. It would take a great physical effort to subjugate the South by bringing the necessary force to bear at the decisive points. A fallacy dogged both sides in the early phases of the war, namely, that armies could be raised within days by bringing together a crowd of men; by virtue of their enthusiasm, pride in their democratic institutions and patriotic zeal, American soldiers could triumph over all obstacles. Such a view represented a perversion of the Napoleonic experience, but the temptation to seek a quick victory would lead to a succession of poorly conceived and ill-organized campaigns, especially on the Confederate side.

Contrary to later impressions, despite the depressed mood in Washington, these months actually experienced a long run of Union victories, including actions in the far west, and a series of successful amphibious operations along the

Southern coastline. These successes on the margins of decisive theaters were *not* due to any significant material or numerical superiority, but better planning and a more methodical approach to supplying armies. Even more significant would be Northern seapower. The federal command of the sea would prove to be one of the most significant foundation stones of the eventual Union victory. Seapower is the basis of strategic mobility, even in operations fought far from the sea.[1] It allows belligerents not only to move their forces over great distances but attain their strategic objectives with greater ease and assurance, particularly if these advantages are simultaneously denied to the enemy.

The Union's ability to blockade the Southern ports, although fitful at first, enabled it gradually to isolate the Confederacy from outside succor and extend control over the numerous great river estuaries opening into the Atlantic Ocean and the Gulf of Mexico. Growing naval strength thus conferred on comparatively small Union forces a tactical edge. Not only did it restrict the Confederacy's ability to equip its forces, but it allowed the Union command to exploit Confederate organizational weaknesses and support expeditions with unmatched weight of firepower. As a result the Confederate heartland, seemingly invulnerable in the spring of 1861, fell prey to invasion, penetration, and occupation only a year later.

Union forces still received a check. The process began in miniature, in a region far away from the power of the federal navy, in the Shenandoah Valley in western Virginia. A Confederate commander, Thomas J. "Stonewall" Jackson, showed clearly that it was possible for Southern forces to defeat Northern troops as they seemed to be marching inexorably toward a crushing victory in 1862. Jackson learned the importance of logistical calculation, local knowledge, and good intelligence. He grasped that a viable and cohesive force could be created by stern discipline, hard marching, and buoyant morale based on a record of success. During these months, superior organization proved to be the key to prospects of Confederate victory rather than reliance on a hazy romantic zeal, wishful attachment to the Spirit of '76, or a list of distinguished Virginians. Dreams of glory led only to reckless gambles and staggering defeats.

In the autumn of 1861 a force of Texans attempted to annex Arizona and New Mexico for the Confederacy. In this instance, the great North American spaces worked against, rather than for, the Confederacy. Texas had nursed a claim to eastern New Mexico since the days of its independence from Mexico.[2] Southerners motivated by the dream of an "imperial Confederacy" could advance two persuasive strategic arguments. First, an advance westward would secure the Confederate western and southern flank; it offered the potential to acquire parts of the Pacific coast and thus stretch federal resources or even break the Union blockade. Second, the raw materials of the western territories could fertilize Southern commerce and thus its war economy.[3]

In June 1861 Brigadier General Henry H. Sibley, who saw himself as the conqueror of the west, received orders to drive federal troops from New Mexico, "securing all the arms, supplies and materials of war," and to establish a military government there. These orders granted Sibley a great deal of latitude. On August 1 John R. Baylor, a violent former Texas Indian agent and future governor of Arizona, declared martial law and claimed Arizona for the Confederate States below 36°30" to the north of the Colorado River (an area including New Mexico). The Union commander of the Department of New Mexico, Colonel Edward R. S. Canby, was a careful and serious-minded man who possessed sober judgment. He had a number of regular units at his disposal, although after some had been siphoned off to the east, he supplemented them with Colorado and New Mexico volunteers.

The operations that took place over the inhospitable terrain of the west took the form of small-scale skirmishes involving on both sides numbers of horsemen, mostly mounted infantry. They used the methods of Indian fighting, darting behind rocks and trees so that it was difficult to see friend or foe. The regiments of Texas Mounted Rifles especially prided themselves on being representatives of the frontier fighting tradition. Every man provided his own horse and weapons and dress was casual and civilian. Such men were largely untrained and resentful of the slightest discipline; they became easily bored and regarded themselves as "warriors" rather than a cohesive, disciplined body. They sometimes described themselves as resembling "excited schoolboys" and in military terms that was exactly what they were.[4]

The initial Confederate force of three hundred men led by Baylor set off from Fort Bliss near Franklin, Texas, and advanced into Arizona intent on capturing Fort Craig, the lynchpin of the Union defenses. Baylor became distracted by Apache raids and turned his attention to extirpating what he regarded as a loathsome tribe. Baylor wanted to get into the field before Sibley arrived and took command. He believed that the Confederacy should develop two thrusts: his own with a thousand men would advance on Tucson, Arizona, and eventually on Sonora and California. Sibley should advance up the Mesilla Valley and occupy New Mexico. When Sibley arrived in San Antonio in July he attempted to bring some order and logistical planning to the bedraggled elements he found.[5]

The problems that Sibley faced had previously been overcome during the thousand-mile march undertaken by Colonel Alexander W. Doniphan in

1846–47, though he took the opposite direction. Doniphan had attempted to penetrate large stretches of Mexican territory before its systematic defense could be organized. Baylor and Sibley faced the same challenge, but their enemy was better posted and equipped than the Mexicans. The main significance of Baylor's movements was that he proved incapable of defeating Canby's 2,500 men at Fort Craig. Time was not on Sibley's side.[6]

Sibley's brigade-sized force of 2,500 men, grandly styled The Army of New Mexico, took the field in February 1862. He intended to take Fort Craig and then occupy Albuquerque and Santa Fe in New Mexico. Sibley was quickly forced to break his force up into mobile columns because the horses suffered from a lack of water and the men had to be put on half rations. As a commander, Sibley proved no advance on Baylor because of his poor health. He endured kidney stones but he unwisely attempted to relieve the pain with copious quantities of alcohol that only made the condition worse. He had to hand over command to his subordinates at crucial moments.[7]

Sibley found Fort Craig too strong, so on February 19 he decided to mask it and move along the high ground to the north and west, and head for the Val Verde fords across the Rio Grande. Canby sallied out and pursued Sibley's column while remaining on the Rio Grande's left bank. As federals crossed the river to seize the fords, the Confederates attacked in a series of disjointed and piecemeal moves. Canby made considerable progress in developing a double envelopment when an impulsive Confederate assault drove in his center and forced him to withdraw. The Texans celebrated their lucky victory but gained no benefit from it. The Army of New Mexico had lost 10 percent of its strength (36 dead and 150 wounded) while Canby had lost 16 percent of his (110 killed and 240 wounded), but he was far from crippled and returned to Fort Craig still astride Sibley's line of supply. Worse, the Confederates had lost a thousand horses, which greatly inhibited their mobility.[8]

The Confederates had no choice but to continue northward with only three days' supplies in hand. On February 28 Baylor sent word that Tucson had been taken. On March 7 Sibley occupied Albuquerque and then Sante Fe three days later. Despite these superficial successes Sibley's fundamental logistical problems remained insoluble and Canby continued to choke his lines of communication; by the third week of March the Union had regained the strategic initiative. Sibley decided to send a column toward Glorietta pass to block the eastern approaches to Santa Fe. On March 27 Union and Confederate forces collided. The Union column had divided into two. The Confederates engaged one, under Colonel John Slough, in obstructed, riven country covered with cedar trees. The

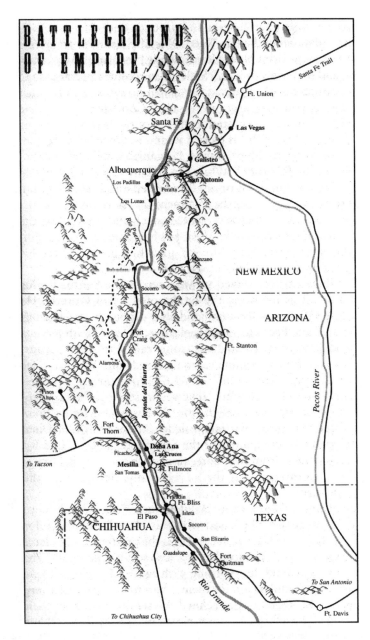

From *Blood & Treasure: Confederate Empire in the Southwest*
by Donald S. Frazier (College Station, TX: Texas A&M
University Press, 1995). © 1995 by Texas A&M University Press.
Reprinted with permission.

Unionists were forced back to a series of defensive positions until they withdrew. The battle of Glorietta had cost the Confederates forty-six killed and sixty wounded, the federals forty-six dead and forty-six wounded, but once again conferred on the victor no advantage. Indeed, they suffered a disaster when the second Union column, whose absence from the battlefield had led to the Union defeat, fell upon the Confederate supply base at Johnson's Ranch and destroyed it, including a train of eighty wagons.[9]

Sibley's troops were strung out over twelve miles and he had no means of feeding them. He decided to evacuate Sante Fe as Union troops were approaching from both north and south. Union forces were also concentrating east of Albuquerque just as he arrived on April 11. Sibley had no choice but on April 12 to continue the withdrawal to Mesilla. Canby pursued and three days later caught the Confederates crossing the Rio Grande at Peralta. They were only saved by a sandstorm that blew up just before Canby could put in a strong attack. Sibley managed to get his force across the river, but his escape route was blocked, and he took flight over the cold and barren wastes of the Magdalena Mountains, a decision that inflicted a great physical ordeal on his men and finished off what remained of their fighting capacity.[10]

The reasons for this humiliating defeat characterize much Confederate military effort at this stage of the conflict; it can be summed up as strategic overextension and logistic underpreparedness. The Confederates needed to demonstrate a strong measure of careful forethought to occupy and hold territory over such distances, and this was wholly absent. The Confederate failure to win an initial decisive success at Val Verde forms an important turning point, rather than Glorietta, as it began a process whereby Confederate logistical sinews were eaten away as they advanced northward. Confederate depredations rendered "these locusts" unwelcome and worsened Sibley's problems. While Union forces remained in the field and could fall back on an invulnerable base, they retained the strategic initiative and the Confederates, despite numerous individual acts of bravery, could not win.

When Sibley issued a proclamation in Arizona denouncing the war as wicked because it was waged "for the subjugation and oppression" of the South, he seemed to be oblivious to the reality that his invasion belied the Confederacy's defensive stance.[11] In the east, the North struggled to land a powerful, offensive blow. The only pressure the Union could bring to bear on the South was not on land but by means of the naval blockade. This policy still presented an enormous challenge both in terms of command and organization. The secretary of the navy, Gideon Welles, set up a group to preside over the coordination of operations along the south Atlantic. Headed by Captain Samuel F. Du Pont of the US Navy, it received the alternative designations of either the Blockade Strategy Board or the Committee of Conference. Its other members included Professor Alexander D. Bache of the US Coast Survey and the treasury department, Major John G. Barnard, and Commander Charles H. Davis.[12]

The Lincoln administration became attracted by the idea of a naval descent on the North Carolina coast, a state with a supposedly significant measure of Unionist sympathy. The original idea for this operation might have begun in the fertile and mischievous brain of Major General Benjamin F. Butler. Butler remained a professional politician to his fingertips, having served as a Democrat congressman from Lowell, Massachusetts. Before 1861 he had been consistently pro-Southern, believing that Democratic Party unity constituted the only "source of safety to the Union." After 1861 he became closely aligned with the Republicans. For Lincoln, Butler served as an important symbol of national unity and cross-party cooperation. But the abandonment of his previous attachment helps explain the peculiar loathing that Southerners especially (but also other Democrats) felt for him.[13]

Butler was not the completely unprincipled opportunist portrayed by his critics, although he certainly appears as a rather sinister figure—an astute lawyer, crafty, evasive, deceitful, and vindictive when crossed. In the early part of the war he had not yet acquired a reputation for military incompetence. He seemed one of the few Northern generals who could show drive and determination. Butler also showed a flair for self-promotion. Hence his appointment to command the Department of Virginia based at the Union enclave around Fortress Monroe, a stronghold that controlled the James River estuary and served as a secure base for mounting amphibious operations.[14]

Butler's most significant act at Fortress Monroe provoked suspicions among the more conservative that his views on slavery were subversive. His keen legal mind led him to deduce that if Virginia was indeed the foreign country claimed by Confederates then the Fugitive Slave Act of 1850 did not apply there; he declared escaped slaves to be "contraband of war," though he only envisaged them as laborers. His actual views were rather less radical than the way he presented them. Still, his approach earned the enmity of McClellan, both men sensing the other as a rival for the 1864 Democratic nomination.[15]

Butler's deficiencies as a tactician were revealed in June 1861 at Big Bethel, a minor but humiliating skirmish into which he blundered impervious to warnings that he lacked sufficient men and equipment to enter Richmond. Butler sought a project that would dispel the cloud hovering over his reputation after

Big Bethel and sent the secretary of war, then Simon Cameron, a memorandum urging an amphibious raid on the Hatteras inlet on the North Carolina coast. Butler claimed that it was a haven for Confederate privateers. He proposed that the US Navy land his men on Hatteras so that it could be destroyed. In August the navy department accepted the idea. Butler would provide 860 men and a company of artillery; the US Navy would provide Flag Officer Silas H. Stringham and a squadron of seven vessels, including the steam frigates *Minnesota* and *Wabash*.[16]

Neither Stringham nor Butler thought in terms of joint action, but in distinct operational phases: Butler would provide the troops and Stringham assumed his ships would do all the rest. Indeed he assumed that Butler would provide his own transports, and he incurred a month's delay when it became clear that Butler had given no thought to the matter. Stringham's squadron did not appear off Hatteras until the end of August. As the ships could only function in waters deeper than twenty feet, they could get no closer to its forts, Hatteras and Clark, than a mile, so they concentrated their fire on each separately. Both forts surrendered after two days and all Butler had to do was occupy them. He then engaged in an acrimonious dispute with Stringham as to who deserved the credit for the success. Simply leaving the forts once they had fallen would do nothing to extirpate privateering and further operations seemed to beckon.[17]

Washington had acquired an appetite for more easy successes along the coastline of the Carolinas. On August 3, prior to the Hatteras victory, Secretary of the Navy Gideon Welles informed Captain Du Pont that the "invasion and occupation of the seacoasts of the states in rebellion" had become government policy. The Blockade Strategy Group Board believed that seizing a port to sustain the blockade along the south Atlantic should also be a priority. A fleet under Du Pont's command to further these aims did not put to sea until October 16, when it had been provided with vague instructions. Du Pont had been given three objectives and allowed to choose the one he deemed most suitable. He selected Port Royal because of the attractions of its great natural harbor.

Du Pont felt the strain of responsibility heavily, and his agitation could hardly have been allayed when his fleet scattered before a storm. He did not arrive in the vicinity of Port Royal until November 4. He found it defended by two forts, Beauregard and Walker, guarding the north and south headlands respectively. Du Pont had planned to land the troops of Brigadier General Thomas W. Sherman on the beaches but could not do so because the surfboats had been lost in the storm. Rather than abandon the operation, Du Pont and Sherman agreed to hazard an unsupported naval assault.

Du Pont formed his squadron into line, sailed into the channel between the ports and opened fire, concentrating initially on Fort Walker. After the squadron passed it five times, Fort Walker surrendered; the garrison of Fort Beauregard, eager to escape similar treatment, did likewise shortly thereafter. Contrary to conventional wisdom, a naval bombardment had overcome land emplacements. Du Pont had enjoyed priceless good luck. Hardly any coordination of effort had been required, and would have been difficult to maintain because Sherman's infantry was short of small arms ammunition as most of this, too, had gone to the bottom of the Atlantic. After two easy victories, the US Navy fell under the spell of a cult of bombardment.[18]

As for the Confederates, General Robert E. Lee was sent hastily to take command of the new military district of South Carolina, Georgia, and north Florida to shore up the coastal defenses. Fortifications at Charleston and Savannah were improved (and neither were taken from the sea). Lee concentrated mobile reserves inland with more works built upstream to protect the railroads beyond the range of Union naval guns. Lee's depression caught the Confederate mood—"another forlorn hope expedition," he confided to his daughter.[19]

The navy department decided to expand its commitment to amphibious operations. Du Pont received the salutations due to a popular hero, and ambitious men on the spot were quick to make claims for opportunities in their own areas. The blockade required a coaling station farther south than Hampton Roads, and Hatteras fit the bill. The Confederates had also been fortifying Beaufort and New Bern in North Carolina. Welles was attracted by an argument that these ports could be seized with small forces before the work could be completed and thus have disproportionate effect on Confederate morale. Initially, Lincoln resisted these claims because he felt that operations in North Carolina could only be mounted at the expense of the overall effectiveness of the blockade. In the event, the decision was taken out of both their hands. After the repulse of an effort to take Roanoke Island, the Confederates threatened to retake Hatteras. The Union high command faced a dilemma: allow Hatteras to be given up, divert Du Pont's squadron from Port Royal, or dispatch another expedition to relieve it? Eventually the last option was chosen.[20]

Union leaders had grasped firmly the value of seapower to the Union war effort. They could see its strategic importance, but it is doubtful whether an overall operational design had been realized to secure their objectives. Historian Rowena Reed argues that Major General George B. McClellan, appointed as general-in-chief in November 1861, had such a well-considered plan.[21] She believes that he utilized his experience in the Crimean War (1853–57) to design a plan whereby amphibious operations would permit the seizure of strategic points inland, cut the railroads between them, isolate and weaken them, and provoke the Confederates to attack strongly posted Union enclaves that could expand once they had been driven back. According to this view, the seizure of Port Royal would permit an advance on Charleston and Savannah; a consolidation at Hatteras would have an equal bonus: the fall of Wilmington and then Raleigh, plus the cutting of the Wilmington–Weldon Railroad, preventing the succor of Richmond from the South.[22]

According to Reed, these operations were important subsidiary elements in his plan to seize Richmond. In a comprehensive statement, McClellan presented these operations as part of an integral scheme, but this scheme is retrospective. The capacity of combined (now defined as "joint") operations to achieve mastery of the coastal waters and the railroads that ran inland, did indeed offer an opportunity to exert pressure on the Confederate flanks, but McClellan failed to distribute his forces adequately to fulfill such ambitions. In short, some elements of a concept can be identified but they were never related or implemented with the rigor or consistency that Reed suggests.[23]

Individual initiatives were just as important as any premeditated design. Brigadier General Ambrose E. Burnside suggested the creation of a specialized division, drawn from the maritime states of New England, dedicated to amphibious operations. Colonel Rush Hawkins, commander of the 90th New York Volunteer Infantry, had become preoccupied by the idea that the counties around Pamlico Sound were predominantly Unionist. He advocated the capture of Roanoke Island, and might have given McClellan the idea.[24]

On January 7, 1862, McClellan issued orders for an attack on Roanoke with Burnside appointed as commander of the Department of North Carolina. McClellan ordered the "crossing" of Hatteras inlet and the capture of Roanoke and New Bern. He made vague references to the subsequent occupation of Goldsborough, Wilmington, and Raleigh, but he did not insist on this aspect. Indeed, he enjoined "great caution in moving so far into the interior as upon Raleigh." He preferred that Burnside take Wilmington and cut the Weldon Railroad. McClellan gave more urgency to the desirability of avoiding proclamations; any issued "should say as little as possible about politics or the Negro." These orders issued to Burnside offer no evidence of a far-reaching strategic design, but merely stipulate the occupation of places and the direction of military and naval movements, without any stress being placed on the roles of the relative parts.[25]

Four days later the expedition put to sea with Commodore Stephen Rowan commanding the naval dimension. They encountered first a ferocious gale that sank five ships, including the *Pocahontas* with all the horses, and then sandbars across the Hatteras inlet that the remaining thirty-six ships could not cross. Rowan and Burnside had little choice but to try and plough their way through or drag the bigger ships over with tugboats. "I have never undertaken a work," Burnside told McClellan, "that has presented so many obstacles." McClellan expressed his faith in Burnside's "energy and pluck" that "will take you through to the end." By the end of January Burnside at last landed troops on Hatteras; but this only compounded his problems because it proved barren and his troops swiftly ran low on water.[26]

The former governor of Virginia Henry A. Wise commanded Confederate troops on Roanoke Island. He had fifteen hundred men and garrisoned its three small sand-and-turf forts with seven hundred men, leaving eight hundred free to resist any landing. On February 7 the Union fleet crossed Pamlico Sound and began bombarding the forts. This proved a less successful gambit; it took two days to finally silence Fort Bartow on Pork Point, and used up much of Rowan's ammunition. A "contraband" teenager called Tom suggested to Burnside that he land at Ashby's Harbor, three miles south of Fort Bartow. He accepted this helpful advice, landing John G. Forster's brigade on February 8, followed by that of Jesse L. Reno. Burnside's view of the fighting was concealed by the thick woods and he delegated tactical authority to Forster. After a brief sanguinary action, Confederate resistance crumbled. Burnside took the surrender of twenty-five hundred men (as Wise had accepted late reinforcement), but their commander did not stay to offer it.[27]

Burnside had secured his lines of communication and he acted quickly to exploit his tactical success. He sailed southwesterly across Pamlico Sound to seize the estuary of the Neuse River. He pillaged and burnt the tiny port of Winton before advancing on New Bern. Its Confederate defenders were commanded by Brigadier General Lawrence Branch, a tactician of some ability. Branch had four thousand men, but had to garrison five forts and man thirty big guns. He had also dug a fortified line called the Croatan breastwork ten miles south of New Bern. Burnside aimed to cut off the latter from the west and the Union fleet continued up the Neuse River to guard the Union right flank even though it was low on ammunition.[28]

Severe storms delayed the joint advance and Burnside did not set off until March 11. He landed unopposed at Slocum's Creek and discovered (thanks again to timely intelligence furnished by "contrabands") that the Croatan breastwork had been abandoned. Branch had pulled back to another line that stretched only

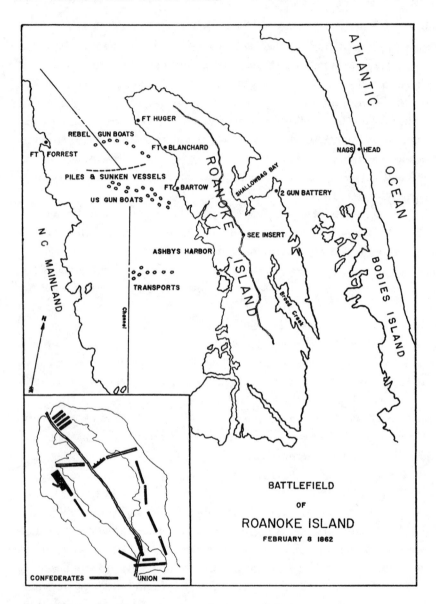

BATTLEFIELD

OF

ROANOKE ISLAND

FEBRUARY 8 1862

From *The Civil War in North Carolina* by John G. Barrett.
Copyright © 1963 by the University of North Carolina Press,
renewed 1991 by John G. Barrett. Used by permission of the publisher.

a mile from Fort Thompson to the Atlantic and North Carolina Railroad where it veered at a right angle. Other than the general wish not to assault this position frontally, Burnside had no plan and simply improvised as circumstances dictated. He decided to attack the militia on the Confederate right who fled as Reno's brigade moved forward. His third brigade, that of John G. Parke, discovered a cavity in the Confederate center and split the Confederate position in two. By 4 PM on March 14 the Confederates had evacuated New Bern after setting fire to its warehouses.[29]

The Confederates could not raise fresh forces to retake New Bern because of the need to defend Richmond. McClellan, removed from the position of general-in-chief so that he could concentrate all his energies on the seizure of the Confederate capital, urged Burnside to consider taking Norfolk, Virginia, as "the best blow to be struck." He acknowledged that Burnside needed reinforcements but he was loath to provide these from his own army. The Confederates eventually evacuated Norfolk on May 9 because they considered it caught in a vice between Fortress Monroe and New Bern. Also significant was the fall of Fort Macon after eleven hours of bombardment on April 25. This uncovered a deep-water port, Morehead City, and the smaller harbor at Beaufort; the former quickly came into operation as a coaling station for the blockading squadron.[30]

Burnside later acquired a reputation as a bungler, but these small-scale operations along the North Carolina littoral suited his talents. He had gained a modest and timely victory. Casualties were minor, 165 killed and wounded and 413 captured (a 15 percent loss) on the Confederate side, to 470 killed and wounded and one captured (a 5 percent loss) on the Union. Burnside had also shown talent as a logistician and he had persevered in overcoming many obstacles. These operations offered few clues as to the talents that might be needed to organize campaigns on a greater scale. Burnside had not yet designed a plan of campaign or showed any ability to allot priorities or make difficult choices. Consequently, he enjoyed an exaggerated reputation. In 1861 and early 1862 the division was the largest formation acknowledged by the Union army; thereafter Burnside would have to adapt to the differing needs of corps and army command.[31]

In the early months of 1862 the federals gained another seaborne triumph —the capture of New Orleans. An attack on the Crescent city—the second-largest port in North America after New York—offered great opportunities. Its exports totaled $105 million annually (compared with Mobile's $39 million and Charleston's $21 million). The loss of New Orleans inflicted a savage blow on the Confederacy's war economy and financial viability.[32]

By comparison with its importance, the city's defenses were fitfully arranged and ill thought out. Since the end of May 1861 New Orleans had been part of Department No. 1, embracing Louisiana and the southern counties of Mississippi and Alabama. It was initially commanded by Major General David E. Twiggs, who entered Confederate service as one of the most reviled senior officers of the US Army to defect, as he had surrendered the nineteen posts of the Department of Texas to state authorities even before an ordinance of secession had been passed. Twiggs was too ill to provide the necessary departmental direction. Defense measures were also subject to the short-term pressures inherent in private enterprise. Jefferson Davis's proclamation of April 17, inviting letters of marque permitting private citizens to arm privateers and realize 20 percent of any cargoes seized, led to a great boom in the construction of privateers that detracted from investment in other defensive measures.[33]

New Orleans suffered from too many conflicting priorities. The Confederate secretary of the navy, Stephen R. Mallory, and other Southerners persisted in the view that a main threat came from north of the city rather than the Gulf of Mexico. Mallory also encouraged the building of rams, like the CSS *Manassas*, ironclad warships like the CSS *Louisiana* (with twenty big casemated guns), and simultaneously a "mosquito" fleet of small cutters. New Orleans should have been defended by an integrated force that embraced the navy, the forts—forts Jackson and St. Philip guarding the Mississippi delta were the most important—fixed linear defenses, the army, and the militia. These elements should have been fused into a system. Twiggs had helped raise 23,557 soldiers but had no contact with the navy and even less interest in its affairs. Consequently, the Confederate defenses broke down once Union forces began to exert multiple pressures; resistance became fragmented and piecemeal.[34]

The true line of defense lay to the south. Should Forts Jackson and St. Philip fall, then the city would become untenable. Morale soared when initial Union incursions up the Mississippi were driven back easily. On October 10, 1861, a small squadron commanded by Captain John Pope of the US Navy occupied Head of Passes, fifteen miles up the delta. Its importance lay as the logistical base for any assault on New Orleans's defenses. On October 12 CSS *Manassas*, supported by "mosquito" ships, caught Pope's squadron by surprise and even forced the temporary abandonment of the nineteen-gun sail sloop, USS *Vincennes*. Amid the panic Pope ordered a humiliating withdrawal to the Gulf—"Pope's Run." The Confederates could have won an even bigger victory, however, they had let slip the chance to sink the *Vincennes* and Pope's flagship, the USS *Richmond* (twenty-two guns).[35]

"Pope's Run" added to the pall of gloom that covered the Union war effort in the autumn of 1861. In November Gideon Welles decided to reinforce the Gulf Blockading Squadron, but this act by itself did not lead inevitably to the decision to launch a powerful attack on New Orleans. Any decision would be the result of a number of factors and the intervention of several powerful personalities with a diverse range of motives.

The advocates for the army and navy respectively were Butler and David D. Porter. Butler had a reputation to retrieve and a fortune to make—for money-making schemes could often be found lurking in the background of his proposals and New Orleans offered rich pickings. Butler persuaded Lincoln that he could raise an army from among New England Democrats. The president gave him command of the Department of New England so that he could organize recruitment. But this position brought him into conflict in September 1861 with the governor of Massachusetts, John A. Andrew, who refused to commission the officers that Butler had selected (mostly Andrew's old political foes); he also supported Thomas W. Sherman for the command. "You mean that General Butler lies?" asked Lincoln in a voice heavy with sarcasm when Andrew's emissaries plead their case at the White House. The dispute could not be resolved until February 1862 when Andrew agreed to commission Butler's candidates in return for the abolition of the Department of New England.[36]

Naval voices also advocated an operation against New Orleans. Butler's old friend, the assistant secretary of the navy, Gustavus V. Fox, enlisted the help of Senator James W. Grimes, the chairman of the Naval Affairs Committee, to persuade the president of the merits of the campaign. Lincoln quickly grasped that the fall of New Orleans could serve as the second prong of a dual thrust both up and down the Mississippi River. Another significant advocate was Captain David D. Porter of the US Navy. He had served in the US Coastal Survey and understood the intricacies of the Mississippi. He favored seizing New Orleans as the simplest and most effective way of blockading it. He had hitched his star unwisely to the ill-fated efforts of William H. Seward to dominate the Lincoln administration as "premier," and was thus automatically suspect in Welles's eyes as "a troublesome fellow." He had also got his fingers burnt serving as an intermediary in Seward's doomed efforts to persuade Samuel Barron to remain loyal; instead Barron defected and eventually surrendered at Hatteras. Lincoln did not trust him either. Sharing so much with Butler and, like him, disliked by so many, Porter and he were destined to squabble.

Porter believed that a Union fleet could pass forts Jackson and St. Philip if the latter were subjected to a long bombardment by mortars. A powerful convert to the argument that naval force conquers while land forces occupy, Porter could bolster his case with the persuasive point that any accompanying land force need only be small. Using deception, Welles gave the impression that his reinforcement of the Gulf Blockading Squadron would lead to attacks on Mobile and Galveston. He distrusted the war department under Simon Cameron because "secrets . . . evitably leaked out. . . ." On November 18 Porter put his case to McClellan, though Welles considered him "indifferent" to the design.[37]

Welles also cast about for a suitable commander. Commodore David G. Farragut seemed to recommend himself, being "capable, energetic and determined" despite his sixty years; but Farragut's Virginian birth raised a significant doubt against the background of the Potter Committee's investigations into treachery in the federal government. Welles recorded that "several members of Congress questioned me closely [about Farragut]." He considered Farragut an officer "of undoubted loyalty." Opinion on his abilities though was not unanimous. An influential lobby backed Silas Stringham, and Seward supported Du Pont thus ensuring that he would be ruled out. Porter, after his own fashion, recommended his foster brother Farragut (they had grown up together as children). Yet during the operation Porter would write a series of snide letters to Gustavus Fox carping about Farragut's inabilities.

Despite the doubts, Farragut would reveal a measure of the "Nelson touch." He believed in the efficacy of combined operations as a means of ensuring that ships could not be cut off during riverine campaigns. He brought healthy skepticism to bear on Porter's "bombardment mania," and enjoyed an instinctive grasp of the elements of command. On January 9, 1862, Farragut formally took up command of the Western Gulf Blockading Squadron, with his flag aboard the wooden steam sloop USS *Hartford*.[38]

The Confederate defenders of New Orleans also witnessed a change of command. On October 17, 1861, Major General Mansfield Lovell arrived to take over Department No. 1. The comparatively youthful Lovell, only thirty-nine, evinced zest in confronting the challenges of his post. These were not slight, as he found forts Jackson and St. Philip dilapidated, a general shortage of powder, and the entrenchments encircling the city incomplete; worse, he discovered that he had a mere twenty scratch companies to hold them.

Lovell expected to be attacked in January 1862. His strongest line of defense remained forts Jackson and St. Philip, guarding the entrance to and from the delta on opposite banks of the Mississippi. The two forts were garrisoned by a thousand men in ten companies. The strongest, Jackson, had been equipped with an array of cannon, six 42-pounders, twenty-six 24-pounders, two rifled 32-pounders, three 8-inch and one 10-inch mortars, plus two 48-pounders and then 24-pounders—a total of sixty-eight guns. St. Philip boasted six 42-pounders, nine 32-pounders, twenty-two 24-pounders and four 8-inch columbiads, one 8-inch and one 10-inch mortars, plus three field guns—an additional forty-three guns to the Confederate tally.

The entrance to Lake Ponchartrain was covered by Fort Macomb, a garrison of 250 men and thirty guns, mostly 32-pounders. Lovell also placed a barrier—a heavy chain secured by fifteen anchors weighing just under two tons and strengthened by several hulks—across the river. He had managed to raise a field force of fifteen thousand men but his real problem remained logistical. Lovell had business experience, having helped manage an iron works, and later worked as superintendent, and eventually as deputy street commissioner in New York City, overseeing road repairs and improvements. But after the boom in priva-teers, he failed to raise the capital to invest in provisions for a long siege. The defeats at forts Henry and Donelson not only depressed morale but distracted the Confederate navy department.[39]

On January 20, 1862, Welles sent Farragut orders for the attack on New Orleans. He indicated that Farragut should not sail until "completely ready"; that is, until the mortars placed under Porter's command were fully prepared for their vital role. The core of the squadron consisted of the sloops *Hartford*, *Richmond*, *Pensacola*, and *Brooklyn*—vessels designed for war in rough seas rather than down great rivers. Once they entered the Mississippi River Farragut's ships were to reduce the defenses that guarded the city, and then "appear off that city." He should retain "possession until troops can be sent to you." Further, Welles looked beyond New Orleans's fall, ordering Farragut "to push a strong force up the river to take all their [Confederate] defenses in the rear" if the naval force sent from Cairo, Illinois, had not arrived.

Welles did not give a moment's thought to the combined aspects and con-fused matters by ordering that Farragut give attention to the seizure of the "for-tifications at Mobile Bay, and turn them over to the army to hold." Welles made it clear that failure had not been contemplated, but his orders's obscurity at key points would force Farragut to use his own initiative.[40]

Welles's neglect of the combined nature of the operation is perhaps not sur-prising as for much of the winter of 1861–62 McClellan had opposed the expe-dition. He thought forts Jackson and St. Philip too strong for ships to "pass." In early 1862 he vetoed any role that Butler might cherish in the scheme and treated him like a carrier of bubonic plague. Over the ensuing weeks McClellan would change his mind. The most persuasive arguments were made by a member of his

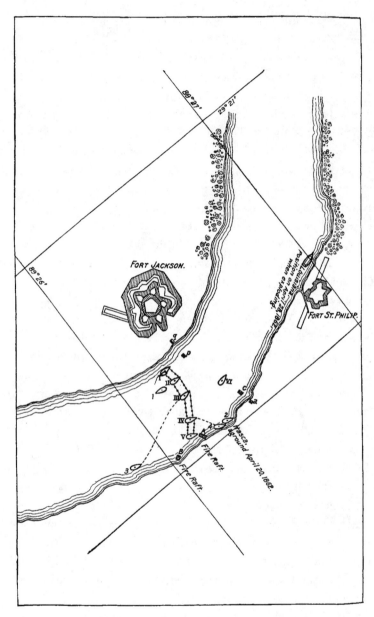

Arrangement of the Confederate barrier below Forts Jackson and St. Philip.
From *Official Records of the Navy*, Ser. I, Vol. 18

From the *Capture of New Orleans, 1862* by Chester G. Hearn
(Baton Rouge: Louisiana State University Press, 1995), p. 210.
© Chester G. Hearn. Reprinted by permission of the publisher.

staff, Major John G. Barnard. Barnard had worked on the construction of the forts before the war and while working on the Blockade Strategy Board had developed a quiet respect for Butler. He believed first that an amphibious operation would succeed if it could exploit surprise; second, he pointed out that given the scale of the problems facing McClellan it would be unwise to oppose an operation that members of the administration and Congress were keen on; third, if successful it could reveal what might be achieved before Richmond by amphibious means and could fit into his strategic design that had yet to be presented at this stage; fourth, Butler was content with his existing force, many of whom he had raised in New England, and he did not need heavy reinforcement from the Army of the Potomac. Besides, New Orleans was far away from Washington, DC, and, McClellan hoped, perhaps Butler could be "buried" there.[41]

As for Butler, he explained his wish to be distant from the biggest Union military effort of the year with characteristic self-righteous hypocrisy. He told fellow Democrat Major General John A. Dix that he was "sick of the intrigues and cross purposes I find here"—activities in which he had participated with such relish. In January 1862 the conniving, lackadaisical Cameron was replaced as secretary of war by Edwin M. Stanton, an old friend of Butler. McClellan acquiesced in his appointment to the New Orleans command. His orders arrived a month after Farragut's. They specified the creation of the Department of the Gulf with Butler as its commander. He was given 15,255 men (14,000 infantry, 275 cavalry, and 580 artillerymen) plus two regiments from the Department of Key West, giving a final total of about 18,000. McClellan required the capture of New Orleans, which Butler should garrison once the navy had taken it. Should the naval effort fail, then Butler should "endeavor to breach the works, silence their fire, and carry them by assault." Rounding out his ambitious plans, McClellan wished to see occupation of Baton Rouge and permitted a feint toward Galveston but he was most interested in capture of rolling stock and "control of the [rail]roads themselves."[42]

On March 7, Farragut sailed from Key West without Porter's mortars and headed for Ship Island, fifteen miles off Biloxi, Mississippi, an outpost midway between Mobile Bay and the Mississippi River delta, that Butler had taken the precaution of occupying the previous November. Butler's force had joined Farragut by March 23. The two commanders were an odd couple, being such a contrast in interests and manner, but worked together surprisingly well. Farragut was loyal and upright and had no interest in politics or his own glorification. Butler made a favorable initial impression by offering Farragut eight hundred tons of army coal when the navy ran low. Farragut, a stickler for orders and adherence to the regulations, queried whether such generosity was not against the regulations, and Butler replied breezily that he never read them. Nor had he bothered to work out a plan, but would rely on circumstances and the opportunities that would come his way.[43]

By contrast, Farragut had given his difficulties considerable thought. He would not repeat Pope's errors and issued orders in meticulous detail. He expected the Confederates to use fire ships but refused to allow any ship to withdraw without his permission. He realized that his predicament would be eased by effective reconnaissance, and he sent steamers upriver to get as much information as they could. In the meantime, Porter's schooners arrived and he had them towed into concealed positions, even though taking the Confederates by surprise could hardly be guaranteed after the delay.[44]

The loss of precious time caused Farragut to fret, but he would benefit from Confederate blunders. Thousands of Louisiana's best troops were sent from New Orleans to Corinth to assist Albert Sidney Johnston's concentration prior to his counterstroke at Shiloh. The Confederate navy department persisted in the error of thinking that the greatest danger came from upriver. On March 13 the barrier broke, but Farragut could not send his ships through because they were stuck attempting to cross mudbars in the delta. The Confederates were offered a chance to disrupt his plans but failed to grasp it. Lovell attempted to organize a devolved system of command but the result proved fractured and inefficient. His biggest weakness lay in poor intelligence, or failing to perceive the mounting federal threat. He seized river schooners to form a defensive squadron but then found that he lacked crews to man them. Lovell surrendered the initiative, invariably forced to respond to Farragut's moves rather than vice versa.[45]

On April 5 a flotilla of federal ships arrived at the barrier and Farragut undertook a personal reconnaissance, but he could not begin operations in earnest until three days later. On April 15 Porter's mortars began their bombardment of forts Jackson and St. Philip. Two days later Confederate fire rafts were released in an effort to break Farragut's tightening grip but caused little damage. The bombardment of the two forts proved more fitful, and Fort Jackson's guns sank a schooner, *Maria J. Coulston*, on April 19, forcing Farragut to order Porter to pull the mortars back. They managed to fire a shot at Fort Jackson every ten minutes, but this rate would not be sufficient to force its surrender within forty-eight hours as Porter had hoped.[46]

On April 20 the naval operation moved toward its climactic phase. Porter had increased the rate of mortar fire but this did nothing to allay Farragut's growing impatience. He had never believed Porter's exaggerated claims and felt that he had to take some urgent action. Farragut had an instinctive grasp of the elements of success at the operational level. He had seven thousand of Butler's men available aboard their transports behind the fleet. He quickly calculated that if the mortars continued at their present rate they would run out of ammunition to no benefit.[47]

Farragut revealed his iron determination to act just as the Confederate naval command fell into disarray. Brigadier General Johnson K. Duncan commanded the fortifications and his hopes rested on the CSS *Louisiana* that had more firepower (sixteen guns) than the rest of the Confederate fleet put together. She was moored just above Fort St. Philip but proved a liability because she could not fire her mortars without the risk of hitting Fort Jackson. Duncan wanted to send the *Louisiana* below the barrier to cause havoc and sink Farragut's wooden ships. Her captain, John K. Mitchell, would not entertain such a dangerous mission because he realized that his scrappily built ship looked more dangerous than she actually was (only ten of her sixteen guns worked). Duncan urged a reluctant Lovell to issue orders to Mitchell directly. Mitchell had no plan and refused to give orders except to four of the eleven available vessels, as he ignored the remainder.[48]

By contrast, Farragut had already made up his mind as to his correct course of action before he consulted his subordinates. Porter opposed any attempt to pass the forts before they had surrendered on the grounds that it would be dangerous to leave a strong enemy in the fleet's rear as it could disrupt the Union line of supply. "I believe in celerity," Farragut snapped. To those captains who offered logistical arguments as a justification for doing nothing, Farragut retorted that they would run out of ammunition, in any case, if they stayed where they were. The fleet, he argued, must pass the forts if New Orleans was to be taken. The sexagenarian Farragut revealed a drive and energy that is not the exclusive preserve of younger commanders. It would provide a refreshing contrast with one such—McClellan's halting procrastination on the Peninsula a month later. Farragut issued an order that urged "whatever is to be done will have to be done quickly."

Butler's desire to cooperate with the navy also proved helpful. Farragut was not blind to the risks that his plans faced. Yet he would not allow a fear of casualties to deter him from increasing the stakes in the pursuit of a greater victory. Confederate use of a fire raft on the night of April 21 might have given him reason to pause, as this single vessel caused panic and several collisions. Farragut gave Porter a further twenty-four hours. He then visited every ship himself to ensure that all captains were acquainted with the plan and knew their part in it. The Union fleet of seventeen ships would sail upriver on the night of April 22.[49]

Farragut's sailing instructions developed a plan for the fleet to sail in three divisions. The first would concentrate on Fort St. Philip on the right bank of the Mississippi. The second division, with Farragut's flagship *Hartford* in the vanguard, would engage the stronger Fort Jackson on the left bank, and the third division would concentrate its fire on Jackson's emplacements, too. The object was not to pulverize the forts into submission but to cover the passage of the fleet. Of course, Farragut entertained doubts about his plan, but his capacity to set them aside provided not just evidence of strength of character, but an ability to garner operational opportunities thrown up by tactical combinations. The material advantage he enjoyed over the Confederates could not be described as overwhelming; what proved to be decisive would be the tremendous advantage he enjoyed in the moral sphere.[50]

After some irritating delays, but buoyed up by the sinking of the barrier on April 20, the fleet raised anchor at 3:30 AM on April 24 and sailed upriver. The Confederates immediately struck back and a series of confused ship-versus-ship encounters developed, shrouded in smoke. The CSS *Manassas* attempted to ram the USS *Pensacola* and the USS *Mississippi* but instead was rammed herself by the latter, caught fire, and drifted downstream helplessly, causing some momentary alarm among Porter's schooners. The USS *Varuna* was rammed and disabled, but despite this setback, the balance of fighting swung in Farragut's favor. The CSS *Governor Moore* caught fire, and Farragut aboard the *Hartford* led the way to engage the forts. Their return fire started fires aboard *Hartford* but they were extinguished. The *Brooklyn* also sustained damage but survived the gauntlet to join the reassembled fleet of fourteen ships north of the forts at Quarantine.

Farragut had shown acute tactical sense. He demonstrated that land-based static defense, unsupported by any interlocking barriers could be bypassed (especially at night) by mobile, naval forces even at close range, and left to "wither on the vine" until forced to capitulate. He had penetrated New Orleans's defenses at the first attempt. As for the CSS *Louisiana*, she remained moored at St. Philip having played no part in the battle. The city itself lay at Farragut's mercy. All the heavy guns had been sent to strengthen the forts, and after the transfer of so many units to Corinth, Lovell had a mere three thousand–man militia to defend New Orleans. He started to evacuate the city as soon as he received word that Farragut's fleet had passed the forts. He believed (rightly) that an early evacuation would grant time to remove all military stores, rolling stock, and factory machinery. In the meantime, Farragut rested his crews and then at 10 AM sailed on, dropping anchor before the Confederate batteries at English Turn. The ships dodged obstacles, including fire rafts, but the farther they sailed the weaker the resistance became. At length New Orleans bristled under their guns.[51]

Farragut sent a small delegation of officers to receive its surrender but Lovell played for time. Farragut responded with a threat to bombard the city that hastened New Orleans's surrender on April 29. The day before, Porter had received the surrender of Fort Jackson after its garrison mutinied and fled en masse; left unsupported, Fort St. Philip followed suit hurriedly; CSS *Louisiana*, in whose guns so much hope had been invested, was ignominiously scuttled.[52]

This brilliant coup de main ended in acrimony as Butler and Porter bickered over the laurels. Butler sent in troops to garrison Jackson and St. Philip and claimed that Porter's bombardment had made no contribution to the success. Porter's officers denounced these opinions in the newspapers. In 1864 Gideon Welles recorded in some exasperation that "Many in this day who read and hear the capture of New Orleans believe it was taken by General Butler" a tribute to his skill at generating publicity. The true victor, Farragut, remained indifferent to the allocation of glory. As for Lovell, he was singled out as the scapegoat for the Confederate defeat; although he commanded a corps at the siege of Corinth six months later, he never held another major command.[53]

The Union had won a notable victory at the cost of 36 killed and 135 wounded. The greatest city in the South had fallen. A financial hub, an industrial center, and the Confederacy's biggest port, its loss would cripple attempts to finance the Confederate war effort and was a blow to Southern pride. The swift reassertion of federal power in the lower Mississippi and Gulf of Mexico would deter any aid from the French puppet regime in Mexico. Northern spirits, buoyant after a series of victories, soared. A rapid victory appeared imminent.

For all this, the premium drawn on the victory, as in North Carolina, appears slight. Whenever Union forces could rely on naval support they triumphed. Important objectives had been gained but their potential had not been exploited. It was not just a question of distance, because Farragut lacked the strength to take Mobile. Raleigh and Wilmington remained well beyond the reach of Burnside. In short, from the spring of 1862 onward the Union's leaders had gained the ability to undermine the Confederacy's strongest front in Virginia, if they chose to use it. Yet, the claims of Rowena Reed notwithstanding, McClellan failed to evolve a coherent, centrally organized strategy. He may have sensed its elements and groped toward a formulation, but no systematic programs emerged. McClellan himself even opposed for a while the most important part of the scheme, the occupation of New Orleans.[54]

This program of amphibious operations was loyal to the precepts of the

Anaconda Plan. Two thrusts up and down the Mississippi River did resemble Scott's concept, relying as much as possible on waterborne lines of communication. In May Farragut occupied Baton Rouge and at the end of the month sailed toward Vicksburg with eight ships and eighteen hundred troops under Brigadier General Thomas Williams. Driven back, he returned in June with mortar schooners and Williams's augmented force of thirty-two hundred men. Although worth making, the incursion was too feeble and Farragut withdrew for a second time. Naval power alone could never be a cure-all and would not solve the strategic dilemmas that the North continued to face.

Nor were these operations "combined" in any real sense. The US Navy interested itself in them as a means of extending the range and power of the blockade. The seaports it wanted were often isolated and poorly suited to the development of operations inland. Technological limitations, such as the difficulty and slowness of getting horses ashore, further restricted the potential of amphibious operations. The telegraph and the railroad conferred on the defender the prospect to concentrate forces far more quickly than the invader, often haphazardly thrown ashore.[55]

In any case, the Confederates had revealed serious weaknesses. They suffered from even more significant strategic lapses, inadequate command systems, poor organization, and ineffective leadership and training. Confederate soldiers had displayed poor fighting spirit, even on the defensive. These weaknesses could not be exploited because a severe deficiency lurked at the heart of McClellan's term as general-in-chief. McClellan could not preside objectively over the Union war effort and adjudicate between commands because, as an army commander, too, he could not be described as a disinterested party. He would not allow any competing military effort to distract attention from his own drive on Richmond. Despite casual promises that both Butler and Burnside would receive reinforcements if successful, McClellan would not make these available. As a result, Union operations along the coastal littoral did not prevent a Confederate concentration before Richmond. McClellan's miserly attitude proved self-defeating.

Federal failure to push matters to the proof created the conditions that increased the likelihood of a Confederate military revival. The Union superiority along the coast resulted not from overwhelming resources, but from an edge in organization, firepower, logistical planning, and Farragut's assertiveness. Without a dynamic leader Union advantages diminished inland, as demonstrated in the operations conducted by Confederate forces in the Shenandoah Valley. There this correlation between force and organization became reversed. The Confederates played to their strong suit, especially a superiority in cavalry;

they also found an effective means to exploit the weaknesses of federal organization. They were also fortunate to identify a commander, Thomas J. "Stonewall" Jackson, who revealed comparable qualities of dynamism and decisiveness to Farragut's. This campaign still retains some of the glamour that raised it to legendary status in the South. It is thus important to emphasize that it was viewed at the time as a secondary theater. Nevertheless, it assumed great importance, and the form this took requires close scrutiny.[56]

The starting point for this discussion lies in Jackson's character and methods. He had graduated from West Point in 1846, seventeenth in his class and had entered the artillery. After serving five years, including service in Mexico, he resigned and took up a professorship at the Virginia Military Institute. His career there reveals that those who are admired in peacetime are not always the ones that thrive in war. The cadets thought him a "hell of a fool": rigid, literal, humorless, and possessing odd personal habits. Jackson came alive in war. He was thirty-eight in 1862, a tough, abrasive, even harsh commander who enforced discipline with a pitiless devotion to the regulations. He had a passionate sense of duty fortified by his strong religious faith that probably imbued him with enormous self-confidence. He proved utterly unrelenting in pursuit of his objectives and desire to carry the war to the enemy. At times, especially in his disregard of sleep, he could overtax his resources. Nevertheless, he proved himself consistently dynamic and an instinctive master of operational art.[57]

Federal military operations had begun in western Virginia from July 1861 with the object of gaining control of the Kanawha Valley and protecting its Unionist counties. Brigadier General Jacob D. Cox commanded in this region but only led eight thousand men. The Confederate response was arthritic and at three battles—Rich Mountain in July, Carnifex Ferry, and Cheat Mountain the following September—failed to make effective use of what military strength could be mustered. By August 23 the thirty-four recalcitrant Unionist counties of West Virginia declared themselves a separate state, though it was not formally admitted to the Union until 1863. The main significance of these operations lay in bringing federal forces onto the flank of the Shenandoah Valley—though west–east movement proved difficult for these columns.[58]

The geography and topography of the Shenandoah Valley explains its strategic significance. It runs for more than 150 miles between the Potomac and James rivers in a northeasterly direction, and is skirted by the Blue Ridge Mountains to the east and the Allegheny Mountains, part of the Appalachian chain, to the west. The valley expanse varies between twenty to thirty miles in width, and its central feature is the Shenandoah River that divides into two, the

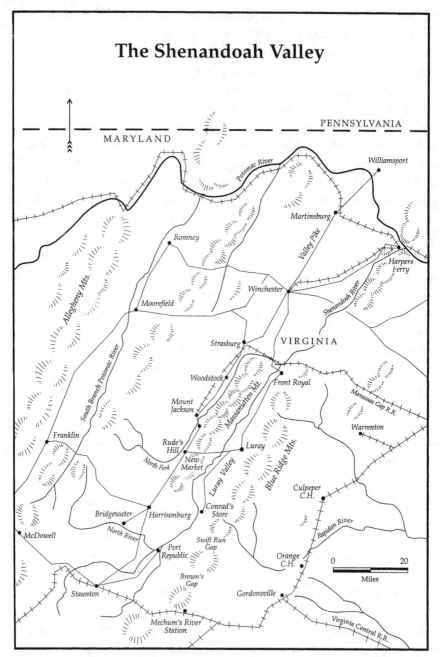

The Shenandoah Valley

From James Robertson, *Stonewall Jackson: The Man, the Soldier, the Legend*, 1st ed., p. 341. © 1997 Gale, a part of Cengage Learning, Inc. Reproduced by permission. www.cengage.com/permissions

north fork that runs west of the Massanutten Mountain, a monumental screen that divides the valley, and the south fork that runs down its eastern face. The confluence of the two forks is located three miles beyond Front Royal and flows northeast to meet the Potomac at Harpers Ferry. River trade explains the language used to describe movements in the valley. As the Shenandoah flows northward, this is *downstream*, and thus movement *northward* is to go *down* the valley, and to travel south is to go *up*. The northern end is thus the *lower* valley, and the southern end the *upper* part.

The Shenandoah Valley points a lance at Washington, DC, and Maryland. An advance by a Confederate force down the valley could bring disproportionate pressure to bear on the soft tissue of the political heart of the Union war effort. Conversely, a Union advance in the opposite direction would be channeled away from the Confederate capital, Richmond, which is shielded, in any case, by the Blue Ridge Mountains. Confederate forces concealed in the valley could debouch through the eleven passes that cut through the Blue Ridge to strike the flank of any Union column advancing on Richmond along the tidewater route via Manassas and Fredericksburg. Union forces were also hampered by the paucity of communications in the valley. Railroads could be found at either end, the Baltimore and Ohio (B&O) Railroad to the north, and the Virginia Central that ran from Richmond to Gordonsville, traversing the Blue Ridge Mountains to Staunton. The only railroad in the valley itself was the Manassas Gap, an unfinished line that ran from Mount Jackson to Strasburg before swinging east to Manassas Junction. This had been the route taken by Joseph Johnston in July 1861 before First Manassas. Confederate control of this line made the coordination of convergent advances from Union-held areas around the valley a haphazard undertaking. Likewise canals ran at either end of the valley, the Chesapeake and Ohio to the north and the James River Canal to the south; but large-scale riverine movement could not be undertaken on the Shenandoah River. Consequently, the most important communications artery was the Valley Turnpike that ran on the west side of the Massanutten Mountain to Winchester, the focal point of nine roads.[59]

The geographic structure of the valley and the resultant warp and weft of its communications offered the Confederates an asymmetric advantage. The concentration of its forces in a central position permitted movement with less difficulty compared with advances undertaken by federal columns denied their customary advantages. The strategic impact of such advances became multiplied as they progressed, not just on Washington, DC, but on the more significant operations in Virginia, not least on the Peninsula. Confederate commanders so far had failed to make any operational use of the valley's strategic potential.[60]

"Stonewall" Jackson did not take up command of the military district of the valley until November 1861. He quickly grasped the opportunities that it offered, especially if he could cross over into Maryland. He did believe, though, that his first act should be to secure his left flank. In January 1862 he undertook an attack against the Union garrison at Romney. His plan enshrined speed, surprise, and concentration: he deployed eleven thousand men and thus effected considerable tactical superiority over a Union force that amounted to no more than three thousand. However, Jackson botched the execution of the operation and set objectives beyond the capacity of his troops, especially in the harsh winter weather. The wagon trains fell eleven miles behind the infantry and the men went unfed. The Confederate force felt the smack of a central firm, commanding presence, but this provoked resentment. "In all his campaigns, too," Colonel Henderson observed, "Jackson was practically his own chief of staff. He consulted no one. He never divulged his plans. He gave his orders and his staff had only to see that orders were obeyed." The Romney campaign revealed this technique's weaknesses.[61]

Jackson quarreled with the commander of a cooperating force from West Virginia, Brigadier General William W. Loring, mainly because of the former's aloofness; the latter complained bitterly about the callous treatment of his exhausted and starving troops. Jackson's northward detour to protect his lines of communication gained its reward on January 3, 1862, with the occupation of Bath; its garrison of two thousand managed to escape when the militia units guarding the Union escape route fled as soon as shots were fired. If this force had advanced toward Winchester, Jackson's entire plan would have been dislocated. Jackson's self-confidence and ability to exploit the lack of Union enterprise allowed him to recover from his own errors. Indeed on January 7 he occupied Romney quickly once he had discovered that it, too, had been abandoned. Jackson seized $60,000 worth of supplies but he could not exploit his advantage because of the demoralization of his troops (18 percent were sick and many more had fallen out of the ranks).[62]

For all the dissension, the operation had been a success. Romney had been taken and Winchester's flank secured, and over one hundred miles of B&O track had been destroyed. Jackson never allowed human weakness or discomfort to distract him from his objectives. In later operations he would give much more attention to logistical coordination. Jackson took steps to solve another problem. When Loring received permission from the Confederate secretary of war, Judah P. Benjamin, to evacuate Romney against Jackson's wishes, which Loring did at once, Jackson resigned. Jackson's political allies, who included the governor of Virginia, John Letcher, got Benjamin's order rescinded and Jackson withdrew his resignation. Loring received promotion and a posting to southwest Virginia, but Jackson retained command of his Virginia troops. There could no longer be any doubt who commanded in the valley, and Jackson emerged as the untrammeled creative force behind the campaign.[63]

The uncovering of Romney left Winchester exposed once more. In March Joseph Johnston, the commander of the Department of Virginia, counseled prudence, enjoining Jackson to keep between Union commander Nathaniel P. Banks and the main Confederate army, still at Orange Court House. Johnston ordered that Jackson should not endanger his force, but "by keeping so near the enemy as to prevent him from making any considerable detachment to reinforce McClellan, but not so near that he might be compelled to fight." Jackson interpreted these orders correctly in the defensive–offensive terms that Johnston intended. He hoped "to inflict a terrible wound and effect a safe retreat in the event of having to fall back." Until Jackson took the field, Confederate commanders had talked grandiloquently but had achieved little offensively. "[T]o move swiftly, to strike vigorously, and secure all the fruits of victory," Jackson claimed "is the secret of successful war." He intended to inflict "all possible damage in the shortest possible time." Jackson's mercilessness was concealed by the small size of his operations, as they so neatly fitted the prewar vision of what war might be like.[64]

By March 7 the Union troops of Nathaniel P. Banks, who had succeeded to Patterson's command in the valley, had advanced within five miles of Winchester. Perhaps scarred by the Romney experience, Jackson submitted his plan to fight for the town to his subordinates assembled in a council of war. Jackson soon learned, as did Vice Admiral Lord Nelson, that "if a man consults whether he is to fight, when he has the power in his own hands, *it is certain that his opinion is against fighting.*"[65] This axiom is not literally true in Jackson's case, but his action encouraged his subordinates to be cautious. They opposed the plan and (perhaps in anticipation of the inevitable) the Confederate supply trains had been sent back eight miles to Newtown. Jackson thus had no choice but to pull out of Winchester. "[T]hat is the last council of war I will ever hold!" he thundered.[66]

Jackson withdrew to the south end of the Massanutten Mountain, and took up position at Rude's Hill. From here he could exploit the "H" of the terrain. Massanutten would screen an advance down the Luray Valley that ran parallel to the main valley, or he could cross the Massanutten Mountain on the crude road between New Market and Luray and outflank Banks's column. When Jackson received news that the division of James Shields had set off to join Irvin McDowell's First Corps at Fredericksburg via Warrenton, bringing its strength to forty thousand men, he grasped instantly that he must attack Banks to retain all his troops in the valley. He built up a strong base in the Mount Jackson area, sorted out his supply lines, and drilled his troops. His irregular cavalry under Colonel Turner Ashby destroyed the bridges between Strasburg and Mount Jackson. Despite poor discipline, Ashby's aggressive screening and audacious scouting, against which Banks's cavalry seemed powerless, proved a major factor in Jackson's success.[67]

At this date, curiously, McClellan felt that the Union could hold the valley with cavalry alone. Jackson's column advanced rapidly toward Banks, covering twenty-one miles on March 22, and a further fourteen miles on March 23, even though his men straggled. As Jackson approached Kernstown, four miles south of Winchester, he received an erroneous report from Ashby that he would encounter only four regiments and two batteries of guns. On March 24, Jackson launched an outflanking attack on the Union right with his Stonewall Brigade, now commanded by Brigadier General Richard B. Garnett. It actually faced three Union brigades and, although Garnett slogged it out for ninety minutes, withdrew on his own initiative. Jackson did not always show good judgment in his views on subordinates and staff and he dismissed the admired Garnett, provoking a controversy that consumed his small command for several weeks.[68]

Jackson had a good plan, chose the best ground, and displayed his customary audacity in the attack, but the whole enterprise rested on a fallacy. His casualties numbered 718 to the Union 574. But although a tactical failure, the battle represents an operational success, as the latter is not invariably dependent on tactical victories. Kernstown contributed to the Union commanders' habit (taking their cue from McClellan) of exaggerating Jackson's strength. This moral victory led to the reversal of the transfer of federal units from the valley.[69]

Jackson had thus succeeded in imposing his own design upon Union commanders, even though Winchester still remained in their hands. Nonetheless, it is unwise to accept the romantic picture of "Lost Cause" writers who tended to present Union generals in this campaign as gibbering incompetents helpless before Jackson's dazzling strokes. Central direction of Union military resources in the Shenandoah Valley was impeded further by McClellan's reduction of authority to command the Army of the Potomac, the creation of the Department of the Rappahannock, based at Fredericksburg, but including Banks's corps, and the Mountain Department under Major General John C. Frémont, stretching from the

Shenandoah to the Ohio valley. Frémont's reassignment had as much to do with political maneuvering in Washington, mainly against Frémont's enemies the Blairs. But Frémont continued to excite hopes that he would bring "vigor" to federal military operations. Lincoln would be sorely disappointed on this score.[70]

On hearing news of Kernstown, McClellan instructed Banks to "push Jackson hard" and then "resume his movement" to Manassas. By April 1, no longer Banks's commander, he offered to reinforce him with Brigadier General Louis Blenker's division, but believed that Banks's main difficulties would be solved by his own movements because they would "have drawn all the rebel forces towards Richmond." He doubted whether Johnston could reinforce Jackson. McClellan hoped for a successful advance on Staunton "to prevent his [Jackson's] return." After Shields's division had been sent to Warrenton, Banks had only 6,500 men available, and the wretched state of the Manassas Gap Railroad made it difficult to supply and reinforce him. Frémont's 15,000 scattered troops were in an even worse condition—dependent on a simple, unsurfaced road to cross the Alleghenies, disrupted by broken bridges caused by swollen floodwaters.[71]

In the meantime Jackson withdrew again to Conrad's Store and Rude's Hill where he could control the Luray Valley and protect his lines of communication through Swift Run Gap to Gordonsville. Robert E. Lee, the Confederate president's military adviser, with Johnston's support, offered Jackson the "use" of Richard S. Ewell's division of four brigades and five batteries. This audacious move enabled Jackson to draw up an ambitious plan. He would attempt to lunge westward, secure Staunton, link up with a small column under Major General Edward "Allegheny" Johnson, knock Frémont off guard, and then return to unite with Ewell to drive Banks back. When Jackson set off at 3 AM on April 30, 1862, he told Ewell nothing of his design.[72]

Two Union brigades—those of Brigadier General Robert H. Milroy and Brigadier General Robert C. Schenck—had occupied an indefensible position at the town of McDowell; they were determined to remain in place with six thousand men until they had ascertained Jackson's strength. On May 7 Jackson united with Johnson, giving him ten thousand men; he favored a rapid, outflanking movement that would allow him to get into the rear of this small Union force. To give it a firm base, he intended to dominate the area by placing his artillery and Johnson's division on Sitlington's Hill. These plans were thwarted on May 8 when Milroy rather inconveniently launched a preemptive attack on Sitlington's Hill. Jackson recalled the outflanking column and personally led it onto the field. After four hours of stubborn fighting the federal troops were repulsed, but Jackson could not throw forward a counterstroke because of nightfall. As Milroy had failed to take Sitlington's Hill he had no choice but to withdraw. Still, Milroy had held his own and had inflicted 416 casualties and a tactical shock on Jackson for the loss of 260 men.[73]

Nonetheless the operational consequences weighed once more on the Confederate side. Jackson's audacious offensive, resulting in Milroy's defeat at McDowell, was used by Confederate propagandists to compensate for the loss of New Orleans, which were in no way comparable. Operations in the Shenandoah Valley came to symbolize Confederate defiance against great odds, even though Jackson outnumbered both Milroy and Schenck. Frémont paid Jackson little attention because he did not think him a serious threat. On May 13 Jackson pulled his troops back to Staunton unmolested and headed off to rejoin Ewell.[74]

Jackson was about sixty-seven miles from his supply base, and Ewell had become increasingly irritated by Stonewall's failure to keep him informed as to his intentions. While en route to join Ewell at New Market, Jackson received a letter from Lee. "A successful blow struck at him [Banks]," Lee intimated, "would delay, if it does not prevent, his moving to either place [Fredericksburg or the Peninsula]." He also emphasized the strategic potential of the valley campaign. "Whatever movements you make against Banks do it speedily, and if successful, drive him towards the Potomac, and create the impression . . . that you design threatening that line." Jackson embraced this scheme enthusiastically because it chimed exactly with his own thinking.[75]

Events seemed to conspire against his plan when Ewell received a letter from Johnston recalling him to Richmond. The Union concentration before Richmond demanded a counterconcentration; as the numerically weaker side, as matters stood, the Confederates risked defeat in detail unless they countered numerical superiority with greater operational velocity. Ewell hastened to confer with Jackson and after the latter asked Johnston for confirmation, received the terse instruction on May 21, "If you and Gen. Ewell can beat Banks, do it." That day Jackson arrived back at New Market. He could field sixteen thousand men with Ewell's division plus twenty-seven guns. He then at once crossed the Massanutten undetected into the Luray Valley. Jackson intended a lightning tactical envelopment of Banks's left flank by driving up from the south via Front Royal. The Union force was scattered over a large area. Banks had divided his forces, and placed a little over 1,000 men at Front Royal, had entrenched 4,476 infantry, 1,600 cavalry and fifteen guns at Strasburg, with a further 1,450 sent to guard the main Union supply base at Winchester. Jackson outnumbered Banks two and a half to one, but local levels of superiority would be much higher.[76]

Jackson had also contrived to get between Banks and the Blue Ridge Mountains. By switching to the Luray side of the Massanutten, Jackson could conceal his advance, hit the point of maximum Union weakness, and simultaneously prevent Banks from either receiving reinforcements or moving away to join McDowell. His close proximity to the Manassas Gap Railroad allowed him to spread alarm along the eastern side of the Blue Ridge. His masterly maneuver had uncovered the Union rear, and unless Banks reacted energetically, he stared disaster in the face.[77]

Banks was only too aware of the dangers of his predicament. He realized that he should "stand firm" but lacked the tactical finesse to extricate his forces; he also lacked intelligence because his cavalry were poor. The Union detachment at Front Royal (mostly Maryland Unionists), commanded by Colonel John R. Kenly, was nothing but a hostage to fortune. Ashby's Confederate cavalry roamed about at will between Front Royal and Strasburg, preventing Banks from moving to relieve Kenly. On May 23 Jackson's column approached within a mile and a half of Front Royal without being discovered. Jackson placed his own division on the left and Ewell's on the right and launched a simultaneous assault. To maintain the momentum of the campaign Jackson's troops had to seize the two road bridges over the south and north forks of the Shenandoah and the railroad bridge over the former. As Ashby galloped to seize the Pike Bridge over the north fork, Kenly realized that to remain stationary meant entrapment. He ordered the retreat and attempted to set the bridges ablaze. He had acted tardily and the Confederates managed to put the fires out; though damaged, the bridges were intact. Seven hundred of Kenly's men surrendered after they were charged by Confederate cavalry, and a supply train carrying $300,000 worth of supplies fell into Confederate hands.[78]

Banks understood that the destruction of Kenly's detachment uncovered Strasburg. He ordered the evacuation of all stores to Winchester, but underestimated the speed and depth of Jackson's thrust. He did not consider trudging west over appalling roads to join Frémont because he feared that Jackson would catch him. The better road, the Valley Turnpike, seemed the best option. But given the space to develop his maneuver, Jackson caught up with the Union column near Middletown. At 3:30 PM the horse artillery unlimbered on a ridge above the road and bombarded the Union trains. Despite the carnage, Banks only lost fifty wagons out of five hundred, and most of his force escaped. Jackson failed to organize a further pursuit because Ashby's cavalry broke up to loot the wagons.[79]

The battle for Winchester that developed during the night and following morning took place on the high ground to the south and west of the town.

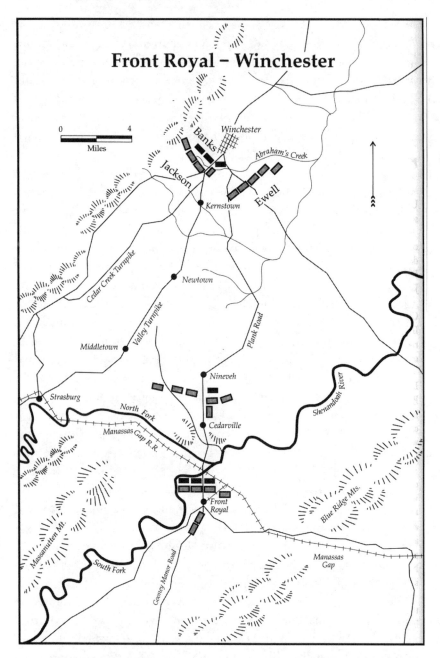

Front Royal – Winchester

Winchester

Banks

Jackson

Abraham's Creek

Ewell

Kernstown

0   4

Miles

Newtown

Cedar Creek Turnpike

Valley Turnpike

Plank Road

Middletown

Nineveh

Strasburg

North Fork

Shenandoah River

Manassas Gap R.R.

Cedarville

Massanutten Mt.

Blue Ridge Mts.

Front Royal

Gooney Manor Road

South Fork

Manassas Gap

From James Robertson, *Stonewall Jackson: The Man, the Soldier, the Legend*, 1st ed., n.p. © 1997 Gale, a part of Cengage Learning, Inc. Reproduced by permission. www.cengage.com/permissions.

Banks could not win this contest, as his position had been turned by Ewell's advance toward the Union left and Ashby's force had cut the Berryville Turnpike running eastward. Banks had no alternative but to conform to Jackson's wishes and withdraw northward back up the Martinsburg Turnpike to the Potomac River. The Confederate victory was consummated, after a halting start, by a simultaneous offensive that began at about 8:30 AM. A double envelopment occurred, distinguished on the Union right where resistance was tough, by the charge of Richard Taylor's brigade. This formation included exotic but undisciplined troops from Louisiana, "the Tigers," that gained the high ground and drove federal troops back into the narrow streets of Winchester.[80]

Jackson could not pursue once more, partly because his cavalry was not in place, but mainly because of the exhaustion of his troops. They had marched a hundred miles in one week and fought two battles plus a series of minor engagements; over the last thirty-five hours the troops had been in action continuously. By May 26 when Banks crossed the Potomac safely, Jackson had advanced 177 miles in seventeen days and had grasped the initiative. The Confederates succeeded in consistently imposing their plans on the federal forces. They had also captured prodigious quantities of supplies, 9,354 small arms, and five hundred thousand rounds of ammunition. Jackson had displayed impressive talents as a field commander at the corps level of command. He committed some errors certainly, especially in the combination of his formations and in all-arms tactical cooperation, but these were more than compensated for by his dynamism, self-confidence, consistency of purpose, and overall grasp of the dimensions of his campaign.[81]

From May 24 onward, Jackson's string of tactical successes began to have an operational impact on the strategy of the war. The main Union weakness in the valley lay in the absence of a single commander and a coherent campaign plan. The president and secretary of war determined to provide both themselves. Lincoln had sent Shields's division back to the valley as soon as it arrived at Fredericksburg.[82] The president urged Frémont to advance on Harrisonburg and thus cut Jackson's lines of communication along the Valley Turnpike. Frémont showed more anxiety for his own rear at this date because the Confederates had attacked a force of nine thousand men commanded by Jacob Cox in the Kanawha Valley. Frémont feared an eastward advance would lead to the uncovering of the Ohio valley "and General Cox also immediately exposed to disaster."[83]

Frémont had reached Franklin and an advance on Harrisonburg, less than forty miles away, looked simple enough. But he had to cross two mountain ranges in execrable weather. Inclined to be high handed, Frémont decided without Lincoln's permission to undertake a detour of a hundred miles via

Petersburg and thence Moorefield, emerging near Strasburg. By the time his force of ten to eleven thousand men arrived at this point of contact where Lincoln hoped he might link up with elements of McDowell's First Corps, it had completely broken down. Union forces lacked Jackson's march discipline and most important, his killer instinct. Instead Frémont pleaded that he faced an enemy thirty to sixty thousand men strong, whereas Lincoln doubted that Jackson's men numbered twenty thousand.[84]

Jackson always believed that the enemy should be pressed hardest at his most vulnerable point. He feinted toward Harpers Ferry while he spirited the captured supplies away. On May 24 Lincoln decided that First Corps should abandon its part in the Peninsular campaign and be transferred to the valley. Lincoln did not succumb to nervousness about the safety of Washington, DC. He had become impatient with the overly cautious and defensive tone of McClellan's dispatches. Lincoln jumped at the chance of taking action against Jackson as a way of forcing McClellan to get on with taking Richmond or face having to abandon the campaign.[85]

The extent to which the North succumbed to attacks of panic by Jackson's feint has been exaggerated. Indeed historian Kenneth Williams argues that Jackson should have concentrated on getting his captured supplies away rather than feinting toward the Potomac. On May 30 Shields's division stormed Front Royal and recaptured a lot of booty. This placed Jackson in a precarious position because he was fifty miles north of Strasburg, while Shields's men were only twelve miles away from this crucial point on the Confederate lines of communication and close to Frémont's column. Jackson's trains were twenty-five miles long, slow, and vulnerable. Jackson still managed to slip between them; Frémont advanced slowly and cautiously lest he be overwhelmed by Jackson (like Banks) unsupported; Shields tarried too long at Front Royal, and then marched down the Luray Valley, so that the Massanutten Mountain remained between him and Frémont.[86]

Jackson sent cavalry to destroy the road bridge over the north fork of the Shenandoah River to prevent Frémont reestablishing contact with Shields. Having secured his left flank, Jackson fell back alert for an opportunity to launch a counterstroke. Matters were complicated by atrocious weather—rain and hail that turned roads into canals of mud and caused floodwaters that endangered bridges. Frémont attempted to complete his circuitous perambulation by marching along the Valley Turnpike toward Harrisonburg. He hoped to push on to Staunton once Shields had joined him there. In the meantime, Jackson maneuvered between them both, attracted by the high ground southwest of Port

Republic at the confluence of the two tributaries of the south fork of the Shenandoah River, as a focal point where he could strike each Union column separately. From Port Republic, the Army of the Valley could shuttle over the two rivers, known as the North and South rivers, as needs dictated. In his turn, Shields's division could turn Jackson's position by crossing the fords south of the town and come up on the bridges from the southwest. Shields did not consider this scheme because he paid too much attention to inaccurate reports that James Longstreet's troops had approached Luray via the passes through the Blue Ridge.[87]

From his central position[88] made possible by the physical geography of the Shenandoah, Jackson could confine Shields to the Luray Valley or strike his exposed flank as his division tried to leave it. The potential of a rapid Union advance though was glimpsed in a nasty shock that Shields planned to give the unsuspecting Confederates. On June 1 he sent a "flying column" of 150 troopers and four guns, commanded by Colonel Samuel S. Carroll, to seize and hold the bridges at Port Republic and to burn the bridge at Conrad's Store ten miles to the northeast. If successful, Carroll's raid would confine the Army of the Valley to the north bank of the Shenandoah.[89]

On June 6 Jackson beat Carroll in the race to occupy Port Republic, though the latter succeeded in destroying the bridge at Conrad's Store. Ewell's division took up a position at Cross Keys, halfway between Harrisonburg and Port Republic. Ashby's cavalry skirmished with Frémont's troops, and this harassment allowed Jackson's men to take up position relatively unmolested; however, Ashby was killed at Chestnut Hill and his absence as an intelligence-gatherer brought Jackson close to disaster. On the morning of June 8 Carroll's small force crossed the lower ford of the South River and entered Port Republic, attacked the trains and Jackson's headquarters, and got between them and the fighting formations to the north. By frantic efforts Jackson brought up some artillery and then infantry and managed to restore the position. Fortunately for Jackson, Carroll did not destroy the bridges.[90]

At about the same time Frémont launched a halfhearted artillery bombardment of Ewell's center at Cross Keys followed by probes with skirmishes. Frémont actually outnumbered Ewell two to one, although he thought the odds the other way around. Individual Confederate brigades advanced as they drove off federal skirmishers, but Ewell recalled them as nothing could be gained by advancing away from Jackson and the point of main effort.[91]

As Shields had done little to support Carroll, Jackson calculated that this lassitude offered him the chance to switch the bulk of his force to the area south and east of Port Republic and attack him. Ewell received orders to pull back at

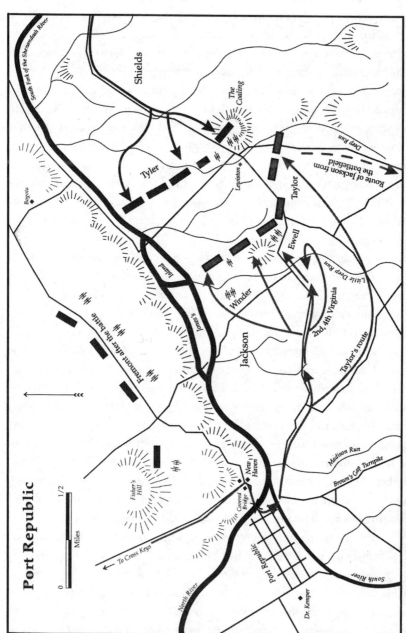

From James Robertson, *Stonewall Jackson: The Man, the Soldier, the Legend*, 1st ed., p. 439. © 1997 Gale, a part of Cengage Learning, Inc. Reproduced by permission. www.cengage.com/permissions.

daylight on June 9 leaving one brigade behind to bluff Frémont that he faced a much larger force. The remaining five brigades (with a sixth guarding Port Republic) would defeat Shields. Jackson had formed an imaginative and audacious plan but to succeed it required a series of rapid and hastily improvised movements. Jackson intended to approach, fight a battle, win, pursue, return whence he came, and fight again—all in eight hours.[92]

The battle of Port Republic got off to an unpromising start for Jackson with Confederate columns stumbling forward in thick fog. Once he engaged Union skirmishers, Jackson impulsively launched an unsupported attack by the Stonewall Brigade in order that he would not lose the benefit of surprise. Jackson had miscalculated because he faced two Union brigades under the command of Brigadier General E. B. Tyler who had occupied a strong position with sixteen guns anchored on a spur called The Coaling. Brigadier General Charles S. Winder's troops were driven back—a modicum of vigor on Tyler's part would have resulted in Jackson being driven from the field. Tyler had prepared a counterstroke but took too long about it. He was knocked off balance by Winder's renewed attack, and the day was saved for the Confederates by an outflanking attack by Brigadier General Richard Taylor's brigade on The Coaling that went in just as Winder concentrated all his fire on it, too.[93]

After 11 AM the federal line crumbled, and although Jackson mounted a pursuit, Union troops maintained cohesion and put up stiff resistance. Confederate casualties were 800 (with 160 in the Stonewall Brigade) to the Union 1,018 (including 450 prisoners of war). During the battle, Frémont drew up his forces along the high ground overlooking the North River and began an artillery bombardment. Anxious lest Frémont might attempt a turning movement via Conrad's Store, Jackson withdrew to Port Republic and then disengaged, heading for Brown's Gap and the Blue Ridge Mountains.

Throughout these operations in the Shenandoah Valley Jackson had shown three central qualities: first, a fine appreciation of position; second, a strategic instinct that frequently transcended the tactical circumstances he confronted, and enabled him to confer on the campaign an operational significance out of all proportion to the small size of his force; third, he developed a technique that would contribute to the later series of Confederate victories in Virginia— namely, he contrived to gain a local, tactical superiority in numbers at the decisive point. From these prime qualities flowed the other elements that allowed him to outgeneral his opponents: secrecy and superior intelligence, mobility, logistical preparation, and an unfailing faith in the offensive.[94]

His Union counterparts labored under organizational and logistical constraints, and a special case can be pleaded for each. In general, though, they lacked enterprise and were long on talk and short on action, especially Frémont. They frequently offered Jackson opportunities that he should have been denied. They lacked confidence and took counsel of their fears. Napoleon once claimed that one bad general was better than two good ones. In the valley a good general was faced by three poor ones, and for the first time in the Civil War a Confederate commander showed himself the superior. Jackson became the most illustrious soldier in the Confederacy, filling that hunger for a hero that the South yearned for.[95]

Efforts to romanticize Jackson's operations are dangerously misleading. Jackson carried out purges of Unionists as he advanced. The ideological forces that had led to the Civil War kept bursting through even in its earliest stages. Union troops had helped themselves to private property (especially in Blenker's division) but Confederates, too, were enthusiastic plunderers. The Union advances, though hesitant, had eroded the vitality of slavery in the valley, with numbers of "contrabands" taking to the roads; conversely, as Jackson returned, so did fears of reenslavement, not least among free blacks. Trains of refugees blocked the roads, adding to the congestion. The campaign in the valley started to wither away distinctions between soldiers and civilians. Union officers complained during the battle of Winchester that civilians (including women) fired on their troops from neighboring houses. Union attempts to stop this practice would lead to controversy later that summer.[96]

The Shenandoah Valley campaign came to an end when Lincoln instructed Frémont to return to Harrisonburg and stand on the defensive. The Mountain and Shenandoah Departments were not amalgamated but they were weakened. Jacob Cox was entrusted with the defense of West Virginia; Frémont and Banks's sphere was limited to guarding the Manassas Gap Railroad. Lincoln returned McDowell's First Corps to McClellan's command from which it had been removed without operational benefit. Still, Lincoln believed rightly that sufficient time still existed to effect a concentration before Richmond. It must be emphasized that the Confederates had not inflicted a permanent operational setback on Union arms.[97]

By the second week of June 1862 the second phase of the Civil War drew to its close. It had been dominated by naval and amphibious operations. The attritional effect of operations along the North Carolina and Louisiana coasts was spasmodic and not the result of any inspired, centrally directed strategy, though they accorded with Lincoln's wishes for a cordon offensive. They did indicate, however, that the balance of probability continued to indicate, especially in economic, organizational, and technological terms, the prospects of a Union victory in 1862.

The main significance of Jackson's victories, when he brought Union forces to battle under conditions that negated their customary features of superiority, lay in underlining that a Union victory would *not* result from an inevitable course of predetermined events. Jackson's actions showed, too, that the Confederacy could mobilize fighting power if a strong character could create a viable military organization. After Jackson's heroics, not only could the Confederate collapse be averted, but even an outright victory was not an impossibility. The Union position could collapse if Confederate forces operated in the vicinity of Washington, DC. They could bring intense pressure to bear on the Lincoln administration with less effect than was required to bring about the fall of Richmond. Other Union successes in North Carolina and Louisiana were much more indirect in their effects; the Confederate disaster in Arizona and New Mexico was almost completely forgotten.

The final aspect of these battles during a nine-month period refers to their small size. They appear halfhearted affairs with a limited social impact and light casualties as many Americans had suspected before April 1861. They manifested much movement but little hard fighting. From the summer of 1862 onward, the face of American battle would be transformed.

NOTES AND REFERENCES

1. Brian Holden Reid, "Enduring Patterns in Modern Warfare," in *The Nature of Future Conflict: Implications for Force Development*, eds. Brian Bond and Mungo Melvin, 25 (Strategic and Combat Studies Institute Occasional Paper No. 36, 1998).

2. Allan Nevins, *The Ordeal of the Union* (New York: Scribner's, 1947), vol. 1, pp. 327–29.

3. Donald J. Frazier, *Blood and Treasure: Confederate Empire in the Southwest* (College Station: Texas A&M University Press, 1995), pp. 21, 36.

4. Frazier, *Blood and Treasure*, pp. 30, 46, 50–51, 53–54, 61, 86, 94–95, 122, 136.

5. Ibid., pp. 54–55, 64–67, 69–70, 76; Jerry Thompson, *Confederate General of the West: Henry Hopkins Sibley* (1987; College Station: Texas A&M University Press, 1996), pp. 221–26.

6. Joseph G. Dawson III, *Doniphan's Epic March* (Lawrence: University Press of Kansas, 1999), pp. 47–48; Frazier, *Blood and Treasure*, pp. 101–106, 110, 114–16.

7. Thompson, *Sibley*, pp. 251–52, 260–61.

8. Frazier, *Blood and Treasure*, pp. 145–54, 160–67, 176–81; Thompson, *Sibley*, pp. 354, 365–66.

9. Frazier, *Blood and Treasure*, pp. 212–15, 216–24.

10. Ibid., pp. 236, 238, 240–49, 249–54, 266–61; Thompson, *Sibley*, pp. 298–300.

11. Thompson, *Sibley*, pp. 218, 237–38.

12. William H. Roberts, *Now for the Contest: Coastal and Oceanic Naval Operations in the Civil War* (Lincoln: University of Nebraska Press, 2004), pp. 12–13.

13. Benjamin F. Butler, *Butler's Book: A Review of his Legal, Political and Military Career* (Boston: Thayer, 1892), pp. 134, 140, 158–59; on his "search for the dramatic," see Hans L. Trefousse, *Ben Butler: The South Called Him Beast* (New York: Twayne, 1957), p. 84.

14. Simon Cameron to Benjamin F. Butler, June 22, 1862, in *Private and Official Correspondence of Benjamin F. Butler*, 5 vols., ed. Jessie Ames Marshall, vol. 1, 631 (Norwood, MA: Privately printed, 1917); Richard J. West, *Lincoln's Scapegoat General: A Life of Benjamin F. Butler* (Boston: Houghton Mifflin, 1965), p. 85.

15. Butler to Cameron, July 30, 1861, in Butler, *Correspondence*, vol. 1, pp. 106–107, 186–87; Kenneth P. Williams, *Lincoln Finds a General: A Military Study of the Civil War* (New York: Macmillan, 1949), vol. 1, p. 148.

16. Rowena Reed, *Combined Operations in the Civil War* (1978; Lincoln: University of Nebraska Press, 1993), pp. 11–12.

17. Roberts, *Now for the Contest*, p. 41.

18. Ibid., pp. 42–44; Reed, *Combined Operations*, pp. 13–14.

19. Robert E. Lee to Mildred Lee, Nov. 15, 1861, in *The Wartime Papers of R. E. Lee* (New York: Bramhall House, 1961), p. 86; Brian Holden Reid, *Robert E. Lee: Icon for a Nation* (2005; Amherst, NY: Prometheus Books, 2007), pp. 69–70.

20. Reed, *Combined Operations*, pp. 15–19.

21. The circumstances of McClellan's appointment are considered above, p. 67.

22. Reed, *Combined Operations*, pp. 36–38; for a reconstruction of McClellan's military outlook, see Roger Spiller, *An Instinct for War: Scenes from the Battlefields of History* (Cambridge, MA: Harvard University Press, 2005), pp. 162–63, 165–66, 172, 174–75, 184–85, 186, 191, 194, 196, 197, 199.

23. George B. McClellan to Stanton, Feb. 3, 1862 (probably drafted Jan. 31), in *The Civil War Papers of George B. McClellan: Selected Correspondence, 1860–1865*, ed. Stephen W. Sears (New York: Ticknor and Fields, 1989), p. 149.

24. William Marvel, *Burnside* (Chapel Hill: University of North Carolina Press, 1991), pp. 32–33.

25. McClellan to Burnside, Jan. 7, 1862, in McClellan, *Civil War Papers*, p. 149.

26. Marvel, *Burnside*, pp. 44–49; John G. Barrett, *The Civil War in North Carolina* (Chapel Hill: University of North Carolina Press, 1963), pp. 67, 70–71; McClellan to Burnside, Feb. 10, 1862, in McClellan, *Civil War Papers*, p. 175.

27. Marvel, *Burnside*, pp. 57–60; Reed, *Combined Operations*, p. 41; Barrett, *Civil War in North Carolina*, pp. 73–74, 77–83.

28. Marvel, *Burnside*, pp. 65–68; Barrett, *Civil War in North Carolina*, pp. 92–94.

29. Barrett, *Civil War in North Carolina*, pp. 96–97, 101–105; Marvel, *Burnside*, pp. 68–76.

30. Barrett, *Civil War in North Carolina*, pp. 113–20.

31. Marvel, *Burnside*, pp. 60, 76.

32. Roberts, *Now for the Contest*, pp. 33, 35.

33. Ezra J. Warner, *Generals in Gray* (Baton Rouge: Louisiana State University Press, 1959), pp. 194–95; Brian Holden Reid, *The Origins of the American Civil War* (London: Longman, 1996), p. 335.

34. Roberts, *Now for the Contest*, p. 35; Chester G. Hearn, *The Capture of New Orleans, 1862* (Baton Rouge: Louisiana State University Press, 1995), pp. 32, 36, 69–79; on the frittering of resources, see Raimondo Luraghi, *A History of the Confederate Navy* (Annapolis, MD: Naval Institute Press, 1996), pp. 48, 104–105, 107–10, 127–31, 155, 157.

35. Hearn, *New Orleans*, pp. 69, 87–95; Luraghi, *Confederate Navy*, p. 159.

36. William B. Hesseltine, *Lincoln and the War Governors* (New York: Alfred A. Knopf, 1955), pp. 186–91. Butler criticized the blockade and argued that the South should be flooded with luxury goods in return for cotton. The US Treasury issued licenses to loyal citizens who seized and sold cotton. Butler would make a fortune if he could seize a port and obtain licenses for his agents. Trefousse, *Butler*, pp. 88–92, 110, 120–22; Reed, *Combined Operations*, pp. 58–60.

37. Gideon Welles, *Diary of Gideon Welles*, 3 vols., ed. Howard K. Beale (New York: Norton, 1960), vol. 2, p. 119 (entry for Aug. 23, 1864); vol. 1, pp. 36–37, 60–61; McClellan to wife, Nov. 18, 1861, in McClellan, *Civil War Papers*, p. 136; T. M. Melia Smith, "David Dixon Porter: Fighting Sailor," in *Quarterdeck and Bridge: Two Centuries of American Naval Leaders*, ed. James C. Bradford, 183–86 (Annapolis, MD: Naval Institute Press, 1997).

38. Welles, *Diary*, vol. 2, p. 117 (entry for Aug. 23, 1864); Hearn, *New Orleans*, pp. 101–104, 125; Reed, *Combined Operations*, p. 61; Smith, "Porter," p. 186.

39. Warner, *Generals in Gray*, p. 194; Hearn, *New Orleans*, pp. 117, 120–21.

40. Welles to Farragut, Jan. 20, 1862, in *The War of the Rebellion: Official Records of the Union and Confederate Navies*, 30 vols. (Washington, DC: Government Printing Office, 1894–1927), series 1, vol. 16, p. 8.

41. Butler to Sarah Butler, Jan. 26, 1862, in Butler, *Correspondence*, vol. 1, p. 337; Hearn, *New Orleans*, pp. 99–100, 133, 173–76; Reed, *Combined Operations*, pp. 60–61; Trefousse, *Butler*, pp. 95–96.

42. Butler, *Butler's Book*, p. 334; McClellan to Butler, Feb. 23, 1862, in McClellan, *Civil War Papers*, pp. 187–88, 189; Trefousse, *Butler*, p. 97.

43. Hearn, *New Orleans*, p. 135; Trefousse, *Butler*, pp. 98–101; Reed, *Combined Operation*, pp. 58–60.

44. Hearn, *New Orleans*, pp. 169–70; William N. Still Jr., "David Glasgow Farragut: The Union's Nelson," in *Quarterdeck and Bridge*, ed. Bradford, p. 128; Edward L. Beach, "David Glasgow Farragut: Deliberate Planner, Impetuous Fighter," in *The Great Admirals: Command at Sea, 1587–1945*, ed. Jack Sweetman, 265 (Annapolis, MD: Naval Institute Press, 1997).

45. Hearn, *New Orleans*, pp. 38–40, 147–49, 154–55; Luraghi, *Confederate Navy*, pp. 159–60.

46. Hearn, *New Orleans*, pp. 177–83; Smith, "Porter," p. 186.

47. Hearn, *New Orleans*, pp. 185–87, 197; Still, "Farragut," p. 128.

48. Luraghi, *Confederate Navy*, pp. 160–61.

49. Still, "Farragut," p. 128; Hearn, *New Orleans*, pp. 198–206.

50. Hearn, *New Orleans*, pp. 201–202, 206–207; Still, "Farragut," pp. 129–30.

51. Beach, "Farragut," p. 266; Still, "Farragut," p. 130.

52. Hearn, *New Orleans*, pp. 234–41, 241–45, 248; Luraghi, *Confederate Navy*, pp. 161–63.

53. Trefousse, *Butler*, pp. 103–104; Welles, *Diary*, vol. 2, p. 114 (entry for Aug. 23, 1864).

54. Richard E. Beringer, Herman Hattaway, Archer Jones, and William N. Still Jr., *Why the South Lost the Civil War* (Athens: University of Georgia Press, 1986), pp. 134–39, 192.

55. Roberts, *Now for the Contest*, pp. 36–37; Barrett, *Civil War in North Carolina*, p. 121; Beringer et al., *Why the South Lost the Civil War*, pp. 187–88.

56. Gary W. Gallagher, "Introduction," in *The Shenandoah Valley Campaign of 1862*, ed. idem. (Chapel Hill: University of North Carolina Press, 2003), p. ix.

57. Charles Royster, *The Destructive War* (New York: Alfred A. Knopf, 1991), pp. 41, 77.

58. Allan Nevins, *The War for the Union* (New York: Scribner's, 1959), vol. 1, pp. 139–44.

59. Robert G. Tanner, *Stonewall in the Valley*, 2nd ed. (Mechanicsburg, PA: Stackpole Books, 1996), pp. 15–18.

60. Herman Hattaway and Archer Jones, *How the North Won: A Military History of the Civil War* (Urbana: University of Illinois Press, 1993), pp. 95, 97, 161–62, 176–77, conveys the tactical potential of Confederate movements in the Shenandoah but not the operational.

61. James I. Robertson Jr., *Stonewall Jackson: The Man, the Soldier, the Legend* (New York: Macmillan, 1997), pp. 284, 287, 294–97; Frank E. Vandiver, *Mighty Stonewall* (1957; College Station: Texas A&M University Press, 1995), pp. 185–88; Colonel

G. F. R. Henderson, *Stonewall Jackson and the American Civil War* (London: Longmans, 1898), vol. 1, p. 181.

62. Robertson, *Jackson*, pp. 306–14; Vandiver, *Mighty Stonewall*, pp. 188–90.

63. Henderson, *Stonewall Jackson*, vol. 1, pp. 192–93; Tanner, *Stonewall in the Valley*, pp. 87–88; Vandiver, *Mighty Stonewall*, pp. 191–95; Robertson, *Jackson*, pp. 314–21.

64. Steven H. Newton, *Joseph E. Johnston and the Defense of Richmond* (Lawrence: University Press of Kansas, 1998), pp. 86–87; Robertson, *Jackson*, pp. 325, 329; Douglas Southall Freeman, *Lee's Lieutenants* (New York: Scribner's, 1943), vol. 1, pp. 306, 328; Gallagher, "Introduction," in *Valley Campaign*, ed. idem., p. xiv.

65. Nelson to Henry Addington, Aug. 21, 1801, in *The Dispatches and Letters of Vice Admiral Lord Viscount Nelson*, ed. Sir Nicholas Harris Nicholas (London: Colburn, 1845), vol. 4, p. 475.

66. Henderson, *Stonewall Jackson*, vol. 1, p. 230; Vandiver, *Mighty Stonewall*, p. 201; Robertson, *Jackson*, pp. 331–34; Tanner, *Stonewall in the Valley*, pp. 106–10.

67. Henderson, *Stonewall Jackson*, vol. 1, pp. 222–24.

68. McClellan to Banks, Mar. 16, 1862, in McClellan, *Civil War Papers*, p. 212; Robertson, *Jackson*, pp. 339–42, 360–67; Freeman, *Lee's Lieutenants*, vol. 1, pp. 312–13; A. Cash Koeniger, "Prejudices and Partialities: The Garnett Controversy Revisited," in *Valley Campaign*, ed. Gallagher, pp. 219–35.

69. Henderson, *Stonewall Jackson*, vol. 1, pp. 247–49, rather overpaints these points; Gallagher, "Introduction," in *Valley Campaign*, ed. idem., p. xiii.

70. William L. Miller, "Such Men as Shields, Banks and Frémont: Federal Command in Western Virginia, March–June 1862," in *Valley Campaign*, ed. Gallagher, pp. 43–44; Allan Nevins, *Frémont: Pathmarker of the West*, new ed. (1933; New York: Longmans, 1955), pp. 550–54.

71. McClellan to Banks, Mar. 24 (telegram), Apr. 1, 1862, in McClellan, *Civil War Papers*, pp. 217, 220–21; Miller, "Federal Command," pp. 54–55, 66–67; Nevins, *Frémont*, p. 555.

72. Newton, *Defense of Richmond*, pp. 162–64; Robertson, *Jackson*, pp. 353–56, 364–70.

73. Robertson, *Jackson*, pp. 375–76; even Henderson, *Stonewall Jackson*, vol. 1, pp. 295–301, regards McDowell as tactically "insignificant"; Tanner, *Stonewall in the Valley*, pp. 194–96.

74. Miller, "Union Command," p. 63.

75. Robertson, *Jackson*, pp. 376–79, 381–85; Lee to Jackson, May 18, 1862, in Lee, *Wartime Papers*, pp. 174–75.

76. Robertson, *Jackson*, pp. 388–89, 859n120.

77. Ibid., pp. 391–92; Tanner, *Stonewall in the Valley*, pp. 246–52.

78. Freeman, *Lee's Lieutenants*, vol. 3, pp. 376–82.

79. Tanner, *Stonewall in the Valley*, pp. 268–71; Miller, "Federal Command," p. 56.

80. Tanner, *Stonewall in the Valley*, pp. 278–86; Terry L. Jones, *Lee's Tigers: The Louisiana Infantry in the Army of Northern Virginia* (Baton Rouge: Louisiana State University Press, 1987), pp. 78–80.

81. Robertson, *Jackson*, pp. 408–11.

82. Abraham Lincoln to McClellan, May 26, 1862, in *The Collected Works of Abraham Lincoln* (Rutgers, NJ: Rutgers University Press, 1953), vol. 5, p. 236.

83. Lincoln to Frémont, May 24, 1862, in ibid., vol. 5, p. 230; Miller, "Federal Command," p. 65.

84. Lincoln to Frémont, May 27–29, 1862, in *Collected Works*, vol. 5, pp. 243, 247; Gallagher, "Introduction," and Miller, "Federal Command," pp. 16, 68–70; Nevins, *Frémont*, pp. 558–60; Williams, *Lincoln Finds a General*, vol. 1, pp. 187–91, doubts that the roads to Harrisonburg were any worse than others used during the campaign.

85. See McClellan to Lincoln, May 26, 27, 1862 (telegrams), in McClellan, *Civil War Papers*, pp. 276, 277; Gallagher, "Abraham Lincoln and the 1862 Shenandoah Valley Campaign," in *Shenandoah Valley Campaign of 1862*, ed. idem., pp. 3–4, 8, 10–11.

86. Williams, *Lincoln Finds a General*, vol. 1, pp. 192, 205–208; Robertson, *Jackson*, pp. 417–22, 423–35; Tanner, *Stonewall in the Valley*, pp. 346–52.

87. Freeman, *Lee's Lieutenants*, vol. 1, pp. 435–36; Miller, "Federal Command," p. 77.

88. Baron Jomini laid it down as a principle "that, if the enemy divides his forces on an extended front, the best direction of the manoeuvre-line will be upon his center." See *The Art of War* (1862; London: Greenhill, 1992), p. 115.

89. Williams, *Lincoln Finds a General*, vol. 1, pp. 200–201; Miller, "Federal Command," p. 76.

90. Tanner, *Stonewall in the Valley*, pp. 375–78, 379–83; Williams, *Lincoln Finds a General*, vol. 1, p. 201.

91. Paul D. Casdorph, *Confederate General R. S. Ewell* (Lexington: University Press of Kentucky, 2004), p. 150; Williams, *Lincoln Finds a General*, vol. 1, p. 202; Nevins, *Frémont*, p. 558. Frémont was proud of having kept "in sight of the enemy."

92. Robertson, *Jackson*, pp. 438, 440; Tanner, *Stonewall in the Valley*, pp. 387–88, 393–96.

93. Freeman, *Lee's Lieutenants*, vol. 1, pp. 454–61; Casdorph, *Ewell*, p. 151; Robert E. L. Krick, "Maryland's Ablest Confederate: General Charles W. Winder and the Stonewall Brigade," in *Shenandoah Campaign 1862*, ed. Gallagher, p. 202.

94. Freeman, *Lee's Lieutenants*, vol. 1, pp. 481–85; see also, Robertson, *Jackson*, pp. 466–68.

95. Miller, "Federal Command," pp. 72–74, 78–79, 80; Robert K. Krick, "the Metamorphosis in Stonewall Jackson's Public Image," in *Shenandoah Valley Campaign of 1862*, ed. Gallagher, pp. 24–42.

96. Jonathan M. Berkey, "In the Very Midst of the War Track: The Valley's Civilians and the Shenandoah Campaign," in *Shenandoah Campaign of 1862*, ed. Gallagher, pp. 88–80, 91–95, 96, 98–101, 103–105.

97. Lincoln to Frémont, June 9, 1862, in Lincoln, *Collected Works*, vol. 5, pp. 264–68.

Chapter Four

UNION FRUSTRATION
APRIL TO JULY 1862

The eyes of politicians were, and would remain, firmly fixed on the course of military operations in Virginia. They were not wrong to do this, but their vision was constricted and it disguised the fact that military operations in the west were important for both sides, but especially for the Union. Indeed, after a slow start, it was in the Mississippi valley that the velocity of land operations began to accelerate, culminating in the next great battle, Shiloh. These operations had surprisingly little political impact in Washington, DC, though the successes of Northern generals put more pressure on McClellan to act (though he gained no credit for those distant operations carried out while he was general-in-chief). He confronted the insuperable difficulty that the theater of military operations in the west was more suitable for mounting offensive operations than the one in the east. This fact likewise presented severe difficulties for Confederate strategic planners, whose discussions were no more ordered and structured than those of the Union. This was despite a self-conscious but ultimately doomed effort to nurture unanimity and patriotic single-mindedness, and rid the Confederate war effort of the curse of self-seeking "politics." If secession was a resolution against "politics," as one historian has claimed, then it had a disappointingly meager strategic dividend.[1]

The fundamental strategic problem faced by the Confederacy was the relative priority to be allotted to the defense of the Mississippi valley and Virginia. The former presented an avenue of advance into the Confederate "heartland," the latter protected the Confederate capital and its attendant war industries. This strategic conundrum has been reflected in the debate among historians over the most beneficial strategy for the Confederacy, and this has become mixed up in one of their favorite controversies, the search for an explanation for why the South lost. Until the 1960s historians (even Southern historians, who tended to dominate the study of the Civil War) were relatively uninterested in the Confederate war effort in the west. The miserable toll of defeats in that theater, and its unedifying crew of senior officers, contrasted so unfavorably with the epic series of victories won by the Army of Northern Virginia under the charismatic and inspired leadership of Robert E. Lee, "Stonewall" Jackson, and "Jeb" Stuart. In the east Lee and his men came to be regarded as the true "cavaliers." They represented all the admirable qualities that Southerners believed were associated with the "Lost Cause" and the "Southern military tradition." By comparison, the Army of Tennessee and the likes of Braxton Bragg were assigned to historiographical oblivion. "Robert E. Lee and the Army of Northern Virginia have been deified by writers such as Douglas Southall Freeman and Clifford Dowday as the epitome of what Southerners like to see in themselves—" writes Thomas L. Connelly with characteristic acidity, "knightly manners, gentleness, planter society."[2]

By the 1960s this preoccupation with the war in Virginia began to change. Increasingly, historians began to understand the importance of the west, and the vital role of its cities—Nashville, New Orleans, Vicksburg, and Chattanooga— in the defense of the Confederacy. If these urban industrial centers were lost, then so was the Confederacy: it could not continue without the foodstuffs from west of the Mississippi, and the loss of the river was a catastrophic strategic blow from which it could not recover.[3] Increasingly, historians blamed the Confederate government for lavishing excessive resources and attention on the war in Virginia, and Robert E. Lee for advocating an offensive strategy that drained the lifeblood from Confederate armies and dissipated resources, especially during his ill-fated adventures in Maryland in 1862 and Pennsylvania in 1863. Properly employed, these troops could have been put to better use shoring up the crumbling Confederate position in the west. Increasingly, too, American scholars have become obsessed with "casualty avoidance" as a strategic panacea, reflecting widespread anxieties about this concern in the media since the end of the

Vietnam War—an anxiety that was not shared in the nineteenth century. Thus the conclusion was reached: the South would have been better advised to adopt a defensive strategy, eschewing wasteful offensive adventures. The main aim of the Confederacy was to survive and persuade the Union that the task of crushing it was too great. Maintaining Confederate armies "in being" was its prime endeavor.[4]

The argument that the South should have traded space for time is not a new one. Major General J. F. C. Fuller, in his very influential books on the Civil War, agreed that the great strategic strength of the Confederacy lay in its size and lack of communications, which would render Union advances difficult. The Confederacy should have concentrated its forces in the west, in Tennessee focused around Chattanooga, leaving a "covering force" in Virginia. A defensive–offensive campaign "if pushed with vigor" would have protected the Deep South, while maintaining "the vital crossings into Missouri, Arkansas and Louisiana," which would have "stretched out a helping hand to Kentucky." It is Fuller, moreover, who is the source of the much-repeated argument that Lee was "heart and soul a Virginian" and that as a strategist he was obsessively parochial.[5]

Discussion of some of these points will have to be deferred until later chapters, but the basic problem must be considered now. Perhaps the most perplexing problem of First Manassas was how to exploit this victory to the fullest. The obsession with the romantic figure of Napoleon prevented a rationalization of strategy. "I always favored a short and quick war, which should be decided by a few Great Battles," P. G. T. Beauregard wrote after the war. Such a policy demanded *concentration*. As Beauregard argued in 1862, "our only success lies in throwing all our forces into large armies, with which to meet and successfully overthrow our adversary. The result of one such victory would be worth more to us than the occupation of all our important cities to our enemies."[6] A victory demanded offensive action; otherwise its advantages, gained at such cost, would be frittered away. Where victories were won clearly has a bearing on the strategic debate.

It is a distorting argument to suggest that because one theater of war, the west, has been neglected, that most resources should have been devoted to it and that Virginia was of less account. Many of the histories that have argued for an increased emphasis on the Mississippi valley, especially the writings of Thomas L. Connelly, reveal a penchant for polemical exaggeration and a one-sidedness that they readily accuse earlier historians of. Virginia was well defended for strong strategic reasons. There was a feeling during the 1970s and 1980s—but especially during the Reagan years—that the "heartland" was intrinsically more valuable than the coastal regions and this tended to percolate into the furthest reaches of Civil War historiography. This is not so; Virginia and the Carolinas contained almost half of the Confederacy's infant industries (49.9 percent), 37 percent of its white population (34.5 percent of its population liable to military service), and Virginia alone enjoyed the benefit of 19.8 percent of the South's railroads. The industrial output of Virginia by itself would ensure that she would be an important defensive priority, as the Old Dominion produced 32.5 percent of the Confederacy's total output of manufactured goods. The factories of Henrico County, Virginia, produced more manufactured goods than Alabama, Arkansas, South Carolina, Mississippi, Florida, and Texas put together. None of this could be given up easily.[7]

All the more severe critics of Confederate strategy agree, even when they advocate emphatically an increased defensive element, that it should still have retained an offensive aspect. The trouble with this criticism is that Confederate grand strategy was based on the *defensive–offensive*. Confederate leaders were much influenced by the experience of the American Revolution. Two generals, Joseph E. Johnston and Maxcy Gregg, carried the swords and pistols worn by their fathers in the Revolutionary War. Thus the experience of George Washington crossing the Delaware at Trenton excited their imaginations, for Washington was faced by great odds yet still prevailed. Keeping their armies "in being," as Washington had managed to do, would go a long way to asserting Southern independence. But the federal armies were more than three thousand miles nearer to the South than the bulk of the British army was in 1775–83. Jefferson Davis calculated that federal penetrations could not be resisted on every front; but he hoped that in launching counterattacks the Confederacy would be able to select "the time and place of the attack." Southern territory could be traded if the opportunity presented itself to strike back effectively. All agreed, however, that their strategy did not depend on an outright strategic offensive *northward*, for "Confederate independence," as Emory M. Thomas has remarked, "did not require Lee to take Boston."[8]

There were two prime difficulties with the way Davis's strategy—which was never codified—worked out in practice. Withdrawals were passionately opposed by the political leaders (who were often also military commanders) of the territory abandoned. The South had selected to defend supposedly endangered property rights—namely slavery. As soon as Confederate forces withdrew, black slaves withdrew their labor from the plantations and many fled to Union camps. This gravely weakened plantation slavery even before the Lincoln administration began to pass legislation against it. The First Confiscation Act, urged on

Congress by the president on March 6, 1862, was aimed against the owners who used their slaves to aid rebellion. The Second Confiscation Act of July 17 decreed that if slaves entered Union camps they would be automatically emancipated. Consequently, during 1862 the approach of Union armies provoked dread among slaveowners. This fanned bitter opposition within the Confederate congress against the Davis administration. So-called Confederate States, such as Missouri and Kentucky, which was abandoned in 1862, produced some of Davis's most venomous critics. General Sterling Price of Missouri, for example, was soon feuding with Davis in June 1862 after Confederate forces had been driven from Missouri and his troops were withdrawn from neighboring Arkansas. Political opposition in the Confederacy assumed a more personal element because of the self-conscious and applauded banishment of party politics from its government. The Confederate president, therefore, could not view the abandonment of territory for long with equanimity.[9]

Secondly, the South's internal lines of communication were not adequate to cope with the movement of forces around the Confederacy that the defensive–offensive demanded. Davis's critics, Beauregard, Johnston, and Price, all of whom soon became the objects of the president's ferocious hatred, demanded concentration at certain points. But Davis realized that the creation of the large field armies they demanded would leave large parts of the Confederacy vulnerable to federal invasion. Davis's own compromise was the distribution of Confederate forces in a series of garrisons in "departments" (in imitation of US military organization) with the understanding that *endangered points* (which, of course, included the field armies) would be reinforced from the safer areas promptly. The Southern railroad system collapsed under the strain; but in any case the strategy, recalling perhaps British logistical struggles of 1777–81, overlooked the possibility that Union material superiority would grow so great that all exposed points could be attacked simultaneously.[10]

It might be asserted that these arguments vindicate those contemporaries (and later historians) who contended that the west was neglected and that Davis and his advisers spent too much time and effort on the war in Virginia. Davis's own property was in Mississippi, so he had no personal reasons for favoring the Old Dominion over the west. But all critics of the priority given to the war effort in Virginia overlook its colossal importance to the Confederacy. The Confederate capital at Richmond could not be given up irrespective of its economic value. Its loss early in the struggle would have been calamitous—especially if the Confederacy was serious in its efforts to persuade Great Britain and France to intervene on its behalf. It is irrelevant to argue that it was a "mistake" to move the capital from Montgomery, Alabama, and that thereafter strategy was distorted by politics; no strategy is ever formulated in a political vacuum. Virginia could offer military resources to the Confederacy that were unmatched by any other Southern state. The plain fact of the matter was that Montgomery was unsuitable in every way to be a capital city. The only other candidates, New Orleans and Nashville, were just as vulnerable as Richmond while lacking its military and geographic advantages.[11]

Virginia enjoyed strategic benefits that would have been foolish to give up voluntarily. It had a strong natural defensive position; the northern part of the state was narrow, confined by mountains which channeled avenues of advance *away* from Richmond, and was crisscrossed by rivers flowing west–east that obstructed an attacker's line of advance. In fact, because of its proximity to the uncensored newspapers and political commotion of Washington, DC, intelligence in this theater was so much better than in the west. In addition, organizing an army here was facilitated by the comparative efficiency of the Virginia militia, with a significantly larger percentage of trained or experienced officers and non-commissioned officers. This provided a cement and hard core around which the aggregate of the esprit de corps of the Army of Northern Virginia could consolidate. The comparative efficiency of Virginia's railroads rendered moving troops around the state more than just a forlorn hope. Virginia thus presented itself as a bastion from which attacks could be launched on the North. In other words, no western state offered comparative advantages that could have come near to compensating for the catastrophic losses should Virginia be given up.[12]

It is also overlooked that the farther south the Union forces advanced into Virginia the more difficult the defense of the Carolinas became. In April 1862, General Robert E. Lee, Jefferson Davis's military adviser, urged a concentration in Virginia. "The need for troops in the vicinity of Fredericksburg is very urgent," he wrote after McClellan had begun his advance on Richmond up the Peninsula, "and they can contribute to the defense of North Carolina as materially at that point, as they would in assisting to prevent an advance from the enemy now occupying the eastern waters of the state." Yet the political ramifications of fighting in Virginia should never be underrated, and Davis did not do so. In short, the strategic advantages of the Virginia theater, and the arguments underpinning it, had been rehearsed *before* Lee took command of the Army of Northern Virginia. Because of the political stakes, as Joseph E. Johnston argued in October 1861, Virginia was the crucial theater. "Success here . . . saves everything; defeat here loses all," he contended passionately. Lee came to argue this case with great authority; but he was not its only advocate nor was he the first to hold this view. If we can consider these strategic debates in a more supple manner, then we should stop personalizing the disputes. If such an approach is adopted, historians might focus on the systems through which they had to work rather than on the merits or faults of Civil War generals.[13]

There can be no doubting the disadvantages under which the Confederacy's western generals labored. The great Mississippi River system offered up a huge avenue of offensive penetration, and scant defense because the streams were easily crossed. Unlike Virginia, the boundaries of the theater of operations were vague and not clearly demarcated by physical geography. Yet few of the advocates of an increased emphasis on the west in Confederate strategy remark on the obvious point that this vagueness should have been a huge advantage for Confederate strategy. Nobody in Richmond, least of all General Lee, needed to be persuaded that "If Mississippi Valley is lost Atlantic states will be ruined." What can be doubted is the ability of Confederate generals in the west to make effective use of what resources and advantages they did enjoy. It is a moot point as to whether they had the capacity to cooperate, put together workable plans, and create armies with a sense of moral cohesion and esprit de corps out of formations that were disparate and inexperienced fragments.[14]

By the spring of 1862 despite its initial failures, Union power was being brought to bear on the margins of the Confederacy. The Confederates tasted defeat at Mill Springs, Kentucky (January 20, 1862) and Pea Ridge, Arkansas (March 7–8, 1862). The latter had been brought on by the advance of Brigadier General Ulysses S. Grant into the Mississippi basin. Grant was an enigmatic personality frequently underrated by those who met him, as he had none of the histrionic qualities associated with Napoleonic warfare by mid-nineteenth-century Americans; as it turned out, Grant had much more in common with Napoleon than all of his latter-day textbook imitators. Certainly Grant had no flair for self-advertisement as they had, and tended to be gruff and taciturn though he was fluent with the pen. His early successes were put down erroneously to his voluble and articulate chief of staff, John A. Rawlins. Grant was a self-assured general; he had immense inner strength and vitality of intellect. He could always see what needed to be done to seize and maintain the initiative.[15]

Grant blooded himself and his troops at the battle of Belmont (November 7, 1861). From his early experiences Grant gained one lesson of immense importance: "I never experienced trepidation upon confronting an enemy, though I always felt more or less anxiety. I never forgot that he [the enemy commander] had as much reason to fear my forces as I had his." This was a lesson—on the need to hit the enemy hard rather than fear when the enemy was going to strike him—that some other Union generals should have learned early on but failed to grasp because they had not enjoyed wide experience of subordinate command.[16]

Grant had clearly given a great deal of thought to the conduct of the war so far (though he gives little indication of this in his *Memoirs*). In February 1862 Grant wrote: "these terrible battles are very good things to read about for persons who lose no friends, but I am decidedly in favor of having as little of it as possible. The way to avoid it is to push forward as vigorously as possible."[17] This is an important clue as to Grant's later, mature military methods: he attempted to use mobility as an antidote to defensive firepower and field fortifications. Even in their early crude form, Grant's methods caught Confederate strategists wrongfooted. The result of Grant's vigor was to stir up a hornet's nest and provoke great battles that would dwarf those he so regretted in 1861 and the early months of 1862.

The inherent vulnerabilities of the Confederate western theater are well exemplified by the experience of General Albert Sidney Johnston when he took over the Second Department on September 1, 1861. Johnston was one of those officers who had a grossly inflated, largely press-sponsored reputation based on little experience. Johnston struggled to impose some kind of strategy on his huge, sprawling department. Political pressure demanded that he defend the area north of Bowling Green, Kentucky, though it had no natural defensive strengths, was damp and unhealthy, and overstretched Johnston's small force of twenty-seven thousand men. Indeed an earlier rash advance here by Leonidas Polk had infringed Kentucky's neutrality and gravely weakened the Confederate position. Johnston thus had a secondary defensive line based on Clarksville, Tennessee, surveyed. There was a good measure of bluff in those dispositions. The flanks were weak, and Johnston had rather blithely assumed that the citizens of Nashville would be keen to assist, with financial contributions and by lending their slaves for labor, in the construction of these defensive lines. Here he was to be disillusioned, for Nashville's leading citizens were prickly, mean, and wholly wrapped up in protecting their prosperous, elegant, and comfortable lives. The two vital outposts that protected the avenue of advance through the secondary line on the Tennessee and Cumberland rivers, Forts Henry and Donelson, were incomplete, undergunned, and undermanned. It was this bubble of bluff and unpreparedness that Grant pricked so abruptly by his sudden advance on the two forts.[18]

Seizure of Fort Henry on the right bank of the Tennessee River would cut the Memphis and Ohio Railroad, and Donelson, placed on the left bank of the Cumberland River, served as the bastion for Nashville. Grant had no elaborate strategic design in mind when making his move. He was keen to maintain the morale and fighting edge of his troops after Belmont. Yet his whole conduct of the campaign revealed an instinctive flair for the operational level of war. Grant was actually ordered by Major General Henry W. Halleck, Commander of the Department of Missouri, to mount a demonstration to enable Don Carlos Buell, the commander of the Department of the Ohio, to attack Johnston's outpost at Bowling Green. Despite appalling weather, a mixture of snow and rain, and bad roads, Grant made good progress in his advance toward Fort Henry; his success was mainly due to his effective use of naval gunboats. A reliance on naval power was a hallmark of Grant's generalship. His personal relations with the naval flag officer commanding the flotilla, Captain Andrew Foote, were warm and harmonious; better, in fact, than they were with his departmental commander, Halleck, who nursed a deep-seated suspicion of Grant, based probably on recollections of his inadequacy as a peacetime soldier.

On February 1, 1862, after some hesitation Halleck gave Grant permission to attack Fort Henry. Grant made maximum use of naval power to land his troops as near to the fort as possible without incurring casualties from its guns. Wartime American wooden ships and ironclads were an entirely coastal fleet, with only a sixteen-foot draught for sea service and even less for this type of riverine operation. They were ideal for the type of operation that Grant envisaged. His tactical plan was consistent with the conclusions he had drawn so far about the nature of the war. The two forts were separated by only eleven miles. Succor would not be long in coming and Grant wished to avoid a stalemate. Thus, as Grant recalled in his *Memoirs*, "the two positions were so important to the enemy, *as he saw his interest*, that it was natural to suppose that reinforcements would come from every quarter from which they could be got. Prompt action on our part was imperative." It is Grant's recognition of the supreme value of military time that so marks him out from other federal generals at this and any stage of the war. Fort Henry was thus seized in a coup de main, gained in a simultaneous assault by the army and the gunboats.[19]

Grant then turned his attention on Donelson. This nut's shell would be much harder to crack. The fort itself was on high ground and its defenses were stronger. "I was very impatient to get to Fort Donelson," Grant recalled, "because I knew the importance of the place to the enemy and supposed he would reinforce it rapidly. I felt that 15,000 men on the 8th [February, 1862] would be more effective than 50,000 a month later." Grant was right; such audacity was so rare among administratively inclined federal generals. Yet Grant's operations did not go like clockwork. He hoped to pin the enemy to his defenses while the gunboats destroyed his guns. But in the artillery duel the gunboats were mauled and forced to withdraw.[20]

On February 14, in chilling cold, naval reinforcements arrived and a fresh division commanded by Major General Lew Wallace who, though his true talents lay in writing novels rather than in tactics, was very welcome. The whole Confederate conduct of the defense of Tennessee was to reveal the systemic and personal paralysis that was to cripple conduct of the war in this region. Johnston had found operations at a high level unduly taxing and often sought refuge in detail. He was surprised by Buell's advance and seemed to duck responsibility for Donelson's defense by devolving command for the fort onto John B. Floyd, former US president James Buchanan's secretary of war; choosing Floyd was a grave misjudgment. A timorous windbag, Floyd was ignorant of tactics and provided no firm or energetic leadership to galvanize the beleaguered garrison. Donelson was actually weakest on the landside, as the initial operations had revealed. Signaling the many disputes that would follow, Floyd quarreled with his subordinates, especially with the Mexican War veteran, Gideon J. Pillow. Floundering in indecision Floyd lost his opportunity to extricate the garrison, which was running low on ammunition; he then compounded his error by launching a preemptive counterattack just at the moment when Grant was reinforced. This was beaten back, whereupon Grant, showing powers of decision beyond his Confederate counterparts, launched a counterstroke and broke inside their lines. Floyd then convened a council of war, that perennial device of Confederate generals in the west when they encountered insuperable difficulties or lacked the confidence to impose their solutions on their subordinates. Floyd, fearful for his own skin, Pillow, plus Nathan Bedford Forrest and the cavalry escaped; the remainder of the garrison, about twenty-five thousand men, surrendered to Grant unconditionally.[21]

The demand for "unconditional surrender" made by Grant and the peremptory tone of his correspondence, "I propose to move immediately upon your works," brought him celebrity at a time when Northern morale was low. But the term was not new and Grant may have followed the precedent set by a Confederate, Sterling Price, when he demanded the unconditional surrender of Lexington, Missouri, in September 1861.[22] Nonetheless the extent of the Confederate disaster in northern Tennessee, exposing Nashville to capture, demanded an immediate counteroffensive. The first effort came in the trans-Mississippi. Major General Earl Van Dorn, an empty-headed adventurer whose roving eye was just as likely to alight on attractive ladies as it was on topography, was placed in command of the Army of the West. Van Dorn and the fractious Sterling Price were keen to create a diversion away from the Cumberland River and launched an attack in northern Arkansas. The Union forces, commanded by

Samuel R. Curtis, took up a strong position behind Pea Ridge covered by trees and dirt breastworks. Van Dorn and Price advanced in two widely converging outflanking columns; separated by Pea Ridge they could not see one another or communicate. The attacks were uncoordinated, defeated in detail, and discipline disintegrated; the Confederates were driven from the field and if a competent pursuit had been mounted, the Army of the West would have been destroyed. Albert Castel argues that at Pea Ridge "a sound strategical concept" was "ruined by poor tactical execution." This is probably correct, but the defeat was symptomatic of a grave Confederate flaw: the inability to mount a cohesive, coordinated offensive blow to strike at the decisive point.[23]

By the spring of 1862 it appeared that the Confederacy might not survive to see another winter. The Mississippi lay open and vulnerable, New Orleans had fallen, and McClellan was about to launch his "grand campaign" that many imagined would bring the war to an end with the fall of Richmond. But despite the very real advances that the Union cause had made, no coherent strategy had yet been imposed on its forces; these advances were made piecemeal, especially in the Mississippi basin, and they were easily frustrated. Union offensives in the west, according to Rowena Reed, were "random, uncoordinated and not tied to any particular intention."[24]

Fortunately for the North, these errors were replicated by the Confederacy. Throughout the remainder of the campaign, Albert Sidney Johnston behaved like a superior army commander. For the first time the Army of Mississippi began to meld as an integral force with an organization of its own. Johnston sought to rectify the strategic disadvantages of the western theater by concentration. On March 23, Van Dorn's forces were summoned by President Davis to the east bank of the Mississippi—although they did not arrive until after the battle of Shiloh had been fought, an exemplification of the weaknesses of the defensive–offensive strategy in practice. But a viable command system was not created to effectively command and control these disparate forces. Johnston has been severely criticized throughout this period. Yet he acted with dispatch and insight, and patched together a strong and enthusiastic army which could have launched an effective counteroffensive. But Johnston could not transcend the command myopia of the time. He could not free himself from detail and take the larger view; the easiest way to do this was by finding a competent army commander who could implement his strategic wishes and free him from the burden of administration.[25]

A candidate was available. On February 4 P. G. T. Beauregard arrived at Columbus to take command of the "left wing." He again became second in com-

mand but with no clear-cut area of responsibility. Yet again Confederate armies suffered from an excess of command and a minimum of control. For once Beauregard's
penchant for the grandiose was appropriate. On February 23, watched by a populace "dumb with apprehension," Don Carlos Buell entered Nashville. Grant, with
120 boats and more than forty thousand men, had passed down the Tennessee
River and formed a menacing bridgehead at Pittsburg Landing, Tennessee.[26] Johnston was at first uncertain of Grant's movements but by March 24 his location was
plain. Beauregard urged a counteroffensive to protect the Mississippi valley; if it
had succeeded, Nashville would have been recovered. The notion that the "heartland" and the Mississippi valley were somehow competing alternatives, as suggested by Thomas L. Connelly, is both parochial and a false antithesis.[27]

The Union tightened its grip on the Mississippi, taking Island No. 10 on
April 1, 1862, brushing aside the Confederate defenders; but the commander of
this minor operation, Major General John Pope, gained from it an inflated reputation which would rebound against him.[28] Further east, General Grant was
eager to attack the enemy again. "I want to push on as rapidly as possible to save
hard fighting," he told his wife. Several weeks later he was of the opinion that,
"With one more great success I do not see how the rebellion is to be sustained."
The latter sentiment indicates how widespread the notion was that the whole war
could be brought to an end by a couple of big battles; it was not just confined to
McClellan, or the politicians in Washington. As he set up camp in southwestern
Tennessee near Shiloh Church, a small, wooden meetinghouse, Grant certainly
exuded a measure of complacency; he did not anticipate being attacked, although
this was far from being a remote possibility. He had been ordered by Halleck to
entrench, but he preferred instead to drill and discipline his raw troops rather
than smother their training prospects with digging details.[29]

The Confederate design, shaped by Beauregard, was an elegant etching.
Beauregard was fascinated by the Waterloo campaign, and the strategic dimen-
sion of the plan reveals a number of striking parallels with that famous clash.
Beauregard had Johnston playing Napoleon, concentrating his forces to strike at
Grant's Wellington and Buell's Blücher in detail, before the latter two could
combine their potentially superior forces. But here any Napoleonic parallel ends.
Because Van Dorn lacked rail transport he had not arrived before the battle and
Johnston thus had not gained local superiority over Grant, with 40,335 opposed
to the latter's 42,682. Moreover, Johnston could not get between Grant and
Buell's twenty thousand men or delay their union because of an amateurish and
chaotic approach march, with straggling and disorder stretching all the way
back to the Confederate base at Corinth, Mississippi. (Buell was encamped at

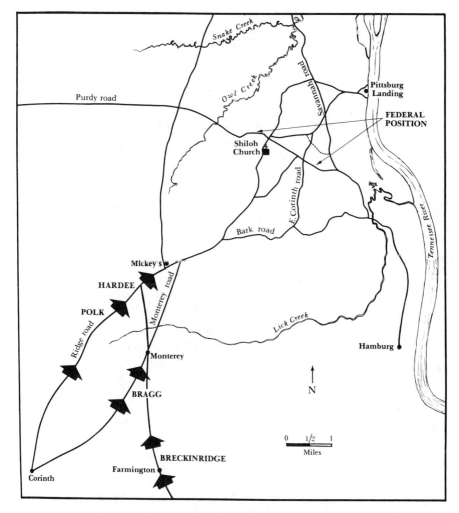

From *Shiloh: In Hell before Night* by James Lee McDonough
(Knoxville: University of Tennessee Press, 1977), p. 71. © 1977 by
James Lee McDonough. Reprinted by permission of the publisher.

Savannah, a few miles farther up the Tennessee River.) Troops on both sides were inexperienced and completely untried. The battle of Shiloh was to be a salutary learning experience for them.[30]

The conduct of the campaigns of the American Civil War has often been judged by theoretical criteria, and its generals have supposedly been "influenced" by military theorists such as Baron Jomini. Jomini was read before 1861 in an army that was entranced by the *image* of Napoleon and his achievements. Beauregard, a French-speaking Louisiana Creole, worshiped at the Napoleonic altar. We shall have occasion to review this question again, but it is important to underline at this juncture that the reading of theorists was *an effort to compensate for a lack of military experience, not supplement it.*

The actual conduct of the battle of Shiloh was a riot of military inexperience on both sides. Even when commanders, such as Beauregard, self-consciously sought to emulate Napoleon, their crude, amateurish execution transformed their mental aspirations into something quite unexpected. In short, we simply cannot assume a simplistic teleology—namely, that an idea for a campaign which resembles one to be found in a book indicates the "influence" of a certain theorist. There is no guarantee of direct influence on the daily, practical thinking behind a campaign, *even if the general concerned had read that theorist's book.* The process of putting together operational plans is a far too complex one for this simplistic link to be made with any measure of competence; and the appalling psychological pressures of command cannot be categorized with a degree of precision by reference to what a general reads (or has not read). The impossibility of documenting "influence" is acknowledged in all other areas of military history, save the American Civil War.[31]

Beauregard's distribution for Shiloh owed nothing to military theory but everything to inexperience. It was faulty in the extreme. He sought to attain concentration, which was unexceptional if vital, and he did this by launching the four Confederate "commands"—they were not organized corps with proper corps staffs, which was regrettable—in a direct frontal assault on Grant's forces, under what can only be described as a queue system. The commands were lined up one behind the other, no reserve was maintained, and the attack was heavily dependent on the weight of the initial shock. Johnston and Beauregard abdicated operational control of their army. But having relinquished control by this bizarre distribution, it was inevitable that the Confederate attack would degenerate into a series of uncoordinated tactical assaults; as the numerically weaker side, it would dissipate the strength of the offensive and reduce the fighting power directed at the decisive point.[32]

Once more strategic advantage was frittered away by faulty operations and naïve tactics. Beaureguard was unnerved by the confusion of the approach march, which he was convinced must have given the attack away. But Johnston showed admirable moral courage in insisting that the attack should be launched on the morning of April 6. "Tonight," he avowed, "we will water our horses in the Tennessee River!" If Johnston had behaved like a commanding general on the battlefield, then his gamble might have paid off. But the plan and its style of execution resulted in great confusion and lack of direction. If Grant kept his head, then greater federal numbers could be organized to throw the Confederate force back.[33]

This was what Grant managed to achieve. The first wave of the Confederate attack caught Grant's troops by surprise at their breakfasts. This caused great panic and some troops ran back toward the river. Here Grant, in great pain from a riding accident, personally rallied them and began to feed them back into the firing line. Instead of concentrating on outflanking and "rolling up" the defenders to break through to the Tennessee River on the right flank, the Confederate attack lost impact as it confronted improvised defensive points in the woods between Shiloh Church and the peach orchard—the most famous being the "hornet's nest" in the center. This was defended stoutly by Brigadier General Benjamin M. Prentiss, a volunteer officer who refused to withdraw and whose division was eventually enveloped and forced to surrender at 5:30 PM; but he had gained for Grant several precious hours. The four Confederate commanders—major generals William J. Hardee, Braxton Bragg, Leonidas Polk, and Brigadier General John C. Breckinridge—lacked divisional organization and their commands consisted of sixteen brigades, which accentuated the fragmentation of Confederate fighting power. Even though Owl Creek on the Union right and Lick Creek on the left were full of water, and thus forced a frontal attack, this does not excuse the faulty Confederate deployment. Johnston himself behaved like a battalion commander and was never available for major decisions; Beauregard was available but did not have the power to make them. Johnston himself was killed at 2:30 PM by a wound in the leg; his life could have been saved by elementary first aid. But for all the direction he exerted over the battle, his unnecessary death had no impact on the fighting. It had degenerated into a "soldier's battle," a euphemism for a shapeless, slogging match.[34]

Grant said of his troops that they were so raw, they "were hardly able to load their muskets according to the manual." Nonetheless, they had resisted stubbornly and a continuous defensive line was maintained as Grant's force was pushed back along the banks of the Tennessee rather than away from it. Grant's

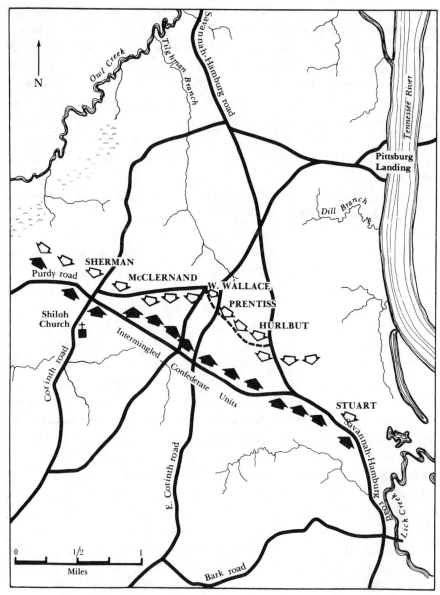

Map 6. Development of the Hornets' Nest, 9–12 A.M., April 6, 1862.

From *Shiloh: In Hell before Night* by James Lee McDonough
(Knoxville: University of Tennessee Press, 1977), p. 121. © 1977 by
James Lee McDonough. Reprinted by permission of the publisher.

attempts to organize his fighting power were initially handicapped by General Lew Wallace inadvertently marching his division *away* from the battlefield, but by evening he had come up, and Buell had pushed troops over Snake Creek and across the Tennessee River. By evening Grant knew that he was able to impose his will on the enemy the following day. His own account, of course, attempts to place his actions in the most favorable light. Yet he was absolutely correct in his confidence "that the next day would bring victory to our arms if we could only take the initiative," and he urged this on all his divisional commanders. On taking over command of the Confederate army after Johnston's death, Beauregard did not attempt to reorganize the attack and place more emphasis on the right; neither did he act urgently in the early evening and try one more throw because he believed mistakenly that Buell was far from the battlefield. This error was typical of faulty Confederate reconnaissance throughout the campaign.[35]

A rainy night interceded and the following morning Grant ordered a general counterstroke all along his line that pushed the Confederates back over the blood-sodden ground they had traversed at such cost the day before. Grant recalled seeing a field, which the Confederates had seized the previous day, "so covered with dead that it would have been possible to walk across the clearing, in any direction, stepping on dead bodies, without a foot touching the ground." Without a reserve at his disposal, and in the absence of Van Dorn, Beauregard had no choice but to give ground. His troops were exhausted by their sterling endeavors, but courage is a wasting asset when it is uncontrolled and rashly expended. By mid-afternoon Beauregard's battered forces were driven from the field. Fortunately for Beauregard, Grant's troops were too weary to pursue. Grant and Buell had not even discussed the detail of the pursuit. Buell just guessed that his advance on the Union left "would be in accord" with Grant's on the right. The Army of the Mississippi marched back in the rain to meet Van Dorn at Corinth.[36]

Shiloh was the first of the truly great battles of the Civil War, and, as a result, would always be remembered as one of the hardest fought engagements of the war. The impact of its casualties was traumatic. Confederate casualties totaled 10,699; the Union's were rather larger, 13,047. In a society comparatively free of the ravages of war, these figures (which combined were less than total French losses at the battle of Waterloo) appeared astronomical. They were greater than the total losses of the American Revolution, the War of 1812, and the Mexican War combined. This initial surprise infuriated many Northern critics and Grant was held to blame. Rumors of his prewar bibulous habits had obviously percolated through to reporters and Whitelaw Reid had telegraphed a report after the first stage of the battle claiming that Grant had fallen from his horse drunk. Grant's reputation was never to fully recover from these wholly unwarranted aspersions.[37]

The real significance of the battle of Shiloh was not just that the Confederate attempt to seize back the valuable counties of west Tennessee and the city of Nashville had been foiled, though this was hardly insignificant. It showed that the war in the west could not be won by a single dramatic battle. General Badeau, in his authorized account of Grant's military career, underlines the extent of Grant's own disillusionment with his earlier optimism. He echoes views that Grant would advance in his own personal memoirs several years later. "There was no course left," Badeau observes, "if the rebellion was to be suppressed, but to annihilate its strength, and root out the resources that supplied that strength." Furthermore, Grant's disillusion was capped by his experience after Shiloh. Halleck came up to take command personally, with Grant as his deputy. Combining the three armies of Grant, Buell, and Pope, he inched nervously toward the town of Corinth, constructing massive fortifications worthy of a Roman Army at every halt, in case Beauregard should be tempted to try to beat him in detail. With an army of almost 130,000 men Halleck made no attempt to destroy the remains of Beauregard's forces and was content to take Corinth at the end of May 1862. A great Union strategic opportunity had been squandered. Grant and his staff "could not see how the mere occupation of places was to close the war while large and effective rebel armies existed." Rapid offensive movement was needed to strike the enemy army, not timorous movements shielded by elaborate entrenchments. Badeau perhaps exaggerates the consistency of Grant's view, but there can be no doubting the prime lesson that Grant drew from Shiloh. Ceaseless attacks on its military strength were the only way to defeat the South: "to find and fight the rebel armies again and again . . . He did not underrate the value of places, but he was always willing to sacrifice them for armies."[38]

The federal offensive in the west had faced a Confederate counteroffensive but had thrown it back; nonetheless, the rebel army remained in being, its discipline and cohesion was unbroken, morale was surprisingly sturdy, and its commanders still cherished ambitious plans. Though significant territory had been lost this could be spared only temporarily; consequently, the strategic initiative in the west was still to be fought for.

In the east the pattern of events was similar. In April 1862 General McClellan at last launched his grand campaign that would bring the war to an end. He exuded confidence in the halls of Washington that he failed to demonstrate on the battlefields of eastern Virginia. So great was the yearning for a dramatic, decisive end to the fratricidal conflict that on the eve of McClellan's campaign, William H. Seward, the secretary of state, informed Senator Charles Sumner that he had "authentic information from Virginia that the Rebellion would be over there in four weeks." This source must have been McClellan, and the expectations he raised would soon become self-defeating.[39]

Like Grant, McClellan made much use of naval power in his advance up the Peninsula between the James and York rivers; this protected his flanks and was vital for logistical support—indeed in this campaign it was more important than the railways. McClellan's supply fleet consisted of 276 barges, schooners, and canal boats, plus 113 ferryboats and packets (chartered at a cost to the War Department of $24,300 per day). These 389 craft moved 121,500 men, 14,592 animals, 1,224 wagons and ambulances, and 44 batteries of artillery. This host required 600 tons of supplies every day. The fighting strength of the Army of the Potomac was sapped by a development that first became evident in the Napoleonic Wars. Simply to keep an army equipped to this level of sophistication, with troops used to a high standard of living, required greater and greater levels of logistical direction and planning. These demands sucked everincreasing numbers from the fighting units at the front to the administrating cadres in the rear, checking their returns, counting their sacks, and sending out memoranda. By the summer of 1862 more than 20 percent of McClellan's troops were involved in jobs that did not require fighting.[40]

McClellan's first priority was to establish a strong, inviolable base from which he could develop the operations of his four corps (whose commanders had been imposed on him just as be embarked). He abandoned his original preference for landing at Urbana and selected Fortress Monroe, which had remained in Union hands since April 1861. McClellan landed without incident and proceeded to fortify his position, an act which would serve as the hallmark of his generalship throughout the campaign. But in establishing himself, McClellan made a number of serious errors. He might have enjoyed an imaginative appreciation of the value of seapower, but he made little effort to cultivate the US Navy and take it into his confidence; as a result, naval operations were invariably muddled and improvised. Thus although he had the potential to outflank Confederate defensive positions across the Peninsula, this potential was never realized; and the slow pace of the land operations permitted the Confederates to build up their artillery batteries on the York River and at Drewry's Bluff on the James River. A naval attack on Richmond thus became out of the question, especially after the repulse of a Union squadron of gunboats before Drewry's Bluff on May 15. Second, McClellan committed a grave error in supposing that the roads in eastern

Virginia were better than those farther north; they were not, and this slowed the advance down even further. Third, he suffered throughout the campaign from a colossal miscalculation about the enemy he faced that distorted all of his plans: he believed he was outnumbered by as much as two to one by "masses" of the enemy. McClellan was a staff officer and an organizer rather than a commander. His idée fixe that he was outnumbered served as a circular, justifying argument for either his cautious advance or, when he was confronted by a perilous course, for choosing a timid response—*when* McClellan was present to make decisions (for he was often absent when decisions were required).[41]

Throughout the campaign, like Albert Sidney Johnston and Beauregard, McClellan's collection of intelligence was appalling and his reconnaissance feeble. Confederate movements were masked by swampy woods, maps were poor, knowledge of the area was nonexistent, and too many federal officers were credulous and gave too much attention to what Virginian civilians told them, comments that were taken out of context or deliberately designed to deceive. The Union cavalry, which should have been the prime reconnaissance arm, lacked a unified system of command, drive, and initiative. McClellan was not unduly concerned; he believed that his firepower, his heavy siege guns, and gunboats would eventually tell; all he had to do was shepherd them into position and shield his "outnumbered" army behind earthworks, then Richmond would fall and victory would be his. He would seek an "American Waterloo"—a defensive victory—on ground of his own choosing. As he approached the Confederate capital, the enemy would be forced to attack him. McClellan envisaged the campaign from the first as a siege, a view revealing so much about his defensive outlook on what was, at its heart, an *offensive* operation. The fundamental question was whether the enemy would permit him to conduct his campaign as he chose.[42]

At first it seemed that he would be given liberty of action. McClellan lay siege to Yorktown on April 4–5. He expected this to be a hard-fought, bitter struggle resembling the siege of Sebastopol during the Crimean War, which he had witnessed himself in 1856. McClellan laboriously brought up his heavy guns and ordered the digging of great works. Alas the Confederate commander, Joseph E. Johnston, ordered a withdrawal on the night of May 3, before they could open fire. McClellan had been warned before setting out that his political enemies were sharpening their knives; McClellan's fussy, excruciatingly cautious tactics and absurd, overly elaborate engineering methods allowed them to vent their spleen on his "cowardice" and fixation with "lines of retreat." McClellan's influence was declining and his political position needed shoring up. He badly needed a great victory to revive his Napoleonic allure. Herman Hattaway and

Archer Jones are quite correct in arguing that McClellan's "Civilian critics confused McClellan's execution with the art of war which he sought to practice. . . . When his plans actually bore fruit, his manner of carrying them out and his unwillingness to follow up made success look like failure."[43] But every field commander knows, as von Moltke truly said, that "no plan survives first contact with the enemy." The real challenge would only come when the Confederates attacked McClellan.

Johnston's strategy was to withdraw from the Peninsula all garrisons, including troops occupying the line built across it, and move all forces from the Carolinas and Georgia northward, concentrating as large a force as possible before Richmond. This policy of giving Virginia priority before all else was opposed by Lee (who has ironically been accused by some historians of being "obsessed" with Virginia and being incapable of taking the larger view) on the grounds that continuing to hold the areas east of the capital and withdrawing slowly would grant valuable time, and that continuing to hold Georgia and the Carolinas would not only reduce the federal concentration against the capital but prevent the federals from seizing valuable strategic points in the Atlantic states. Lee had just come from commanding in South Carolina and was making effective use of that experience. In Virginia itself, to achieve the concentration before Richmond, Lee wrote, "they [the federals] must weaken other points, and now is the time to concentrate on any that may be exposed within our reach." It was not at all clear from Johnston's advocacy of concentration whether he intended to hold the city of Richmond, or what he would do with the army when it was finally organized. Johnston, like McClellan, did not hold his political master in high regard and avoided his company as much as possible. He did not treat the president with the deference he deserved or inform him of his plans. Johnston was irritable and prone to stand on his dignity; he was a capable defensive commander but one who was not good at communicating his wishes to either his subordinates or his superiors. The result was that Lee, who was tactful and respectful, with a political guile that could be easily underestimated, gained great influence over Davis while Johnston lost it.[44]

McClellan's utter disregard of the time factor permitted the Confederates to build up their forces around Richmond. After two months' campaigning he had only reached Williamsburg by May 5. The roads were poor but he could have made more effective use of command of the sea and outflanked Johnston's forces; Johnston had been very worried by this possibility. The Confederate forces in the Peninsula giving ground before McClellan were commanded by John B. Magruder. Magruder's only military attribute was bluff, of which he had had years of experience. By ruse and theatrics Magruder (unknowingly) played up to McClellan's illusion that he faced an overwhelming host, and the latter gingerly fed units into the battle of Williamsburg on May 5, 1862. The total federal casualties of 2,283 to 1,560 Confederate in this comparatively minor engagement indicated the ferocity of the fighting to come; but it also revealed McClellan's fumbling and hesitant command methods. The battle, in Major General William F. Smith's view, was "a beastly exhibition of stupidity and ignorance."[45]

The main object of Johnston's retreat was to withdraw behind the Chickahominy River. Secure behind this sluggish stream, whose width varied due to sudden and quite unexpected floods so that it could become a mile wide, and here allied with armies of mosquitoes and the junglelike woods, Johnston intended to fight for Richmond. By concentrating on this line, however, Johnston had seriously foreclosed his strategic alternatives; he could no longer retreat without giving up Richmond, and that would be a catastrophic blow to the Confederacy with Britain and France looking on. But neither did Johnston give any sign that he was undertaking preparations that would drive McClellan away from the city: crisis approached.

The Chickahominy was important for McClellan, too. It had taken him more than three weeks to advance toward this river. It was his intention to move his main supply base from West Point to the White House plantation on the Pamunkey and use the York River Railroad to bring up his heavy guns. Once these deliberate movements had been completed and his lines secured by entrenchments, McClellan would cross to the south bank of the Chickahominy and batter Richmond into surrender from the east. On arrival in the Peninsula McClellan had created two further corps, the Fifth and Sixth, commanded by his own protégés—major generals Fitz John Porter and William B. Franklin—thus diluting the predominantly Republican group which had been imposed on him by the president before setting out. Fitz John Porter, the most northerly corps commander, engaged in a skirmish at Hanover Court House on May 27 which delayed McClellan's concentration to the south of the Chickahominy. By that date two corps, the Third and Fourth, one third of the Army of the Potomac, were south of the river.[46]

Johnston had decided on an audacious plan to strike at this exposed southern flank of McClellan's army, destroy it, and force McClellan to withdraw. He had concentrated two-thirds of his army to attack this exposed third, some twenty-two of his twenty-nine infantry brigades then serving in the Army of Northern Virginia. But Johnston had communicated his desires indifferently and his personal weaknesses were accentuated by the complete lack of any trained staff who were not only fully versed in the details of the plan, but could advise and inform generals of formations as to their part in it. Consequently, the execution of the battle of Seven Pines was completely botched. Johnston had intended to deploy his forces on three parallel roads. They would strike the front and flanks of the two Union corps simultaneously. Instead, three divisions were crowded in unwieldy echelons on one road. Consequently, no coherent offensive utilizing the full fighting power of the Confederate concentration was achieved; only nine brigades (and part of a tenth) did all the fighting—12,500 of the 30,000 men Johnston had mustered. Artillery firepower was badly coordinated and squandered. The battle degenerated into a series of small-scale skirmishes between minor units, which made no coherent contribution to the operational design. A great Confederate opportunity had been missed.[47]

Joe Johnston, like his colleague and namesake at Shiloh, had been wounded in the battle. But, unlike Albert Sidney, he survived. He was replaced in command of the Army of Northern Virginia by General Robert E. Lee, who had been orchestrating strategy in Virginia as Jefferson Davis's military adviser. Lee was the greatest field commander of the American Civil War. He was a general of flair, imagination, and real artistry. His early experience in the war had been disappointing and frustrating. Lee was held responsible for the loss of West Virginia, his preference for digging field entrenchments had been ridiculed, and as the president's adviser Lee had responsibility without power. He had been dismissed as "Granny" Lee by the Southern press. Despite all, what Edith Wharton in *The Buccaneers* (1938) called "some secret thread of destiny" brought Lee to the fore. Aged fifty-five, he was appointed to field command for the first time, and his generalship was to display a dynamism and a powerful determination to impose his will on the enemy that belied Lee's serene, mild, affable, and gentlemanly manner. His greatest attribute as a commander was his concern to impose his designs on the enemy rather than worry about what the enemy was going to do to him. This was a quality he shared with Grant. By sheer power of personality and exemplary qualities of leadership, he created a cohesion and esprit de corps in the Army of Northern Virginia that was to elude all other Confederate field commanders. Although the Virginian's army witnessed disputes, the crippling quarrels between generals that brought the Army of Tennessee to the brink of destruction were avoided. It would never have occurred to Lee to call a council of war, that refuge of those bereft of confidence or ideas, and the result was that Lee *commanded*; though even great commanders make mistakes, as Lee sometimes did.[48]

Lee did not avoid some of Johnston's mistakes, for he too was inexperienced, and the quality of his staff work (especially in drafting orders) remained poor. Errors of communication and deployment were still committed, and for the remainder of the campaign the use of artillery remained execrable. Yet Lee's tenure of command revealed that he made improvements in five important areas. The first was the care he devoted to his relations with the president. Lee gained Davis's trust and support, not his venom and suspicion. Lee was able to concentrate on important questions, not become distracted by unseemly quarrels—a cardinal error committed by both Joseph Johnston and Beauregard. These two commanders pursued their vendettas with the president with an unremitting ferocity that would have been better directed at the enemy. Second, having selected his objectives, Lee was determined not only to seize the initiative but to gain a powerful psychological ascendancy over his opponent. Lee sensed McClellan's caution, timidity, and his failure to command (which had been evident again at Seven Pines), and Lee was minded to exploit them to the fullest.[49]

Third, Lee appreciated Magruder's skill at deception, and this was to play a crucial part in his evolving concept for a counteroffensive. The least popular of Lee's changes was a fresh emphasis on field fortification. "It will require 100,000 men to resist the regular siege of Richmond," which perhaps would only prolong its defense, not save the city. "I am preparing," Lee informed the president, "a line that I can hold with part of our forces in front, while with the rest I will endeavor to make a diversion to bring McClellan out." Fourth, the most important improvement that Lee instituted was in reconnaissance. All Confederate offensives thus far had exhibited lamentable reconnaissance, and an error once compounded can never be retrieved on the battlefield. Lee intended to improve reconnaissance by exploiting the undoubted superiority of Confederate cavalry. On June 11 Major General J. E. B. Stuart was dispatched on an expedition to McClellan's right flank and enjoined to "remember that one of the chief objects of your expedition is to gain intelligence for the guidance of future movements." Stuart was given the responsibility of establishing whether McClellan's right flank was vulnerable and whether a scheme to bring Jackson from the Shenandoah was possible.[50]

Finally, from the first Lee had realized that the paramount operational requirement was to weaken McClellan's concentration. His first thought was to reinforce Jackson so that he could advance into Maryland or Pennsylvania and thus force withdrawals not only from the Peninsula but from the Atlantic coast. But Lee soon changed his mind. He was rightly convinced that "McClellan will make this a battle of posts. He will take position from position, under cover of his heavy guns, and we cannot get at him without storming his works, which

From *An Atlas of American Military History* by James C. Bradford (New York: Cynthia Parzych Publishing, 2003).

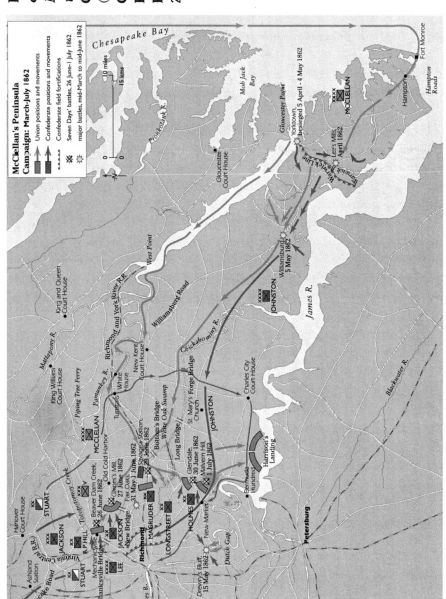

McClellan's Peninsula Campaign: March-July 1862

Union positions and movements

Confederate positions and movements

Confederate field fortifications

Seven Days' battles, 26 June-1 July 1862

major battles, mid-March to mid-June 1862

with our new troops is extremely hazardous." If McClellan could be winkled out of his positions, then Lee hoped that he could be paralyzed and defeated in detail. The solution would be to find an open flank, move around it, and mount a strategic thrust at McClellan's lines of communication along the York River Railroad. Lee would thus attempt to concentrate his army *north* of the Chickahominy, just as McClellan was concentrating his *south* of it. Magruder would thus have a vital role disguising this deception. But what of Irvin McDowell's First Corps? Should he return to his encampments at Fredericksburg and then march south toward Richmond, his corps would completely outflank the defending Confederate army and render their own outflanking maneuver impossible. McDowell had been withdrawn to the Shenandoah Valley on May 24; that is, before the battle of Seven Pines. Jackson was to be further reinforced so that McDowell could be kept there. And the nerves of politicians in Washington were to be jangled by his lightning maneuvers in their direction.[51]

In his posthumously published apologia, *McClellan's Own Story*, the Union commander was to make much of Lincoln withholding McDowell's First Corps just as the spires of Richmond came in sight. He argued that it was a fatal weakening of his forces by the president just as he was poised to strike the culminating blow of the campaign. It certainly complicated his dispositions, but McClellan was suffering from the extraordinary and crippling delusion that he was outnumbered when he had the superior force. He therefore had ample resources to seize the city if he only showed the mental resilience to deploy efficaciously the forces under his command. The campaign had been launched on condition that Washington be protected safely. Lincoln was therefore justified in retaining the corps; competent generalship offered the hope that Jackson would be surrounded and crushed, and thus render Lee's offensive impossible.[52]

In a carefully thought-out operation ("Every chance had been carefully calculated," wrote Major H. B. McClellan, a cousin of the Union commander, who also had three brothers serving in the Union army, and who served as Stuart's chief of staff), from June 12–15 Stuart not only located the exposed right wing of the Union army but operated astride its communications and rear and rode "around" it. This operation was not only valuable for the information it imparted but as a propaganda coup.[53] Stuart also reported that McClellan's concentration south of the Chickahominy was continuing and confirmed that the weaker part of his army (approximately one-third) lay north of the river. The Confederate counteroffensive thus became a preemptive strike before McClellan was able to launch his final assault on Richmond. By the third week of June 1862 Lee commanded 92,400 men; the Confederate's concentration had been successful. He would never again command so large an army. To recapitulate: Lee would launch a great envelopment of McClellan's right, empowered by the sudden removal from the Shenandoah Valley by both road and rail of Jackson's Army of the Valley, and force him to fight for his lines of communication once he had withdrawn from his entrenchments. Lee's concentration north of the Chickahominy has become a textbook example of economy of effort because, though he was marginally inferior overall, he gained an advantage of twelve to seven in the decisive sector. Jackson would continue to distract attention to the Shenandoah and then at the last moment move his troops to Ashland, advance on McClellan's right, and drive into his rear. The object was to maneuver around McClellan in a series of phased, elegant echelons.

The plan has been likened to Napoleonic warfare and the battle of Austerlitz (1805). These analogies are superficial and misleading. There is no evidence that Lee was influenced unduly by Napoleon's example in his correspondence. An envelopment is not a unique Napoleonic device; indeed Napoleon's defeated enemies at Austerlitz attempted just what Lee aimed to do, and he did not want to emulate them. The plan was a specific response to certain unique conditions, not an attempt to repeat an academic formula. If Lee was attempting to repeat any previous military move, it was Joseph E. Johnston's maneuver from the Shenandoah Valley to Manassas the previous July. In any case, Lee's prime objective remained driving McClellan back and relieving Richmond. Any further objectives would depend on the reaction to the Confederate offensive.[54]

Lee's plan was too ambitious and elaborate for his keen but utterly untried army to carry out. In a series of battles known as the Seven Days', fought in a great arc from northeast to southeast of Richmond June 26 to July 1, 1862, Lee struggled to bring the full weight of his concentrated fighting power to bear on the Union forces. Fitz John Porter's Fifth Corps bore the full weight of the attack. Yet though Porter succeeded tactically in repulsing the Confederate attacks, Lee seized the initiative and consequently, as McClellan misread the entire battle and thought in terms of salvaging from defeat what he could rather than defeating Lee, the Army of the Potomac's successes could not add up to an operational triumph. Certainly, staff work in the Army of the Potomac was better (though McClellan's erroneous conclusion was that the Peninsula campaign demonstrated that an operational branch of the staff was unnecessary), but this could not prevent the spread of demoralization through its ranks. McClellan did not show the character that is demanded of a commander in the field to enforce his will on his subordinates, and he virtually allowed his corps commanders to do what they pleased. Fitz John Porter was the de facto commander throughout the Seven Days' battles. Furthermore, McClellan refused to take responsibility for his actions and sought to blame his political superiors; this abdication of responsibility reduced their confidence in him even further.[55]

Lee's main problem was bringing a sustained, coordinated offensive against the decisive point. At Mechanicsville (June 26, 1862) only one division attacked Porter's position; this assault was repulsed and surprise had been given away, but Lee gambled on continuing the offensive for he had now exposed Richmond to McClellan's riposte. Throughout the campaign he gambled that McClellan would not act boldly and he was proven correct. At Gaines Mill (June 27, 1863), mainly because of a brilliant feat of arms by John B. Hood's Texas Brigade in seizing Turkey Hill, the two divisions of James Longstreet and A. P. Hill drove Porter's troops from their positions and south of the Chickahominy. But still Jackson, who did not come into action until June 27, remained inert and uninterested in the proceedings. The contrast between his lethargy in the Seven Days' and his dynamism in the Shenandoah Valley has excited much comment, some highly critical. Perhaps Jackson did not understand Lee's plan; more likely he obeyed orders that should have been changed, for communications in the Seven Days' battles were execrable; he may have disliked a strictly subordinate role, whereas in the valley he had been his own master; more to the point he was simply, after his recent exertions, an exhausted husk of a man, badly in need of rest and refreshment. At any rate, at Gaines Mill, Lee achieved the nearest he came to a coordinated, well-orchestrated offensive, and Porter was forced back in full retreat. Yet he did not achieve the devastating envelopment that his plan, and his growing ambition, demanded.[56]

McClellan at this point made a decision that helped Lee achieve the design that his own subordinates seemed incapable of realizing. He ordered a full-scale withdrawal and a "change of base" to the James River where he could shelter under the protection of the guns of the Union navy. The Army of the Potomac, though it was by no means defeated (indeed only one corps had been fully engaged), thus retreated in increasing disorder to the James River. Lee's attack on McClellan's lines of communication had been successful; he abandoned his fortifications and ordered forward the three divisions entrusted with Richmond's defense to attack the Union rearguard. Lee was offered the chance of cutting up McClellan's army while it was on the march, a chance to completely destroy its cohesion, perhaps trapping it entirely.

McClellan, in his turn, had completely succeeded in forcing the Confederates to attack him on ground of his choosing; but he did not fight an "American Waterloo" because he failed to show Wellington's presence of mind and tactical acumen; the next three days resembled a *déroute*. At Savage's Station (June 29, 1862) Union troops repelled more frantic Confederate assaults but did not feel pride in themselves, so low had their morale fallen. More opportunities for envelopments were offered to Lee. Such was his superlative skill at concentration that despite the setbacks and casualties he had sustained in the intense fighting in the previous two battles, Lee outnumbered McClellan at Fraser's Farm (June 30, 1862) 71,000 to 61,500. But Jackson did not cross the White Oak Swamp and fall on McClellan's rear, even though the opportunity to cleave the Army of the Potomac in two tantalized Lee's eager and bright brown eyes. Then, the following day, instead of destroying McClellan in the open, Lee's army was repulsed in a series of undisciplined, chaotic, unordered, exuberant waves of small formations, attempting to assault McClellan's artillery posted along Malvern Hill, who replied with devastating fire. "It was not war: it was mass murder," is Freeman's solemn judgment.[57]

Malvern Hill was actually vulnerable to a well-coordinated attack. Why had the Confederate offensive degenerated into such confusion? First and foremost, as Douglas Southall Freeman emphasizes, because of lamentable staff work. Staff officers themselves lacked military knowledge and training and could not act on behalf of their commanders. Consequently, if Jackson was exhausted, or Magruder confused—as he was before Malvern Hill—then a staff officer could not make decisions on Lee's behalf or authoritatively advise befuddled commanders on Lee's intentions. The Confederates possessed no concept of a modern general staff; even in the Army of the Potomac staff duties and operations were inextricably confused, although staff officers were more proficient at the clerical, administrative side of their duties. Even in the role of superior clerks, Confederate staff officers performed poorly. Orders were badly drafted, not drafted at all, or not sent. Lee's chief of staff, Colonel Robert H. Chilton, made no contribution to this and later successes; an old hand from Lee's time as second in command of a cavalry regiment in Texas, Chilton had long ascended past his command ceiling.[58]

Second, subordinates acted unilaterally or failed to understand the overall plan; they launched crude, unimaginative, weak frontal assaults on Union positions. As in the west, the profusion of independent brigades added to this fragmentation of offensive power. It was not uncommon for units to lose 25–30 percent of their fighting strength in this litany of confused, courageous but rash, and wholly unnecessary actions. General Fitzhugh Lee, in his biography of his uncle, wrote, "It has been said we were lavish of blood in those days, and it was thought to be a great thing to charge a battery of artillery or line of earthworks with infantry." The result was a series of disparate, small-unit, piecemeal assaults, conducted in an ill-disciplined, irresponsible manner. Southern armies would continue to exhibit this weakness throughout the war. It is this systemic structural weakness that accounts for Southern offensive failures during the Civil War. Such structural weakness was due to lack of discipline among senior officers and their subordinates, the lack of experience and military knowledge of their staffs, and an inability to coordinate with pinpoint timing the movement of large fighting formations. There is little evidence to support the fanciful notion (which stands on very shaky historical foundations) that a penchant for the offensive was due to the "Celtic" ethnic background of many Southerners, which impelled them toward rash attacks.[59]

McClellan's troops fought most of their actions behind field fortifications. At this stage in the war they were not the elaborate entrenchments that covered every battlefield. They were more frequently abatis that could be constructed easily in the thick undergrowth of the Virginia woods, rifle pits, and breastworks; in other words, soldiers intent on protecting themselves with fieldworks tended to build up rather than dig down. Breastworks were sometimes vulnerable to cannon, but this was canceled out during the Seven Days' by feeble Confederate artillery fire. Faced by the challenge of breastworks, Southern brigade and regimental commanders simply charged straight at them in long, unwieldy lines with no reserve. Almost all commentators stress "the tactical advantages of fighting on the defensive . . . indicating the wisdom of the turning strategy which had worked so well in the West." This is, of course, correct up to a point, for Lee had no intention of directly assaulting McClellan in his works but to get behind them; yet it by no means follows, as Hattaway and Jones argue, that "the Seven Days' Battles again displayed the relative invulnerability of the armies engaged."[60]

This assumption that, because the tactical defensive was strong, an American Civil War army could not be destroyed in the field is unproven, and is misleadingly circular. It by no means follows that because there are few examples of Civil War armies being subject to shattering defeat until the end of 1864, that such an outcome was beyond each side's resources and could not be achieved before that date. The Seven Days' was the nearest that each side came to realizing the prevailing image that an apocalyptic, decisive battle would decide the war. It had not been Lee's initial intention to destroy the Army of the Potomac, but McClellan's blunders were exploited ruthlessly by him. McClellan's army of 110,000 men was considerably smaller than many of Napoleon's armies; his frontage (despite the extension permitted by the railroad) was no more than five to eight miles. It was not beyond the strength of Lee's 92,000 men to entrap and annihilate such a force; what was required was a measure of calculation in planning and execution that would make the most of his army's fighting power. Gaines Mill showed that even if a modicum of such an orchestration of fighting power was achieved, that stout defenders could be driven from their positions. But consummating this complex maneuver required standards of command and control completely lacking in the Army of Northern Virginia in the summer of 1862. This weakness was accentuated by Lee's own command system, which imitated that of his mentor, Winfield Scott, in the Mexican War. Although Lee was firm and decisive in elucidating his operational objectives, he left it to his subordinates to find their own tactical solutions. This would now be called "mission command"; but in the absence of any accepted doctrine or body of experience, it could lead to confusion and tactical defeat. It was amateurishness in the *offense*—the product of a wholly unrealistic and sentimental prewar vision of war, which saw the officer waving his sword and leading his heroic troops, running at the enemy—that stymied Lee's ambitious and elegant maneuvers, not an inherent superiority of the defense in 1862. Lee's operational objectives—first, the relief of Richmond and later, the destruction of McClellan's army—were not in themselves unattainable, and he came so near to attaining them in full.[61]

As for McClellan, Major General Fitzhugh Lee observed that, "It can not be denied that the retreat of McClellan from his position in front of Richmond to the James River was cleverly executed." Throughout the Seven Days' battles, the Army of the Potomac operated organizationally in a more professional and cohesive manner. The "change of base" did not result in disaster, although a staff muddle resulted in the loss of almost 50 percent of McClellan's five thousand wagons; even with this setback, and the loss of much materiel as the line of the York River was abandoned and the Army of the Potomac moved toward Harrison's Landing, it remained well administered and supplied. But field commanders cannot be judged by their administrative capacity and the distribution of bread alone. McClellan later justified his failure to seize Richmond after Lee had taken the offensive on grounds of logistics over insurance; he feared the Confederates had cut his supply lines. He refused to give any thought to the opportunity granted to cut theirs.[62]

Throughout the campaign McClellan had abdicated his responsibilities as a commander. He had been outclassed at the operational level and he had left tactics to the discretion of his corps commanders. Although he had studied Napoleon's campaigns, he had forgotten one of the emperor's most important maxims—namely, "Hesitation and half-measures lose all in war." Even though he had wanted the Confederates to attack him, when they did so at Seven Pines and in the Seven Days', he was taken wholly by surprise and had failed to *act*. Indeed, at Gaines Mill and Malvern Hill he was absent from the battlefield. Strategically, his offensive had failed: Richmond was relieved and McClellan's credibility with the Lincoln administration was low, remained low, and continued to diminish. On July 8 McClellan foolishly handed the president his famous letter written at Harrison's Landing during a visit Lincoln paid the Army of the Potomac. He pleaded that the war continue to be fought "upon the highest principles known to Christian Civilization." It was not so much the contents of the letter as the timing of its composition that is open to criticism. Military withdrawals, no matter how cleverly executed, do not serve to advance political goals. McClellan had not taken Richmond and he had lost the initiative. The president looked around for somebody else who could regain the initiative and take Richmond.[63]

The main significance of the Seven Days' battles was that, like Shiloh, they demonstrated that the war would not end with one "grand campaign." The stalemate was mainly due to technical factors, especially the lack of basic training and military doctrine, and the absence of a general staff. These serious structural weaknesses prevented commanders from realizing the opportunities that were offered up on the battlefield. But if victory is not gained in an early phase, then wars are inclined to assume an attritional form, and time was not really on the side of the Confederacy; the big battalions were certainly not.

Yet the relief of Richmond was a crucial turning point in the Civil War. It offered the Confederacy hope and the prestige of maintaining its capital inviolate. Furthermore, the city's infant industries, as well as the manpower resources of the upper South, could be more effectively mobilized, turning out desperately needed munitions. The Seven Days' battles ensured the survival of the Confederacy to mobilize forces sufficient to resist attempts to crush it. But the victory was not decisive enough to achieve outright independence for the South.

In short, the war would continue. The South had suffered a long series of defeats; the arrival of news of the fall of New Orleans on May 1 had depressed the Confederate cause further. The Seven Days' seemed to indicate the turning of the tide. Once more the price had been high, a total of 20,204 Confederate casualties or 22 percent of the Army of Northern Virginia. McClellan's casualties were 15,885. Given the emphasis of previous historians on the superiority of the defensive this is not a staggering margin. Indeed it becomes less significant under close scrutiny. Because of McClellan's abdication of command the great brunt of the fighting had fallen on the Fifth Corps, which had fought behind strong defenses. Porter suffered 7,575 casualties or 28 percent of his total force. In intensive fighting the offensive and defensive tend to inflict equal casualties, with no great margin of advantage either way. In short, the passion of American historians for identifying a strategy that would avoid these casualty bills is not only a chimera, but misguided. Twenty-two percent casualties were average for battles between great powers in the nineteenth century. But they were not commonplace in the American military experience. And, despite all the promises, the war had still not ended.[64]

NOTES AND REFERENCES

1. Emory M. Thomas, *The Confederate Nation, 1861–1865* (New York: Monticello Edition reprint, 1993), p. 44; George C. Rable, *The Confederate Republic* (Chapel Hill: University of North Carolina Press, 1994), pp. 1–3.

2. Thomas L. Connelly, *Army of the Heartland: The Army of Tennessee, 1861–1862* (Baton Rouge: Louisiana State University Press, 1967), p. x; Richard M. McMurry, *Two Great Rebel Armies* (Chapel Hill: University of North Carolina Press, 1989), pp. 3–9.

3. Archer Jones, *Confederate Strategy: From Shiloh to Vicksburg* (Baton Rouge: Louisiana State University Press, 1961), pp. 28–29.

4. Archer Jones, "Military Means, Political Ends: Strategy," in *Why the Confederacy Lost*, ed. Gabor Boritt, 47 (New York: Oxford University Press, 1992).

5. Major General J. F. C. Fuller, *Grant and Lee: A Study in Personality and Generalship* (London: Eyre and Spottiswoode, 1933; Spa Books reprint, 1992) pp. 41, 95, 255–58.

6. T. Harry Williams, *P. G. T. Beauregard: Napoleon in Gray* (Baton Rouge: Louisiana State University Press, 1955), p. 94.

7. McMurry, *Two Great Rebel Armies*, pp. 24–26.

8. Emory M. Thomas, *The Confederacy as a Revolutionary Experience* (Columbia: University of South Carolina Press, 1971, 1991 reprint), pp. 44–50; Craig L. Symonds, *Joseph E. Johnston* (New York: Norton, 1992), p. 172.

9. Phillip S. Paludan, *The Presidency of Abraham Lincoln* (Lawrence: University Press of Kansas, 1994), pp. 127, 145–46; Albert Castel, *General Sterling Price and the Civil War in the West* (1968; Baton Rouge: Louisiana State University Press, 1993 reprint), pp. 87–92. In Price's case these feelings were exacerbated by doubts about his loyalty. See ibid., pp. 30–31, 188–96, 259–61.

10. McMurry, *Two Great Rebel Armies,* pp. 58–60.

11. Ibid., p. 56; Thomas, *Confederate Nation*, pp. 39–41. Montgomery, Alabama, was little more than a village of nine thousand people and two hotels, which "adjusted their bills to match the congressmen's salaries." The sting of Montgomery's mosquitoes also had a depressing effect on morale.

12. McMurry, *Two Great Rebel Armies,* pp. 14, 15–17, 60, 77, 80, 110.

13. Robert E. Lee to Holmes, Apr. 28, 1862, in *The Wartime Papers of R. E. Lee*, eds. Clifford Dowdey and Louis H. Manarin (New York: Bramhall House, 1961), pp. 159–60; Symonds, *Johnston*, pp. 130–31.

14. McMurry, *Two Great Rebel Armies*, pp. 10–12, 15–17; Lee to Pemberton (telegram), Apr. 10, 1862, in Lee, *Wartime Papers*, p. 145.

15. Brian Holden Reid, "The Commander and His Chief of Staff: Ulysses S. Grant and John A. Rawlins," in *Command and Leadership: Anglo-American Military Experience since 1861*, ed. G. D. Sheffield, 18 (London: Brassey's 1996).

16. Ulysses S. Grant, *Personal Memoirs* (London: Sampson Low, 1886), vol. 1, p. 250.

17. Grant to Julia D. Grant, Feb. 24, 1862, in *The Papers of Ulysses S. Grant*, ed. John Y. Simon (Carbondale and Edwardsville: University of Southern Illinois University Press, 1972), vol. 4, p. 284.

18. Connelly, *Army of Heartland*, pp. 62, 66–75; Peter Maslowski, *Treason Must Be Made Odious: Military Occupation and Wartime Reconstruction in Nashville, Tennessee, 1862–65* (Millwood, NY: KTO Press, 1978), pp. 3–7, 12–18.

19. Donald L. Canney, *The Old Steam Navy*, vol. 2, *The Ironclads, 1842–1885* (Annapolis, MD: US Naval Institute Press, 1993); Grant, *Memoirs*, vol. 1, pp. 284–86, 291; J. F. C. Fuller, *The Generalship of Ulysses S. Grant*, 2nd ed. (Bloomington: Indiana University Press, 1957), pp. 145–46.

20. Grant, *Memoirs*, vol. 1, pp. 296–98, 302–304; the best account is Benjamin Franklin Cooling, *Forts Henry and Donelson: The Key to the Confederate Heartland* (Knoxville: University of Tennessee Press, 1987).

21. Connelly, *Army of the Heartland*, pp. 109–25; Grant, *Memoirs*, vol. 1, pp. 305–15; Bruce Catton, *Grant Moves South* (Boston: Little, Brown, 1960), pp. 160–76.

22. Castel, *Price and the Civil War in the West*, p. 55.

23. Ibid., pp. 70, 71, 73, 75, 78–79; William J. Shea and Earl J. Hess, *Pea Ridge: Civil War Campaign in the West* (Chapel Hill: University of North Carolina Press, 1992).

24. Rowena Reed, *Combined Operations in the Civil War* (Lincoln: University of Nebraska Press, 1978, 1993 edition), p. 50.

25. Castel, *Price and the Civil War in the West*, pp. 81–82. On Johnston, Connelly, *Army of the Heartland*, pp. 59–65, 74–77, 85, 99, 108–13, 142–46 is too censorious, though Connelly is correct in describing him as having the mentality "of a post commander" (p. 62). Charles P. Roland, *Albert Sidney Johnston: Soldier of Three Republics* (Austin: University of Texas Press, 1964), pp. 287–88, is a corrective.

26. Connelly, *Army of the Heartland*, p. 141, 147–48.

27. Maslowski, *Treason Must be Made Odious*, p. 15; James Lee McDonough, *Shiloh: In Hell before Night* (Knoxville: University of Tennessee Press, 1977), pp. 60–69; Connelly, *Army of the Heartland*, pp. 147–53. My differences of interpretation with Connelly

are obvious. Connelly believes that "Johnston's failure to stand up to his lieutenant [Beauregard] still left him commander in name only." I believe it would have been better if he had given Beauregard full powers as field commander.

28. Wallace J. Schutz and Walter N. Trenerry, *Abandoned by Lincoln: A Military Biography of General John Pope* (Urbana: University of Illinois Press, 1990), pp. 77–78, 82–84, 88–89, 170; Larry J. Daniel and Lynn Bock, *Island No. 10: Struggle for the Mississippi Valley* (Tuscaloosa: University of Alabama Press, 1996).

29. Grant to Julia D. Grant, Feb. 24, Mar. 18, 1862, in *Grant Papers*, vol. 4, pp. 284, 389; Roland, *Johnston*, p. 328; Edward Hagerman, "From Jomini to Dennis Hart Mahan: The Evolution of Trench Warfare and the American Civil War," *Civil War History* 13 (1967): 216; Grant, *Memoirs*, vol. 1, pp. 359–68.

30. Williams, *Beauregard*, pp. 77, 126–27; McDonough, *Shiloh*, pp. 70–75; for Buell's approach see Larry J. Daniel, *Days of Glory: The Army of the Cumberland, 1861–1865* (Baton Rouge: Louisiana State University Press, 2004), pp. 78–81; Connelly, *Army of the Heartland*, pp. 152–54.

31. For problems of "influence," see Brian Bond, *Liddell Hart* (London: Cassell, 1977), p. 215. For a simplistic approach, see Thomas L. Connelly and Archer Jones, *The Politics of Command: Factions and Ideas in Confederate Strategy* (Baton Rouge: Louisiana State University Press, 1973), although by p. 31 they are candid (if inconsistent) enough to admit, "this was true [the influence of Napoleon and Jomini] even though it is uncertain whether many of the participants were explicitly guided by a knowledge of Napoleonic or Jominian concepts."

32. Williams, *Beauregard*, pp. 127–28; Connelly, *Army of the Heartland*, pp. 154–55.

33. McDonough, *Shiloh*, pp. 77–84; Williams, *Beauregard*, pp. 131–32.

34. Grant, *Memoirs*, vol. 1, pp. 339, 344; Williams, *Beauregard*, pp. 138–39; Connelly, *Army of the Heartland*, pp. 162–67. When Johnston was shot he did not have a single staff officer with him to convey his instructions.

35. Grant, *Memoirs*, vol. 1, pp. 432, 348; Brooks D. Simpson, *Ulysses S. Grant: Triumph over Adversity* (New York: Houghton Mifflin, 2000), pp. 132, 134.

36. Grant, *Memoirs*, vol. 1, pp. 354–66; Connelly, *Army of Heartland*, pp. 171–75; Williams, *Beauregard*, pp. 142–47; Daniel, *Days of Glory,* pp. 81–84.

37. Simpson, *Grant*, pp. 134–36; Paludan, *Presidency of Lincoln*, p. 129; Adam Badeau, *Military History of Ulysses S. Grant* (New York: Appleton, 1881), vol. 1, p. 72n; Holden Reid, "Grant and Rawlins," pp. 24–25.

38. John F. Marszalek, *Commander of All Lincoln's Armies: A Life of General Henry Halleck* (Cambridge, MA: Belknap Press of Harvard University Press, 2004), pp. 123–26; Badeau, *Military History of U. S. Grant*, vol. 1, pp. 95–96; Grant, *Memoirs*, vol. 1, p. 381.

39. David Donald, *Charles Sumner and the Rights of Man* (New York: Alfred A. Knopf, 1970), p. 53.

40. James A. Huston, "Logistical Support of Federal Armies in the Field," *Civil War History* 7 (1961): 46–47; Stephen W. Sears, *To the Gates of Richmond: The Peninsula Campaign* (New York: Ticknor and Fields, 1991), pp. 23–24, 173.

41. President's General War Order No. 3, Mar. 8, 1862, in *The Collected Works of Abraham Lincoln*, ed. Roy P. Basler (New Brunswick, NJ: Rutgers University Press, 1953), vol. 5, p. 151; Robert M. Epstein, "The Creation and Evolution of the Army Corps in the American Civil War," *Journal of Military History* 55 (January 1991): 30–34; Sears, *Gates of Richmond*, pp. 8–9, 10–11, 18, 35, 36–37, 61, 98, 108–109, 353–54; Reed, *Combined Operations in the Civil War*, pp. 164–69.

42. Stephen W. Sears, *George B. McClellan: The Young Napoleon* (New York: Ticknor and Fields, 1988), pp. 172–73, 189, 192, 200–202; idem., *Gates of Richmond*, pp. 29–30, 54, 57–59, 98, 113, 170.

43. Hattaway and Jones, *How the North Won*, p. 173.

44. Steven H. Newton, *Joseph E. Johnston and the Defense of Richmond* (Lawrence: University Press of Kansas, 1998), pp. 35–36, 57–58, 82–83; Lee to Jackson, Apr. 25, 1862, in Lee, *Wartime Papers*, p. 156. The genesis of Johnston's feud with Davis is discussed in Symonds, *Johnston*, ch. 10; see also ibid., pp. 147–53, 170; Brian Holden Reid, *Robert E. Lee: Icon for a Nation* (2005; Amherst, NY: Prometheus Books, 2007), pp. 74–75.

45. Sears, *Gates of Richmond*, pp. 70–83, 85, 163; although errors were found on the Confederate side, too, see Douglas Southall Freeman, *Lee's Lieutenants*, 3 vols. (New York: Scribner's, 1942), vol. 1, pp. 190–91.

46. Sears, *Gates of Richmond*, pp. 95–96, 105, 113, 117.

47. Clifford Dowdey, *The Seven Days* (Wilmington, NC: Broadfoot reprint, 1964, 1988), pp. 69–70, 78, 85–86, 109–10, 114–15; Sears, *Gates of Richmond*, pp. 123, 128, 130, 133, 136, 138; Symonds, *Johnston*, pp. 162–74.

48. Clifford Dowdey, *Lee: A Biography* (London: Gollancz, 1970), pp. 229, 235; Steven E. Woodworth, *Davis and Lee at War* (Lawrence: University Press of Kansas, 1995), pp. 157–58; for a development of these points, see Holden Reid, *Lee*, pp. 246–50.

49. Dowdey, *Lee*, pp. 215–16, 235; Sears, *Gates of Richmond*, pp. 151–52.

50. Sears, *Gates of Richmond*, p. 154; Lee to Davis, June 5, 1862, in Lee, *Wartime Papers*, p. 184; H. B. McClellan, *I Rode with Jeb Stuart: The Life and Campaigns of Major General J. E. B. Stuart* (Secaucus, NJ: Blue and Grey Press, 1993 reprint), p. 53.

51. Lee to Davis, June 5, 1862, in Lee, *Wartime Papers*, p. 184; Sears, *Gates of Richmond*, pp. 174, 176, 211, 249; Holden Reid, *Lee*, pp. 86–89.

52. T. Harry Williams, *Lincoln and His Generals* (New York: Alfred A. Knopf, 1952), pp. 93–100; Sears, *McClellan*, pp. 104–107, 172, 175–76; idem., *Gates of Richmond*, pp. 157–58; Kenneth P. Williams, *Lincoln Finds a General* (New York: Macmillan, 1949), vol. 1, pp. 216–17, argues against the notion that Lincoln's decision weakened McClellan.

53. McClellan, *Stuart's Campaigns*, pp. 62, 67; Emory M. Thomas, *Bold Dragoon: The Life of J. E. B. Stuart* (New York: Harper and Row, 1986), pp. 113–24.

54. Freeman, *Lee's Lieutenants*, vol. 1, pp. 490–94, 504–506; Brian K. Burton, *Extraordinary Circumstances: The Seven Days Battles* (Bloomington: Indiana University Press, 2001), pp. 232–35; Sears, *Gates of Richmond*, pp. 156, 192–95; Major General Sir Frederick Maurice, *British Strategy: A Study of the Application of the Principles of War* (London: Constable, 1929), p. 117; Russell F. Weigley, *American Way of War* (New York: Macmillan, 1973), p. 106; William L. Miller, "'The Siege of Richmond Was Raised': Lee's Intentions in the Seven Days Battles," in *Audacity Personified: The Generalship of Robert E. Lee*, ed. Peter S. Carmichael, 27–56 (Baton Rouge: Louisiana State University Press, 2004).

55. Sears, *McClellan*, pp. 172, 225–26, 230–37, 268; idem., *Gates of Richmond*, pp. 187, 190–91, 200, 215, 265, 280–82, 309, 314, 338–39; Burton, *Extraordinary Circumstances*, pp. 390–91; Dowdey, *Seven Days*, pp. 89, 178, 182, 190–92; see McClellan to Stanton, June 28, 1862, in *The Civil War Papers of George B. McClellan*, ed. Stephen W. Sears (New York: Ticknor and Fields, 1989), p. 323.

56. James I. Robertson Jr., *Stonewall Jackson: The Man, the Soldier, the Legend* (New York: Macmillan, 1997), pp. 467, 468, 495–98; Dowdey, *Seven Days*, pp. 184, 187–88, 192; idem., *Lee*, pp. 234–50; Richard M. McMurry, *John Bell Hood and the War for Southern Independence* (Lincoln: University of Nebraska Press reprint, 1982, 1992), pp. 45–50; Douglas Southall Freeman, *R. E. Lee*, 4 vols. (New York: Scribner's, 1933), vol. 2, appendix 3, pp. 572–82; Sears, *Gates of Richmond*, pp. 288–89.

57. Burton, *Extraordinary Circumstances*, pp. 314–15, 325–40; Freeman, *Lee's Lieutenants*, vol. 1, pp. 589, 591–92, 536–602; Sears, *Gates of Richmond*, pp. 279, 301–302.

58. Freeman, *Lee*, vol. 2, pp. 199, 233–37; idem., *Lee's Lieutenants*, vol. 1, p. 604; Dowdey, *Lee*, pp. 252–53; idem., *Seven Days*, 267, 320, 330–31, 341, 345; Sears, *Gates of Richmond*, pp. 234, 268, 274, 306–307, 317, 323.

59. Sears, *Gates of Richmond*, pp. 201, 226, 227, 236–37, 242, 326, 330, 335; Fitzhugh Lee, *General Lee* (1894; New York: Da Capo reprint, 1994), p. 161; Grady McWhiney and Perry D. Jamieson, *Attack and Die: Civil War Military Tactics and the Southern Heritage* (Tuscaloosa: University of Alabama Press, 1982), pp. 7–9, 172–80.

60. Hattaway and Jones, *How the North Won*, pp. 199–200.

61. Freeman, *Lee*, vol. 2, pp. 239–40; see also Williams, *Lincoln Finds a General*, vol. 1, p. 237; Burton, *Extraordinary Circumstances*, pp. 394–95.

62. See McClellan's report in *The War of the Rebellion: A Compilation of the Official Records of the Union and Confederate Armies*, 128 parts in 70 vols. (Washington, DC: Government Printing Office, 1880–1901), series 1, vol. 11, part 1, pp. 53–54, 60. McClellan claimed erroneously "that almost everything was saved"; his ultimate aim remained to "get a position whence a successful advance upon Richmond would be again possible." He does not clarify how this could have been done without a railroad to carry his heavy siege guns.

63. Lee, *General Lee*, p. 166; Edward Hagerman, *The American Civil War and the Origins of Modern Warfare* (Bloomington: Indiana University Press, 1988), p. 51; Brian Holden Reid, "General McClellan and the Politicians," *Parameters* 17 (September 1987): 108; for Napoleon's maxims, see *Jomini, Clausewitz and Schlieffen* (West Point, NY: USMA, 1948), no. 134, p. 92; McClellan to Lincoln, July 7, 1862, in *Civil War Papers*, pp. 344–45.

64. Sears, *Gates of Richmond*, pp. 343, 345.

Chapter Five

CONFEDERATE FRUSTRATION
JULY TO SEPTEMBER 1862

G eneral Lee's accession to command of the Army of Northern Virginia resulted in a great increase in the velocity of the Civil War. After the Seven Days' battles he fought a further three great battles in the six months before Christmas 1862, all dwarfing those engagements—Ball's Bluff, Yorktown, and Williamsburg—that had brought forth so much earlier exaggerated comment. The war was entering a new phase of dynamic offensive movement. Lee believed profoundly that the Confederacy had to *seize* its independence itself. It could not wait for the great powers, Great Britain and France especially, to intervene on its behalf as so many Southerners complacently assumed because they had been starved of cotton. In short, the strategy followed by the rebel colonists of 1779–81 of relying on an alliance with France, culminating in the surrender of Lord Cornwallis at Yorktown in 1781, could not be repeated. Consequently, the Confederacy needed dramatic victories; it needed to demonstrate a measure of aggression and boldness. The strategic defensive could not be passive. If foreign intervention followed a victory so much the better; but the South could not wait on foreign intervention to win such victories. Time was not on its side as much as is commonly supposed. Failure to seize the initiative would allow the North time to mobilize its resources, and the South could not hope to match these. Lee constantly warned against allowing the war to degenerate into a siege. There was an element of shrewd political calculation in his view that is frequently overlooked.[1]

Lee's experience in routing McClellan had convinced him of the practicality of his strategy. Moreover, it had to be executed in the theater which was *politically the most sensitive*, and that was Virginia—so near Washington, DC, and where foreign eyes were focused. Lee had seized the initiative in Virginia and he was determined to make the most of it. There was still time to repair defenses in the west; indeed all it required was a modicum of competent generalship. If a great success could be achieved in the east, the west would be saved. The two theaters were intimately related and stood or fell together. Lee also calculated that the Confederacy was large enough to give ground in one area if the result was a striking success in another. Dissipating the initiative in one just to shore up defenses in the other was not an adequate response to the great crisis in the South's fortunes. In any case, the western Confederacy had adequate military resources; all they needed were to be properly organized and distributed.[2]

This strategy has been severely and unfairly criticized by certain historians. Lee's critics tend to oversimplify a complex strategic equation. It is unhelpful to presume that Virginia was unimportant, and simultaneously suggest that the west was just more important.

But why was Lee able to achieve such success in Virginia while his counterparts in the west were driven back? In the first instance, he created a real army with cohesion, a sense of loyalty, and an articulation that was wholly lacking in the west. Staff officers who were inadequate, such as R. H. Chilton, were discreetly bypassed or removed. Lee was quite ruthless in assessing the capability of his subordinates for formation command; if they were found wanting, then they were tactfully removed. The artillery was reformed and its command more closely centralized. Lee devoted much attention to the higher organization of his army because its skill in maneuver depended upon excellence in command. He created two wings (or corps), the first under James Longstreet and the second under Stonewall Jackson. Despite the latter's disappointing performance in the Seven Days', Lee had not lost faith in his abilities. But more than anything else, Lee by his quiet, dedicated example, worked to create the right harmonious atmosphere in his army. There would be disputes between his generals—mainly involving the unpredictable and harsh Jackson (who quarreled with A. P. Hill, among others). However, there was little friction between unit commanders at corps level, even though there were quarrels within formations. When these broke out Lee acted as an arbitrator and, where possible, mollified the antagonists. The acrimonious and intensely personal feuds that split the Army of Tennessee asunder were avoided; Lee never quarreled with his subordinates. Those historians who criticize him for being excessively mild in his command methods tend to ignore the importance he attached to harmony between his senior officers. The alternative did not beckon as an attractive one.[3]

There was a further reason for Lee's success, and that had to do with the psychological outlook of Northern commanders in the east. Before 1861 eastern intellectuals had become anxious concerning the damage inflicted on the Northern character by materialism, bribery, and corruption. They warned that courage and vitality were being sapped; "manliness" was on the wane and selfish cowardice was on the increase. From this debilitating process the South was excepted. The South, it was believed, was a rural society in which the martial virtues were cultivated, especially those involving horsemanship. The notion of a Southern "military tradition" was widely accepted. By the beginning of 1862 it was assumed that Southern forces were inherently superior to those of the North: their officers were better; their men enjoyed superior skills with the rifle and in the saddle; they were also tougher, and could march or ride faster.[4]

The notion that secession was the product of a deeply laid conspiracy also gained ground. Thus Northern generals could attribute (and so excuse) their failures by reference to Southern "preparation" and the "war machine" that had been put in place before 1861. McClellan greatly admired Southern military gentlemen. This is clear from his early correspondence. These attitudes combined to produce distinct feelings of inferiority in the Army of the Potomac. This had not occurred in the west. The hard-fought victory at Shiloh "was a Union victory that gave the men . . . great confidence in themselves ever after." Grant concluded that Southern soldiers "must have gone back discouraged and convinced that the 'Yankee' was not an enemy to be despised." McClellan's "change of base" became the butt of numerous Southern jokes between pickets at Harrison's Landing; Northern offensive efforts, especially if they involved cavalry, were treated with derision. Morale, and a consequent sense of superiority in the Army of Northern Virginia, soared; the converse was true in the Army of the Potomac even though these attitudes were based on no objective evidence whatsoever.[5]

McClellan had a further problem in that such views concerning Northern military inferiority were widely shared in the North. They produced a reaction that exalted the importance of moral forces in war—especially brazen courage and the attack *à l'outrance*. Critics ridiculed McClellan's preference for making war by engineering methods and entrenchments. McClellan had been right to use them, but the manner of the execution of his battles had discredited them.

"McClellan's forte is digging not fighting," complained Senator Benjamin F. Wade, "Place him before an enemy and he will burrow like a woodchuck. His first effort is to get underground." McClellan's failure in the Peninsula led to a wide-ranging reappraisal of Union priorities and the ridicule heaped on him by political enemies led to a public discrediting of entrenchments, which was unwise; aspirants for high command tried to distance themselves from McClellan's methods. But anxieties about the fighting qualities of Union troops continued to fester. Salmon P. Chase was appalled to hear General George W. Cullum complain, "Our men won't fight." Chase reflected, "The style of that remark does not suit me; but it is too common among our generals. In my opinion the soldiers are better than the officers." On the evidence of the Peninsular campaign Chase was probably right, but it by no means followed that, in the struggle to cope with the problems of mass involvement, Confederate generals were automatically superior. In the west they manifestly were not. Thus a pervasive sense of inferiority was only one factor, albeit an important one, that explains Union failures before Christmas 1862.[6]

McClellan's strategic and operational failures on the Peninsula resulted in a wide-ranging debate over the future of Union strategy. Given yet another failure this was hardly likely to be conducted in a calm, detached atmosphere; on the contrary, passions were high and tempers bad. For the first time, President Lincoln turned to the more successful generals in the west to invigorate the eastern army. On the strength of Grant's victories, Halleck was called from the west to become general in chief and to fill a vacuum since McClellan's demotion the previous March. The president had never had much faith in the peninsular concept, a prejudice reinforced by his visit to the Army of the Potomac on July 8, penned up in its disease-infested base at Harrison's Landing. Halleck was immediately dispatched there and ordered a withdrawal. Lee had been watching the Army of the Potomac warily; McClellan was pressing for reinforcements and demanding a continuation of the campaign, yet showed no disposition to act. McClellan's strategic concept was undoubtedly sound; his execution of it puerile. Halleck was unconvinced by McClellan's rather petulant entreaties and ordered a concentration in northern Virginia. Another commander, John Pope, had been brought to Virginia from the west and a new Army of Virginia was being created; Fitz John Porter's Fifth Corps was moved to reinforce it.[7]

The debate revolved around much more than who commanded what; it concerned the very nature of the war itself. The duration and scale of the conflict was wholly unexpected and an unpleasant shock. McClellan's halting and indecisive generalship was self-defeating. He could only succeed in his aim of limiting the ferocity of the war if he could bring the war to an end dramatically and cleanly. In July 1862 McClellan had taken advantage of Lincoln's visit to Harrison's Landing and gave him a considered statement of his strategic view. "It should not be a war looking to the subjugation of a people of any state," he urged Lincoln in his Harrison's Landing letter. "It should not be at all a war upon population, but against armed forces and political organizations." But this could only be achieved if the war was going well; success was not as self-evident as many would have hoped and McClellan was blamed for this state of affairs. "Neither confiscation of property," he averred, "political executions of persons, territorial organization of states, or forcible abolition of slavery should be contemplated for a moment." These views might have been an initial manifesto for the 1864 presidential election. Yet they flew in the face of political reality. Lincoln had already signed two bills confiscating property, approved the emancipation of slavery in the District of Columbia and in the territories. The president was already beginning to agree with Senator Wade's view that "you cannot escape from this war without the emancipation of Negroes." Increasingly, therefore, the protection of Southern property—and slavery in particular, which underpinned the Confederate war economy—had already become a low priority.[8]

The Joint Committee on the Conduct of the War was briefed on the contents of the Harrison's Landing letter by Stanton, who had also read it out at a cabinet meeting. Denunciations of McClellan followed, including the shameful allegation that he was a traitor. By comparison, "Old Brains" Halleck was a canny operator. From the first he grasped the social implications of the war. "The North," he wrote, "will become ultra anti-slavery, and I fear, in the course of the war, will declare for emancipation and then add the horrors of a servile to that of a civil war." The Joint Committee on the Conduct of the War was composed of radical Republicans and their war Democrat allies such as Tennessee Senator Andrew Johnson who, due to the exigencies of the war, were temporarily allied with them. Its members now more than ever demanded a "vigorous" war effort and the setting aside of delicate sensibility about carrying the war to Southern civilians and protecting their private property. The committee was most effective when it enjoyed a clear-cut foe (and scapegoat) like McClellan, whose generalship it damned. By the use of gossip, exploitation of newspaper headlines, and collaboration with sympathetic cabinet members like Stanton, it became a much-feared body. Yet it lacked real executive authority. Senator Wade, the chairman, had introduced Rule 22 in the Senate in January 1862, which permitted the Senate or the House of Representatives to move into secret executive session should the president require urgent or drastic measures. But Lincoln did not avail himself of this expedient, which would have granted Congress a measure of executive authority sufficient to challenge the power of the presidency to conduct the war. Consequently, throughout the Civil War the committee enjoyed influence rather than power. It pursued a series of issues in such a forthright manner that commanders (and their political leaders) could not afford to ignore them. And the longer the war continued the greater the weight its case carried. The committee thrived on bad news from the front and there was no shortage of this in the summer and autumn of 1862.[9]

The members of the committee were not a very pleasant group of people. Snarling, uncouth, their breath often smelled of whisky; they were garrulous, zealous, dogmatic, and self-righteous. They lacked basic military knowledge. But they were excited by the immense material superiority of the North and were fearful that it was being frittered away by poor leadership; in truth there were good grounds for this suspicion, in Virginia at least. Wade's biographer defends his ruthlessness. If his "zeal sometimes led him to questionable methods," writes Professor Trefousse, "the desperate situation of the government gave him all the excuse he needed. Wade believed that unusual times called for unusual devices." The committee provided a forum for the justification of these inquisitorial instincts of members of Congress. It called for "action" and "fighting men" and advocated the emancipation of slavery. It also gave voice to the fear that Lincoln was in thrall of his generals.[10]

Witnesses before the committee were invited to give their opinions on virtually all matters relating to the Army of the Potomac irrespective of the plans of their superiors. Some refused to answer, claiming with justification that to do so would break army regulations. Wade and Senator Zachariah Chandler (Republican, Michigan) believed that "independent opinion" improved rather than impaired military discipline. But some ambitious commanders, especially John Pope and Benjamin F. Butler, pandered to the committee's prejudices and began to advocate strategies of which its members approved. Their main targets were McClellan's conduct in the Peninsula and his Harrison's Landing letter. The committee met in secret and before it received a conservative general, scores of witnesses sympathetic to its own aims were heard. Testifying generals were not informed that some of their peers had made serious charges impugning their integrity and motives. They appeared alone without counsel and Wade, Chandler, or Congressman Daniel Gooch (Republican, Massachusetts) would ask vague or leading questions. Conservative witnesses were also lulled into a false sense of security by the assurance that Wade was compiling an account of the war.[11]

Such a measure of importunate interference in the conduct of the war has provoked a good deal of denunciation, especially among those writers favorable to McClellan. Well-intentioned but ignorant interference that hamstrung McClellan for base "political" motives, critics claim, cost thousands of lives and millions of dollars. The verdict of most historians is now more favorable though occasionally equivocal. The committee provided a justification for punitive strategies of annihilation just as McClellan was maneuvering to justify his own limited strategy. Pope told the committee that he was in favor of emancipation and abrasive treatment of Southern civilians. Two days after his appearance before the committee he announced his General Order No. 7. The safety of civilians behind Union lines, he proclaimed, "depends upon the peace and quiet among themselves and upon the unmolested movements through their midst of all pertaining to the military service." Any damage to railroads or telegraphs in the Shenandoah Valley would be punished by a levy to pay for the damage and any houses containing snipers would be razed to the ground. Pope then announced that "as far as practicable" the Army of Virginia would subsist on the country.[12]

It was politicking in Washington that formed the most important source of punitive strategies in the Civil War. These were developed by Halleck, fertilized by his acute political sense and disseminated by him down the chain of command. Sensing the drift of the political breeze after hearing of the committee's deliberations, and testimony like Pope's, Halleck was now more likely to support calls for punitive measures. These were not the unique inspiration of commanders in the west but the product of a widespread and, on the whole, constructive debate that focused on the conduct of operations in Virginia. The committee was much less interested in the more successful operations in the west. Grant claimed that "the Congressional Committee for investigating the Conduct of the War will have nothing to enquire about in the West." He was largely right. The most significant feature of its activities was that it channeled discontent, disaffection, and sheer rumor mongering, sometimes mischievous and sometimes not, into constitutional and political channels that upheld the party system. In the Confederacy, which had set its face against "parties" and factionalism, disputes about the war became bitter and intensely personal. The personal element was hardly lacking in the committee's vendetta against McClellan. When Wade and Chandler visited the Army of the Potomac, McClellan had them chased away from a shelter of trees during a shower of rain. Nevertheless in the North the political system was made to work, and for all its bluster and misguided activity, the committee did make a positive contribution to the war effort and did not simply indulge in personal spite. The party system and its ethos were not so pernicious as contemporaries were prone to claim.[13]

The limitations of the committee's authority becomes clear when its relations with the executive branch are considered. Earlier historians considered it an infernal nuisance, waging an incessant guerrilla war on the administration's policies. Other scholars have viewed it as a valuable ally, a "vanguard" for the administration. This latter interpretation assumes perhaps too much common ground between Lincoln and his radical critics. In September 1862 the president would ignore their ferocious invective and restore McClellan to favor; control of appointments remained firmly in his grip. If Lincoln did consider this committee a valuable ally then it might be retorted that he never recorded this view. It is more likely that he regarded their voluble heckling and exhortation with the stoic, and rather bemused, tolerance that he treated the many importunate and patriotic petitioners who trespassed on his good nature. The significance of the Joint Committee lay not so much in its relationship with the executive as what it indicated about the ambitions of the legislature. With a general in command, Pope, who was moving swiftly away from the limited strategies of Winfield Scott and McClellan, congressional hopes soared. They were to be brutally dashed.[14]

John Pope, who is hardly an overpraised figure among military historians, got off to a good start in field command. He had a fine presence and impressed politicians and reporters. His energy contrasted with McClellan's constant whining and tactical torpor, and Pope was determined to impress his dynamism on his command. Despite his sympathy for emancipation, he did not repeat Frémont's error of interferring with Lincoln's prerogative by issuing edicts on slavery. Pope understood the limits of the committee's power but appreciated that it was an agency working to his advantage. In his much ridiculed general order, he declared robustly that:

> The strongest position a soldier should desire to occupy is one from which he can most easily advance against the enemy. Let us study the probable lines of retreat of our opponents, and leave our own to take care of themselves. Let us look before us, and not behind.

This was clearly a coded attack on McClellan's generalship and indicated a desire to draw a line under it and start afresh. Pope was pandering to the deepest prejudices and desires of committee members. The order contains much sense but its rhetorical effectiveness was reduced by a throwaway line that his "headquarters were in the saddle." This led to much ridicule at the time, which has percolated into a historiography that frequently reflects Confederate biases and one of Lee's most frequently repeated jokes as to the location of General Pope's brains.[15]

It was said unkindly of General Pope that if his house had been emblazoned with a coat of arms, then "it would have been bombast rampant upon an expansive field of incompetence." Such ridicule is exaggerated. Pope revealed himself a commander of energy but his great fault was inexperience. He lacked skill in deploying an army in excess of five corps and his subordinates knew this. Consequently his confident and dogmatic pronouncements were undoubtedly tinged with bluff and provoked skepticism. Worse, one of these which particularly irritated his corps commanders—"I have come to you from the West where we have always seen the backs of our enemies; from an army whose policy has been attack and not defense"—Pope claimed had actually been dictated by Secretary of War Stanton, a stalwart ally of the Joint Committee on the Conduct of the War. The specter of political interference seemed to haunt his period of command; consequently, his subordinates did not respect him. Stanton earned McClellan's undying hatred as a traitor to the Democrat cause. McClellan cared nothing for Pope's predicament and, despite orders to withdraw from the Peninsula, he organized the evacuation of the Army of the Potomac in his customary leisurely fashion, gruffly remarking that Pope should get out of his "scrape" as best he could. This was a disgraceful attitude to adopt but, in the annals of war, was not unique.[16]

Pope therefore did not enjoy the confidence of his subordinates, notably those, like Fitz John Porter, who were protégés of McClellan. He had problems enough in adjusting his command horizons to a higher level. Pope's basic instinct was to act at the corps level of command and this explains his bewilderment in the face of Lee's maneuvers. His more experienced subordinates, furthermore, were not disposed to help him. Porter, who was ordered to join Pope's Army of Virginia on August 17, was soon writing to his old chief, McClellan, scorning his new commander.

> I wish myself away from it [Army of Virginia], with all our old Army of the Potomac, and so do our companions. . . . Most of this is private, but if you can get me away please do so. Make what use of this you choose, so that it does good.

With such a measure of disloyalty, the auspices for the new campaign did not look encouraging.[17]

With a new army organizing in northern Virginia Lee was placed in an unenviable strategic position, for he was uncertain as to whether McClellan would renew his assault on Richmond. When it became plain by August 14 that units of the Army of the Potomac were being withdrawn by water, Lee began to transfer units northward. "I suppose he [McClellan] is coming here too," Lee wrote to his wife, "so we shall have a busy time." The operations that he contemplated, however, were not of a decisive nature. Once Lee received confirmation that McClellan was abandoning the Peninsula, he felt "a great relief" yet he regretted that McClellan "ought not to have got off so easily." Nonetheless, the object of the operations he undertook in August 1862 was to consolidate the Confederate grip on the capital. He intended to strengthen the defense of the city's logistical lifelines, especially the Virginia Central Railroad, over which Richmond drew supplies from the fertile Shenandoah Valley. It is probable that Lee envisaged these moves as a preliminary to an advance on Northern soil from which he could draw supplies, relieve Virginia of the burden of war, and then engage the enemy in a humiliating defeat that would erode Northern fighting power and prompt foreign powers to intervene in the conflict on the Southern side. Lee intended to move onto the offensive, concentrate his forces, and "baffle the principal efforts of the enemy." On August 19 Stuart was dispatched with the cavalry. "Get what information you can of fords, roads & position of enemy," he was instructed, "so that your march can be made understandingly & with vigor." Lee was not keen that McClellan and Pope should join forces on the Rappahannock River for another massive drive on Richmond, which would undo the success of the Seven Days'.[18]

With something less than eighty thousand men he intended to move around Pope's left flank and drive into his rear, strike at his lines of communication, and force him to withdraw from northern Virginia. Federal forces captured a letter from Lee to Stuart outlining the campaign almost as soon as it began; such operational bonuses were a feature of the campaigns of August and September 1862 and denote a certain casualness toward staff work. Yet the improvement in technique exhibited by the Army of Northern Virginia since the Seven Days' battles (let alone the fumbling of First Manassas) is impressive. The division of the army between Longstreet and Jackson gave it a flexibility previously lacking and allowed Confederate forces to fulfill the *operational* aims of the campaign with fluency, sophistication, and a measure of speed wholly lacking on the federal side. There were rumblings of disagreement between some Confederate generals over seniority: between Stuart and Brigadier General Isaac R. Trimble, and between D. H. Hill and Longstreet, and the latter and the boastful but ineffective former Confederate secretary of state and now brigadier general, Robert Toombs. Toombs was arrested by Longstreet, but the latter was far too ambitious to antagonize a powerful politician from his native state of

Georgia and earned Toombs's thanks by ordering his release. Lee's exercise of quiet authority and the success of his generalship seemed to restrict the ferocity of these disagreements in his army.[19]

As his army moved northward with Jackson's corps of twenty-three thousand men in the van and Stuart operating on his right, Lee hoped to "turn his [Pope's] position at Warrenton &c, so as to draw him out of them. I would rather you have easy fighting and heavy victories." Jackson obliged by attacking individual unsupported Union corps, as he had in the Valley campaign, but the result at Cedar Mountain (August 9, 1862) was a messy battle that offered no clear-cut tactical victory but a further glittering opportunity. Lee, angered by Pope's threats to Virginia's civilian population, felt a personal contempt for Pope that was not transferred to his successors. He wanted to "suppress" him. An opportunity seemed to present itself for suppression after Cedar Mountain by trapping the Army of Virginia in the triangle formed between the Rapidan and Rappahannock rivers. But the capture of Lee's orders alerted Pope to his danger and he hurriedly withdrew north of the Rappahannock. Lee observed ironically to Longstreet, "General, we little thought the enemy would turn his back upon us thus early in the campaign."[20]

A new offensive on Richmond was the last thing that Halleck wanted in August 1862. As a scholar Halleck was highly conscious that Lee enjoyed interior lines and a central position between the two federal armies, "ready to fall with his superior numbers upon one or the other, as he may elect." Although acknowledging the difficulties of reinforcement, Halleck told Pope to wait for McClellan and his army; but Pope was not anxious to share any glory with the "Young Napoleon," the unrelenting enemy of his most enthusiastic political backers. In any case, he was too aggressive and impulsive to obey Halleck's instructions that he was not to expose himself to any disaster. Halleck was studiously vague about who was to command whom. McClellan was obviously the senior and had more experience; yet Halleck was acutely aware that Pope enjoyed influential political support, which would not tolerate him being elbowed aside.[21]

Such disputes were brushed away by Stonewall Jackson's thrust toward Manassas Junction, the nerve center of Pope's supply line, which he captured on August 26. Pope had erroneously believed that Jackson was heading for the Shenandoah Valley. Jackson's corps gorged like locusts on Pope's bountiful supplies and destroyed what they could not move. A further bonus was Stuart capturing Pope's letter book, which was passed to General Lee—although the importance of this prize has been exaggerated. Pope now faced two stark alter-

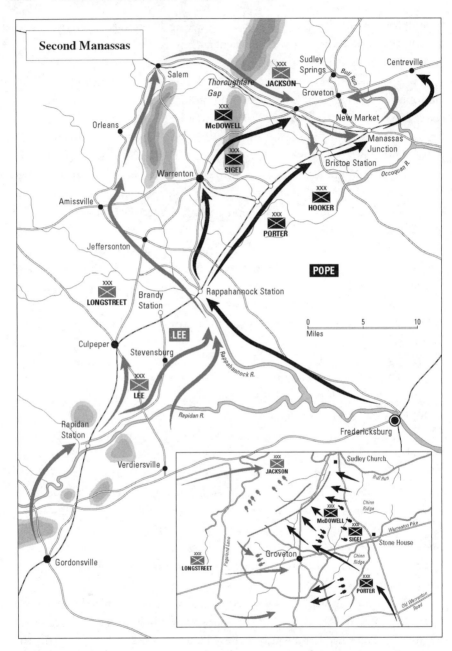

Second Manassas

From Brian Holden Reid, *Robert E. Lee: Icon for a Nation* (London: Weidenfeld & Nicolson, 2005). Map © Peter Harper. Reprinted by permission of The Orion Publishing Group.

natives. He could either withdraw into the Washington defenses or seek out Jackson and destroy him. Pope enjoyed overwhelming superiority, and facing down a single corps was an object and level of military activity which gave him confidence. He decided to seek and destroy Jackson.

The campaign so far had proved a conspicuous success for the Army of Northern Virginia. Lee had divided his army into four parts: Longstreet, Jackson and Stuart, with D. H. Hill commanding his own division, plus McLaws's and the artillery reserve hastening to join the main body. These units, on home territory surrounded by a sympathetic population, were often separated by more than fifty miles. Pope seemed incapable of turning and acting upon these dazzling maneuvers; he invariably drew wrong deductions as to Lee's intentions. Pope "did not appear to be aware of his situation," reported the Confederate commanding general. The strategic object of transferring the theater of war northward as a prelude to a crossing of the Potomac north was rapidly being achieved. In an echeloned envelopment reminiscent of the Seven Days', Longstreet was now wheeled to Jackson's left as he plunged eastward and crossed the Bull Run Mountains, advancing to support Jackson. Lee had hoped "to consume provisions and forage now being used in supporting the enemy . . . [and] prevent so great a draft upon other parts of the country." The object of the campaign was to guarantee the security of the Confederate capital as a strong base from which to launch an offensive movement and an ambitious program was ordered "to insure the safety of Richmond." It was *not* to seek out a decisive battle. Therefore the many parallels that are frequently made with the campaigns of Napoleon, often with an implication that Lee was somehow imitative (based on no evidence), are not only superficial but also misleading. In detail the campaign has little in common with Napoleonic practice, although it does demonstrate a growing mastery of a technique attempted in a rather fumbling manner during the Seven Days'. It is with these operations that Lee's August 1862 campaign should be compared. They were a rationalization of Lee's earlier military experience in Mexico adapted to the peculiar American conditions of the 1860s. Lee's technique of war elevated the strategic importance of railroads as the operational imperative and furthermore, the division of the army in the face of a superior enemy (not just for tactical but for logistical reasons).[22]

The opportunity to fight a great battle was made available by John Pope, Lee had not sought it out. Pope's crucial error was in failing to gauge the extent of the threat he faced. He failed myopically to enlarge the sphere of his thoughts beyond a keen desire to get even with Jackson and destroy his corps. Longstreet's corps, two days behind Jackson's (contrary to the suggestions of Longstreet's many postwar critics), advanced with alacrity: his thirty thousand men covered thirty miles on the first day. Traversing Thoroughfare Gap, Longstreet's troops encountered opposition. This was the crucial moment; had Pope risen to the occasion and sent substantial reinforcements to prevent Longstreet from marching the last twenty-two miles to join Jackson at Groveton, then with his concentrated army now consisting of six corps (three had arrived from the Army of the Potomac), Lee could have been beaten in detail. But Pope did nothing for he believed erroneously that McDowell's First Corps had driven Longstreet back. Instead Longstreet's corps brushed aside the single division that opposed their advance.[23]

Tired but triumphant on August 29 Longstreet's corps linked up with Jackson's, whose command had occupied a strong defensive position along Stony Ridge above Groveton. Jackson had resisted Pope's attacks all that day. The Army of Northern Virginia now resembled an open nutcracker with Pope's Army of Virginia caught between its jaws. Here was an extraordinary opportunity. Lee had effected an uninterrupted concentration and was now poised to envelop Pope's left flank. The only question left unanswered was deciding on the timing of the counterstroke. Longstreet opposed an immediate attack on the grounds that it would be risky to launch his corps without even an elementary reconnaissance. Lee relented; the recollection of many shattered and uncoordinated attacks during the Seven Days' must have been uppermost in his thoughts. Longstreet's reluctance to attack, which was voiced on two further occasions, has been seized upon by an earlier generation of Southern historians as the roots of "the disaster at Gettysburg." They picture Longstreet like the Prince of Darkness standing obstinately at Lee's ear, whispering prudence and delay. In that image, he personified the pernicious spirit of fatal hesitation when immediate action was required. Yet after the Civil War, Fitz John Porter was confident that Longstreet would have been repulsed had he attacked on August 29.

Lee's style of command, by which subordinates were given their missions and then expected to seek out by their own devices how best to fulfill them, invited this kind of intervention, which Lee was free to accept or reject as he saw fit. Operations in the Peninsula clearly had left their scars because he accepted this advice without demur. Longstreet was the only subordinate to emerge from the Seven Days' with his reputation enhanced and Lee took notice of his views. As Jeffrey Wert, Longstreet's most impartial biographer, comments, "to argue that Longstreet dominated Lee is to presume that Lee could be controlled. It would be accurate to say that the commanding general utilized Longstreet's talents, listened to his counsel and concurred." Certainly during the Seven Days' the dynamic and decisive Lee had given no hint that he was impressionable and easily swayed.[24]

During the night Lee considered moving against Pope's rear to get between him and Washington. That night he wrote to President Davis a letter that was much preoccupied with logistical matters: "I hope every exertion will be made to create troops and to increase our strength and supplies. Beef, flour and forage may be obtained in the back country by proper exertions . . . and it will be far better for us to consume them than to leave them for the enemy." Having successfully forced the Union forces to concentrate around Centreville, Lee repeated "My desire has been to avoid a general engagement, being the weaker force, and by maneuvering to relieve the portion of the country referred to." He continued: "we shall be able to relieve other portions of the country, as it seems to be the purpose of the enemy to collect his strength here." This letter shows without doubt that it was not Lee's intention to use the campaign to fight a climactic, decisive battle pursuing some neatly worked out design of "Napoleonic strategy," with Jackson as the fixing force and Longstreet as his maneuver force.[25] If this had been Lee's design, surely he could have reversed the roles of the two commanders. But the results of his maneuvers had so outgeneralled Pope that he was offered an opportunity he could not ignore.

With his thoughts directed toward avenging many indignities on Jackson, Pope neglected his left flank and allowed himself to be persuaded that Lee was retreating northward. He ordered a general attack on Jackson's position by Porter's Fifth Corps supported by two divisions, deaf to the pleas that the Confederate line had extended to the south and that his flank would be exposed. "The enemy is massed in the woods in front of us," he informed Porter hours after Longstreet's arrival. The level of Union intelligence gathered by the cavalry, as in the Peninsula, was puerile. Due to muddle and confusion it took Porter three hours to organize this assault and it did not begin until shortly after 3 PM on August 30. The Army of Northern Virginia had displayed one further improvement that would have a major impact on the conduct of the second battle of Manassas. This was in the deployment of artillery. Longstreet had set up a massed battery of artillery upon arriving on the field. In addition, Colonel Stephen D. Lee had concentrated the reserve artillery in the center between the two Confederate corps. This force comprised about twenty-two guns that played havoc with Porter's advancing infantry. This intense, concentrated fire uncontested by the Union artillery ensured that Porter's first line could neither advance further after reaching Jackson's position nor escape. An observer recorded that "the first line of the attacking column looked as if it had been struck by a blast from a tempest and had been blown away." Porter's force recoiled before the ferocity of the Confederate defense and the moment was propitious for a counterstroke.[26]

Lee gave the order, taking the opportunity that could not be neglected. "My whole line was rushed forward at a charge," Longstreet wrote, along the axis of the Warrenton Turnpike Road toward Centreville. But the country was broken and wooded; and effective though the attack was, it had the effect of pushing the enemy back toward his lines of communication rather than shattering his cohesion. Artillery was hurriedly sent forward to maintain the momentum. Much praise has been lavished on this counterstroke; in its exploitation of concentration, tactical surprise, and mobility, it does indeed serve as an object lesson in tactics. It brought maximum strength to bear on weakness, which is the ultimate object of economy of effort. One of Longstreet's divisional commanders, John B. Hood, described the action as "the most beautiful battle scene I have ever beheld." His division, "true to their teaching," took the fight to the enemy and captured five cannon and fourteen battle flags. But this tactical emphasis—which was right and proper for a divisional commander—denoted a weakness.[27]

Pope was routed but not crushed. In attempting to seek an explanation for this failure, many of the interpretations most favored by historians need to be reviewed. These touch upon some of the outstanding issues in Civil War historiography that are central to an understanding of the conflict. General Lee himself, in a letter to the Confederate president a few days after the battle, averred that "the darkness of the night, his [the federal] destruction of the Stone Bridge [over Bull Run] after crossing, and the uncertainty of the fords stopped the pursuit." The armies had also been drenched by rain, which always slows those who are merely taking lives more than those who are frantically trying to save theirs. Lee also conceded Pope's success at "masking his retreat." Getting the Army of Northern Virginia moving again after its triumph had not been easy as rainfall, Lee reported, "threatened to render Bull Run impassable and impeded our movements." Stuart's cavalry had located Pope at the strong position of Centreville, "about four miles beyond Bull Run." An attempt to bring sequential blows to bear on Pope's fleeing forces had failed because of the exhaustion of Jackson's corps, "who, in addition to their arduous marches, had fought three severe engagements in as many days." Thus, despite every valiant effort, Lee remarked with no little sarcasm that the pursuit could not be sustained because "the enemy had conducted his retreat so rapidly that the attempt to intercept him was abandoned." Pope successfully sought refuge behind the Washington defenses.[28]

Later historians have developed Lee's line of reasoning. Douglas Southall

Freeman lamented the lateness of the hour, about 4 PM, at which Longstreet's counterstroke was launched, which even with long summer evenings meant that the amount of time available for developing truly decisive operations was limited. Hence the criticism of Longstreet's overweening pigheadedness in resisting Lee's plans for an assault on August 29, which Freeman depicts as downright obstructionism.[29] Other historians of the Confederacy view Lee's strategy with disdain and are not perplexed by his failure to crush Pope's army. Their interpretation is simple. Lee was too fond of battle; he sought at every opportunity to seek out and win a Napoleonic decisive battle, was reckless in the defense of his precious Virginia, and his strategy was self-defeating because he wore down the fighting power of his splendid army in search of a chimera. The second battle of Manassas was yet another step on this bloody and futile path. Technological improvement of weapons had rendered battle indecisive, and the pursuit impossible.[30]

A much more considered explanation is offered by Herman Hattaway and Archer Jones in their comprehensive history of the war. Lee "failed to destroy Pope because the maneuverability and defensive power of Pope's troops enabled him promptly to cover his exposed flank and withdraw during the night." Thus "the movement to the rear to threaten something vital had given the army on the strategic offensive the opportunity to fight on the tactical defensive and so have an advantage." This argument is certainly worthy of respect. But Hattaway and Jones conclude by observing that Pope's retreat illustrated a "mid-nineteenth-century army's virtual invulnerability to destruction in 'the open field.'" This seems to be rather overstating the case.[31]

Were mid-nineteenth-century armies "invulnerable"? Surely not. Lee's entire front covered slightly more than three miles.[32] This hardly represents an expansion of the size of the battlefields or a great extension of the span of command. Indeed the field of Second Manassas is comparable in size to Waterloo. Thus Lee could have controlled the battlefield and managed his forces so as to bring about a decisive victory. The topography of the battlefield did not work against this and his army was responsive to his will (indeed over great distances); furthermore, he had a clear-cut objective in Pope's rear to aim for—the Stone Bridge over Bull Run, the capture of which would have forced Pope's surrender in the field. Although Lee was outnumbered, his army of sixty thousand could have overwhelmed and forced the surrender of one of eighty thousand men, especially given the disparity of *fighting power* revealed by the campaigns in the Peninsula and Second Manassas. This concept does not refer to combat *potential*, but to the degree of success in which this capacity is organized and directed. Despite their numerical and material superiority, the Union armies of Virginia and the Potomac were poorly commanded and ill directed, often at the wrong level. Federal commanders proved inept at concentration, failed to utilize the full strength of their forces, and allowed outnumbered fragments to engage superior Confederate forces. Under these circumstances a complete envelopment of the Union army, or splintering it into smaller pieces, or launching a devastating pursuit were certainly not beyond the bounds of possibility. Mid-nineteenth-century armies were far from invulnerable.

This whole question is usually discussed without reference to morale. Union morale had certainly suffered since the Seven Days' and the conduct of Second Manassas had weakened it further. Union troops fled the field in panic, "like dogs," admitted Private Richard Ackerman. Their confidence had been further weakened and that of the Confederates boosted. It was an army, recalled General Oliver O. Howard, "with broken ranks and haggard looks come straggling and discouraged to the protection of the encircling forts of Washington"; "some for the first time," admitted a private soldier, Warren Lee Goss, "began to regard our cause as a losing one. Most of the soldiers believed the Confederate armies were more ably commanded than our own." Under these conditions—when soldiers feel that they have not been defeated but their commanders have—they are most likely to surrender because they lack confidence in the higher leadership. Yet Michael Adams's challenging analysis of the sense of inferiority that was pervasive in Union forces perhaps overstates a plausible case. He argues that these troops placed too much faith in McClellan's sense of his own destiny and showed an excessive contempt for Pope. Such attitudes "profoundly influenced the senior officers [of the Army of the Potomac], who were the nervous system of the army, giving it life and tone." But there were several Union generals who loved fighting. Philip Kearny informed George A. Custer, "I love war. It brings me indescribable pleasure, like that of having a woman." Alas, Kearny was killed at Chantilly, September 1, 1862, shielding Pope's retreat.[33]

Yet Adams's thesis strengthens an argument advanced here, namely that the *organization* of the Army of Virginia was far from invulnerable; on the contrary, wracked by internal divisions and a lack of confidence, it was ripe for capitulation in the field. Then why did it escape? It is true that for nineteenth-century armies pursuits at night were extremely hazardous. Waterloo offers a rare example of a successful night pursuit in June 1815. Yet it is too often forgotten, especially by zealous and misguided historians who are in such a hurry to slap erroneous, theoretical labels on Lee's generalship, that he did not launch the campaign with decisive objectives in mind. It was intended only as a transitional phase of maneuver that would consolidate the Confederate hold on northern Virginia before launching an offensive into the North, which had been in Lee's mind since the spring of 1862. The attack at Second Manassas was a demonstration of Lee's opportunist philosophy. As he had instructed Stonewall Jackson almost three months previously, "should an opportunity occur for striking the enemy a successful blow do not let it escape you."[34]

The term "blow," which as Hattaway and Jones emphasize, was Lee's preferred term for offensive action (not the modern parlance of "annihilation" or "destruction"). This term clearly demonstrates the importance of the psychological and political influence of his operations, especially on those powers abroad that sympathized with the Confederacy. We may therefore locate the failure to destroy Pope's army in the nature of the "blows" inflicted upon it, not in its inherent defensive strength. The prime Southern difficulty of organizing, coordinating, and sustaining offensive action on the battlefield has already been discussed in an analysis of the Seven Days' battles.[35] The source of Lee's operational failure lay in the excessively tactical character of Longstreet's counterstroke after Fitz John Porter's repulse on August 30. Admirable though it was, Longstreet's thrust was too concerned with engaging enemy positions frontally instead of going around them. Once it was clear that Pope was defeated, organizing the pursuit should have become a top priority because it is a *separate act* of battle. As much thought should have been devoted to it as the break-in battle; failure to devote sufficient attention to the pursuit accounts for the comparatively few number of successful examples in military history, not just in the American Civil War.[36]

Yet such difficulties do not render the pursuit impossible. The effect of Longstreet's counterstroke was to dissipate his own strength over a large area; advancing toward Henry House Hill, for instance, took him away from the decisive point. The prime objective was the stone bridge that would have cut Pope's line of retreat. By shifting frontally instead of pivoting on his right, Longstreet drove Pope's forces back toward the stone bridge and thus enabled him to rally a defense that prevented an improvised pursuit from gaining momentum. Lee was also culpable in allowing Longstreet to conduct this operation without guidance, and in failing to conserve a pursuit force. The long approach marches also took their toll because any pursuit had to be carried out by infantry chasing beaten infantry and not, as during the Napoleonic Wars, by heavy cavalry. Stuart's cavalry was posted on Longstreet's right and tried to maneuver toward the bridge. But the Confederate cavalry was forced into the secondary role of fighting Union cavalry, adopting a column formation. Stuart "wheeled by fours, and charged at full gallop." At other times it merely escorted the artillery forward to maintain the bombardment of Pope's disintegrating left flank. The Army of Northern Virginia thus lacked a *corps de chasse*. Pope's army was given time to organize its withdrawal. Union troops stoutly defended a perimeter around the stone bridge; Stuart's troopers only crossed it after the Union forces made good their escape.[37]

This study thus argues that, far from being hypnotized by the illusion of an impossible Napoleonic-styled decisive battle, Lee devoted *insufficient* attention to the problem of shattering the Union army in the field. At Second Manassas Lee might have secured a capitulation in the field that would have had incalculable political consequences both within North America and in Europe. Yet Lee was satisfied with the results of a highly successful campaign: Virginia was cleared of Union forces, the enemy had been severely defeated, and the reorganization of the Army of Northern Virginia had been triumphantly vindicated, all for less than ten thousand casualties. Pope's casualties were more than sixteen thousand. To secure a campaign north of the Potomac River had been the main object. This could now be launched without hindrance. As for Pope, abandoned by the president, his congressional allies defended him; he was revenged on Porter, whom (as McClellan's "pet") he blamed for the defeat. Hounded by Stanton and Wade, Porter was court-martialed and cashiered. Despite this Pope could not be saved and he languished in Minnesota fighting Indians. Still, he bequeathed an enduring legacy. His introduction of punitive measures supported by members of Congress had long-term effects. Even some of McClellan's allies realized after Porter's fate that these could not be ignored, let alone spurned.[38]

Lee had seized the initiative after Seven Days' and was determined to keep it in his hands. Liberty of maneuver was his watchword because he realized that the Confederate war effort could not survive should the war become a huge siege. The experience of the Franco-Prussian War more than justifies Lee's reasoning. In 1870 the French armies were by no means worsted in the field. Yet they foolishly and voluntarily gave up their freedom of maneuver and withdrew into fortresses at Sedan and Metz. Those mid-nineteenth-century armies were not invulnerable and were forced to surrender. Lee hoped to escape a similar fate. But the fundamental question was *how?*

His answer was to cross the Potomac and invade Maryland. This decision has been much criticized, too, often with an excess of wisdom after the event. Some historians have also pointed out that Lee voluntarily gave up the advantages of the strategic and tactical defensive. It is not quite clear why these advantages were so much more powerful in devastated Virginia than they were in bountiful Maryland, though the move was hardly without risk. Yet the risk was hardly negligible in Virginia either, given the paramount object of defending Richmond, because the factors of time and space in this theater of operations did not favor such a strategy; Confederate armies would get weaker as their opponents got stronger and they would be worn down in an attritional siege. Furthermore, Lee's critics do not always argue consistently. Longstreet afterward declared that he regarded Second Manassas as the model of an offensive strategy with defensive tactics—a battle culminating in a powerful counterstroke. One of Lee's most acerbic critics, Alan T. Nolan, writes that a "defensive grand strategy within the context of which Lee could on occasion have undertaken offensive thrusts, appropriate operationally strategic and tactical offensives while avoiding the costly pattern of offensive warfare that he pursued in 1862 and 1863" should have been adopted. How this would have differed from the measures actually adopted by Lee is difficult to discern.[39]

The advance across the Potomac was perfectly consistent with the defensive–offensive grand strategy advocated by the Confederate government. The autumn of 1862 thus witnessed what amounted to a counteroffensive by the Confederate armies. This was not a predetermined, well-thought-out strategy, but an opportunistic thrust over a front of some six hundred miles. In addition, this happy turn of events in the autumn of 1862 was advantageous to Jefferson Davis politically. Lee was, of course, the most powerful voice supporting the strategy; but he was an army commander and inevitably his perspective was influenced by the direct burdens of his field command. Davis had not yet shown any capacity to view the conflict as a whole, and was prone to overwork and immerse himself in detail. Although his command of what was happening on all the war fronts was impressive, he had difficulty in distinguishing what was crucial and what was inconsequential. He was also much less decisive than he appeared. The result was, in his biographer's words, that he "put bits of himself into all those offensives" launched in the autumn of 1862. His behavior was symptomatic of basic structural flaws in the Confederate higher conduct of the war.[40]

Lee provided the most detailed rationale for the strategy and his correspondence reads like that of a grand strategist rather than a field commander. This combination of two demanding roles is illustrative of the increasingly impossible position in which he found himself. In the first instance, he looked "to the safety of our own frontiers, and to operate untrammeled in an enemy's territory"; this was hazardous, but Lee had calculated the time factor and argued that the reinforcements brought to Washington "are not yet organized, and will take some time to prepare for the field." This confusion would give Lee an initial advantage and allow him to keep a tenacious grip on the initiative. Lee realized that his army was not equipped for a full-scale invasion of the North and he pleaded for a strengthening of the Richmond defenses. Yet to maintain—and vigorously demonstrate—the territorial integrity of the Confederacy was an important motive behind the invasion. Second, sustaining the Army of Northern Virginia logistically impelled Lee to move north. Virginian crops could be harvested unmolested and supplies could be drawn from a plentiful and untouched Maryland countryside.

But it was the political motive that was uppermost in Lee's mind. He intended "to annoy and harass the enemy." Lee also urged Davis to offer the United States government peace terms. With a shrewd eye on Northern discontent with the war, Lee averred that "the rejection of this offer would prove to the country that the responsibility of the continuance of the war does not rest upon us." Those who thought it should end would use their vote in the November 1862 midterm elections to bring pressure on the Lincoln administration to accept the terms. Giving the lie to those historians who have argued erroneously that Lee's strategy lacked an all-important political dimension, and that he failed "to grasp the vital relationship between war and statecraft," Lee elaborated his position.

> Such a proposition coming from us at this time, could in no way be regarded as suing for peace, but being made when it is in our power to inflict injury upon our adversary, would show conclusively to the world that our sole object is the establishment of our independence, and the attainment of an honorable peace.

Lee sensed that time was not on the side of the Confederacy; opportunities had to be seized at once and risks had to be accepted in making the most of them.[41]

Lee was using the Army of Northern Virginia in an attempt to resuscitate the secessionist fervor that had been stamped out by the Lincoln administration in the spring of 1861. He wanted to take with him the prosecessionist former governor of Maryland, Enoch L. Lowe, and on September 8 Lee issued a proclamation assuring the people of the Old Line State that the Confederate army "is prepared to assist you with the power of its arms in regaining the rights of which you have been despoiled." He also assured them that "no constraint upon your free will is intended, no intimidation will be allowed." Undisciplined marauding and looting was, of course, counterproductive. However, as the Confederates were to discover in all the border states, substantial effort on their behalf was in rather short supply as pro-Confederate sympathy was more apparent than it was real. (Lee had been briefed on this on September 4.) Supplying the army was not as easy as Lee thought and, although he wrote that "we have had no difficulty in procuring provisions in the country," he relied heavily on supplies drawn from the Shenandoah Valley. Furthermore, in his zeal to garner all he could from the initiative, Lee overlooked the strain that it would impose on his men and his letters are full of complaints about straggling. The campaign itself would add to those strains quite unexpectedly. But it is quite clear that Lee planned to withdraw to Warrenton should he be forced back. Yet he aimed to defy federal military power and to remain on Northern soil while the November elections were held. These ambitious plans were to be rudely interrupted.[42]

Lee took the calculated risk of dividing his army into three in pursuit of his logistical objectives. Stonewall Jackson, with five divisions, was to "intercept" federal garrisons retreating from Martinsburg and Harpers Ferry that lay astride Lee's lines of communication with the Shenandoah Valley. Should Lee continue his advance into Pennsylvania, as he had suggested to Jefferson Davis on September 4, they could not be permitted to operate in his rear; but initially he saw no reason for a siege of Harpers Ferry. Longstreet would advance northward toward Boonsboro and then on to Hagerstown while D. H. Hill with the rearguard would follow with the reserve artillery, ordnance, and the supply trains. The cavalry scouted to the east and would form a screen along the passes of South Mountain. The Army of Northern Virginia was broken into three and stretched out over a front of some twenty-five miles. Longstreet disapproved of the risk and it is possible that Jackson, too, had severe reservations about such a wide dispersal. Lee had calculated that McClellan would be too preoccupied with his favorite task of reorganizing the federal forces to take advantage of his indisposition. Under normal circumstances this gamble might have paid off.[43]

Despite ferocious opposition from radical Republicans, notably the members of the Joint Committee on the Conduct of the War, Lincoln had reappointed McClellan to command all the troops in the Washington defenses. McClellan had, of course, never been relieved from his post as commander of the Army of the Potomac but was given authority over Pope's men on September 2. As for Halleck, he dealt with a president experienced in military affairs and (rightly) had come to have confidence in his own military judgment. Halleck appeared to recoil at the political pressures he encountered in the byzantine and often overheated atmosphere in Washington, DC. "There are so many cooks," he complained, "they destroy the broth." In truth, for all his complaints about wishing to return to private life, never seeing another politician, and never stepping foot in Washington again, Halleck rather enjoyed the political cut and thrust. He protested rather too much. The president and the general-in-chief were complementary; the former was by far the senior partner, and though he complained that Halleck did not command, in truth he did not wish him to because he exerted his prerogatives as commander-in-chief to the full. As for McClellan, he commanded on sufferance. Lincoln believed that Lee's move northward offered the North a splendid opportunity; McClellan's political position would be fully restored should he make the most of it.[44]

The momentum of the campaign quickened dramatically when, on September 13, a soldier of the 27th Indiana picked up a copy of Lee's Special Order No. 191 wrapped around three cigars in an envelope. The best-laid plans are often thwarted by quirks of fate. The discovery soared up the chain of command and McClellan, ecstatic with joy, realized that he had captured a copy of Lee's plan detailing his scattered distribution over a swath of western Maryland. The culprit was never identified, but such carelessness on the part of a Confederate staff officer was typical of the amateurish staffwork exhibited at this stage of the war. H. B. McClellan (J. E. B. Stuart's chief of staff) wrote later that "No general could hope for a greater advantage over his adversary; and yet the mountain gaps were not forced until the evening of the 14th [of September]."

Actually McClellan had already set his columns in motion westward to Frederick before Special Order No. 191 had been handed to him, and units of Ninth Corps entered Frederick on September 12. Union troops were closer to the Confederate flanks than they were to one another. A persuasive case has been made that McClellan's benefit from the "lost order" has been exaggerated. Should McClellan seize the passes through the long, elongated South Mountain at Turner's Gap and Crampton's Gap, the Army of Northern Virginia would be split in two and McClellan could destroy its constituent parts piecemeal at his leisure. Longstreet, who had never been keen on Lee's plan, was particularly vulnerable beyond Boonsboro. The defense of Turner's Gap in the battle of South Mountain on September 14 forms D. H. Hill's finest hour, and with the cavalry he mounted a stubborn rearguard action, not only to prevent McClellan breaking through South Mountain, but to allow the ordnance trains to escape. Perhaps for once, McClellan's critics are too severe on the battle of South Mountain. Considering the demoralized state of his army just two weeks previously, it took him just over a day to seize these passes, which was lightning quick by his standards. Lee's army remained in mortal danger.[45]

Longstreet advanced rapidly to D. H. Hill's support and Lee decided to withdraw these elements of his army toward the small town of Sharpsburg north of the Potomac. Its location allowed him to screen the rear of McLaws's two divisions in Pleasant Valley that had participated in the operations around Harpers Ferry. He hoped that by withdrawing southward he could reunite with

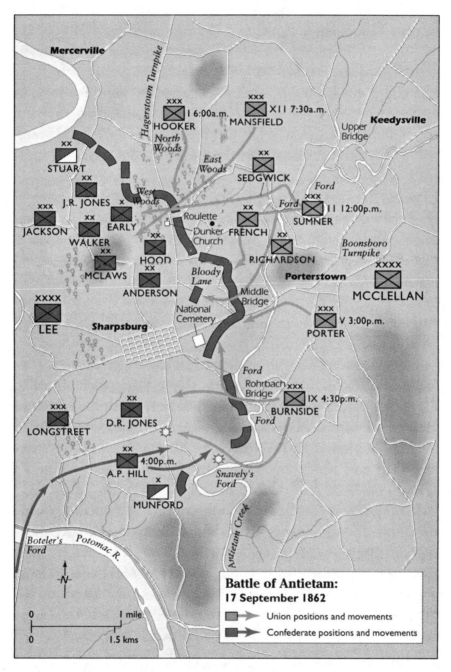

Battle of Antietam:
17 September 1862

Union positions and movements

Confederate positions and movements

From *An Atlas of American Military History* by James C.
Bradford (New York: Cynthia Parzych Publishing, 2003).

Stonewall Jackson en route. On September 15 Lee's mood lightened after he received news of the success of the siege of Harpers Ferry that had been forced on Jackson unexpectedly. The Confederate lines of communication with Virginia were safe. The danger that McClellan might occupy Sharpsburg before Jackson could be extricated had passed. Lee then decided to risk confronting McClellan in the hope that Jackson could reach him before the two armies were fully engaged. Lee could not bring himself to abandon all the ambitious hopes he had cherished for the campaign. His decision has been much criticized but an uncontested withdrawal would have been highly damaging to Confederate prestige, even though the booty from Harpers Ferry was a great prize. Lee did not commit himself to fighting a battle before Sharpsburg until the very last minute. It is possible that he planned to bluff McClellan into holding off until his army was reunited by maneuvering his small force vigorously behind the rolling undulations of the Maryland countryside. In short, to repeat Magruder's maneuvers in the Peninsula. Certainly he managed to do after the battle what he had planned to do before it.

Lee's position west of Antietam Creek was more suited to lateral defensive maneuver than to the tactical defensive. Close study of the ground reveals that it is not as strong as it appears. That Lee might have thought in terms of bluffing McClellan behind these rolling crests rather than in fighting him there is confirmed by Lee's decision not to order the digging of entrenchments, which was unusual for him. A circuitous country road, "Bloody Lane," running between the Boonsboro Turnpike and the Hagerstown Pike in the center of the position, appeared superficially to give protection comparable to entrenchments; but if Lee believed this he erred, because the undulations offered the attackers protection until they were almost on the position and then were actually above it, and could fire into the sunken road from a vantage point, leaving the Confederate center vulnerable to enfilade and fire from the front. Furthermore, the undulations served to segment the battlefield into three parts; those on the right could not see what was happening in the center, let alone observe developments on the left.[46]

In the event, the weakness of Lee's position was more than compensated for by the ineptitude of McClellan's offensive order. He, to all intents and purposes, abandoned his role as commanding general as he had during the Peninsular campaign. He let things roll forward according to the dictates of fate. On the field of Antietam McClellan exerted little tactical control over the forces he deployed, just over 75,300 to Lee's 51,800—although McClellan persuaded himself that he faced a rebel host of 120,000. The result resembled, though for different reasons, the series of wild, uncoordinated, and unsupported attacks that had characterized Southern efforts in the Seven Days' battles. This allowed Lee, who was fighting his first battle at the tactical level, to concentrate all his energies and resources at repulsing each of these successive isolated attacks.

McClellan did not arrive on the battlefield until approximately 2 PM on September 16. He then gave Lee's army a whole afternoon and evening's rest. It may have been this delay that persuaded Lee that McClellan would keep tarrying, so that Lee could wait for all of Jackson's units to come up, and that a good deal could yet be salvaged from this unexpected setback, the cause of which he by now had more than an inkling. At any rate, thanks to the delay parts of Jackson's command took their position on Lee's left. Other elements, however, notably McLaws's and A. P. Hill's Light Division, had not yet arrived, and the former wearily marched onto the field early in the morning of September 17.[47]

At 4 PM on September 16 Joseph Hooker's First Corps crossed Antietam Creek, followed that night by Major General Joseph Mansfield's Twelfth Corps. Ten batteries of First Corps's artillery were placed on the Union right on Potfenberger Hill behind the north woods. McClellan's position appeared strong—no mean achievement considering that when he had taken up command a week before, the best that he hoped to achieve might be to force the Confederates to withdraw from Maryland. He had seized back the initiative; Lee's army lay in disarray and he had won a tactical success at South Mountain. He had yet to prove that he had the ruthlessness of decision to consummate the successes that his clever combinations had thrown up and attain an operational triumph.[48]

The ground at Antietam made it difficult for McClellan to discover Lee's positions. Fog had shrouded the battlefield on the morning of September 16, and for several hours McClellan believed that Lee had slipped away again. But Lee stood his ground. His right rested on the Antietam Creek; sharpshooters had occupied its bluffs above the Rohrback (now Burnside's) Bridge. Consequently, Union troops on the left, comprising Burnside's Ninth Corps with Porter's Fifth Corps to their right, would have to fight their way over Antietam Creek with terrain favoring the defenders. Still, this appeared the most promising line of advance because the Union left lay closest to the town of Sharpsburg and the Confederate lines of communication, dependent on a single road to the lifeline at Boteler's Ford. For all the topographical disadvantages, this sector should have been selected as McClellan's point of main effort.[49]

However, an attack made by the Union right promised much too as the ground favored McClellan's artillery, being open with broad fields of fire. As Lee had pulled his left flank back to Nicodemus Hill overlooking the Potomac River—that is, refused it—McClellan could not launch a turning movement;

but Lee had given up the line of the Antietam as a result and offered McClellan the space to strike him hard.

McClellan decided initially that he would assault the Confederates with his right. But the ghosts of Lee's hidden legions unveiled their hideous faces. Throughout the battle McClellan labored under the delusion that he was outnumbered. This fallacy distorted his calculations because he feared for the safety of his army and failed to commit overwhelming strength when it mattered. He kept waiting to see how his attacks progressed before committing more formations to them. In the event he attacked *both* flanks, but not simultaneously. McClellan issued no directives detailing his intentions and specifying roles. He designated Franklin's Sixth Corps as the reserve, but this remained some miles away at Keedysville. McClellan would wait on events, but would he wait too long?

At 5 AM on September 17 Hooker opened the great battle of Antietam by throwing First Corps forward. Although he had been granted authority over the entire right wing, he did not wait for Twelfth Corps to come up in support. He had received no precise instructions from McClellan except to attack the Confederate left. Hooker's troops pushed through and around the north woods and entered a thirty-acre wheat field. They headed for a small, white-washed timber chapel known as the Dunker Church. This lay atop a finger of high ground behind Lee's left flank. Its seizure would allow Hooker to roll up the entire Confederate left and unhinge the Confederate center anchored on the sunken lane.[50]

Stuart's horse artillery on Nicodemus Hill succeeded in breaking up the cohesion of Hooker's formations as his own powerful corps artillery concentrated their fire on the Confederate line of battle. Hooker's failure to deal with this thorn in his side is inexplicable. The troops of Jackson's wing resisted the Union attacks fiercely. His front extended perhaps five hundred yards and both federals and Confederates were in close proximity. Under such conditions, as one side advanced, fell back, and the other advanced to drive them back further, often provoking countercharges, the distinction between defensive and offensive melted away. Some five thousand Confederates and 8,700 federals slogged it out and sustained additional casualties from artillery fire. By 7 AM of the 13,682 men that became engaged, 4,368 had become casualties.[51]

Two questions immediately suggest themselves. First, why did the Confederates not entrench? Second, why did they not enjoy the benefits supposedly inherent in the defense? Lee, of course, hoped on September 17, once the concentration of his army had been completed, to slip around the Union right flank and maneuver toward Hagerstown. Hooker's advance across the Antietam had ended this hope.

The second issue is related to the first and has much to do with the weapons used by the Confederates. The great majority of Lee's infantry were equipped with smoothbore muskets that had an effective range of a hundred yards. To gain the most from any volley the troops had to mass and stand up to deliver concentrated fire. Similarly, a lot of Lee's artillery pieces were short-range smoothbores; only five of the fifty-three Confederate batteries had uniform equipment and the variety of guns caused severe supply problems. Confederate artillery was inferior in both range and weight of fire. It still made an effective contribution to the Confederate defense though by riding across the battlefield in small numbers, dividing the fire of the more concentrated federal batteries while focusing their effort against Union infantry.[52]

Eventually a well-timed counterattack by Hood's division threw back First Corps and restored the Confederate line. At 7:30 AM Hooker ordered the two divisions of Mansfield's Twelfth Corps, who were mostly "green," unseasoned troops, forward. They attacked piecemeal and Mansfield fell mortally wounded within minutes of leading them forward. McClellan took a snooze during Hooker's fight but had actually witnessed the repulse of First Corps before the Twelfth had been committed. During this lucid interval he ordered Major General Edwin V. Sumner to support Hooker with two of the divisions of Second Corps. This move forced Lee to respond by sending first McLaws's division and then that of John G. Walker to help shore up Jackson's line. This left only one small division, J. R. Jones's 2,400 men, to cover the entire right flank.

McClellan's conduct of the battle had proved so far lethargic. By comparison, even though he had injured his hands and found riding a horse difficult, Lee seemed to be everywhere and always made himself available to deal with all emergencies. It has been argued that McClellan had succeeded in imposing his will on Lee by forcing him to commit all his reserves to defend the Confederate left. But the aim of the onslaught that McClellan had so halfheartedly unleashed appears quite unclear. Was it a feint designed to draw Confederate forces northward, or should it be deemed a decisive attack aimed to pulverize Lee's army and roll up his entire line? If the former, then the number of troops allotted to it was excessively large—almost three corps. If the latter, then the force given to Hooker was insufficient. The scheme, whatever it was, demanded tight control and neat timing. McClellan provided neither. Indeed he succumbed to a temptation that he thought he had avoided by not attacking on September 16, namely that his attack degenerated into a series of piecemeal lunges that were not strong enough to land a crippling blow. McClellan granted Lee enough time to muster his reserves and then throw them forward just at the right moment.[53]

McClellan's errors were compounded by the decision to send much of Second Corps to the right. Sumner thought that a victory was imminent on this sector. After conferring with Hooker (who had been wounded in the foot) he hurriedly led John J. Sedgwick's division forward without the benefit of reconnaissance. He led it toward the west woods in the expectation of rolling up the whole Confederate line. He had left just five minutes before the arrival of an order from McClellan enjoining prudence. But he entered the west woods at an unpropitious moment—just as the Confederates fired into it from three sides. "My God, we must get out of this," exclaimed Sumner, ending yet another piecemeal effort.[54]

The "fits and starts" identified by historian Stephen W. Sears are evidence of McClellan's failure to maintain overall tactical control and shape the battle to meet his desired operational ends. The confusion continued when Sumner's second division, commanded by William French, mistook elements of Twelfth Corps for Sedgwick and advanced by mistake to join him. At about 10 AM French attacked in what he presumed to be the direction of the Dunker Church, but blundered into the Confederate center. D. H. Hill's troops, supported by R. H. Anderson's division, repulsed him without difficulty.[55]

The air of operational bewilderment permeating McClellan's conduct is conveyed in a message sent at about 11:45 AM to Alfred Pleasonton, commanding the cavalry division in the center. "How goes it with you [?]" And then as a postscript, "Can you do any good with a cavalry charge?" In the meantime, Sumner's last division under the command of Israel B. Richardson attacked the sunken lane without orders. The weight of numbers began to tell and eventually at about 1 PM Richardson seized it. But a breakthrough by one division made no signal contribution to any coherent design, for although a dale ran through the Confederate center, the success could not be exploited. McClellan's army had not been positioned to do this, for as he complained to Halleck later in the afternoon "thus far it looks well but I have great odds against me."[56]

An indication of the pernicious effect of this misconception can be measured by McClellan's fear, once the fighting had ground to a halt at about 2 PM on the right, that Lee would launch a massive counterstroke. McClellan's right had been damaged and Lee hoped to move around it. But the aim of Lee's mooted counterstroke was to escape McClellan's blows. The mission was placed in Stuart's hands and he had about four thousand men and twenty-one guns to try and find a way around. By 4 PM Stuart abandoned what he regarded as an impossible mission in the face of overwhelming federal firepower. But in McClellan's topsy-turvy world, this feeble move became a mortal threat.[57]

At 2:30 PM, for the first time, McClellan went to the front to confer with Sumner and Franklin who had just arrived. The latter expressed some uncharacteristic optimism concerning the potential for a fresh attack on the right. By the time McClellan arrived to take a decision, Franklin's enthusiasm had been diluted by Sumner's tart observation that all previous troops had been "all cut up and demoralized." McClellan temporized, not wishing to risk the right as "things had gone so well on all the other parts of the field," and indeed the Dunker Church had fallen (temporarily) into Union hands a couple of hours before.[58]

The evidence supported McClellan's optimistic view to a degree. But at about 2:30 PM A. P. Hill rode onto the battlefield and reported that his division, marching from Harpers Ferry seventeen miles away, might be an hour behind him. "General Hill, I was never so glad to see you," remarked a delighted Lee, "you are badly needed. Put your division on the right as soon as they come up." Hill's arrival would throw McClellan's calculations into confusion.[59]

McClellan's decision to place Burnside's Ninth Corps on the left had been fraught with difficulty from the first, especially as reconnaissance had been feeble, and McClellan's own staff was unsure as to the location of the fords. Burnside had only received the order to attack at 10 AM (McClellan later claimed that it had been sent at 8 AM). Burnside was delayed for three hours at Rohrback Bridge and made three unsuccessful attempts to cross Antietam Creek. Burnside's crowded and frustrated troops made easy targets for several hundred Georgians who had occupied the bluffs above the bridge. Burnside made little progress until Snaveley's Ford had been located and the small Confederate force had been brushed aside. McClellan and Burnside exchanged a series of increasingly irritable messages. It is probable that Burnside's caution had been influenced by McClellan's curious assumption that he was outnumbered.[60]

When Burnside began his assault he thought he was carrying out a feint designed to draw rebel strength from the north, not the decisive blow that would bring victory. The confusion over McClellan's priorities helps account for Burnside's lack of urgency. But by 3 PM Burnside's advance began to menace Sharpsburg and Lee's escape route to Boteler's Ford. But Ninth Corps's flank was attacked by A. P. Hill's division in a tactical meeting engagement. Burnside had no warning of Hill's approach because McClellan had placed the cavalry in the center of his position ready for the pursuit. Ninth Corps's rout began amid the ranks of the 16th Connecticut Volunteer Infantry, a green regiment that had suffered 25 percent casualties in its first battle. Panic spread to the rest of Rodman's division and as this pulled back, Burnside had no choice but to abandon the attack, return to the Antietam, and screen the Rohrback Bridge.[61]

Burnside pleaded for support, but McClellan had already sent Franklin to the right and had only one division of Porter's Fifth Corps and the cavalry to hand. McClellan decided again not to reinforce a sector where success had been temporary and the attacking force inadequate to gain its objectives. He was fearful, too, that the right might be overwhelmed, as he could hear the exchange between Stuart and the federal artillery on Poffenberger Hill. His imagination fell victim to this specter and his deep-seated failure to lay down clear priorities and stick to them.[62]

In one of his coolest and most audacious decisions of the war, Lee stood his ground on the night of September 17–18, and defied McClellan to attack again. He argued that he should claim the battlefield; in short, win a *moral* victory. The extra day, moreover, would enable the staff to organize a well-executed withdrawal. A hurried, chaotic, and humiliating evacuation in Lee's view could be worse in the propaganda war than the catastrophic defeat on the battlefield that he had so skillfully avoided. Perhaps an opportunity could be found to renew the campaign of maneuver, and Lee took the time to search for this in vain. "Under these circumstances," Lee wrote later, "it was deemed injudicious to push our advantage further in the face of the fresh troops of the enemy." Lee could claim a tactical victory but nothing more.[63] He decided to withdraw.

McClellan congratulated himself after Lee's retreat for saving the Union. Yet he had failed to seize the greatest single opportunity handed on a plate to a federal general to destroy a Confederate army. Such opportunities were far from uncommon in the Civil War; what was more rare was the single-mindedness, forethought, and courage to seize such chances. Antietam, therefore, was a strategically significant success for the Union because it frustrated Lee's far-reaching design to strike at the North's political vulnerabilities and its determination to carry on the war. That the battle was decisive sprang more from political action the president decided to take on hearing news of Lee's withdrawal rather than from McClellan's halting indecisiveness on that bloody field.[64]

The battle of Antietam also revealed starkly that fighting on the defensive —and this was Lee's first defensive battle—did not offer any magic formula that would avoid casualties. The Army of Northern Virginia suffered 13,724 to the Army of the Potomac's 12,469. The disparity was not great but it showed that an army that had high morale and was well commanded could not magically escape the carnage that results from tactical meeting engagements, even when it stands on the defensive. To suggest that it could do so is to attempt to build castles in the clouds. Historians are fascinated by the discussion of why the South lost. They are equally fascinated by the search for a solution to its intractable dilemmas, a formula whereby the Confederate defeat could have been avoided. The new panacea is "casualty avoidance" and standing on the defensive. Yet the Antietam campaign also revealed that defensive successes were not sufficient to realize Lee's important political objectives. In October 1862 Great Britain decided not to recognize the Confederacy or attempt to mediate. "These last battles in Maryland have rather set the North up again," Lord Palmerston, the prime minister, wrote to his foreign secretary, Lord John Russell. "The whole matter is full of difficulty, and can only be cleared up by some more decided events between the contending armies." Repulsing Union forces on any individual field was not enough; vigorous offensive action would be required to convince the British that they should take a great risk and intervene.[65]

NOTES AND REFERENCES

1. See T. Harry Williams's verdict in "The Military Leadership of North and South," in *Why the North Won the Civil War*, ed. David Donald, 48–49 (New York: Collier, 1962 paperback).

2. Richard M. McMurry, *Two Great Rebel Armies* (Chapel Hill: University of North Carolina Press, 1989), pp. 62–63, 90, 142, 151–52.

3. Thomas L. Connelly and Archer Jones, *The Politics of Command* (Baton Rouge: Louisiana State University Press, 1973) is critical of Lee; McMurry, *Two Great Rebel Armies*, pp. 134–35, 141–50, is a valuable corrective. For the reforms, see Douglas Southall Freeman, *R. E. Lee*, 4 vols. (New York: Scribner's, 1933), vol. 2, pp. 417–19.

4. See Brian Holden Reid, *Origins of the American Civil War* (London: Longmans, 1996), pp. 192–96; Marcus Cunliffe, *Soldiers and Civilians: The Martial Spirit in America, 1775–1865*, 3rd ed. (London: Gregg, 1993), pp. 337–40.

5. Michael C. C. Adams, *Fighting for Defeat: Union Military Failure in the East, 1861–1865* (Lincoln: University of Nebraska, 1992), ch. 5; Ulysses S. Grant, *Personal Memoirs* (London: Sampson Low, 1886), vol. 1, pp. 356–57; Stephen W. Sears, *To the Gates of Richmond: The Peninsula Campaign* (New York: Ticknor and Fields, 1991), p. 348.

6. Brian Holden Reid, "General McClellan and the Politicians," *Parameters* 17 (1987): 108; *Inside Lincoln's Cabinet: The Civil War Diaries of Salmon P. Chase*, ed. David Donald (New York: Alfred A. Knopf, 1954), p. 139.

7. Kenneth P. Williams, *Lincoln Finds a General* (New York: Macmillan, 1949), vol. 2, pp. 254–57; Stephen E. Ambrose, *Halleck: Lincoln's Chief of Staff* (Baton Rouge: Louisiana State University Press, 1962), pp. 64–69; John F. Marszalek, *Commander of All Lincoln's Armies: A Life of General Henry W. Halleck* (Cambridge, MA: Belknap Press of Harvard University Press, 2004), pp. 140–41.

8. *War of the Rebellion: A Compilation of the Official Records of the Union and Confederate Armies*, 128 parts in 70 vols. (Washington, DC: Government Printing Office, 1880–1901) [hereafter *O.R.*], series 1, vol. 21, part 1, pp. 73–74; *McClellan's Own Story* (New York: Webster, 1881), pp. 487–88; Hans L. Trefousse, *Benjamin Franklin Wade: Radical Republican from Ohio* (New York: Twayne, 1963), p. 186.

9. Marszalek, *Commander of All Lincoln's Armies*, p. 109; Allan G. Bogue, *The Congressman's Civil War* (New York: Cambridge University Press, 1989), pp. 74–75, 79, 101–102, 103–104; Brian Holden Reid, "Historians and the Joint Committee on the Conduct of the War," *Civil War History* 38 (December 1992): 337–38; for a critical view of its influence, see Bruce Tap, *Over Lincoln's Shoulder: The Committee on the Conduct of the War* (Lawrence: University Press of Kansas), pp. 164–66.

10. Trefousse, *Wade*, pp. 144, 158, 186; Theodore Clarke Smith, *The Life and Letters of James Abram Garfield* (New Haven, CT: Yale University Press, 1925), vol. 1, pp. 240–41; T. Harry Williams, *Lincoln and the Radicals* (Madison: University of Wisconsin Press paperback edition, 1965), p. 195.

11. Elizabeth J. Doyle, "The Conduct of the War, 1861," in *Congress Investigates: A Documented History*, eds. Arthur M. Schlesinger Jr. and Roger Bruns, vol. 2, 1198–1211 (New York: Chelsea House, 1975).

12. Tap, *Over Lincoln's Shoulder,* pp. 127–29; Holden Reid, "Historians and the Joint Committee," pp. 336–37; *O.R.*, series 1, vol. 12, part 2, pp. 49–50; Williams, *Lincoln and the Radicals*, p. 142; Wallace J. Schutz and Walter N. Trenerry, *Abandoned by Lincoln: A Military Biography of General John Pope* (Urbana: University of Illinois Press, 1990), pp. 104–105.

13. Halleck's initial position resembled McClellan's, see Marszalek, *Halleck*, p. 140; Grant to Julia D. Grant, Feb. 24, 1862, *Grant Papers*, vol. 4, p. 184; Eric L. McKitrick, "Party Politics and the Union and Confederate War Efforts," in *The American Party Systems,* eds. William N. Chambers and Walter Dean Burnham, 120–25 (New York: Oxford University Press, 1967); Hans L. Trefousse, "The Joint Committee on the Conduct of the War: A Reassessment," *Civil War History* 10 (March 1964): 9, 11–13, 19; for the view that political strife impeded the Union war effort, see Mark E. Neely Jr., *The Union Divided: Party Conflict in the Civil War North* (Cambridge, MA: Harvard University Press, 2002).

14. Compare Williams, *Lincoln and the Radicals*, pp. 65, 224, with Hans L. Trefousse, *The Radical Republicans: Lincoln's Vanguard for Racial Justice* (New York: Alfred A. Knopf, 1969), p. 265; Holden Reid, "Historians and the Joint Committee," p. 335.

15. *O.R.*, series 1, vol. 12, part 3, pp. 473–74; Clifford Dowdey, *Lee: A Biography* (London: Gollancz, 1970), p. 288, although Dowdey attributes the hilarity to officers around Lee rather than the commanding general himself.

16. Herman Hattaway and Archer Jones, *How the North Won* (Urbana: University of Illinois Press, 1983), pp. 211–12; Benjamin P. Thomas and Harold M. Hyman,

Stanton (New York: Alfred A. Knopf, 1962), pp. 217–18; T. Harry Williams, *Lincoln and His Generals* (New York: Alfred A. Knopf, 1952), p. 150. For a highly critical view of McClellan's conduct, see John J. Hennessy, *Return to Bull Run: The Campaign and Battle of Second Manassas* (New York: Simon and Schuster, 1993), pp. 90–91, 241–42. McClellan's behavior can be compared with Montgomery's slowness to advance the Eighth Army to the aid of the beleaguered Fifth Army at Salerno in September 1943. See Nigel Hamilton, *Monty: Master of the Battlefield* (London: Hamish Hamilton, 1983), p. 412.

17. Porter to McClellan, Aug. 17, 1862, in *The Civil War Papers of George B. McClellan*, ed. Stephen Sears (New York: Da Capo, 1989, 1992 paperback ed.), pp. 393–94; *O.R.*, series 1, vol. 12, part 3, p. 700.

18. Lee to Mrs. Lee, Aug. 17, Lee to Davis, Aug. 17, Lee to Stuart, Aug. 19, 1862; Battle Report of Second Manassas Campaign, June 5, 1863, in *The Wartime Papers of R. E. Lee*, eds. Clifford Dowdey and Louis H. Manarin (New York: Bramshall House, 1961), pp. 258, 260, 275; Hattaway and Jones, *How the North Won*, pp. 220–21; Freeman, *R. E. Lee*, vol. 2, pp. 269–77; Joseph L. Harsh, *Confederate Tide Rising: Robert E. Lee and the Making of Confederate Strategy* (Kent, OH: Kent State University Press, 1998), pp. 58–60, 62–73.

19. H. B. McClellan, *The Life and Campaigns of J. E. B. Stuart* (Secaucus, NJ: Blue and Grey Press, 1993 reprint), pp. 90, 99–100; Jeffry D. Wert, *General James Longstreet* (New York: Simon and Schuster, 1993), p. 159.

20. Brian Holden Reid, *Robert E. Lee: Icon for a Nation* (2005; Amherst, NY: Prometheus Books, 2007), pp. 106–107, 108–10; Douglas Southall Freeman, *Lee's Lieutenants*, 3 vols. (New York: Scribner's, 1944), vol. 2, pp. 44–47; Dowdey, *Lee*, pp. 283–85, who reflects Lee's contempt (see p. 279); Wert, *Longstreet*, p. 160.

21. *O.R.*, series 1, vol. 12, part 2, pp. 9–11; Marszalek, *Halleck*, pp. 142, 144, 145; Williams, *Lincoln and His Generals*, pp. 154–56.

22. Hennessy, *Return to Bull Run*, pp. 22–31, 66–67, 74–81, 92–94, 108, 113–15, 117–18, 129–30, 135; Freeman, *Lee's Lieutenants*, vol. 2, pp. 82–83, 89–90, 102–107, 113; Dowdey, *Lee*, pp. 287–88; Lee to Davis, Aug. 23, Lee to Gilmer, Aug. 25, 1862, Battle Report of Second Manassas Campaign, June 5, 1863, in Lee, *Wartime Papers*, pp. 262, 265, 279; Kenneth P. Williams, *Lincoln Finds a General* (New York: Macmillan, 1949), vol. 1, pp. 282–83; Russell F. Weigley, *The American Way of War* (New York: Macmillan, 1973), p. 109.

23. Hennessy, *Return to Bull Run*, pp. 225–31; Wert, *Longstreet*, pp. 164–67; Williams, *Lincoln Finds a General*, vol. 1, pp. 298–302, 316–21, 325.

24. Freeman, *R. E. Lee*, vol. 2, p. 325; Gary W. Gallagher, *Lee and His Generals in War and Memory* (Baton Rouge: Louisiana State University Press, 1998), pp. 139–57; Dowdey, *Lee*, pp. 291–92; Wert, *Longstreet*, pp. 172–73.

25. As argued by Weigley, *American Way of War*, p. 109; also Peter S. Carmichael,

"Lee's Search for the Battle of Annihilation," in *Audacity Personified: The Generalship of Robert E. Lee*, ed. idem. (Baton Rouge: Louisiana State University Press, 2004), pp. 1–26.

26. Wert, *Longstreet*, pp. 175–77; Hennessy, *Return to Bull Run*, pp. 332–34, 350–55, 361; Williams, *Lincoln Finds a General*, vol. 1, p. 328.

27. Hennessy, *Return to Bull Run*, pp. 362–66, points out that Longstreet knew little about federal strength beyond Porter; Wert, *Longstreet*, p. 177; Dowdey, *Lee*, pp. 293–94; Richard M. McMurry, *John Bell Hood and the War for Southern Independence* (1982; Lincoln: University of Nebraska Press paperback reprint, 1992), p. 55.

28. Lee to Davis, Sep. 3, 1862, Battle Report of the Second Manassas Campaign, June 5, 1863, in Lee, *Wartime Papers*, pp. 269, 284. Because of the imputations made about Longstreet, Wert (*Longstreet*, p. 178) makes much of Jackson's slowness, "[f]or reasons unexplained." But they are obvious. See Freeman, *Lee's Lieutenants*, vol. 2, pp. 128–34.

29. Freeman, *R. E. Lee*, vol. 2, pp. 322–25, 335, 347–48.

30. Thomas L. Connelly and Archer Jones, *The Politics of Command* (Baton Rouge: Louisiana State University Press, 1973), pp. 32–34. See also Alan T. Nolan, *Lee Considered* (Chapel Hill: University of North Carolina Press, 1991), pp. 81, 89.

31. Hattaway and Jones, *How the North Won*, p. 229.

32. Wert, *Longstreet*, p. 168. The author can personally vouch for this, having walked the field in November 1990 accompanied by his long-suffering friend and battlefield tour companion, Lieutenant General Sir Alastair Irwin KCB CBE; few Americans could be found walking similar distances!

33. Hennessy, *Return to Bull Run*, p. 371; Adams, *Fighting for Defeat*, pp. 101–102; Gerald F. Linderman, *Embattled Courage: The Experience of Combat in the American Civil War* (New York: Free Press, 1987), p. 74.

34. Lee to Davis, June 5, 1862, Lee to Jackson, June 8, 1862, in Lee, *Wartime Papers*, pp. 184, 187.

35. See pp. 148–49, 155–57.

36. See Brian Holden Reid, *Studies in British Military Thought: Debates with Fuller and Liddell Hart* (Lincoln: University of Nebraska Press, 1998), pp. 85–86.

37. McClellan, *Campaigns of Stuart*, pp. 106–107; Emory M. Thomas, *Bold Dragoon: The Life of J. E. B. Stuart* (New York: Harper and Row, 1986), p. 157.

38. This whole question requires reassessment. Otto Eisenschiml, *The Celebrated Case of Fitz John Porter* (Indianapolis: Bobbs-Merrill, 1957) is now very dated. See also, Schutz and Trenerry, *Abandoned by Lincoln*, pp. 167–69, appendix A, pp. 189–213.

39. Nolan, *Lee Considered*, p. 100.

40. William C. Davis, *Jefferson Davis: The Man and His Hour* (New York: HarperCollins, 1991), pp. 468–69.

41. Lee to Davis, Sep. 3, 5, 6, 12, 13, 1862, Battle Report of Sharpsburg Campaign, Aug. 19, 1863, in Lee, *Wartime Papers*, pp. 282–306, 312; Williams, "Military Leadership North and South," pp. 48–49; Dowdey, *Lee*, pp. 297–98.

42. "To the People of Maryland," Special Orders No. 191, Sep. 8, 9, 1862, ibid., pp. 299–301; Lee to Davis, Sep. 8, 13, 1862, in ibid., pp. 300, 307; Dowdey, *Lee*, p. 300; see Brian Holden Reid and John White, "'A Mob of Stragglers and Cowards': Desertion from the Union and Confederate Armies, 1861–1865," *Journal of Strategic Studies* 8 (March 1985): 68–69; Joseph L. Harsh, *Taken at the Flood: Robert E. Lee and Confederate Strategy in the Maryland Campaign of 1862* (Kent, OH: Kent State University Press, 1999), pp. 124–28.

43. Special Orders No. 191, Sep. 9, 1862, Battle Report of Sharpsburg Campaign, Aug. 19, 1863, Lee, *Wartime Papers*, pp. 301–302, 314; Wert, *Longstreet*, pp. 182–83; Harsh, *Taken at the Flood*, pp. 141–42, 152–67.

44. Williams, *Lincoln and His Generals*, pp. 161–62; Ambrose, *Halleck*, pp. 65–66, 93, 102–103; Marszalek, *Halleck*, pp. 146, 149, 153–54; Ethan S. Rafuse, *McClellan's War* (Bloomington: Indiana University Press, 2005), pp. 273–74.

45. McClellan, *Life and Campaigns of Stuart*, pp. 118–19; Dowdey, *Lee*, pp. 304–308; Harsh, *Taken at the Flood*, pp. 229–52, 263–97; Rafuse, *McClellan's War*, pp. 294–99.

46. Harsh, *Taken at the Flood*, pp. 229–308, 346; Robert K. Krick, "It Appeared as though Mutual Extermination Would Put a Stop to the Awful Carnage: Confederates in Sharpsburg's Bloody Lane," in *The Antietam Campaign*, ed. Gary W. Gallagher, 231–33 (Chapel Hill: University of North Carolina Press, 1999). See also Freeman, *R. E. Lee*, vol. 2, pp. 378, 384–86; and Major General J. F. C. Fuller, *Grant and Lee* (Stevenage, UK: Spa Books reprint, 1992), pp. 269–70.

47. Harsh, *Taken at the Flood*, pp. 242–44, 248–49; James M. McPherson, *Crossroads of Freedom: Antietam* (New York: Oxford University Press, 2002).

48. Rafuse, *McClellan's War*, pp. 308–309, stresses his achievements.

49. McClellan to Franklin, Sep. 16, 1862 (7:45 AM), in McClellan, *Civil War Papers*, p. 466; Rafuse, *McClellan's War*, pp. 310–12.

50. Stephen W. Sears, *Landscape Turned Red: The Battle of Antietam* (New York: Ticknor and Fields, 1983), pp. 180–91.

51. Robert E. L. Krick, "Defending Lee's Flank," in *Antietam Campaign*, ed. Gallagher, pp. 198–203; Harsh, *Taken at the Flood*, pp. 372–73.

52. Harsh, *Taken at the Flood*, pp. 330–33; Keith S. Bohannon, "Dirty, Ragged, and Ill-provided For: Confederate Logistical Problems in the 1862 Maryland Campaign and Their Solution," in *Antietam Campaign*, ed. Gary W. Gallagher, pp. 105–106.

53. Rafuse, *McClellan's War*, pp. 315–16; Holden Reid, *Lee*, p. 133; also see D. Scott Hartwig, "Robert E. Lee and the Maryland Campaign," in *Lee: The Soldier*, ed. Gary W. Gallagher, pp. 349–50; Sears, *Landscape Turned Red*, p. 234.

54. Harsh, *Taken at the Flood*, pp. 385–87; Sears, *Landscape Turned Red*, pp. 222–30; Rafuse, *McClellan's War*, pp. 315–17.

55. Sears, *Landscape Turned Red*, pp. 237–42.

56. McClellan to Pleasonton and Halleck (telegram), Sep. 16, 1862, in McClellan, *Civil War Papers*, p. 467.

57. Harsh, *Taken at the Flood*, pp. 408–12.

58. Rafuse, *McClellan's War*, pp. 322–24; Sears, *Landscape Turned Red*, pp. 271–73.

59. Holden Reid, *Lee*, pp. 132–33.

60. Rafuse, *McClellan's War*, pp. 312, 320–21; William Marvel, *Burnside* (Chapel Hill: University of North Carolina Press, 1991), pp. 132–39.

61. Lesley J. Gordon, "All Who Went into That Battle Were Heroes: Remembering the 16th Regiment Connecticut Volunteers at Antietam," in *Antietam Campaign*, ed. Gallagher, pp. 176–77; Sears, *Landscape Turned Red*, pp. 276–90; Marvel, *Burnside*, pp. 142–45.

62. For a defense of McClellan, see Rafuse, *McClellan's War*, p. 326, but his analysis treats his fantasy as an objective factor rather than the root of error.

63. Sears, *Landscape Turned Red*, pp. 303–304; Wert, *Longstreet*, pp. 193–202; Battle Report of Sharpsburg Campaign, Aug. 19, 1863, in Lee, *Wartime Papers*, pp. 320–21; Freeman, *R. E. Lee*, vol. 2, pp. 395–402; Harsh, *Taken at the Flood*, pp. 426–28.

64. Hattaway and Jones, *How the North Won*, pp. 243–44; Wert, *Longstreet*, p. 200; James M. McPherson, *The Battle Cry of Freedom* (New York: Oxford University Press, 1988), p. 557.

65. Frank L. Owsley, *King Cotton Diplomacy*, 2nd ed. (Chicago: Chicago University Press, 1959), p. 351.

Chapter Six

THE CONFEDERACY FUMBLES
AND A BOLD UNION MOVE

SEPTEMBER TO OCTOBER 1862

In September 1862 Lee had urged Davis to persuade General Braxton Bragg to mount a thrust similar to his own toward the Ohio River. This evidence of grand strategic thinking beyond the confines of his immediate responsibilities seems to be contradicted by his call for reinforcements from Bragg's army. This is indicative of the impossible position that Lee's success had put him in. He remained a field commander whose first responsibility was to his own army; yet he was called upon to make judgments on questions beyond his immediate purview by a president who failed to evolve an adequate system for the conduct of the war as a whole. Lee's call for reinforcements was qualified, "should General Bragg find it impracticable to operate to advantage," and Bragg had been nursing plans for a sweeping counterattack since June that Lee knew nothing about. Bragg had been instructed by President Davis to take over command of the Army of Tennessee in July 1862 after Beauregard had earned presidential displeasure by absenting himself from the army without permission. Beauregard was ill and recuperated at Mobile and Bladon Springs, where he took a rest cure. It was rather typical of the self-centered Beauregard, whose relations with Davis were already poor, that he spent his leisure organizing anti-Davis newspaper editors to attack the president rather than reorganize the formations of his army. To this task Bragg devoted himself with formidable energy and dispatch.[1]

Bragg was a friend of Davis's but had managed to stay on good terms with Beauregard. Bragg is in some ways the Confederate version of McClellen, save that he has found no admirers. He was, like McClellan, an organizer and strategist of considerable acumen and should have been appointed to the equivalent position of chief of the general staff, orchestrating the entire war effort. Despite his gifts, he was temperamentally unsuited to field command. Yet the prevailing ethos of the day required that this be his *métier*. Bragg was moody, morose, tense, and querulous. A much-repeated anecdote among officers of the "old" army told of the agonies that Bragg brought upon himself while a young officer, when he occupied simultaneously the positions of company commander and company quartermaster. These two personified in one officer nonetheless punctiliously exchanged memoranda on the necessary requisitions. Bragg could not reconcile the demands of these two positions as the memos came hurtling back to him like boomerangs. He sought the advice of his commanding officer. "My God, Mr. Bragg," he replied rather wearily, "you have quarreled with every officer in the army, and now you are quarrelling with yourself."[2]

Bragg lacked self-confidence and was prone to indecision. He sought refuge from the responsibility of making great decisions by immersing himself in detail, even trivia. Although he pursued ferocious quarrels with his subordinate commanders he nonetheless virtually threw himself on their mercy by convening councils of war—the refuge of those commanders who either lack self-confidence or ideas. Bragg provoked vitriolic dislike; he lacked charisma and failed to bind his army to him. His soldiers feared him but did not respect him. A significant reason for the comparative failure of the Army of Tennessee was that its commander failed to create what Field Marshal Montgomery called the "right atmosphere." On the contrary the intriguing, feuding, and open quarrels between the generals severely eroded morale. Another source of Bragg's unpopularity was his determination to impose strict standards of discipline on his soldiers. Bragg insisted on the death penalty for desertion and his zeal in carrying out executions was rather exaggerated in the telling by camp rumor. Lee, too, took a very firm line with desertion, and argued continually for the imposition of the death penalty. But he had a more subtle understanding of the informal and voluntary character of Southern discipline. He realized that Southern troops could not be bludgeoned into submission and he hastened to sweeten the bitter taste of his remedies by agreeing to increased furloughs.[3]

Bragg, influenced by Beauregard, had become an exponent of concentration in the west and trading space, if necessary, to achieve it. Certainly, the fragmentation of Confederate military power in the west was to do so much to reduce his capacity to launch a counteroffensive. Bragg was offered an opportunity because the great Union host that Halleck had shepherded to Corinth had not made the most of its strategic opportunities. Gradually his army broke up and its parts went their separate ways. Bragg argued that the Confederacy should concentrate military force in its turn to take advantage of this diffusion of effort. The Lincoln administration was extremely keen that succor should be brought as rapidly as possible to the Unionists of east Tennessee. Don Carlos Buell and the Army of the Cumberland were ordered to occupy this part of the state and advance to Chattanooga. Buell assured Halleck that this could be done quickly; but they had both overlooked the damage wreaked on the East Tennessee and Virginia Railroad.

Buell was in any case a fussy, meticulous administrator, like McClellan, and simply lacked the imagination and dash to defy what he believed to be overwhelming administrative realities; he could not, or would not, act incautiously. Furthermore, his stern attempts to discipline and restrict the depredations of his troops provoked a Washington whispering campaign, stirred up by the Joint Committee on the Conduct of the War, casting doubt on his loyalty. As a slave-owner and brother-in-law to Confederate General Daniel E. Twiggs, Buell was very vulnerable to this kind of gossip; but it only seemed to reinforce his obstinacy not to move before he was ready. Buell was—rather like Bragg—cold, austere, and branded a "martinet" by his troops. He gave the impression that he was more worried about his supply lines than the enemy's movements. It was rumored that he had told his aunt who lived near Nashville "that everything was right; that special protection would be given to the peculiar institution." Buell was, claimed the *New York Tribune*, "pro-slavery to the core." This was an equation with ominous implications. Laggard movements, it was claimed, resulted from a lack of enthusiasm for the war. Antislavery fervor was being equated with patriotism and to oppose emancipation meant "weak-backed Union" feeling.[4]

Buell contemptuously disregarded this feeling; but increasingly those commanders who failed (or were perceived to have failed) could no longer afford to do so. Buell was certainly cautious to the core. This was shown up to disadvantage by the launching of two audacious Confederate cavalry raids to wreak further havoc on his vulnerable supply lines. Nathan Bedford Forrest inflicted a million dollars' worth of damage on these in central and southern Tennessee, and captured over two thousand prisoners, including a general. John Hunt Morgan raided Kentucky and it was feared that he would strike at Cincinnati, Ohio. Morgan had about nine hundred men with him and, like Forrest, used his cavalry as mounted infantry, relying on their mobility to arrive at the most advantageous and vulnerable of the enemy's points. Engagements were sudden and could be broken off if danger threatened. His men had the firepower of infantry and thus considerable Union reinforcements were required to destroy them. While the men fought, the horses rested; while they rode their horses the men rested; Morgan's force could thus travel considerable distances. His first Kentucky raid, and Forrest's into Tennessee, starkly contrasted Confederate audacity, imagination, and mobility, with Union inertia, overcaution, and bureaucratic fussiness. Consequently, President Lincoln was not best pleased with his generals.[5]

While the destruction of the railroads stymied Buell's advance on Chattanooga, Bragg exploited them to effect a brilliant concentration at this railway junction, menacing Buell's left flank. His first plan was to move directly with his army into central Tennessee. It was wholly characteristic of this campaign that Bragg then changed his mind. The whole enterprise was aimless, with no clear objectives set down. The Confederate president, Davis, did not lay down what it was supposed to achieve and the individual commanders involved participated when they saw fit, when it touched upon their selfish or parochial interests. This weakness was exacerbated by Bragg's foolish decision to act as his own chief of staff, so that he became absorbed by minor detail and was too busy to give the movement of other armies his full attention. The command system that was supposed to execute it was a shambles. The campaign was waged over three departments and involved six different forces, commanded for the most part by quarrelsome and vain prima donnas with huge but empty heads on their shoulders. Jefferson Davis did not impose a broad policy or a clear strategy on the operation and failed to rationalize the levels of command responsibility. He signally failed to distinguish between field command and garrison command (which demanded different talents) and sort out who enjoyed seniority when two armies combined. Furthermore, concentrating sufficient force by utilizing the forces scattered among the various departments was more easily talked about than achieved. Clearly, Bragg's offensive should have enjoyed an intimate relationship with Lee's move into Maryland. A move northward would have offered Bragg similar logistical advantages and would have contributed to the erosion of Union morale. But Davis failed to coordinate these movements, and he should have found a general-in-chief who could. Either Lee or Bragg could have carried out these duties splendidly; but neither could assume higher strategic duties while subject to the enormous strain of field command. Davis consistently vetoed efforts by the Confederate congress to establish the rank of general-in-chief. Bragg's offensive was a great raid but its object was not so well thought out as Lee's, though in the event it was better executed.[6]

In the first place Bragg, by dint of sheer hard work and administrative ingenuity, managed to overcome the structural weaknesses of the departmental command arrangement by transferring the thirty thousand men of the Army of Mississippi from Tupelo in northern Mississippi to Major General Edmund Kirby Smith's department in east Tennessee via Mobile, Alabama, and Atlanta, Georgia. The troops covered 776 miles over six different railroads and arrived at their destination within six days of the orders being issued. It says much for Bragg's abilities as an organizer and trainer that such a complex turning movement over the South's incomplete railway system could be carried out just over two months after the Shiloh setback. Two small forces were left in Mississippi: sixteen thousand men under Sterling Price and a further sixteen thousand under Van Dorn at Vicksburg. Combined, this force was larger than Bragg's army. These two commands were to attack western Tennessee and prevent Grant from reinforcing Buell. Van Dorn had not been given unambiguous orders and the headstrong and pompous Price (who had recently quarreled bitterly with Jefferson Davis) soon showed a disinclination to take orders from him (his main priority was to return to his home state of Missouri). Bragg had seized the initiative from fumbling Union hands. He was poised to win back all that had been lost in the spring. Union armies could be engaged separately, their flanks and rear had been exposed by his shrewd move, and should Bragg move north, the western Union armies' lines of communication with the east could be disrupted.[7]

Yet Bragg failed to achieve the concentration by which he set so much store. While he waited for his wagon train and ordnance to arrive by road (the delicate Southern railroad system could not cope transporting such heavy artifacts), Kirby Smith (whose "cordial cooperation" Davis had promised), although he made cooperative noises, took his force of some twelve thousand men off on a separate expedition toward Knoxville, Tennessee. He successfully eluded Bragg's control because he was the departmental commander; he actually secured Bragg's acquiescence in this move, which resulted in his independent thrust into Kentucky. Bereft of a clear aim or a thoroughly thought-out plan, Kirby Smith occupied Lexington after a short but tough fight on September 1. Taking the town seemed to satiate Kirby Smith's lust for fame; in truth, he lacked any strategic sense. Despite his exposed position and small force, he scattered it across Kentucky, adopted a defensive stance, and suggested it was now time for Bragg to do something. "[I]f Bragg pushes him [Buell] and gains a victory we will have made the most brilliant campaign of the war," he claimed. The superficial understanding of the conduct of war revealed by his actions and obsession with "brilliant" operations is self-evident. Thus Confederate forces were tempted into overly ambitious operations they could not sustain. The ratios of small forces to large distances against a numerically superior foe operated to their disadvantage.[8]

Without a single guiding hand such strategic advantages as Bragg had gained were frittered away. His two feckless lieutenants in the west, Van Dorn and Sterling Price, attempted to distract Grant and ensure he sent no reinforcements to Buell. Price entered Tennessee in September. On hearing news that Major General William S. Rosecrans, one of Grant's corps commanders, had sent three divisions to aid Buell, Bragg urged Price, once he had failed to retain Grant's forces on his front, to attack. Price was "to keep his men well in hand, and ready to move north at a moment's notice." The "road was open" into west Tennessee. The whole campaign foundered on the Confederate high command's inability to allot a priority as to which was most important, the defeat of federal armies or the occupation of territory for political reasons. Bragg informed Price (who was waiting to join Van Dorn) that Buell was withdrawing toward Nashville and that Rosecrans should at all costs be prevented from joining him; he should be pushed northward. Not overly keen to wait on Van Dorn and in all probability lose his independence, Price moved on Iuka. It was typical of the besetting sin of federal logistical waste that Price's move was sustained by the great quantities of stores that he seized *en route*.

Grant, restored to command of the Army of the Tennessee, reacted to this raid energetically by attempting to envelop Price, attacking simultaneously from the northwest with Ord's corps of eight thousand men and from the southwest with Rosecrans's force of nine thousand men. Such moves, however, demand clear control, full understanding of the part played by each force, and impeccable timing. On all these counts, Grant failed; coordination was impaired by a freak wind which blew so strongly from the north that Ord could not hear firing, and Rosecrans's thrusts were piecemeal and unsupported. Price's force retreated, hurt but not fatally wounded. There was no pursuit, for which Grant blamed Rosecrans, probably unfairly. A Confederate general commented that "pursuit . . . can amount to little in a country like that of northern Mississippi, heavily wooded and with narrow roads, when the enemy has time to get his artillery and trains in front of his infantry." This is special pleading for the geographic factors affect the retreating quarry as well as the predatory pursuer, and he is in a state of greater psychological disarray than the victor. The plain fact of the matter was that Grant's fresh troops, Ord's corps, were too distant to strike, and Rosecrans's forces were too worn out by ferocious fighting. The battle of Iuka was, Price claimed, "waged with a severity I have never seen surpassed."[9]

The tactical advantage had lain with Price and he had taken much persuading before he would abandon the field, although he refused to relinquish the stores seized from the federals. The battle illustrated the power and rapidity with which the federals could concentrate strong forces to repel scattered, fragmented, and piecemeal Confederate offensive efforts. On September 28 Price at last joined forces with Van Dorn. This combined force was now dubbed by Van Dorn the "Army of West Tennessee." But despite the quality of its veteran troops, and the strength of its artillery, it was an army in name only. There was great tension between the commanders and the staffs of its constituent elements. Price particularly resented the way Van Dorn appropriated the stores that were intended for his own men. The casual cavalier had not deigned to make any effort to provide for his own troops.[10]

Van Dorn, with his penchant for melodrama, now decided upon an immediate assault on Corinth, which had fallen to Halleck the previous May. Price argued against this on the grounds that the Army of West Tennessee lacked the power to take the fortified town. Van Dorn should, he argued, await the arrival of a further twelve to fifteen thousand exchanged prisoners still in Mississippi. Van Dorn retorted that Corinth, with its two strategic railroads, was so important that it "warranted more than the usual hazards of battle"—another example of how Confederate armies oscillated between geographical and military objectives. On October 3 Van Dorn launched a frontal assault on the town's outer defenses and Price's men, showing great vigor and courage, took them at the first assault. The weather was oppressive and some succumbed to sunstroke in temperatures in the upper ninety degrees Fahrenheit range. Van Dorn then made excessive demands on the morale of his men. This early success led him to underestimate Rosecrans's determination to hold this important communications center on Grant's extreme left flank. Van Dorn decided on a further frontal assault the following day by the same troops of Price's corps. Van Dorn did not seem to have gained his subordinates' agreement to this attack, nor their basic understanding of the part allotted to each unit. The result was yet another rashly directed, impulsive, and badly coordinated Southern attack which went forward piecemeal, each unit being driven back separately by the overwhelming firepower of the Union artillery. Bravery was not enough against overwhelming defensive firepower; it needed husbanding and concentration. Brigadier General Dabney H. Maury's division of four thousand men suffered more than two thou-

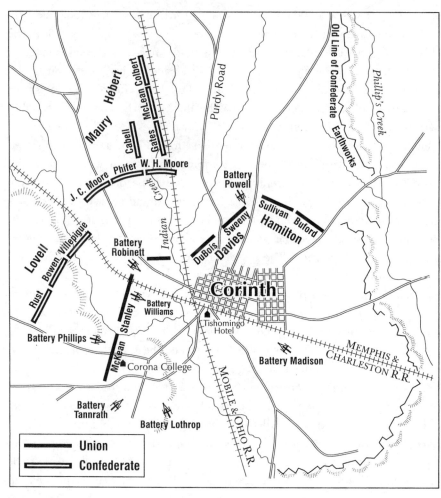

8. Corinth, October 4, 1862

Reprinted from *Banners to the Breeze: The Kentucky Campaign, Corinth and Stones River* by Earl J. Hess, by permission of the University of Nebraska Press. © 2000 by the University of Nebraska Press.

sand casualties. The Union infantry then moved forward to drive Price's shattered units from the field. A cooperation of arms invariably destroys a force that advances in a fragmented manner.[11]

Logistics were crucial to organizing the pursuit. Rosecrans, worn out by the psychological demands of battle, showed his usual torpor immediately after its conclusion. The pursuit did not start until October 5 and then was botched, Rosecrans cramming too much traffic on the Chewalla Road. On October 13 Grant decided to discontinue the pursuit on the grounds that it was no longer sustainable because the Army of the Tennessee had advanced beyond its lines of supply. Rosecrans pleaded that the pursuit be allowed to continue. He touched upon themes that reflected on the indecisiveness of battle and the limitations of strategic and operational mobility. He wrote to Grant that to halt "would permit them [the Confederates] to recruit their forces, advance and occupy their old ground, reducing us to the occupation of a defensive position, barren and worthless, with a long front, over which they can harass until bad weather pre vents an effectual advance except on the railroads, when time, fortifications, and rolling stock will again render them superior to us."[12] But Rosecrans's plans illustrated the need for Union commanders to treat the pursuit as a separate action that demanded forethought and planning before a general engagement began, and the need to *not* wait, as Rosecrans did, an entire day before beginning it thus failing to gain maximum benefit from the enemy's disarray after being beaten. It was this factor far more than the logistical that persuaded Grant to bring the operation to an end. "Two or three hours of pursuit on the day of battle," Grant wrote in his *Memoirs*, "without anything except what the men carried on their persons, would have been worth more than any pursuit commenced the next day could have possibly been."[13]

Yet logistics was crucial to the outcome of Bragg's campaign in Kentucky. Bragg enjoyed the initiative but the need to subsist his army forced him to make deployments that might forfeit it. With less than thirty thousand men, opposed to Buell's Army of the Ohio of fifty thousand, Bragg had fewer mouths to feed than Lee in Maryland, but his army was too small for decisive operations. His force, in short, was simultaneously too large to ignore logistics but too small to destroy Buell's army. His men were also worn out by long marches and inadequate food stocks: "With but one suit of clothes, no vests, nothing to eat but meat and *bread*, or when we can't get that *roasting ears* from the corn fields along the road, we have made the most extraordinary campaign in military history," Bragg wrote to his wife, Elise.[14]

Buell was fearful that Bragg would attack his vulnerable lines of communi-

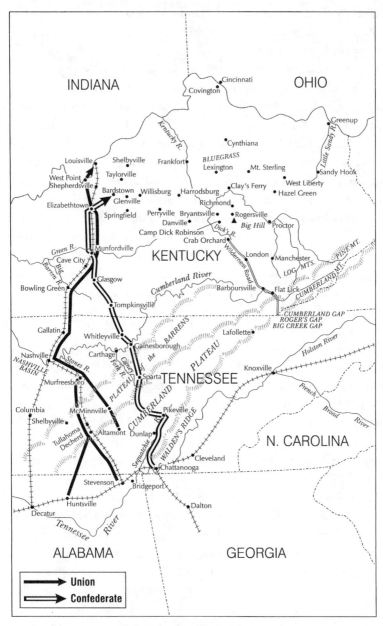

2. Bragg's campaign and Buell's retreat

cation, especially the rail junction at Nashville. The Confederates had no such vulnerability. Yet Buell understood that Bragg's offensive was essentially a raid and that he would be forced to retreat eventually. Buell played a waiting game. "Nashville can be held and Kentucky rescued," he decided. In the defense against a foe who was desperate for sustenance, Buell's obsession with logistics turned out to be the saving grace in the autumn campaign in Kentucky. Buell had 1.2 million rations at Bowling Green and he was planning to create another supply base at Louisville, which he was keen to defend for this reason. Even should Louisville fall, Buell calculated that Bragg would have to disperse his army. The stolid, unglamorous, unimaginative Buell was certainly not psychologically paralyzed by Bragg's deft maneuvers; his limitations were his greatest strength in this campaign.

Bragg's advance into Kentucky was distracted by the surrender of Munfordville, on the Bowling Green–Louisville Railroad, which a subordinate had rashly and unsuccessfully attacked without permission. Bragg could not ignore this unwonted repulse for political reasons and brought his whole army up to surround the town, forcing its capitulation. On September 17 he announced Munfordville's fall and also, foolishly, that he had already joined forces with Kirby Smith even though Smith was still one hundred miles distant. This bulletin was a product of the propaganda war, and Bragg's desire to give his raid some psychological "momentum" after this delay. Yet he appreciated that he "could not prudently afford to attack" Buell, and for the time being Buell refused to attack him. Certainly logistical weakness accounts for Bragg's failure to seize Louisville and its rich supplies before Buell's arrival. Bragg remarked, "this campaign must be won by marching, not fighting." Yet his troops needed wherewithal to keep their legs moving. Neither could he solve his problem by remaining on the defensive. Bragg urgently needed reinforcement by Kirby Smith's troops. Only this could give him the strength to maintain the initiative. Yet he acquiesced in Smith's independence. "Nashville is defended by only a weak division; Bowling Green by only a regiment. Sweep them off and push up to the Ohio," Kirby Smith was informed by a (for once) excessively polite Bragg.

The nearer he got to the enemy, the more irritable, discouraged, and weary Bragg became; he was always prone to hypochondria and his self-confidence seemed to desert him. He certainly suffered from lack of sleep. Two other matters agitated his temper. The Kentuckians refused to rally to his banner. Like Lee in Maryland and Price in Missouri, he found that the border states were full of men expressing sympathy, but few could be persuaded to do anything for the cause they cheered so enthusiastically. He imitated Lee and issued a stirring proclamation. The response was disappointing. "Enthusiasm runs high, but exhausts itself in words," he complained. The pocketbook spoke louder than romantic yearning and impulsive emotion. "Their hearts are evidently with us, but their blue-grass and fat cattle are against us," Bragg lamented. The sight of dirty, bedraggled, poorly shod Confederate soldiers could not have inspired enthusiasm among prosperous Kentuckians. Kirby Smith planned to have recruited a brigade but Bragg found himself in the embarrassing position of having fifteen thousand rifled muskets and no soldiers to hand them out to. He had hoped to recruit several Kentucky divisions. This failure made a union with Kirby Smith the more urgent. Yet the latter's flamboyant spirit could not be pinned down and he ingeniously avoided Bragg's suggestions for a meeting.[15]

Nonetheless, as his biographer suggests persuasively, Bragg had committed no major errors as yet, and the campaign had gone reasonably well. Grady McWhiney is also right to defend Bragg stoutly for his decision to attend the inauguration of the Confederate "governor" of Kentucky, Richard C. Hawes, at Frankfort on October 4. Like Lee in Maryland, Bragg promised to respect property rights and pay adherence to civil supremacy; militarily, his most significant promise was to "defend your honor and your territory." He had another, less noble motive in setting up a Confederate government in Kentucky—this was the only way he could conscript Kentuckians legally. Even before the inauguration, Bragg had inclined increasingly toward a defensive strategy. He had decided that the only way to persuade Kentuckians to join his army was by demonstrating its power to hold their state; this required seeking a defensive line, and the dispersal this involved eased the logistical difficulty. The whole strategy assumed that the federal forces would remain inert. Bragg was to be quickly disillusioned.[16]

Historians have been critical of Bragg's attendance at Hawes's inauguration (which overlooks the political dimension of the campaign) because it resembled the rather frivolous and stubborn appearance of the Duke of Wellington at the Duchess of Richmond's ball before the battle of Waterloo. Alas, Bragg had not been so well served by his subordinates as the great duke. Bragg's army was far too small to defend Kentucky unaided. Once more he hoped to involve the elusive Kirby Smith in his schemes. Two days before the inauguration, Bragg received warning that the plodding but pertinacious Buell had completed his concentration at Louisville and was advancing in an unhurried manner on a broad front. With Leonidas Polk's corps at Danville, near Kirby Smith, a substantial force could be concentrated against him. Bragg thought that if they moved in combination quickly enough he could strike Buell's exposed and unsupported right flank. Such a move was worthy of Robert E. Lee, but Bragg had to rely on Polk, Bishop of Louisiana, rather than Stonewall Jackson. Bragg had no great respect for Polk's abilities and this scornful attitude was not unjust, as Polk bristled with self-importance, was slow, and lacked tactical flair. Like many senior clerics, Polk was rather more fond of giving his views than listening to those of others.[17]

Thus Bragg attended Hawes's inauguration in the belief that he had organized an imaginative counterstroke. However, his complacence was shattered during the ceremony itself, and so was his steadiness of judgment, when couriers arrived informing him that Buell was bearing down on Frankfort unimpeded. Polk had not bothered to move because be believed that the Confederate army was too dispersed, and he had not hurried himself to keep Bragg apprised of the fate of his cherished counterstroke. It is revealing of Kentucky's ambivalent sympathies that throughout the campaign, Bragg's intelligence was poor. Bragg panicked, abandoned Frankfort, and decided to retreat south to effect a concentration with Polk. When Bragg recovered his balance, he changed his mind; he decided to expose his base at Bryantsville and his line of retreat via the Cumberland Gap and move north. All of these moves resemble the last phase of the Antietam campaign, during which Lee decided to fight rather than give up the objectives of the campaign. Yet unlike Lee, Bragg had to cope with the aloof and elusive Kirby Smith and the obstructive Polk. Bragg struggled to effect a concentration of the Confederate forces.[18]

Criticism of Buell's sluggish performance reached a crescendo, and on September 24 Lincoln relieved him and offered command of the Army of the Ohio to George H. Thomas. Thomas, wary of taking over command under such circumstances, declined the offer. Lincoln had no choice but to reinstate Buell. Buell had seventy-five thousand men concentrated and had anticipated a Confederate retreat from Frankfort. On October 1 Buell's army continued its advance from Louisville. He intended to strike at the Confederate left in the hope that Bragg would concentrate as far distant from the Cumberland Gap as possible. Buell intended to mount a strong demonstration against Bragg's right, partly to confuse Bragg but also to protect his own rear and lines of supply back to Louisville. Buell was now enjoying logistical plenty thanks to his intricate preparations, while the Army of Mississippi found it difficult to subsist on the countryside and the abandonment of Frankfort had resulted in a dislocation of the reserve stocks which Bragg had hoped would sustain a union with Kirby Smith. Bragg's forces also suffered from poor logistical transport that failed to distribute the food stocks adequately. The real Confederate logistical difficulty was not so much gathering foodstuffs or even storing them, but in distributing them to the field armies, especially in the front line.[19]

Given the broad distribution on both fronts, indifferent intelligence, poor reconnaissance, and that the forte of both commanders was administration and strategy rather than tactics, it is not surprising that the two armies collided in a classic meeting engagement at Perryville on October 8, 1862. Union soldiers were searching for water. "There is no water here," an anxious Buell wrote, "and we will get but little, if any, until we get to Perryville." The battle escalated from skirmishing by pickets, which drew in formations bit by bit; tactical control on both sides was minimal. Communication was not impressive either. Alexander M. McCook on Buell's left failed to inform the commanding general that he was engaged by the bulk of the Army of Mississippi. Thus Buell did not realize the magnitude of his opportunity and could not bring his overwhelming numbers to bear until the late afternoon. Coordination was not easy on the four lateral roads over which Buell's corps were advancing because there were few connecting lanes. Buell was forced to rely heavily on the signals corps in communicating with his commanders. Yet this expedient did not prevent Bragg from withdrawing Major General Benjamin F. Cheatham's division from his left, and transferring it to his right to mount a strong assault on Buell's exposed left over Doctor's Creek. This succeeded in driving the federal infantry back a mile and three batteries of artillery were seized. Bragg threw in his last reserves in an attempt to drive McCook's corps from the field.

This action seems to sustain Grady McWhiney's claim that Bragg's earlier attempt to combine Polk with Kirby Smith might have succeeded the previous week before the fall of Frankfort. By 8 PM the battle came to a halt. A tactical Union victory of sorts had been won. But Buell had retired for dinner and was in no position to exploit it. "It was also evident that the main body of the [federal] enemy was in our front, our intelligence from prisoners, of whom we had a number, giving us needed information." And what they told Bragg and his staff was not encouraging. After convening a council of war, and faced by Buell's virtually unscathed main body, Bragg realized that should he remain stationary, he could suffer the same fate as Beauregard at Shiloh. He ordered a withdrawal to Bryantsville and then, fearing that the autumn rains would damage his lines of communication and in lieu of the lack of Kentucky recruits, decided to abandon the campaign. Logistics were again the crucial factor in his final decision. Due to an administrative blunder the Bryantsville depot was found to contain only four days' supplies. News of Van Dorn's defeat at Corinth had, in Bragg's view, rendered the expedition fatally exposed as Buell could be rein-

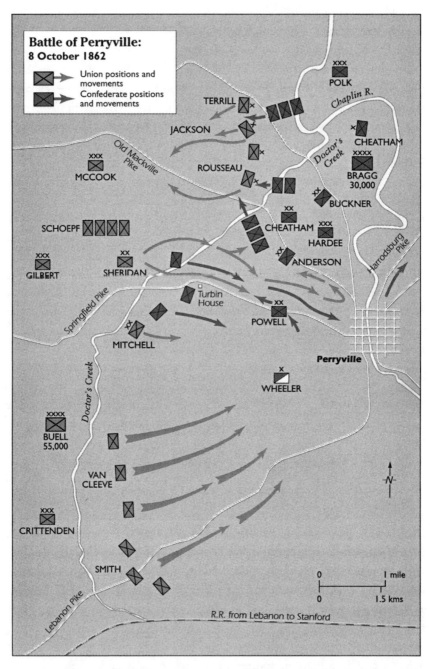

Battle of Perryville:
8 October 1862

Union positions and movements

Confederate positions and movements

POLK

Chaplin R.

TERRILL

JACKSON

CHEATHAM

Doctor's Creek

ROUSSEAU

BRAGG
30,000

BUCKNER

Old Mackville Pike

MCCOOK

SCHOEPF

CHEATHAM

HARDEE

ANDERSON

GILBERT

SHERIDAN

Harrodsburg Pike

Springfield Pike

Turbin House

POWELL

MITCHELL

Perryville

WHEELER

Doctor's Creek

BUELL
55,000

VAN CLEEVE

CRITTENDEN

SMITH

0   1 mile

0   1.5 kms

Lebanon Pike

R.R. from Lebanon to Stanford

From *An Atlas of American Military History* by James C. Bradford (New York: Cynthia Parzych Publishing, 2003).

forced by Grant at his leisure. "Jaded, hungry, and tired," the Army of Mississippi withdrew back into Tennessee through the Cumberland Gap.[20]

With Bragg's retreat in October 1862 the frustration of the Confederate counteroffensive was complete. In Maryland, Lee's strategy was frustrated but his army was saved by his tactical excellence; in Kentucky, Bragg's acumen as a strategist was undoubted but his opportunities at the operational level were squandered by poor, unimaginative tactics. At Perryville Bragg repeated the errors of Shiloh. He employed crude frontal assaults, relied excessively on the bayonet charge, and threw his men into the attack piecemeal. The main reason for the continuing strength of the defensive was not so much any supposed "invulnerability" of mid-nineteenth-century armies, but the inability of Southern armies to combine their full strength in the attack. Corinth was an object lesson in frittering away offensive strength. Both the offensives in Maryland and Kentucky were examples of turning movements on a great scale. Yet the conduct of offensive operations made severe demands on the Confederacy's capacity to make war. Command and control were quite inadequate in the west. Intelligence in the border states was not so reliable as in the seceded states. Command was the responsibility of the field commanders, but control was ultimately the responsibility of the Confederate president, Davis. He failed to fashion a coherent grand strategy in practice. Offensive operations demand a measure of planning, forethought, and an ability to perform skillfully in the field that Confederate armies failed to demonstrate in these campaigns. Davis failed to provide a single guiding hand, clear objectives, and firm coordination. On the contrary, his attempt to placate all his old friends smacked of cronyism and led to a fragmentation of the offensive, especially in the west.[21]

Are those critics who condemn the offensives of 1862 correct? Should the South have remained on the defensive? The answer must be an emphatic negative. To recapitulate: victory in war demands offensive action. A defensive strategy would have required offensive action of some kind at some date. The summer and autumn of 1862 provided the best conditions the South would ever encounter. In 1864 Lee reflected on its dilemma. "Our safety depends on ourselves alone. If we can defeat or drive the armies of the enemy from the field, we shall have peace." All states that aspire to independence *must* demonstrate martial power, especially when confronting the forces of those who seek to extinguish that independence. Such efforts involve high levels of risk; indeed they are axiomatic. The South felt the hard hand of fate in the autumn of 1862. As Emory M. Thomas has put it, "the fates frowned upon rising Southern hopes." Bad luck and accidents played an important part, as they always do in war. 1862 was the crucial year. The frustration of the Confederate counteroffensive cemented the attritional deadlock. Such an unwelcome development demanded a new form of war, and to this urgent requirement President Lincoln had been devoting much thought during the summer months of 1862 and in the autumn he at last decided to act.[22]

This was clearly the decisive year of the Civil War because it saw the frustration of both sides' offensives and confirmed the deadlock. Major General Montgomery C. Meigs said of Antietam that it "was not such a victory as Napoleon had accustomed the world to demand." Attrition set in and with it came an expansion of war aims. Each step forward in the war, each acceleration in its intensity, had been preceded by an outburst of popular enthusiasm or fury. The channels of democratic procedure had directed the velocity of military force aimed at the Confederacy, as before First Manassas. But after that battle, and again after Second Manassas, despite the shock attendant on unexpected defeats, political conservatism had reasserted itself. In the congressional resolutions on war aims, presidential use of the war powers, and the passage of the two confiscation acts, war aims were changing but still remained restricted. All this ground shifted because of McClellan's failure to win a decisive victory at Antietam and revive faith in the conservative view of war aims.[23]

The main problem that Lincoln faced in the first year of the war was that the North had not resigned itself to the kind of intense, arduous conflict that we readily associate with the American Civil War. The popular expectation was of a massive federal victory by the summer of 1862. McClellan coached Northern public opinion to expect a tremendous success. The bloody battle of Shiloh in April was a portent of things to come, a portent confirmed by the great disappointment at McClellan's failure in the Peninsular campaign, the setback at Second Manassas, and the lost opportunity at Antietam. These general engagements indicated that far from suppressing a rebellion, the federal government would have to brace itself to wage a full-scale civil war. Such a realization came slowly and took just over twelve months from the firing of the opening bullets at Fort Sumter.

The increasing favor of public opinion toward adopting more destructive and punitive military measures could be gauged by the increasing attacks on private property. The defense of private property is, after all, one of the prime duties of a nation-state. Once such a duty is jettisoned, however gradually, then it is clear that any pretense at harmony between conflicting polities has been abandoned. All barriers to the escalation of organized violence and brutality have been swept away until the end of "total" victory has been achieved. The

July 1861 resolution passed by the House of Representatives had stated that soldiers were under no compulsion to return runaway slaves. The Confiscation Act
of August 6 declared that any slaves found undertaking military labor for the
enemies of the United States would be forfeit. Such measures did not impugn
the Fugitive Slave Act of 1850 because they were worded in such a way as to
avoid reflecting on the liberty of the broad mass of slaves. The moot point here
was an assumption that confiscation of private property could take place in wars
between nations, but not in a war *among* Americans.

Following the furor after Ball's Bluff in October 1861 and the attempt to
mount a purge of generals sympathetic to slavery, a new article of war was passed
by Congress on March 13, 1862, which forbade the return of slaves to Confederate masters. A more all-embracing document, the Second Confiscation Act,
followed on July 17, 1862. This empowered the chief executive to employ
negroes in uniform to put down the rebellion as all slaves, whether escaped, captured, or simply abandoned by fleeing owners were "forever free of their servitude and [were] not again [to be] held as slaves." Slavery was abolished in the
District of Columbia in April, and in all territories the following June. Lincoln
was insistent that commitments to compensate owners be included in these
latter two measures so that Maryland slaveowners would not be alarmed. Also,
in May 1862 Great Britain and the United States signed a treaty designed to
eradicate the slave trade. These events form the background to Lincoln's own
initiatives on emancipation, which gathered pace after March 1862. As with
most of his executive acts, Lincoln moved toward a resolution of the problem
slowly and cautiously; but once he had decided on a solution he acted boldly and
resolutely. In his special message to Congress on the subject, Lincoln stressed
that emancipation would be gradual and voluntary (with compensation) and
would not be completed in a hurry; 1900 was his chosen terminal date. He was
anxious, moreover, that emancipation would not be misconstrued as an attack
on private property. Many of these assumptions would be challenged over the
next few months.[24]

In May 1862 Lincoln was forced, in a rerun of the Frémont controversy, to
rescind an order hailing from General David Hunter based at Port Royal, South
Carolina. Hunter saw that martial law and slavery were irreconcilable. He issued
an edict based on his own authority that the slaves in his department were "forever free." Lincoln was irritated that once again the issue of emancipation was
nibbling at his executive powers. He believed it should not be regarded as akin
to "police regulations in armies and camps." In a proclamation he warned the
slave states of the consequences if they did not return to the Union of their own

volition and accept compensated emancipation. "You cannot . . . be blind to the signs of the times. . . . [The change] would come gently as the dews of heaven, not rending or wrecking anything. Will you not embrace it? . . . May the vast future not have to lament that you have neglected it." Lincoln was still mindful of the value of a cautious strategy, that Maryland would have no cause for alarm. Yet for all his cautious instincts, by June 1862, with the failure of McClellan's offensive in the Peninsula, Lincoln realized that he would have to take more drastic measures to weaken the Confederate war effort. He had received no response from his conciliatory gestures; therefore, more draconian measures would be required. Turning this way or that, as circumstances dictated, Lincoln not only grasped opportunities but created them. He began scribbling a draft emancipation proclamation in the War Department telegraph office at the end of the Seven Days' campaign. Based on the First Confiscation Act, this initial document was discussed at a cabinet meeting on July 22, 1862.[25]

Lincoln still held to the view that compensation for slaveowners would be required. The strategic element remained uppermost in his thoughts. "Things had gone from bad to worse, until I felt that we had reached the end of our rope on the plan . . . [we] must change our tactics or lose the game." The formulation of the policy was entirely the president's and he told the cabinet "that I had resolved upon this step, and had not called them together to ask their advice, but to lay the subject-matter of a proclamation before them, suggestions as to which would be in order after they had heard it read."

As the psychological impact of an edict of proclamation would be enormous, Lincoln acted with great prudence and gave only the most oblique hint of the way the policy would develop. Senator Charles Sumner, for instance, tried to wear the president down with interminable sermons on the desirability of emancipation. Lincoln had already made up his mind on this matter.

Yet during Sumner's second visit on July 4, 1862, after another bout of tedious sermonizing, Lincoln conceded that he would consider freeing slaves in the war zone of eastern Virginia but a wholesale declaration of emancipation would be "too big a lick." Acting as a devil's advocate, he aired a worry that could not be gainsaid, namely that an emancipation proclamation would not be popular save among committed abolitionists: "half the officers would fling down their arms and three more States would rise." But as Lincoln soon grasped, even conservatives now realized that attacking slavery was an indispensable weapon in bringing down the Confederacy. That if a shattering victory could not be attained in the first phase of the conflict, then in the later phase more drastic measures would be required to attack the South's sources of warmaking. As

Horace Birney, a traditional conservative, admitted, emancipation was a *military necessity*. "The Negroes are part of the enemy. . . . We shall be whipped as sure as fate, if we fight with one of our hands tied behind our backs." Members of the cabinet tended to echo this view. But Seward was fearful that coming after two successive defeats, Seven Days' and then Second Manassas, that issuing the proclamation in August would have the ring of wailing despair rather than the triumphant shout of battle. Lincoln was immediately struck by the force of this argument and decided to withhold it until Union armies won a victory.[26]

Whereas the first six months of the war had seen only one great battle, First Manassas, the second campaign season of six months from March 31, 1862, had seen a clutch of great battles—Shiloh, Seven Days', Second Manassas, and then, in September 1862, Antietam. Perryville followed in October. Although Perryville was a significant action and confirmed the failure of the Confederate counteroffensive, it was the decisive events in the east that stimulated truly important political measures that determined the character of the war. It was these battles in the east that agitated the thoughts of the politicians in Washington. Lincoln complained of this tendency and that success in the west received insufficient attention; but his attention, too, was centered on Virginia. These battles not only transformed the face of war in North America, but the unprecedented scale of death and destruction inflicted on American society had important political consequences. The very indecisiveness of these great battles led to a recourse to punitive war measures. As Lincoln warned the influential Democrat August Belmont, "this government cannot much longer play a game in which it stakes all, and its enemies stake nothing."

After Lee's withdrawal from Maryland, on September 22 Lincoln presented to his cabinet the text of the preliminary Emancipation Proclamation. This august occasion was enlivened by Lincoln reading an amusing passage from Artemus Ward's the "High Handed Outrage at Utica," which affronted the sensibilities of the pompous secretary of the treasury, Salmon P. Chase. He thought it too frivolous for such a solemn occasion. Turning more gravely to the necessity he had been forced to confront, Lincoln observed, "I think the time has come. I wish it were a better time. The action of the army against the rebels has not been quite what I should have best liked." Nonetheless, Antietam had driven Lee from Northern soil and restored some credit to the Northern cause. The indecisive action at Perryville and Bragg's withdrawal from Kentucky seemed to confirm the impression that a decisive corner had been turned.[27]

The entire document was justified as an exercise of the presidential war powers. In this way Lincoln attempted to sustain the proclamation's authority as an exercise in executive power sanctioned by the Constitution; otherwise Lincoln feared it could be overturned in the courts. The reference to the president as commander-in-chief, which prefaced it, did not appear in the proclamation calling out the militia in April 1861. All slaves held as chattels in states "in rebellion against the United States" from January 1, 1863 were "then, thenceforward, and forever free." All federal agencies were to recognize this freedom and not discourage chattel slaves from seeking it. If the Confederate states returned to the Union, however, then Lincoln would ensure that loyal slaveowners would "be compensated for all losses by acts of the United States, including the loss of slaves." If they remained outside the Union then they risked losing all. For the preliminary Emancipation Proclamation applied only to areas not occupied by Union forces. Slaveowners residing in areas occupied by Union troops would be able to keep their slaves, at least for the time being, and would receive compensation after a due process of gradual emancipation. Montgomery C. Blair and Seward were still worried about the reaction of the border states; but Lincoln now felt confident in their loyalty. The federal government "must make the forward effort. . . . They [will] acquiesce, if not immediately, soon." This emphasis on "forward movement" is significant. Lincoln realized that a means had to be found, as the war had moved into a defining phase, of striking at the Confederacy rather than sitting back and allowing the South to strike at the Union (which it had been allowed to do over the previous two months). Given the adamant Confederate refusal to make any concessions, Lincoln realized that he had no choice if he was to achieve a reunion of the states but to wage a punitive war against the South and its social system. He was candid in agreeing that after January 1, 1863, "the character of the war will change. It will be one of subjugation . . . The [old] South is to be destroyed and replaced by new propositions and ideas."[28]

The fearful cost of the war, which would be multiplied many times before it came to an end, not only supported those who called out for more drastic war measures, but lent credence to an increasingly strong cry that the South be punished for bringing the curse of fratricidal conflict upon the United States. The North, furthermore, should be punished by providence, too, for tolerating the evil of slavery for so long. Even soldiers who had objected to the Emancipation Proclamation realized as they advanced onto Southern soil how slavery sustained its war economy. By striking at slavery Lincoln aimed to root out the fundamental cause of the war, the paramount issue that had tempted the South to seek its independence. Some conservative members of his cabinet were still fearful that the outbreak of a servile rebellion in the Confederacy would tempt foreign intervention. Yet the South's greatest opportunity to demonstrate the integrity of its independence and seek foreign assistance had passed by. Its military power had now to be isolated, enveloped, and crushed. Lincoln had already warned, "I shall not surrender this game leaving any available card unplayed."[29]

NOTES AND REFERENCES

1. Clifford Dowdey, *Lee: A Biography* (London: Gollancz, 1970), p. 300; Lee to Davis, Sep. 3, 1862, in *The Wartime Papers of R. E. Lee*, eds. Clifford Dowdey and Louis H. Manarin (New York: Bramshall House, 1961), p. 293; T. Harry Williams, *P. G. T. Beauregard: Napoleon in Gray* (Baton Rouge: Louisiana State University Press, 1955, 1989), pp. 158–65; Grady McWhiney, *Braxton Bragg and Confederate Defeat*, 2 vols. (Tuscaloosa: University of Alabama Press, 1969, 1991), vol. 1, pp. 260–61. Beauregard decided to take four months sabbatical leave. See William C. Davis, *Jefferson Davis: The Man and His Hour* (New York: HarperCollins, 1991), p. 405.

2. McWhiney, *Bragg*, vol. 1, pp. 33–34. When the Confederate government was being organized, Bragg was considered as a candidate for the cabinet portfolio of secretary of war. See Davis, *Jefferson Davis*, p. 311.

3. Brian Holden Reid and John White, "'A Mob of Stragglers and Cowards': Desertion from the Union and Confederate Armies, 1861–1865," *Journal of Strategic Studies* 8 (March 1985): 70–71; McWhiney, *Bragg*, vol. 1, pp. 258–59; Lee to Davis, Aug. 17, 1863, *Lee's Dispatches: Unpublished Letters of General Robert E. Lee to Jefferson Davis*, eds. Douglas Southall Freeman and Grady McWhiney (New York: Putnam's, 1957), pp. 123–24; Thomas L. Connelly, *Army of the Heartland* (Baton Rouge: Louisiana State University Press, 1967, 1986), pp. 205–206.

4. Stephen D. Engle, *Don Carlos Buell: Most Promising of All* (Chapel Hill: University of North Carolina Press, 1999), pp. 57, 66–67, 116–17, 201–203, especially controversial was Buell's zeal to return runaway slaves to their masters; T. Harry Williams, *Lincoln and His Generals* (New York: Alfred A. Knopf, 1952), p. 151; idem., *Lincoln and the Radicals* (Madison: University of Wisconsin Press paperback edition, 1965), pp. 193–94; *War of the Rebellion: A Compilation of the Official Records of the Union and Confederate Armies*, 128 parts in 70 vols. (Washington, DC: Government Printing Office, 1880–1901), series 1, vol. 19, part 2, pp. 135–38.

5. James A. Ramage, *Rebel Raider: The Life of General John Hunt Morgan* (Lexington: University Press of Kentucky, 1986), pp. 91–92; J. H. Mathes, *General Forrest* (New York: Appleton, 1902), pp. 78–79; Herman Hattaway and Archer Jones, *How the North Won* (Urbana: University of Illinois Press, 1983), p. 216.

6. Connelly, *Army of the Heartland*, pp. 208–209; Davis, *Jefferson Davis*, pp. 464–66; McWhiney, *Bragg*, vol. 1, pp. 279–80; Steven E. Woodworth, *Jefferson Davis*

and His Generals (Lawrence: University Press of Kansas, 1990), pp. 22–25, 160–61, 183–84.

7. McWhiney, *Bragg*, vol. 1, pp. 268–70; Albert Castel, *General Sterling Price and the Civil War in the West* (Baton Rouge: Louisiana State University Press, 1968, 1993), pp. 92–95; Davis, *Jefferson Davis*, pp. 461–62, 464.

8. Connelly, *Army of the Heartland*, pp. 209–20; Earl J. Hess, *Banners to the Breeze: The Kentucky Campaign, Corinth and Stones River* (Lincoln: University of Nebraska Press, 2000), pp. 121, 124–25.

9. Catton, *Grant Moves South* (Boston: Little, Brown, 1960), pp. 307–11; Castel, *Price*, pp. 94–103; Ulysses S. Grant, *Personal Memoirs* (London: Sampson Low, 1886), vol. 1, pp. 410–13. Grant "found no fault at the time" but this failure contributed to his later disillusion with Rosecrans's abilities. See also, Hess, *Banners to the Breeze*, pp. 129–40.

10. See Castel, *Price*, pp. 104–106.

11. Ibid., pp. 106–108, 111, 114–19, 123; Hess, *Banners to the Breeze*, pp. 141–47; also see Peter Cozzens, *The Darkest Days of the War: The Battles of Iuka and Corinth* (Chapel Hill: University of North Carolina Press, 1997)

12. Quoted in Edward Hagerman, *The American Civil War and the Origins of Modern Warfare* (Bloomington: Indiana University Press, 1988), p. 188.

13. Grant, *Memoirs*, vol. 1, p. 418.

14. McWhiney, Bragg, vol. 1, p. 284.

15. McWhiney, *Bragg*, vol. 1, pp. 285–88, 290–91, 294–96; Hess, *Banners to the Breeze*, pp. 56–62; Engle, *Buell*, pp. 287–94; Hagerman, *American Civil War*, pp. 178–79; Kenneth Williams, *Lincoln Finds a General* (New York: Macmillan, 1956), vol. 4, pp. 125–28; Connelly, *Army of the Heartland,* pp. 228–30, 231–34.

16. McWhiney, *Bragg*, vol. 1, pp. 297–99; see also, Connelly, *Army of the Heartland*, pp. 250–52. It is characteristic of Connelly's extreme ambivalence toward Confederate history, combining censoriousness with a barely concealed exasperation at its failure to gain independence, that he should describe Bragg's contribution to the inaugural (p. 251) as "pathetic, hopeful, and even amusing . . ."

17. General Richard H. Taylor was horrified by the candor with which Bragg derided his subordinates. See McWhiney, *Bragg*, vol. 1, p. 278; see also ibid., pp. 298–301.

18. Connelly, *Army of the Heartland*, pp. 252–57; McWhiney, *Bragg*, vol. 1, pp. 301–10. McWhiney makes an interesting case (pp. 303–306) that Bragg's attack on Buell's right could have succeeded even though it was based on erroneous information.

19. Major General D. C. Buell, "East Tennessee and the Campaign of Perryville," *Battles and Leaders of the Civil War*, eds. Robert V. Johnson and Clarence C. Buel, vol. 3, 46 (New York: Century, 1956 edition); Engle, *Buell*, pp. 294–306; Larry J. Daniel, *Days of Glory: The Army of the Cumberland, 1861–1865* (Baton Rouge: Louisiana State University Press, 2004), pp. 134–36.

20. Kenneth W. Noe, *Perryville* (Lexington: University Press of Kentucky, 2001), pp. 143, 242–55; McWhiney, *Bragg*, vol. 1, pp. 314–23; Connelly, *Army of the Heartland*, pp. 256–67.

21. McWhiney, *Bragg*, vol. 1, p. 320; Wordworth, *Davis and His Generals*, pp. 166–68; Davis, *Jefferson Davis*, pp. 470–73.

22. Lee to Davis, July 6, 1864, in *Lee's Dispatches*, p. 368; Nolan, *Lee Considered*, pp. 102–106, invariably deprecates "risk"; Emory M. Thomas, *The Confederate Nation, 1861–1865* (New York: Monticello, 1979, 1993), p. 164.

23. Montgomery C. Meigs, "On the Conduct of the Civil War," *American Historical Review* 26 (1921): 291.

24. David Donald, *Charles Sumner and the Rights of Man* (New York: Alfred A. Knopf, 1970), pp. 52–53; James G. Randall, *Lincoln the President* (London: Eyre and Spottiswoode, 1947), vol. 2, pp. 132–43 is still the best account of the evolution of Lincoln's thinking if the prejudices of the author are discounted; also see Benjamin P. Thomas and Harold M. Hyman, *Stanton* (New York: Alfred A. Knopf, 1962), pp. 10–11, 232–33; Glyndon G. Van Deusen, *William Henry Seward* (New York: Oxford University Press, 1968), pp. 330–31; Allen C. Guelzo, *Lincoln's Emancipation Proclamation: The End of Slavery in America* (New York: Simon and Schuster, 2004), pp. 37–42, 64–65, 81–89, 111–13.

25. Randall, *Lincoln the President*, vol. 2, pp. 148–50, 154–56; Guelzo, *Lincoln's Emancipation Proclamation*, pp. 73–73, 108–109, 114–22, 126–30; Message to Congress, Mar. 6, 1862, in *The Collected Works of Abraham Lincoln*, ed. Roy P. Basler (New Brunswick, NJ: Rutgers University Press, 1953), vol. 5, pp. 145–46.

26. Randall, *Lincoln the President*, vol. 2, pp. 154–55; Donald, *Sumner and the Rights of Man*, p. 60 (though it is likely that Stanton warned Sumner that an emancipation proclamation would be issued within two months [see Thomas and Hyman, *Stanton*, p. 238]); George M. Fredrickson, *The Inner Civil War: Northern Intellectuals and the Crisis of the Union* (New York: Harper and Row, 1965), p. 114; Van Deusen, *Seward*, p. 331; James M. McPherson, *The Battle Cry of Freedom* (New York: Oxford University Press, 1988), p. 496; Guelzo, *Lincoln's Emancipation Proclamation*, pp. 120–23, 171.

27. Guelzo, *Lincoln's Emancipation Proclamation*, pp. 153–56; *Inside Lincoln's Cabinet: The Civil War Diaries of Salmon P. Chase*, ed. David Donald (New York: Alfred A. Knopf, 1954), pp. 149–52 (entry for Sep. 22, 1862); Lincoln to Belmont, July 31, 1862, in Lincoln, *Collected Works*, vol. 5, p. 350.

28. Guelzo, *Lincoln's Emancipation Proclamation*, pp. 197–200; Randall, *Lincoln the President*, pp. 162–65; McPherson, *Battle Cry of Freedom*, p. 558.

29. See Peter J. Parish, "The Instruments of Providence: Slavery, Civil War and the American Churches," in *The Church and War*, ed. W. J. Sheils, 291–320 (Oxford: Basil Blackwell, 1984); Van Deusen, *Seward*, pp. 330–34. The initial reaction to the proclamation, however, was not enthusiastic. See Holden Reid and White, "'A Mob of Strag-

glers and Cowards,'" p. 63. The consensus was that it would provoke Southerners to fight harder than ever. Lincoln to Reverdy Johnson, July 26, 1862, in Lincoln, *Collected Works*, vol. 5, p. 344.

Chapter Seven

ERRORS IN THE ATTACK

NOVEMBER 1862 TO MARCH 1863

T he frustration of the Confederate counteroffensive in the autumn of 1862 had one rather unexpected result: the frustration was felt more in the North than in the South. The two commanders who had led what in retrospect (though not at the time) looked like raids remained in command of their respective armies. Lee remained unassailable as commander of the Army of Northern Virginia; Bragg remained, too, at the head of the Army of Tennessee, although he had generated much dislike among his subordinates and his relations with his senior corps commander, Lieutenant General Leonidas Polk, had deteriorated ominously. The stage was set for their feud, which would have such calamitous consequences. Both men were friends of Jefferson Davis. Whatever his other numerous deficiencies, Davis was tenaciously loyal to friends. Polk was a much older friend than Bragg. Polk and Davis had been affectionate members of the same "set" at West Point, a loyalty that transcended all others. A blind faith in the ability of friends must surely be included in any list of weaknesses. Bragg had no choice but to acquiesce in Polk's presence in his army; but he hardly made the best of it.[1]

On the Union side, Lincoln conducted what amounted to a purge of his generals. After Antietam the Army of the Potomac made no offensive moves and, as always, this had deleterious effects on the Union war effort. Halleck complained of the Union's premier fighting force that "It requires the lever of Archimedes to move this inert mass. I have tried my best, but without success." Halleck ordered an advance lower down the Potomac, but McClellan was fearful of Lee's strong position on his right flank in the Shenandoah Valley, and found all kinds of reasons to procrastinate. The president was convinced that a great opportunity had been missed in Maryland: "[If] we cannot beat him when he bears the wastage of coming to us," he claimed, "we never can when we bear the wastage of going to him." It was easier to defeat the Confederates in northern Virginia or Maryland than when they had retired "within the entrenchments of Richmond." Lincoln wanted another drive on Richmond from the north; given his central position, McClellan could get between Lee and the city, indeed beat him to it. McClellan pleaded logistical difficulties, especially the fatigue of his horses. Lincoln replied sarcastically, "I have just read your dispatch about sore-tongued and fatigued horses. Will you pardon me for asking what the horses of your army have done since the Battle of Antietam that fatigues anything?" McClellan did not seem to be able to learn from experience; he did not mature as a commander. In the offensive he lacked drive, failed to deploy so as to maximize the fighting power of his army, and quailed before the enemy's every move. Lincoln concluded that he must be dismissed. Yet there were two political considerations uppermost in Lincoln's mind. The order superseding him was dispatched on November 7. This was after the midterm congressional elections, so that voters who admired McClellan would not be antagonized; and the order was sent at night to minimize the possibility that his troops might sway McClellan to march on Washington and strike against his political enemies in the Republican Party.[2]

Ambrose E. Burnside was prevailed upon to take the command although he protested at his lack of capacity for it, of which, alas, he gave all too much evidence over the next two months. Don Carlos Buell had also been dismissed a couple of weeks previously. He had certainly missed a heaven-sent opportunity at Perryville to crush Bragg, but what the president really held against him was a refusal to occupy east Tennessee before he had straightened out his line of supply; he resolutely refused to live off the country. In this he was probably right. The Confederates had stripped the country during the occupation. Yet it was political imperatives that pressed the hardest. Buell refused to understand or acknowledge these. The strongly pro-Unionist counties of east Tennessee were suffering from Confederate oppression and Lincoln was anxious to relieve them; he was certainly feeling the pressure of intense lobbying from Unionist Tennesseans in Washington led by Andrew Johnson, the state's war governor. That Confederates could behave in a brutal fashion, and that Lincoln's anxieties were well founded, is confirmed by the mass execution of Unionists at Gainesville, Texas, in October 1862. Secessionist strength was based on force and intimidation, not merely on an exercise of constitutional niceties. That strength could only be broken by physical occupation by Union armies. The president lost patience and thus Buell joined his friend McClellan on the list of unemployed Union generals.[3]

The dismissal of both these conservative generals overjoyed radical Republicans. They saw an opportunity to impress their views about the conduct of the war on the administration and its generals. Burnside made some genuflections in their direction. Halleck had urged on Buell that the Emancipation Proclamation had transformed the nature of the war. When Buell had complained that east Tennessee was the heart of the enemy's resources, he retorted, "Make it the heart of yours. Your army can live there if the enemy's can." It is unlikely that, as a field commander, Halleck would have contemplated such action if he had been given a choice; but being a political realist he was now signaling a change of policy. This had much to do with the failures of McClellan and Buell, and the hardening of political attitudes in Washington. The president was now tending to agree with his radical critics and his frustration stemmed from the failures of his field commanders. This momentous alteration in policy thus sprang from the interchange of views springing from the clamor and maneuvering of party politics in Washington; this was the vital focal point of thought and deed. Some historians, like Stephen E. Ambrose, tend to argue that it was the product of soldiers in the field. "New approaches to tactics and strategy did come during the war," he writes, "but the originators were field commanders operating in practical situations, not theorists in Washington." This view is overly simplified and divorces the conduct of the war from its political context.[4]

Once the cloak of presidential approbation had been removed peremptorily from McClellan's shoulders, he became the target for savage criticism. Ancient historians tell us that the Carthaginians crucified failed generals. The members of the Joint Committee on the Conduct of the War were certainly determined to crucify McClellan's reputation, and kill him "deader than the prophets," as Senator Zachariah Chandler put it with his usual pungency.[5]

This change in the climate of opinion, which affected soldiers as well as civilians, is illustrated by the views put forward during a court of inquiry demanded by General Buell to clear his name. Buell unexpectedly did not go as quietly as McClellan. After the battle of Perryville, and Bragg's escape before a fraction of Buell's army was engaged, disaffection with their commander by certain vocal elements spread throughout the Army of the Ohio. The court of inquiry was convened in November 1862 and dragged on into the summer months of 1863. It served as a forum for justifying the increasingly punitive measures needed to be taken to defeat the South. During the inquiry, Buell asked the provost marshal, James B. Fry, "whether the disposition to plunder and pillage . . . was not encouraged by the popular idea . . . of living upon the enemy, as it was called and regarded . . . as constituting a vigorous prosecution of the war?" Fry replied that such a disposition had not been spread by officers; they had never attempted "to advance the idea that it was proper" to plunder. At this, the judge advocate general, Joseph Holt, a prewar Democrat and Stanton appointee, intervened and asked, "Has not the jealous care of rebel property impressed upon our forces that our generals were really sympathizing with that side?" Fry had to agree. Such exchanges served to damage Buell and the outlook on the war he sought to defend.[6]

Buell then changed tack and asked Major General Thomas L. Crittenden whether "the tone of a considerable portion of the public press [which supported the radical Republicans] encouraged in the minds of the men the idea that they were more or less at liberty to make use of private property . . . ?" Crittenden agreed. He claimed many soldiers "adopted this idea" and orders to the contrary were "disagreeable to them." Colonel Marc Mundy's testimony revealed that the newspapers most widely circulated among the troops were those most closely associated with Senators Wade and Chandler and their allies. They included the Cincinnati *Times*, *Gazette*, and *Commercial*, and the Chicago *Tribune*. According to Mundy the "burden of [their] complaint" was that "General Buell was protecting the [Southern] people, rather than punishing them . . . that he did not devastate the country and destroy all the rebel sympathizers, and that he treated the people generally too kindly . . . ." In other words, they seemed to advocate what they called a "vigorous war policy," by which they seemed to mean general devastation.

Mundy then made a significant remark. He attached great weight to "the general applause of the press for the orders and policy pursued by General Pope in Virginia, which the troops and papers construed into a right on the part of our soldiers to appropriate all the rebel goods they could find." These orders clearly had more influence than has been recognized by historians. The radicals were not surprised by this. They had always believed that the generals would be forced to fight a "vigorous" war by the true instincts of the "natural genius" of the American people.[7]

The further discrediting of the reputations of McClellan and Buell, and their simultaneous removal, ushered in a period of upheaval in Union strategy in the east that was not to subside until the appointment of Major General George G. Meade to command the Army of the Potomac in June 1863. It was not to finally quiet until the Grant-Sherman partnership gained control in 1864 (with Lincoln's support) of federal warmaking. But the coming months would represent the crisis of the federal war effort. They were months of commotion that damaged but did not rupture discipline among senior ranks in the Union army, as generals struggled to exploit the rapidly changing circumstances.

Throughout this period Lincoln acted as his own general-in-chief. Halleck was a staff officer with shrewd political instincts. He was not a commander. The constitutional provision that designates the president as commander-in-chief of the armed forces is vague. The partnership of Lincoln and Halleck, though not without its virtues, brought to the fore the ambiguities of the relationship between the president and the general-in-chief. The latter was a military position that simultaneously combined the position of a supreme commander in the field with staff control. The latter position most suited Halleck but he did not control a general staff responsive to his wishes, and he had to impose his operational views by acting as a superior field commander, the role that contemporaries exalted more than any other. Yet if he did so he trespassed on the constitutional prerogatives of the president, and in dealing with such a confident and masterful chief executive as Lincoln, Halleck shrank from commanding. He adopted a profile that was so low as to be almost indiscernible. Halleck received a stern rebuke from Lincoln in January 1863 urging him to *command*: "gather all the elements for forming a judgment of your own; and then tell General Burnside that you *do* approve, or that you do *not* approve his plan. Your military skill is useless to me, if you will not do this." Halleck complained, coached, tutored, and nagged, but he did not command.[8]

Yet Halleck's record was not undistinguished. He took greater interest in the war in the west. It was he who urged on the administration and the field commanders the importance of Vicksburg (the president was inclined to give the Mississippi basin a lower priority than east Tennessee). He helped to improve logistical support and the appointment of officers. But he conceived his position as essentially *managerial*. Neither was the informal system he presided over in any sense "modern." Hattaway and Jones, in their judicious and favorable assessment of Halleck's activities, argue, "This staff effectively performed most of the duties of a modern general staff with Halleck as its de facto chief." They go on to claim (despite a recognition that the American staff system is French in provenance) that, "The contemporaneous Prussian general staff closely approximated that of the Union."[9] Such comparisons with the Prussian general staff have been almost obligatory in the literature.

This comparison is almost wholly misconceived. The purpose of a modern general staff, to use a term popularized by the British military writer Spenser Wilkinson, is to provide the "brain of an army." It integrated operations, intelligence, training, personnel, and logistics as *tools* for the use of the commander. In short, training, logistics, and the forces raised were the means by which victory could be organized by placing them at the disposal of the commander. In Prussia the chief of the general staff orchestrated the forces at his disposal while in attendance with the head of state, the king. The elder von Moltke brought this system to a peak of efficiency during the Franco-Prussian War of 1870–71. It assumed a level of staff training, a doctrinal commonality, and an acquaintance with the chief of the general staff's plans and intentions so great that staff officers could advise field commanders accordingly and, if necessary, supersede them should this drastic expedient be necessary. The whole military instrument thus reacted to the will of the chief of the general staff, who was *not* a field commander in the American sense.[10]

These conditions were wholly lacking in the American context of the 1860s. It was not that American generals or staffs were inferior to their Prussian counterparts; in some ways, especially logistically, they were superior organizers. Yet this ingenuity and organizing capacity was not tied to a *system* that elaborated military doctrine and integrated it into a clear-cut and universally accepted military *practice*. On the contrary, research has shown that the United States Army lacked the mechanism to produce doctrine, learn from its mistakes, and restructure itself in accordance with experience for the rest of the nineteenth century. Such manuals as it produced were essentially drills; even the Leavenworth series published in the 1890s hardly rose above the level of minor tactics.[11]

Moreover, the rank of general-in-chief, with all its contentious ambiguities, not least in the relationship between the senior general and the president and secretary of war, did not provide the impetus for directing a general staff in the modern, operational sense. Halleck increasingly saw his prime duty as "to strengthen the hands of the President as Commander-in-Chief." He drafted orders for the president, liaised with field commanders, and translated the president's very real strategic and operational insight into military jargon. This was a very limited, not innovative, approach to his duties. Staff officers lacked the training and authority to issue commands. Halleck also adopted Winfield Scott's practice, while a field commander in Mexico, of not interfering with subordinate commanders. "I have always, wherever possible," he explained to Lincoln, "avoided giving positive instructions to generals commanding departments, leaving them the exercise of their own judgment while giving them my opinion and advice." There is some anticipation of Moltkean practice here—not least allowing subordinates discretion. But Moltke laid down firmly and decisively the mission and expected it to be carried out at the earliest opportunity. He gave "positive advice." The lack of aim, coordination, and direction that was produced under the American system was inimical to "modern" general staffs; but then Halleck was not the chief of a general staff. This position did not exist in the United States; he was simply a clever, fussy staff officer carrying out instructions as bidden. What can be claimed for the system that emerged in 1862–63 is that for all the stresses and strains, Lincoln had a closer working relationship with his generals than either James Madison in the War of 1812 or James K. Polk in the Mexican War of 1846–48.

The improvement in personal relations could not compensate for structural weaknesses. Consequently, the huge logistical resources built up by the United States in 1862 were not linked to any overarching strategic design or operational focus; indeed the latter is conspicuous in its absence. Significantly, Halleck put the weakness of Union forces in the pursuit down to their excessively large "baggage and supply trains and to a want of training in making marches." Grant had made the same point. The inability of the Lincoln administration to decide on whether it should pursue a strategy of annihilation or exhaustion is a moot point and, in a casual fit of absentmindedness, seemed to adopt both. In 1862 the North had witnessed four battles, Antietam, Perryville, Corinth and Iuka, which should have offered up great strategic dividends, yet they were barren. This whole issue of "decisive" battle illustrates the doctrinal vacuum that the conduct of great operations in the Civil War highlighted. Civilians and some generals (mainly those who had acquired commissions through political influence) believed that the object of the war was to fight great battles. The radical critics of the war effort also thought largely in these terms. Professional soldiers increasingly stressed the results that could be gained from campaigns. Halleck was by far the most sophisticated spokesman of the latter school. Yet the actual conduct of professional soldiers was so halting and inept that their credibility was damaged. Buell at Perryville had suffered from some bad luck but the effect was the same, for he showed himself incapable of profiting from his campaigns whatever his fortunes.[12]

Halleck's main contribution to the conduct of war was *political*. He served Lincoln as a variety of personal chiefs of staff akin to Admiral William D. Leahy to Franklin Delano Roosevelt, 1941–45. Halleck conducted the president's enthusiasm into regular military channels, restricted the activities of military "entrepreneurs" like John A. McClernand, and managed to divert criticism of fumbling West Pointers—sometimes onto himself. Such criticism was by no means restricted to the radicals; the secretary of the navy, Gideon Welles, was especially caustic by December 1862. Halleck also signaled to field commanders the increasingly attritional character of Union strategy. The president on a number of occasions had indicated how the Emancipation Proclamation had ushered in a new emphasis on a strategy of exhaustion; but this had yet to take a coherent form. The army "has become demoralized," Lincoln complained "by the idea that the war is to be ended, the nation united, and peace restored . . . by *strategy*, and not by hard desperate fighting." The president had been inclined to shield the South from the horrors of servile war. However, a combination of stronger Southern resistance than expected and the failure of Northern generals to win a decisive success left him little choice but to adopt harsher measures. Lincoln emphasized: "They [Southerners] very well know the way to avert all this is simply to take their place in the Union upon the old terms. If they will not do this, should they not receive harder blows rather than lighter ones?" For, as he told August Belmont, a leading Democrat, "they cannot experiment for ten years trying to destroy the government, and if they fail still come back into the Union unhurt."[13]

Thus as 1862 came to an end, the president had not yet shaken off a tendency to translate strategy into the fighting and winning of battles. The weaknesses of the rank of general-in-chief were still unresolved; they would remain so until a general-in-chief was appointed who behaved like the field commander that American military culture demanded. "Unless we have some success soon—I mean real substantial success—the ultra radicals will force us to yield," Halleck warned. This search for success led to the launching of the ill-fated Fredericksburg campaign, which would precipitate the administration into its greatest crisis, a crisis that threatened to weaken the hold of the executive branch over the conduct of the war, reduce the prerogative of the president to construct his cabinet as he saw fit, and force him to rebuild it on radical lines. As always, it was the course of the war in Virginia that determined the ability of the president to dominate the government. No wonder he paid such close attention to the affairs of the Army of the Potomac. Halleck was the ostensible general-in-chief but failed to assert himself, so Lincoln assumed the prime responsibility for the central strategic and operational decisions and almost paid the consequences for the campaign he launched. The president was Halleck's last line of defense against untrammeled congressional interference in strategy and command appointments. This was undoubtedly an important reason for the unstinting loyalty Halleck accorded his brilliant, exacting, and occasionally exasperating master.[14]

The new commander of the Army of the Potomac, Ambrose E. Burnside, was hearty, genial, and much liked. In seeking out a fresh alliance with the Joint Committee on the Conduct of the War, Burnside showed himself capable of acting in an underhanded way. On the whole, however, his appointment was an unmitigated disaster. Although Lincoln had little inkling of Burnside's weaknesses before the appointment was made due to his strong record in North Carolina (perhaps for once he had been misled by appearance), it soon became clear that Burnside had been moved above his command ceiling, had no original military ideas of his own, and continually deferred to Lincoln or Halleck for advice. There was a lot of the bluffer about Burnside; he looked good, but was neither as self-assured nor as intelligent as he seemed. Perhaps Lincoln had calculated that having a field commander carrying out his instructions might not be a bad idea, considering the lethargy and stubbornness of his immediate predecessor; but if so, Lincoln gambled on a tactical craftsmanship which was wholly lacking in Burnside. He spent the month of November 1862 in a state of blind depression; he lacked confidence and, like other commanders who seek a refuge from their responsibilities, began a drastic bout of reorganization and renaming of formations. The existing corps structure was scrapped and replaced by three "grand divisions," the left under William B. Franklin, the center under Joseph Hooker, and the right under Edwin V. Sumner. With this expedient he attempted to tighten command and control by coordinating several corps under the control of one general officer. The idea made a lot of tactical sense because the fighting power of individual Union corps was far inferior to Confederate ones, but such reorganizations always damage morale and the men were soon ill disposed toward their new commander. Another perhaps more pressing matter irritated them—they had not been paid for several months.[15]

Before his dismissal, McClellan had begun to advance southward, hugging the Blue Ridge Mountains, and had reached Warrenton. Burnside disliked this avenue of approach because it served to expose his lines of communication to the kind of depredation that had so infuriated and unhinged John Pope. Furthermore, the president had urged on McClellan the desirability of taking an indirect approach on Richmond that would force Lee to leave the Shenandoah Valley.

Burnside followed this advice and transferred operations to the tidewater coast and advanced toward the pretty town of Fredericksburg on the sinuous Rappahannock River. The Virginia roads were, as usual, glutinous and movement was not easy. On November 12 Burnside sent his plan that would involve a rapid advance on Fredericksburg and thence to Richmond, with feints toward either Culpeper or Gordonsville, to Halleck. He did not approve, perhaps because the Army of the Potomac was abandoning its central position. Halleck also had the military bureaucrat's talent for ensuring that his opposition to any venture was well recorded, so that in the event of a disaster, he could not be held accountable. Further limitations on this supposed "modern" general staff system would be revealed by the campaign. One further legacy of the Pope regime was noted: a tendency toward lawlessness and plundering that went far beyond merely "subsisting off the country."[16]

The president approved Burnside's plan, though not with an excess of enthusiasm, mainly because he preferred his own more audacious and imaginative scheme. This had not gained the approbation of Halleck or Burnside, mainly because it required the cooperation of the US Navy in transporting troops down the Rappahannock and up the Pamunkey in an attempt to break the defensive power of the Virginia river system. Lincoln nonetheless said on November 14 that Burnside's plan would succeed if he moved rapidly. This Burnside managed to do, arriving at Fredericksburg on November 17. Then his advance ground to a halt, due to staff inefficiency that resulted from confusion over precise roles. Burnside believed that forwarding the pontoon bridges to Falmouth should have been Halleck's responsibility, but Burnside was ultimately responsible for all the preparations for the campaign of the army under his command, not Halleck. They had been left on the upper Potomac and were not dispatched from Washington until November 19. It was a classic staff blunder all too characteristic of cross purposes and amateurishness. Burnside could not cross the river in force and many men were to pay for this carelessness with their lives. Although the south back of the Rappahannock was unguarded, Burnside foolishly decided not to hold it. Once more feeble intelligence and poor reconnaissance were to fail a Union commander, and Burnside sat down and waited.[17]

Rain fell in torrents, slowing all movement. Some of Burnside's grand divisional commanders, notably Joseph Hooker, began to mutter complaints about the whole design. General Lee, although initially caught off guard, had reacted with dispatch to the federal movement. In a perceptive report to Jefferson Davis, he predicted that Burnside would have little alternative but to continue with his movement, for to "change his base of operations the effect produced in the

United States would be almost equivalent to a defeat." Thus Burnside would "persevere . . . and the longer we can delay him and throw him into the winter, the more difficult will be his undertaking. It is for this reason that I have determined to resist him at the outset, and to throw every obstacle in the way of his advance." The Army of Northern Virginia had recovered from its ill-fated Maryland venture; on November 6 the corps structure had been formalized and Jackson and Longstreet acquired the rank of lieutenant general; the huge number of stragglers and lightly wounded (Antietam had produced a disproportionate number of these in the large casualty bill) had returned to the ranks (twenty thousand in the first eight days of October alone) and morale was high. By November 10 the army numbered 70,909 men with the promise of six thousand reinforcements. "It was never in better health or in better condition for battle than now," Lee reported proudly. In short, the damage inflicted by Antietam has been much exaggerated by Lee's critics.[18]

Lee had long believed that the Union forces would advance southward. Longstreet was set in motion for the tidewater and by November 5 he had reached Culpeper Court House. Stonewall Jackson was left in the valley, mainly for logistical reasons; Jackson could subsist comfortably there and those resources could be denied to the enemy. Yet Lee hoped to dislocate Burnside's movements by maintaining this strong flanking position—"to threaten the enemy's flank and rear"—especially if Jackson could strike at Manassas Junction, which would force Burnside to retreat. But it was never Lee's intention to seek any decisive military decision on the Rappahannock line. "I now do not anticipate making a determined stand north of the north Anna [River]," he confided to Jackson. Thus Lee had decided on what Hattaway and Jones correctly describe as a "Fabian" strategy. But Lee could not afford to give up the area of the Rappahannock and its communications with the Shenandoah for logistical reasons. Consequently, he would time Jackson's removal from the valley carefully, oppose Burnside for as long as possible, and then withdraw southward. "I think it more advantageous" he argued, "to retire to the Annas and give battle than on the banks of the Rappahannock." Ultimately, logistical weakness was the decisive factor that governed Lee's operational distribution.[19]

The other notable factor was reconnaissance. Here the Army of Northern Virginia's cavalry excelled. Burnside's cavalry by comparison proved feeble and ineffective. Stuart had been warned of "the necessity . . . of watching him [Burnside] closely," and buoyed up by another "ride" around McClellan's army before the latter's dismissal, he did so. On November 18, Stuart crossed to the north bank of the Rappahannock and found the Army of the Potomac moving eastward. Leaving Jackson full discretion as to the timing of his movements, Lee apprised him of this urgent intelligence. Longstreet was ordered to Fredericksburg and Jackson was ordered to join the army on November 27, arriving on December 1. It is clear from this distribution that if Burnside had crossed the Rappahannock on November 17, he would have caught Lee wrongfooted. What has been less well known is the extent of the tensions and jealousies that seethed under the placid calm of military efficiency in the Army of Northern Virginia. It had been claimed, mainly prompted by D. H. Hill, that Jackson felt some irritation with Lee throughout this campaign for supposedly favoring Longstreet; and the latter, with a keen eye to his future, was writing sycophantic letters to Joseph E. Johnston, now recovering from wounds suffered at Seven Pines. For should this senior general return to command, either in the west or in Virginia (Lee was, after all, his temporary replacement), he could have an important influence on Longstreet's hopes for future promotion. It was a tribute to Lee's tact, guile, and force of personality that these tensions were not allowed to break out into the open as they did all too frequently in the west.[20]

For ten days the two armies faced each other across the Rappahannock. Lee occupied a series of elongated hills on the south bank, the strongest of which was Marye's Heights, a low ridge running behind the town. There were few trees on this position, though many on the hills stretching southward. Longstreet occupied Marye's Heights, Jackson the high ground around Prospect Hill further to the south. The position was strong, but not that strong; in short, though it was more formidable than at Antietam, it was far from being impregnable. It is interesting (or surprising) to note, following the harsh criticism of Grant for not putting his army behind field fortifications at Shiloh, that Lee did not immediately dig in. Braxton Bragg repeated the error at Murfreesboro at about the same time. The Confederates invested much labor in cutting roads through the woods (the Military Road that ran parallel along the hills helped to integrate the position), digging gun pits, and constructing lateral communications, but Lee's headquarters issued no order requiring the army to entrench. Longstreet partly did so on Marye's Heights, but Jackson did not. Much use was made of a stone wall in front of a road running parallel along the heights; soldiers dug rifle pits on their own initiative, constructed abattis, and exploited railroad cuts. Jackson enjoyed the advantage of thick woods, which many considered impenetrable, an excessively sanguine opinion. Lee has been criticized for not entrenching and after Antietam it has weight. Yet he never *planned* to fight a serious engagement at Fredericksburg. He did not think that Burnside would be so foolish as to attack him in a frontal assault; and he believed that Burnside was waiting for further operations to develop. Lee thus gave lateral communications a higher priority than entrenchment. In addition, he may have thought it more politic to let Jackson go his own way if he had heard hints of his disaffection.[21]

In the event, the decision as to whether a battle should be fought at Fredericksburg was taken out of Lee's hands. If he was to attack Lee and build the necessary bridges, then Burnside needed to occupy the town and cross to the south back of the Rappahannock. Confederate pickets and snipers had occupied houses in Fredericksburg. Doubtless with a nod toward his backers in the Joint Committee on the Conduct of the War, Burnside bombarded the town on December 11 and then occupied it. Having contemplated but then rejected turning Lee's right by seizing Hamilton's crossing, Burnside believed that an assault on the Confederate position would be so unexpected as to take Lee by surprise; in this he was probably correct. But in unraveling Burnside's intentions the historian must distinguish between what he intended at the time and how he explained away his colossal failure later. This failure was excused by the Joint Committee and, as was customary with its judgments, a subordinate was blamed for the failures of the commanding general (who tended to be a protégé of McClellan). The unlucky scapegoat on this occasion would be Major General William B. Franklin.[22]

Thanks to lamentable reconnaissance Burnside was under the impression that he faced only a fragment (perhaps Longstreet's corps) of the rebel army. Burnside commanded a force of 120,000 men; each "grand division" contained approximately forty thousand men. Sumner's grand division was to take Marye's Heights, while that of Franklin moved to the south to ascertain the position of the enemy. This latter move was represented by Burnside in his testimony before the Joint Committee as an outflanking move that should have struck Lee's right and rolled it up as Franklin swung north, thus making Sumner's mission easier. Franklin denied hotly that it was ever agreed that such was his task. The evidence supports him, as Burnside's orders stipulated an attack with one division with "its line of retreat open." This later unseemly exchange illustrated another grave defect. Burnside was inarticulate—he could not communicate; neither his superiors nor his subordinates were very clear as to what his precise intentions were. Hooker denounced the plan to cross and attack at Fredricksburg. Sumner proved more supportive but the exchanges among senior officers further undermined confidence in Burnside's judgment. Doubt and misunderstanding seemed to be the order of the day.[23]

At about 10 AM on December 13 the mist cleared over the battlefield revealing the Army of the Potomac then arrayed for battle, a sight of such

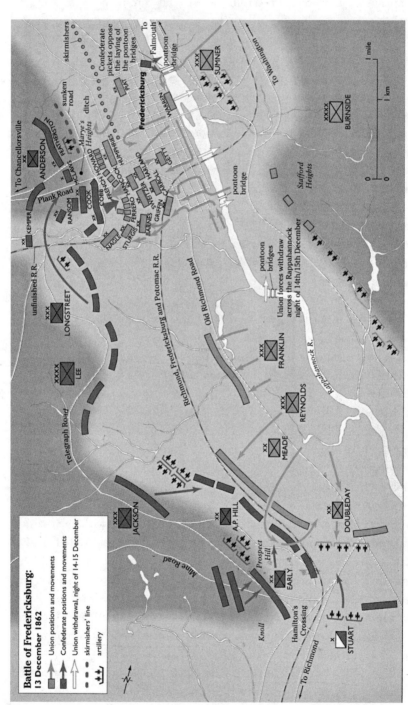

From *An Atlas of American Military History* by James C. Bradford (New York: Cynthia Parzych Publishing, 2003).

splendor that it made a deep impression on both Lee and Longstreet. By comparison, the Confederate army was concealed, doubtless adding to Burnside's confusion. With such a level of disorder and ambiguity, the battle moved forward, toward its hardly preordained but grim conclusion. The federal soldiers showed astonishing bravery as their lives were paid forfeit for the absence of sensible tactics. The Union artillery managed to suppress Confederate artillery fire, especially on the Union left where the Confederates lost eleven guns in the exchanges, so that the infantry could advance; once they were deployed, however, hedges, fences, and ditches broke up unit cohesion and the tightly packed formations became easy and inviting targets for Longstreet's artillery. Lee and his generals were amazed that Burnside's main thrust was being made on the Union right against the rock of the strongest part of Lee's line. No attacks were made in the vicinity of Deep Run, the weakest part of the Confederate line, a potential fissure between the two Confederate corps. Burnside might have intended this as demonstration. Yet riddled with indecision, Burnside pleaded that the assault was neither a feint nor a full-blooded assault. At noon Sumner's entire "grand division" was thrown forward on the Union right, but its units were sent into the attack piecemeal; the great fighting power of this magnificent but ill-used Union force was frittered away. No less than six great assaults diffused in time and space were sent forward at Marye's Heights (individual units made many more charges), and these waves of blue were swept back by volleys of such ferocity, supported by artillery fire, that they never got closer to the stone wall than a depression in the ground one hundred yards distant. "It seems as if our Company and Regiment were all gone," wrote one Connecticut soldier. The 5th New Hampshire, 7th New York, and 81st Pennsylvania infantry regiments all lost two-thirds of their strength.

Burnside then seemed to lose his head. He had thrown Sumner's troops forward early in the hope of aiding the advance on the Union left when Sumner's advance should have been dependent on Franklin's progress—not a means of securing it. The logic of Burnside's plan lay in ruins. Like a neurotic, compulsive gambler who knew the stake was beyond his resources, Burnside kept expending more and more of his capital with increasingly frantic throws of the dice. His only response to the repulse of Sumner's "grand division" was at about 2:30 PM to commit Hooker's "grand division" in further headlong attacks. Hooker made no attempt to conceal his contempt for these dispositions. Nonetheless, the surge of federal infantry toward Longstreet's corps looked impressive. Lee observed to Longstreet, "General, they are massing very heavily and will break your line, I am afraid." To which Longstreet replied, "if every man on the other side of the Potomac" approached his corps "give me plenty of ammunition, I will kill them all before they reach my line." He then warned, "Look to your right; you are in some danger there but not on my line."[24]

Longstreet was correct. The Confederate triumph on this sector could easily have been negated by failure to the south. Momentarily the situation on the right flank caused Lee some anxiety. There was more space on the right for maneuver and should this flank be turned, the Army of Northern Virginia would be cut off from the Telegraph Road. The Telegraph Road ran at a forty-five-degree angle across the Confederate position and headed southwest from Lee's Hill, occupied by the commanding general. It intersected with the Military Road that ran along the spine of Jackson's line at a ninety-degree angle. If Franklin had seized this point and driven in the Confederate center from the rear, then Lee's army could have been destroyed.

In the first significant move of the battle at about 10:30 AM, Meade's Third Division of "Baldy" Smith's Sixth Corps crossed the Rappahannock south of Fredericksburg and then the Richmond–Fredericksburg–Potomac Railroad line held by skirmishers and horse artillery. It advanced up the ridge behind the railroad so quickly that it caught Gregg's South Carolinian brigade by surprise. Part of two of Jackson's divisions still moving into place, Gregg had carelessly relied on the troops in front to give him warning of an enemy approach, which was not forthcoming. By midday Meade's men reached the top of Prospect Hill and cut the Military Road that ran along it. A breakthrough seemed likely and Gregg paid for the error with his life. Franklin was ordered by Burnside to push on but dallied. (Burnside's plan had not specified a great onslaught.) Jackson sent in reserves, including Hood's division loaned by Longstreet, and Meade was forced back. It was the rushing forward of one of Hood's North Carolinian brigades that prompted Lee's famous observation, "It is well that war is so terrible—we should grow too fond of it." For most of the battle, unlike at Antietam, Lee was a spectator. Fredericksburg shows his devolved system of command working at its best.[25]

The completeness of Lee's victory—having inflicted terrible damage on the Union army for such comparatively light losses (12,600, to Lee's 5,300, with a high percentage of lightly wounded)—has led to suggestions that he should have launched an immediate counterattack. The morale of Burnside's army was so shattered that a decisive victory was in Lee's grasp. This claim seems rather exaggerated. Lee had won Fredericksburg with a slender margin for error. "The slightest straw," Meade wrote with asperity, "would have kept the tide in our favor." The federal army's position on the Stafford Heights was stronger than Lee's, and its artillery remained powerful. Lee was still greatly outnumbered. On the contrary, he expected the attack to be renewed, and the night of December 13 was spent entrenching. Burnside had indeed ordered a renewal of the assault; at one point he contemplated leading his old Ninth Corps himself on a suicide charge up Marye's Heights but he was dissuaded by cooler and more prudent voices. On December 15 Burnside withdrew the Army of the Potomac to the north side of the Rappahannock. The main reason for the defeat was himself. The casual approach to planning and operations that had served him so well in North Carolina was quite out of place in operations of this scale and intensity. His indecision and fumbling had led to frontal assaults of the crudest kind. Faith in the potency of the frontal assault would die hard in the Civil War. In truth, something resembling the frontal assault was always necessary in nineteenth-century warfare. However, sending troops forward in uncoordinated torrents—in which overall fighting power became fragmented by allowing brigades to advance unsupported—was not the solution to the tactical conundrum.[26]

The battle of Fredericksburg was not devoid of strategic benefit for the South. It threw the Union cause into disarray and the Lincoln administration was plunged into despair. Burnside's conduct of affairs was severely criticized by Franklin and Major General W. F. Smith in a letter to the president; other senior officers actively voiced the view that the army had no faith in Burnside. He obstinately planned to renew operations on the Rappahannock but his subordinates feared another disaster. The poor opinion of the soldiers was not retrieved by these moves, derided as "Burnside's Mud March." Burnside demanded that the president relieve his critics forthwith (as well as Halleck and Stanton). Burnside was in no position to make such demands and he was relieved instead. Lincoln also had to face simultaneously a cabinet crisis. His adroit tactics foiled an attempt, orchestrated by the treasury secretary, Salmon P. Chase, to remove the secretary of state, William H. Seward. This would have resulted in a cabinet more attuned to the radical view of war aims and strategy. Lincoln was determined not to allow one faction or lobby to dominate his cabinet and restrict his room for maneuver.[27]

But in this tough struggle to keep his head above the surging water thrown forward by a sea of troubles, Lincoln turned to affairs in the west to seek relief and succor. He was determined on an offensive in Tennessee to relieve Unionists from secessionist persecution. The new commander of Union troops, shortly to be designated the Army of the Cumberland, William S. Rosecrans, was an efficient organizer and strategist of some insight; but like his antagonist Bragg, he found the conduct of battles an intolerable strain and was subject to a degree of indecision that sometimes resulted in command paralysis. Here was another general who found the burden of responsibility of commanding at the higher level not an easy load to carry. Nonetheless, he sought to please by engaging the Confederates as close to Nashville as he could contrive, and to "crush them in a decisive battle."

Yet Rosecrans faced very real logistical problems in advancing through the inhospitable country before Chattanooga, and even allowing for the logistical self-indulgence and waste to which Union armies were prone, he was quite correct to insist on sustainable supply lines for his troops. This necessity seems to have been too casually brushed aside by critics such as T. Harry Williams. Furthermore, the priority given to Rosecrans's advance is not evidence that the Lincoln administration saw the east as merely a holding operation to keep Lee away from Washington while "They looked to the West, particularly to Grant, for their important achievements." This was how matters turned out but things were not consciously planned that way, let alone foreordained. Comparative lack of success in the east had more to do with weaknesses of command and personality than from any lessening of the demands made upon the generals; on the contrary, Lincoln made demands on them that were beyond their capacity to fulfill. In short, by the turn of the new year in 1863, the Lincoln administration was still demanding that its generals on all fronts simultaneously implement a strategy of annihilation and exhaustion.[28]

Bragg's reputation had been clouded by the outcome of the Kentucky campaign. Much criticism had resulted from his cantankerous behavior and acid tongue. The most bitter denunciation, however, came from Kentuckians who deplored the abandonment of their state even though their fellow citizens had shown such a marked reluctance to be "redeemed." They particularly resented some acerbic remarks Bragg had made about Kentuckians' lack of enthusiasm for fighting. Bragg's insistence on shooting Corporal Asa Lewis of the 6th Kentucky Infantry for desertion, which came near to provoking a mutiny among Kentucky troops, further poisoned relations; it added John C. Breckinridge to Bragg's formidable list of enemies. Bragg was undeterred and demonstrated his customary administrative zeal: the troops were reorganized, reequipped, and deserters returned to the ranks. Despite the storm of abuse, President Davis stood by his commander and then turned his attention to the command system.[29]

To give operations in the west some semblance of unity, the now-convalesced Joseph E. Johnston was given command of the newly created Department of the West. Bragg was in favor of this appointment; he even claimed that he had suggested it. Yet the old deficiencies were not removed. Johnston's powers were defined ambiguously. "The arrangement," Davis explained afterward, "was intended to secure the fullest cooperation of the troops in those departments and at the same time to avoid delay by putting the commander of each department in direct correspondence with the War Office." The last phase indicated that the administration (which meant Davis) was determined to reserve to itself the final decision on everything. The established bureaucratic procedures, which hampered dynamic military decision making but to which Davis was so dedicated, remained in force and hedged Johnston's authority about with significant qualifications. Johnston reacted to these limitations by complaining persistently that he felt inadequately supported by his political masters. Furthermore, the structure was muddled by a persistent expectation that Johnston would assume field command of either the forces in Mississippi or Tennessee when he deemed it appropriate. This is, of course, a very significant misconception of the period. Davis, after two and a half years of war, still failed to distinguish between the talents and duties required of the commander of an army, and those required of a commander of a group of armies. This failure indicates the severely constricted insight that he enjoyed not only of the very different qualities that these positions demand, but of the adjustment of thought and perspective that they dictate.[30]

The winter months of 1862–63 had witnessed the growing influence of what was later called the western concentration bloc. The intellectual inspiration of this group, which was very critical of Davis's conduct of the war, was Beauregard. Beauregard had made something of a fetish of concentration, which the Southern armies sorely needed. His strategic nostrums made some sense but his demands were excessive and his claims extravagant. He argued that the Confederacy should concentrate its strength against Union weakness. This weak link he perceived was Rosecrans's Army of the Cumberland. The object must be the occupation of Kentucky. Needless to say, this ultimate goal sounded like the sweet strains of a Mozart piano concerto in the ears of the vociferous Kentucky lobby. To fulfill this concentration Beauregard sought troops from the Army of Northern Virginia, thus endangering a concentration already successfully made. Beauregard, by exploiting his powerful political and newspaper contacts, including Texas Senator Louis T. Wigfall, perhaps Davis's most unrelenting critic, intended his plans to serve as a springboard to prepare the ground for his own triumphant return to field command.[31]

This whole question raised the problem of competing strategic priorities, the resolution of which the Confederate military system (like that of the Union) was so ill equipped to achieve. In the first instance the plan overlooked the very real problem that the seizure of Richmond was a pressing objective of the Lincoln administration; its loss would be an irretrievable catastrophe. A significant reduction in the size of the Army of Northern Virginia would render holding Richmond as well as Virginia and the Carolinas, in face of overwhelming superiority, well nigh impossible. Any hope of foreign intervention would be dashed, and the loss of prestige would sound the Confederacy's death knell. However important objectives were in the west, Virginia remained *politically* the most sensitive theater. It could not be risked, and Beauregard simply ignored this urgent grand strategical reality, as indeed have those historians who see the west as the key to the Confederacy's survival.[32]

The demand for concentration in Tennessee, which Johnston enthusiastically took up, also blurred any solution as to what should be done about the deteriorating position in Mississippi and especially around the city of Vicksburg. Johnston regarded Tennessee as his primary concern. Vicksburg and the control of the upper Mississippi were relegated to secondary status. In fashioning the new Department of the West, Davis had wanted Johnston to coordinate both theaters of operations based on the "security in the concentration and rapid movement of troops." Yet the departmental system of command, the poor state of Southern railroads, and the need to constantly defer to Richmond all slowed down the process by which these disputes were considered and decisions made. Indeed, these structural deficiencies were exacerbated by Davis's dispute with his secretary of war, George W. Randolph. Randolph paid close attention to affairs in the west. But he chaffed under Davis's relish for paperwork, his failure to distinguish between the important and the trivial, and his overbearing ways.

In particular, he disliked Davis's penchant for innumerable and interminable meetings—a device so often preferred by the insecure, who instinctively wish to delay the making of decisions. Inevitably the most powerful member at any meeting, namely its chairman, had the last word on matters of vexed controversy, even if that word was to decide not to make a decision. Obviously, other members called to the meeting could contribute to the discussion, but Davis's conciliar approach was essentially a device that promoted cumbersome overcentralization and stifled initiative. The departmental heads were not allowed to get on and run their departments. Moreover, it fed Davis's passion for detail. Randolph was called to account for his attempts at independence in giving orders in the Trans-Mississippi Department and he finally resigned in November 1862. By this date war department business had ground to a halt.[33]

In December 1862 Davis conferred with Johnston and Bragg at Murfreesboro, Tennessee. Despite their pleas, Davis decided to send most of Kirby Smith's corps of twelve thousand men to Mississippi and ordered Johnston there. Davis had a far keener appreciation of the military importance of Vicks-

burg than any of his generals. This was not just another example of Davis
wanting to defend everything for political reasons. Johnston opposed the
decision on the grounds that the Mississippi was a more effective defensive line
than it was avenue of advance and he was uninterested in the affairs of the Trans-
Mississippi. Bragg was opposed to reductions in the strength of his army.
Although his troops enjoyed control of the Cumberland Gap, they only
numbered forty-seven thousand before Kirby Smith was detached. Beauregard
had paid little attention to Vicksburg because it contradicted his cry of concentration (which became something of a sacred cow). When in May 1863 the
deterioration of affairs in Mississippi demanded Beauregard's attention, he
merely adjusted his plan so that, once Rosecrans had been defeated, Bragg's
forces would sweep triumphantly westward and cut Grant's communications.
Beauregard seemed to envisage the movement of armies as akin to an army of
ants, munching as they moved. He always neglected logistics in his grandiose,
unrealistic conceptions.[34]

After the Kentucky setback Bragg had turned his face against another offensive. He awaited Rosecrans's move at Murfreesboro, but not passively. In
December 1862 six thousand cavalry were dispatched under brigadier generals
John Hunt Morgan and Nathan Bedford Forrest to attack the Union lines of
communication west of Nashville. Johnston hoped these raids would disrupt
Grant's advance on Vicksburg. Morgan's "Christmas Raid" was a great success;
it was directed just as much against private property as against military property, as retaliation for Union attacks on Southern civilians and their homes that
had been increasing since the summer. This success was due to the continuing
weaknesses of Union cavalry; it was futile pursuing cavalry with infantry, and
Rosecrans immediately addressed the problem by organizing dragoons—
mounted infantry. These would greatly reduce Morgan's effectiveness in 1863.
Like several other Confederate commanders, the upheaval of war provided
Morgan with marital opportunity and he married a young woman much his
junior. The charms of matrimony weakened his attachment to guerrilla warfare.
He became less dedicated to hit-and-run tactics, of eluding a stronger foe, and
minimizing casualties, and more to reducing the length of his raids, to taking
greater risks, and to attacking the enemy frontally so that he could return to his
beloved at the earliest opportunity. Forrest, with vigor and determination,
struck railroads; and Van Dorn (with Pemberton's cavalry) hit Grant's supply
base at Holly Springs, completely destroying his stocks and forcing him to
abandon his first attempt against Vicksburg.[35]

On learning news of Rosecrans's advance from Nashville on December 26,

1862, Bragg took up a defensive position in front of Murfreesboro where he could control the road junctions. But the position lacked naturally strong geographical features: The fields were open, the woods could conceal an attacker's advance, and he had his back to Stones River. Yet he did not entrench his position—a significant blunder. Bragg was still effectively his own chief of staff and prone to overwork, and this error exacerbated his limitations as a tactician. Fortunately for Bragg, his error was matched by Rosecrans. The Union general's advance had caught Bragg napping with his army subsisting, spread out over a front of thirty-five miles. Yet Rosecrans had logistical problems of his own. The roads were poor, he lacked staff officers and adequate maps, and he was dependent on vulnerable railroads. He also, like Buell, found it difficult to coordinate his columns with semaphore in the wooded terrain. He had been put under pressure to advance by Halleck. "If you remain one more week at Nashville," he had been warned by the general-in-chief, "I cannot prevent your removal." Rosecrans was thus keen to bring matters to the proof at the earliest opportunity.[36]

In the same way that the commanders' errors canceled one another out, so did their respective inspirations. Rosecrans intended to hold with his right, strike Bragg's army with his left, and seize the high ground that enclosed the Confederate right flank. He placed great faith in the moral power of his troops in the attack. Nonetheless, like Burnside, he had communicated his plans indifferently and his subordinates were unclear on the details. Rosecrans had organized his army into three "wings," the right under Alexander McCook, the left under Thomas Crittenden, and in the center the largest (32,936 men) under George H. Thomas. He issued a general order imploring soldiers to "Keep ranks. Do not throw away your fire. Fire slowly, deliberately. . . . Close steadily in upon the enemy, and, when you get within charging distance, rush on him with the bayonet."

Bragg issued what amounted to a carbon copy of this order. His actual scheme of attack was audacious and imaginative. Joseph Wheeler and the cavalry were to strike at Rosecrans's vulnerable lines of communication. Eighty percent of his remaining thirty-five thousand men would pivot on his right flank and strike a powerful blow against Rosecrans's right flank; it was Perryville in reverse. The object was the Nashville Pike Road, the seizure of which would cut off Rosecrans's retreat. Bragg's order declared, "the general desires that your attack shall be vigorous and persistent. In so doing, keep up the touch of elbows to the right, in order that the line may be unbroken." Given that the operational designs of both commanders were moving in diagrammatically opposite directions in what B. H. Liddell Hart would later call a "revolving door," it was just a matter of who struck first. Bragg gave evidence of greater audacity when his

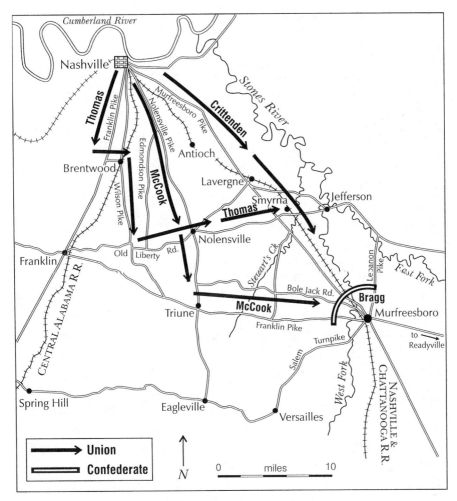

9. The Stones River campaign

Reprinted from *Banners to the Breeze: The Kentucky Campaign, Corinth and Stones River* by Earl J. Hess, by permission of the University of Nebraska Press. © 2000 by the University of Nebraska Press.

cavalry commander, Joseph Wheeler, emulated Stuart and "rode around" the Army of the Cumberland. Bragg then launched his attack on Rosecrans's position west of Murfreesboro at 6 AM on December 31.[37]

Tactically, it was perhaps unwise of Bragg to strike first. The broken ground disrupted the cohesion of Bragg's attack despite the importance he attached to it. Stones River also flows through the middle of the battlefield with operations being mounted on both banks. The real fault was a repetition of the errors of Perryville: clumsy, ill-coordinated, and rash attacks were thrown forward, which dissipated Confederate fighting power for no commensurate gain. The artillery was also mishandled, not opening fire until the infantry had occupied positions for it, and it spent hours moving uselessly around the battlefield. The attack took Rosecrans's army completely by surprise. Yet despite Bragg's skillful husbanding, his strength was eroded rapidly as the Union right was forced back but not broken. The Confederate attack then ran up against Rosecrans's center, which had prepared for the onslaught by strengthening a disused railway embankment. Rosecrans showed great moral courage and powers of leadership in holding his army together. As at Shiloh, the Union forces were pushed back but their cohesion was not shattered. There was nothing inevitable about this process; it was the result of Bragg virtually abdicating tactical control of the attack. Bragg needed reinforcements to maintain the momentum; he intended to draw these from the right but they took several hours to arrive from Major General John C. Breckinridge's division that had been posted to guard the flank; then they were wasted in driblets. After the war, there was talk of lost opportunities as Liddell's brigade claimed to have cut the Nashville pike. Yet Grady McWhiney is justified in supposing that even if reserves had been found they would have been frittered away in weak and unsupported attacks. Murfreesboro once again illustrates the fundamental weakness of Southern generalship throughout the war: its inability to make the most of its offensive power. Thus by common consent, amid mutual exhaustion, the first day's fighting ended.[38]

That night Rosecrans summoned a meeting of his wing commanders and asked them whether he should pull back to Nashville. Accounts of its deliberations vary, but Rosecrans decided to stand and fight it out. On the second day, January 1, 1863, Bragg renewed the contest and after much hard fighting his troops seized most of the Round Forest, which served as the pivot of Rosecrans's tenacious defense, but this success did not prove fatal to the Union position. On January 2 the battle continued once more and Bragg decided to attack again. This time he shifted his attack to the right bank of Stones River, ordering Breckinridge's division forward to strike the Union left. Its initial progress was

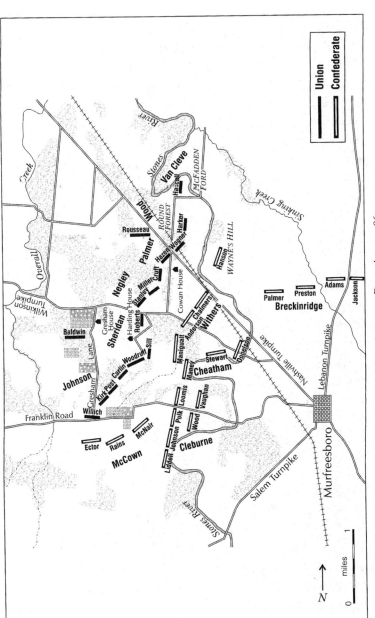

10. Stones River, 6:30 A.M., December 31, 1862

Reprinted from *Banners to the Breeze: The Kentucky Campaign, Corinth and Stones River* by Earl J. Hess, by permission of the University of Nebraska Press. © 2000 by the University of Nebraska Press.

good and drove Brigadier General John Beatty's federal brigade back. But Rose-crans had massed a grand battery of fifty-seven guns in the center of his position at McFadden's Ford on Stones River. From this bluff the Union artillery could enfilade Breckinridge's troops with impunity. Colonel Brent, who acted as Bragg's chief of staff throughout the battle, recorded in his diary that "A mur-derous fire was opened upon them. . . . It was a terrible affair, although short." The Union divisions of brigadier generals Jefferson C. Davis and Milo S. Has-call quickly restored Rosecrans's line. Breckinridge's ill-fated attack fitted the pattern of piecemeal Confederate assaults that so disfigured this battle. "From a rapid advance," Crittenden wrote, "they broke at once into a rapid retreat." Bragg's army was simply too small, as before Perryville, to launch operations of a decisive nature. If Bragg's intention had been to guard east Tennessee, then it would have been better to await Rosecrans's attack and then launch a counter-stroke. As matters turned out, to paraphrase Siegfried Sassoon, he did for his army by his mode of attack. His men had been in the open for five days; they were wet, exhausted, and outnumbered. Polk and Hardee urged him to with-draw. By noon on January 3 Bragg ordered a retreat east of Stones River.[39]

The messy tactical handling of Murfreesboro on both sides—though on Rosecrans's it was characterized by a stubborn tenacity that does him credit—is illustrative of what occurs when two generals who have an aptitude for opera-tional artistry are mediocre tacticians: their two armies simply collide in confu-sion. Yet another drawn, indecisive battle illustrates the question of deadlock in the American Civil War. Although the news of Bragg's withdrawal came as sweet tidings to the beleaguered Lincoln,[40] it was an encounter bereft of strategic results. It is now appropriate to review tactical developments at this midpoint in the war's course and discuss the reasons for the many changes that had been forced on the generals.

The development of tactics is based on weapon power, those weapons that are available and deployed. Because of the impact of the Industrial Revolution and the technological improvement that was in the vanguard of this upheaval, in the opinion of Major General J. F. C. Fuller, "tactics when compared to strategy have become the more uncertain branch of the art of war." The most important point arising out of this flux was that it both enhanced and ham-pered the utility of fighting power. The other important factor bearing on tac-tics was mass involvement. Both the Union and the Confederacy raised huge armies. Yet their actual forces in the field were smaller than Napoleonic armies, often even smaller than Wellington's army in the Peninsula. The inherent problem of communication and coordination of these forces can be exaggerated.

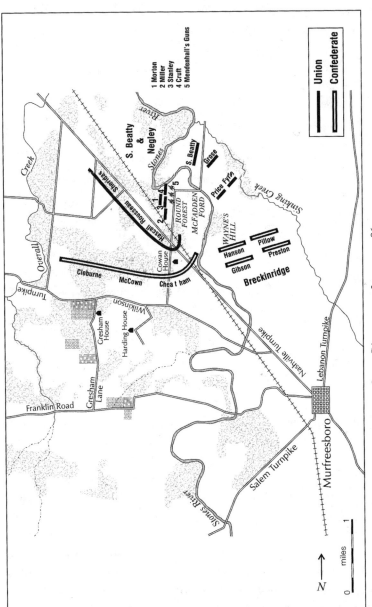

II. Stones River, 4 P.M., January 2, 1863

Reprinted from *Banners to the Breeze: The Kentucky Campaign, Corinth and Stones River* by Earl J. Hess, by permission of the University of Nebraska Press. © 2000 by the University of Nebraska Press.

Of the 350,000 men mustered into the Confederate service in 1863, Lee's Army of Northern Virginia rarely fielded more than 75,000, Bragg often 20,000 to 40,000. The generals demanded larger armies but a combination of political factors, high wastage rates arising from the dual system of raising armies and competition between federal and state authority, and the intensity of operations combined to keep Civil War armies small by comparison with the numbers of troops raised. Certainly on the Union side there were no logistical reasons for this restriction, though as logistics were constantly neglected in the Confederate war department, this is patently a factor reducing the size of Southern concentrations.[41]

Nonetheless, the Union troops had no decisive advantage over Confederate troops in weaponry. Both sides were equipped largely with the rifled musket, which had increased both the range and the intensity of infantry fire. Thus, although the skirmish line and loose formations had increased in importance before 1861, the main tactical act remained bringing a well-aligned mass of infantry onto the battlefield, sending forward the charge so that it would close with the enemy's position, punish him with a volley, and then close with the bayonet. The moral power of the charge was elevated and "manly": this was obviously a legacy of prewar sentimentality; yet it was pervasive. At Fredericksburg Hooker ordered that his "grand division" was not to load its rifled muskets and would attack only with the bayonet. Dense, close-order formations remained important. The favored formation for an attack was in two lines. If the attackers paused on the open ground to get a shot in, they exposed themselves even longer to the defender's fire. Therefore, although the shock of the assault still remained important, large-scale bayonet fights remained largely a product of the imagination.[42]

Because of the avalanche of projectiles thrown at them, soldiers sought out shelter: sunken lanes, stone walls, rail fences, and railway embankments were favorites. At Second Manassas and Murfreesboro, Confederate and Union troops respectively had made effective use of railway embankments; at Fredericksburg four lines of infantry deployed in four brigades sheltered behind the stone wall and lost less than eight hundred men. Lee became so impressed by the effectiveness of fieldworks that he issued an order that the entire army entrench along the Fredericksburg position after the battle. Sunken roads were far less effective, as the "bloody lane" at Antietam showed. Until 1863 entrenching was the exception rather than the rule. It was resorted to as a base from which to launch an offensive, as Lee had before the Seven Days' battles, but until Fredericksburg he seemed to believe that entrenching impeded the offensive. The most important exception was McClellan's use of breastworks in the Peninsula. Jefferson Davis immediately discerned McClellan's intention. "We must find if possible the means to get at him without putting the breasts of our men in antagonism to his heaps of earth," he explained to his wife. Yet McClellan's halting and fumbling advance discredited entrenchments and engineers and led to a renewed emphasis, especially among politicians, on the moral strength of the bayonet attack. This influence was seen at its most crass during the battle of Fredericksburg.[43]

The artillery remained a most powerful weapon on Civil War battlefields. Napoleon had strengthened the attack by concentrating his guns and sending them forward with the infantry charge. Braxton Bragg attempted to repeat these tactics at Murfreesboro without success. The prime reason for his failure was that long-ranged massed artillery had become a devastating weapon in defense against the infantry charge. By sending the infantry forward without artillery support but with their guns, Bragg permitted Rosecrans's grand battery to devastate Breckinridge's division with impunity, thus greatly increasing the barrage of fire that his infantry faced in the assault. Using rifled muskets, which had longer range than smoothbore muskets of the Mexican War, any defending infantry could also pick off enemy gunners quite easily as they sat on limbers or horses moving their pieces forward. After they unlimbered and set up their cannon, artillerists offered even better targets for the rifled muskets, at ranges up to six hundred yards. Thus centralized artillery tactics would punish severely any breakdown in the cooperation of arms or in the cohesion of the attack on both sides, for feebly organized offensive efforts were all too numerous in 1862. Yet artillery was far from omnipotent. The campaigns of 1862 would demonstrate that, though rifling had increased the range of artillery fire, it could do little damage to men sheltering behind entrenched positions; this would require shrapnel that was not introduced until after the Civil War.[44]

All of these significant tactical developments have led to a certain pessimistic strain in American historiography. The most important themes of some works are the invulnerability of Civil War armies in the defense; the strength of the tactical defense; the corresponding importance, for the Confederacy especially, of the strategic defense; the unassailable character of entrenched defenses; and, consequently, the utter indecisiveness of battle. The majority of Civil War historians seem to have concluded that the attack was a hopeless affair. Clearly, these themes cannot be airily disregarded. Yet they have attained a degree of universal and uncritical acceptance that has had a distorting effect on the subject. Nothing seems to have depressed more than failure. *If* Lee had shattered

McClellan's cohesion in the Seven Days' battles, as he came within an ace of doing, or if McClellan had shattered Lee's beleaguered army at Antietam, needless to say, this argument would not have become so favored. The *decisiveness* of Civil War military operations would have become the conventional wisdom.

In a welcome corrective to so much somber hand wringing, Paddy Griffith raises questions about the pervasive power of the defense in the Civil War. Although he concedes the defensive power of artillery and the omnipotence of entrenchments, he shows that shock action *did* succeed. Moreover, Griffith questions whether rifled-musket fire was that potent beyond Napoleonic ranges; the artillery was the main killer at longer ranges. One could advance a further argument, namely that the fault was not merely tactical; operational deficiencies also played a major role in numerous campaigns.

Commanders and their staffs on both sides lacked the experience and doctrine to mount offensive operations successfully in the first half of the Civil War. Hence their reliance on historical precedent, the half-remembered nostrums of Jomini, and other European military pundits. Staff officers could not make up for the deficiencies of their commanders because they were just as callow and untrained. This factor is often overlooked because of the continuing but erroneous insistence of historians that a "modern-style" general staff was created by 1863. An increase in tactical defensive power required more than anything else a streamlining of offensive measures; but the American military system was incapable of achieving this because of its amateurishness and the pressures resulting from hurried improvisation. Consequently both Union and Confederate commanders repeatedly failed to achieve *tactical concentration* supported by a firm cooperation of arms in the attack at the decisive point. Opportunities were thus wasted because they did succeed often enough at achieving a strategic concentration. On so many fields, attacks failed even when conditions (like the attainment of surprise) favored them because of poor technique in the attack, not because of any impregnability of the defense.[45]

One development that had an important influence on the outcome of battles was the changing role of the cavalry. Heavy cavalry were not needed in North America and increasingly they were regarded as dragoons—mounted infantry. They assumed an essentially supplemental role. The prime duty of cavalry was strategic and operational, not tactical: reconnaissance was its prime function though some cavalry commanders, like Stuart, chaffed against this marginalization on the battlefield. In addition, cavalry could carry out large-scale operations against the flank and rear of the enemy (though these should not have been conducted at the expense of reconnaissance). Cavalry could mask the movements of armies and seize and hold ground until the arrival of the infantry. The narrow roads and low, thickly wooded country in the south and west made the creation of a *corps de chasse* on Napoleonic lines a wholly impractical expedient. Cavalry charges during the Peninsular campaign of 1862 had been virtually suicidal affairs. In short, the cavalry had been driven from the battlefield. Indeed during most of the great battles when cavalry units were engaged, they fought separate battles between themselves on battlefields apart from the main field. The superiority of Confederate cavalry was a product of a centralized command system and the use of dragoon tactics. The decline in the importance of old-style cavalry did reduce the mobility of the pursuit, but not fatally.[46]

The essential problem could be found in the failure to think through operational and tactical problems in terms of all-arms cooperation. The key to so many failures was an overreliance on direct attacks to carry the day without coordinating them *effectively* with turning movements or serious and credible threats to the rear at about the same time. Even the Confederate superiority in cavalry could not be made to weigh successfully in the balance. For instance, Stuart preferred to seek out some kind of *independent* assignment *away* from the main army. Stuart remained ambivalent about the true use of cavalry and dismounted reluctantly. A truly significant shift in understanding that cavalry should "ride to the battle and fight on foot" only came in 1864–65. It would be advocated by Union commanders like Philip H. Sheridan and James Harrison Wilson. Such a transformation would depend on the introduction of the repeating carbine that greatly increased cavalry firepower. In 1862–63 an ambivalence about the role of cavalry and a general failure to secure a cooperation of arms contributed to the indecisiveness of battle.

NOTES AND REFERENCES

1. William C. Davis, *Jefferson Davis: The Man and His Hour* (New York: Harper-Collins, 1991), pp. 28–29. The most heated criticism of Bragg came from the vocal Kentucky lobby. See ibid., pp. 449, 465, 472–73.

2. Benjamin P. Thomas and Harold M. Hyman, *Stanton* (New York: Alfred A. Knopf, 1962), pp. 223–25; Stephen W. Sears, *George B. McClellan: The Young Napoleon* (New York: Ticknor and Fields, 1988), pp. 332–41; Herman Hattaway and Archer Jones, *How the North Won* (Urbana: University of Illinois Press, 1983), pp. 264–66; T. Harry Williams, *Lincoln and His Generals* (New York: Alfred A. Knopf, 1952), pp. 172–77; idem., *McClellan, Sherman and Grant* (New Brunswick, NJ: Rutgers University

Press, 1962) pp. 11–15. Williams is right in suggesting, in *Lincoln and His Generals* (New York: Alfred A. Knopf, 1952), p. 172, "He [McClellan] was not the stuff of which dictators are made."

3. Williams, *Lincoln and His Generals*, pp. 183–85; Richard B. McCaslin, *Tainted Breeze: The Great Hanging at Gainseville, Texas 1862* (Baton Rouge: Louisiana State University Press, 1994), pp. 66–71; Stephen D. Engle, *Don Carlos Buell: Most Promising of All* (Chapel Hill: University of North Carolina Press, 1999), pp. 312–14, 318.

4. Stephen E. Ambrose, *Halleck: Lincoln's Chief of Staff* (Baton Rouge: Louisiana State University Press, 1962), pp. 88, 92, 208.

5. Brian Holden Reid, "General McClellan and the Politicians," *Parameters* 17 (September 1987): 110; Bruce Tap, *Over Lincoln's Shoulder: The Committee on the Conduct of the War* (Lawrence: University Press of Kansas, 1998), pp. 162–64.

6. *The War of the Rebellion: A Compilation of the Official Records of the Union and Confederate Armies*, 128 parts in 70 vols. (Washington, DC: Government Printing Office, 1880–1901), series 1, vol. 16, part 1, pp. 135–38.

7. Ibid., pp. 231–32, 541, 639–41; Hans L. Trefousse, *Benjamin Franklin Wade: Radical Republican from Ohio* (New York: Twayne, 1963), p. 195.

8. Williams, *Lincoln and His Generals*, pp. 176, 188–89, 203–204; Lincoln to Halleck, Jan. 1, 1863, *The Collected Works of Abraham Lincoln*, ed. Roy P. Basler (New Brunswick, NJ: Rutgers University Press, 1953), vol. 6, p. 31.

9. Hattaway and Jones, *How the North Won*, p. 285; for their shrewd appraisal, see ibid., pp. 285–89, 291–97; see also Ambrose, *Halleck*, pp. 102–107; John F. Marszalek, *Commander of All Lincoln's Armies: A Life of General Henry W. Halleck* (Cambridge, MA: Belknap Press of Harvard University Press, 2004), p. 197, persists with this line of argument.

10. Andrea Bucholz, *Moltke, Schlieffen and Prussian War Planning* (New York: Berg, 1991), pp. 49–53.

11. Perry D. Jamieson, *Crossing the Deadly Ground: United States Army Tactics, 1865–1899* (Tuscaloosa: University of Alabama Press, 1994), pp. 20, 37, 40, 111–12.

12. Hattaway and Jones, *How the North Won*, pp. 288, 328.

13. Ibid., pp. 288–89; Williams, *Lincoln and His Generals*, pp. 188–89; Lincoln to Reverdy Johnson, August Belmont, July 26, July 31, 1862, in Lincoln, *Collected Works*, vol. 5, pp. 343, 350; Philip S. Paludan, *The Presidency of Abraham Lincoln* (Lawrence: University Press of Kansas, 1994), pp. 100, 218, 265–66.

14. Hattaway and Jones, *How the North Won*, p. 248; Williams, *Lincoln and His Generals*, p. 195; Paludan, *Presidency of Lincoln*, pp. 236–37.

15. William Marvel, *Burnside* (Chapel Hill: University of North Carolina Press, 1991), pp. 164–65, 171; Williams, *Lincoln and His Generals*, p. 194; Edward Hagerman, *The American Civil War and the Origins of Modern Warfare* (Bloomington: Indiana University Press, 1988), p. 79; Bruce Catton, *Glory Road* (London: White Lion reprint, 1952, 1977), p. 31; Williams, *Lincoln Finds a General* (New York: Macmillan, 1957), vol. 2, p. 483.

16. Catton, *Glory Road*, pp. 18–19, 21; George Rable, *Fredericksburg! Fredericksburg!* (Chapel Hill: University of North Carolina Press, 2002), p. 57.

17. Marvel, *Burnside*, pp. 165–66, and Williams, *Lincoln and His Generals*, pp. 196–97, blame Halleck; Williams, *Lincoln Finds a General*, vol. 2, pp. 497–98; Catton, *Glory Road*, pp. 22–23; Rable, *Fredericksburg*, 59, 87. Halleck issued the order on November 12 but it was put in the mail rather than sent by faster means, such as by courier.

18. Williams, *Lincoln Finds a General*, vol. 2, p. 518, estimates the Army of Northern Virginia at eighty-five thousand men; Catton, *Glory Road*, pp. 27, 30; Lee to Davis, Nov. 25, Dec. 6, 1862, in *The Wartime Papers of R. E. Lee*, eds. Clifford Dowdey and Louis H. Manarin (New York: Bramhall House, 1961), pp. 345, 353; Jeffry D. Wert, *General James Longstreet* (New York: Simon and Schuster, 1993), pp. 204–205; Alan T. Nolan, *Lee Considered* (Chapel Hill: University of North Carolina Press, 1991), pp. 81–84; Brian Holden Reid, *Robert E. Lee: Icon for a Nation* (2005; Amherst, NY: Prometheus Books, 2007), pp. 136–38.

19. Lee to Jackson, Nov. 9, 10, 14, 19, 23, 1862, Lee to J. A. Seddon, Dec. 16, 1862, *Wartime Papers*, pp. 330, 332, 335, 340, 344, 363; Wert, *Longstreet*, p. 213; Douglas Southall Freeman, *R. E. Lee* (New York: Scribner's 1933), vol. 2, pp. 429–32; Clifford Dowdey, *Lee: A Biography* (London: Gollancz, 1970), pp. 326–27; Hattaway and Jones, *How the North Won*, p. 304.

20. Lee to Stuart, Nov. 9, 1862, Lee to Jackson, Nov. 19, 23, 1862, in *Wartime Papers*, pp. 340, 343–44; Rable, *Fredericksburg*, p. 146; H. B. McClellan, *Life and Campaigns of Major General J. E. B. Stuart* (Secaucus, NJ: Blue and Grey Press reprint, 1993), pp. 186–88; Emory M. Thomas, *Bold Dragoon: The Life of J. E. B. Stuart* (New York: Harper and Row, 1986), p. 191; Wert, *Longstreet*, pp. 206–208; James I. Robertson Jr., *Stonewall Jackson: The Man, the Soldier, the Legend* (New York: Macmillan, 1997), pp. 631, 649, casts doubt on any tension between Lee and Jackson.

21. G. F. R. Henderson, *The Campaign of Fredericksburg* (1886; Fall's Church, VA: Old Dominion reprint, 1984), pp. 42–47, 63, is still a model study; Hagerman, *American Civil War*, pp. 122–23; Wert, *Longstreet*, p. 218. Hagerman points out (p. 318n55) that Freeman's interpretation that Lee failed to entrench because he did not wish to deter an attack on a strong position "is speculation." Maybe so, but he took the idea from G. F. R. Henderson, *Stonewall Jackson* (London: Longman, 1898, 1911), vol. 2, p. 330; see Freeman, *R. E. Lee*, vol. 2, pp. 441–42.

22. Catton, *Glory Road*, pp. 34, 40–41; Marcus Cunliffe, *Soldiers and Civilians: The Martial Spirit in America, 1776–1865*, 3rd ed. (London: Gregg 1993), p. 324; Rable, *Fredericksburg*, pp. 162–65.

23. Marvel, *Burnside*, pp. 171–73, 185; Catton, *Glory Road*, p. 21; Williams, *Lincoln and His Generals*, p. 195; Kenneth Williams, *Lincoln Finds a General*, vol. 2, pp. 528–29, has some trenchant observations on Burnside's indecision and failure to pass the "acid test" of a general; also see Rable, *Fredericksburg*, pp. 185–91.

24. Douglas Southall Freeman, *Lee's Lieutenants*, 3 vols (New York: Scribner's, 1944), vol. 2, pp. 361–68; Henderson, *Fredericksburg*, pp. 69–75; Wert, *Longstreet*, pp. 220–21; Hagerman, *American Civil War*, p. 123; Rable, *Fredericksburg*, pp. 199–203, 221–26, 228, 235–36, 255–67.

25. Dowdey, *Lee*, pp. 329–30; Henderson, *Fredericksburg*, pp. 88–95; Richard M. McMurry, *John Bell Hood and the War for Southern Independence* (1982; Lincoln: University of Nebraska Press, 1992), p. 65; Freeman, *R. E. Lee*, vol. 2, p. 462; Rable, *Fredericksburg*, pp. 192, 205–209, 210–16.

26. Rable, *Fredericksburg*, pp. 215–16, 263–72, 281; Battle Report of Fredericksburg Campaign, Apr. 10, 1863, in Lee, *Wartime Papers*, p. 373; Hattaway and Jones, *How the North Won*, p. 308; Catton, *Glory Road*, pp. 48–62; Russell F. Weigley, *History of the United States Army* (New York: Macmillan, 1967), p. 237; the best discussion of the prospects of a Confederate counterattack is Daniel E. Sutherland, *Fredericksburg and Chancellorsville: The Dare Mark Campaign* (Lincoln: University of Nebraska Press, 1988), p. 66.

27. Williams, *Lincoln and His Generals*, pp. 201–206; Paludan, *Presidency of Lincoln*, pp. 171–77; also see the accounts of J. G. Randall, *Lincoln the President* (London: Eyre and Spottiswoode, 1947), vol. 2, pp. 242–49, and Allan Nevins, *The War for the Union* (New York: Scribner's 1959–60), vol. 2, pp. 352–62. Paludan is an essential corrective (see p. 143) to those historians, like Randall, who see the radical Republicans, and not the Democrats, as Lincoln's most bitter foes; Rable, *Fredericksburg*, pp. 410–22.

28. Williams, *Lincoln and His Generals*, pp. 206–207; Richard E. Beringer, Herman Hattaway, Archer Jones, and William N. Still Jr., *Why the South Lost the Civil War* (Athens: University of Georgia Press, 1986), p. 252; also see Ludwell H. Johnson, "Civil War Military History: A Few Revisions in Need of Revising," *Civil War History* 17 (1971): 123; Hattaway and Jones, *How the North Won*, p. 309; Larry J. Daniel, *Days of Glory: The Army of the Cumberland, 1861–1865* (Baton Rouge: Louisiana State University Press, 2004), pp. 181–84.

29. Grady McWhiney, *Braxton Bragg and Confederate Defeat* (Tuscaloosa: University of Alabama Press, 1969, 1991), pp. 332–33; William C. Davis, *Breckinridge: Statesman, Soldier, Symbol* (Baton Rouge: Louisiana University Press, 1974, 1986), pp. 331–33.

30. Craig L. Symonds, *Joseph E. Johnston* (New York: Norton, 1992), p. 188; Davis, *Jefferson Davis*, pp. 475–76, 493; Archer Jones, *Confederate Strategy: From Shiloh to Vicksburg* (Baton Rouge: Louisiana State University Press, 1961), pp. 193–97; Steven E. Woodworth, *Jefferson Davis and His Generals* (Lawrence: University Press of Kansas, 1990), pp. 181–84.

31. Thomas L. Connelly and Archer Jones, *The Politics of Command* (Baton Rouge: Louisiana State University Press, 1973), pp. 53–54, 182–83; T. Harry Williams, *P. G. T. Beauregard: Napoleon in Gray* (1955; Baton Rouge: Louisiana State University Press, 1989), pp. 181–83; Woodworth, *Davis and His Generals*, pp. 228–29.

32. See especially, Connelly and Jones, *Politics of Command*, pp. 193–95.

33. Davis, *Jefferson Davis*, pp. 474–76, 485; Woodworth, *Davis and His Generals*, pp. 123–24, 173, 179–80.

34. McWhiney, *Bragg*, vol. 1, pp. 335, 344–45; Williams, *Beauregard*, pp. 181, 215; Symonds, *Johnston*, pp. 191–92; Robert L. Kerby, *Kirby Smith's Confederacy: The Trans-Mississippi South, 1863–1865* (1972; Tuscaloosa: University of Alabama Press, 1991), pp. 52–53. Kirby Smith arrived on March 7, 1863.

35. McWhiney, *Bragg*, vol. 1, pp. 340–41; Ramage, *Rebel Raider*, pp. 143, 145–47; for their impact and Rosecrans's response, see Daniel, *Days of Glory*, pp. 197–200.

36. McWhiney, *Bragg*, vol. 1, pp. 346–48; Hagerman, *American Civil War*, pp. 192–93; Williams, *Lincoln Finds a General*, vol. 4, pp. 241–42, 255, 258; Daniel, *Days of Glory*, pp. 194–96.

37. McWhiney, *Bragg*, vol. 1, pp. 348–50; Hagerman, *American Civil War*, p. 195; Williams, *Lincoln Finds a General*, vol. 4, pp. 230–32, 264–65; Daniel, *Days of Glory*, pp. 190–91, 202–206 is critical of Rosecrans's cumbersome approach.

38. McWhiney, *Bragg*, pp. 352–64; Williams, *Lincoln Finds a General*, vol. 4, pp. 272–74, 275–76; Hagerman, *American Civil War*, p. 194; Davis, *Breckinridge*, pp. 337–38; Daniel, *Days of Glory*, pp. 208–17.

39. Williams, *Lincoln Finds a General*, vol. 4, pp. 278–81, 284–85; McWhiney, *Bragg*, vol. 1, pp. 359–71; Davis, *Breckinridge*, pp. 339–46. Davis (p. 345) makes clear Breckinridge's opposition to Bragg's misguided artillery tactics; Daniel, *Days of Glory*, pp. 219–23.

40. Williams, *Lincoln and His Generals*, pp. 208–209. The extent to which Lincoln attached fond remembrance of this battle is illustrated when he revealed on the day of his assassination that before each Union success he had a dream of "a phantom ship, moving towards a dark, indefinite shore." He had had it before all the great Union triumphs, including Murfreesboro. Grant, who was present at the cabinet meeting and was then not well disposed toward Rosecrans, immediately interjected, pointing out that Murfreesboro was no victory. See Benjamin P. Thomas, *Abraham Lincoln* (London: Eyre and Spottiswoode, 1952), pp. 337–38.

41. Major General J. F. C. Fuller, *The Generalship of Ulysses S. Grant*, 2nd ed. (Bloomington: Indiana University Press, 1957), p. 200; Paddy Griffith, *Rally Once Again: Battle Tactics of the American Civil War* (Ramsbury, UK: Crowood Press, 1987), p. 59; McWhiney, *Bragg*, vol. 1, p. 201; Hattaway and Jones, *How the North Won*, pp. 278, 280.

42. Grady McWhiney and Perry D. Jamieson, *Attack and Die: Civil War Military Tactics and the Southern Heritage* (Tuscaloosa: University of Alabama Press, 1982), pp. 44, 78–79. For a defense of the bayonet, see Griffith, *Rally Once Again*, pp. 140–42. But he fails to distinguish clearly between shock action and bayonet fighting (the two are not synonymous), cannot explain away the absence of bayonet wounds, and that in hand-to-

hand fighting American soldiers did not use it. I emphatically agree (p. 141) that "the key word . . . was not so much 'bayonet' as 'shock.'" See also John Buechler, "'Give 'em the Bayonet': A Note on Civil War Mythology," *Civil War History* 7 (1961): 128–32.

43. Hagerman, *American Civil War*, pp. 88, 117, 123; Davis, *Jefferson Davis*, p. 430; Rowena Reed, *Combined Operations in the Civil War* (Lincoln: University of Nebraska reprint, 1978, 1993), p. 35.

44. Williams, *Lincoln Finds a General*, vol. 4, pp. 279–80; Sears, *McClellan*, pp. 113–14; Hagerman, *American Civil War*, pp. 65, 145; McWhiney and Jamieson, *Attack or Die*, pp. 112–14; Jennings Cropper Wise, *The Long Arm of Lee*, 2 vols. (1915; Lincoln: University of Nebraska Press, 1991), vol. 1, pp. 238–39, 243–44, 264–65, 275–76.

45. Griffith, *Rally Once Again*, pp. 52, 65–66, 137–52, 170–71, 190–91. I do not always agree with the details of Griffith's interpretation and its belligerent tone does not aid persuasiveness, but it is certainly stimulating.

46. Griffith, *Rally Once Again*, pp. 181–84; Hagerman, *American Civil War*, pp. 145–46; Stephen Z. Starr, *The Union Cavalry in the Civil War*, 3 vols. (Baton Rouge: Louisiana State University Press, 1979–85), vol. 3, pp. 109–14.

Chapter Eight

THE EBB AND FLOW OF BATTLE

APRIL TO JULY 1863

Whatever its weaknesses, cavalry action provided Lee with his great opportunity in the spring campaign of 1863. And in the summer it was to help wreck his hopes of reversing the bad luck that had dogged the Maryland campaign of the previous year. The campaign was prefaced by the appointment of yet another commander of the Army of the Potomac, Major General Joseph Hooker. Hooker's appointment was the product of skillful lobbying on his own part; he was plausible, articulate, and had no mean opinion of himself. He exploited Burnside's downfall and made his own contemptuous opinion of his former chief abundantly clear in a number of barrooms; he also exploited the somewhat frenetic activity of the Joint Committee on the Conduct of the War in its attempt to utterly demolish McClellan's reputation. A string of McClellan's enemies were summoned to give testimony, including corps commanders Edwin V. Sumner, Samuel P. Heintzelman, and Ethan A. Hitchcock, who had acted as Stanton's military adviser.

Few of McClellan's allies were called, and of these only General William B. Franklin carried any weight. Franklin himself was in a tight corner over his conduct at Fredericksburg and had to put up a good performance. Four members of the Joint Committee even visited the Army of the Potomac at Fredericksburg. Both there and in Washington, Hooker made a strong impression. He ridiculed McClellan's siege of Yorktown and thus distanced himself from their archenemy. "I would have marched right through the redoubts," he boasted, sending a thrill down the backs of the Committee members, "and into Richmond in two days." Hooker had thus positioned himself as the inevitable choice for the command, his only rival being the comparatively colorless Major General George G. Meade. The choice was Lincoln's, and he made the decision without consulting any member of the cabinet, including Stanton. Nonetheless, after the cabinet crisis Hooker's appointment on January 26, 1863, can be viewed as an effort to placate the president's radical critics.[1]

Hooker at any rate had been appointed with what amounted to a mandate for vigorous action. As for the hapless Burnside, he was restored to the command of his Ninth Corps and moved west. His superficially courageous refusal to abdicate responsibility for his errors (he soon found Franklin to blame) "disarmed all criticism," recalled Congressman George Julian, and the Joint Committee stood by him. Franklin had been one of McClellan's "pets" and they were pleased that Burnside had given them the opportunity to discredit him. But Hooker was a more exciting prospect. He had a strong personality, an engaging presence, and good looks. Politicians in the United States took some time to learn that there was no equation between a pleasing appearance and performance in the field: good looks alone do not a good general make. Hooker's boisterousness and his capacity for intrigue provoked distrust. His brash self-advertisement coupled with a predilection for the bottle perhaps concealed a deeper insecurity. Only the strain of a campaign would reveal the extent to which Hooker could withstand the stress of high command when there was nobody else around to blame except himself.[2]

Hooker's appointment thus signaled that the radical view of war aims was preeminent. The president had indicated his flexibility on this question when he had written before the battle of Fredericksburg, "I needed success more than I needed sympathy, and that I have not seen the so much greater evidence of getting success from my sympathizers, than from those who are denounced as the contrary. It does seem to me that in the field the two classes have been very much alike in what they have done, and what they have failed to do." Congressman Julian in late 1862 had tried to convince General Burnside that his troops should "adequately hate" their enemies. The 1862 senatorial reelection campaigns had led to denunciation of Democrat moderation as "Copperhead treachery." *The Report of the Joint Committee on the Conduct of the War* was published in April 1863, greeted by a deftly orchestrated newspaper fanfare, and hundreds of copies were distributed to the Army of the Potomac. Senator Wade concluded that "More than any other wars, rebellion demands rapid measures. . . . Though delay might mature more comprehensive plans and promise greater results it [the Civil War] is not the first case in which it has been shown that successful war involves *something more than abstract military principles*." The political pressure which all this investigatory steam had built up thus rendered it impossible for Lincoln to stand on the defensive in the east by "relying on Scott's anaconda plan," as suggested by Hattaway and Jones. "The main Union effort centered in Grant on the Mississippi, just as Scott had recommended." Politically this course was impossible. A great effort would have to be made in Virginia in 1863.[3]

Despite his radical support, the new commander of the Army of the Potomac did not issue any orders like John Pope's. Hooker had received instructions from Lincoln via Halleck indicating that Lee's army, and not Richmond, should be his objective. Operational concerns from the first dominated Hooker's thoughts. This document also revealed the lasting damage that McClellan's sluggish drive on Richmond had inflicted on the Union war effort. Halleck was now of the view that a successful siege of the Confederate capital was all but impossible. Halleck deplored operations on exterior lines while Lee occupied a central position. Lee had exploited this advantage to the fullest during the Second Manassas campaign the previous summer. Lincoln had never been persuaded of this dogma; but he saw that Richmond would fall if Lee's army was destroyed, not before. As always, Lincoln believed that the quickest and simplest way of effecting this was by a direct approach across northern Virginia. Grant in 1864 was to reveal Halleck's pessimism and fears quite groundless.

Yet Hooker was prevented from employing the tidewater Virginian rivers as an avenue of approach, relying on Union seapower. He had to cross them; Burnside had had his difficulties with the Rappahannock and Hooker was determined to avoid his fate. Lincoln granted Hooker a great measure of freedom from Halleck's hectoring, and he drew up an impressive plan based on a dual envelopment of Lee's left flank along the Rappahannock and Rapidan rivers, crossing at Kelly's Ford, and Germanna Ford, and at US Ford. Rivers are far from insurmountable obstacles unless a crossing is opposed by the full weight of the enemy's fighting power. The final stroke, designed to cause paralysis of decision and mayhem in Lee's rear areas and cut his lines of communication to Richmond, would be delivered by a federal cavalry raid. Hooker's rejuvenated army (six months' back pay had been disbursed, diet had been improved, and new uniforms issued so morale had soared) carried out this maneuver with dispatch despite heavy spring rains.[4]

Improvements in morale were matched by a major structural overhaul of the army that Hooker had undertaken in February and March of 1863. He wished at all costs to avoid the wasteful frontal assaults that had disfigured Antietam and Fredericksburg. He sought greater flexibility by dismantling the grand divisions. Seven infantry corps were deployed, each sporting a new badge to boost formation pride. Hooker placed the cavalry in a single corps, centralizing its command and conferring on it greater cohesion and tactical power. He had committed a signal error, though, in decentralizing the command of his artillery among the separate brigades just at a time when the Confederates, utilizing a battalion system, were centralizing theirs at the corps level. Hooker's measure did much to reduce the federal superiority in this arm.

Hooker understood that the deployment of up to eight corps over considerable distances would stretch his span of command. He proposed to coordinate his army by taking the field himself, but using army headquarters at Falmouth under the direction of his chief of staff, Major General Daniel Butterfield—equipped with the new Beardslee field telegraph equipment—as a clearinghouse through which all messages should be passed. This imaginative scheme failed because the US Military Telegraph (USMT) lacked sufficient wire to cover such long distances, the new machines broke down, the operators were untrained in their use, and the system became dangerously overloaded. It took up to five hours for telegrams to reach Butterfield. During two crucial days in the Chancellorsville campaign, April 30 and May 1, communications failures help explain the tardy response of the Army of the Potomac to Confederate countermoves.[5]

The most impressive part of Hooker's plan though was that he had managed to keep it out of the newspapers. Lee was momentarily baffled by his design. Hooker had originally thought in terms of driving Lee out of northern Virginia and back toward Richmond. As Hooker's columns converged on the crossroads at Chancellorsville, marked by a large brick house that served as his field headquarters, he became more sanguine. If he could get through the wilderness, a large, clotted, virtually impenetrable wooded area, then he was confident that he could win the decisive victory for which the president hankered. His orders began to assume that rather bombastic tone which was so approved of by radical Republicans. "Let your watchword be fight, fight, fight," the commander of his cavalry, Major General George Stoneman, was instructed. Yet Hooker's plans and hopes had rather left out of account what the enemy would do. When Lee eventually struck, his savage rapier thrusts pricked the inflated bubble of Hooker's overvaluation of his own accomplishment, and so much rodomontade.[6]

The deployment of Stoneman on a cavalry raid similar to those carried out by Stuart, Morgan, and Bedford Forrest effectively blinded Hooker. It aimed to strike at Lee's lines of communication and cause alarm and despondency in Richmond, but any damage it caused was more than canceled out by his loss of reconnaissance and intelligence gathering. Hooker had 130,000 men but they stumbled about like partygoers pushed from a brightly lit anteroom into a deep, pitch-black cellar. Even when the cavalry returned to the main body they were of little use. General Fitzhugh Lee, recalling his experience with Stuart, wrote that "Cavalry raids are dazzling, but do not generally accomplish enough to compensate for the number of broken-down horses and men." His misuse of the mounted arm was perhaps Hooker's single most significant error in an otherwise well-planned maneuver.[7]

Hooker had divided his army of 130,000 men into three parts. Major General John Sedgwick remained at Fredericksburg with a force almost the size of Lee's entire army while the remaining seventy-three thousand, in two columns, converged on Chancellorsville. Hooker had turned Lee's flank and had so distributed his forces that he could strike Lee in the rear whichever way he turned. Lee's predicament was indeed baleful, but his resourcefulness was equal to its challenges. The strength and vigor of the Union's offensive in Virginia had given the lie to the western (that is, Tennessee) lobby that the Virginian theater could be downgraded. In April 1863 Lee had to fight off suggestions that troops be sent from his army to reinforce Bragg. This has been denounced by a number of historians, who accept the arguments of the western concentration lobby, as "parochialism," an "obsession" with Virginia, and an inability to come to terms with the fundamental grand strategic problems that faced the Confederacy. This argument, which has its origins in the pungent criticisms of Major General J. F. C. Fuller, is quite misconceived. There are at least two grand strategic reasons for Lee's position, and they deserve no less respect than the western option.[8]

The first was the assumption that for a variety of reasons, many of which had little to do with military affairs, the east was the politically decisive theater. Lee's defensive-offensive strategy, which was not inspired by Napoleonic models,[9] was grounded on a desire to maintain the integrity of the Confederacy's frontiers; this could be achieved by pivoting his army on the rich, fertile, logistically abundant Shenandoah Valley. This deployment would allow him to strike at the flank of any forces invading Virginia and, moreover, bring pressure on the federal government by moving northward when it was propitious to do so. Alert to broader applications of military power, Lee wanted to wage war on Northern public opinion. If the Confederacy was successful in 1863, "next fall will be a great change in public opinion at the North. The Republicans will be destroyed and I think the friends of peace will become so strong as that the next administration will go in on that basis. We have only to resist manfully." Lee was the only one of Jefferson Davis's generals that thought in these terms. Virginia was the only theater of operations where such benefits could be gained. One of the motives behind Beauregard's planning was to divorce operations and tactics from such political complications and, of course, from Davis himself.[10]

The other weakness of the western concentration bloc (including those historians who support its view but rather gloss over its myopia toward the fate of Vicksburg) is that it tended to ignore the plans and the movements of the enemy. This was characteristic of Beauregard's military planning; he always assumed that the enemy would behave as he calculated and that he could do as he pleased. The plain fact of the matter that cannot be shunned is that a drastic weakening of Lee's army would expose Virginia and the Carolinas to occupation and the loss of the Confederate capital. It would result in the grand strategic loss of all that had been gained since the Seven Days' battles, with no promise of any commensurate gain elsewhere. The moral injection this would give to the Northern war effort would be rejuvenating. As Lee wrote in February 1863, "General Hooker has many strong reasons to induce him to take this step [advance on Richmond], and if he believes that but feeble resistance can be made to his advance he will more likely do so." The onslaught that Lee now faced could not be written off as a minor incursion.[11]

The most difficult obstacle Lee encountered in trying to resist Hooker was that his urgent need for subsistence had led to an operational dispersal of the Army of Northern Virginia. In February 1863, Lee had moved Longstreet's corps south of the James River and thence to Suffolk in an effort to throw back federal amphibious penetration of the North Carolinian hinterland. The Confederate commissary department in Richmond was hopelessly clogged, and no less a priority for Lee was the collection of supplies from rich agricultural areas; it was not lack of subsistence from which the Confederacy suffered but proper *logistical organization*—the ability to collect, transport, and distribute resources. Though Lee had implored Longstreet to deploy his troops so that "they can be readily moved to resist an advance upon Richmond," he was granted, as was Lee's custom, a fair measure of latitude. This Longstreet enjoyed. He sympathized with the western concentration bloc, and saw himself as Bragg's successor after Murfreesboro, especially since Johnston's appointment to the overall western command. It is therefore perhaps not strange that Longstreet opposed a concentration in Virginia—preferring to remain at Suffolk: "If we cripple him

[the enemy] only, a little at one place and then another, we may mutually produce grand results"—while advocating a concentration in Tennessee, where he
hoped to command. His self-interested formula was simply a recipe for piecemeal assaults and the attrition of Confederate strength that Longstreet was supposedly anxious to avoid.[12]

The result of these dispositions was that Lee lacked two divisions of
Longstreet's powerful corps when he fought at Chancellorsville. He had 61,500
troops with him at Fredericksburg. That he could field an army in the region of
eighty thousand men is further illustration of the exaggeration by Lee's critics
of the harmful effect of the Maryland campaign; hence envious eyes were
directed by other Confederate commanders toward his capable veterans. But he
fought the campaign outnumbered by more than two to one, a serious disadvantage. Longstreet was en route but not available for the action itself. This
peculiar situation may account for the risks that Lee took. He could not allow
himself to be passively crushed between the vice devised by Hooker; he knew,
too, that Longstreet was coming up should a setback occur. What Hooker could
not calculate for was Lee's gambling instinct. As a response to the division of the
Army of the Potomac, Lee intended to divide his weaker force again to turn the
flank of the stronger, as Hooker simultaneously struggled to envelop Lee.
Despite his earlier failure to discern Hooker's opening gambit, his recovery was
impressive. It was a masterly demonstration of bold calculation and operational
skill. No less impressive was Lee's control of the battle, his orchestration of its
constituent parts, and his cool nerve. Hooker had shown himself an intelligent
planner. Preparation is, of course, crucial; but on campaign what counts is execution, the capacity to put thought into practice, and on this count Hooker was
quite outclassed.[13]

Convinced that Sedgwick was feinting at Fredericksburg, on April 29 Lee
moved west with the bulk of his army. He left behind a division supplemented
by a brigade commanded by Major General Jubal A. Early to guard the Freder-
icksburg position. His movements were shielded by the thick woods and
Hooker was incapable of detecting them. Indeed, despite stealing a march on
Lee, the Army of the Potomac had still not cleared the wilderness. On May 1
Confederate cavalry supported by infantry encountered Major General George
Sykes's division of Meade's Fifth Corps in a tactical meeting engagement before
Chancellorsville. In many ways, this preliminary encounter was the decisive
moment of the battle. Hooker rapidly lost his jaunty confidence. In reality, his
plan included a strong defensive element. Hooker wished to force Lee to retreat
or attack him. The ghost of McClellan materialized, for all of Hooker's earlier

ridicule. He determined quickly to call off the offensive movement, bring back all the army to Chancellorsville, and dig in to await the rebel attack. "It's all right, Couch," Hooker assured one of his corps commanders, "I've got Lee just where I want him." But behind the empty boasting, Hooker had surrendered the initiative. What would Lee do with it?[14]

That evening General Lee and Stonewall Jackson met beside the Plank Road; Jeb Stuart soon joined them. Lee sat on a tree stump and spread out his maps on the ground. He was in a dilemma. The Union troops had dug formidable works supplemented by the plentiful timber to form abattis. "It was evident that a direct attack upon the enemy would be attended with great difficulty and loss," Lee wrote later. "Now," he said quietly, "how can I get at those people?" Here was striking evidence of Lee's keenness to retain the initiative and preoccupation with what he was going to do to the enemy, rather than with what the enemy was going to do to him. Drawing upon an important, even vital use of cavalry, Stuart reported that his patrols had discovered that Hooker's right flank was exposed. Jackson indicated his willingness to carry out anything that Lee ordered. The plan the latter came up with relied heavily on Jackson's audacity and trustworthiness, for he would be charged with working out the detail.

Lee's basic concept was "to endeavor to turn his [Hooker's] right flank and gain his rear, leaving a force in front to hold him in check and conceal the movement." In short, Lee proposed to divide his army of forty-three thousand men again in face of seventy-three thousand Union troops. Lee's plan was a response to a grave emergency and the unusual topographical conditions of northern Virginia; it was the logical fulfillment of the measures he had introduced since the previous spring. On Napoleon's inspiration the sources are silent. Jackson rather shocked Lee, though he accepted the gamble with a shrug, when he suggested taking his entire corps of twenty-six thousand men, leaving Lee only seventeen thousand. Should Hooker become aware of the division he could smash each part of the Confederate army with great ease. But he had already given evidence of timidity, and Lee moved to exploit this ruthlessly.[15]

Jackson had promised to move at 4 AM, but did not actually get all his troops off on this "long and fatiguing march" along the dark, gloomy Brock Road until 9 AM. This ensured that his men would not arrive too exhausted for battle in the afternoon. The tree line was so thick that it provided a protective arch under which his corps moved. Yet Jackson did not move undetected. His wagon train was attacked. Major General Daniel E. Sickles of Third Corps reported seeing Confederate columns moving on his front and reported his discovery to headquarters. He was told by Hooker that Lee was retreating and that he should advance cautiously to seize his artillery. Hence the attack on Jackson's supply train, which had to be rescued by two brigades. Observation balloons also spotted dust clouds wafting above the trees along Jackson's line of march. Information was thus available but Hooker made poor use of it.

Alas, Hooker's whole conduct of the battle was crippled by communication difficulties. It took hours for Butterfield's messages to reach his commander. Hooker needed reliable intelligence, which was not forthcoming because of the absence of the cavalry. His communications broke down mainly because of the inexperience of the signalers, but also because of the short range of the equipment. Yet such was Hooker's state of mind that even had both these assets been working efficiently in his favor, they would have made little difference. Hooker's span of command was simply too great for his experience or his headquarters staff to cope with; consequently, he merely indulged in wishful thinking, namely that Lee was retreating.[16]

Jackson arrived in Hooker's rear three miles behind Chancellorsville at 4 PM on May 2; he then waited two hours for his entire corps to come up before launching the attack. He struck Major General Oliver O. Howard's Eleventh Corps, largely composed of Pennsylvania Germans, "an outcast from the spirit and affection of the army," in Bruce Catton's apt description. The Germans (or "Dutch" as Deutsch was willfully mispronounced by Americans) were branded as cowardly incompetents and derided by the whole Army of the Potomac in a fit of "Know-Nothing" enthusiasm.[17] (The reputation of the Germans for martial excellence is a post-1870 development.) The Eleventh Corps's sense of isolation was now given a tactical expression by Sickles's advance that opened up a gap of a mile between it and the main body; furthermore, its flank was completely exposed. However, the precarious position of the Corps did not seem to invite drastic measures from its officers and the soldiers stacked arms and began preparing their evening meal. "Their situation invited a catastrophe," writes Bruce Catton.[18]

And catastrophe was visited upon them by an avenging prophet, Stonewall Jackson. Pandemonium broke out as Jackson's troops hurled themselves down the Orange Court House Turnpike toward an unsuspecting foe. Jackson had attacked in two waves of divisional strength with A. P. Hill's division as reserve. It took Jackson fifty-four minutes to rout Eleventh Corps; but as Lee reported, once Hill was committed, the troops "were completely blended and in such disorder from their rapid advance through intricate woods and over broken ground that it was necessary to reform them." By the time the advance was moving forward again it was nearing 8 PM, and as Jackson prepared to redirect his advance toward Chancellorsville, he was shot and mortally wounded by a Confederate

From *An Atlas of American Military History* by James C. Bradford (New York: Cynthia Parzych Publishing, 2003).

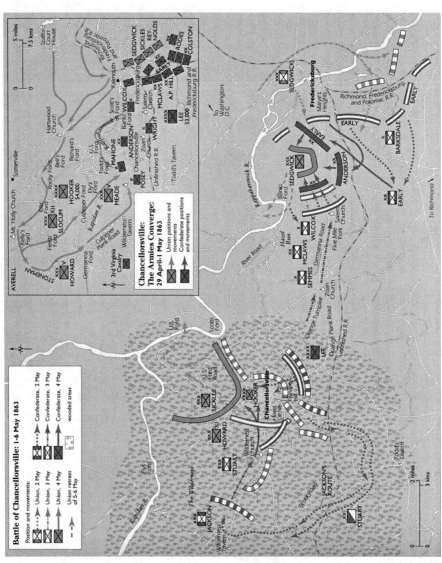

picket (although it is likely that the true mortal wound occurred later during his evacuation from the battlefield) who had mistaken him, in the bad light, for a Union officer. Thus ended the career of Lee's great executive officer, the dynamic and diligent subordinate who made Lee's loose command system work, Lee's "right arm." Intensely secretive to the end, Jackson had given no hint of his plans. Hill had also been slightly wounded; Stuart, who had accompanied the march, took command of Jackson's corps. Darkness now intervened.

As the third day of the battle dawned, Stuart faced an unenviable task. Deprived of its commander at such a moment when it had still failed to link up with Lee, disaster or triumph stared Jackson's corps in the face. Stuart got a grip on his divisions and began to locate his scattered units. During the early hours of the morning of May 3, Lee issued orders requiring a renewal of the attack "with the utmost vigor." Stuart ordered a frontal assault on the Union breastworks but progress was slow as the Union troops were prepared and their resistance stout. At last, inspired by Stuart's flamboyant leadership, Hazel Grove, a critical piece of high ground commanding Chancellorsville, was taken by Confederate troops. Stuart concentrated fifty of Jackson's guns there and began to bombard the center of gravity of the Union army, covering his own advance on the left and Lee's on the right. The Chancellor family's house was hit and Hooker wounded, but he refused to relinquish command. His position was far from inextricable: he had a cohesive line and could still destroy the separated wings of Lee's army. Hooker needed to show leadership and a determination to wield the fighting power of his army, but the effort was beyond him.

Lee had ordered an attack as soon as firing was heard from the left the previous day. His force was pitifully small but progress was good, mainly because Hooker had ordered a withdrawal to the Rappahannock to another redoubtable fortified position protected by the convergence of the Rappahannock and Rapidan rivers. At 10 AM General Lee rode into the clearing at Chancellorsville by the burning house to meet Stuart—the two small halves of the Army of Northern Virginia had at last joined. Lee's magnificent presence and soldierly bearing produced among his soldiers, a member of his staff, Charles Marshall, wrote many years later, "one of those uncontrollable outbursts of enthusiasm which none can appreciate who have not witnessed them." It was his greatest moment as a field commander; but the triumph was far from complete: tactically Lee had succeeded, but operationally the issue was still in doubt.[19]

On receiving news of Jackson's attack, Hooker telegraphed Sedgwick at Fredericksburg on the night of May 2 (as he had repeatedly the day before) to attack Early's troops and thus strike Lee in the rear. This part of Hooker's plan was still intact and offered a chance on May 3 of retrieving victory from defeat by operational maneuver outside the wilderness. But it took hours for the message to get through; the Union rear echelons themselves were in terrible confusion and telegraph lines were cut. Sedgwick's own communications were faulty. He did not know that Early had been mistakenly ordered to evacuate his position by Lee's chief of staff, Colonel R. H. Chilton, on the morning of May 2. Lee reversed the order and Early had successfully reoccupied his lines along Marye's Heights at about 10:30 PM.

It took three assaults the following day to finally drive Early away from his defenses in the second battle of Fredericksburg. Sedgwick's men were deluded as to the real size of the Confederate force opposing them. Once more the myth of Southern numerical superiority had worked in the Confederates' favor. Yet Lee's rear was now exposed, and he was forced to call off his attack on Hooker and to turn units around to confront Sedgwick at Salem Church. Confronted by Lee himself, Sedgwick's timorousness matched that of his commanding general; he went over to the defensive, determined to hold his line of retreat over the Rappahannock against Lee's ferocious attacks. On the night of May 4, even though his force was numerically superior to Lee's, Sedgwick withdrew across the Rappahannock. Lee then fell back whence he came to confront Hooker with his reunited army. Hooker still had double Lee's number of troops south of the Rappahannock, and Sedgwick north of it, but he had lost his appetite for battle. Longstreet had yet to arrive (and Hooker became increasingly anxious at the prospect), but Lee concentrated to attack. On the night of May 5 Hooker abdicated the operational initiative that was his for the taking and withdrew northward before Lee had time to strike.[20]

Lee's victory at Chancellorsville is the greatest achievement of American generalship in the nineteenth century. The design underlying the operation is smoothed by the polish of an unsurpassed intellectual elegance carried through with cool, brilliant execution. The confidence of Lee and Jackson is all the more impressive because they so completely lacked the material and numerical superiority that is such a feature of successful American generalship thereafter. Given the virtually unanimous salutations of Lee's skill, the literature is permeated by frustration, especially among Lost Cause writers, that the battle was not more decisive.[21] Hooker had been driven back, but Chancellorsville was bereft of strategic advantages. Herman Hattaway and Archer Jones, and Edward Hagerman also, in their authoritative studies emphasize the power of the tactical defensive. Hattaway and Jones suggest that any real decision in this battle was impossible. They make much of Lee's total casualties of 12,764 against the

Union loss of 17,728, a proportionate loss of 21 percent to 15 percent. But these figures are misleading because this loss is not 21 percent of Lee's entire army, because Longstreet's two divisions of men were not engaged, while it is based on an aggregate of Union troops who were very intermittently engaged.

Such figures would not lend such authority to the supposed supremacy of the tactical defensive if they were based around Hooker's core fighting force of seventy thousand men. Hagerman does not go so far as this gloomy prognosis, and shows how the Confederate cooperation of arms both on May 2 and 3 allowed first Jackson and then Stuart to take Union defensive lines without the loss inflicted on Union arms at Fredericksburg. Indeed, Hattaway and Jones develop their basic argument to the degree that they claim it is "an unrealistic assumption" to believe that Hooker could have destroyed the Army of Northern Virginia. Needless to say, the growing strength of the tactical defensive cannot be ignored; but though it is permissible to acknowledge its growing influence on Civil War battlefields, it by no means follows that historians should deduce from this premise that all tactical decision lay beyond the bounds of possibility. Such an argument verges on the circular and is excessively influenced by historians' knowledge of the conduct of the battles of the First World War.[22]

The reasons for the comparative indecisiveness of Chancellorsville have more to do with the tactical execution of the battle, especially in the offense, than any profound changes in the structure of warmaking itself. In the first place, Lee's field army of forty-three thousand, like that of Bragg before Perryville and Murfreesboro, was too small for truly decisive operations, given comparative levels of armament. Without a reserve, that is to say lacking Longstreet's corps or even part of it, Lee could not hope to do more than drive Hooker back; under the circumstances, even this was a tremendous achievement and does much to discredit the notion that nothing positive could be gained by fighting a great battle.

In the second place, great opportunities were created by operational maneuver, but the time in which to exploit these had been reduced by long approach marches. Once more a crucial tactical thrust was launched in the late afternoon or evening; once more the interruption of night prevented decisive operations from developing. Finally, truly decisive operations demand incredibly high levels of good fortune; certainly the goddess seemed to smile on Lee's endeavors considering the risks he had taken; but she suddenly frowned and the mortal wounding of Jackson was a savage blow just as he was moving forward to regain control of his divisions. The very high level of casualties inflicted on Confederate senior officers is certainly a hint of the future influence of firepower on the place of the commander in battle and his ability to exert tight tactical control at moments of crisis.[23]

Historians have also been concerned to explain Hooker's loss of nerve. The reasons are probably a compound of the personal and institutional. Hooker was not a general to be despised: he was a talented administrative innovator who centralized the command of the Army of the Potomac's cavalry. Yet he showed no flair for field command at the higher level, though he was highly capable at directing a corps. The Union high command in the east was hardly characterized by an excess of moral courage. His psychological inadequacies were aggravated by an earnest decision to give up drinking. This perhaps accounts for the swings in Hooker's mood. Yet at the moment of crisis his resolve folded, and armies tend to respond to the mood of their commander. "There was a want of nerve somewhere," suspected Major General Gouverneur Warren, and that paralysis had crept down the army's backbone from its directing brain. Armies that are constantly outmaneuvered by a more nimble adversary are prone to crises of confidence. Hence Hooker and his subordinates were receptive to suggestions of Southern martial superiority. Thus, although he had publicly ridiculed McClellan, Hooker increasingly came to resemble the creator of the Army of the Potomac and its "lost" leader. He exaggerated Southern numbers, shied away from launching an offensive, and fundamentally mismanaged his superior resources.[24]

The pace of the war in the east now quickened toward its dramatic climax with Lee's second invasion of the North. Lee hastened to remove federal forces from the rest of northern Virginia by advancing up the Shenandoah Valley toward the Potomac. Hooker, who still remained in command of the Army of the Potomac, had no choice but to follow him. At Winchester (June 14–15) the Army of Northern Virginia swept aside all opposition, taking over five thousand prisoners; but in a cavalry battle fought earlier at Brandy Station (June 9, 1863), the smooth articulation of Lee's preparations was disrupted when Stuart was surprised by another federal cavalry raid of eleven thousand troopers. Although Stuart retrieved the situation, the moral victory lay with the new Union cavalry commander, Major General Alfred Pleasonton. Stuart was criticized in the Southern press, and he began the new campaign determined to restore his flagging reputation. Because of the distraction of this separate cavalry action, Lee had difficulty screening his advance as he proceeded up the valley. Brandy Station rather than Winchester set the mold for the forthcoming campaign. Both sides were unaware of the presence of the other, collided, and were forced to fight battles they had not planned for.[25]

Hooker's confidence had not recovered after Chancellorsville and he had to be coached like a schoolboy by the president. He was a downcast and beaten man, and quickly subject once more to Halleck's authority. His demise was only a matter of time. On June 28, after an unseemly exchange over the scope of the general-in-chief's powers and an exhibition of McClellan-like tricks, including a call for reinforcements, Hooker was relieved and replaced by the senior corps commander, George G. Meade. Meade was a Pennsylvanian and potentially an asset should the decisive battle be fought in his native state. He was tall and rather severe, but lacked charisma. He was cautious and eminently safe: a solid and careful tactician. But he was highly strung and prone to outbursts of bad temper. He had been on the receiving end of too many of Lee's ruses to take a detached view of his opposite number and remained much in awe of him. His greatest weakness as a commander was an inability to rise to the challenges of conducting war at the higher level. He could not infuse the army with a grand purpose; his strategic thoughts were pedestrian and his operational execution halting. For all his irascibility, Meade was essentially a pleasant, mild gentleman; in short, he lacked the killer instinct. But he had the resolution to halt Lee, even though he could not outwit him.[26]

Meade had one further attraction. He had been born abroad and was thus ineligible for election to the presidency. He would not, therefore, be tantalized by presidential ambitions; and in any case, he had limited political interest. The decision to appoint him was made by the president in consultation with Stanton. The congressional radicals, whose influence usually thrived when the news from the front was bad, exerted no sway over the decision. Having supported Pope, Burnside, and Hooker, the Joint Committee's credibility had been damaged in all eyes save its own. Henceforth, few generals allied with it were appointed to high command. Despite the Emancipation Proclamation, the sidelining of radical favorites worried Senator Charles Sumner. Sumner and those who thought like him feared Union victories more than defeats. If military success came too rapidly, he feared that members of the administration, like Democrats, Copperheads, and William H. Seward, would insist upon an amnesty and allow the South to return to the Union with slavery intact.[27]

Lee's offensive onto Northern soil had begun brilliantly, even more auspiciously than the comparable invasion of September 1862. In a series of engagements in the Shenandoah Valley, more than seven thousand Union soldiers were put *hors de combat* (at a time when trained soldiers were in short supply and badly needed by Hooker and Meade), and the Army of Northern Virginia seized two hundred thousand rounds of ammunition, twenty-three pieces of artillery, and much foodstuffs as well as horses. This was a logistical bonus of great value. Lee's army seemed to be operating at a high level of proficiency and delivering well-executed attacks based on an efficient cooperation of arms with impeccable timing. This was all the more impressive because the death of Stonewall Jackson had forced Lee to institute a major organizational overhaul which would inevitably have an impact on his hitherto successful system of command.[28]

General Lee had decided that the existing corps structure, without Jackson's drive and experience, was too unwieldy. The two existing corps contained in excess of thirty thousand troops each and the span of command was too broad. It expected too much of one man to keep all these troops "under his eye in battle in the country that we have to operate in. They are always beyond the range of his vision, and frequently beyond his reach." A third corps was organized, commanded by A. P. Hill. Richard S. Ewell, rather than Stuart, also received promotion to lieutenant general and was appointed to replace Jackson in command of the Second Corps.

Ewell had served under Jackson since the Valley campaign of 1862. He had shown himself a vigorous divisional commander and was regarded as Jackson's heir. But he had lost a leg at Second Manassas and was suspected of being under the sway of a new bossy wife; doubts about his psychological and physical stamina for high command—especially that he lacked self-confidence—were dispelled somewhat by the Winchester operation. Nonetheless, Ewell was just as eccentric as his late and much lamented chief. He had a jerky, birdlike demeanor that encouraged him to draw the conclusion occasionally that he actually was a bird, and would disconcert subordinates with parrotlike squawkings when under pressure. A. P. Hill's metier, too, was divisional command. He was impetuous and subject to hypochondria—although, in truth, his health was uncertain. There can be no doubt that at a time when Lee was embarking on an operation pregnant with risk, that half of his army was entrusted to untried senior officers. Douglas Southall Freeman may exaggerate when he considered that this reorganization was sufficient to explain the defeat at Gettysburg, but it certainly underlines the incalculable loss represented by the death of Jackson.[29]

One aspect of this reorganization has provoked comment, namely that Ewell and Hill were both Virginians and thus, combined with Lee himself and Stuart, it confirmed the domination of a Virginia clique at the head of this army. Much of this comment relies on innuendo unworthy of serious historians.[30] Certainly there was grumbling at the promotion of two more Virginians, as such upheavals tend to lead to complaints from the disappointed and those who are temperamentally disinclined to welcome reorganization. Nonetheless, compared with the volcanic eruptions that overwhelmed the Army of Tennessee, these were mild ripples. Virginia had produced more trained officers than any other state and they were likely to be disproportionately represented in the higher ranks of senior officers. Lee's guarded appointment of Ewell and Hill was qualified by numerous complaints about the quality of Confederate generals and he clearly felt they were the best of a very restricted pool of talent. A. P. Hill was preferred over his morose namesake, the North Carolinian D. H. Hill, because of his long service with the Army of Northern Virginia and his acquaintance with Lee's working methods.

The continuance of this successful system was Lee's most important priority but he was much too sanguine in thinking that no modifications would be required in it, even though the men he had selected had been present during some of his greatest triumphs. Furthermore, any notion that Lee favored Virginians is controverted by the great favor bestowed on the Georgian, Longstreet, who was taken into Lee's confidence more warmly than any other general. Longstreet informed Lee of P. G. T. Beauregard's desire to serve in the Army of Northern Virginia. Beauregard's seniority rendered this impossible, but Lee urged on the Confederate president (in a move that he must have known would be unwelcome to Davis) that the Creole be given a separate force based at Culpeper Court House to menace Washington, DC. This could be organized out of the scattered garrisons of North Carolina, which Lee wanted to see concentrated at the decisive point.[31]

Lee's rationale for the Pennsylvania campaign has also been the subject of much debate and criticism. The whole question of his motives in launching an invasion of the North needs to be carefully drawn, for it reflects on two broader questions, namely how did the Confederate government react to an increasingly unenviable strategic dilemma and how did strategic policy contribute to the ultimate Confederate defeat? Lee's rationale was quite simple. His idea was to draw the Army of the Potomac away from its strong position on the Rappahannock, north of Fredericksburg, "where it could not be attacked except at a disadvantage." As in September 1862, Lee hoped "if practicable to transfer the scene of hostilities beyond the Potomac." That he should return to this fundamental idea is important because it confirmed Lee's belief that the vicinity of the Potomac *was the political center of gravity of the war*. Here the eyes of the world were focused, and only in this theater of operations could a victory be won with great political and international resonance. This was proven in reverse by Antietam, when a tactical repulse of a Union army had led Lincoln to issue the preliminary Emancipation Proclamation. Lee now sought a clear-cut Confederate victory on Northern soil to reverse the ill fortune that had dogged the earlier campaign. But its course had confirmed Lee in his view of the importance of moving north. Here was a priceless opportunity afforded by Chancellorsville to seize the political initiative; it should not be wasted.[32]

Lee might attempt to conceal the degree of risk involved in another invasion of the North from Davis and his cabinet when he sought their sanction, but he did not delude himself. His army had just escaped destruction in September 1862. "There is always hazard in military movements," he explained, "but we must decide between the positive loss of inactivity and the risk of action." Lee demanded concentration of effort at the decisive point and immediate action; these were the two vital elements of a defensive–offensive strategy. Lee's strategy was not blindly offensive or bullheaded.[33] "As far as I can judge there is nothing to be gained by this army remaining quietly on the defensive, which it must do unless it can be reinforced," he wrote.

The main priority on the Virginia front, he felt, must be to avoid another siege of Richmond. Given an inferiority of resources, a passive defensive policy would allow the Union to muster its great strength undisturbed, which could only lead inexorably to the Confederate loss of Richmond. "This may be the result in any event," Lee wrote with an ominous hint at the possibility of defeat, "still I think it is worth a trial to prevent such a catastrophe." Lee's argument for immediate action was strengthened by the assertion that "We should not therefore conceal from ourselves that our resources in men are constantly diminishing, and the disproportion . . . between us and our enemies, if they continue united in their efforts to subject us, is steadily augmenting." Lee was already alarmed at the reduction in strength of the Army of Northern Virginia. As it numbered about eighty thousand in December 1862 this was hardly evidence of a dramatic decline, but such a state of affairs required that the Confederacy *maintain* initiative and this could be done only by a forward movement. The alternative, frequently advocated by modern historians, that Lee should remain on the defensive hugging strong positions in northern Virginia, is based on an assumption of the utility and economy of the defensive that is frequently asserted but not proven.[34]

Moreover, Lee demonstrated his awareness of the declining strength of the Confederate political position. This understanding was given point by his recommendation that every overture for peace terms should be encouraged whatever its form, in order "that we should at least carefully abstain from measures or expressions that tend to discourage any party whose purpose is peace." The Peace Party in the North must be strengthened and the quickest way to do this was to occupy Northern territory and defy Union military strength. Pennsylvania was vulnerable and some counties showed disaffection with the war. Consequently, the more resources the North mobilized to resist invasion, the greater the psychological effect of defying it. Thus Lee's army had to be as strong as possible and not weakened by diversions or the defense of static points like the city of Richmond. Lee drew the logical deduction, namely that material weakness denotes offensive *movement* rather than inertia.[35]

It was the political dimension of the projected invasion that most appealed to the Confederate president. Davis wished to strike at Lincoln's rear and exacerbate growing war weariness in the North. In May 1863 Lee had been invited to a series of meetings in Richmond, including one with the full cabinet. Davis, always less decisive than he seemed, at first supported the scheme for an invasion of the North and then prevaricated. Although some criticisms were expressed, the rest of Davis's cabinet mostly supported Lee; the president, still anxious over the fate of besieged Vicksburg, then swung back to support his only consistently successful field commander. Nonetheless, neither Lee nor Davis could agree over what had actually been decided, and this was characteristic of Davis's diffuse but bossy direction of affairs. It was characteristic, too, of his failure to impose a consistent and unambiguous grand strategy on the Confederate war effort. A marked increase in tension arose between Lee and Davis, especially when Lee attempted to draw troops from other departments ("I cannot operate in this manner," he telegraphed in exasperation).[36]

The tension also illustrates grave structural weakness in the Confederate higher direction of the war, weaknesses that were already apparent the previous year.[37] Jefferson Davis had consistently opposed the appointment of a general-in-chief with real executive power, preferring an "adviser." That office had fallen vacant with Lee's appointment to command the Army of Northern Virginia and would not be filled until February 1864. With the president overburdened with too many problems to attend to, the central direction of the war suffered and Confederate strategy became the victim of lobbies that gained and then lost influence. These disputes were also marked by an intense personal antagonism, which was not so strong on the Northern side. One of these lobbies, obviously, was Lee. Lee enjoyed great prestige because of his long string of victories and because he had served as Davis's military adviser. He had much influence. But influence is not power, and Lee was *not* a de facto general-in-chief. He was too busy commanding an army and too distant from the other theaters to provide authoritative advice, as he continually reminded Davis. Davis should have either appointed him general-in-chief with clear-cut authority or stopped badgering him. By trying to get the best of both worlds, Davis put Lee in an impossible position. That both emerged with credit says much for the essential integrity of their working relationship.

When generals assume field command they identify with their army. Lee was no exception; he was immensely proud of his army and its achievements. This pride influenced the view he took of strategic matters. To argue in this way is not to accept the oft-repeated criticism that Lee was "parochial" in his strategic concerns, only to point out that he cannot be judged adequately as a grand strategist because, even taking informal influence into account, he was not serving in an appointment that gave him scope to direct affairs at this level. Nor does it follow necessarily that because Lee advocated the Northern expedition as an army commander, it was wrong. It was strategically sound, politically shrewd, and preferable to remaining on the defensive. Yet, because gifted soldiers adjust their thoughts in accordance with the level of their command and responsibilities, we cannot assume glibly (as Connelly does) that had Lee been appointed general-in-chief, he would have acted in the same way he did as an army commander in June and July 1863. What Davis was offering Lee in 1862 and 1863 was responsibility without power and Lee has suffered censure for assuming this burden.[38]

In their judicious account, Herman Hattaway and Archer Jones suggest that Lee's "enthusiasm" for garnering the opportunities arising from his invasion led him, "as he focused his attention on his own army," to lose "his appreciation of the realities of the total Confederate strategic situation."[39] But the real weakness here is *systemic*, not personal—the Confederate confusion of grand strategic direction with field command—and this has been disguised by the zeal of Civil War historians to criticize individual commanders rather than focus on the systems they operated under. They are excessively preoccupied with exalting their heroes and condemning those opposed to them. The man ultimately responsible for these systemic weaknesses was the Confederate president.

Davis worried, and rightly, about the fate of Vicksburg. Failures in the west, too, had more to do with weaknesses in command responsibility and organization. Confederate generals floundered in their efforts to muster fighting power out of barely adequate resources. The crisis in the west did not wholly result from inadequate resources but from an inability to organize them. Therefore, as both Joseph Johnston and Beauregard (the one responsible for its defense, the other as self-appointed spokesman for western affairs) had neglected Vicksburg in their strategic thinking, it seems perverse and hypercritical to blame Lee for its fall—a general whose connection with the problems of Mississippi was at best indirect.

Lee agreed with Johnston on the need for concentration. "It should never be forgotten that our concentration at any point compels that of the enemy, and his numbers being limited, tends to relieve other threatened localities." What the Confederate direction of the Vicksburg campaign needed was dynamic action and firm control, *not* reinforcements that would probably have arrived too late to affect the campaign and would have left Lee too weak to seize the initiative offered up by his victory at Chancellorsville. In strategy, as in stock investments, good money should not be thrown after bad. Lee was prepared to act and the Confederate secretary of war, James A. Seddon, told him to court risk if the outcome warranted it. The Pennsylvania expedition was the logical result of a policy that sought to avoid transforming the war in Virginia into the equivalent of a second Vicksburg siege—the siege of Richmond.

In Mississippi the South had lost the initiative, its logistics were a mess, and fragments of Confederate forces were too weak to throw Grant back. Those of Johnston and Pemberton combined could have achieved more than they managed when divided. Davis was determined to maintain the military capability to launch counteroffensives. The result was an unsupported invasion of the North by the Army of Northern Virginia. Although Davis did his best to reinforce it, his actions fell far short of the Herculean efforts that Lee demanded in order that he might gain his ambitious objectives. Not far beneath the exhilaration that characterized Lee's conduct at the end of June 1863 can be found a thick layer of despondency over the future of the Confederacy: a melancholy that induced desperation. Clifford Dowdey has shrewdly etched this dimension of Lee's strategic thinking. But it was more than the impulse of an ardent nature. The Gettysburg offensive was typical of the Confederate higher direction of war, with inadequate, poorly organized resources expected to accomplish great ends.[40]

Armies cannot fight without the necessary logistical support—especially American armies which, even in the South in the nineteenth century, enjoyed comparatively high standards of living. Armies that maneuver and thus expend high levels of physical energy demand even greater logistical resources. There was a tension latent in Lee's chosen mode of warfare. In order to keep his army mobile, he needed large logistical stocks. As the war continued he found it difficult to obtain these from northern Virginia and the only real solution was to cross the Potomac River and live off the country. This increased the risk of mounting defensive–offensive operations. But guarding the Shenandoah Valley was crucial. Here was Lee's prime source of supply that should be conserved at all costs; one of the most effective ways of doing this was to draw supplies from Maryland and Pennsylvania so that reserves could be built up. Yet if Lee went over to what really amounted to a passive defensive, relinquishing the initiative, and allowing his army to become a pool of reinforcements for other fronts, he ran the real danger of losing this area. Alan Nolan sorely neglects the importance of logistics when he advances the case for a purely defensive strategy.[41]

Lee's army finally crossed the Potomac on June 15 using Ewell's corps as an advance guard. Lee with Longstreet's corps followed on June 19, with A. P. Hill's corps following several days later. The temptation that must be resisted at all costs in appraising this campaign is the assumption that because the campaign ended in defeat, therefore disaster was foreordained. This is the worst kind of pseudo-Tolstoyan wisdom after the event. "Win, lose, or draw, the Gettysburg campaign was a strategic mistake because of the inevitable casualties that the Army of Northern Virginia could not afford," observes Nolan in his counsel of despair. Even though the Army of Northern Virginia was an excellent force, it would only be capable of achieving a victory on Northern soil if operational forethought and execution were of a high order. Yet significant errors were made which greatly increased the risk of the operation.[42]

The most serious error was Lee's decision to give Stuart discretionary orders to mount a raid, with more than half of his command, into the Union rear. Stuart, on the prompting of John S. Mosby, suggested a deep raid—in effect another "ride" around the Army of the Potomac. Lee's order was very vaguely worded; he laid down no clear-cut objectives or dates by which Stuart should return to the army. As the Army of Northern Virginia was moving out of territory with which it was familiar, the reconnaissance duties of cavalry would increase in importance, even become crucial to the operation. Stuart's division of five brigades was at its peak strength but Lee was proposing to divest himself of Stuart's incomparable talents, and those of his three best subordinates, just at the time when, as he admitted to Ewell, "I cannot give definite instructions, especially as the movements of General Hooker's army are not yet ascertained . . . carry out the plan you proposed so far as in your judgment may seem fit." He was therefore advancing blindly. In his decision to send Stuart on another raid that he hoped would demoralize the federals even more, Lee showed excessive disdain for his enemy.

Lee was an immensely self-confident general and an opportunistic virtuoso, but at the beginning of the campaign he failed to mark out a clear-cut concept of what the campaign was designed to achieve militarily; this is quite frequent in the nineteenth century and Grant, too, liked to keep his options open. Lee, however, asked too much of his inexperienced subordinates. In failing to modify his system of command, he risked losing control of his army. The number of formations needing coordination had also multiplied and Lee could no longer take the cooperation of units for granted.[43]

Lee's essential difficulty was that by his own volition he had changed the conditions of war. As Peter Parish has observed, Lee was essentially a counterpuncher of supreme skill. Under these conditions, in which Lee improvised expedients to foil Union moves, the enemy himself provided a clear-cut, unambiguous objective. In an offensive operation the enemy is not so obliging. Lee was under no illusions that he could advance into the enemy's own country without encountering opposition, though he hoped to avoid battle under disadvantageous circumstances. He would fight when it suited him. Nevertheless, as a prime objective was logistical, and the Army of Northern Virginia was subsisting in rich agricultural land, the army had to disperse to live off the country. As in September 1862, concentration became problematical. Unless Lee exerted a measure of tight control over his scattered units, he was risking a meeting engagement before he was ready and his army was concentrated, and without most of his cavalry to give that measure of advantage in securing reliable intelligence that had so distinguished his earlier campaigns. Consequently, his lack of trustworthy information impaired his ability to perform effectively at the operational level.[44]

Before his relief, Hooker had hoped to strike at Lee's lines of communication. He sought "elbow room" in which to maneuver. Lee's army was scattered throughout southern Pennsylvania from Chambersburg to Heidlersburg; his wagon trains stretched back a hundred miles into Virginia. Lee had lost contact with Stuart's cavalry as Hooker's army had moved north with unexpected rapidity, blocking Stuart's attempts to send him intelligence. This move redounds to Hooker's credit. Whereas in 1862 the Army of the Potomac had averaged sluggish marches of only six miles per day, in June 1863 it had transferred its base of operations smoothly and advanced forty-five miles in two days, concentrating five corps, three cavalry divisions, plus the artillery reserve east of South Mountain. But Hooker instinctively shied away from confronting Lee again. His plan to attack Lee's lines of communication is a case in point. The decision to stab at Lee's long, vulnerable lines was only made after Lee's own decision on June 25 to do away with them and live entirely off the country. Winfield Scott had done this in Mexico. Lee reflected the practice of an earlier campaign in which he had been a participant. He also anticipated the methods that Sherman would adopt in 1864. (We may therefore dispose of the judgment rendered by T. Harry Williams that Lee "was the last of the great old fashioned generals."[45]) The use that Lee had in mind for Beauregard and his second army now becomes apparent—it could guard Lee's rear (including Richmond) as well as play on fears for the security of Washington. At any rate, Lee felt that if they were to play no role in his invasion, these troops should be sent to reinforce Johnston in Mississippi; they were useless as garrisons.[46]

Lee issued strict orders to prevent marauding while he lived off the country. Uncontrolled plundering would rot the discipline of the army; in any case it would be counterproductive, for stealing would stimulate resistance while Lee's main priority was nurturing Northern disillusion with the war, of which Pennsylvania gave abundant evidence. All requisitions were to be paid for with "Confederate money or certificates." As this currency was worthless, Lee was simply offering a quasi-legal gloss on an act of acquisition, but the gloss was vital to Confederate propaganda. As he wrote to Davis, "I do not know that we can do anything to promote the pacific feeling, but our course ought to be so shaped as not to discourage it." Such hopes have encouraged claims that Southern troops behaved with more restraint than Northerners. The evidence does not bear this out, and Confederates continued "foraging" even during the last hours of the retreat.

It was a logistical move—a search for shoes in the little town of Gettysburg, which lay at the hub of a network of roads—that began the famous battle. On June 30 a brigade of Henry Heth's division collided unexpectedly with John Buford's brigade of Union cavalry and withdrew. Heth then brought up his entire division on July 1, followed by two more of A. P. Hill's divisions. Neither of the commanding generals were involved in these meeting engagements, or even knew that the enemy was present in the vicinity.[47]

Meade had been ordered to "maneuver and fight in such manner as to cover the capital and also Baltimore. . . . Should General Lee move upon either of these places, it is expected that you will either anticipate him or arrive with him so as to give him battle." Meade was given unprecedented powers to appoint or dismiss subordinates irrespective of seniority. The instruction to "cover" Washington, DC, lent Meade's strategy a defensive hue from the outset; he had inherited no plan from Hooker but he felt obliged to retain Hooker's clever but insincere, manipulative, and duplicitous chief of staff, Daniel Butterfield, because nobody else would take the job. Meade was anxious lest Lee cross the Susquehanna River because such a move would greatly complicate his task of simultaneously covering Washington and bringing the Confederates to battle. He thus maneuvered the Army of the Potomac toward the Baltimore-Harrisburg Road, placing emphasis on his right flank. This would give him a central position from which he could guard all three of these cities and perhaps strike at "Lee's army in detail." His relations with Halleck were much better than Hooker's and he hastened to keep the general-in-chief apprised of his movements.

On June 30 Meade discovered a Confederate "disposition" to move toward Gettysburg. His planning required a change of emphasis. The Second and Third Corps were moved toward Taneytown and Emmitsburg to strengthen his left and Meade gave command of this force (plus the First and Eleventh Corps), the entire left wing of his army, to Major General John F. Reynolds. Reynolds was a reliable and aggressive corps commander, and a fellow Pennsylvanian whom Lincoln had considered for the chief command. Meade became increasingly sensitive to the unwisdom of making the smallest error and paid closest attention to the movement of his formations. He admitted that he felt "much oppressed with a sense of responsibility and the magnitude of the great interests entrusted to me." Fortified by Buford's superb reconnaissance, Meade moved two of his corps to the environs of Gettysburg with four others nearby.

He also issued the Pipe Creek Circular that day outlining a strong position in Maryland, which the Army of the Potomac could withdraw to, should circumstances dictate, and fight a defensive battle. This document was later used by Butterfield before the Joint Committee on the Conduct of the War to besmirch Meade's reputation in a crafty effort to exculpate its favorite and Butterfield's friend, Hooker. This document merely canvassed possibilities and the need to consider how circumstances might change. Meade was still undecided about the wisdom of the concentration in the direction of Gettysburg, for he did not know the ground there. His decision to give command of half his army to the trusted Reynolds is evidence that Meade was determined to fight at the earliest opportunity under conditions that were advantageous to him. If Reynolds decided to fight, Meade would be content in the knowledge that Reynolds thought it was the right place for a battle, and one where the Army of the Potomac had a strong chance of winning.[48]

It was unwise of Lee to allow himself to be dragged so unexpectedly, though hardly reluctantly, into a battle before he was fully prepared. The fundamental fault that disfigured his conduct of the campaign was that Lee was overly confident and expected too much of his marvelous troops. He was ready to seize on any opportunity that came his way and turn it to his advantage. But was it the right opportunity? "Tomorrow, gentlemen," Lee told his staff casually, "we will not move to Harrisburg as we expected but will go over to Gettysburg and see what General Meade is after." Lee should have set the objectives of the campaign, not allowed the Union commander to set them for him. Lee had received no firm intelligence as to the movements of the Army of the Potomac until June 28. This came from a source he distrusted, a spy in Longstreet's pay named Henry T. Harrison. He brought news of the crossing of the Potomac by the

Union army and the concentration of five corps east of South Mountain. As it was imperative to keep the Union army as far east as possible, both to enlarge the foraging area and protect the line of retreat, Lee decided to temporarily hold back the northward advance—which aimed to cross the Susquehanna River and take the state capital at Harrisburg (an objective of political significance). Instead Lee sought to concentrate southward and eastward at Cashtown. His realignment of the army represented a drastic alteration of his plans based on weak intelligence and taken at short notice.[49]

Of the bulk of his cavalry, Lee knew nothing. Stuart had disappeared and remained unaware of the moves that had led to the opening of the battle. Lee feared lest his cavalry had been overcome by disaster. He had two other cavalry brigades with him but these lacked an enterprising commander. What he really missed was Stuart himself, his drive and initiative. It was therefore not audacious but foolhardy to precipitate a battle without the "eyes and ears" of his army.

Yet despite these handicaps, the first phase of the battle went well for the Confederates. Two Union corps, the First and the Eleventh, were thrown back by a closely coordinated attack by Ewell and Hill's corps and Gettysburg was taken (this was important because seven of Lee's nine divisions needed to use roads converging on Gettysburg in order to effect a concentration). Lee ordered a pursuit with the proviso that high ground south of the town, Cemetery Hill and Culp's Hill, should be taken "if practicable." Hill's third division was delayed in arriving on the field by traffic congestion. An outright victory could not be achieved and the responsibility for this failing has led to much criticism of Hill and Ewell by Lee's admirers, and of Lee himself by his more zealous detractors.[50]

Much of this latter criticism is misconceived. Lee had thought that should the Army of the Potomac still be in position the following day, he would attack it. In a meeting with his generals he thrust his fist into the air in a rather melodramatic gesture. Lee thought he had encountered an unsupported fragment of the Army of the Potomac and, as he enjoyed a local superiority of force on the field, he could smash it before Union reinforcements arrived. That is to say, Gettysburg would resemble Second Manassas in reverse. There is an element of desperation in Lee's gesture as described by Longstreet: an overeagerness to move and garner opportunities without being fully apprised of the facts. Yet Lee had good grounds for confidence. The two corps (almost half of Meade's available force) had been severely defeated, losing fifteen thousand casualties (including more than four thousand prisoners); the First and Eleventh Corps could muster only about five thousand men on the evening of July 1. The redoubtable Reynolds had also been killed; the loss of his sound tactical advice was a grave blow for Meade. Furthermore, Lee had concentrated his army rapidly and was posed to strike an overwhelming blow—perhaps at the north end of the Gettysburg position, perhaps farther south.[51]

As Lee was struggling to impose an operational design on events it is by no means evident that failure to take the high ground south of Gettysburg, Cemetery Hill and Culp's Hill, was as serious an error as some historians have suggested. Therefore who was responsible for it is a question of minor significance. Lee had decided to renew the attack on the following day in any case, so it is the relevance of these operations to his overall concept that really counts. Judging from past experience, even if Ewell and Hill had been successful in driving the First and Eleventh Corps from the high ground, these operations with tired troops could not possibly have reached their full potential until 7:30–8:00 PM. Thus even if the Confederates could have gained the tactical advantage of occupying the high ground, driving Union forces back on advancing formations, and dislocating Meade's concentration, the hour was too late to consummate this success decisively. Successful military operations do not consist merely in occupying significant topographical points, but rather in how such movements contribute to the defeat of the opponent's army. By leaving these hills in Union hands, Lee left ground that Meade could not abandon without inviting disaster. Thus if Ewell and Hill were to launch diversionary assaults, Cemetery Hill and Culp's Hill would act like magnets drawing in previously engaged Union units irresistibly from other parts of the front.

During the evening of July 1 Lee decided, after much debate and some changes of mind (not least the rescinding of a decision after Ewell had personally appeared at his headquarters), to move Ewell's corps around west of Gettysburg. The prime responsibility for the attack the next day was given to Longstreet's First Corps who would advance against Meade's left. Ewell had not shown Jackson's dash and initiative. One of his defenders argues that "the fair question is whether Hill and Ewell discharged their duties reasonably well . . . not whether they matched the standard of excellence set by Stonewall Jackson." But regrettably this momentous campaign demanded such a standard of excellence. Certainly Lee was to blame for not gripping his subordinates and giving them firmer direction. One of his most impressive characteristics as a commander was granting his subordinates the benefit of the doubt. At Gettysburg this tendency was to bring him to grief.[52]

Meade's position at Gettysburg was strong defensively but far from invulnerable, for the simple reason that most of it was unoccupied. It has been likened on numerous occasions to a fishhook. Cemetery and Culp's Hills pro-

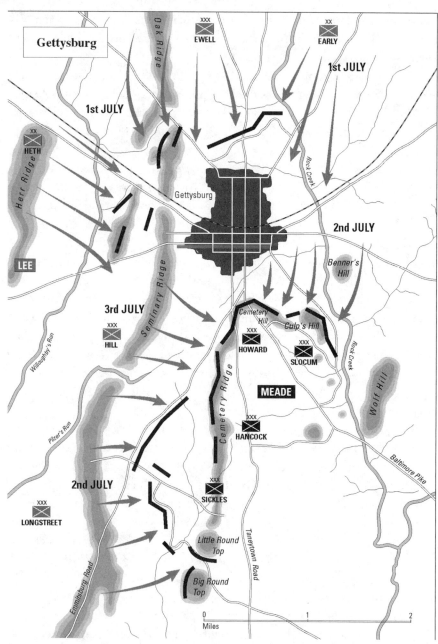

Gettysburg

From Brian Holden Reid, *Robert E. Lee: Icon for a Nation*
(London: Weidenfeld & Nicolson, 2005). Map © Peter Harper.
Reprinted by permission of The Orion Publishing Group.

vided the protrusion, Cemetery Ridge the spine, and with two conical hills, Big and Little Round Top, as the base. The Emmitsburg Road, running from the town, ran parallel with Cemetery Ridge. The latter did not look imposing from a distance, for the country was lush and undulating: the defensive position had good, open fields of fire. Opposite lay the much shallower Seminary Ridge, which was thinly covered with woods; Cemetery Ridge, utilized mainly as arable farmland, had been cleared of most of its tree cover; so another geographical feature, dense forest that had done so much to screen Lee's attacks in Virginia, was missing in Pennsylvania.

The great weakness of Southern generalship during the Civil War was in launching offensives; so many of these had been ill directed and piecemeal, mainly due to impulsive indiscipline. Lee had done much to reduce this tendency in the Army of Northern Virginia since the Seven Days'. A successful attack is a compound of exact timing, concentration of firepower and movement, and an efficient cooperation of arms. The challenge faced in combining these elements in his second attack at Gettysburg was complicated by a need for hurried improvisation arising out of an unexpected meeting engagement and from the distribution of his three corps. Lee was on exterior, not interior, lines. He occupied the outer edge of a concave position five miles long. His nine divisions in thirty-four brigades of infantry and two of cavalry averaged ten thousand men per mile (six to each yard). Meade deployed fifty-one brigades of infantry and seven of cavalry along a three-mile line. He also enjoyed an advantage in artillery, with 354 guns to Lee's 272; he could push forward 118 guns per mile of front, while Lee could only oppose him with 54. In sum, Meade fielded a total of 88,289 men and Lee 73,280. As the attacker, Lee was numerically inferior; but this might be a far from insuperable obstacle. The odds were less, for example, than Napoleon faced in the Waterloo campaign.[53]

As the federal position combined narrowness with defense in depth, Lee had to organize his blows from a base that was both broad and shallow. His fundamental tactical problem has been well expounded by Jennings Cropper Wise: Lee needed "the utmost cooperation between the various parts of the exterior line, together with the concentration of its fire effect"; this was crucial because he needed to weaken the enemy's strength on the inner line. If he failed to achieve this precondition, his attack would fail "for the lack of momentum of a superior mass at any given point of assault."[54] This Lee failed to achieve, but it should not be deduced from his failure that defeat was inevitable. The decision to strike Meade's right, toward the peach orchard and the high ground to the south, was not a headstrong, crude, frontal assault against a well-posted and prepared enemy. When the idea was mooted on the evening of July 1, this flank was open with two already beaten Union corps pinned down on Culp's and Cemetery Hills. If the ground to Meade's right could be seized rapidly and *early enough* the following day, then not only could Confederate artillery shatter the First and Eleventh Corps from the rear but the cohesion of Meade's army could also be shattered. It would be defeated piecemeal as individual corps rushed to relieve their beleaguered comrades. In short, the concept was representative of Lee at his scintillating best. But the execution was fatally flawed and the responsibility for this was Lee's, too.

The concept resembled Second Manassas; this had always been held up by James Longstreet as the model that all Confederate planning should attempt to emulate. His opposition to Lee's plan is therefore inexplicable. Throughout his memoir, *From Manassas to Appomattox*, Longstreet exaggerates the strength of the Union position and conveys the impression that it was as strong on July 2 as it had become on July 3.[55] Longstreet's role in the campaign has been the subject of heated controversy. Much of it was motivated by postwar animosity toward his apostasy in embracing the cause of the Republican Party and joining the ranks of the "Scalawags" during Reconstruction. Nonetheless, his role in the campaign had probably more to do with the internal politics of the Army of Northern Virginia than any other factor. Longstreet's post facto rationalization (which is really a didactic effort to explain Confederate defeat in general) dwells on operational and tactical factors in an effort to disguise his personal ambitions.[56]

Longstreet was a vain, opinionated, imposing, and rather difficult man. He had no small opinion of his own abilities and he nursed ambitions that he should succeed Jackson as Lee's right-hand man. Before 1863 it had been Jackson, rather than Lee, who had been the illustrious popular hero of the Confederacy and his role in Lee's triumphs had been greatly exaggerated by newspaper reports. This is surely the root of Longstreet's extraordinary misconception that his agreeable intimacy with Lee, and his obvious seniority vis-à-vis Ewell and Hill, made him cocommander of the army with some kind of right of veto over decisions. This was not Lee's style, as Longstreet would soon discover. Lee often asked the opinion of his subordinates but never sought a sharing of responsibility for his decisions. Unlike President Davis, Lee was much more decisive than he actually appeared. But for Lee's political skill and the extraordinary strength of his personality, which seemed to compel admiration and a dominating sway by the most understated methods, Longstreet's ambitions could have rent the Army of Northern Virginia thoroughly, as they were to cleave the Army of Tennessee on more fertile ground for mischief after the battle of Chickamauga.[57]

Longstreet had begun to develop some airy ideas about combining defensive tactics with an offensive strategy. These were half baked and by no means as fully developed as he later made out. He would claim, too, that he had secured Lee's assent to pursue this policy during the Pennsylvania incursion, as Lee had recognized its desirability. This is more evidence that he thought he had gained ground as Lee's *Svengali*. Given the opportunistic nature of the campaign on which Lee had embarked, he would never have given any such undertaking to a subordinate. He might have listened politely and even agreed that under certain circumstances such a policy had much to commend it. But those circumstances did not prevail on July 1 and 2. Moving around Meade's left flank would surrender the initiative to the federals, sacrifice the concentration achieved by July 1, and expose the Army of Northern Virginia to defeat in detail as its own flank would be exposed before a strong defensive position could be located. Here was the rub. Lee had few cavalry at hand because of Stuart's absence; to undertake this kind of movement without decent intelligence while tactically blind would be foolish. Finally, such a maneuver was logistically unsustainable.

It is thus hard to reconcile Longstreet's postwar rationalization of his lack of enthusiasm for an attack and his contemporary enthusiasm for Second Manassas. The defensive element in this battle was actually small and Longstreet had launched the offensive element. The only answer to the conundrum must be that Longstreet sought, by exaggerating his military differences with his chief, to disguise the real point at issue. As this had more to do with their personal relationship and working methods, his resultant behavior was characterized by wounded pride and pique.[58]

This behavior notwithstanding, Longstreet had not provided any realistic solution to the tactical dilemmas facing Lee. The latter was determined to launch an attack; he believed that he was so near victory and that the Army of the Potomac was a vulnerable target. Lee sought to strike the individual corps with concentrated force as they approached Gettysburg and Longstreet agreed with this plan. Lee had already made a promising start on July 1. However, the elements that had brought success in his earlier battles were breaking down.

In the first instance, the speed of improvisation demanded by the sudden battle led to defective cooperation exacerbated by faulty staffwork. At this stage of the war this must be condemned as a serious weakness. Lee relied heavily on oral orders and these resulted in much misunderstanding and action taken at cross-purposes. Longstreet used this as an excuse for dilatoriness. First thing on the morning of July 2 Lee reaffirmed that the First Corps would strike Meade's exposed flank. Shortly after 8 AM Lee left Longstreet and rode around north of his position to confer with Ewell, who was to launch a diversionary attack from the north. During the morning a reconnaissance had discovered the camps of the Union Third Corps behind the position. Longstreet took alarm at this but they were not dug in and formed an inviting target for a sudden attack, like the Eleventh Corps at Chancellorsville. Longstreet's infantry had already been delayed in their approach march by congestion on the roads; the corps commander decided to wait for the arrival of Major General George E. Pickett's division that had to march all the way from Chambersburg.

The attack was due to be launched at 11 AM. When Lee returned to Longstreet's command post shortly after 11 AM he found that his preparations had been all but desultory. Longstreet was habitually deliberate in preparation, but this was perversely so. "I never like to go into battle with one boot off," he said. "Longstreet is a very good fighter when he gets into position and gets everything ready," Lee is supposed to have complained, "but he is *so slow*." Jubal A. Early was the dubious source for this complaint and Longstreet's most ferocious postwar critic. It cannot be construed as a judgment on Longstreet's overall style. On this occasion, however, Longstreet found every excuse to delay. When all factors are considered and taking all the evidence into consideration (and certainly resisting any attempt to make Longstreet the scapegoat for the defeat), Longstreet did not act on July 2 with the vigor, efficiency, and loyalty that Lee had the right to expect from his most senior subordinate.[59]

Second, the course of military operations are not decided only by the mistakes of one side, they are determined also by the corresponding action of the other. If Lee had calculated that Meade's accession of command would lead to a prolonged period of study and adjustment, he was mistaken. Meade acted with a volcanic energy and determination belied by his professorial appearance. He had been taken by surprise when his troops collided with Confederates at Gettysburg, but he was not thrown off balance. He was a cautious tactician, but unlike McClellan knew his own mind and did not abdicate his responsibilities. He was a proficient defensive commander and, after his arrival from Taneytown in the early hours of July 2, knew a strong position when he saw one. He rushed the Second, Third, and Fifth Corps onto Cemetery Ridge and ordered that they entrench. Thus during the long delay that morning, Meade was given the priceless opportunity of transforming the Gettysburg position into the immensely strong shield that Longstreet had feared to attack; but Longstreet had summoned up images of its formidable power before it was prepared. "Well," said Meade after casting an experienced eye over the position, "we may as well fight it out here just as well as anywhere else."[60]

Meade's position along Cemetery Ridge had one grave weakness that Lee's engineer's eye readily spotted. Because of undulations the ground at the peach orchard in front of Cemetery Ridge was actually higher than the ridge itself. The commander of the Third Corps, the raffish, conceited, and petulant Major General Daniel E. Sickles, immediately realized the danger to his corps if it remained stationary. He took the wholly understandable step of advancing his troops forward to this higher ground. Tactically, Sickles's action was justified; but operationally he had weakened Meade's defensive line. Meade did not hold Sickles in high regard, considering him an ignorant, vain *poseur* of dubious morals. Sickles did not bother to explain to his commander that he had moved beyond his allotted position, and Meade was so preoccupied with the imminence of Ewell's attack to the north that he could not inspect his front. By making this unilateral move Sickles had broken the cohesion of Meade's line; he had advanced almost half a mile beyond it, exposing his own flanks, and had placed his corps in a salient vulnerable to converging fire. This did much to negate the advantages of making the move in the first place as the length of the front he had to cover was doubled. Meade's left flank was thus still vulnerable to a strongly executed attack. Failures in communication during this campaign were not a Confederate monopoly.[61]

Meade ordered Sickles to withdraw his corps to Cemetery Ridge but then changed his mind when Longstreet's much-delayed assault opened. This was the real crisis of the battle, not the symbol-laden Confederate attack on the third day. Confusion continued to prevail. Lee had rather publicly corrected Longstreet as to the direction of his corps's attack, which he wanted perpendicular and not parallel to the Emmitsburg Road. This had put Longstreet in his place and afterward he appeared very grumpy. Longstreet, in turn, sternly refused to permit Major General Lafayette McLaws to personally conduct a reconnaissance of the unfamiliar ground over which his division was to advance. Lee had intended that McLaws and John B. Hood's divisions would strike an open flank. Instead, by 3:30–4:00 PM Union forces occupied Little Round Top and the steeper broken ground, peppered with large rocks, surrounding Plum Run. Furthermore, Lee had insisted that the advance be made without risking discovery by a Union signal station on Little Round Top. The threat of discovery forced a confused countermarch that agitated Longstreet's temper further and added to the delay. Lee's orders to Longstreet were then eight hours old.[62]

As Hood's troops prepared to attack, his skirmishers discovered that the flank toward the big Round Top was unguarded. Hundreds of wagons were packed there and the route to Meade's rear was completely open. Hood asked

Longstreet for permission to turn this flank. As seeking an open flank was the object of the operation, Longstreet's refusal seems incredible. In a rebuke to Hood, Longstreet snapped, "It is General Lee's order—the time is up—attack at once." This contravenes the very spirit of Lee's system of command and indeed contradicts Longstreet's (and Lee's) own view of proper Confederate strategy— namely that the Confederacy should oppose Union numbers and *materiel* with operational skill that wore away at federal morale. Longstreet must have been anxious at the passage of time, but this does not excuse his rejection of this extraordinary opportunity; his conduct was reprehensible. It is a measure of the personal pique he felt that in his memoirs, *From Manassas to Appomattox*, he conflates Hood's request to turn Meade's left—an adjustment of operational direction—with Lee's refusal to countenance his own plan to move *around* Meade's left, a change of strategic direction in order to seek a new defensive position. Lee, he claimed, had refused at least twice to accept such a move. The two schemes were completely separate acts of war, and should not be confused.[63]

Despite the delay, the attack of two divisions amounting to 14,500 infantry in oblique order, striking Meade's front at a refused angle, was not well executed. McLaws and Hood attacked separately and the fighting power of their divisions became diffused as Hood's brigades found it difficult to cooperate over the rough terrain broken by small hills. The wheat field south of the peach orchard exchanged hands six times; the fighting was ferocious and unremitting. Sickles's position was not a strong one, but his corps was fortunate (especially after Sickles was carried wounded from the field—Meade's second corps commander rendered *hors de combat*) that Longstreet's corps had only managed to get forty-eight of its more than eighty cannon into action. The Union troops had dug rifle pits and made good use of low stone walls and farm buildings. Union counterbattery fire was especially accurate and reduced the potency of Confederate covering fire.

Lee had hoped that, once Longstreet had gained the high ground of the peach orchard, then Sickles's infantry and the Second Corps to the north could be driven from their positions. If all went as Lee planned, Longstreet's infantry could sweep all before it and take the defenders of Cemetery Hill and Culp's Hill in the rear. The role of artillery in the successful Union defense was vital. Skillful use was made of the reserve artillery and devastating fire brought to bear on exposed infantry lines and the outgunned Confederate artillery. Brigadier General Henry J. Hunt, restored by Meade to the command of the Army of the Potomac's artillery, dislocated the fundamental elements of Lee's plan based on a cooperation of arms and prevented him from securing the victory he so badly needed. By 7 PM Longstreet's troops had become bogged down in separate, unrelated fights. He had failed to take Little Round Top but had taken Devil's Den, much of the peach orchard, and the bases of both the round tops. The federal Third Corps fell back to Cemetery Ridge in confusion. Thanks to the inspired tactical direction of Major General Winfield Scott Hancock, who was entrusted with command of the Third Corps in addition to the Second Corps, Meade still held Cemetery Ridge intact and controlled the summits of the round tops. Despite some incursions he still held the Plum Run inviolate. Fighting ceased on this front at 9 PM.[64]

Longstreet had succeeded in getting some of his troops up on Cemetery Ridge before they were driven back. His attack was unsupported; indeed, Longstreet's entire thrust was crippled by a failure to organize concentrated blows at the decisive point. The vitality of the Army of Northern Virginia was drained by the perennial Southern weakness of launching disjointed, piecemeal attacks. Lee had failed to orchestrate his moves in an operational sequence. Longstreet had been supported on his left flank by Anderson's division of Hill's Third Corps. It might have been better to have left this division in reserve to give any breakthrough a real punch and drive Sickles's Third Corps completely from the field. "Each Division had fought its battle almost alone and in no case with its full strength exerted," concludes Freeman.

This experience was repeated before Cemetery and Culp's Hills. Henry Hunt had succeeded in replenishing the ammunition stocks of the First and Eleventh Corps. Lee had hoped that a demonstration on the Union right would draw reserves north and facilitate a breakthrough on the Union left. Ewell's attack actually began after Longstreet's, rather than before it; as Meade was most fearful for this part of the line the converse would have been preferable. When his artillery opened fire, Ewell found that it provoked furious Union counterbattery fire. Under these inauspicious circumstances he decided to launch a major assault. Powerful Union artillery fire drove back Confederate batteries and thus denied Ewell's infantry covering fire. Ewell asked for support from Hill's corps to the right, but launched his attack before he received notification of its availability. Ewell's divisions attacked separately. The attack was poorly timed and Ewell's coordination was lamentable. Consequently, Ewell's divisions could not overcome breastworks and Union infantry posted behind stone walls, although they did succeed in taking some of these works at the base of Culp's Hill.[65]

The second day at Gettysburg was a near Confederate victory. It had been marred by poor coordination and the cooperation of arms had broken down. The essential problem was one of communication. The Confederates had not established a system of visual signaling that was immune from Union interception and relied too much on word of mouth. Lee concluded from his experience "that with proper concert of action, and with the increased support that the positions gained on the right would enable the artillery to render the assaulting columns, we should ultimately succeed, and it was accordingly determined to continue the attack." In short Lee hoped to restore both the breakdown of cooperation between the arms and his formations; the latter had been riven especially by hasty improvisation. One development, however, helped restore the cooperation of arms. Stuart and his cavalry had at last returned to Lee's army on the morning of July 2.[66]

The battle of Gettysburg was undoubtedly the worst Lee directed because the fighting power of his army was dissipated. This had occurred during the battle of Malvern Hill, but then Lee attacked an opponent who refused to face up to his responsibilities as a commander. Meade was in a superior category as an operational commander: his skillful combinations had resulted, for the first time in the history of the Army of the Potomac, in an efficient concentration of its formidable fighting power. Lee's decision to renew the attack was therefore a blunder; it was a desperate gamble. Lee decided to strike Meade's center with fresh troops including Pickett's division, which arrived on the battlefield during the night. His tactical problem was that Meade's position along Cemetery Ridge was now formidable—as formidable as Longstreet had erroneously claimed it was on July 1. Consequently, if his aim was to destroy a fragment of the Union army, or destroy it piecemeal, he had to create an open flank first. He decided to do this by striking at the comparatively fresh Second Corps, commanded by Winfield Scott Hancock, rather than by renewing the effort against the weakened Third Corps.

This was the attack that came to be immortalized as "Pickett's Charge." It has been severely censured, especially by interwar writers such as General Fuller, Captain B. H. Liddell Hart, and those influenced by them as foreshadowing the bloody, inept, and futile offensives along the western front in the First World War.[67] As on the second day, "Pickett's Charge," indeed, the whole of Longstreet's assault, was never designed to be an unsupported frontal assault. Lee intended to use the captured breastworks on Culp's Hill to strike at Meade's rear and force him to rush reserves from the center to his right. Stuart, moreover, was dispatched with his exhausted troopers to Meade's center rear; there was some further cavalry skirmishing on the Union right flank with both sides attempting to strike at their enemy's soft rear echelons. Such operations represented a much greater danger to either side as they were firmly established in positions from which they showed no inclination to move.[68]

Lee's plan broke down immediately on the morning of July 3. Meade was determined not to stand by and passively permit Lee to strike his blows with impunity. For one thing, the quality of his intelligence remained far superior. Despite his reputation as a hard taskmaster with a savage temper and cruel tongue, Meade invariably took his subordinates into his confidence so that they fully understood their parts in the plan. On the evening of July 2 Meade held a meeting at the small, simple, whitewashed Leister farmhouse that served as his headquarters. He did not intend that this gathering should act as a council of war, but as a means of discovering the army's fitness for offensive operations. As Lee had already committed the bulk of his strength, all corps commanders agreed that they should continue to stand and fight. The meeting denoted, it has been suggested, a certain lack of confidence in the new commanding general, if not a wobbly spine. Meade's willingness to break off the battle has been undoubtedly exaggerated and so has his lack of resolve; Meade's position was strengthened by the unanimous support of his subordinates. Major General John Newton, Reynolds's successor at the First Corps, declared, "They have hammered us into a solid position they cannot whip us out of."

Early the following morning Ewell launched a further attack on Culp's Hill; only after his men had been sent forward did he receive a message from Lee that Longstreet would not be ready until 10 AM. But it was too late to recall the troops, who advanced piecemeal. At 8 AM Newton's First Corps launched counterattacks on Ewell's troops and they were driven from the breastworks they had captured the previous day. The pattern of muddled planning and execution, indifferent communication, and execrable timing thus persisted. Meade had strengthened an exposed flank without endangering his center.[69]

Thus Lee's design to launch a simultaneous converging attack collapsed. His system of combining oral orders with the delegation of all tactical detail to his subordinates was disintegrating under the combined weight of time pressures, instant improvisation, the inexperience of Ewell and Hill at the corps level, and the tensions resulting from the recalcitrance of Longstreet. Lee was unduly complacent and should carry the full responsibility for not imposing firmer direction on the course of operations. There is no evidence from his correspondence to confirm the claim that Lee had fallen victim to illness.

Should he thus have abandoned his offensive and waited in position along Seminary Ridge in the hope that political pressure would force Meade to attack him? Lacking lines of communication and living off the country, the one thing he could not do was remain stationary. Seminary Ridge, in any case, was far from an ideal defensive position. Preparations for the reckless gamble of striking at

302   AMERICA'S CIVIL WAR

Meade's center were allowed to continue. But Longstreet was now right in
thinking that Cemetery Ridge was too formidable to be taken by the troops
available unless cooperation of the attacking elements worked perfectly. As Lee
later admitted, "It's all my fault; I thought my men were invincible."[70] Yet he
had pulled off the "impossible" before and he never flinched from a challenge.
Ultimately, decisions in battle defy the neat, rational categories imposed on
them by historians because war is not an academic business.

Lee's admission, furthermore, does not excuse Longstreet from launching a
very shabbily directed assault. Pickett was not informed that his division would
be required and this led to the delay that stymied Ewell's earlier assault.
Longstreet was still too preoccupied with pressing his own cherished design to
attend to his proper job. He urged a move around Meade's left again on the
morning of July 3, despite Lee's increasing impatience. "Pickett's Charge" actually comprised troops from three other divisions. Although the deployment of
this force greatly impressed onlookers on Cemetery Ridge, with flags flying, officers and men smartly accoutered, and lines well dressed, the formation was
faulty. The troops from the Third Corps were not properly aligned with those of
the First, so that when the advance began Pickett's flank was grievously exposed.
Longstreet did not give these troops the attention they deserved and Hill did
not interfere in what was Longstreet's business—another piece of fatal noncoop-
eration. Confusion also resulted from doubt as to whether the divisions of
McLaws and Hood were to support the assault.[71]

The other area of neglect lay in the failure to oversee adequately First
Corps's artillery and ensure that it had enough ordnance to support the attack.
Lee had ordered an artillery bombardment to preface it. First Corps mustered
172 guns in this bombardment, although 56 guns were left unused. The guns
were not deployed skillfully so that enfilading fire could be brought to bear on
the focus of the attack. They were dispersed in a straight line so that the range
increased to the north—where fire was most needed. Consequently, the massed
batteries that Henry Hunt had mustered—some 220 guns—were virtually
untouched by this inept distribution. Here was yet another disadvantage
resulting from Lee's practice of delegating so much of the conduct of his battles
to his subordinates. At Antietam Lee had personally supervised minor tactics
and he succeeded. At Gettysburg, despite warning shots, he failed to exert himself and paid the price. The overall effect of the artillery fire was very disappointing. A high percentage of the balls fell "short" or went "over" the Union
positions, hitting wagon trains and "soft" targets in the rear; Meade's defenses
were hardly touched.[72]

At the end of the bombardment, Longstreet discovered that the batteries were running out of ammunition. The attacking Confederate infantry thus lacked effective covering fire. The effect of Union artillery fire on them was devastating: "canister" blew great holes in their ranks as they walked toward a clump of four trees on Cemetery Ridge that served as the focal point of the attack. As at Malvern Hill, Union rifled-musket fire shattered what remained of Pickett's cohesion (Alexander Hay, for instance, packed every rifle in his division in the front line) and the bayonet delivered the coup de grâce. Only perhaps a dozen cannon went forward with the Confederate infantry, whereas Lee expected a high measure of guns to accompany the advance. Hancock's tactical grip was firm and well controlled. The federal defensive line overlapped the Confederate by eight hundred yards and enfilading fire was thrown on Pickett's exposed left. The Confederate repulse began here and spread to the center and right. Pickett's command ceased to exist as an organized force, and its remnants were driven back to Seminary Ridge.[73]

The Union victory at Gettysburg cannot be explained exclusively by Confederate errors. It was a noted Union triumph built on solid strengths. While Stuart revealed weaknesses of judgment in his raid, the performance of Union cavalry was creditable. The contribution of Buford was especially valuable because he maintained such a tight cavalry screen around Meade's right flank that prevented Lee from gaining intelligence. Throughout the battle Union artillery, concentrated and devastatingly effective against infantry, was superior to the Confederates'. Its role on the third day of the battle was crucial. Although Lee was a greater general than Meade, like other commanders of the highest ability, when it was bad Lee's generalship was deplorable. Meade had a steadier, if more prosaic talent. He had adjusted well to his responsibilities and had reacted to Lee's moves sensibly and without hesitation; he was rarely caught off balance. He had deployed his available fighting power judiciously, but ultimately his caution would tell against him. Above all, it was the dogged tenacity and endurance of Union infantry that saw them through to a victorious conclusion. Their skill had often been concealed by halting generalship. Under Meade they had shown what they could do, but they had yet to be tested on the offensive under this new leader.

Meade was urged by both Hancock and Pleasonton, the cavalry commander, to launch an immediate counterattack. He spurned this advice. He was a prudent commander and was determined not to hazard his success. His corps had, in any case, got broken up and scattered all over the battlefield. A fundamental question remained unanswered. *Where* would Meade strike? Union casualties were 23,049, Confederate 28,063—considering that they were attacking consistently for three days this margin does not denote a tremendous advantage for the defensive. Lee's failure had as much to do with errors in the attack and his inability to impose a unified operational design on his efforts as it did with the inherent superiority of defensive action. The Confederate total was proportionately much higher because of their smaller aggregate numbers. At this stage, Meade's army was probably not strong enough to destroy the Army of Northern Virginia. Lee's army was wounded, but not fatally. The issue was not put to the test so we cannot tell for certain. At any rate, Meade was offered a great opportunity that surely Grant would not have passed up. Lee's army was hardly invulnerable, yet Meade was too cautious to put matters to the proof.[74]

A distracted President Lincoln urged him to destroy Lee's army while he had the chance. Lincoln thought the end of the war was imminent. Lee had had no alternative after the repulse on July 3 but to retreat. This began in stages on July 4 back toward Hagerstown, Maryland. Lee hoped at least to salvage from the campaign his dominance of the Potomac flanking position based on the Shenandoah Valley. As the pontoon bridge over the Potomac had been destroyed by federal cavalry and flood waters had swollen the river, Lee could neither withdraw back to Confederate territory nor draw supplies northward. On July 14 Lincoln sent Meade an order instructing him to attack Lee while absolving him from responsibility. Lee entrenched between Falling Waters and Williamsport to shield the building of pontoon bridges at these two points and defied Meade to attack; despite Lincoln's blandishments, Meade resisted the temptation. This whole incident explains Lincoln's desperate search for decisive battles, because only by winning them could he convey to a skeptical public the military achievements of his administration.[75]

When the floodwaters fell Lee crossed unmolested back into Virginia; but he could not bluff Meade as he had McClellan the previous October, who crossed lower down the Potomac and forced Lee to withdraw to the line of the Rappahannock. By the end of July the campaign ended with the two armies back where they had started.

There is a tendency among some historians to underrate the significance of the Gettysburg campaign. This is perhaps an understandable reaction to an earlier, obsessive preoccupation with it. The Gettysburg campaign wore down Lee's offensive capability. He could no longer strike effectively at the political center of gravity of the war, and hence this battle was a decisive turning point in the Civil War.[76]

Unlike at Antietam Lee had been beaten tactically. His troops had been repulsed. His image as a "winner" had been tarnished although the damage to his prestige did not endure. At the time, the battle of Gettysburg lacked the significance later conferred on it. The reputation of the Army of the Potomac surged even though Meade himself did not acquire heroic status. Lee had fought the campaign for numerous sound military and political reasons and had gained none of them. Within days news of the fall of Vicksburg could be linked with the victory at Gettysburg to form a tandem set of triumphs denoting solid progress toward a Union victory. Northerners as well as Southerners could discern these portents. For over a year the one theater where hopes of winning could be entertained, the east, suddenly tasted sour to Confederate enthusiasts.[77]

NOTES AND REFERENCES

1. *Report of the Joint Committee on the Conduct of the War* (Washington, DC: Government Printing Office, 1863), vol. 1, pp. 635–41; Brian Holden Reid, "McClellan and the Politicians," *Parameters* 17 (September, 1987): 110; Marcus Cunliffe, *Soldiers and Civilians: The Martial Spirit in America 1775–1865*, 3rd ed. (London: Eyre and Spottiswoode, 1968), p. 324; T. Harry Williams, *Lincoln and His Generals* (New York: Alfred A. Knopf, 1952) pp. 210–11.

2. George W. Julian, *Political Recollections, 1840–1872* (Chicago: Jansen McClurg, 1884), p. 225; Walter H. Hebert, *Fighting Joe Hooker* (Indianapolis: Bobbs-Merrill, 1944); Williams, *Lincoln and His Generals*, pp. 213–14.

3. Lincoln to Carl Schurz, Nov. 24, 1862, in *The Collected Works of Abraham Lincoln*, ed. Roy P. Basler (New Brunswick, NJ: Rutgers University Press, 1953), vol. 5, pp. 509–10; Joint Committee, *Report*, vol. 1, pp. 3–4; Julian, *Political Recollections*, p. 133; Herman Hattaway and Archer Jones, *How the North Won* (Urbana: University of Illinois Press, 1983), p. 350.

4. Williams, *Lincoln and His Generals*, pp. 211–12, 232–35; Hattaway and Jones, *How the North Won*, pp. 348–50, 379–80; Bruce Catton, *Glory Road* (1952; London: White Lion reprint, 1977), pp. 156–58; Kenneth P. Williams, *Lincoln Finds a General* (New York : Macmillan, 1949), vol. 2, pp. 566–70. Compare this plan with Hooker's posturing before Stanton the previous November (*Glory Road*, p. 30) and after Fredericksburg (Benjamin P. Thomas and Harold M. Hyman, *Stanton: The Life and Times of Lincoln's Secretary of War* [New York: Alfred A. Knopf, 1962], pp. 252–53).

5 . Stephen W. Sears, *Chancellorsville* (New York: Houghton Mifflin, 1996), pp. 52, 57, 63, 67, 194–96; John J. Hennessy, "We Shall Make Richmond Howl: The Army of the Potomac on the Eve of Chancellorsville," in *Chancellorsville: The Battle and Its Aftermath*, ed. Gary W. Gallagher, 1–27 (Durham: University of North Carolina Press, 1996).

6. Catton, *Glory Road*, pp. 160–62; Williams, *Lincoln Finds a General*, vol. 2, pp. 575–78.

7. Williams, *Lincoln Finds a General*, vol. 2, pp. 603–604; Fitzhugh Lee, *General Lee* (1894; New York: Da Capo reprint, 1994), pp. 266–67; A. Wilson Greene, "Stoneman's Raid," in *Chancellorsville*, ed. Gallagher, pp. 98–99, argues that it marks a significant step in the revival of federal cavalry.

8. Brian Holden Reid, "British Military Intellectuals and the American Civil War," in *Warfare, Diplomacy and Politics; Essays in Honour of A. J. P. Taylor*, ed. C. Wrigley, 47 (London: Hamish Hamilton, 1986). Thomas L. Connelly and Archer Jones, *Politics of Command* (Baton Rouge: Louisiana State University Press, 1973), p. xi; Thomas L. Connelly, "Robert E. Lee and the Western Confederacy," *Civil War History* 15 (1969): 116–32; Alan T. Nolan, *Lee Considered* (Chapel Hill: University of North Carolina Press, 1991), pp. 100–101.

9. This persistent error is repeated frequently. See David G. Chandler, *The Campaigns of Napoleon* (London: Weidenfeld and Nicolson, 1966), p. 180: the defensive-offensive "found no place in the Napoleonic repertoire." As I have pointed out in my *J. F. C. Fuller* (London: Macmillan, 1987, 1990), p. 67, if there is a historical precedent for the strategy, it is Wellington in the Peninsula. His was the weaker side, standing on the defensive 1808–11, but had command of the sea that the Confederacy lacked. Yet see Hattaway and Jones, *How the North Won*, p. 351.

10. Hattaway and Jones, *How the North Won*, pp. 351–54, 362–64; T. Harry Williams, *Beauregard* (1955; Baton Rouge: Louisiana University Press, 1989) pp. 201–202; though Beauregard had no distaste for party politics when they served his interests. Lee, quoted in Brian Holden Reid, *Robert E. Lee: Icon for a Nation* (2005; Amherst, NY: Prometheus Books, 2007). See Cunliffe, *Soldiers and Civilians*, pp. 298–99.

11. Lee to Seddon, Lee to Davis, Feb. 4, 26, 1863, in Lee, *Wartime Papers of R. E. Lee*, eds. Clifford Dowdey and Louis H. Manarin (New York: Bramhall, 1961), pp. 397–98, 410; Williams, *Beauregard*, p. 149. It was *the strength* of Lee's army that deterred Halleck from besieging Richmond; obviously that objection would wither once the army had been broken up. There is no evidence of any "obsession" with Virginia in Lee's correspondence; see his judicious response, in Lee to Cooper, Apr. 16, 1863 in *Wartime Papers*, pp. 433–34.

12. Lee to Longstreet, Feb. 18, 1863, in Lee, *Wartime Papers*, p. 406; Douglas Southall Freeman, *R. E. Lee*, 4 vols. (New York: Scribner's, 1934–35), vol. 2, ch. 32; Jeffry Wert, *General James Longstreet* (New York: Simon and Schuster, 1993), pp. 226–33, 238–39; on earlier efforts against Suffolk and Norfolk, see Rowena Reed, *Combined Operations in the Civil War* (1978; Lincoln: University of Nebraska Press, 1993), pp. 140–42; Sears, *Chancellorsville*, p. 53.

13. Freeman, *R. E. Lee*, vol. 2, pp. 513–18; Lee to Davis, May 2, 1863, in Lee, *Wartime Papers*, p. 450; Sears, *Chancellorsville*, pp. 96–97, 113–14.

14. Gallagher, "East of Chancellorsville: Jubal A. Early at Second Fredericksburg and Salem Church," in *Chancellorsville*, ed. idem., pp. 40–41; Battle Report of Chancellorsville Campaign, Sep. 23, 1863, in Lee, *Wartime Papers*, p. 460; Williams, *Lincoln Finds a General*, vol. 2, pp. 576–78; Catton, *Glory Road*, pp. 166–70; Sears, *Chancellorsville*, pp. 118–20, 181–82; Daniel E. Sutherland, *Fredericksburg and Chancellorsville: The Dare Mark Campaign* (Lincoln: University of Nebraska Press, 1988), pp. 139–40, is more skeptical of the "defensive" interpretation.

15. Battle Report of Chancellorsville Campaign, in Lee, *Wartime Papers*, p. 462; Emory M. Thomas, *Bold Dragoon: The Life of J. E. B. Stuart* (New York: Harper and Row, 1986), pp. 208–209; Freeman, *R. E. Lee*, vol. 2, pp. 518–24, appendix II-5, pp. 584–89; Clifford Dowdey, *Lee: A Biography* (London: Gollancz, 1970), pp. 345–47; Frank E. Vandiver, *Mighty Stonewall* (New York: McGraw-Hill, 1957), pp. 464–65; John Selby, *Stonewall Jackson as Military Commander* (London: Batsford, 1968), pp. 191–92; Sears, *Chancellorsville*, pp. 230–37, 240.

16. Battle Report of Chancellorsville Campaign, in Lee, *Wartime Papers*, p. 463; Douglas Southall Freeman, *Lee's Lieutenants* (New York: Scribner's, 1944), vol. 2, pp. 548–55; Sears, *Chancellorsville*, pp. 191–92, 200–201, 202, 210–11, 212–13, 223–24, 228; James I. Robertson Jr., *Stonewall Jackson: The Man, the Soldier, the Legend* (New York: Macmillan, 1997), p. 704.

17. Know-Nothing was a nickname for the anti-immigration Nativist, or American Party. See Brian Holden Reid, *The Origins of the American Civil War* (London: Longman, 1996) pp. 137–39.

18. Battle Report of Chancellorsville Campaign, in Lee, *Wartime Papers*, p. 463; Catton, *Glory Road*, pp. 175–81; Freeman, *Lee's Lieutenants*, vol. 2, pp. 555–57; Sears, *Chancellorsville*, pp. 241–48, 254–55, 257–59.

19. Freeman, *Lee's Lieutenants*, vol. 2, pp. 561–73; Vandiver, *Mighty Stonewall*, pp. 472–80; Battle Report of the Chancellorsville Campaign, in Lee, *Wartime Papers*, p. 464; Thomas, *Stuart*, pp. 210–11; Freeman, *R. E. Lee*, vol. 2, pp. 548–56; Dowdey, *Lee*, pp. 353–54; Williams, *Lincoln Finds a General*, vol. 2, pp. 586–90, 593–94, 600–602; Robert K. Krick, "The Smoothbore Volley That Doomed the Confederacy," in *Chancellorsville*, ed. Gallagher, pp. 132–33.

20. Edward Hagerman, *The American Civil War and the Origins of Modern Warfare* (Bloomington: Indiana University Press, 1988), pp. 84–85; Williams, *Lincoln Finds a General*, vol. 2, pp. 595–99; Hattaway and Jones, *How the North Won*, pp. 381–82; Sears, *Chancellorsville*, pp. 226, 248–49; Freeman, *R. E. Lee*, vol. 2, pp. 552–56; Gallagher, "East of Chancellorsville," in *Chancellorsville*, ed. idem., pp. 43–53; Sears, *Chancellorsville*, pp. 420–30.

21. Freeman, *R. E. Lee*, vol. 3, pp. 1–8, devotes an entire chapter to "The 'Might-Have-Beens' of Chancellorsville."

22. Hattaway and Jones, *How the North Won*, pp. 383–84, 416n12; Hagerman, *American Civil War*, pp. 134–35; Holden Reid, "British Military Intellectuals and the American Civil War," pp. 43–46.

23. Freeman, *Lee's Lieutenants*, vol. 3, p. xiii; John Keegan, *The Mask of Command* (London: Jonathan Cape, 1987), pp. 208–209; Holden Reid, *Fuller*, p. 126.

24. Hagerman, *American Civil War*, p. 92; Michael C. C. Adams, *Fighting for Defeat: Union Military Failure in the East, 1861–1865* (Lincoln: University of Nebraska Press reprint, 1978, 1992), pp. 141–43.

25. Steven Z. Starr, *The Union Cavalry in the Civil War*, 3 vols. (Baton Rouge: Louisiana State University Press, 1979), vol. 1, pp. 385–95; Edwin B. Coddington, *The Gettysburg Campaign: A Study in Command* (New York: Scribner's, 1968, 1979), pp. 86–87; Thomas, *Stuart*, pp. 219–31; Stephen Sears, *Gettysburg* (New York: Houghton Mifflin, 2003), pp. 66–74, 78–82.

26. John F. Marszalek, *Commander of All Lincoln's Armies: A Life of General Henry W. Halleck* (Cambridge, MA: Belknap Press of Harvard University Press, 2004), pp. 173–75; Coddington, *Gettysburg Campaign*, pp. 128–33; Williams, *Lincoln and His Generals*, pp. 250–61; Freeman Cleaves, *Meade of Gettysburg* (Norman: University of Oklahoma Press, 1960, 1991), pp. 122–26; Sears, *Gettysburg*, pp. 30–32, 39, 86–89, 93–94, 121–23.

27. Hans L. Trefousse, *Benjamin Franklin Wade: Radical Republican from Ohio* (New York: Twayne, 1963), pp. 204–206; Thomas and Hyman, *Stanton*, pp. 272–73; David Donald, *Charles Sumner and the Rights of Man* (New York: Alfred A. Knopf, 1970), pp. 117–18. See below, p. 405.

28. Coddington, *Gettysburg Campaign*, pp. 89–91; Battle Report of Gettysburg Campaign, Jan. 20, 1864, in Lee, *Wartime Papers*, pp. 570–72. Lee himself (p. 572) puts the number of artillery pieces taken at twenty-eight.

29. For the psychological effects of amputation and his marriage, see Paul D. Casdorph, *Confederate General R. S. Ewell: Lee's Hesitant Commander* (Lexington: University Press of Kentucky, 2004), pp. 210–12, 217–19; Wert, *Longstreet*, pp. 247–48; Freeman, *R. E. Lee*, vol. 3, pp. 14–17; Dowdey, *Lee*, pp. 358–60; in addition, Thomas, *Bold Dragoon*, p. 239, suggests that Stuart underwent a crisis of confidence in himself during this campaign.

30. See especially, Connelly and Jones, *Politics of Command*, pp. 45–52.

31. James Longstreet, *From Manassas to Appomattox* (New York: Da Capo reprint, 1896, 1992), pp. 332–33, 336–37; Wert, *Longstreet*, pp. 248–50; Richard McMurry, *Two Great Rebel Armies* (Chapel Hill: University of North Carolina Press, 1989), pp. 110–11; Lee to Davis, May 20, Lee to J. B. Hood, May 21, 1863, in Lee, *Wartime Papers*, pp. 488–89, 490; Lee to Davis, June 23, 25, 1863, ibid., pp. 527–31; Coddington, *Gettysburg Campaign*, pp. 11–12.

32. For a sample of the criticism see Connelly and Jones, *Politics of Command*, pp. 40–41, 45–46, and Archer Jones, *Confederate Strategy: From Shiloh to Vicksburg* (Baton Rouge: Louisiana State University Press Report), pp. 92–96; also see Battle Report of Gettysburg Campaign, in Lee, *Wartime Papers*, p. 569; Coddington, *Gettysburg Campaign*, pp. 4–9.

33. As characterized by Nolan, *Lee Considered*, pp. 76–83.

34. Lee to James A. Seddon, June 8, Lee to Davis, June 10, 1863, in Lee, *Wartime Papers*, pp. 504–505, 507–509; Nolan, *Lee Considered*, pp. 79–80, 82, draws opposite conclusions from this correspondence.

35. Lee to Seddon, June 13, 1863, in Lee, *Wartime Papers*, p. 513; Coddington, *Gettysburg Campaign*, pp. 138–45, 151–52, 157–62, is candid on the degree of collaboration proffered by Pennsylvanians and their reluctance to give information to the Army of the Potomac.

36. Jones, *Confederate Strategy*, pp. 211–18; Davis, *Jefferson Davis*, pp. 504–505; Lee to Davis, May 29, 30, 1863, in Lee, *Wartime Papers*, pp. 495–96. The general complained: "I fear the time has passed when I could have taken the offensive with advantage." For more detail on the debates before the opening of the Gettysburg campaign, see Brian Holden Reid, *Robert E. Lee: Icon for a Nation* (2005; Amherst, NY: Prometheus Books, 2007), pp. 163–67.

37. See Stephen E. Woodworth, *Davis and Lee at War* (Lawrence: University Press of Kansas, 1995), pp. 160, 161, 197–98; Coddington, *Gettysburg Campaign*, pp. 5, 18.

38. Connelly and Jones, *Politics of Command*, pp. 35–37; Connelly also ignores the distinction between influence and command responsibility, or simply assumes that informal influence can be equated with it, in *The Marble Man: Robert E. Lee and His Image in American Society* (New York: Alfred A. Knopf, 1977), pp. 202–203, and "Robert E. Lee and the Western Confederacy," *Civil War History* 15 (1969): 120–22. So too does Nolan, *Lee Considered*, pp. 62–63, who conflates field command and grand strategy. Some of these points in Lee's defense are hinted at in Albert Castel, "The Historian and the General," *Civil War History* 16 (1970): 55–60, and Charles Roland, "The Generalship of Robert E. Lee," in *Grant, Lee, Lincoln and the Radicals*, ed. Grady McWhiney (Evanston, IL: Northwestern University Press, 1964). See also the later qualification in Jones, *Confederate Strategy*, 2nd ed. (1991), p. xi.

39. Sears, *Gettysburg*, pp. 38–41; Hattaway and Jones, *How the North Won*, p. 402; also see, Woodworth, *Davis and Lee at War*, pp. 220–29, for this and the next paragraph.

40. Ibid., pp. 384–85; Lee to Davis, June 25, 1863, in Lee, *Wartime Papers*, p. 533; Davis, *Jefferson Davis*, p. 505; Dowdey, *Lee*, pp. 359–60; Connelly, *Marble Man*, pp. 154–55, gives some good examples of personal criticisms of Lee as an *individual* rather than on failures of *the system*, although his own book should be included with them.

41. Nolan, *Lee Considered*, ch. 4.

42. Alan T. Nolan, "R. E. Lee and July 1 at Gettysburg," in *The First Day at Gettysburg: Essays on Union and Confederate Leadership*, ed. Gary W. Gallagher, 12 (Kent, OH: Kent State University Press, 1992). The two concepts of command and leadership, which are quite distinct, are confused throughout this chapter.

43. Coddington, *Gettysburg Campaign*, pp. 108–13; Lee to Stuart, June 22, 23, 1863; Lee to Ewell, June 19, 1863, also see Lee to Seddon, June 13, 1863, in Lee,

Wartime Papers, pp. 513, 520–21, 523, 526–27; H. B. McClellan, *I Rode with Jeb Stuart: The Life and Campaigns of Major General J. E. B. Stuart* (1885; Secaucus, NJ: Blue and Grey Press, 1993), pp. 315–19; Thomas, *Bold Dragoon*, pp. 240–42; Nolan's criticisms of command and control are better founded, see "R. E. Lee and July 1 at Gettysburg," *First Day at Gettysburg*, 12, 17, 19, 21; Sears, *Gettysburg*, pp. 105–106.

44. Peter J. Parish, *The American Civil War* (London: Eyre Methuen, 1975), p. 582; Coddington, *Gettysburg Campaign*, pp. 105–106. "The difficulty of procuring supplies retards and renders more uncertain our future movements," wrote Lee to Davis, June 19, 1863, in Lee, *Wartime Papers*, p. 52; Jay Luvaas, "Lee at Gettysburg: A General Without Intelligence," in *Intelligence and Military Operations*, ed. Michael I. Handel, 133 (London: Frank Cass, 1990); Sears, *Gettysburg*, pp. 138–41.

45. Sears, *Gettysburg*, pp. 38–41; Williams, *Lincoln and His Generals*, p. 314.

46. Thomas, *Bold Dragoon*, p. 242; Coddington, *Gettysburg Campaign*, pp. 118, 125–26, 130, 133. Coddington is full of praise for Lee's scheme to use Beauregard (p. 116) but criticizes its timing. In fact Lee had mentioned it on June 7. Longstreet pointed out that Lee dealt "cautiously" with Richmond, mainly to secure confidentiality "so that his plans were disclosed little at a time," see *From Manassas to Appomattox*, p. 337; Lee to Davis, June 7, 23, 25 (two letters), 1863, Lee, *Wartime Papers*, pp. 503, 527–28, 531, 532.

47. Sears, *Gettysburg*, pp. 107–13; Lee to Ewell, June 17, 1863, Lee to Imboden, June 20, General Orders No. 73, June 17, 1863, in Lee, *Wartime Papers*, pp. 518, 522, 530, 533–34; Coddington, *Gettysburg Campaign*, pp. 153–55, 175; Nolan, "R. E. Lee and July 1 at Gettysburg," *First Day at Gettysburg*, pp. 21–22; Kent M. Brown, *Retreat from Gettysburg* (Chapel Hill: University of North Carolina Press, 2005), p. 333.

48. Cleaves, *Meade of Gettysburg*, pp. 129–34; Sears, *Gettysburg*, pp. 142–52; Coddington, *Gettysburg Campaign*, pp. 214–20, 225, 230–40; Williams, *Lincoln Finds a General*, vol. 2, pp. 655, 673–80, is much more critical.

49. Wert, *Longstreet*, p. 256; Longstreet, *From Manassas to Appomattox*, pp. 340, 346–48; Jennings Cropper Wise, *The Long Arm of Lee* (Lincoln: University of Nebraska Press reprint, 1915, 1991), vol. 2, p. 162.

50. Coddington, *Gettysburg Campaign*, pp. 181–86, 194–95, 198–99; Thomas, *Bold Dragoon*, pp. 241–42; Edward G. Longacre, *The Cavalry at Gettysburg* (Lincoln: University of Nebraska Press reprint, 1986, 1993), pp. 160, 202; Wert, *Longstreet*, p. 257; Freeman, *Lee's Lieutenants*, vol. 3, pp. 102–103; Nolan, "R. E. Lee and July 1 at Gettysburg," *First Day at Gettysburg*, pp. 27–28; David G. Martin, *Gettysburg, July 1* (Conshohocken, PA: Combined Books, 1995), pp. 557–63.

51. Longstreet, *From Manassas to Appomattox*, pp. 358–59. Longstreet, of course, intended to convey his superior wisdom. The conversations here recorded should be treated with the same caution as speeches detailed in Livy. Wert, *Longstreet*, p. 257; Hattaway and Jones, *How the North Won*, p. 405; Catton, *Glory Road*, p. 282; Coddington, *Gettysburg Campaign*, p. 558; the best analysis is Gary W. Gallagher, *Lee and His Generals in War and Memory* (Baton Rouge: Louisiana State University Press, 1998), pp. 47–76.

52. Gary W. Gallagher, "Confederate Corps Leadership on the First Day at Gettysburg," in *First Day at Gettysburg*, ed. idem., p. 40; Freeman, *Lee's Lieutenants*, vol. 3, pp. 100–105; Dowdey, *Lee*, pp. 371–72; Sears, *Gettysburg*, p. 232.

53. Hattaway and Jones, *How the North Won*, p. 406; Thomas L. Livermore, *Numbers and Losses in the Civil War in America, 1861–1865*, 2nd ed. (Boston: Houghton Mifflin, 1901), pp. 102–103.

54. Wise, *The Long Arm of Lee*, vol. 2, p. 630.

55. See Longstreet, *Manassas to Appomattox* p. 358, where he describes the position parallel to the Emmitsburg Road, omitting to mention that it was not occupied by the enemy with his main force.

56. Connelly, *Marble Man*, pp. 83–84.

57. Thomas L. Connelly, "The Image and the General," *Civil War History* 19 (1973): 53, 55–56; Dowdey, *Lee*, pp. 373–75; Freeman, *R. E. Lee*, vol. 3, pp. 87–95.

58. Wert, *Longstreet*, pp. 258–59; Dowdey, *Lee*, p. 374; Freeman, *R. E. Lee*, vol. 3, pp. 149–50; Coddington, *Gettysburg Campaign*, pp. 10–11; Noah Andre Trudeau, *Gettysburg: A Testing of Courage* (New York: HarperCollins, 2002), p. 284, shows that Lee did not rule out completely turning the Union left; Sears, *Gettysburg*, pp. 6–8, 236–38.

59. Gallagher, *Lee*, p. 68; Wert, *Longstreet*, pp. 268–69; Freeman, *Lee's Lieutenants*, vol. 3, pp. 110–12, 114–15; Dowdey, *Lee*, pp. 375–76; Coddington, *Gettysburg Campaign*, p. 190; Wise, *Long Arm of Lee*, vol. 2, p. 631; Stephen E. Woodworth, *Beneath a Northern Sky: A Short History of the Gettysburg Campaign* (Wilmington, DE: S.R. Books, 2003), pp. 164, 190, 209–10.

60. Cleaves, *Meade of Gettysburg*, pp. 138–44; Sears, *Gettysburg*, pp. 240–44, 247; Coddington, *Gettysburg Campaign*, pp. 196–97; Gabor S. Boritt, "'Unfinished Work': Lincoln, Meade and Gettysburg," in *Lincoln's Generals*, ed. idem. (New York: Oxford University Press, 1994), pp. 86–87.

61. Kenneth P. Williams, *Lincoln Finds a General*, vol. 2, pp. 698–99, 721; Coddington, *Gettysburg Campaign*, pp. 341–51; Catton, *Glory Road*, pp. 286–89; W. A. Swanberg, *Sickles the Incredible* (New York: Scribner's, 1956), pp. 208–12; Sears, *Gettysburg*, pp. 249–52.

62. Wert, *Longstreet*, pp. 269–71; Coddington, *Gettysburg Campaign*, pp. 368–76; Dowdey, *Lee*, p. 378; Sears, *Gettysburg*, pp. 254–56, 257–60.

63. Wert, *Longstreet*, pp. 272–73; Longstreet, *From Manassas to Appomattox*, pp. 366–68; Freeman, *Lee's Lieutenants*, vol. 3, pp. 115–21; Wise, *Long Arm of Lee*, vol. 2, pp. 640–44; Sears, *Gettysburg*, p. 262, is in error in supposing that this "was exactly what Old Pete earlier had urged on Lee."

64. Williams, *Lincoln Finds a General*, vol. 2, pp. 700, 705–706; Catton, *Glory Road*, pp. 290–301; Wise, *Long Arm of Lee*, vol. 2, pp. 645–51; Hagerman, *American Civil War*, p. 95; Wert, *Longstreet*, pp. 274–79; Sears, *Gettysburg*, pp. 281–83, 298–302, 313–14, 355.

65. Freeman, *Lee's Lieutenants*, vol. 3, pp. 128–35; Wise, *Long Arm of Lee*, vol. 2, pp. 665–66; Casdorph, *Confederate General R. S. Ewell*, pp. 260–62; Sears, *Gettysburg*, pp. 326–31, 333–40.

66. Hagerman, *American Civil War*, p. 140; Battle Report of Gettysburg Campaign, in Lee, *Wartime Papers*, pp. 578–79; Sears, *Gettysburg*, pp. 257–58, 349–50.

67. Fuller, *Grant and Lee* (Stevenage: Spa Books, 1992 reprint), pp. 198–200; B. H. Liddell Hart, "Why Lee Lost Gettysburg," *Saturday Review* 11 (March 23, 1938), and idem., *Memoirs* (London: Cassell, 1965), vol. 1, pp. 165–66.

68. Wise, *Long Arm of Lee*, vol. 2, p. 660; Longacre, *Cavalry at Gettysburg*, pp. 222, 237.

69. Williams, *Lincoln Finds a General*, vol. 2, pp. 696–97, 706–707 is excessively critical; Sears, *Gettysburg*, pp. 342–45, 355–56; Casdorph, *Ewell*, pp. 262–64; Coddington, *Gettysburg*, pp. 235–36; Longacre, *Cavalry at Gettysburg*, pp. 212–13; Wise, *Long Arm of Lee*, vol. 2, pp. 660–61.

70. Sears, *Gettysburg*, pp. 357–59, 360, 364–71; Lieutenant Colonel A. J. L. Fremantle, *Three Months in the Southern States, April–June 1863* (Lincoln: University of Nebraska Press, 1991), p. 269, is the original source for Lee's admission that "All this has been *my* fault—it is *I* that have lost this fight." Longstreet, *From Manassas to Appomattox*, pp. 385–88; Wert, *Longstreet*, pp. 281–82.

71. Freeman, *Lee's Lieutenants*, vol. 3, pp. 180–86; Wert, *Longstreet*, pp. 286–92.

72. Sears, *Gettysburg*, pp. 377–82, 396–97; Wise, *Long Arm of Lee*, vol. 2, pp. 665–90; Catton, *Glory Road*, pp. 309–14; Longacre, *Cavalry at Gettysburg*, p. 226.

73. Sears, *Gettysburg*, pp. 376–77, 406–407, 419, 424–26, 428–29, 430, 440.

74. Carol Reardon, "I Think the Union Army Had Something to Do with It," in *The Gettysburg Nobody Knows*, ed. Gabor S. Boritt, 122–24 (New York: Oxford University Press, 1997); Cleaves, *Meade of Gettysburg*, pp. 170–75; Williams, *Lincoln Finds a General*, vol. 2, pp. 722–23.

75. Sears, *Gettysburg*, pp. 465–66; Livermore, *Numbers and Losses*, pp. 102–103; Boritt, "Lincoln, Meade and Gettysburg," pp. 96–100; for a detailed account, see Kent Masterson Brown, *Retreat from Gettysburg: Lee, Logistics and the Pennsylvania Campaign* (Chapel Hill: University of North Carolina Press, 2005), pp. 322–32.

76. See, for instance, Hattaway and Jones, *How the North Won*, p. 415, and the view that its "strategic impact . . . was . . . fairly limited."

77. On the symbolic significance the battle later acquired, see Carol Reardon, *Pickett's Charge in History and Memory* (Chapel Hill: University of North Carolina Press, 1997).

Chapter Nine
GRANT TRIUMPHS OVER ADVERSITY
JULY 1862 TO JULY 1863

The twelve months prior to the fall of Vicksburg in July 1863 saw the emergence of a single dominating personality in the west—Ulysses S. Grant. Braxton Bragg could have had the position but the test of battle found him timorous and incapable of seizing his opportunities. Unlike many of his contemporaries, Grant was a modest and taciturn man. He did not look the part of a great commander, did not strike fashionable Napoleonic attitudes, or make stirring speeches. Charles Francis Adams Jr. (the grandson of the sixth president) saw Grant later in the war during the battle of the Wilderness. He was not impressed. Grant seemed "a very ordinary looking man," "a dumpy and slouchy little subaltern," a rather "comical" figure, who in "walking leans forward and toddles." He may have lacked a dazzling appearance but he developed real strength of character and impressive powers of decision. He also had the good fortune of serving in various subordinate formations, so that unlike McClellan (or Lee), he started at regimental level and moved to the command of armies, learning and mastering his trade as he was promoted. He was not thrust in at the top with little inkling of how lower formations contributed to the power of the greater whole.

Grant's military philosophy was deceptively simple. "Find out where your enemy is. Get at him as soon as you can. Strike at him as hard as you can and as soon as you can, and keep moving on." Consistently aggressive and dynamic, Grant effectively utilized the abundant Union material and numerical superiority. All other Union commanders enjoyed a material superiority; such an advantage did not automatically confer success. Grant was a confident commander who invariably took the offensive and made the most of the resources at his disposal; in short he effectively exploited the initiative. In the field he often rode alone unaccompanied by escorts or his staff. "If he had studied to be undramatic," claimed General Lew Wallace, "he could not have succeeded better."

Grant did not court risks and rarely led troops beyond the front line. As B. H. Liddell Hart observed in his study of Scipio Africanus, it was not necessary for the general "to be a platoon leader, thrusting himself into the fight at the expense of his proper duty of direction." Grant spent most of his time in quiet contemplation. He did not interfere unduly in the affairs of his subordinates, making time for his own thoughts. "He talked less and thought more than any one in the service. He studiously avoided performing any duty which someone else could do as well or better than he," wrote Horace Porter, a member of Grant's staff. Out of this deep capacity for uninterrupted reflection, free of routine and distractions, grew Grant's promptness of decision and his overall grasp of the campaign.

Grant had tremendous powers of concentration, always kept his own counsel, and remained imperturbable. "His speech was never hurried," recalled Porter, "and his manner betrayed no trace of excitability or even impatience." But this power of decision did not lead to arrogance. Grant "always invited the most frank and cordial interchange of views, and never failed to listen particularly to the more prominent members of his staff." It was this technique that led some to conclude erroneously that he was in thrall to his staff. On the contrary, he was one of those rare individuals who come alive and exhibit greatness of an elevated kind when confronted by the moral and intellectual challenges posed by war.[1]

In the autumn of 1862 Grant was faced with one of the great challenges of his career—overcoming the almost insuperable obstacles presented by the reduction of the Confederate stronghold of Vicksburg. Geography shaped the course of this campaign but did not predetermine its outcome.

The town of Vicksburg enjoyed strategic significance because it occupied the only high ground that abutted the Mississippi River south of Memphis. The town itself was small and had little industry; but it was a communications center of some importance. A railroad ran east via Jackson, Mississippi, and thence to Chattanooga and the other main centers of the Confederacy. Another ran west to Shreveport, Louisiana. Vicksburg was thus the vital link between the Confederate states along the Atlantic seaboard and those west of the Mississippi. Consequently, as General Grant observed later with his usual concision, "So long as it was held by the enemy, the free navigation of the river was prevented." Should Vicksburg fall, all other Confederate strongholds on the river could be isolated and picked off; the Union would enjoy undisputed mastery of the Mississippi; and the Confederacy would be denied effective access to the huge stocks of foodstuffs provided by Texas and Louisiana.[2]

It was one of Henry W. Halleck's major achievements as general-in-chief during the Civil War that he recognized the importance of the Mississippi theater of operations, and that he eventually persuaded the president of its importance. Lincoln tended to regard a campaign in east Tennessee as second only in importance to the occupation of Richmond. Halleck soon grasped that a naval expedition would not suffice to take Vicksburg, and contemplated the need for "a land expedition . . . against Vicksburg as soon as troops can be spared for that purpose." Thus by the autumn of 1862 Halleck was determined that "The great object is now to take and hold the Mississippi." Despite his earlier hostility toward Grant, Halleck now became one of his keenest supporters. The two main problems any Union commander faced in mounting an attack on Vicksburg were identical to those faced by Confederate generals responsible for defending it. The first was logistical; the second was the organization of the forces in the theater.[3]

The logistical difficulty that Grant faced—the supply of his scattered forces over huge distances—was compounded by the inhospitable, unhealthy, and largely untamed country over which he had to operate. The roads were bad and the railroads few. Consequently, the Confederates could fall back on their lines of communication, destroying the railroads as they went. Union columns had to stop their advance to build railroads, and complete even more ambitious engineering projects, such as canals. Large numbers of troops had to be siphoned off to garrison the lines of communication. This fitted in with the conventional military wisdom of the day that was "regarded as an axiom . . . that large bodies of troops must operate from a base of supplies which they always covered and guarded in all forward movements." During the Vicksburg campaign Grant, under Halleck's coaching, was to step decisively away from this concept. But for the moment Grant systematically built up huge logistic stocks to support an overland march on Vicksburg due south from Memphis. Grant laid up two hundred thousand rations at Holly Springs, Mississippi, and eight hundred thousand at La Grange, Tennessee. He was cautioned by Halleck, "Do not go too far";

but should he lose touch with his supply lines he was given permission to take supplies from the country.[4]

The organizational setup appeared to take an important step forward when in October 1862 Grant was given command of the Department of West Tennessee. Yet, the opposite was true: Grant's problems were only just beginning. In September 1862 the former Democrat congressman John A. McClernand approached Lincoln with a plan to sweep down the Mississippi and take Vicksburg from the north. His plan was typical of those concocted by generals with little command experience. To them war consisted of lightning marches, sweeping advances, and glorious charges; organization, logistic calculation, and careful planning counted for nothing. Desperate for success and impressed by McClernand's confidence, in October 1862, Lincoln gave McClernand the command.

The president saw the chance for a double envelopment being organized in the Mississippi Valley. Major General Nathaniel P. Banks would advance northward from New Orleans as McClernand, supported by Admiral Porter's naval squadron, came down from the north, took Vicksburg, and then moved on Grand Gulf. Lincoln saw a further, crucial political bonus arising from this scheme. McClernand proposed raising a "legion" from among his political supporters in Illinois. Lincoln saw this as a valuable expedient in placating and retaining the support of war Democrats in his adopted state. It would preempt any disaffection with his administration's conduct of the war.[5]

Equipped with a lawyer's gift for semantic ambiguity, Secretary of War Edwin M. Stanton drew up an order giving McClernand authority over the process of raising troops. He was directed to send them to Memphis and Cairo, both of which were in Grant's department, and presumably McClernand's troops then came under Grant's authority. Stanton then stipulated that once McClernand had raised enough troops for an "expedition," which were thus surplus to Grant's requirements, McClernand was to be given command of the move against Vicksburg. To suggest that this order was detrimental to military efficiency is an understatement. However, Stanton then included "a let-out clause" worthy of a corporate lawyer who had negotiated many a contract.

The order did not specify that McClernand should be given an independent command, though McClernand thought it did and Grant suspected that it did. The whole enterprise would remain subject "to the designation of the general-in-chief," although it appears that Halleck was unaware of this stipulation until the new year. Nonetheless, he soon picked up intelligence about McClernand's design in conversation, and hastened to warn Grant of its dangers. On November 11, 1862, he informed Grant of the nature of his authority, which was to prove the final means of thwarting McClernand's pretensions. "You have command of all troops sent to your department, and have permission to fight the enemy where you please."[6]

Grant learned of McClernand's command through the newspapers. He received no guidance from the president or secretary of war. Yet the McClernand affair revealed the true extent of Grant's political acumen, which was belied by his modest, unassuming manner and shabby appearance. Although McClernand was a professional politician, at every turn Grant outmaneuvered him. Grant wrote no impassioned protests, nor shouted outrageous demands. He did not antagonize his political masters, he simply got on with his job. He had a lot of thinking to do. The obstacles to be faced in taking Vicksburg had multiplied during the autumn of 1862. There was no doubt that the best opportunity to strike at the city had occurred in the summer when General Earl Van Dorn had moved against Corinth.[7] But Grant had been unable to take advantage of this vulnerability. He had been forced to send reinforcements to the east, and half the remainder of his command was on guard duties.

Grant now divided the Army of the Tennessee into three wings of corps strength. He had fifty thousand men, by no means a colossal force. Sherman was given command of the right, Major General James B. McPherson the center, and Major General Charles S. Hamilton the left. The three corps were to move in unison along the lines that Grant had sketched at Iuka. Sherman would distract while Grant pinned the enemy down with the center and left or *vice versa*, should circumstances dictate. This design crumbled as soon as it was erected. Grant moved south toward Grenada, crossing the Tallahatchie River, while Sherman took command of the force moving down the Mississippi. But on December 20 Van Dorn and his cavalry arrived in the streets of Holly Springs causing pandemonium. He took 1,500 prisoners and $1.5 million worth of war stores were put to the torch. Grant rightly blamed the garrison commander for this disaster. Van Dorn's cavalry raid, which was followed by another led by Nathan Bedford Forrest on Grant's communications in Tennessee, "demonstrated," the latter concluded, "the impossibility of maintaining so long a line of road over which to draw supplies for an army moving in an enemy's country."[8]

Grant invariably moved with rapidity, but the speed with which he launched his first campaign to take Vicksburg had been accelerated by the knowledge that John A. McClernand was on his way with plans to take command. He had been warned by Halleck that the president "may insist" that McClernand be given a separate command. Thus Grant was anxious to get Sherman underway down the Mississippi before McClernand arrived and complicated matters. Sherman had thirty-two thousand men in the Thirteenth Corps aboard sixty transports and escorted by seven gunboats. He was instructed to move south of the Yazoo River and was given discretionary orders. It was evidence of the growing warmth, trust, and harmony of the Grant-Sherman partnership that the commanding general gave Sherman orders to carry out his mission as he saw fit: "move your troops," he was told, "as you may deem best to accomplish the great object in view."[9]

The speed of Sherman's advance caught the Confederates in Vicksburg completely unawares. The commander of the city's defenses did not arrive until after the campaign had opened. Brigadier General Stephen D. Lee hurried to put together a scratch defense. The Confederate commander, Lieutenant General John C. Pemberton, enjoying interior lines, was at least successful in concentrating twelve thousand men to face Sherman. The thirty-two thousand men of Thirteenth Corps disembarked in very difficult country, which split the troops into four columns; these had to be moved over a single bridge. Lee occupied the right back of the Mississippi on Chickasaw bluffs. Sherman knew that time was of the essence yet the risk of attacking this strong position was great. He was forced to make a hasty decision and, unwisely as it turned out, delayed the attack for a further day until December 29. When he finally advanced, Sherman was beaten back as much by topography as by Lee's resolute defense. The broken country rendered coordination of the attacking troops almost impossible and the formations went forward piecemeal. Sherman's troops were repulsed at the total cost of 1,776 casualties; Confederate losses were only two hundred. With this further setback—and McClernand's arrival on January 2, 1863—the first campaign against Vicksburg was brought to an end.[10]

The imminence of McClernand's arrival had persuaded Grant to take command in the field himself. He had well-founded doubts about McClernand's abilities for an independent command. On December 18 Grant received orders from Halleck to organize the Army of the Tennessee into four corps, with General McClernand commanding one of them (the Thirteenth). Sherman was given command of the Fifteenth Corps. But the problem did not end there. McClernand was the senior major general in the department after Grant himself, and he had more in mind than the command of a mere corps. He went south of the Yazoo to take command of all the forces under Sherman, a move in which Sherman acquiesced reluctantly. It was illustrative of McClernand's lack of fixity of purpose and how easily he was seduced into flitting from one idea to another, that he was attracted by Sherman's suggestion of a diversion up the Arkansas. Sherman was keen to retrieve his reputation from the stigma of defeat at Chickasaw Bluffs and set aside his contempt for McClernand in supporting this chimerical scheme. Grant objected to the lack of concentration, believing that this was not "a military movement looking to the accomplishment of one great result, the capture of Vicksburg." Thanks to this diversionary move, McClernand failed both to impose himself on his troops and to stamp his own authority on the design to take Vicksburg. Grant discerned a deep distrust of McClernand's capacity among his subordinates and men. His suspicion was deepened by McClernand's request for further reinforcements to continue his diversion up the Arkansas River.[11]

Grant's decision to take personal command of the expedition inaugurated a period of intense reconsideration of the basis of the campaign. Every conceivable expedient was examined and tried. The actual object of the campaign was simple. The city of Vicksburg lay on the east bank of the Mississippi. To render it untenable Grant had to cut the railroad running east to Jackson. But getting there was immensely difficult. Rains turned the country south of Holly Springs into a sea of mud, and this complicated the logistical problem because overland communications were so poor. Perhaps the solution lay in river transport. One valuable byproduct of McClernand's venture down the Arkansas was that Admiral Porter's gunboats had fought their way through to the Yazoo River. Grant thus placed his faith initially in fighting his way through to Vicksburg from the Yazoo. But if he did, he would have to overcome the olympian power and willful perversity of the Mississippi River, which defies engineers to this day.

As a prelude to military operations, Grant in his common-sense, methodical way, began to consider the logistical problem. Grant intended to strike at Confederate logistical resources. He intended to cut the railroad running east from Vicksburg to Jackson. The city could then be completely isolated from succor and starved into surrender. Alternatively, the Confederate garrison would be forced to leave its defenses and fight in the open, trapped against the Mississippi, while Grant dominated its communications: this was the objective that Napoleon strove for, and Grant did so also. But Grant's options were limited during the winter months and he was restricted to the Mississippi because of the sea of mud and poor communications. Time in Grant's calculations was essential, and even in the spring his advance could be hindered by the nature of the country. Yet Grant's spring campaign presented a puzzling dilemma for his Confederate opponents. The further Grant advanced into the Confederate hinterland the less vulnerable his communications became, and the more the Confederates fell back on theirs, the more vulnerable they became—the reverse of the usual state of affairs. The Confederate command system never quite grasped the subtlety of Grant's scheme and how it limited their ability to launch a counterstroke.[12]

Grant's keen understanding of the logistical factor was also a reflection of changing attitudes toward the nature of the Civil War. Such attitudes were profoundly influenced by political and social considerations, not least the extremity of the measures that would be required to finally defeat the South. Dissatisfaction with the current rate of progress throughout 1862 led to a much broader contemplation of harsher measures. Grant was not in the vanguard of this change of opinion. In December 1862 he still insisted that "The country does not afford supplies for troops, and but a limited supply of forage." Grant attempted to shield families in Mississippi from the worst ravages of war and stated that "humanity" demanded "that in a land of plenty no one should suffer the pangs of hunger"; consequently, at all military posts, southern Unionists were empowered to sell "provisions and absolute necessaries for family use." Special funds, closely monitored by the departmental inspector general, were made available for the purchase of foodstuffs for starving families.[13]

At this stage, also, Grant was not too keen on allowing blacks to enter federal service, "or be enticed away from their homes except when it becomes a military necessity." Yet he was a much more sophisticated political animal than he appeared. Unlike Sherman, Grant was not obdurate and was sensitive to the ebb and flow of political intercourse. Grant very sensibly turned to Halleck for advice on the ticklish problem of handling the increasing numbers of blacks entering Union camps. Halleck was a political weather vane. He fully appreciated the effect that inflammatory newspaper accounts and congressional hearings were having on public opinion and the discrediting of conciliatory military approaches. In April 1863 the Joint Committee on the Conduct of the War's first *Report* was published. Congressmen were flooded with requests for it; many used it as the basis for their speeches in the congressional elections of 1863 and 1864. Halleck shared their frustration. Some "harsh measures are required," he bluntly informed Major General Horatio G. Wright, then commanding a division in the Army of the Potomac.[14]

Increasingly inclined to take Grant into his confidence and having assured him earlier that "the opening of the Mississippi River will be to us of more advantage than the capture of 40 Richmonds," Halleck was prompted to provide for Grant a full statement of administration policy. This was pregnant with implications for his conduct of the Vicksburg campaign. Halleck wrote:

> Every slave withdrawn from the enemy is equivalent to a white man put *hors de combat*. . . . It certainly is good policy to use them to the very best advantage we can. . . . In the hands of the enemy, they are used with much effect against

us; in our hands, we must try to use them with the best possible effect against the rebels.[15]

He had developed these points steadily over the course of the previous six months.

> The character of the war has changed very much within the last year. There is now no hope of reconciliation with the rebels. . . . There can be no peace but that which is forced by the sword. We must conquer the rebels or be conquered by them. The North must conquer the slave oligarchy or become slaves themselves, the manufacturers mere "hewers of wood and drawers of water" to the Southern aristocrats.

The conclusion that Halleck drew from his gloomy survey was firm and unequivocal: "we must live upon the enemy's country as much as possible and destroy his supplies. This is cruel warfare, but the enemy has brought it upon himself by his own conduct."

This letter from Halleck to Grant is one of the central military documents of the Civil War. It signals the acceptance by the United States military of a strategy of attrition, although individual field commanders would still seek to secure decisive victories by pursuing a strategy of annihilation. But it is more than this. It also denotes an acceptance by the Lincoln administration of the basic values of the radical Republicans and their allies. Federal armies should seek nothing less than unconditional surrender and the destruction of plantation slavery, and the conduct of the war should take on an increasingly punitive character. The troops should be allowed to forage liberally from the countryside, although the Confiscation Acts had not granted license to individual soldiers to commit crimes. Halleck was acknowledging, furthermore, that soldiers had been keen to commit such depredations even *before* General Pope's General Order No. 7, and that it was counterproductive trying to restrain them. This letter also reveals how far Halleck's own views had shifted since 1861.[16]

What Halleck did not say, but could have said, was that because the conservative generals who championed moderation and conciliation had failed to win the victories expected of them, they had done much to bring punitive war on the South. It is a curious irony, however, that the general most connected with this important change in the Northern military outlook, Halleck, has received virtually none of the credit for it; Grant has certainly received too much. Grant's eventual decision to abandon his lines of communication south of

Vicksburg was a brilliant and audacious move, but it was made under coaching from Halleck. The political environment does more to shape military decisions —even strokes of genius—than historians are prone to admit. Nonetheless, Grant's role was crucial in transferring political views into military practice. He was sufficiently flexible, shrewd, and imaginative to grasp, interpret, and express vague political desires operationally. It was not just humility but profoundly good sense for Grant to assure Halleck, "You may rely on me carrying out any policy ordered by proper authority to the best of my ability."[17]

Assured of the government's confidence, Grant gave renewed thought as to how he could overcome the numerous obstacles that blocked the road to decisive victory. Grant himself had been the victim of much unjust criticism since the setback at Holly Springs. He needed to gain a foothold on the high ground east of the Mississippi without conceding what he calls in his *Memoirs* "an apparent retreat," which would invite further invective and perhaps weaken the confidence of his political masters. He still had to sort out the problem of McClernand, but he was content to let McClernand pull on more and more rope; precipitate action here, too, was ill advised politically. McClernand reluctantly accepted command of the Thirteenth Corps. Instead of focusing on the complex Vicksburg problem, he turned about and pursued Sherman's scheme of advancing up the Arkansas River, taking Sherman and the Fifteenth Corps with him, and fought the battle of Arkansas Post (January 14, 1863).

This modest victory cost McClernand 1,032 casualties, although 4,701 Confederate prisoners were captured and much ordnance and stores. The battle terminated any danger that this small Confederate force might present to the Union rear during the Vicksburg campaign and thus served some public relations value after the setbacks at Chickasaw and Fredericksburg. Yet it was a diversion from the central task for McClernand was moving away from Vicksburg rather than advancing toward it. Grant thereupon decided to end all such distractions and concentrate his force.[18]

One way of helping to effect this concentration was by making the maximum use of his command of the rivers. Relations between the United States Army and Navy were always tinged with distrust, but there was less distrust between Grant and Admiral David D. Porter than between other commanders of the two services during the Civil War. The sailors certainly did not like McClernand. Grant would later use this knowledge to bring about his removal. Grant urged Porter to send his ironclads past Vicksburg, assaulting the city's batteries and destroying river commerce and supply wharves. The USS *Queen of the West* was dispatched successfully on just such a raid. She severely damaged the CSS *Vicksburg* and arrived safely in the Red River. The *Queen* should have thus ensured communications along the Yazoo and Steele's Bayou. However, on arrival in the Red River she ran aground, was captured by the Confederates, and then used against the federal naval forces.[19]

At this stage Grant sought every means to turn the Confederate right. He aimed to establish a secure line of communications based on linking the Mississippi, Yazoo, and Tallahatchie Rivers. The gunboats could then pass through the tangled, swampy vegetation that harbored many enemies other than Confederate soldiers, including legions of snakes. A canal was built from Young's Point above Vicksburg to the river below; it was a mile long and ten to twelve feet wide; hopes that with a rise in the river level it would gouge out a navigable channel were dashed on March 8, 1863, when the waters instead swamped a dam at the Young's Point end.

The other route that promised much stretched via Lake Providence. Bayou Baxter, Bayou Macon, and the Tensas, Washita, and Red rivers that flowed from it were encased with heavy timber, and the whole area was surrounded by swampland covered by an average depth of two feet of water. The trees themselves had to be cut under water. Small groups of Confederate skirmishers and sharpshooters disrupted the work of the four thousand soldiers that were cutting and hewing in the already torrid heat. Work here came to a halt when the cutting of a levee built by the state of Mississippi led to a rise in the water level which made the cutting of timber even more arduous. The troops also encountered a fortified meander, Fort Pemberton, which was so tight it was virtually an island. Grant calculated that a further rise in the water level would drive its garrison out, so the levee was cut a second time; but perversely it contributed to a further rise in the waters drenching Grant's troops without affecting Fort Pemberton. Had more resources been devoted to this route earlier, the island might have been cleared before it was fortified.

Grant himself "never felt great confidence that any of the experiments resorted to would prove successful. Nevertheless I was always prepared to take advantage of them in case they did." Consequently, he turned to a third route via Steele's Bayou. Should a way forward be found along this route then Grant could advance on Vicksburg from the north by seizing Haynes Bluff below the navigable Sunflower River. The gunboats sailed on but the transports carrying the soldiers were delayed. Porter's squadron of eleven ships got within a few hundred yards of getting to water unimpeded by low-lying timber when four thousand Confederate troops attacked his slow-moving vessels. Only a dramatic, candlelit night march by Sherman saved the squadron from complete destruction. Faced by frustration at every turn, Grant's troubles were not lightened when he received another irritating request from McClernand to continue his advance toward Pine Bluff, Arkansas, with twenty thousand men. Grant replied coolly yet tactfully that such an advance would detract from "the one great object, that of opening the Mississippi." Halleck agreed to Grant's request that his authority be extended to Arkansas and the west bank of the Mississippi. But Grant was careful not to antagonize McClernand, who received reinforcements and remained the overall commander in Grant's absence.[20]

A further three failures were now added to the humiliating end of the first Vicksburg campaign. Criticism of Grant—especially that he was an incompetent drunkard—grew in intensity. Had Grant buckled under this it would not have been surprising. Sylvanus Cadwallader, a reporter then working for the *Chicago Times* who was virtually adopted by Grant's staff as one of their own, reported that in the spring of 1863 Grant went on a drunken binge. Cadwallader dates this incident at about June 1863, that is, after the investment of Vicksburg. Grant's admirers have responded to his charges with the defensiveness to which they are prone, and also scorn and innuendo, which Cadwallader does not deserve.

A full treatment of the issue of Grant's predilection for drink is unnecessary here. Yet though it can be conceded that Cadwallader's memoirs are unsatisfactory in many respects, and he confuses details and dates, his story is probably true. Like many reporters, Cadwallader could write with concision, color, and cogency in a few hundred words, but writing a sustained piece in many thousands was beyond him. To concede the general truth of Cadwallader's recollection is not to join in any conspiracy to denigrate Grant, as so many of his biographers too hastily assume, but on the contrary to evince increased admiration for him. That a general, who had endured so many disappointments before 1861 and was now faced by setbacks at every turn, could overcome these and advance to victory while simultaneously conquering grave weaknesses verging on alcoholism, is reason to salute his phenomenal strength of character and will. Any attempt to conceal Grant's struggles to overcome his own inner torment does him a fundamental disservice.[21]

Nevertheless, the Lincoln administration became worried about vicious rumors concerning Grant's character and his halting progress, and dispatched the assistant secretary of war, Charles A. Dana, to Grant's headquarters. A former newspaperman, Dana was instructed not to interfere in operations but to report daily to Secretary Stanton. In short he was to verify the truth of the many aspersions that had been laid on Grant's competency. Dana quickly became an admirer of Grant and a firm ally—another factor undercutting McClernand's favor in the War Department. The key figure in Dana's conversion was Grant's chief of staff, Colonel John A. Rawlins.

Rawlins has almost completely disappeared from the historical record. His contribution to Grant's success is acknowledged in one meager paragraph in the general's *Personal Memoirs*. His friends (including Cadwallader), stung by this neglect, were wont to exaggerate his role and suggest that he was "one half" of Grant and made a decisive contribution to the evolution of Grant's campaigns. This claim is untrue. Rawlins's role was personal and political rather than operational. It illustrates once more the underdeveloped character of the American staff system and the overwhelmingly civilian style in which the Civil War was fought. Rawlins's main aims were to protect Grant from himself, advance his cause in the patronage stakes (which meant lavishing time and attention on correspondents, like Cadwallader, because it was in the columns of newspapers that reputations were embellished), and develop Grant's political networks in Washington. Rawlins succeeded brilliantly. Dana was welcomed in Grant's camps and proffered every courtesy. This small investment would reap huge dividends for Grant after the fall of Vicksburg.[22]

Observers tended to assume that because Rawlins was a handsome man, articulate, and forceful in speech, that he exerted a magnetic hold over the reserved, gruff, shambling figure of Grant. Despite impressions to the contrary, Grant dominated his staff and not vice versa. Yet he succeeded in creating an atmosphere in which even the most junior staff officer felt that he could speak his mind without fear of retribution—unless he offered Grant a drink, for then the miscreant would face the wrath of Rawlins. It cannot be emphasized too strongly that Grant did all his own work as a general. He wrote out all his reports and orders first in his own hand. He had a marvelous memory and could synthesize powerfully all the conflicting issues, drawing them together into one simple, easily understood concept—a task of crippling difficulty. These papers were then checked, edited, and if necessary, extended by his staff. Unlike Rawlins, Grant was a natural writer. "His thoughts flowed as freely from his mind," recalled Horace Porter, "as the ink from his pen; he was never at a loss for an expression, and seldom interlined a word or made a material correction." Rawlins was no Gneisenau. His role as chief of staff was more akin to a twentieth-century chief of staff in the White House. Yet his contribution was vital. Grant could not have succeeded without him.[23]

Stuck in the bayous, Grant now contemplated turning the Confederate left, moving down the Mississippi, linking up with Nathaniel P. Banks's army

advancing north from Baton Rouge, and taking Grand Gulf. This would complete the isolation of Vicksburg from the south, and was the course most favored
by President Lincoln. Sherman began to urge on Grant the necessity of cooperating with Banks's thirty thousand men, because he thought the Army of the
Tennessee too weak to take Vicksburg unaided. He also believed, at this stage,
that the logistical problem was insuperable. Sherman argued fiercely that a
thrust southward could not be made without a strong line of communications,
a conclusion that demonstrated a traditional line of thought. Banks was
advancing to besiege Port Hudson but communications with him were haphazard. Grant thus decided to move south but kept his options open as to
whether he should advance beyond Grand Gulf or shift south and eastward to
strike at Vicksburg's communications.

On the very day that Grant decided to send his gunboats south of Vicksburg, April 16, Colonel Benjamin H. Grierson led a Union cavalry raid of 1,700
troopers into northern Mississippi from Tennessee in an attempt to strike at
Pemberton's communications and repeat Van Dorn's coup at Holly Springs in
reverse. Grierson caused confusion in Pemberton's rear areas and diverted scant
Confederate cavalry units away from looking for Grant. This was not the only
surprise that Grant had in store for Pemberton. On the evening of April 16
Pemberton and his officers attended a ball in Vicksburg to celebrate Grant's
defeat. The violins were disturbed by the roar of the Vicksburg batteries firing
at Porter's ships heading south.

Letters were taking more than a month to reach General Banks. Grant felt
the attractions of taking Grand Gulf, but was increasingly inclined to bring the
campaign to a climax and move on Vicksburg unaided. Banks, in any case,
became distracted by an incursion into western Louisiana. Using river transport
Grant concentrated his army, calling McClernand and his troops to join
McPherson's corps on the west bank of the Mississippi opposite Grand Gulf.
Sherman carried out a feint toward Haynes Bluff to the north. Porter's gunboats
then attacked Grand Gulf on April 29; the bombardment was fierce though no
boats were lost and the Confederate batteries remained intact.

The gunboats sailed on but, as the transports carrying Grant's infantry
could not pass without grave risk, the troops were disembarked at Hard Times.
A runaway slave then told Grant that a good road existed running easterly from
Bruinsburg, opposite Hard Times on the dry east bank, to Port Gibson in the
hinterland south of Vicksburg. "Finding the position too strong, late in the day
I decided again to run the blockade," he informed Sherman, "which has been
successfully done." Halleck was also informed succinctly: "A landing will be

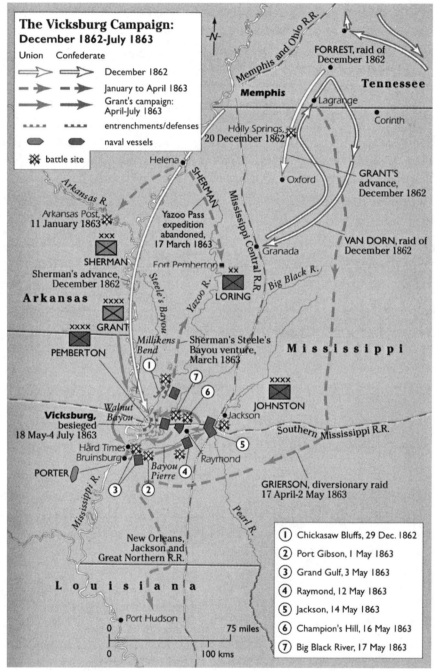

The Vicksburg Campaign:
December 1862-July 1863

Union   Confederate

⟹   ⟹   December 1862

- ‑ ›   - ‑ ›   January to April 1863

→   →   Grant's campaign:
April-July 1863

▪▪▪▪   ▪▪▪▪   entrenchments/defenses

⬮   ⬮   naval vessels

✖ battle site

FORREST, raid of
December 1862

Memphis and Ohio R.R.

Tennessee

Memphis   Lagrange

Corinth

Holly Springs,
20 December 1862

GRANT'S
advance,
December 1862

Helena

Oxford

Arkansas R.

Arkansas Post,
11 January 1863

Yazoo Pass
expedition
abandoned,
17 March 1863

Granada

VAN DORN, raid of
December 1862

xxx

SHERMAN

Sherman's advance,
December 1862

Fort Pemberton

xx

LORING

Big Black R.

Arkansas   xxxx

xxxx GRANT

PEMBERTON

Millikens
Bend

Sherman's Steele's
Bayou venture,
March 1863

Mississippi

xxxx

JOHNSTON

Vicksburg,
besieged
18 May-4 July 1863

Walnut
Bayou

Jackson

Southern Mississippi R.R.

Hard Times
Bruinsburg

PORTER

Bayou
Pierre

Raymond

GRIERSON, diversionary raid
17 April-2 May 1863

New Orleans,
Jackson and
Great Northern R.R.

Louisiana

Pearl R.

Port Hudson

0   75 miles
0   100 kms

① Chickasaw Bluffs, 29 Dec. 1862
② Port Gibson, 1 May 1863
③ Grand Gulf, 3 May 1863
④ Raymond, 12 May 1863
⑤ Jackson, 14 May 1863
⑥ Champion's Hill, 16 May 1863
⑦ Big Black River, 17 May 1863

From *An Atlas of American Military History* by James C.
Bradford (New York: Cynthia Parzych Publishing, 2003).

effected on the east bank of the river tomorrow. I feel that the battle is now more than half won." With such confidence and decisiveness Grant moved to follow up his hard-won advantage.[24]

In April 1863 the Confederate high command was still confident that geography and the weather were their greatest allies and that any federal thrust could be thrown back. The commander at Vicksburg, renegade Pennsylvanian John C. Pemberton, enjoyed an inflated reputation after the first Vicksburg campaign, and it was boosted by Grant's later frustrations in the bayous. Nonetheless, Pemberton was sensitive to protecting his lines of communication with Grand Gulf and batteries of heavy guns were dispatched thence. President Jefferson Davis had taken a close personal interest in these developments and congratulated Pemberton for foiling "every attempt [by Grant] to get possession of the Mississippi River." Pemberton then jumped to the false conclusion that Grant's army would be transferred to Tennessee. This was a rumor that Grant's deception plan encouraged. Pemberton was so confident that he offered to send eight thousand men to reinforce Braxton Bragg in Tennessee. Pemberton was already displaying that fatal tendency to presume that federal generals would readily do what he expected them to do—what Napoleon called "painting pictures." The emperor believed that a general's "intelligence should be as clear as the lens of a telescope." Throughout the campaign Pemberton suffered from lamentable intelligence even though he was operating in his own country.[25]

This weakness would prove fatal as the climactic stage of the campaign got underway. Superficially, Pemberton's position appeared strong. His total strength was 61,495 men, but he could never muster anything like this number in the field. Confederate forces were scattered and ill organized, and Pemberton had sent his cavalry to General Joseph E. Johnston who was attempting to build up a force under his personal command. Although Davis had sent Johnston to command all Confederate forces in the west, in reality unity of command was lacking. The boundary of Johnston's department was the Mississippi River; Edmund Kirby Smith, who commanded the Trans-Mississippi Department, declined to cooperate with Pemberton even though Davis had ordered that his highest priority should be protecting the Mississippi basin. At one stage Smith suggested that Pemberton reinforce him. Even within his department Johnston refused to accept the responsibility of his position. He acted hesitantly and uncertainly toward his subordinates and churlishly toward the Confederate president. Stephen Woodworth calls this "sheer contrariness born of resentment of any higher authority."

Johnston was also confused because Davis expected him to act like a field commander rather than a theater commander, when his true role was to direct the armies under his command. Yet, in truth, he felt more at ease with and hankered after field command. He made no effort to coordinate the movements of Bragg's troops with Pemberton's, nor to reduce the undue attention lavished by Beauregard and his acolytes on the war in Tennessee. Because responsibility was so diffused and direction so muddled, it is not surprising that the Confederate command system reacted so inefficiently when confronted with Grant's dynamic and concentrated thrusts.[26]

The other major problem was President Davis himself. Although he took a close personal interest in his adopted state for much of the campaign, the president was bedridden and so stricken with illness he could not even speak. Johnston believed that Davis denied him intelligence and freedom to command while at the same time demanding he take what Johnston believed were essentially "political" decisions. The latter complaint is perhaps symptomatic of Johnston's refusal to accept responsibility. But it has a certain validity in that the chaotic command system needed a general-in-chief who could concentrate on military affairs in a way that the president was unable to do and stamp military decisions with clear-cut authority.

Davis tended to procrastinate and hated Johnston; yet he would not countenance any diminution of his own constitutional military prerogatives inherent in the appointment of a general-in-chief. Davis had faith in Pemberton but this was wholly misplaced. Pemberton was diligent and eager to please, but he was timid and lacked a firm sense of direction. Martin van Creveld has observed that for a Hannibal to win a Cannae, he needs to be faced by a Varro. Pemberton was well qualified to fill Varro's shoes. Temperamentally better suited to the position of chief of staff rather than army commander, he proved indecisive or neglectful over great matters but stubborn and opinionated over small ones; but Davis remained convinced that his performance was worthy of Fabius and therefore not deserving of censure.[27]

Yet Pemberton's conviction that he could strike at Grant's exposed supply lines when he chose was completely dislocated when on April 30 Grant crossed the Mississippi to the east side, and at last, the men of the Army of the Tennessee placed their feet on terra firma. Grant was now prepared to abandon strict reliance on his lines of communication and advance into the enemy's heartland. Only five day's rations had been issued. In sustaining Grant's decision Halleck's letter detailing administration policy, written in April, was crucial. Grant now indicated his intention to "immediately follow the enemy, and, if all promises as favorable hereafter as it does now, not stop until Vicksburg is in our possession." Pemberton was to be persuaded to keep his strength in the environs of Vicksburg so that Grant could strengthen his force of twenty-three thousand men and then move onto the high ground east of the river. Once this was achieved, Sherman and his Fifteenth Corps were recalled to join the main body, arriving on May 6. "I was now in the enemy's country, with a vast river and the stronghold of Vicksburg between me and my base of supplies."[28]

Grant's advance had nonetheless placed him in an extremely advantageous position vis-à-vis Pemberton and Johnston. The further he advanced on the same bank as his enemies, the easier it became to dislocate their movements. Grant could divide their forces and thus guarantee that he could concentrate greater force at the decisive point; and he could make decisions more quickly. In short, Grant gained liberty of maneuver which is surely the operational object of all generalship. He achieved this virtually unaided; Rosecrans made little attempt to draw the enemy's attention toward Tennessee, and Banks had but a slight effect in Louisiana. Thus Grant's first priority was to delude Pemberton into thinking that he intended to move on Vicksburg via the Big Black River, when he actually intended a much more sweeping maneuver via the Mississippi state capital, Jackson. The ferries over the Big Black were held in strength to confirm this impression.[29]

Port Gibson had fallen easily on May 1 and Grant's force fanned out east of the Big Black with McClernand's Thirteenth Corps on the left, Sherman's Fifteenth Corps in the center, and McPherson's Seventeenth Corps on the right. The Army of the Tennessee was now forty-three thousand strong with more reinforcements en route. Grant had instructed that "We must fight the enemy before our rations fail, and we are equally bound to make our rations last as long as possible." Foodstuffs were collected from the country. As many horses, mules, and oxen as could be found in local plantations were gathered so that Grant could transport ammunition forward as the columns advanced eastward. Sherman was still at this stage skeptical that Grant could pull his gamble off. But by May 12 he had brushed aside desultory Confederate resistance and had seized Raymond ten miles southwest of Jackson. Rowena Reed might criticize Grant's campaign for its administrative overlap, wasted effort, and fumbled expedients—certainly McClellan's operations were more meticulously staffed—but planning alone does not make a general: he must decide and act. Grant had no fear in taking advantage of opportunities as they arose and integrating them into his overall plan. Grant bore down on Jackson in overwhelming strength.[30]

Throughout the climactic period of the campaign the overall Confederate commander, Joseph E. Johnston, was plagued with defeatism. He wished to avoid "some great blunder." Once he had arrived in Jackson on May 13 still suffering from bad health and heard the news that Grant was approaching, Johnston deduced that this blunder had already occurred. He instructed Pemberton that their only chance was to unite their forces and concentrate to face Grant in the open field. If Grant could be driven back, then any towns that had been evacuated could be reoccupied. This was straightforward military sense, which would have done much to negate Grant's advantage over the divided Confederate forces. But it overlooked the disastrous political consequences—especially for the Davis administration—of giving up a stronghold in which so much political capital had been invested. Pemberton, who bore the responsibility for this act, was inclined to ignore Johnston's instructions. He could only see that if he moved south of the Big Black he could attack Grant's slender lines of communication.[31]

Pemberton did not relinquish Vicksburg but he did his best to concentrate a field force of some twenty-three thousand men around the city; Johnston only had six thousand troops with him in Jackson but fifteen thousand men were rushing to join him, with nine thousand more behind them. If this entire force could be concentrated, the Confederates would be strong enough to attack Grant. But Pemberton was timorous; he was also one of those men who the more he thought about a problem, the more likely he was to reach the wrong conclusion. Pemberton then convened a council of war, which groped for unsatisfactory compromises. His subordinates urged on Pemberton the view that it was preferable to force Grant back without confronting his army directly. Pemberton agreed to attack Grant's supply lines that had recently begun to sprout from Grand Gulf. He decided to advance into the open, but he would not abandon Vicksburg. Yet the price of his decision was to advance south, and not east, and away from Johnston rather than toward him. He thus rendered a Confederate concentration impossible.[32]

President Jefferson Davis had played a part in marking out Pemberton's wavering course by ordering that under no circumstances were Vicksburg and Port Hudson to be abandoned. He also ordered that Grant's supply lines be severed. Pemberton then ordered the Port Hudson garrison to return to their lines and remain there "to the last." So the unhappy compromise was compounded. Pemberton was prepared to advance from Vicksburg but not too far. He moved cautiously toward the Big Black but he had difficulty locating Grant because he had no cavalry. Grant's troops could not take ammunition from the country but Union lines of supply did exist, as wagon trains lumbered northeastward from Grand Gulf. Pemberton spent much time trying to locate them. All he achieved was to waste several days in inconsequential activity. Grant did not waste time. He advanced straight into Jackson on May 14 and drove Johnston out. Johnston remained ignorant of Pemberton's advance and withdrew northward, in the opposite direction. Grant was kept informed of this confusion of cross purposes by a Confederate courier who worked as a Union spy.[33]

Pemberton at last received word from Johnston of the fall of Jackson, his northward retreat, and the consequent hazard of any southerly advance. Johnston hoped to link up with Pemberton via the northerly route on May 14 and summoned Pemberton north. Grant soon deduced Johnston's intent. McClernand's Thirteenth Corps was instructed, "We must not allow them to do this. Turn all your forces toward Bolton Station and make all dispatch in getting there." McPherson was also ordered to Bolton Depot on the Jackson to Vicksburg railroad. Grant had been worried by the concentration of Confederate reinforcements and was determined to bring the campaign to a conclusion before they could make their influence felt. Sherman's Fifteenth Corps would remain in the environs of Jackson to destroy Confederate stores, the railroad, and to guard the rear of the Army of the Tennessee.[34]

It was a measure of Grant's success in dividing the Confederate forces that, despite his rapid advance, he still had not fought a major battle, though he had won a number of minor engagements against greatly outnumbered detachments. As Grant thrust westward at great speed, Pemberton's fumbling and halfhearted move north to link up with Johnston would inevitably produce a collision with the Union army. Johnston in the meantime hoped to funnel five thousand of his reinforcements through to Pemberton. He continued to suggest that a concentration of the scattered fragments of the Confederate army in Mississippi was vital. He also continued to issue vague generalities, such as the desirability of assembling a force "that may be able to inflict a heavy blow upon the enemy." Yet he did not specify how this was to be achieved.

Johnston was recovering from illness, and he failed signally to grip the operations for which he was responsible and issue clear orders; but effective communication had never been his strong point. In any case, by the time Pemberton received General Johnston's thoughts on their joint predicament, they were valueless. The only clear stipulation Pemberton received was the order to move north. Johnston realized that such a maneuver entailed a risk of bringing on a battle with Grant before a concentration with Pemberton could be effected, but he calculated that this was less dangerous than continuing to allow the two forces to move away from each other.[35]

Pemberton hurriedly occupied a ridge called Champion's Hill facing Grant's columns marching westward. This was a strong position running north to south. If held resolutely, Pemberton could have delayed Grant here and allowed Johnston to join him or even fall on his flank. Pemberton fielded twenty-three thousand men; Grant's two corps, over twenty-nine thousand. Grant estimated Pemberton's strength at twenty-five thousand. Thus his decision to attack Champion's Hill on May 16 was not based on any calculation of great numerical superiority. The battle opened haphazardly with the dynamic but circumspect Grant prepared instantly to take advantage of any opportunities that might accrue from vigorous offensive action. Pemberton, by contrast, fumbled because he had been taken completely by surprise. McClernand's Thirteenth Corps arrived at the position first. Grant hurried to the front and ordered McClernand several times to attack forthwith Pemberton's right. By 11 AM the skirmishing on Pemberton's left had already become very severe. The divisions of Brigadier General Alvin P. Hovey and Major General John A. Logan had pinned Pemberton's force to their position, and Logan was successfully working his way round their left flank on the summit of Champion's Hill, south of the railroad. But McClernand's failure to launch a similar fixing operation on Pemberton's right allowed Stephen D. Lee to grasp the import of Grant's tactics. He was the only one of Pemberton's generals with any shred of ability and he persuaded his chief to hurriedly transfer units from the Confederate right to the hard-pressed left.[36]

This Confederate movement represented the crisis of the battle for Grant because Hovey and Logan were both driven back. But Grant had gauged accurately the state of Confederate morale, which had been eroded by the inept mismanagement of Pemberton, who had failed to take advantage of his opportunities—mainly because of the execrable state of his intelligence. Grant decided instantly "If we can go in again here [on Pemberton's left] and make a little showing, I think he will give way." Union artillery had thrown back Confederate counterattacks and Hovey's division was reinforced by two regiments from Brigadier General Marcellus M. Crocker's division. Hovey advanced successfully over ground that had already been fought over twice and, finding no evidence of the "invulnerability" of the defense along Champion's Hill, drove the Confederates from their position.

Indeed, Grant was somewhat taken by surprise by the extent of his success. By 4 PM not only were the Confederates retreating but Logan, by far the most tactically astute of all "political" generals, had outflanked them. The complete annihilation of Pemberton's army was now a distinct possibility. But Grant later admitted that he lacked knowledge of the country behind Champion's Hill, and he was unprepared to take advantage of this glittering opportunity. Furthermore, because of McClernand's laggard behavior he lacked a fast-moving reserve to send to Logan's aid. Pursuits cannot simply be improvised, they have to be thought through. Grant had not been given the time to think about and organize an effective pursuit. If he had, Grant would have been quite justified in claiming that "I cannot see how Pemberton could have escaped with any organized force."[37]

Nevertheless, although the tremendous dividend of the complete destruction of Pemberton's field army had not been earned, the battle of Champion's Hill had been a complete success for Grant and virtually sealed Vicksburg's fate. Union casualties were 2,441, while Confederate casualties totaled 3,851 and eleven cannon; again, these indicate no automatic advantage for the army standing on the defensive. Indeed, it is worth reiterating that the primary factor promoting deadlock in the east was morale. The sense that the Army of Northern Virginia was a corps d'elite, with a moral cohesion and a strong sense of its identity transmitted by the excellent standard of its regimental and brigade commanders, was wholly absent among Confederates in the west. Johnston and Pemberton did not lack resources but they utterly failed to master the fighting power of the units under their command. Consequently, as Grant's campaign developed, he maximized the fighting power of the units in his army, which did not greatly outnumber the Confederate forces, at their expense. The Army of the Tennessee grew in fighting power as the Confederates grew weaker; this process is as much moral as it is material. Grant's determination to renew the assault at Champion's Hill is strong evidence of his discernment of the psychological factor; but Grant was not always right in his assessments of the enemy's morale, as the final stage of the campaign would show.[38]

Pemberton's divisions withdrew back to another entrenched defensive line on the Big Black River ten miles east of Vicksburg from which the Army of the Tennessee had no difficulty in evicting them. Pemberton was outraged by the lack of fighting spirit evinced by his men and criticized them in his report. Yet it never occurred to him that his own lack of leadership had something to do with this unhappy state of affairs. Pemberton then had to force his thoughts to embrace the higher conduct of the campaign. He withdrew back into Vicksburg. Johnston had throughout May 1863 stipulated that the survival of his army was more important than holding on to Vicksburg. Pemberton's perceived earlier success in the campaign had led him into believing the town impregnable and therefore giving it up voluntarily was unthinkable. Johnston's pleas for him to move and join forces were most unwelcome. "[If] you are invested in Vicksburg, you must ultimately surrender," Johnston pointed out. "Under such circumstances, instead of losing both troops and place, we must, if possible save the troops. If it is not too late, evacuate Vicksburg and its dependencies, and march to the north east."[39]

This was the course that Grant thought the most sensible, and Pemberton for the first time in the campaign showed resolution—but he was resolved to do the wrong thing. He called another council of war and urged his generals that Vicksburg must be held. He could not afford to lose control of the Mississippi, permit the fall of Port Hudson, and lose all the stores gathered to sustain the defense of the river centers. The political results of such an act would indeed have been severe. But Johnston was right in thinking that the loss of Vicksburg *and* Pemberton's army was an even greater loss than just the city itself. Certainly Pemberton could have escaped Grant's clutches at this point if he had had a mind to. The consensus reached by the council of war, however, that an evacuation of Vicksburg would be hazardous, smacks of a self-fulfilling prophecy. Pemberton thus told Johnston that he had "decided to hold Vicksburg as long as is possible, with the firm hope that the Government may yet be able to assist me." Pemberton justified this rank disobedience to Johnston's orders on the grounds that he believed Vicksburg "to be the most important point in the Confederacy." In truth, fortifications have a distorting effect on weak military minds. Pemberton feared the risk of maneuvering in the open against Grant but felt resolute while remaining stationary behind his defenses. The onus was thus placed on others to save him.[40]

This put Johnston in a quandary because he had tarried in moving to take up his command in the west and had neglected to build up a large force under his personal command. His small force of about ten thousand men was far too weak to cut through Grant's lines and relieve the city. Johnston therefore had to await reinforcements. "They come too slowly," he pleaded with Richmond. "Do urge them forward." By the beginning of June he had managed to field twenty-three thousand men. Yet Grant now had invested Vicksburg with forty-three thousand and Sherman had been recalled to the Big Black with thirty-four thousand, facing eastward to guard against Johnston's relief attempts. This is a fine example of how Grant's effective concentration, while the Confederates remained divided, added to his fighting power while that of the Confederates diminished. Yet President Davis blamed Johnston rather than Pemberton for this deterioration. After Vicksburg's surrender, he put the failure down to a "want of provisions inside, and a general outside who wouldn't fight." But the time for fighting was now past and the responsibility for this failure lay more with Pemberton than Johnston, for all the latter's deficiencies.[41]

Grant had moved to invest Vicksburg on the evening of May 18. He had hoped to gain the maximum effect from the demoralization of the Confederates and advanced in three columns. The most northerly, Sherman's Fifteenth Corps, got between Vicksburg and the forts at Haynes Bluff, in front of which Sherman had been demonstrating only weeks before. The forts were abandoned and Grant was able to open up a new line of supply via the Yazoo, his main concern being ammunition. Sherman then admitted to Grant, with his beguiling candor, that he had been wrong and Grant right as to the wisdom of living off the country; Sherman had just learned the most important military lesson of his life.

By the morning of May 19, Vicksburg was invested entirely on the east side of the Mississippi from Mint Springs in the north to Stout's Bayou in the south; Sherman's Fifteenth Corps occupied the northern lines, McPherson's Seventeenth Corps the center, and McClernand's Thirteenth Corps the southern. Grant thereupon ordered an all-out assault on the town's defenses, supported by Admiral Porter's gunboats. But Grant had exaggerated the demoralization of the Confederate defenders and lost 950 men to the Confederate 200 for no gain. Vicksburg was an entrenched camp rather than an elaborately fortified town so characteristic of the military history of northern France and Belgium. Grant attacked a second time on May 22 with 34,446 men against Pemberton's 22,301, but by attacking all along the line his margin of superiority was simply too slender and his thrusts were repulsed. A misleading message from McClernand suggesting success on the left, persuaded Grant to order Sherman and McPherson to repeat their attacks; but this was wasted effort. His failed assault was the first setback Grant had faced since crossing to the east bank of the Mississippi on April 30. It cost him 3,052 casualties while Pemberton's losses were comparatively small, fewer than 500.[42]

Grant then settled down to besiege Vicksburg determined to tighten his grip on the beleaguered Confederate garrison. He methodically set about seizing the Confederate positions one by one without exposing his men unduly. The terrain was very rugged and trenches and breastworks were built with difficulty. Union forces were rarely harassed by Confederate artillery because any rash firing provoked an avalanche of federal shells and these were not popular with the good citizens of Vicksburg. A buffer zone—a "no-man's land"—divided the trenches across which raids were launched. Grant also strengthened lines of communication with Hard Times and Grand Gulf. The siege became a contest of determination and stamina. Although Grant worried whether he was strong enough to reduce Vicksburg, Halleck steadfastly acquired reinforcements for him. Pemberton was now completely trapped in the town, and the only effort made on his behalf was an ineffective assault on New Carthage by Kirby Smith and a raid toward the Mississippi by Sterling Price in Arkansas. These moves were too small and too late; they were symptomatic of a crippling Confederate failure to concentrate its resources in the west. Johnston was urged by Davis to relieve Vicksburg but he remained too weak.[43]

Now that the object of the campaign was in sight, Grant at once moved to solve the McClernand problem. McClernand's long-term political enemy, Frank Blair Jr., had noticed a congratulatory order issued by McClernand's headquarters published in the *Memphis Evening Bulletin*. He reported this to Sherman who, in turn, sent it to Grant with a reminder that the publication of such documents was forbidden by the War Department. Grant inquired as to whether this was a correct copy and when he discovered that it was, he coolly relieved McClernand. He could rely on Halleck's support, and Charles A. Dana mollified Stanton. Always prepared to back a winner Lincoln rather brutally dropped McClernand, who was left expostulating on the margins, wailing that he was sacked for an omission of his adjutant.[44]

Over the next five weeks the position of Pemberton's army within Vicksburg deteriorated gravely. He was not popular or respected and, being a Northerner, was suspected of treachery. Desertion bled his forces white. He was warned starkly by a private soldier, "This army is now ripe for mutiny, unless it can be fed." Supplying his troops was Pemberton's central problem. He calculated that he had enough food to last until the end of June. He implored Johnston to relieve him, warning that the federal lines had crept ever nearer to the city; whereas they had started out twenty-five yards distant from his own trenches, they were now only twenty-five feet away. Pemberton also discovered that Grant was acquainted with his problems, thanks to his excellent intelligence service, because Grant's signals to Admiral Porter were intercepted.[45]

As Grant's troops closed on the rebel units, two mines were exploded on June 25 and July 1. These foreshadowed the experience of the much more famous "crater" at the siege of Petersburg a year later. Artillery opened fire at the same time as the explosion occurred. "The effect," Grant recalled, "was to blow the top of the hill off and make a crater where it stood." Neither of these two mines had decisive results. "The breach was not sufficient," Grant decided, "to enable us to pass a column of attack through." Close cooperation with the US Navy allowed Grant to dominate the west bank of the Mississippi should Pemberton seek to slip out that way. But Pemberton was bereft of ideas and merely pleaded for Johnston to rescue him. General Richard Taylor marched from Louisiana to Milliken's Bend opposite Vicksburg; but he found trying to cooperate with Kirby Smith as frustrating as everybody else had. Taylor had hoped also to strike at Grant's line of supply, and thus offered Pemberton no relief.[46]

Jefferson Davis was becoming so desperate that he contemplated going to Mississippi himself and taking personal command: an impossible option given the demands of his health and many other duties; but it was symptomatic of his excessive centralization. Johnston in the meantime was thinking more about protecting his reputation than saving Vicksburg, which he now thought as good as lost. When Pemberton suggested a desperate scheme whereby Grant would be offered Vicksburg in return for letting Pemberton leave Vicksburg unmolested, Johnston retorted that should the town be surrendered, then this should be done by the general who had insisted on holding it. Still, Johnston hoped that Pemberton's force could be saved. He reoccupied Jackson and hoped to divert Grant's attention by a move timed for July 7 into his rear toward the Big Black River. Pemberton would then be encouraged to break out to the northeast and then the two forces would combine west of Jackson. Yet the logistical and transport difficulties Johnston faced in this ravaged country hindered him at every turn. Grant had, if anything, been oversensitive to such a maneuver on Johnston's part, and Sherman's Fifteenth Corps was positioned ready to resist it. In any case, Pemberton did not receive warning of this intended move until after he had surrendered.[47]

Thoroughly apprised of Pemberton's baleful situation, Grant intended to bring the siege to an end before Johnston could interfere. He had forty-three thousand men around the city, in twelve miles of trenches, supported by 220 guns in eighty-nine batteries, and Admiral Porter's squadron of gunboats. At ten points around Grant's lines the distance between the trenches was less than five yards and never more than a hundred yards. Preparations were made to attack Vicksburg's defenses on July 6. The levels of Union improvisation shown in siegecraft were very impressive. Convening yet another council of war, in this case a council of despair, Pemberton agreed with his commanders that Vicksburg could no longer be held and that, in the absence of outside help, the town should be surrendered. On July 3 Pemberton ordered the raising of white flags and asked Grant to appoint commissioners for the discussion of terms. This Grant adamantly refused to do, pointing out that the ordeal of Vicksburg could be ended immediately by surrendering. Grant then offered to parole Confederate troops, which clinched Pemberton's agreement because throughout the discussions he remained undecided to the last. On hearing of Vicksburg's capitulation, Grant with an eye on future operations, ordered Sherman to drive Johnston from Jackson, inflicting "all the punishment you can."[48]

Thus ended Grant's brilliant Vicksburg campaign, which has been so highly praised by technical military authorities. Colonel Conger calls it "a campaign as brief and as brilliant as is to be found in military annals." General Fuller is no less effusive.[49] The fall of Vicksburg had punished the Confederate war effort severely. Port Hudson was untenable once Vicksburg had been occupied, and surrendered shortly after July 4. The Confederate Department of the Trans-Mississippi was strategically cut off from the remainder of the South; some movement and smuggling across the river was still possible but this detracts little from the massive strategic reverse inflicted on the South. The troops lost, including Port Hudson's garrison, in excess of forty thousand men, plus 172 guns, and sixty thousand rifled muskets; the latter were of superior quality to his own and Grant distributed them among his infantry. Grant's own casualties were 9,362 (more than half sustained during Champion's Hill). Set against such a triumph—the most complete victory yet won by the North in the Civil War—no wonder Grant was so indifferent to the rudeness of Pemberton and his generals when he met them to finalize terms on entering Vicksburg on July 3.[50]

Often hailed as the turning point of the war, the importance of the fall of Vicksburg has sometimes been exaggerated. The isolation of the Trans-Mississippi made conducting the war much more difficult for the Confederacy. But it could continue to field armies so long as its Southern forces maintained a tentative hold on Tennessee and Virginia—and the Confederacy was forced to surrender only once these had been irrevocably lost, almost two years after Pemberton was bottled up in Vicksburg. Nonetheless, the town's loss was a signal success for Grant. His generalship was of a Napoleonic order—a label often applied erroneously only to defeated Confederates. But Grant's generalship can be described accurately as Napoleonic because of the brilliant use he made of surprise and mobility in exploiting systemic Confederate weaknesses, especially in terms of command and control. Yet such labels should not be employed indiscriminately. Grant effectively exploited his command of the Mississippi River and, by the speed of his advance, not only outmaneuvered his opponents, he outthought them.[51]

Grant did enjoy certain superiority in materiel, which allowed him to exercise the initiative, but this was far from overwhelming. It was his skill in outmaneuvering the enemy that rendered local Union superiority at the decisive point while Confederate strength was dispersed in weak fragments. Another way in which Grant's generalship resembled Napoleon's was in his tendency to exploit Confederate weak points by attacking; he would then look for his opportunity and pursue it with utter ruthlessness. No general had a more highly developed instinct to strike at his enemy's jugular than Grant. Whether this technique was the result of continuous study it is now impossible to say; probably not. It was more likely a result of an adaptation to circumstances and the benefit of the material abundance that Grant enjoyed.

Grant's generalship was a compound of opportunities successfully exploited. Rowena Reed has persuasively argued that Grant did not "cut loose his communications [South of Vicksburg] intentionally . . . nor is it technically true that he had no supply line after leaving the river," for Grant soon reknitted a line with Grand Gulf once Vicksburg was invested. But by stressing the "impulsive" nature of this decision, she underrates the amount of calculation that Grant invested in his risky maneuver. She also forgets that generalship consists not only in planning but in carrying out the tasks set. By his amazing power of decision and eagerness to exploit any expedient that came to hand, Grant displayed his infinite superiority to Reed's hero, McClellan. For McClellan, despite all the forethought and elegance of his planning, showed himself on so many occasions incapable of seizing even the most glittering opportunities that the goddess Fortune placed in his path.[52]

NOTES AND REFERENCES

1. T. Harry Williams, *McClellan, Sherman and Grant* (New Brunswick, NJ: Rutgers University Press, 1962), pp. 82, 105; John Keegan, *The Mask of Command* (London: Jonathan Cape, 1987), pp. 195–96, 198–99; Horace Porter, *Campaigning with Grant*, with an introduction by Joseph G. Dawson III (New York: Bantam Books abridged edition, 1991), pp. 8, 30–31, 36–37, 45, 47, 102–103, 169–70, 174–76; Brian Holden Reid, "The Commander and Chief of Staff: Ulysses S. Grant and John A. Rawlins, 1861–1865," in *Command and Leadership in War*, ed. G. D. Sheffield, 25 (London: Brassey's, 1996); also B. H. Liddell Hart, *A Greater Than Napoleon: Scipio Africanus* (London: Greenhill reprint, 1992), p. 11.

2. U. S. Grant, *Personal Memoirs* (London: Sampson Lowe, 1886), vol. 1, p. 422; Samuel Carter III, *The Final Fortress: The Campaign for Vicksburg, 1862–1863* (New York: St Martin's Press, 1980), pp. 8–18.

3. John F. Marszalek, *Commander of All Lincoln's Armies: A Life of General Henry W. Halleck* (Cambridge, MA: Belknap Press of Harvard University Press, 2004), p. 161; Herman Hattaway and Archer Jones, *How the North Won* (Urbana: University of Illinois Press, 1983), pp. 292–95, are among the very few general historians of the war who recognize Halleck's achievement.

4. Ibid., p. 327; Grant, *Memoirs*, vol. 1, p. 424; Kenneth P. Williams, *Lincoln Finds a General* (New York: Macmillan, 1956), vol. 4, p. 167.

5. Williams, *Lincoln Finds a General*, vol. 4, pp. 144, 150, 504n1; T. Harry Williams, *Lincoln and His Generals* (New York: Alfred A. Knopf, 1952), pp. 191–92; Benjamin P. Thomas and Harold M. Hyman, *Stanton* (New York: Alfred A. Knopf, 1962), pp. 265–66; Richard L. Kiper, *Major General John Alexander McClernand: Politician in Uniform* (Kent, OH: Kent State University Press, 1999), pp. 138–39.

6. Williams, *Lincoln Finds a General*, vol. 4, pp. 147–48, 162–63; Williams, *Lincoln and His Generals*, pp. 192–93; Stephen E. Ambrose, *Halleck: Lincoln's Chief of Staff* (Baton Rouge: Louisiana State University Press, 1962), pp. 109–13; Kiper, *McClernand*, pp. 140–43.

7. Michael B. Ballard, *Vicksburg: The Campaign That Opened the Mississippi* (Chapel Hill: University of North Carolina Press, 2004), pp. 78–79.

8. Grant, *Memoirs*, vol. 1, pp. 426–30, 432; Williams, *Lincoln Finds a General*, vol. 4, pp. 150, 196–97; Hattaway and Jones, *How the North Won*, p. 311.

9. Grant, *Memoirs*, vol. 1, p. 429; Williams, *Lincoln Finds a General*, vol. 4, pp. 168–69; Kiper, *McClernand*, pp. 147–49, makes it clear that McClernand lacked the "wholehearted support of the entire command structure," including Lincoln.

10. John F. Marszalek, *Sherman: A Soldier's Passion for Order* (New York: Free Press, 1993), pp. 205–207; Williams, *Lincoln Finds a General*, vol. 4, pp. 211–18; Hattaway and Jones, *How the North Won*, pp. 312–14.

11. Kiper, *McClernand*, pp. 155–61; Grant, *Memoirs*, vol. 1, pp. 426, 432; Williams, *Lincoln Finds a General*, vol. 4, pp. 292–94, 324; Marszalek, *Sherman*, pp. 207–208; Carter, *Final Fortress*, pp. 104–105.

12. On the "convoy system" based on Memphis, see Warren E. Grabau, *Ninety-Eight Days: A Geographer's View of the Vicksburg Campaign* (Knoxville: University of Tennessee Press, 2000), pp. 30–34; Grant, *Personal Memoirs*, vol. 1, p. 433.

13. Quoted in Bruce Catton, *Grant Moves South* (Boston: Little, Brown, 1960), p. 342; Williams, *Lincoln Finds a General*, vol. 4, p. 174; Brooks D. Simpson, *Let Us Have Peace: Ulysses S. Grant and the Politics of War and Reconstruction* (Chapel Hill: University of North Carolina Press, 1991), pp. 33–36.

14. Williams, *Lincoln Finds a General*, vol. 4, pp. 178–79; Simpson, *Let Us Have Peace*, pp. 28–32, stresses also the role of Grant's mentor, Elihu B. Washburne, in keeping him informed about developments in Washington, and also shows his increasingly independent outlook; *The War of the Rebellion: A Compilation of the Official Records of the Union and Confederate Armies*, 128 parts in 70 vols. (Washington, DC: Government Printing Office, 1880–1901) [hereafter *O.R.*], series 1, vol. 16, part 2, p. 421.

15. *O.R.*, series 1, vol. 24, part 3, p. 157.

16. Ambrose, *Halleck*, pp. 119–20; Hattaway and Jones, *How the North Won*, p. 343; *O.R.*, series 1, vol. 24, part 1, p. 31; Williams, *Lincoln Finds a General*, vol. 4, p. 179; Simpson, *Let Us Have Peace*, pp. 38–39; Mark Grimsley, "Conciliation and Its Failure, 1861–1862," *Civil War History* 39 (December 1993): 320, 328–29.

17. Simpson, *Let Us Have Peace*, pp. xv–xvii, 39–41, 45.

18. Grant, *Memoirs*, vol. 1, pp. 443, 446; Williams, *Lincoln and His Generals*, p. 226; Williams, *Lincoln Finds a General*, vol. 4, pp. 294–300; Catton, *Grant Moves South*, pp. 343–46, 374–76; Marszalek, *Sherman*, pp. 209–10; Kiper, *McClernand*, pp. 162–93.

19. For a critical account of Grant's operations, see Rowena Reed, *Combined Operations in the Civil War* (Lincoln: University of Nebraska Press, 1978, 1993), pp. 239–40, 242–43. These strictures seem too severe.

20. Grant, *Memoirs*, vol. 1, pp. 446–55; Williams, *Lincoln Finds a General*, vol. 4, pp. 311–14, 318–28; Catton, *Grant Moves South*, pp. 377–87. Kiper, *McClernand*, pp. 189–94; Marszalek, *Sherman*, pp. 214–15.

21. Sylvanus Cadwallader, *Three Years with Grant*, ed. Benjamin P. Thomas (New York: Alfred A. Knopf, 1956), pp. 103–11; Williams, *Lincoln Finds a General*, vol. 4, pp. 318, 439–51; Catton, *Grant Moves South*, pp. 368–71, 463–65; but also see James M. McPherson, "Ulysses S. Grant's Greatest Victory," in *The Experience of War*, ed. Robert Cowley, 222–31 (New York: Norton, 1992); Brooks D. Simpson, *Ulysses S. Grant: Triumph over Adversity* (New York: Houghton Mifflin, 2000), pp. 206–208, considers the incident a "fable," and if Grant did drink, it was an effort to dull pain—probably of a migraine.

22. Thomas and Hyman, *Stanton*, p. 267; Holden Reid, "Grant and Rawlins," pp. 20, 25–26; Catton, *Grant Moves South*, pp. 388–90; Simpson, *Let Us Have Peace*, pp. 37–38.

23. Holden Reid, "Grant and Rawlins," pp. 22–23, 31–34; Catton, *Grant Moves South*, p. 389; Williams, *Lincoln Finds a General*, vol. 4, p. 302; William S. McFeely, *Grant: A Biography* (New York: Norton, 1981), p. 146.

24. Williams, *Lincoln Finds a General*, vol. 4, pp. 333–35, 337–39, 343–44, 345, 355; Catton, *Grant Moves South*, pp. 416–25; Marszalek, *Sherman*, pp. 219–20.

25. Steven E. Woodworth, *Jefferson Davis and His Generals: The Failure of Confederate Command in the West* (Lawrence: University Press of Kansas, 1990), pp. 200–203; Williams, *Lincoln Finds a General*, vol. 4, pp. 349–50; J. F. C. Fuller, *The Conduct of War, 1789–1961* (London: Eyre and Spottiswoode, 1961), p. 45.

26. Woodworth, *Davis and His Generals*, pp. 199, 205, 207; see Craig L. Symonds, *Joseph E. Johnston* (New York: Norton, 1992), pp. 199–203, for a defense.

27. Martin van Creveld, *Air Power and Maneuver Warfare* (Maxwell, AL: Air University Press, 1994) p. 209; William C. Davis, *Jefferson Davis: The Man and His Hour* (New York: HarperCollins, 1991), pp. 491–507; Michael B. Ballard, *Pemberton* (Jackson: University of Mississippi Press, 1991), pp. 116–17, 132–33, 135, 136–39.

28. Grant, *Memoirs*, vol. 1, pp. 435, 478, 480; Williams, *Lincoln Finds a General*, vol. 4, p. 360; A. L. Conger, *The Rise of U. S. Grant* (New York: Da Capo, 1931, 1996), p. 289.

29. Conger, *Rise of Grant*, p. 289; Williams, *Lincoln Finds a General*, vol. 4, pp. 355, 364.

30. Marszalek, *Sherman*, pp. 221–22; Catton, *Grant Moves South*, pp. 426–40; Williams, *Lincoln Finds a General*, vol. 4, pp. 366–68.

31. Archer Jones, *Confederate Strategy: From Shiloh to Vicksburg* (1961; Baton Rouge: Louisiana State University Press, 1991), p. 226; Woodworth, *Davis and His Generals*, p. 205; Symonds, *Johnston*, pp. 205–207; Ballard, *Pemberton*, p. 147.

32. Symonds, *Johnston*, pp. 207–208; Catton, *Grant Moves South*, p. 440; Ballard, *Pemberton*, pp. 146, 156–57.

33. Williams, *Lincoln Finds a General*, vol. 4, p. 373; Kiper, *McClernand*, p. 235; Woodworth, *Davis and His Generals*, pp. 206–208; Symonds, *Johnston*, p. 208.

34. Catton, *Grant Moves South*, pp. 441–42; Marszalek, *Sherman*, pp. 222–23.

35. Symonds, *Johnston*, pp. 208–209.

36. Thomas L. Livermore, *Numbers and Losses in the Civil War in America, 1861–1865* (Boston: Houghton Mifflin, 1901), p. 99, puts Pemberton at around twenty thousand, which is probably too low an estimate; Grant's strength he gives at 29,373. Grant, *Memoirs*, vol. 1, pp. 511, 513–16; Williams, *Lincoln Finds a General*, vol. 4, pp. 376–77; Woodworth, *Davis and His Generals*, p. 208; Ballard, *Pemberton*, pp. 162–63, Kiper, *McClernand*, pp. 244–48, offers a fair estimate of his errors.

37. Grant, *Memoirs*, vol. 1, pp. 517–21; Catton, *Grant Moves South*, pp. 442–45; Williams, *Lincoln Finds a General*, vol. 4, pp. 378–79; Ballard, *Vicksburg*, pp. 305–309, defends McClernand.

38. Livermore, *Numbers and Losses*, pp. 97–98; Williams, *Lincoln Finds a General*, vol. 4, p. 379.

39. Symonds, *Johnston*, p. 210; Ballard, *Vicksburg*, pp. 310–18, he also (p. 318) emphasizes Johnston's detachment.

40. Ballard, *Pemberton*, pp. 165–74; Woodworth, *Davis and His Generals*, p. 210.

41. Symonds, *Johnston*, p. 211; Davis, *Jefferson Davis*, p. 509; Pemberton's motives had also been influenced by the accusations of treachery thrown at him by his own soldiers. See Ballard, *Pemberton*, p. 168.

42. Williams, *Lincoln Finds a General*, vol. 4, pp. 383–89; Marszalek, *Sherman*, pp. 222–27; Livermore, *Numbers and Losses*, p. 100; Catton, *Grant Moves South*, pp. 445–53; Grant, *Memoirs*, vol. 1, pp. 528–31. On the other hand the assaults of Grant's troops may well have further undermined Pemberton's psychological outlook and reduced the chance that he would attempt a breakout. See Ballard, *Pemberton*, pp. 169–72.

43. See Ballard, *Vicksburg*, pp. 360–70, for a detailed account; Williams, *Lincoln Finds a General*, vol. 4, pp. 397–404, 414; Albert Castel, *General Sterling Price and the Civil War in the West* (Baton Rouge: Louisiana State University Press, 1968, 1993), pp. 142–43, 145.

44. Kiper, *McClernand*, pp. 265, 268–73. Rawlins had been calling impetuously for McClernand's dismissal for weeks but when it came to the moment of decision he was much less cool than Grant. See Holden Reid, "Grant and Rawlins," pp. 27–28;

Williams, *Lincoln and His Generals*, pp. 230–32; Grant, *Memoirs*, vol. 1, pp. 546–47; Marszalek, *Sherman*, pp. 227–28; Ballard, *Vicksburg*, pp. 349, 358–59, argues that McClernand came closer to a breakthrough than anybody else.

45. Williams, *Lincoln Finds a General*, vol. 4, p. 416; Woodworth, *Davis and His Generals*, p. 214; Ballard, *Pemberton*, pp. 175–78.

46. Grant, *Memoirs*, vol. 1, pp. 549–53; Woodworth, *Davis and His Generals*, p. 216; Ballard, *Vicksburg*, p. 391.

47. Davis, *Jefferson Davis*, p. 499; Woodworth, *Davis and His Generals*, pp. 215–16; Grant, *Memoirs*, vol. 1, pp. 548–49; Edward Hagerman, *The American Civil War and the Origins of Modern Warfare* (Bloomington: Indiana University Press, 1988), p. 206.

48. Catton, *Grant Moves South*, pp. 471–77; Williams, *Lincoln Finds a General*, vol. 4, pp. 416–19; Hagerman, *American Civil War*, pp. 204–206; Marszalek, *Sherman*, pp. 229–31; Ballard, *Pemberton*, pp. 175–80.

49. Conger, *Rise of U. S. Grant*, p. 291; J. F. C. Fuller, *The Generalship of Ulysses S. Grant* (New York: Da Capo, 1929, 1952, 1991), p. 188.

50. Catton, *Grant Moves South*, pp. 476, 479.

51. For the Napoleonic analogy, see Hattaway and Jones, *How the North Won*, p. 145.

52. Reed, *Combined Operations in the Civil War*, pp. 255–56.

Chapter Ten

BREAKING THE DEADLOCK
IN TENNESSEE

JUNE TO DECEMBER 1863

I f there was another federal general in the Civil War who promoted the same cries of exasperation from Northern politicians as McClellan, it was William S. Rosecrans. Grant had complained during March and April 1863 of Rosecrans's failure to attack and draw off Confederate strength from Mississippi. In June Rosecrans and the Army of the Cumberland, by then prepared to its commander's satisfaction, set off from Murfreesboro toward the rail junction of Tullahoma. He sought to turn the Confederate right, get around behind Braxton Bragg's entrenchments, and strike at his communications. Once he had attained control of the railroads, Rosecrans thought that he could bring Bragg to battle at a great disadvantage.

A deluge of rain halted the Union advance but Bragg was not prepared to fight for his communications and retired to Bridgeport and from thence back to Chattanooga, a vital rail junction in east Tennessee. Moving via Bragg's right, Rosecrans advanced on Manchester and then toward Chattanooga from the northwest. The whole of middle Tennessee was occupied at the cost of 560 Union casualties and the Confederate hold on Tennessee dangerously weakened by two

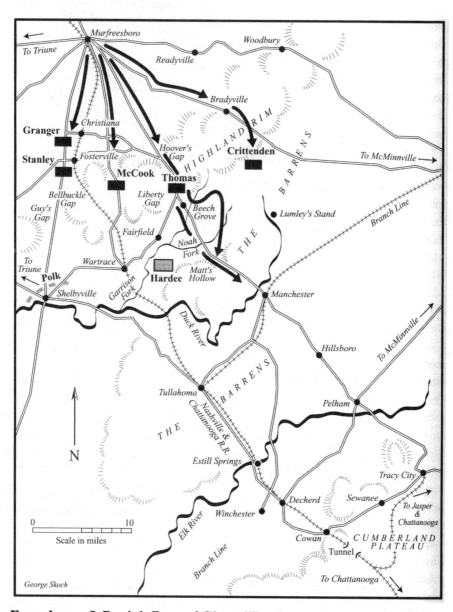

From Larry J. Daniel, *Days of Glory: The Army of the Cumberland, 1861–1865* (Baton Rouge: Louisiana State University, 2004). Map © George Skoch. Reprinted by permission of the illustrator.

impressive outflanking movements, for which Rosecrans got little credit. Rosecrans observed cynically that his success was overlooked "because it is not written
in letters of blood." But the battle for control of Tennessee was just moving
toward its climactic phase and letters of blood would be daubed before its end.[1]

The outcome of the campaign in Tennessee was influenced decisively by
events in Virginia. Here the conclusion of the Gettysburg campaign had
brought another period of inactivity. Meade, unlike McClellan in October 1862,
had adopted a deep counterthrust through Maryland, forcing Lee out of the
Shenandoah Valley and into his lines along the Rappahannock near Culpeper
Court House. All passion for a federal offensive action was now spent.[2] Anxious
about the deterioration of affairs in Tennessee, President Davis summoned General Robert E. Lee to Richmond to discuss the strategic predicament. Having
refused to accept Lee's resignation after Gettysburg, Davis offered Lee Johnston's
command in the west. Lee preferred to stay with the army he had built up. But
Davis was running out of troops and asked for units from the Army of Northern
Virginia to be sent to Tennessee. Lee had always opposed allowing his army to
be frittered away as a source of piecemeal reinforcements; the dispersal and
fielding of weak, underequipped columns were the besetting sin of Confederate
military organization. Given circumstances in the east on this occasion, however, he agreed that Longstreet's First Corps should be sent west.

Using a reinforced Army of Tennessee to strike a blow against Rosecrans's
Army of the Cumberland seemed to be the only avenue available to retrieve the
South's fortunes. Rosecrans had failed to mount a vigorous pursuit after
Murfreesboro, despite his best intentions to the contrary, and Bragg had successfully disengaged without incurring further damage to his army. The Army
of Tennessee had 31,924 infantry available for duty and a cavalry force of 15,625
troopers. The cavalry had been augmented by General Earl Van Dorn, who had
left Mississippi and was sorely missed by Pemberton. Bragg could still field the
core of a powerful army, and reinforced by Longstreet's Corps, could match
Rosecrans in numbers. For although Rosecrans enjoyed an aggregate strength of
98,073 men, his field strength was 80,124 and this was further diminished by
the numerous garrisons he had to provide. The present-for-duty strength of the
Army of the Cumberland in the field was 75,752. Rosecrans's field army was
thus strong, but it did not enjoy overwhelming superiority. Premature news of
Longstreet's arrival in Tennessee in exaggerated strength was already causing
alarm and despondency in Rosecrans's department, even though the movement
of more than twenty thousand men put the Confederacy's ramshackle railway
system under grave strain.[3]

Even with Longstreet gone Lee could not be encouraged to stand idle and he yearned to go on the offensive again. But his continued desire to strike at the Army of the Potomac was only practicable if that force showed enterprise, and little of significance occurred in the eastern theater once the Confederacy had decided to send reinforcements to Tennessee. Under Meade, however, it acted very cautiously. Meade had seen many times how Lee had ruthlessly exploited errors. As Meade grew in confidence and experience he determined not to make any mistakes. Such a negative policy, similar to McClellan's approach, could not serve as a means of winning the war. For all his gifts, Meade lacked the inspiration and the force of personality to impose himself as "the coming man." This was revealed later in the Mine Run campaign of November 1863, launched once Meade was sure that Longstreet had been sent west. Meade advanced gingerly into the wilderness. Lee discovered that the Union left flank was exposed to another riposte and as he moved to strike, in the nick of time Meade discovered his error and withdrew. Unlike Hooker, he avoided defeat but lacked the flair to spring a trap on Lee.[4]

Thus in the autumn of 1863 the Confederacy's main strategic effort was focused where Beauregard and his acolytes had long argued it belonged—in Tennessee. The problem was that Bragg, unlike Meade, wanted to spring traps on his enemies but he failed to close them and secure victories. His two previous forays had shown imagination, but on the battlefield he fumbled. Despite the numbers of cavalry available, and its quality, Bragg's setbacks can in part be explained by the comparative weakness of Confederate cavalry in the west. The individual cavalry commanders, especially Morgan, Wheeler, and Forrest, were first rate (Van Dorn had more flamboyance than skill). Yet these individual talents were not harnessed to a centralized command system and failed to act as the "eyes" or talons of the Army of Tennessee, as Stuart demonstrated so effectively in Virginia. Cooperation from subordinates was, in any case, difficult with a commander as cantankerous as Bragg. The campaign of autumn 1863 would continue to highlight this intelligence-gathering deficiency. Bragg's acquiescence in John Hunt Morgan's overly ambitious "Great Raid" through Kentucky, Indiana, and Ohio, which resulted in the destruction and surrender of a large cavalry division of two brigades (2,500 men), is symptomatic of the casualness with which he erred, allowing his strength in cavalry to ebb away.[5]

Bragg was also plagued by desertion. The Confederate defeats in the summer of 1863 were a watershed not just in the South's strategic fortunes: the morale of her armies suffered severely. The Gettysburg and Vicksburg campaigns demonstrated that the war would not be ended soon. The Lincoln administration encouraged Confederate desertion by offering amnesties; although some deserters returned to their own homes, others much preferred to enter Union lines.[6]

The autumn campaign in Tennessee, which was to be disfigured by the most acrimonious disputes between Braxton Bragg and his subordinates, had been preceded by an unedifying, petty dispute between Jefferson Davis and Joseph E. Johnston over areas of responsibility during the late campaign in Mississippi. Whenever he was under pressure, Davis invariably sought refuge in the intricate interpretation of regulations that appealed to his legalistic frame of mind. Johnston was no less tenacious in the defense of any matter that seemed to impugn, however remotely, his precious reputation. The result was a bitter, detailed, and time-wasting correspondence—as if the parlous state of Confederate fortunes did not demand that both men expend their energies on more urgent and weighty matters. Through the offices of Johnston's ally and Davis's enemy, Senator Louis T. Wigfall, this dispute found its way into the newspapers. The Richmond *Examiner* led the assault on the Davis administration.

Throughout, this small-minded affair reveals Davis's indecisiveness. Davis did not relieve Johnston; nor did he issue abrupt, unbrookable commands as a response to Johnston's bleating over the load of responsibility that the president was asking him to unfairly carry. Davis insisted on a policy of "noninterference" in the business of field commanders, while simultaneously hampering almost all these commanders (except Lee) with restrictions because he did not trust them to use their initiative. Davis's halting methods were to reappear with disastrous results in October 1863.[7]

General Rosecrans, for his part, was irritated that his successful Tullahoma campaign had not received the attention and praise that he thought it deserved from the authorities in Washington. Rosecrans displayed just as baffling a mixture of impressive ability, bumbling hesitancy, and petty littleness as his opponent, Bragg. High handed and unable to appreciate the difficulties of other commanders, Rosecrans had refused to launch an attack to aid Grant during the Vicksburg campaign on the spurious grounds that two battles should not be risked simultaneously. Moreover he elevated sophistry into an elaborate art form. He was flippant, moody, fussy, and prone to boast when things went well or blame subordinates when they did not. Unlike Grant, Rosecrans failed to cultivate amicable relations with the US Navy and the sailors were not prepared to help him improve his lines of supply, over which he lavished a justified but probably exaggerated care. Rosecrans's greatest weakness as a commander was his disingenuousness; he did not inspire trust.[8]

After the Union disaster at the battle of Chickamauga, Rosecrans's chief of staff, James A. Garfield, was inclined to blame the radical Republicans for his chief's downfall. The radicals thought briefly that they had found a suitable candidate to run against Lincoln in the 1864 presidential election. "If the President hunters had left him alone," commented Garfield later, "he might have been at the head of our armies today but in the fatal summer of 1863 he was enveloped in clouds of incense—and visions of the Presidency were constantly thrust upon him." To his credit, Rosecrans spurned these approaches. If he showed a lack of balance under pressure, it had more to do with military rather than political factors. Rosecrans certainly did not lack political gifts: he was a good talker and an opaque writer, with a considerable talent for ambiguity. Yet the latter attribute proved fatal militarily because Rosecrans failed to communicate his intentions effectively. Kenneth P. Williams calls him a "master of deceptive and ambiguous sentences"; subordinates out of his hearing tended to misunderstand his orders and the result was near catastrophe on the field of Chickamauga.[9]

Rosecrans, however, was overly confident. Although Bragg had been all but driven out of Tennessee by the Tullahoma campaign, little injury had actually been inflicted on his army. Bragg's troops had been thrown back on their supply lines while Rosecrans's were stretched to breaking point. Strategic maneuver, as Sherman discovered, can only be carried out with impunity if the enemy vacates the theater of operations or his forces are destroyed. Neither of these conditions prevailed for all of the skillful outflanking marches carried out by Rosecrans before Tullahoma. Bragg's reorganization of his forces after Murfreesboro had created, by Confederate standards, a well-disciplined and supplied fighting force. Retreating into north Georgia on September 6, the Army of Tennessee was poised to launch a counterstroke.[10]

Rosecrans had advanced on a wide, dispersed front of about twenty-five miles. This scattered distribution had been forced on him in part by logistics. After arriving in Chattanooga, Rosecrans needed to improve the railroads so that his base could be advanced from Murfreesboro. The Union advance ground to a halt. Mobility was also reduced by the besetting Union sin of transporting excessive baggage, especially among officers. This did not prevent Rosecrans from reporting untruthfully, "We never think of moving with any but the minimum baggage." But geography had also imposed itself on Rosecrans's designs. Once the advance was renewed in September, Major General Alexander McCook's Twentieth Corps crossed the Tennessee River at Bridgeport and advanced south toward a gap in Lookout Mountain about forty miles southwest of Chattanooga. Major General George H. Thomas's Fourteenth Corps advanced

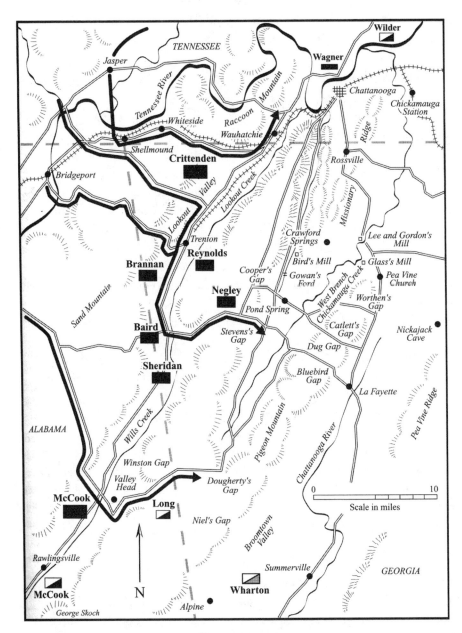

From Larry J. Daniel, *Days of Glory: The Army of the Cumberland,
1861–1865* (Baton Rouge: Louisiana State University, 2004). Map ©
George Skoch. Reprinted by permission of the illustrator.

southeasterly, twenty miles to the north through Stevens gap. Major General Thomas L. Crittenden and his Twenty-first Corps crossed the Tennessee River from the north and occupied Chattanooga. Crittenden was then ordered to advance eastward toward Ringgold on the Chattanooga-Atlanta Railroad. Rosecrans's frontage extended along some thirty-five miles.[11]

The picturesque setting of this campaign, with long sinuous columns of toiling troops marching up winding roads surrounded by splendid scenery, should not conceal the hardships the troops faced. It rained incessantly and the soldiers could not cook their rations; the roads were muddy, slowing movement to a crawl. Halleck was fearful that if Rosecrans halted, Bragg would be reinforced by Johnston. It came as a relief to Halleck when on September 9 Major General Ambrose E. Burnside and his Ninth Corps began its advance toward Knoxville; this distracted Bragg and offered to Rosecrans's scattered columns a measure of security (especially after the surrender of Confederate forces covering Cumberland Gap). For at least a day after the fall of Chattanooga on September 9, Rosecrans still believed he was pursuing a broken enemy. He cherished a design to attempt an envelopment on a grand scale, get into Bragg's rear, and destroy his army. McCook was ordered to press on to Alpine and Summerville in Georgia and intercept Bragg's long columns. Rosecrans persisted in believing that even an unsupported corps, like McCook's, could wreak havoc in Bragg's rear. Garfield estimated that Bragg was only a two days' march in front of Twentieth Corps.[12]

Garfield was right but for all the wrong reasons. Bragg had concentrated the Army of Tennessee at Rome, Georgia, near Chickamauga Creek. He intended to strike individual corps with overwhelming strength one by one. The first target was Thomas's Fourteenth Corps at McLemore's Cove on September 10. A council of war convened by Bragg's subordinates decided to ignore his orders to outflank Thomas's exposed lead division. But this staggering blunder was made worse by Bragg's own lack of decision and fumbling the following day; he seemed perplexed by the mental effort required to combine enveloping forces on the battlefield itself. Though the main culprit was Thomas C. Hindman, the divisional commander—a strutting *poseur*, but one who did not lack ability—who should have struck Thomas's flank as D. H. Hill's corps attacked in front, Bragg's own incapacity rendered his strictures against his subordinates seem like bluster designed to shift the blame. The Confederates repeated this ridiculous exercise in fumbling, military amateurism on September 12. Bragg planned to strike Crittenden's Twenty-first Corps in the north with Polk's corps, destroying him in detail. Always recalcitrant, Polk refused to attack that morning without stronger forces in case the enemy attacked him. Once again a council of war intervened and decided to do nothing. The harmony and trust vital to mounting complex offensive operations was singularly lacking in the Army of Tennessee. Bragg's own indecision hardly helped him overcome the lethargy of his subordinates. "The truth is," General Hill averred dryly, "General Bragg was bewildered by 'the popping out of the rats from so many holes.'"[13]

Thanks to this comedy of errors, rather than his own exertions, Rosecrans had gained a lucky escape. By September 11 he began to divine the danger facing the Army of the Cumberland. He issued orders for the concentration of his forces southeast of Chattanooga. He had ten days' supply of food and forage in hand, and his immediate priority was launching an attack on Bragg. During the concentration Thomas was empowered to order McCook to come to his aid should he be attacked. This move injected a measure of confusion as McCook had two commanders. Rosecrans was warned by Halleck that Longstreet had been sent west with three divisions (in fact only two were dispatched). Although Rosecrans had blithely disregarded Grant's predicament during the Vicksburg campaign, he immediately demanded that he be reinforced from the Army of the Tennessee. Burnside was also castigated for advancing eastward, even though he had been assured on September 10 by Crittenden that Bragg was on the verge of defeat. For once Burnside was in the right and his accusers in the wrong. Rosecrans was always ready to blame everyone but himself for any setbacks.[14]

The Union decision to concentrate in northern Georgia, southeast of Chattanooga, made the forcing of a general engagement near Chickamauga Creek unavoidable. On the evening of September 18 Rosecrans dithered over whether to attack and then thought better of it, shifting Thomas's Fourteenth Corps to the left flank. Crittenden's Twenty-first Corps occupied the center and McCook's Twentieth Corps guarded the right flank. Rosecrans fielded just under fifty-four thousand men. The first day of the battle of Chickamauga resembled Bragg's two earlier great battles, Perryville and Murfreesboro. He launched the opening attack audaciously and then hesitated timorously, confused as to what to do next. Bragg intended to seize the bridges over Chickamauga Creek at Lee and Gordon's Mill, Reed Bridge, Alexander's Bridge, and take Thedford's Ford, then attack with his right in the hope of driving Rosecrans back into McLemore's Cove where he could be entrapped and destroyed. He would then cut the road back to Chattanooga and round up the remnants of the Army of the Cumberland. But Bragg's hopes of gaining this objective were reduced when Thomas extended his defenses to the left, protecting the vital road link to Chattanooga, the LaFayette Road. The Union forces thus outflanked the Confederates and could bring enfilading fire to bear on the attackers. Bragg was unaware of this adverse development, mainly due to faulty deployment of cavalry, but also because the tangled terrain impeded visibility. Striking a concentrated blow at the Union forces became an even more difficult task because they kept changing position, and did so at the same time that the Confederates changed position, too.[15]

Bragg's initial attack on September 19 was as mismanaged and as poorly coordinated as at Murfreesboro. It featured similar clumsy, heavy linear formations in frontal assaults. Taken aback by the strength of the federal position, Bragg succumbed to gloom. Amidst the chaos and lack of higher direction, a dangerous gap opened between Cheatham's division and Hood's division in the center, which formed the advance guard of Longstreet's Corps. If Rosecrans had shown more enterprise, and this cavity had been exploited, then Bragg could have been driven back; but tactically, Rosecrans preferred standing on the defensive. It was a measure of Bragg's depression that his bête noir, Polk, previously in command of the left, was now ordered to take command of the right where things were going wrong. Cheburne's division was also moved from the left and eventually drove Thomas's troops back. This success, however, was counterbalanced by the Union advance of Brigadier General James S. Negley's division on the right, which advanced half a mile. Despite the confusion, the Confederates remained in possession of the ground. But the deadlock remained unbroken.

The overnight pause that ensued ushered in the decisive phase of the battle. Although Bragg's haste in attacking Rosecrans is understandable, in retrospect the decision was mistaken. Bragg still wanted to make the most of his rapid concentration while the Union commander was in a state of mental disarray having just escaped narrowly from utter defeat. This haste was the crucial error that ultimately cost Bragg the campaign and the Confederacy its last opportunity to regain the initiative in the war in the west. By attacking prematurely, Bragg frittered away his strength for no commensurate benefit. When the decisive moment came he had no reserve to complete Rosecrans's destruction. On the evening of September 19, James Longstreet himself arrived with most of the remainder of his infantry (though not his artillery and other stores). He was seriously discommoded by the failure of any of Bragg's staff to meet him. The arrival of yet another general with a high opinion of himself, and his troops who continually reminded their hosts how things were done in the Army of Northern Virginia, was hardly conducive to a restoration of harmony and affability in Bragg's command.[16]

Bragg treated Longstreet gruffly, as he did everyone else, but told him that he had decided to reorganize the army into two wings. The timing of this rearrangement was unfortunate. It would have been better had this change been made before the battle had started. Longstreet was to be given command of the left wing of the army while Polk retained command of the right. Longstreet commanded Buckner's corps of two divisions and the two divisions of Hindman and Bushrod R. Johnson, plus most of Hood's division from his own corps. This kind of ad hoc organizational arrangement was typical of Bragg's Army of Tennessee. Longstreet was then given a map to orientate himself and virtually told to get on with it. He did not know the ground and had to wait until daylight before he could see it; then he was perplexed to discover that it consisted of "a heavy woodland, not adapted to the practice of artillery." He could not find Buckner's chief of artillery and rations had gone missing. Under these circumstances his imaginative solution to the tactical problem he encountered was little short of miraculous.[17]

Longstreet was not impressed either by the professionalism or the cohesion of the Army of Tennessee. He could not locate the inner flank of Polk's wing, "but when arranged for battle," he recalled, "it was about half a mile in rear of the line upon which the left wing was established." The arrival of Longstreet had led to the effective demotion of D. H. Hill, his equal in rank, a corps commander who now found himself under the overall command of Polk. Hill resented this, rightly believing that Polk was his inferior as a tactician as well as being lazy and contrary. Thus was added a further personal tension to a command structure already seething with resentment and incipient hatred. Within hours Polk and Hill were quarreling because of the latter's failure to appear at a meeting arranged at the former's headquarters. The root of the difficulty was Bragg's abdication of command. Had he spent less time niggling and finding fault in the arrangement of trivial matters and more time impressing himself as a commanding general, giving dynamic and clear directions to his four corps commanders directly, and seeing that they were carried out, then these tensions could have been overcome. As it was, by introducing a wholly superfluous layer of command—the two "wings"—Bragg only ensured that he inflamed the exposed and tender sensibilities of the corps commanders subordinated to it. The only matter on which Hill and Polk agreed was that they would not obey Bragg's orders.[18]

On the evening of September 19 General Rosecrans convened a council of war. It is testimony to the lack of confidence of generals on both sides, and their lack of training and experience for senior command responsibilities, and their excessive awareness of the numerous errors that had been made by their predecessors, that commanders convened these councils so frequently in 1863. Their interventions were never happy; their repercussions, as General Meade was shortly to discover, rarely redounded to the benefit of the reputation of the commander who called them. Rosecrans asked his corps commanders where they expected Bragg to renew his attack. General George H. Thomas was so exhausted by his exertions that he kept dozing off. In his rare lucid intervals, Thomas muttered, "I would strengthen the left." Rosecrans then implored the sleeping Thomas, "Where are we going to take it from?" There was only one answer to this question that Rosecrans need not have asked anybody: troops would have to come from the right. Garfield issued written orders stipulating that McCook's Twentieth Corps would close to the left to guard the Widow Glenn's house that shielded the Dry Valley Road to Rossville and thence to Chattanooga. Crittenden was ordered to pull back two divisions to guard the inner flank of the Twentieth and Fourteenth Corps. This deployment was simultaneously the source of the misunderstanding that led to defeat and the means by which the Army of the Cumberland was saved.[19]

Bragg had intended to renew the battle on September 20. Thanks to Longstreet's arrival, for the first time as a field commander he enjoyed a numerical superiority over the enemy, fielding 66,326 men, but the margin of superiority was not great. Polk was to attack Thomas's Fourteenth Corps, shielded by Forrest's cavalry on the right, and fix him to his position. Longstreet expected to pivot on Polk's wing and strike Rosecrans's right flank just as he was denuding it of troops to succor his hard-pressed left. Next, Longstreet wanted to gain the Dry Valley Road and move on the gaps through Missionary Ridge. Rosecrans would then, Bragg at last hoped, at the third attempt be driven in hopeless chaos into McLemore's Cove where he would be forced to capitulate or be annihilated. There are two striking features about this plan. The first is that Longstreet found no cause to complain about the untrammeled offensive he was being asked to carry out over unfavorable terrain; his previous whining about defensive tactics in pursuit of an offensive strategy was conspicuous in its absence. Second, it placed a heavy burden of responsibility on the ample Episcopal shoulders of General Polk. By allowing Polk a major part in the attack, Bragg took a huge gamble that past experience indicated was unjustified.[20]

By 8 AM Bragg was riding along the Confederate line waiting once more in his bad-tempered way to hear the sound of Polk's cannon open the battle. Once more he was to be disappointed by silence. Polk, in his typically indolent fashion, had delayed issuing orders for the renewal of the assault and then once he had found the time to attend to his prime responsibility, did not bother to check to ensure that his orders were carried out. Bragg, incensed by the delay, sent a staff officer to the right to find out what was happening. Polk was discovered sitting on the porch of a farmhouse sheltering from the sun, resting complacently reading the newspaper; the smell of his substantial breakfast wafted from the nearby kitchen. Polk, on being asked why his troops were not firing, replied simply but truthfully that he did not know. When the staff officer reported back to General Bragg, the commanding general let out "a terrible exclamation." Bragg at once rode over to Polk's headquarters. Polk thought it best to vacate the premises before his expected arrival and sought out Hill in order to launch the attack. But he left a message for Bragg telling him, it intoned, "that my heart is overflowing with anxiety for the attack. Overflowing with anxiety, sir." If command of florid speech could make a fine tactician, General Polk would have been among the South's best generals.[21]

Polk could not find Hill and issued orders to his divisional commanders directly. When he discovered this action, Hill was furious. In the meantime Bragg found Hill and ordered the assault. No preparations had been made, and these would take time. Hill also insisted that the attack be delayed until the men had consumed their breakfasts. The specter of breakfast again rose to haunt Bragg's ambitious schemes and frustrate them. In the event, the right wing did not mount its attack until 10 AM. Four hours had been wasted. The attack was also typical of the kind of offensive launched by Southern armies, especially in the west. It was poorly organized and uncoordinated. Polk threw his troops at the Union entrenchments—which largely consisted of breastworks formed by logs and railway timbers—in a single line lacking any kind of reserve. The assaults were smashed in detail and thrown back with unnecessarily heavy casualties.[22]

Bragg had planned that the attacks by the two wings of his army should be made in a synchronized sequence, one following immediately after the other in a concentrated, concerted blow striking Rosecrans's defenses. Considering his difficulties it is not surprising that Longstreet was still not ready by 10 AM, even after the troops on the right wing had eaten their breakfasts. Longstreet seems to have learned the real lesson of Gettysburg: his two assaults on that field had been insufficiently concentrated. Longstreet sought to avoid dispersal by adopting a deep column focused on a narrow front with eight brigades. Longstreet managed to avoid overcrowding while not presenting too fat a target; the latter consideration was important. Although the woods would shield the attackers, they could also break up their cohesion and Rosecrans's position favored his infantry because it had a clear field of fire once the Confederate artillery emerged from the woods, while the weaker Confederate artillery (minus Longstreet's own guns) were correspondingly hampered. Longstreet aimed to maximize his hitting power with a numerically strong and deep assault formation.[23]

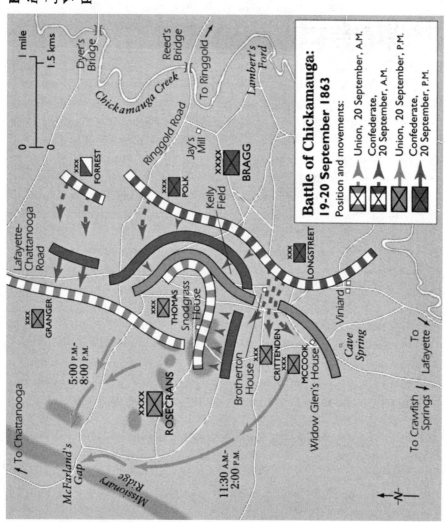

From *An Atlas of American Military History* by James C. Bradford (New York: Cynthia Parzych Publishing, 2003).

Longstreet's assault at Chickamauga has been likened to a "giant lance." It was the first time in the Civil War that a Southern general combined velocity in the attack with concentration. The power of Longstreet's tactics of penetration (the turning movement that he thought so essential to success in war had been forgotten, perhaps because its efficacy he later exaggerated for other reasons) received an unexpected supplement thanks to an error on the Union side. After Polk's attack had gone in, Rosecrans inspected all of the line, and ordered McCook to send Thomas reinforcements. McCook then found himself the subject of Rosecrans's displeasure when the latter discovered that McCook's corps had not realigned to offer increased protection to the Widow Glenn's house and the Dry Valley Road. Rosecrans then took up position on this flank to ensure that his orders were carried out.[24]

A fatal failure in communication then intervened like the goddess Nemesis to curse Rosecrans's hopes of a resolute defense. A report arrived that the division of Brigadier General John M. Brannan had moved out of line. This report was erroneous though Brannan had sought additional cover in the woods behind McCook's main position. In an act of carelessness rather typical of Chickamauga, Rosecrans acted hurriedly without thinking or checking. He issued orders to the division on Brannan's right, that of Brigadier General Thomas J. Wood, to immediately close up to the right flank of the next division in line, that of Brigadier General Joseph J. Reynolds. Wood was understandably perplexed by these contradictory orders, as there was no space available to occupy and his division was already aligned with Brannan's. He deduced that the only way he could carry out Rosecrans's peremptory order and "close up on Reynolds" was moving behind Brannan. Some of his subordinates questioned the wisdom of the order but Wood did not want to provoke the anger that had been directed toward his corps commander. This maldeployment was made doubly worse because the reinforcements being dispatched to Thomas were from Brigadier General Philip H. Sheridan's division protecting Rosecrans's right flank. By his vague, ill-thought order that bypassed the corps commander responsible for this sector, Rosecrans had placed his entire right flank in jeopardy.[25]

The goddess Fortune then intervened on the Confederate side. If Longstreet had attacked in sequence with Polk he would have faced a cohesive Union defense. It is not clear from his memoir, *From Manassas to Appomattox*, even whether he was aware that Rosecrans had so conveniently created a gap in his defenses just at the moment Longstreet was about to strike. At about 11 AM, that is, an hour after Polk had attacked, the order to advance was given and Hood's division moved forward. Longstreet remembered that they "came under the fire of this formidable array of artillery and infantry, and found his [Hood's] lines staggering under their galling missiles, and fast losing strength as the fire thickened." The advance was certainly not an easy one—testimony to Rosecrans's skill as a defensive commander despite his blunder. Confederate infantry moved into the woods east of LaFayette Road and Longstreet ordered up his reserve, Hindman's division, and threw this into the attack. Under such pressure Rosecrans's weakened right collapsed and Union fugitives streamed away north in a state of panic.[26]

Longstreet was almost embarrassed by the extent of his success. The plan had required that he move southward toward the Dry Valley Road, the cutting of which would block Rosecrans's retreat to Chattanooga. Yet as at Second Manassas, the securing of such objectives while maintaining an operational envelopment aimed at the destruction of the entire Union army was subordinated to chasing the enemy troops immediately in front of the attackers away from the battlefield—the two are not synonymous. Under these circumstances, the breakthrough battle degenerates into a series of uncoordinated tactical actions that tend, over time, to favor the defender because offensive momentum is lost. Longstreet gave permission for his troops to continue their advance northward. To make matters worse, Hood was wounded again and, without his driving presence, cohesion in the attack was frittered away.[27]

Rosecrans seems to have lost his head during the *déroute* of his right flank and fled with his troops back to Chattanooga. McCook and Crittenden accompanied him in breathless haste. Confederate attempts to cut the road were feeble. Instead Confederate units crowded toward centers of Union resistance rather than masking them and then moving on. Any kind of disciplined, controlled movement in the pursuit was beyond Confederate armies even at this stage of the Civil War. General George Thomas managed to keep his head while all others around him (including his commander) lost theirs. He calmly withdrew Fourteenth Corps back across the LaFayette Road and occupied a piece of high ground between Snodgrass Hill and Horseshoe Ridge. Thomas brought down powerful fire on the disorganized Confederate attackers and forced a lull in the battle wherein he could strengthen his defenses and provide a rallying point for Union stragglers. The battle was not resumed until after 3 PM. By his skillful defensive action and imperturbable presence Thomas saved Rosecrans's disintegrating army; the fissiparous process was stopped by one man who had the confidence to command. The personal factor made itself felt just as the federal units were beginning to recover and a defensive line began to congeal.[28]

No viable pursuit was organized. Why was this so when a powerful assault had driven the defenders from the field and they fled in the open, at the mercy of the attackers? The answer is simple: an effective pursuit demands thought and planning, and this had not been forthcoming. Devastating pursuits are rarely improvised, especially with tired, battle-spent troops. They also demand a measure of discipline and operational understanding among commanders that was not to be found in the Army of Tennessee. It is striking that no senior officer suggested masking Thomas's Fourteenth Corps while striking at the remnants of Twentieth and Twenty-first Corps and cutting the vital roads. Even Longstreet missed the significance of the half-mile gap between Horseshoe Ridge and Kelly Field, through which Confederate forces could have passed in pursuit of Rosecrans, leaving Thomas bypassed and isolated. This lapse is all the more surprising in Longstreet because he was an experienced commander who had witnessed several failed pursuits in previous campaigns. Yet he did not give his full attention to this tactical problem. The "set-piece" attack and the counterstroke were Longstreet's forte, not the pursuit.[29]

In short, given the delays, the failure to seize operational opportunities while concentrating on unimportant tactical targets, and the worsening supply situation, Bragg who (as usual) was "pale and careworn" after a battle, was right in postponing the pursuit. An effective pursuit could not, in any case, be attempted. The fruitless, wasteful attacks launched on September 19 and repeated again the following day by Polk had eroded Bragg's strength. He simply lacked the fresh and powerful reserve necessary to consummate his victory. The cost of Chickamauga, the most signal Confederate success won in the war in the west, was indeed prodigious. Although Bragg took eight thousand prisoners and seized fifty-one cannon, his own casualties were great: 16,986 total casualties (of which 2,312 were killed and 14,674 wounded). Twenty-five out of Bragg's total of thirty-three brigades suffered an average of 33 percent casualties (individual formations registered up to 40 percent losses). Bragg lost 25 percent of his total force engaged. Rosecrans sustained 11,413 casualties, 19 percent of the Army of the Cumberland (though this last figure excludes the prisoners taken—if these are included then Union losses standing on the defensive are comparable with Confederate casualties).

Yet it cannot be emphasized too strongly that the high Confederate casualty bill had more to do with the way attacks were carried out, rather than any weakness inherent in the offense. What counts is battle management. Success in battle—which includes the pursuit—can be measured by a general's skill in organizing and judiciously expending the forces under his command. Battle management was hardly one of Bragg's gifts and he neglected it. And consequently even his greatest tactical successes, such as Chickamauga, did not garner their full operational fruits.[30]

Thus Thomas, who had been reinforced by Major General Gordon Granger on September 20, was allowed to execute a well-organized delaying action and eventual disengagement that permitted him to withdraw back to Chattanooga with the Fourteenth Corps. His movement began at 6 PM on the evening of September 21 and Thomas arrived in the town the following morning. He then dug in, judging his position "strong enough for all defensive purposes." Bragg, for his part, thought in terms of entrenching. He was anxious about a shortage of wagons for moving supplies, and Longstreet's two divisions had added significantly to the number of mouths to be fed. Bragg ruled out the possibility of moving past Rosecrans's flank and into the Tennessee hinterland. He occupied the high ground around Chattanooga and commenced a siege. Confederate troops moved up the wooded slopes of Missionary Ridge to the east of the town, into the valley dividing Missionary Ridge and Lookout Mountain, and occupied the summit of the mountain, covering the ground down to the Tennessee River. This was the crucial sector because Rosecrans could only draw supplies over the railway running to the west via Bridgeport. The wagon route over Walden's ridge to the north was out of range of Confederate fire but too difficult to carry the quantity of provisions that resisting a siege demanded. Soon Rosecrans's force was on the verge of starvation. He was having major difficulties finding fodder for his horseflesh and the many thousands of mules that he had collected for mountain operations. The Army of the Cumberland appeared trapped and Rosecrans befuddled and powerless to extricate it.[31]

How Bragg was to sustain a siege logistically should the Union forces continue to hold out was not a question that agitated many minds. For at the very moment when all thoughts should have been directed toward bringing the campaign to a victorious conclusion, attention was diverted from the decisive point. The personal disaffection that had so disrupted the efficiency of the Army of Tennessee and reduced its recent operations to the level of an amateurish, comic farce, now reached a pitch of astonishing pettiness. The arrival of Longstreet in the west, truly a stormy petrel flying over treacherous and unpredictable waters, was the catalyst for a renewed outburst of quarreling. Bragg hastened on September 22 to move against Polk and demanded an explanation for his slowness on the second day of Chickamauga. Polk stalled and met with Longstreet and Hill and they agreed that Bragg should be removed from command. Longstreet became the leader of the anti-Bragg faction because of his military reputation, and also because he coveted Bragg's command. He wrote to James A. Seddon, the Confederate secretary of war, requesting that he urge the president to remove Bragg; Polk wrote directly to his old friend more explicitly.[32]

In the meantime after Polk had replied to Bragg's curt inquiries and put the blame on Hill, he was dismissed and took himself off to Atlanta. Polk demanded a court of inquiry and all the victims of Bragg's wrath determined on further insubordination. All of his twelve senior generals signed a petition to the president, actually drafted by Buckner, demanding Bragg's removal. This explosion of disaffection and rancor against Bragg, who doubtless returned it in full measure, is difficult to explain rationally. It is in part an unhappy conjunction of incompatible personalities and frustrated ambition. Yet this touchy rather histrionic anxiety over precedence, place, and personal reputation is characteristic of all Southern armies. Senior commanders in the Confederacy were excessively prickly about matters touching upon their "honor," and this resulted in confrontations of consuming pettiness. They brought the Army of Tennessee to the brink of disintegration and their machinations soon affected the morale of the fighting troops. Their disputes were also a reflection of the paucity of command talent in the Confederacy, or at any rate, talented generals who could work effectively with Davis. Such convulsions demonstrate some of the worst aspects of the Southern code of "honor" that were manifest before 1861.[33]

President Davis himself then stepped into the controversy. Taking a remarkable trip away from Richmond on October 9, 1863, he arrived at Bragg's headquarters in an attempt to sort out the matter once and for all, having talked to Polk en route. Both of Davis's friends, Bragg and Polk, expected him to take their side in the feud. Davis also spoke to Longstreet and John C. Breckinridge privately about the affair; the former was scathing about his commander, the latter more balanced. Davis then convened a meeting of the corps commanders and after a desultory discussion on the future of the Tennessee campaign, Davis invited them to express their views. First Longstreet and then Hill called for a change of commander. Davis had no intention of sacking Bragg; he had made this clear to Seddon before leaving Richmond. Bragg was probably told this by Davis on his arrival at headquarters. By organizing this meeting, Davis was probably trying to be too clever. He believed wrongly that criticism of Bragg had been exaggerated. Surely in such a meeting he surmised, even Bragg's critics in his presence would proffer loyalty for the good of the cause. Bragg would then be comforted by such sentiments and be more tolerant in the future. This miscalculation is an indication of how ignorant Davis was of the true state of affairs in the Army of Tennessee. He found the ill-tempered scene embarrassing, especially as Bragg was present, and brought the meeting to an end.

Although the initial design had miscarried, Davis nonetheless obstinately adhered to his plan. He pretended that he was still openminded but noticed that whenever Bragg was present the soldiers refused to cheer. Yet there were only three alternatives available to replace Bragg: Johnston, Beauregard, and Longstreet. The first two were anathema to the president, and Davis had disapproved of Longstreet's disloyalty during the whole unhappy affair. John C. Pemberton had also accompanied Davis on the trip, but the president was warned that if he attempted to give him any command in Tennessee the army would mutiny. He then issued his decision: Bragg would remain in command and Polk was reinstated and given command of his own department in the comparatively becalmed Mississippi; but Bragg succeeded in removing D. H. Hill, who became a scapegoat for the errors at Chickamauga. Davis always stood by his friends and he did so now. But he did not eradicate the sources of friction within the Army of Tennessee. This would have required either a purge of the senior commanders or the replacement of Bragg by a commander that Davis hated. Davis would not sample these two sour alternatives. Thus the disaffection remained. It resembled a dormant virus that would spread at a later date and have crippling effects on the campaign that had started so well for the Southerners.[34]

The real victors were the Union forces defending Chattanooga. They had been given three precious weeks to organize their defense and this time it had not been wasted.

The collapse of the Union position in northern Georgia found the Lincoln administration cool and decisive. The president believed that Chattanooga had to be held at all costs. Its capture had disrupted Confederate east-west rail communications and provided a bulwark against a further effort by Bragg to reoccupy Tennessee. Lincoln also grasped immediately that Chattanooga served as an advance base whereby Union forces could gather strength and then strike at Bragg's exposed columns at a time and place of their choosing. Rosecrans showed rather less decisiveness, save in his search for a scapegoat to blame for the disaster. (McCook was selected, although after a court of inquiry he was acquitted of all blame.) Rosecrans first of all indicated that it was doubtful whether he could hold Chattanooga; but on September 23 he wrote that he could. But Rosecrans did not inspire confidence for his actions certainly lacked resolution.[35]

The crisis at Chattanooga was Stanton's finest hour as secretary of war. On the night of September 23 he convened a conference to consider what action could be taken to redress the deteriorating situation. Those present included the president himself, Seward, the secretary of state, Chase, the treasury secretary, and General Halleck. Stanton announced that "I propose then to send 30,000 men from the Army of the Potomac," and he expected them to arrive within five days. Halleck was doubtful whether this could be achieved and Lincoln was not enthusiastic about weakening Meade. In a gloomy moment he predicted that it would take five days to get the troops to Washington. A compromise was reached whereby Rosecrans would be reinforced but by a smaller force.

The entire move was an excellent example of the manner by which a combination of the centralization of the telegraph and the railroad in the hands of an efficient war department made possible the direction and coordination of a complex military movement on a great scale over huge distances. At 2:30 AM the following morning Halleck wired Meade telling him that the Eleventh and Twelfth Corps should be ready to leave for Washington within twenty-four hours. Charles A. Dana, who had accompanied Rosecrans throughout the campaign, was telegraphed on September 24 informing him that fifteen thousand men were on their way. General Hooker was to command this force, and Stanton and his staff spent the following day poring over maps and railway timetables. Stanton then telegraphed all military commanders instructing them that for the duration of the movement the railway officials were in charge. Later that day an order was issued by which the government took control of all the railroads over which the troops would move. On September 25 at 5 PM the first trains began leaving Washington's Union Station. At 11 AM the following day the initial three trains with 2,000 men on board had reached Martinsburg. By September 27, 12,600 men were in transit via Indianapolis and Bridgeport. By October 3 over 20,000 men, ten batteries of artillery, plus their horses and ammunition, had arrived in Bridgeport; the remainder of their impedimenta were following on later trains. Hooker had been given firm orders permitting him to arrest anybody that obstructed the journey. It was, as Thomas and Hyman acknowledge, "the fastest mass movement of troops in history." Indeed it was a magnificent achievement, a model of the effective utilization of command, control, and communications. It was not the first time in history that the telegraph and railway had been used in this way, but it was a significant, evolutionary step forward in military technique.[36]

Rosecrans's position was unenviable but not fatal. His horses and mules were starving and his men were on half rations. Chattanooga was under constant bombardment. The sound of the bombardment was impressive, its execution less effective. "All the execution I ever heard of those guns doing," an Ohio captain remarked sardonically, "was to kill a mule that would have died of starvation later on." Bragg was too preoccupied with feuding with his subordinates to give his attention to any plan that might lead to the rapid fall of Chattanooga.

The longer he dallied the stronger the federals would become and the harder his task. Yet he believed the ground surrounding the town was so strong that he was virtually invulnerable to attack. He was quite wrong. For his part, Rosecrans seemed incapable of organizing his thoughts in order to effect a relief of his beleaguered forces. The future of the command of the Army of the Cumberland was one matter that Lincoln and Stanton had not as yet addressed. With confidence in Rosecrans evaporating each day, they hastened to settle it.[37]

Ulysses S. Grant had spent the late summer of 1863 preparing a plan to strike at the port of Mobile, Alabama. He then intended using it as a base to strike at Georgia. Grant's plan aroused little enthusiasm in Washington. Lincoln was too preoccupied with securing Tennessee to be attracted by such a scheme, though it certainly confirms the range and scale of Grant's strategic imagination. On October 17 Grant, then in Cairo, was ordered to Louisville to await orders. Stanton hurtled at great speed westward in a special train (which the engineers feared would leave the tracks on steep mountain bends). By coincidence, the two met for the first time en route at Indianapolis. A comic interlude then ensued. Stanton rushed up to Grant's chief of staff, Rawlins, instead of the general himself, shook him vigorously by the hand and said how like his photographs Grant was. Grant was not nettled by this minor if unfortunate error, but it does indicate how he was continually underrated because he did not "look like a general."[38]

Grant was handed two orders. Stanton told him that he should accept the one he found most agreeable. Both stipulated that on October 24 he should assume command of all military departments west of the Allegheny Mountains (except Banks's) in the newly created Military Division of the Mississippi. The second order also specified a change in the Department of West Tennessee, with Thomas promoted to replace Rosecrans. Grant accepted the latter order.

Rosecrans later charged that his removal from command was the result of one of Stanton's nefarious and elaborate plots. This seems rather exaggerated—though certainly Dana's reports of Rosecrans's psychological collapse appear overstated. Rosecrans's days were already numbered. Grant had little respect for Rosecrans's military ability and once lost in his eyes, it was rarely regained. The dramatic telegram received from Dana on the night of October 18, warning that Rosecrans intended to give up Chattanooga, only sped up the process of removal. Grant, with characteristic decisiveness, assumed command of the military division at once and telegraphed Thomas to take command immediately. Thomas replied equally characteristically, "We will hold the town till we starve." Grant wrote later, "I appreciated the force of this dispatch later when I witnessed the condition of affairs which prompted it"—a clear indication that Grant would have relieved Rosecrans as soon as he arrived in Chattanooga.[39]

Grant was anxious to take command and left for Chattanooga on October 20 still in great pain from a recent fall from his horse in New Orleans. He arrived in Nashville that afternoon and conferred with Andrew Johnson, Tennessee's war governor. He then pushed on to Chattanooga the following day. Grant had consulted with Rosecrans, who had left the day before, en route to Chattanooga. He recollected that Rosecrans "made some excellent suggestions as to what should be done. My only wonder was that he had not carried them out." Grant received a frosty reception, not from Rosecrans but from Thomas. This is not mentioned in Grant's *Personal Memoirs* but is detailed by other eyewitnesses. As much as Thomas would have welcomed reinforcements, he did not welcome the arrival of his commander. Thomas felt that his achievements on the field of Chickamauga had been sufficient for the relief operation to be entrusted to him, and that he did not need Grant's help. He must also have recognized that henceforth he would be overshadowed by the victors of Vicksburg. That night Grant telegraphed Halleck requesting that Sherman and the Army of the Tennessee be sent at once to Chattanooga.[40]

Thomas's pique was perhaps understandable. He was now subject to a measure of supervision that Rosecrans had not endured. Yet he seems to have ignored the political consequences of the defeat at Chickamauga that he had done so much to mitigate. The dire state of affairs at Chattanooga was now the source of political anxiety and Grant could not afford to ignore it. Grant fully understood and sympathized with Lincoln's desire to protect the Unionists in east Tennessee. His personal presence was vital, and Lincoln had been impressed by his drive and decisiveness. Thomas should have made much more of his predicament because Grant was initially well disposed toward him. However, his display of bad manners almost fatally undermined their relations and they never fully recovered from it. Grant from about 1863 onward never forgot a slight of this kind. Thomas was also very jealous of Grant's friendship with Sherman and showed it rather too openly.

Grant had also taken the opportunity before arriving in Chattanooga of impressing his new authority on General Hooker, who had had the temerity to invite his commander to come and visit him at his headquarters in Stevenson, Alabama (where he had met Rosecrans). Grant snapped, "If General Hooker wishes to see me he will find me on this train." Hooker was standing at attention in front of his commander within minutes. Grant was not a general who permitted any dispute over his status and authority to go unchecked. But by comparison with the ructions that engulfed the Army of Tennessee, the tensions that lurked under the surface of the Union command relationships were insignificant.[41]

Grant's first priority on arrival in Chattanooga was to break the state of siege and open up an improved line of supply. This was a matter of pressing urgency because, should Hooker and his two corps be concentrated at Chattanooga, they would only help consume the dwindling stocks of food at a faster rate. In any case, Grant had been deeply shocked at what he saw of the state of affairs in Chattanooga and was determined to improve them at the first opportunity. Sylvanus Cadwallader noticed soldiers wandering about "with their eyes fixed on the ground as if searching for some lost valuable" but they were really searching "the street [for] one or two more grains of corn or oats which had jolted out of the wagons." A harrowing sight were the "many hundreds of mules lying where they had been chained to trees, till they starved to death." This baleful situation had to be rectified before the arrival of Sherman and a counteroffensive was launched.[42]

Hooker's troops remained at Bridgeport, some seventeen miles west of Chattanooga. Major General W. F. Smith urged on Grant an ingenious plan whereby Hooker should cross to the south side of the Tennessee River with his rear protected by a division of the Fourteenth Corps of the Army of the Cumberland. This was one of the schemes that Grant had discussed with Rosecrans on his arrival. He gave orders for it to be carried out at once. Smith with four thousand men would operate from Chattanooga, placing eighteen hundred men on sixty pontoon transports. At night on October 27 these troops sailed down the river while the bulk of Smith's troops marched west overland to Brown's Ferry to support them. Engineers hurriedly built a pontoon bridge. A line of communication was now protected running across the two widths of river arising from the great westward meander of the Tennessee River. Hooker's troops marched around Raccoon Mountain near the road and rail junction of Wauhatchie and into Lookout Valley. The new line of supply running via Brown's Ferry could no longer be interdicted from Lookout Mountain. Grant at once telegraphed for a supply of vegetables. The arrival of this food was a major tonic to morale. Hooker's trains were now available, and they were far fresher than the worn-out and starving teams of horses in Chattanooga. "Neither officers nor men," Grant recorded, "looked upon themselves any longer as doomed."[43]

The Confederate conduct of these initial operations was singularly inept. It would presage low levels of military competence shown by the Army of Tennessee for the rest of the campaign. Longstreet was in command of this sector and he was at his obdurate worst. He was sulking after the failure of his attempt to remove Bragg. He had not approved of the attempt to besiege Chattanooga and took little interest in the operation. But the prime reason for the setback was due to the dispute over command relationships within Longstreet's corps. Longstreet's tactless handling of this dispute tends to indicate that, had he replaced Bragg in October 1863, he would not have been an emollient presence able to soothe the outraged sensibilities inflamed by Bragg. After Hood's wounding Longstreet favored as his replacement not the ranking brigadier general, Evander McIvor Law, but his own protégé, Micah Jenkins. Jenkins was distrusted by the officers and disliked by his troops. Longstreet insisted on Jenkins's appointment (even though Jefferson Davis had said that Law should get the command). The relations between the new commander of Hood's old division and his subordinates were far from harmonious.

Law had repeatedly warned that an attack was afoot but Longstreet ignored his blandishments. Law's brigade had only two regiments available—perhaps Law's weakness was deliberate and that Longstreet and Jenkins hoped he would be defeated. When the federals struck at Brown's Ferry, Law was too weak to resist them. Longstreet then failed to inform Bragg of the defeat. When Bragg discovered what had happened, he ordered an immediate counterattack. Longstreet ignored this order on the night of October 27. The following morning Bragg went himself to order an attack, but Longstreet said that he needed another division. Bragg provided this, but the attack was eventually launched by only two weak brigades. Longstreet seems to have failed to grasp the true strategic significance of Lookout Valley. Smith had no difficulty in throwing these puny attacks back. If Longstreet had calculated that these mismanaged efforts would benefit Jenkins he was mistaken. This small operation was a disaster for the Confederates. Not only had the state of siege ended and Grant was free to build up his forces, but Bragg concluded that Longstreet was such a nuisance, it would be better if he was rid of him.[44]

The arrival of General Sherman with four divisions of the Army of the Tennessee on the evening of November 14 provided a major supplement to Grant's strength. The Union forces numbered 56,359, while Bragg fielded perhaps 36,000. Grant was very pleased to see Sherman and offered him an easy affability and influence over the planning process that was denied to his other subordinates. Sherman's march to Chattanooga was itself an impressive achievement that prefigured his later marches through Georgia and the Carolinas. He was to be given the major role in the forthcoming battle. Grant distrusted Hooker, who still had to live down his defeat at Chancellorsville. He had made mistakes during the march to Wauhatchie and had dispersed his forces too widely, but his position astride Brown's Ferry and the Confederate left flank on Lookout Mountain was potentially very strong.

Grant's relations with Thomas were also continuing to deteriorate. The week before, under considerable pressure from Washington, Grant ordered the Army of the Cumberland to attack the northern slopes of Missionary Ridge and advance on the railroad junction of Dalton. Thomas objected strongly to this and on November 7 the order was rescinded. Grant had perhaps overestimated the speed of the Army of the Cumberland's recovery; he was anxious, moreover, to help Burnside at Knoxville. Grant's left flank was vulnerable should Burnside be defeated. But Grant concluded that Thomas was a laggard old fusspot who would never be ready to attack.[45]

By the time Sherman arrived, Grant's plans were recast so that his point of main effort was on the Union left flank. Sherman's Army of the Tennessee was to advance into the hills north of Chattanooga and cross over the Tennessee River. Then Sherman was to close up to South Chickamauga Creek and strike Bragg's right flank with a concentrated blow against Tunnel Hill on the north edge of Missionary Ridge. Rapidity of approach was the key, because the Army of the Tennessee had to get up on the ridge before Bragg could concentrate to throw Union troops off it. Thomas and the Army of the Cumberland were to demonstrate before Missionary Ridge. Bragg believed that his left flank was most vulnerable. Grant was keen to give the impression that Sherman's troops were en route to that sector, while they actually advanced to the Confederate right flank over hidden roads that had been especially prepared for the purpose. At this stage Hooker and his two corps of "eastern pimps" (as they were branded by Thomas's men) would attack Lookout Mountain, seize it, and then hit at Rossville to the south. Grant stressed the paramount need to strike at Confederate lines of communication behind their defenses and Sherman was ordered to push on to Cleveland to cut the Chattanooga–Cleveland Railroad.[46]

On November 15 after a detailed reconnaissance, Grant made a number of changes to the plan. Sherman was very confident of his ability to get over Tunnel Hill and onto Missionary Ridge. "I can do it," snapped Sherman with typical vigor. He even claimed it could be done before 9 AM. But he was keen to concentrate as much strength for the northern operation as he could. Thus Grant canceled the move against Lookout Mountain. He believed that "The possession of Lookout Mountain was of no special advantage to us now." Howard's Eleventh Corps was thus allotted as a reserve to aid either Sherman or Thomas. Hooker's operations in Lookout Valley were thus downgraded to subsidiary status.[47]

From the first Grant's plans went awry. Sherman was not at his best as he was grieving over the loss of his son, Willie, a few weeks earlier. His advance to South Chickamauga Creek was slowed down by heavy rain. Grant, who had hoped to begin the offensive on November 21, had to postpone it for a further two days. Thomas then intervened in an to attempt to persuade Grant to allow Hooker to continue to use Howard's corps to assault Lookout Mountain because Sherman's movements would have alerted Bragg to his attack and that he would have stripped the Confederate left to meet it. Grant dismissed these suggestions, indicating that Howard's position around Chattanooga would distract Bragg from the peril about to engulf his right. Grant's faith in Sherman's move at this date was actually justified because Bragg had deduced erroneously that the Army of the Tennessee would strike his left flank. Nonetheless Sherman's move would not go according to the plan and Grant would be forced to reexamine its assumptions.[48]

The disparity between what Grant had planned and how the battle would actually develop would lead to some harsh postwar exchanges between the partisans of Grant and Thomas as to who had thought up the moves that led to victory. Grant's supreme attribute as a general was his opportunism. He had the immense self-confidence to strike, wait and see what happened, assess what changes needed to be made, improvise during the battle itself, and then go on and win. One suspects that there would be rather fewer candidates stepping forward to claim the credit for the ideas enshrined in Grant's plans had he been defeated. Chattanooga was to see him win the battle with the stunning self-assurance that a numerical superiority affords. Whether Grant himself thought up the expedients that he then put into practice is a matter of great insignificance.

In a sense, much of the postwar controversy as to who deserved the credit for thinking up and suggesting various moves to Grant illustrates the crudeness of the workings of American staffs in the 1860s and the wide measure of misapprehension which existed as to their role in war. It is the prime duty of a staff to serve as a source of suggestions for the commander; the main function of the commander is to put the ideas (which often seem obvious not just to the officers who suggest them, but to many others who simply may not have voiced their thoughts to their commander, or who did so with more subdued voices) into practice—a task of infinitely greater difficulty. Seeing ideas carried out at the right place and at the most propitious time is a task of fiendish complexity, tricky timing, and awesome responsibility. Carrying out those ideas was a task that Grant found easy, but that generals like McClellan, who appeared at first sight more intellectually impressive than Grant, found so taxing. Grant made decisions with alacrity and accepted the responsibility for acts that were sometimes (but not invariably) based on the vague suggestions of his subordinates. And, as Colonel Conger concludes, "when the decision was forthcoming, it came out . . . with a torrent of energy, and was speedily clothed by Grant himself in concise and forceful orders."[49]

Fortunately for the Union, Grant was aided in his task of improvising a new plan by the blunders of Braxton Bragg. Not only did Bragg miscalculate the direction of Grant's main attack, but he committed the signal blunder of drastically weakening his own forces just at the time when Grant was able to make use of the Army of the Tennessee. Bragg gave command of all his cavalry to Joseph Wheeler (which led to another disagreement with Forrest) and sent them on a raid into Tennessee that inflicted damage on the federal rear. However, Wheeler's raid mainly succeeded in wrecking his command, which was unfit for further operations with the main army. But Bragg's most significant and perplexing error was his decision to dispatch Longstreet and his corps to besiege Burnside in Knoxville. Bragg later explained this away by reference to a desire "to get rid of him and see what he could do on his own resources." The logistical factor is perhaps not irrelevant, as Bragg was having difficulty supplying his besieging forces. But it is difficult to accept Judith Lee Hallock's view that Bragg "probably did not injure his chances any more by sending him than by keeping him." Furthermore, by worrying that Grant's move toward his right would get between Longstreet and the main body, on November 22 Bragg withdrew Cleburne's division from Missionary Ridge and sent it to help Longstreet. Bragg was so confident in the strength of his position that the following day a party of fourteen ladies was invited to visit his headquarters; their visit was to be an eventful one.[50]

The other important reason for the defeat was Bragg's lack of experience or skill as a defensive general. This was to be his first battle in which he did not attack. He was not an engineer and he evinced a blind faith in the massive strength of the terrain, especially Missionary Ridge, which was not borne out by events. His attention was diverted to either flank when it would have been better to focus on the center. Bragg's force, numbering approximately thirty-six thousand men, was overstretched to defend the center of his position, which ran for four miles; he could muster only three divisions in Breckinridge's corps—about sixteen thousand men. He then divided each regiment in two with one half defending the top of the ridge, and the other half the base. Bragg had issued secret orders to the officers commanding the units in the valley to withdraw back up the ridge after they had fired one volley. This effectively masked the Unionist attackers because the defenders could not fire on them for fear of hitting their own men. As for the defending units on the crest, each soldier stood more than a yard apart in Breckinridge's breastworks; the intervals were as large as seven or eight feet in the weakest parts. Breckinridge did not approve of the decision to stand on Missionary Ridge and had warned his divisional commanders that they might need to withdraw. This admonition did not fortify confidence.[51]

The defensive strength of Missionary Ridge was more apparent than it was real. The actual construction of breastworks in this sector was a hurried, last-minute affair, with artillery officers reconnoitering gun positions in the dark the night before the battle began. The overall layout was inept. The defenses had been placed right at the top of Missionary Ridge, but nobody bothered to notice that there was a large area of dead ground below the crest, so that if attackers could clear the lower slopes their advance to the top was effectively covered. Confederate guns could not be depressed far enough to hit attacking infantry at that close range and, overall, the defensive firepower of the Confederate artillery was squandered by the dispersal of batteries all along the line; some guns were not even in place when the Union attack began.[52]

Though Grant was uninterested in the Lookout Mountain flank, he adjusted the orders so that Thomas and the Army of the Cumberland would demonstrate toward Orchard knob to convince Bragg that Thomas's move, and not Sherman's, was the point of main effort. Grant had got word on the night of November 22 that Bragg was retreating and Thomas was ordered to conduct a reconnaissance in force in case Bragg had weakened his defensive lines. Overall, progress on the first day, November 23, was satisfying to Grant. Orchard knob was the strongest of the Confederate positions lying beneath Missionary Ridge. Thomas arrayed his rejuvenated army on parade, ready to move forward and exploit any opportunities, with "the ringing notes of the bugles, companies wheeling and counter-marching, and regiments getting into line," wrote one eyewitness. "It was an inspiring sight. Flags were flying; the quick, earnest steps of thousands beat equal time." Thomas's troops moved with vigor and overran with ease the Confederate first-line positions in well-timed stabs. What was Thomas to do? The operation was not designed as a decisive attack. Deaf to the blandishments of his noisy staff, Grant barked laconically: "Intrench them and send up support."[53]

This move certainly succeeded in convincing Bragg that his center on Missionary Ridge was the prime Union objective. A division was moved from Lookout Mountain and a further two divisions (including Cleburne's) were retained on the north end of Missionary Ridge instead of being transferred to Longstreet's corps. But this deployment rebounded against Sherman's progress. Sherman's troops closed up to the Tennessee River in the pouring rain and were concealed in the woods on the north side by the evening of November 23. He crossed the Tennessee River, built a pontoon bridge, and by the afternoon of November 24 the Army of the Tennessee was ready to move forward on a three-division front. Sherman advanced onto the high ground in front of the river and was then shocked to discover that this was not Tunnel Hill, which lay behind this ridge separated by a steep ravine.

Sherman's reconnaissance had not been as thorough as he had presumed and, furthermore, he could not tell how strongly the tunnel was held. This was a difficult obstacle because the railroad ran through it, linking Tunnel Hill with Missionary Ridge. Sherman decided to consolidate his position rather than attack rashly; a sharp recollection of Chickasaw bluff perhaps pressed on his imagination. It is possible that, had Sherman pressed on, he might have turned Bragg's right and cut his rail communications, thus meeting all of Grant's high expectations for his move. But having received one severe shock during his advance, to have plunged on without firm intelligence as to Confederate strength with his back to the river, would have been imprudent in the extreme. Sherman's caution certainly does not deserve the censure that it has received. That Sherman did not win the battle singlehandedly was a blow to his pride; he was later to claim in his *Memoirs* that he had nonetheless drawn Bragg's strength to his front; this is slightly exaggerated, yet his troops' dogged fighting with Cleburne's division did perform an important service, for the latter—after its hurried return to the position on November 24—would have greatly strengthened Bragg's defensive power in the center.[54]

In short, Sherman's tactical setback was disappointing but did not have an adverse effect on the orchestration of the battle at the operational level. Bragg had neglected his right at the expense of his left, which he had visited at the same time that Sherman's troops attacked Tunnel Hill. The ground was shrouded in fog on November 24 and Bragg, despite his prominence, could not see what was going on. General Hooker's role on this flank was also diversionary. But he had benefited from a stroke of good luck when the pontoon bridge at Brown's Ferry collapsed, stranding one of Sherman's divisions on the south side of the Tennessee River. Grant had ruled the previous day that if this division could not be crossed then it was to serve under Hooker's command, which went a long way to compensate for the loss of Howard's troops. Hooker was also keen to learn from his errors in the first stage of this (and also the Chancellorsville) campaign. He thus concentrated his artillery for an overwhelming blow against the weakened Confederate defenders.[55]

The fighting was harsh and difficult, but the Confederates on the summit of Lookout Mountain could not depress their guns low enough to help the infantry on the slopes and hinder the Union assault. Hooker's attack hit the west side of Lookout Mountain while a bridge was simultaneously seized over Lookout Creek. These maneuvers permitted a frontal assault to be combined with an outflanking move. The west side of Lookout Mountain was slowly cleared and Hooker concentrated to strike at the northern end, which would expose the left flank of Missionary Ridge and the Confederate line of communication to Rossville. In a dramatic moment during the afternoon the fog cleared suddenly, revealing Hooker's progress and this excited a great cheer from Thomas's men watching from Orchard Knob.[56]

Grant rode back to the center from the left of Thomas's flank. A relative said of Grant that he looked like a farmer out on a horse inspecting the progress of his crops. He remained, as always, perfectly calm, and wrote to Hooker, ensuring that he got any reinforcements that he needed. Grant was satisfied with progress on this flank, too. He predicted that Confederate troops would be gone from Lookout Mountain the following morning. He was correct: they would all be evacuated that night. Grant was thus free on November 25 to strike at both of the flanks of Bragg's enfeebled army while Thomas pinned him down in the center. Hooker's unenviable reputation as a braggart and intriguer rebounded on him. Always alert to the subtleties of military politics, Grant tended to downgrade the importance of Hooker's advance in his report and later in his *Personal Memoirs*, to ensure that Hooker did not use this success at the expense of Sherman. Grant's assessment was slighting and unfair, and Hooker certainly did not appreciate having his own tactics turned against him.[57]

The progress on Hooker's flank pleased Thomas because he believed that Missionary Ridge could not be assaulted successfully until Bragg's two flanks had been smashed. Despite his unexpected success, Grant did not allot Hooker's three divisions a clear role on the third day. Thomas suggested to Hooker that he move into the valley of Chattanooga Creek and close up to Missionary Ridge and link with Thomas's right flank, thus enhancing cooperation. This Hooker was keen to do, although he was frustrated in his efforts to get across Chattanooga Creek. Grant's relations with Thomas had cooled further. Rawlins and other members of Grant's staff had uttered tactless remarks that conveyed an unmistakable impression that they looked forward to Sherman's success on the left because it would be made at the expense of Thomas and the Army of the Cumberland. But Sherman's attack on the morning of November 25 on Cleburne's breastworks running across Tunnel Hill had not been a success: two brigades had gone forward in piecemeal, poorly managed actions, and these had been driven back easily. Sherman rarely thrived as a commander when his space for maneuver was limited. Within the confines of Tunnel Hill the outnumbered Confederate defenders could muster greater fighting power than Sherman could throw against them.[58]

From *An Atlas of American Military History* by James C. Bradford (New York: Cynthia Parzych Publishing, 2003).

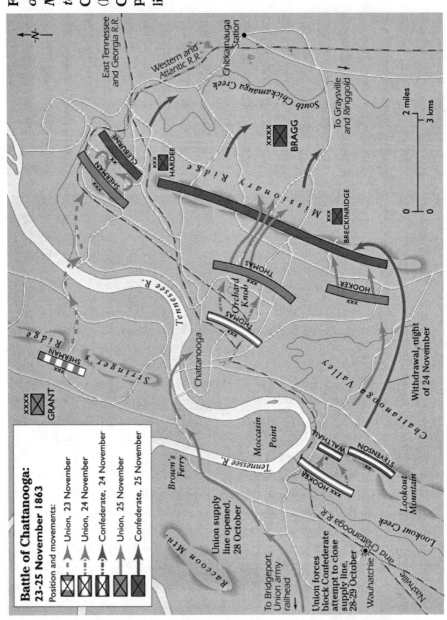

Battle of Chattanooga: 23-25 November 1863

Position and movements:

— Union, 23 November
— Union, 24 November
— Confederate, 24 November
— Union, 25 November
— Confederate, 25 November

Sherman began to ask Grant, "Where is Thomas?" The commanding general enjoyed an excellent view of the entire panorama of fighting at Chattanooga as he had moved his command post to Orchard knob. Yet he believed mistakenly that Bragg was strengthening his right flank. One of Thomas's divisions was sent to reinforce Sherman. By the afternoon of November 25 Grant muttered, "General Sherman seems to be having a hard time." He then proposed that Thomas's troops assault the entrenchments at the base of Missionary Ridge "directly in front of them or move to the left, as the presence of the enemy may require." Thomas objected, possibly because at that point Hooker had not yet moved toward Bragg's left. Grant did not overrule him until he was prevailed upon by Rawlins to issue a peremptory order stipulating the seizure of "the enemy's first line of rifle pits." Nothing happened. General Granger, whose Fourth Corps was to lead the assault and who had come to Thomas's aid at Chickamauga, had a rather tiresome habit in moments of strain of resuming the outlook of a junior officer, and sought solace in siting batteries of artillery. "If you will leave that battery to its captain, and take command of your corps, it will be better for all of us," roared Grant. With this injunction ringing in his ears, Granger ordered his two divisions forward in what Thomas believed bitterly was a futile effort to sacrifice the Army of the Cumberland for the sake of the Army of the Tennessee.[59]

The assault on Missionary Ridge, rather like the charge of the Light Brigade at the battle of Balaclava in 1854, was an attack that nobody ordered, though with a much happier outcome for the attackers. Grant held and exercised the initiative; in typical opportunistic fashion, he was attempting to relieve the pressure on Sherman by a limited push in the center. Thomas did not approve of this advance and wanted to see greater use made of Hooker's troops on his right. Neither foresaw the consequences of this move—a full-blooded assault on Missionary Ridge itself. Both Grant and Sherman were prone to claim that all these individual operations had "gone according to plan," and Thomas was inclined to complain that their postwar rationalizations slighted his own contribution and the magnificent efforts of his troops. Certainly, Bruce Catton's biography of Grant confers on these moves a coherence that they lacked at the time. Grant still thought of Sherman's move as the point of main effort and Thomas's advance was considered subsidiary to it. Yet, despite all the errors that were committed and the false suppositions that rested on faulty intelligence, both writers who favor Grant and Sherman's version and those who take Thomas's side underrate the importance of the degree of successful *improvisation* that Grant and his subordinates managed to achieve.[60]

Yet there can be no doubting that the assault on Missionary Ridge was based on a misunderstanding. Not for the last time in his military career, Grant did the right thing for the wrong reasons. On the face of it, after the failures before Fredericksburg and Gettysburg, the attack seemed impossible. Many commentators later detected the finger of providence. Charles A. Dana, for example, celebrated one of "the great miracles of military history." The sheer exhilaration of the experience was another factor, the inexplicable levels of adrenaline released and the unlooked-for good luck. "A scene never to be forgotten," recalled one participant, "a panorama to stir the blood into a wild tumult." Cadwallader, an observer rather than a participant, expressed these intangible feelings well when he wrote, "the fascination of the great battle wholly overcame all prudential considerations. There is nothing on earth approaching it in sublimity." In short, the irrational always lurks not far from the surface in war, and historians should beware of delivering judgments that are too neat, too rational, and too deterministic.[61]

Grant with Thomas and their staffs took up their posts on Orchard knob to observe the proceedings. The battle opened shortly after 4 PM. Thomas's troops easily seized the rebel rifle pits at the base of Missionary Ridge, and with few casualties despite the cacophony of fire that had greeted the Union advance. The Confederate defenders had no clear idea what to do, and some simply abandoned their positions and ran back up the ridge. Confusion also prevailed on the Union side. Orders were vaguely worded; no explicit instruction had been issued requiring Thomas's troops to halt at the rifle pits. In any case, they had become easy targets for the one hundred Confederate guns on Missionary Ridge. The troops would rather hazard running in the open rather than become sitting targets for fire they could not return. An officer of Granger's staff then said to Sheridan, whose division was in the van, that the corps commander was of the view that if Sheridan thought the ridge itself could be taken, then he should move forward and take it. Sheridan instantly issued orders to advance. Most other commanders issued similar orders; those troops who received none, buoyed up by their success, simply followed those who had. "Groupthink" took over with a vengeance: all four of Thomas's divisions, a total of twenty-three thousand men, moved forward with a splendid cohesion.[62]

The cohesion was not of the parade-ground order because many units had got mixed up, but it was of a moral order, with the soldiers cheering and urging one another on. Confederate fire seemed to have no effect. The moral effect of the charge that so many generals had previously relied on and found elusive (including Lee) now began to undermine the fighting spirit of Confederate troops. Those retreating from the rifle pits "went scurrying up the ridge like a flock of sheep with dogs at their heels." Inexorably, and without orders, the Union troops began to run up Missionary Ridge. Grant's initial reaction to these unexpected events was amazement. "Thomas, who ordered those men up the ridge?" he snapped. "I don't know; I did not," Thomas replied. Another of Granger's divisional commanders, Brigadier General Thomas J. Wood, then sent back an excited message: "Tell Granger, if we are supported, we will take and hold the ridge!" Neither Grant nor Thomas were sanguine about the prospects. "If Wood fails, by God he'll pay for it," Grant vowed.[63]

Missionary Ridge is five hundred feet high, and though the Union troops were "fagged and blown" when they arrived at the top, and were thus vulnerable to a counterattack, no such effort greeted them at the crest. The Confederate defenders were utterly demoralized by their failure to prevent the successful Union assault—and the sudden realization that their position was not as invulnerable as so many had smugly assumed threw them into panic. Missionary Ridge was not one huge chunk of rock, but a series of interconnected ridges marked by deep undulations. As on Lookout Mountain, Confederate generals had difficulty depressing their guns and the undulations offered cover. This depressed the Confederates but encouraged the Union attackers who felt "a feeling of new confidence . . . always too fast for the Confederates' depressing of their pieces." The top of Missionary Ridge was too narrow to regroup and the artillery was vulnerable. The Confederate gunners experienced difficulties in getting their guns away and entire batteries were captured intact, as the teams were cut loose in a frantic effort to escape the advancing Union infantry.[64]

Throughout the climax of the battle Grant remained calm despite his anger, and made no decisions that redounded either to his discredit or the successful outcome of the battle. The same could not be said for Braxton Bragg and his subordinates. Bragg had conferred with Cleburne that morning and was content with the position on the right flank. Yet in the center the Confederate line was shattered—with six simultaneous penetrations of the Army of Tennessee's trenches—with the Union troops moving through the position and veering left and right. Bragg attempted to emulate Lee's example at Gettysburg and rally his shattered formations. He was insulted and humiliated for his pains. Bragg simply lacked the charisma for this kind of melodramatic gesture to work; yet it is testimony to the fear that his presence still aroused that he rode away from these encounters unharmed; oaths not blows (nor bullets) were aimed at him. Bragg's left disintegrated. It was the weakest part of the Missionary Ridge position with "long intervals [sic] between brigades which the Federals soon discovered." Many defenders were surrounded because of the speed of the Union advance.[65]

Breckinridge, responsible for the left of the position while Bragg concentrated on the center, shouted: "Boys, get away the best you can." Both commanders narrowly escaped capture themselves. Breckinridge had failed to organize a reserve should the position be penetrated, and had gone missing for some hours before the attack while Bragg was visiting the right. Although later successes would redeem his military career, at Chattanooga he had signally failed to impose himself on events. Even if the faulty defensive arrangements were not his brain-child, he had simply acquiesced in them. After the battle, Bragg claimed that Breckinridge had been drunk and utterly incapable of directing his corps. Breckinridge's biographer, William C. Davis, defends his subject from what he suggests is Bragg's spite, but the evidence is strong that Breckinridge was incapable. During the retreat the commander of the rear guard was ordered "under no circumstances to leave the drunken general or permit him to give an order." Such orders could not simply be manufactured after the event. Bragg had made no attempt to use accusations of drunkenness to undermine his critics after Chickamauga. Breckinridge was a heavy drinker and had succumbed at the moment of greatest psychological pressure. When the Army of Tennessee fell back to Dalton, Georgia, Breckinridge was relieved of his command. But even if the charge is true, it reflects badly on Bragg's judgment for retaining an incompetent sot in command, even if it was in a sector he was less worried about. The incident is another example of the shallow depth of the Confederate pool of senior commanders of any ability. Bragg retained Breckinridge because he had nobody else to replace him with.[66]

The harsh reality was that the constant bickering between Bragg and his generals had slowly trickled down the chain of command and had fatally eroded the faith of the men in their commanders. Bragg was, in any case, not a leader and could not present himself to inspire his troops, as his appearance during the crisis on Missionary Ridge had convincingly shown. After the battle his own morale was as badly shattered as that of his men. He looked frightened, a soldier reported, "hacked and whipped and mortified and chagrined at defeat." The bungling at Chattanooga irreparably shattered what was left of Bragg's reputation. Henceforth he became a byword for military incompetence in the South. A few days later he tendered his resignation and, to his amazement and discomfiture, Jefferson Davis accepted it.[67]

The only element of the Army of Tennessee that left the battlefield in any semblance of order was Cleburne's division on the right flank. Cleburne had soon realized his danger after the collapse of Breckinridge's corps as Union troops streamed northward along Missionary Ridge. He issued orders to all Confederate units for a rapid withdrawal and led the retreat southeast toward Chickamauga. Troops from Sheridan's division had made their way down the other side of the ridge and urged a pursuit toward Chickamauga Station to cut Cleburne off. But the evening was drawing to a close—it was about 7:30 PM. Grant and Thomas had made their way up onto Missionary Ridge. Yet it was not surprising that Grant failed to organize a pursuit after Chattanooga. Although a series of unforeseen contingencies and unplanned events had set at naught the preferred, deterministic explanations—that armies on the defensive were "invulnerable" or automatically superior to those that attack—Grant could not overcome the inertia that surrounded the pursuit. The hour was late and the ground very difficult to traverse. The advance that had brought decisive success was spontaneous and unexpected. No fresh reserve was available. All troops were committed and after the strenuous exertions of the day they were tired and hungry. By Civil War standards the fighting had not been of great intensity. The morale of Bragg's troops had been eroded by the ructions in the chain of command and by boredom. They were half beaten before the coup de grâce on Missionary Ridge was delivered. Consequently, Grant lost 5,495 casualties (less than 10 percent of his total) and Bragg 2,521 (about 16 percent, as in addition 4,146 were missing).[68]

But Grant had an even more pressing reason for calling off the pursuit. The plight of his left flank was causing him a lot of anxiety. Having advanced into east Tennessee, Burnside believed strongly he could not abandon it. He was moved by the heartfelt pleas of Tennessee Unionists that they should not be abandoned and left to Confederate retribution. Burnside's Army of the Ohio was a small force of about eight thousand men built around the Ninth Corps. Its central weakness was a lack of cavalry. Burnside's lines of supply, already unreliable because of the dreadful state of east Tennessee roads, were vulnerable to the depredations of Wheeler's Confederate horses. Nonetheless, the corps level of command was the one at which Burnside felt most comfortable, and he conducted the campaign competently. It is unlikely that Grant felt so sanguine. Although Burnside had sent several messages indicating his resolve to hold Knoxville, which sat on the high ground above the Holston River, Grant hastened to send him aid. Telegraph communications had been cut several times and a misunderstanding had arisen. Grant (probably influenced by his recent experience at Chattanooga) gained the impression that Knoxville's garrison was on the brink of starvation. He and Burnside were communicating at cross purposes. At any rate, Grant could not risk letting Knoxville fall. The Confederate reoccupation of Unionist east Tennessee would be a political catastrophe for the Lincoln administration, and would be no less a blow to Grant's burgeoning reputation with the president.[69]

Sherman's Army of the Tennessee plus Granger's Fourth Corps were dispatched to relieve Knoxville. Sherman's men were already tired after their long march to Chattanooga immediately followed by the battle. His troops then marched rapidly for six days. On December 5 Sherman arrived at the outskirts of Knoxville. Burnside had created a strong position and had sought to fix Longstreet far distant from Chattanooga. Longstreet had obligingly assaulted Knoxville on November 29 and was repulsed. The following day Longstreet got news of Bragg's defeat. He later received instructions from Bragg either to join him at Dalton, Georgia, or fall back to Virginia, depending on circumstances. Looking at the picture another way Longstreet concluded that he could serve as a distraction that would allow Bragg to reorganize his forces unhindered. But by December 3 the true magnitude of his isolation and vulnerability dawned on him with news of Sherman's rapid approach. By December 4 he withdrew along the roads to Virginia.[70]

Sherman was far from pleased when he entered Knoxville. Burnside's troops were on half rations but comfortable. His own troops were worn out, hungry, and their feet were bleeding, often "wrapped in old clothes or portions of blankets that could be ill-spared from shivering shoulders." Sherman's temper was not improved when Burnside (not a man to deny himself comfort) laid on a lavish dinner for him that evening. The misunderstanding—that Burnside would be starved into surrendering by December 4—was hardly Burnside's fault. It reveals that, even with the telegraph, the conduct of operations over so great an area could still lead to errors of deduction and distribution.[71]

This messy siege brought to an end a campaign marked by improvisation and the unexpected. Bragg had made many errors and Grant had taken full advantage of them. Despite Bragg's stunning success at Chickamauga, his failure at Chattanooga sealed the end of his career as a field commander. As for Grant, he emerged from the campaign not only the dominant military personality of the war in the west but of the entire Union war effort, and he began to enlarge the sphere of his thoughts accordingly. He began to proffer opinions on the strategy of the war as a whole and on command appointments. On the field, Grant's success at Chattanooga was due to his ability (whatever the personal tensions) to allow his subordinates a great measure of discretion to carry out their missions as they saw fit. He watched, waited, and then acted, confident that his subordinates would provide the opportunities that he could exploit with lightning speed and heavy force.[72]

The prime results of Grant's victory were twofold: first, Grant had finally brought to an end Confederate efforts to regain Tennessee, and Unionists in the state's eastern third were at last succored; second, an advance base—Chattanooga—had been secured which would allow Union armies to strike at the Deep South and the secessionist heartland. Yet before this opportunity could be exploited to the uttermost the Union command system had to be reordered to give Grant the scope to dominate Union strategy.[73]

NOTES AND REFERENCES

1. Herman Hattaway and Archer Jones, *How the North Won* (Urbana: University of Illinois Press, 1983), p. 404; Stephen E. Ambrose, *Halleck: Lincoln's Chief of Staff* (Baton Rouge: Louisiana State University Press, 1962, 1996), pp. 150–52.

2. Though Lee hoped to change this state of affairs, see Lee to Longstreet, Aug. 31, 1863, in *The Wartime Papers of R. E. Lee*, eds. Clifford Dowdey and Louis H. Manarin (New York: Bramhall House, 1961), p. 594.

3. Even though Bragg had successfully done it in July 1862. See above, pp. 206–209, but he had not faced a change of railroad gauge at Lynchburg and the destruction of bridges. See Kenneth P. Williams, *Lincoln Finds a General* (New York: Macmillan, 1959), vol. 5, pp. 145–46, 149, 162, 172.

4. Freeman Cleaves, *Meade of Gettysburg* (Norman: University of Oklahoma Press, 1960), pp. 212–13; T. Harry Williams, *Lincoln and His Generals* (New York: Alfred A. Knopf, 1952), pp. 285–89; Douglas Southall Freeman, *R. E. Lee* (New York: Scribner's, 1934–35), vol. 3, pp. 184–87.

5. James A. Ramage, *Rebel Raider: The Life of General John Hunt Morgan* (Lexington: University Press of Kentucky, 1986), pp. 158–60, 178–82.

6. Judith Lee Hallock, *Braxton Bragg and Confederate Defeat* (Tuscaloosa: University of Alabama Press, 1991), vol. 2, pp. 22, 35, 52, 60, 115; Brian Holden Reid and John White, "'A Mob of Stragglers and Cowards': Desertion from the Union and Confederate Armies, 1861–1865," *Journal of Strategic Studies* 8 (March 1985): 73–74; Mark A. Weitz, *More Damning Than Slaughter: Desertion in the Confederate Army* (Lincoln: University of Nebraska Press, 2005), pp. 51–52, emphasizes the reluctance of Southern deserters to go home; on the loyalty oaths, see pp. 117–22.

7. Craig L. Symonds, *Joseph E. Johnston* (New York: Norton, 1992), pp. 220–26; Steven E. Woodworth, *Jefferson Davis and His Generals* (Lawrence: University Press of Kansas, 1990), pp. 216–21; William C. Davis, *Jefferson Davis: The Man and His Hour* (New York: HarperCollins, 1991), pp. 510–12.

8. This is denoted by the nature of Lincoln's assurances. See his letter of August 10: "I think of you in all kindness and confidence: and that I am not watching you with an evil-eye." *The Collected Works of Abraham Lincoln*, ed. Roy P. Basler (New Brunswick, NJ: Rutgers University Press, 1953–55), vol. 6, p. 378.

9. Williams, *Lincoln and His Generals*, pp. 249–51, 278–79; Theodore Clarke Smith, *The Life and Letters of James Abram Garfield* (New Haven, CT: Yale University Press, 1925), vol. 1, pp. 845–46; Kenneth P. Williams, *Lincoln Finds a General*, vol. 5, pp. 211–18. Garfield's moralizing should perhaps not be taken too seriously. He, too, had sedulously cultivated Salmon P. Chase as a political ally and was unpopular among his subordinates. Garfield was thought too "ambitious." See Peter Cozzens, *This Terrible Sound: The Battle of Chickamauga* (Urbana: University of Illinois Press, 1992), pp. 10–13.

10. Halleck claimed that the crushing of Bragg in the Tullahoma campaign was not expected. See K. P. Williams, *Lincoln Finds a General*, vol. 5, p. 239; T. H. Williams, *Lincoln and His Generals*, p. 279; Thomas L. Connelly, *The Autumn of Glory: The Army of Tennessee, 1862–1865* (Baton Rouge: Louisiana State University Press, 1971), pp. 127–34; Cozzens, *Terrible Sound*, pp. 21–33.

11. Williams, *Lincoln Finds a General*, vol. 5, p. 243.

12. Ibid., vol. 5, pp. 240–41, 244–47; Cozzens, *Terrible Sound*, pp. 45–48.

13. Hallock, *Bragg*, vol. 2, pp. 54–62; Connelly, *Autumn of Glory*, pp. 175–85.

14. Cozzens, *Terrible Sound*, pp. 78–79; Williams, *Lincoln Finds a General*, vol. 5, pp. 248, 251–52; William Marvel, *Burnside* (Chapel Hill: University of North Carolina Press, 1991), p. 287.

15. Williams, *Lincoln Finds a General*, vol. 5, pp. 253–54; Hallock, *Bragg*, vol. 2, pp. 67–68, 70; Connelly, *Autumn of Glory*, pp. 201–10; Steven E. Woodworth, *Six Armies in Tennessee: The Chickamauga and Chattanooga Campaigns* (Lincoln: University of Nebraska Press, 1988), pp. 81–82, 87.

16. Cozzens, *Terrible Sound*, chs. 8–15, gives a detailed account of the first day's fighting; James Longstreet, *From Manassas to Appomattox* (New York: Da Capo, 1895, 1992), pp. 437–39.

17. Longstreet, *Manassas to Appomattox*, pp. 440–41; Cozzens, *Terrible Sound*, pp. 299–302.

18. Hallock, *Bragg*, vol. 2, p. 71; Cozzens, *Terrible Sound*, pp. 301–10.

19. Williams, *Lincoln Finds a General*, vol. 5, pp. 254–55; Cozzens, *Terrible Sound*, pp. 294–98.

20. Longstreet, *From Manassas to Appomattox*, p. 442; Hallock, *Bragg*, vol. 2, pp. 71–72; Thomas L. Livermore, *Numbers and Losses in the Civil War*, 2nd ed. (Boston: Houghton Mifflin, 1901), p. 106.

21. Woodworth, *Davis and His Generals*, pp. 235–36; Connelly, *Autumn of Glory*, pp. 201–203, places the blame for the delays on Bragg's shoulders.

22. Ibid., p. 236; Hallock, *Bragg*, vol. 2, pp. 73–74; Longstreet, *From Manassas to Appomattox*, p. 443.

23. Jeffry D. Wert, *General James Longstreet* (New York: Simon and Schuster, 1993), pp. 311–12; Longstreet, *From Manassas to Appomattox*, p. 444.

24. Williams, *Lincoln Finds a General*, vol. 5, p. 257.

25. Ibid., vol. 5, pp. 257–58; Cozzens, *Terrible Sound*, pp. 363–67.

26. Longstreet, *From Manassas to Appomattox*, p. 447; Wert, *Longstreet*, pp. 312–15; Grady McWhiney and Perry D. Jamieson, *Attack and Die: Civil War Military Tactics and the Southern Heritage* (Tuscaloosa: University of Alabama Press, 1982), p. 90, stress luck as a factor in Longstreet's success. But Longstreet might not have been so lucky had he not deployed the best formation. He would merely have repeated his near success on the second day of Gettysburg.

27. Wert, *Longstreet*, pp. 313–14; Richard M. McMurry, *John Bell Hood and the War for Southern Independence* (Lexington: University Press of Kentucky, 1982), pp. 76–77.

28. Freeman Cleaves, *Rock of Chickamauga: The Life of General George H. Thomas* (1948; Norman: University of Oklahoma Press, 1996), pp. 171–76; Woodworth, *Six Armies in Tennessee*, pp. 121–22, although my conclusions about the pursuit are very different from the latter.

29. Wert, *Longstreet*, pp. 315–19; Cozzens, *Terrible Sound*, pp. 454–56.

30. Hallock, *Bragg*, vol. 2, pp. 75–78. Even McWhiney and Jamieson concede the latter point. See *Attack and Die*, p. 11.

31. James L. McDonough, *Chattanooga: A Death Grip on the Confederacy* (Knoxville: University of Tennessee Press, 1984), pp. 45–48.

32. Woodworth, *Davis and His Generals*, pp. 238–39; Wert, *Longstreet*, pp. 302–305, 323–36.

33. Brian Holden Reid, *The Origins of the American Civil War* (London: Longmans, 1996), pp. 184–86, 210.

34. This unedifying affair can be followed in Woodworth, *Davis and His Generals*, pp. 241–43; Davis, *Jefferson Davis*, pp. 518–22; Wert, *Longstreet*, pp. 326–30; Hallock, *Bragg*, vol. 2, pp. 89–99; William C. Davis, *Breckinridge: Statesman, Soldier, Symbol* (Baton Rouge: Louisiana State University Press, 1974), pp. 381–84; McDonough, *Chattanooga*, pp. 25–37, 37–39; Connelly, *Autumn of Glory*, pp. 240–47.

35. Williams, *Lincoln and His Generals*, pp. 281, 283; McDonough, *Chattanooga*, pp. 44–45.

36. Benjamin P. Thomas and Harold M. Hyman, *Stanton: The Life and Times of Lincoln's Secretary of War* (New York: Alfred A. Knopf, 1962), pp. 285–89; David Donald, *Lincoln* (London: Jonathan Cape, 1995), p. 458; Brian Holden Reid, "The Commander and His Chief of Staff: Ulysses S. Grant and John A. Rawlins," in *Leadership and Command: The Anglo-American Military Experience Since 1861*, ed. G. D. Sheffield (London: Brassey's, 1997).

37. Peter Cozzens, *The Shipwreck of Their Hopes: The Battles for Chattanooga* (Urbana: University of Illinois Press, 1994), pp. 28, 31, 32–33, 36–37, 103, 125, 306; for Dana's warnings of a want of "system" and that "catastrophe is close upon us," see Thomas and Hyman, *Stanton*, p. 290.

38. Bruce Catton, *Grant Takes Command* (Boston: Little, Brown, 1968), pp. 12–13;

Williams, *Lincoln and His Generals*, pp. 291–92; Ambrose, *Halleck*, pp. 154–55. On Grant's frustration over Mobile, see *Personal Memoirs* (London: Sampson Low, 1986), vol. 2, pp. 21, 519. Also see Thomas and Hyman, *Stanton*, p. 290; McDonough, *Chattanooga*, pp. 50–51.

39. The decision to remove Rosecrans was Lincoln's and it arose from direct correspondence with him, not at Stanton's urging. See Williams, *Lincoln and His Generals*, pp. 284–85; Grant, *Memoirs*, vol. 2, pp. 18–19, 26–27; Thomas and Hyman, *Stanton*, pp. 290–92; McDonough, *Chattanooga*, pp. 48–49; Catton, *Grant Takes Command*, pp. 33–35; Thomas resented this telegram, especially its implication that he might abandon Chattanooga, see Woodworth, *Six Armies in Tennessee*, p. 152.

40. Grant, *Memoirs*, vol. 2, pp. 27–30; Horace Porter, *Campaigning with Grant* (New York: Century, 1898), pp. 3–5; Catton, *Grant Takes Command*, pp. 23–25, 35–37, 38–41; McDonough, *Chattanooga*, pp. 49–50.

41. Brooks D. Simpson, *Let Us Have Peace: Ulysses S. Grant and the Politics of War and Reconstruction* (Chapel Hill: University of North Carolina Press, 1991), p. 50. Grant's later feud with Charles Sumner reached ferocious proportions. See David Donald, *Charles Sumner and the Rights of Man* (New York: Alfred A. Knopf, 1970), pp. 444–47. Catton, *Grant Takes Command*, pp. 15–16, 36–37; Cozzens, *Shipwreck of Their Hopes*, pp. 43–44. For Grant's view of Hooker's penchant for insubordination, see John J. Hennessy, "We Shall Make Richmond Howl: The Army of the Potomac on the Eve of Chancellorsville," in *Chancellorsville*, ed. Gary W. Gallagher, 8 (Chapel Hill: University of North Carolina Press, 1996).

42. Grant, *Memoirs*, vol. 2, pp. 34–35; Sylvanus Cadwallader, *Three Years with Grant*, ed. Benjamin P. Thomas (New York: Alfred A. Knopf, 1956), pp. 138–39. Cadwallader also tells an amusing anecdote of a fraudulent photographer selling snaps which he claimed were of Grant. Grant's appearance was not yet well known. Cadwallader immediately recognized the fraud and demanded that the photographer refund the money to his customers.

43. Grant, *Memoirs*, vol. 2, pp. 35–38; Catton, *Grant Takes Command*, pp. 46–56; McDonough, *Chattanooga*, pp. 76–85; Livermore, *Numbers and Losses*, p. 107.

44. Woodworth, *Davis and His Generals*, pp. 246–48; Hallock, *Bragg*, vol. 2, pp. 122–24; Longstreet, *From Manassas to Appomattox*, pp. 473–77; Wert, *Longstreet*, pp. 331–39; Woodworth, *Six Armies in Tennessee*, pp. 155–67.

45. John F. Marszalek, *Sherman: A Soldier's Passion For Order* (New York: Free Press, 1993), pp. 240–42; Cozzens, *Shipwreck of Their Hopes*, pp. 74–75, 106–108; Catton, *Grant Takes Command*, pp. 59–62, 68–69; McDonough, *Chattanooga*, pp. 106–108; Marvel, *Burnside*, p. 306; Cadawallader, *Three Years with Grant*, pp. 154–55. For a defense of Thomas, see Cleaves, *Rock of Chickamauga*, pp. 190–91.

46. Cozzens, *Shipwreck of Their Hopes*, pp. 111–12, 115–16; Catton, *Grant Takes Command*, pp. 64–65; McDonough, *Chattanooga*, pp. 108–109; Marszalek, *Sherman*, p. 243.

47. Cozzens, *Shipwreck of Their Hopes*, pp. 114–15; Marszalek, *Sherman*, p. 243.

48. Cozzens, *Shipwreck of Their Hopes*, pp. 122–25; Cleaves, *Rock of Chickamauga*, pp. 195–96.

49. Holden Reid, "Grant and Rawlins," pp. 23–24, 28; A. L. Conger, *The Rise of U. S. Grant* (New York: Da Capo, 1931, 1996), p. 299; also see Brooks Simpson's remark in his introduction to the latter that, "At times participants in these discussions claimed pride of authorship as if that in itself was sufficient to assure their successful implementation" (p. xiv). For the claim that Rawlins was "unquestionably entitled to one-half the praise, for the strategy" of Grant's campaigns, see Cadwallader, *Three Years with Grant*, p. 140.

50. McDonough, *Chattanooga*, pp. 68–72; Hallock, *Bragg*, vol. 2, pp. 125–26; Davis, *Breckinridge*, p. 385; Wert, *Longstreet*, pp. 338–39. Bragg reported to Jefferson Davis that Longstreet's move constituted a "great relief to me." It was a relief to Longstreet also. No agreement was made as to whether Longstreet should return to the Army of Tennessee. See Longstreet, *From Manassas to Appomattox*, pp. 481–83.

51. Hallock, *Bragg*, vol. 2, p. 136; Livermore, *Numbers and Losses*, p. 107; Davis, *Breckinridge*, pp. 385, 387; McDonough, *Chattanooga*, pp. 25, 35.

52. Cozzens, *Shipwreck of Their Hopes*, p. 141; Davis, *Breckinridge*, p. 387; Hallock, *Bragg*, vol. 2, p. 137.

53. Craig L. Symonds, *Stonewall of the West: Patrick Cleburne and the Civil War* (Lawrence: University Press of Kansas, 1997), pp. 162–65; Cozzens, *Shipwreck of Their Hopes*, pp. 124, 128–33; Catton, *Grant Takes Command*, pp. 71–72; McDonough, *Chattanooga*, pp. 108–13; Holden Reid, "Grant and Rawlins," pp. 23–24.

54. McDonough, *Chattanooga*, pp. 113–14, 118–28; Cozzens, *Shipwreck of Their Hopes*, pp. 148–51, 154, 157, 241; even Marzalek, *Sherman*, pp. 243–45, seems too censorious.

55. Hallock, *Bragg*, vol. 2, pp. 132–34; Cozzens, *Shipwreck of Their Hopes*, pp. 162–63, 187.

56. Catton, *Grant Takes Command*, pp. 73–74; McDonough, *Chattanooga*, pp. 135–42.

57. Brooks D. Simpson, *Ulysses S. Grant: Triumph over Adversity, 1822–1865* (New York: Houghton Mifflin, 2000), p. 239; McDonough, *Chattanooga*, p. 142.

58. Symonds, *Cleburne*, pp. 167–69; Cleaves, *Rock of Chickamauga*, pp. 197–98; Cozzens, *Shipwreck of Their Hopes*, pp. 200–203, 218, 232; McDonough, *Chattanooga*, pp. 146–59; Woodworth, *Six Armies in Tennessee*, pp. 191–93.

59. McDonough, *Chattanooga*, pp. 162–63; Cozzens, *Shipwreck of Their Hopes*, pp. 245–48. Grant had been greatly annoyed by Granger's antics throughout the afternoon, and thereafter his military career entered terminal decline. After this campaign he never again commanded a formation in one of the important armies. See Ezra J. Warner, *Generals in Blue* (Baton Rouge: Louisiana State University Press, 1964, 1989), p. 181.

60. Catton, *Grant Takes Command*, pp. 79–85; Cleaves, *Rock of Chickamauga*, pp. 198–200; McDonough, *Chattanooga*, pp. 161–64.

61. McDonough, *Chattanooga*, pp. 165–67, 169; Cozzens, *Shipwreck of Their Hopes*, p. 268; Cadwallader, *Three Years with Grant*, p. 152.

62. McDonough, *Chattanooga*, pp. 171–75, 179–80; Cozzens, *Shipwreck of Their Hopes*, pp. 259–63.

63. Cozzens, *Shipwreck of Their Hopes*, pp. 269, 265, 282–83.

64. Ibid., pp. 290, 295, 301; McDonough, *Chattanooga*, p. 182.

65. Symonds, *Cleburne*, pp. 165–66; Hallock, *Bragg*, vol. 2, pp. 138–42; McDonough *Chattanooga*, p. 184, rightly points out that accounts of very long intervals in the Confederate line are often exaggerated.

66. Davis, *Breckinridge*, pp. 388–91, 393–96. Breckinridge was not, as Davis claims, "a moderate drinker" (p. 394); Woodworth, *Davis and His Generals*, pp. 250, 360–61n192; Hallock, *Bragg*, vol. 2, p. 147.

67. Cozzens, *Shipwreck of Their Hopes*, p. 346; Hallock, *Bragg*, vol. 2, pp. 149–45; William C. Davis, *Jefferson Davis*, p. 528.

68. Symonds, *Cleburne*, p. 170; Cozzens, *Shipwreck of Their Hopes*, pp. 337–42, 349–52; McDonough, *Chattanooga*, pp. 228–29; Livermore, *Numbers and Losses*, pp. 107–108.

69. Marvel, *Burnside*, pp. 302, 306, 307–309, 314, 317; Catton, *Grant Takes Command*, p. 88; Simpson, *Grant*, pp. 236, 242–43.

70. Grant, *Memoirs*, vol. 2, pp. 92–95; Marszalek, *Sherman*, p. 246; Douglas Southall Freeman, *Lee's Lieutenants* (New York: Scribner's, 1944), vol. 3, pp. 288–97.

71. Marszalek, *Sherman*, p. 246; Marvel, *Burnside*, pp. 522–33.

72. Hallock, *Bragg*, vol. 2, pp. 152–53; Catton, *Grant Takes Command*, pp. 93–100; Simpson, *Grant*, pp. 231, 239.

73. McDonough, *Chattanooga*, p. 230.

Chapter Eleven

HALFTIME

THE TRANSFORMATION OF A WAR

In his *English History 1914–1945* (1965), A. J. P. Taylor placed a chapter in the middle of the book where the author paused "for refreshment" and contemplated the general themes that influenced his account.[1] When considering a conflict of such broad sweep and tremendous scale as the Civil War it is appropriate to do likewise. Although not an exact halfway point, the autumn of 1863 does represent a natural break; fighting did not cease, but the great decisive campaigns did not resume for a further six months. The political and social forces that shaped the Civil War must now be brought into sharper focus. The nature and impact of any war, even one as destructive as the Civil War, cannot be measured by the sum of its military operations. Forces that operate beyond the battlefield are just as potent in framing strategy and military policy as the ceaseless engagements led by rival commanders in the field.

This chapter and the next will be concerned preeminently with the harnessing of resources and the way in which they were used. The deployment of military force in a democracy is a complex affair. In 1861–65 men and women had to be persuaded to support the war effort on both sides. Throughout these two chapters the concept of consent—or the withdrawal of consent—will be employed to underpin the discussion of the raising and deployment of armies. "On the battlefield or elsewhere," Peter Parish reminds us, "this was a highly individualistic society where individual initiative and commitment really mattered."[2] As well as reviewing what has already occurred, this chapter will look forward to cover developments that will have an impact on events considered in a successor book covering the years 1864–65.

Armies are just figments of the imagination without men. The size of armies cannot be estimated unless commanders and their staffs have a clear idea of the size of the military tasks they are going to be set by political leaders, and the potential duration of the war. The political leadership must be willing to sanction the former and demonstrate toughness of fiber should the contest be prolonged. The entire problem of organizing armies either to subdue the Confederacy or gain Southern independence was complicated (or confused) by the widespread assumption that the war would be short. Huge efforts and expense were required to put in place armies of sufficient size and power to secure victory for either side.

The American military tradition rested on a profound hostility to standing armies and an elevation of the status of the nonregular. Free men would zealously protect their liberties; the self-government of individuals, communities, and the volunteer military forces they raised, lay at the very heart of the American concept of liberty. Consequently, the American military tradition conferred on the white, male population an obligation to undertake military service; yet it failed to create any central, institutional machinery to coordinate and administer it. The organization of militia forces was the business of the separate states. It was not unusual for militia organization to be subject to individual whims or even entrepreneurial initiatives. An informal approach to military structures was a basic and powerful ingredient of American democracy; it rendered any imposition of a centralized form of conscription during the Civil War both a political impossibility and counterproductive because it would dissuade men from coming forward to join the colors if they suspected any central authority of attempting to prune their liberties for administrative convenience.[3]

Nevertheless, should the military tasks facing both the Union and Confederacy be so great that armies would have to be raised by other, more draconian means, then the existing system could not be set aside—its deficiencies would have to be demonstrated. As Secretary of State William H. Seward admitted, if some form of draft was considered necessary the need would have to be demonstrated, "we . . . first prove it is so, by trying the old way."[4]

Authority to call forth militia forces could be sought in the Militia Act of 1792. The power was placed in the hands of the state governors. The militia, composed of white men aged eighteen to forty-five, were organized into companies; only the governors were empowered to bring them together into larger units. In a second militia act three years later, the president was permitted (with the permission of state legislatures, or governors if legislatures were not in session) to bring the militia into federal service for three months every year.[5]

During the first half of the nineteenth century a distinction gained strength between the "common" or "beat" militia (in which military service was obligatory) and the volunteers (who chose to serve and were generally much keener). Volunteers were sometimes given militia designations, but they selected their own uniforms and arranged their own organization and training; they often elected their own officers and noncommissioned officers. Such volunteer units could be socially exclusive. By 1840 the great majority of volunteer regiments had been incorporated into the militia—indeed confirmed as the effective militia of the states. The volunteer system was most highly developed in the North, especially in Massachusetts.[6]

The raising of Civil War armies depended on a similar dual system of regulars and volunteers. Local officials called for volunteers, and if insufficient numbers came forward, they were empowered to draft or impress men. In 1846 on the outbreak of the Mexican War, rather than use existing militia units Congress attempted both to enlarge the regular army and volunteers simultaneously. It failed to reach its quota for the regulars, but enthusiasm to join fresh volunteers units was buoyant. Congress gave the authority for 50,000 volunteers to serve for twelve months or for the duration of the war, supposedly at the president's discretion. Actually, 73,532 men served in units outside the regular army. The president was also empowered to call the militia into federal service for six rather than three months. But many anticipated that the military operations would be on Mexican soil, and the common militia could not be employed beyond the borders of the United States; hence the necessity for new volunteer units. Volunteers were organized according to the militia laws of the various states. Despite the acknowledgment of presidential authority, the incumbent, James K. Polk, committed an error in delegating to the states the option of enlisting for twelve months or for the duration of the war.[7]

The powers to raise troops inherited by the Lincoln administration in the spring of 1861 were diffuse and poorly coordinated. In the closing months of James Buchanan's administration, an effort was made to expand the clauses of the 1795 Militia Act so that it covered "insurrections." Buchanan warned that, as it stood, the militia could only assist a US marshal to execute the due process of law and "disperse hostile combinations." It could not be used to suppress rebellion. The case was debated in Congress but not put to the vote. When the Civil War broke out in April, Lincoln's proclamation calling for seventy-five thousand volunteers for three months represented his correct, legal, but incredibly limited entitlement to call volunteers into federal service while Congress was not in session. Those who criticize this act for its pitiful inadequacy overlook the traditional subordination of the executive to Congress in this distribution of the war powers.[8]

Lincoln called Congress into special session on July 4, 1861, but he could not afford to wait nearly three months before federal military power was mobilized to crush the Confederacy. On his own responsibility, he took the unprecedented step of organizing an army and paying for its armament without the sanction of Congress. Lincoln justified this strictly unconstitutional behavior by virtue of the war powers conferred on him by the Constitution as commander-in-chief of the army and navy. The first wave of three-month volunteers was reinforced by a further forty-three thousand in 40 regiments, who had signed on for three years. By July 1 three hundred thousand men had been raised for a total of 208 regiments, including the previous 40. Some sentiment had been expressed calling for a draft, but this had been drowned out by the hubbub generated by a patriotic zeal to volunteer.[9]

By comparison with previous American armies, the initial waves of Northern volunteering had been large. The stress throughout the Union's recruiting process had been on the individual's willingness to volunteer—reflecting the egalitarian ethos of the society from whence the recruits came. Patriotic sentiment was reinforced by a number of financial and other inducements. These offers—or bounties—were designed to counteract a diminution in volunteering experienced after the summer of 1862 and especially after May 1864. They had their origins in the colonial period. During the American Revolution bounties had been paid if men volunteered to serve in the Continental Army, plus a promise of one hundred acres of land after the war had been won. Such inducements were, in effect, a bonus either pecuniary or in kind. For example, those who volunteered for three years received a hundred-dollar bounty on discharge. Bounties were often supplemented by state committees who supplied soldiers with home comforts—quilts, socks, dried fruit, and the like. Soldiers' pay might be supplemented. For instance, Wisconsin paid an extra fifteen dollars per month to those with dependents. Vermont and New Jersey similarly paid an extra seven and six dollars respectively.[10]

The bounty system led to widespread abuses after the summer of 1862 because an alteration was made whereby the bounty was received on joining the colors. "Bounty jumpers," who received their cash and then deserted to be paid to join up again, excited much scorn. One managed to desert and be paid thirty times before he was arrested and shot. Such a mercenary attitude was a product of Union setbacks in the summers of both 1861 and 1862. Widespread denunciation in the newspapers of abuses of the system discouraged recruiting and encouraged a desire to be recompensed for the dangers, discomfort, and inconvenience of soldiering. Altogether, three hundred million dollars were lavished on the bounty system (equal to the total pay of the Union army or five times the cost of its ordnance).

Manpower shortages were accentuated by the impulsive decision of the secretary of war, Edwin M. Stanton, in General Order No. 33, to close all recruiting offices on April 3, 1862. Stanton's order represented an excessive confidence in imminent victory. When the War Department realized that recruiting would have to continue, the states were asked to take up the burden; but Stanton stamped the authority of the national government on the system by coordinating the process tightly and setting the states strict quotas. Previously the governors had suggested the administration had not asked them to do enough; after the spring of 1862 they moaned that they were doing too much—but the balance of power had shifted away from the states to the federal government.[11]

Ulysses S. Grant might well have been right when he complained that because of the bounty system the Union army only received 20 percent of all men recruited. Nonetheless confidence in it remained undiminished because the US Treasury preferred not to raise pay overall, and was satisfied that local communities bore a greater proportion of the cost. Periodic financial difficulties encouraged the treasury to defer payments to the troops as frequently as possible. Soldiers' families thus came to depend very heavily on state bounties.[12]

Despite the criticisms directed at the system of volunteering, legislators in Washington, DC, led by Senator Henry Wilson, chairman of the Senate Military Affairs Committee, resolved to stand by the traditional ways. The Militia Act of July 1862 was designed to give the federal government power to order a draft in states where the militia system was working inefficiently. It required the enrollment of all male citizens aged eighteen to forty-five for future draft calls made by their state governors. The levies were calculated according to the population of the states. Further, Lincoln was granted authority to call the militia into federal service for nine months. This militia act also attempted to guarantee black emancipation in exchange for service (as laborers) in the Union army, but opposition to manumission delayed the passage of the act.

Wilson made little effort to eradicate the weaknesses of the existing system of raising troops or outrage the opinion of those who cherished the principle of individual volunteering. Persuading more men to consent to volunteer counted more with him. In this act the relationship between the chief executive and the war governors remained ill defined. It was quite unclear when the president enjoyed authority to interfere in the affairs of individual states and could override the authority of the governor.[13]

The need for more men after the failure in the Peninsular campaign awakened calls for a draft. Both Democratic and Republican newspapers believed this would enable the Lincoln administration to wage war "in earnest." On August 4, 1862, Stanton issued a call for a further 300,000 volunteers to be drawn from the militia. His action duplicated an earlier call made on July 1, 1862, also for 300,000 volunteers. Confusion resulted because the July 1 call asked for men to serve three years while that of August could only ask militiamen to serve nine months. Consequently, the troops raised only amounted to the equivalent of 375,000 three-year men. The federal government then raised the total figure to 669,670 for both calls. Amid a sea of administrative confusion, the total numbers raised amounted to 87,588 nine-month men and 421,465 three-year men— a total of 509,053 that still remained far below the total stipulated by the initial calls. A tension had thus developed between the demands of a long war and the reluctance to coerce citizens into offering their services to fight it.[14]

The problems faced by the Confederacy in raising—and sustaining, often a more difficult task—sizeable field armies resembled the Union's both in degree and in kind. In contrast to the stress often placed in older accounts on the constraints imposed by localism and states' rights, the Confederacy revealed in its preparations for war a tendency toward centralization and national planning. The Confederacy would certainly start by advancing boldly. It would create powerful organizations and then, alarmed by what had been created, scurry back down the track, qualifying the authority of this central agency. So it was with manpower. The original Confederate armies raised in 1861 were predominantly composed of one-year volunteers. They had been authorized by the Confederate congress but controlled by the states. After a series of setbacks in the early months of 1862, not least the fall of forts Henry and Donelson and the loss of New Orleans, the Confederacy faced the dissolution of its armies. Agitation for the draft became more vocal; volunteering slowed and men who did come forward showed a disinclination to sign on for three years even though they enjoyed the privilege of electing their own officers. In March 1862, 148 regiments were due to dissolve within thirty days.[15] Disaster loomed.

The Confederate secretary of war, George W. Randolph (supported by the president's military adviser, Robert E. Lee), believed that some form of conscription was the only method whereby the Confederacy's armies could be sustained. "Despotism is the soul of efficient military organization," opined one colonel, "and our people must be made to feel that the whole country needs their services as soldiers, they must temporarily submit to absolute discipline, as a part of the price of permanent civil liberty."[16] The argument that any accretion of central authority would be temporary grew in persuasiveness.

The result was the first Conscription Act of April 16, 1862. It was not only the first Confederate but the first national conscription act in American history. Seemingly eager to enhance the power of the Confederate government, the law made available all able-bodied white men aged eighteen to thirty-five for a three-year period of military service unless they could gain an exemption. The act also prohibited those already in the Confederate army from leaving; volunteers were allowed a thirty-day period of grace to take their place in the ranks and enjoy the privilege of electing their officers (the act assumed that many would wish to escape the taint of being drafted). No commutation fees were permitted. The whole process was coordinated by a bureau of conscription that was empowered to release men from military service even if they had been drafted, and direct their skills to the areas of the war economy where they were needed.[17]

The Confederacy might have taken a determined step forward in bringing some central direction to the management of war resources, but it took two steps back with the two exemption acts that followed on April 21 and October 11, 1862. Although these were supposed to be based on the importance of certain occupations to the war effort (pharmacists, miners, foundry workers, and those involved with cotton and wool), they gave the impression of favoring the upper classes. Men supervising twenty or more slaves were also excused from military duty. This provision was justified on the grounds of being able "to secure the proper police of the country"; but it gave rise to the virulent Southern claim that the Civil War amounted to "a rich man's war and a poor man's fight." The number of slaveowners exempted was fairly small (but it was a high proportion of a given class): 200 in Virginia, 120 in North Carolina, 301 in South Carolina, and 201 in Georgia. The payment of substitutes was also permitted, which lent further evidence to support the view that the First Conscription Act favored the wealthy. The Confederacy lacked the money to pay lavish bounties to encourage volunteers to join the colors (although it did pay ten dollars to permit volunteers to travel to their assembly camps).

Pressure developed immediately to reduce the number of exemptions. A favorite "dodge" was to set up a "drug store" at a convenient point on the road-side stocked with several boxes of castor oil, hair restorer, and bogus pills, and thus claim an apothecary's exemption. On December 28, 1863, and January 5, 1864, the Confederate congress abolished the right to pay a substitute. In 1864 the number of exemptions were halved in number. The Second (September 1862) and Third (February 1864) Conscription Acts extended the age of those liable to be conscripted first to forty-five and then to between seventeen and fifty. The number of Confederate soldiers enlisted through conscription num-bered 82,000 or 10.9 percent of the total. The Confederacy had access to approx-imately 1,140,000 men of military age. Of these about 750,000 served in the Confederate army. Its strength reached a zenith in June 1863 when 261,000 men were present for duty. As in the North, the overwhelming majority, 78.9 percent, were volunteers; but unlike the North, the number of foreign-born sol-diers was negligible. After the summer of 1863 the manpower pool of the Con-federacy dried up much more drastically and quickly than the resources avail-able to the Union.[18]

Despite the formal adoption of centralized powers, the attitude of the majority of Southern politicians to conscription was ambivalent. If they had favored conscription more wholeheartedly they might have forged a more effi-cient, less divisive system. Although most agreed on the need to deploy "heavy battalions," and thus "necessity" demanded intrusive laws, Confederate nation-alism was equated with constitutional purity and therefore self-conscious patriots tended to denounce conscription, or condemn it with faint praise. The governor of Virginia, John Letcher, believed it an "alarming" development, but "harmony, unity and conciliation are indispensable to success just now." The spokesmen for states' rights, especially Governor Joseph E. Brown of Georgia, denounced conscription; but they were by no means as obstructive to the cen-tral war effort as sometimes depicted later, although often inconsistent and exas-perating to Jefferson Davis. Brown improved the quality of Georgia's militia and dispatched a division drawn from it to the Army of Tennessee.

A widespread dedication to individual, traditional liberty was too strong for even the supporters of the Davis administration to make a positive virtue out of embracing, however reluctantly, the principle of conscription. Conversely, in the propaganda war the Confederacy's speed in adopting a limited form of con-scription undercut efforts to present itself as the guardian of pristine, constitu-tional liberty.[19]

The Confederacy's political and cultural heritage might have prevented it from making the most effective use of conscription, but the failure of the Union to win the war in the summer of 1862 forced it, even more unwillingly, to tread a similar road. The North, too, resorted to a limited form of conscription. In a renewed effort to revitalize volunteering, Congress passed the Enrollment Act on March 3, 1863. The main idea behind this legislation required the enrollment of all male citizens aged twenty to forty-five as eligible for the draft (including those foreigners who intended to seek citizenship). They were divided into two classes; first, those aged twenty to thirty-five were to be drafted before the second category, men aged thirty-six to forty-five. The Enrollment Act granted to "the national government" authority to "raise and support armies" without state involvement.[20]

The draft itself was a simple mechanism whereby all eligible names were written on slips of paper and placed in a mixing container. They were plucked out at random by a blindfolded citizen of good character. Indeed, Utica, New York, took the precaution of entrusting this duty to a blind man, blindfolded. The whole process resembled a lottery. All draft legislation had permitted exemptions, and the 1863 Act was no exception. The numbers allowed were fewer than the First Confederate Conscription Act and were restricted to government employees (including customs clerks, postmasters, and transport workers); exemptions were also granted to men who supported families, the physically infirm, and the mentally ill. Substitutes could be presented or a commutation fee of three hundred dollars paid in lieu of service; but men could not plead their case for exemption until they had answered the draft call.[21]

Under the Militia Act of July 1863, the provost marshals of each state were responsible for the pursuit and arrest of deserters and for deciding who was exempt. The 1863 Enrollment Act attempted to reduce the intrusion of state authority in ensuring that drafted men serve; it was to be replaced by federal authority. A federal provost marshal's bureau was set up run by the provost marshal general; he carried the responsibility for enforcing the draft. The post was given to Colonel James W. Fry, a zealous and diligent officer. He directed provost marshals in every congressional district to enforce the draft and arrest both evaders and deserters. In effect, these federal officials slowly but surely replaced the existing state authorities in an effort to increase the flow of men into the Union army.[22]

Exemptions led to abuses and efforts to juggle the system in the favor of individuals. A professional class of brokers grew up who found substitutes and those willing to fill quotas set by a state government by bringing in men from poorer areas attracted by bounties. Poorer areas were forced to draw more frequently upon their numbers of physically fit men than the more prosperous because they could not afford to pay commutation fees or provide substitutes. In 1865 the governor of Ohio, John Brough, criticized the federal government for failing to establish a residency requirement and tolerating inequitable local bounties. Certainly local businesses throughout the North became vocal supporters of the draft as they wearied of paying state taxes needed to finance bounties. The cost of bounties and exemptions escalated after July 1864.[23]

This informal, contradictory, and often ramshackle system of raising armies —one that reflects a society dedicated to laissez faire—led to widespread draft evasion. Clever and numerous means of deception bamboozled the officials who were responsible for listing all the men eligible for the draft; these often took the opportunity to ensure that their own names were omitted from the lists; they were open to bribes to remove the names of others. The 1863 Enrollment Act provoked a stampede for federal political appointments such as postmasterships. The greatest ingenuity was employed against doctors responsible for verifying the health of draftees. Deafness, bad backs, and game knees were examined in profusion; some members of the medical profession appeared open to financial inducement to provide exemption certificates.[24]

Resistance to the federal draft stiffened in the spring of 1863. Ever greater levels of violence and abuse were encountered by the provost marshals. Some draftees fled to Canada. Unscrupulous agents of substitute brokers were not averse to crossing the Canadian border, drugging or getting British soldiers drunk, and hurriedly transporting them back to the US to enlist them in the Union army while they were still unconscious.[25]

The number of federal draft evaders has been estimated as large as 161,244; perhaps 40,000 to 50,000 evaded the state authorities before 1863. Governor Buckingham of Connecticut was excoriated for sending his two sons abroad to escape the draft. In general, governors were disinclined to interfere with local customs, traditions, and usage, or trample upon treasured liberties. Even the mild provisions of the July 1862 Militia Act were challenged in the Wisconsin state courts. The much greater coercive power embodied in the 1863 Enrollment Act provoked far more ferocious resistance.[26]

By far the most significant act of resistance against the expansion of federal authority occurred during the New York City draft riots, July 13–17, 1863. This extraordinary outburst of urban violence (that left several hundred dead and many more injured) represented much more than just a tumultuous rejection of the draft. It enshrined widespread revulsion by Democrats against the Republican Party's objectives and the social upheavals unleashed by the Civil War (not the least, emancipation); the insurrection took the form of a strike as well as riots: factories were closed and lines of communication (railroads, streetcar tracks, and telegraph lines) damaged. By threatening ferries and bridges the rioters attempted to take control of the entire city rather than only ethnic neighborhoods. The New York City draft riots were a far more complex conflagration than antebellum urban violence directed mainly against blacks.[27]

Even so, there were important links with pre-1861 attitudes. First, abolitionists were associated with outsiders, seen as dangers to the community, and subject somehow to "foreign" influences. In 1856 the rise of the Republican Party had provoked hysterical outbursts of violence, mainly in the South. Seven years later, pro-Confederate, anti-Republican antagonisms triggered off rioting in New York City. In short, Republican efforts to improve the draft levy brought together a whole series of anxieties about Republicans governing the country and what might happen if Republicans extended their authority into the Democrats' bastion of New York City. Their reactions ignited a most violent response.[28]

In the winter of 1862–63, opposition to the draft in Maryland, Wisconsin, and Pennsylvania probably delayed the extension of the draft to New York State. Discontent was exacerbated by whispers of the terrible carnage on the battlefields and complaints about irregular pay; 1863 was a time of full employment and high wages. The disappointing conduct of the war in the east and the efforts to maintain a substantial field army at a time of poor morale allowed Democrats to raise the political issue of the basic competence of the Lincoln administration and the legitimacy of Republican policies—especially on emancipation. Critics of the president and the Republican Party hurled the wild accusation of "dictatorship" at their political rivals. Democrats expressed a fear that the creation of the Provost Marshal's Bureau would neuter Democrat state governments. The recruitment machinery of 1861–62 had grown out of the mechanisms of the Republican Party (which were more highly developed than the administrative machinery of the federal government). Democrats feared that efforts to enforce the draft would lead to the persecution of Democratic critics of the war in the name of extirpating "treason." To some it appeared that a threat was posed to the very survival of the Democratic Party, summoning up the specter of one-party dominance. In hindsight these threats seemed contrived and unrealistic, but many Democrats gave credence to them.[29]

There was also an important social aspect. The 1863 Enrollment Act permitted the federal government to interfere in unprecedented ways in both the workplaces and homes of the prosperous working class. It intensified three controversial issues within New York City. First, relations worsened between the wealthy and the poor, between blacks and whites, and between city and nation.

The three-hundred-dollar commutation fee, in particular, excited criticism by appearing to favor the wealthy. Democratic critics claimed that it served as a crude Republican device to load the burdens of war on the backs of the poor. Fears surfaced that whites would face competition for work from freed slaves encouraged to migrate to the North. The "laboring classes," it was reported, believed their status was diminished by the draft. "[T]hey say that they are sold for $300 whilst they pay $1000 for [N]egroes." New York's Democratic politicians, like Governor Horatio Seymour, were alert to the worries of their constituents. In words that later could be used to question his devotion to the Union, Seymour stated that he would not enforce the draft.[30]

The early months of 1863 witnessed a rise in the influence of peace Democrats in New York State, reaching its peak in June. Nonetheless, President Lincoln remained confident that he "apprehends nothing from the Peace Party"— even as Lee's invasion of Pennsylvania reached its climax. In May and June preparations for the draft went ahead; on July 6 Colonel Fry received notification that the lotteries were ready to begin the allocation of names. The populace over the next few days—especially in New York's uptown tenement districts— realized that the city's politicians had failed to protect them from federal authority. Seymour and other spokesmen warned of the threat of mob violence, but the outbreaks that ensued were spontaneous, not preplanned. An anxious air of crisis brewed over the weekend of July 10–11.[31]

Like other insurrections, the New York City draft riots moved through different phases and expressed different layers of distress as different groups of rioters with different grievances moved against shifting targets. The violence erupted suddenly on July 13 after a crowd assembled in Central Park carrying "No Draft" placards. They were joined by groups from other parts of the city: private and federal property was plundered and set ablaze, police officers were assaulted, and Horace Greeley and leaders of the New York *Tribune* were threatened. Even women were prominent in the tumult and used crowbars to pull up streetcar tracks. Firemen were conspicuous in the crowds on the first day, but withdrew their support and worked against the mob thereafter.

As the violence escalated, the racial assaults on the city's blacks proliferated. The supposed revolution in race relations promoted by the Republican Party received a symbolic rejection in a welter of lynchings and mutilations. Stanton was urged not to send a black regiment, the 55th Massachusetts, to the city. Many rioters were under eighteen and thus not eligible for the draft. Extortion was commonplace and crossed ethnic lines. Irish rioters attacked German and Jewish shops. The New York police despaired of preventing the mobs from seizing weapons in a temporary arms factory; women were "very desperate," attacking the police with clubs and stones. A company of the 12th US Regular Infantry only drove the mob back by firing repeated volleys into the mass swirling about the streets.[32]

The insurrection came to an end at last with the arrival of three regiments from Gettysburg, amounting to six thousand veteran troops. Throughout the violence the police rather than the army were targets, as they were regarded as Republican lackeys. The police superintendent, John A. Kennedy, had been appointed as a special provost marshal; he was badly beaten up on the first day.[33]

The New York City draft riots fall naturally into two phases. The first was dominated by the antidraft demonstrations; the second involved rioters of far greater violent (even anarchic) intent who sought out any evidence of a Republican presence and attempted to destroy it. The great majority of the rioters were not the dregs of the slums, vagrants, thieves, or drunks. They were usually prosperous members of the working class, artisans, and industrial workers.[34] They were diverse anti-Republican groups who represented what historian Iver Bernstein labels "a fractured and unstable political order." The war, far from releasing a uniform patriotic response to its utility, had instead thrown up divergent and combustible attitudes. This can be observed in the ambivalent response of the most prosperous citizens to the disorders. Conservative Democrats (fearful of emancipation) assumed a benign attitude and opposed any declaration of martial law. Republicans, although more sympathetic to the plight of the working class, took a much more severe view: they denounced the rioters and called for stern measures to suppress them, including the use of troops. In the event, the violence was suppressed without recourse to martial law—but at a price. A leading war Democrat and former member of President James Buchanan's cabinet, John A. Dix, was appointed to command the Department of the East. New York City remained a Democratic bastion.[35]

The draft riots revealed, although fleetingly, the true extent of Democratic and ethnic dissatisfaction with the war. It indicated a measure of weakness that the Confederates could have exploited if they had been more proficient at propaganda, subversion, and diplomacy. If the Union's conduct of the Civil War in the last resort depended on the consent of the populace, then the months between November 1862 and July 1863 indicate that a significant minority did not proffer their consent. They did not necessarily withdraw it in the sense that they openly sympathized with the Confederacy, but substantial groups took the view that the conduct of the war and the Republican leadership were antipathetic to them. The peace Democrats profited not at all from the riots because they were associated with sedition. The lack of consent extended to soldiers in the ranks. During the winter of 1862–63, the Union army sustained one hundred thousand desertions, amounting to several hundred every day. The problem was worsened by the simultaneous attractions of the bounty system and the failure of the US Treasury to find the money to pay the troops.[36]

Despite all these difficulties and ructions, it should be remembered that the Enrollment Act had been designed to resuscitate volunteering; draftees were, in any case, the object of scorn and ridicule from volunteers. As a means of raising troops the draft was inefficient. The quotas consequently were raised higher (sometimes by as much as 50 percent) in an effort to get the men needed; these were based on an estimate of the number of men available rather than the numbers of physically qualified men. In July 1864 Congress doubled the size of the quotas. If the numbers summoned were considerable so were the groups excused from duty. In 1863 65 percent were released; some 88,171 were inducted into federal service, but of these 52,288 paid the commutation fee, and 26,002 provided substitutes. In all, only 9,881 were conscripted from the 292,441 names called in the draft.[37]

A total of 2,690,401 men served in the Union army during the Civil War, although not all at the same time or for the same periods of time. Of this host, 86,724 paid the commutation fee, so that 1,261,567 served in the ranks. The potential military strength of the North numbered about 4,500,000 white men of military age. So the number available for the draft can be estimated at 2,250,000, but many of these names failed to be drawn. Of the fighting troops, just under 75 percent were volunteers, 13.02 percent entered the ranks via the draft (9.35 percent were substitutes and only 3.67 percent federal conscripts). The remaining 12 percent were black troops, whose contribution will be considered in the next chapter. The chances of being conscripted, despite the exertions invested in getting draftees into the service, were only one in a hundred. One quarter of the Union army consisted of recent immigrants; but as these formed 30 percent of the antebellum population, contrary to the impression often given in some Southern accounts, immigrants were *underrepresented*. German Protestants showed greatest keenness to fight, German and Irish Catholics rather less; the latter were at the forefront of the New York City draft riots, while the Germans sought to protect private property.[38]

Due to a reluctance to volunteer or a frantic desire to evade the draft, the Union army faced real problems meeting its commitments after the summer of 1863. The numbers of men needed to sustain its gigantic war effort were huge and the draft system failed to furnish them. The majority of the men already in the military system were enthusiastic to continue the war until final victory. The problem lay in consolidating and reinforcing numbers of veteran troops. This perspective contrasts sharply with the view propounded in so many Confederate accounts that they were overwhelmed by Union "hosts" or "hordes." The Confederates were outnumbered, but the margin was not that great. In the winter of 1864–65 Grant took the calculated risk that he could win the war by the spring of 1865 with the existing system. On February 24, 1865, the payment of a commutation fee was abolished—a measure of the dwindling pool of manpower that could be tapped by the provost marshal general.[39]

In any war the heroism, stoicism, and self-sacrifice found in some can always be matched by the selfish "skulking" of those who are prepared to let others pay the necessary costs; the Civil War is no exception. Men evaded the draft for a variety of reasons, some because of political beliefs, suspicion, and hatred of the Republican Party; revulsion at the consequences of slavery emancipation; a basic lack of patriotism and a tendency to allow private concerns to outweigh national ones; finally, rank cowardice should not be forgotten: "In a world of petty conning and compromise and calculation, of often grossly self-serving self-righteousness and sentimentality," as David Grimsted describes mid-nineteenth-century America, we should not be surprised if large numbers—certainly, a sizeable minority—made a supreme effort to ensure the safety of their own skins.[40]

The constraints on Union and Confederate manpower help explain, despite an initial outburst of enthusiasm and a large population, why the armies of the Civil War were considerably smaller than European conscripted armies in the same period. The Prussian and Austrian central state authorities were more capable of putting men into their armies than the US in the 1860s. Certainly, Prussian and Austrian authorities functioned in nations that were smaller *geographically* than the US. In the American Civil War, the multiplicity of small commands maintained for political reasons, the duration and intensity of the conflict, plus the need to garrison a huge theater of war, all contributed to a diffusion of federal military strength. The largest Union force raised in the Civil War was the Army of the Potomac before the Chancellorsville campaign— 130,000 men in April 1863. By their failure to concentrate overwhelming resources at the decisive point both North and South placed a ceiling on the size of Civil War armies. Compare the Army of the Potomac with the Prussian and Austrian armies in the War of 1866. Admittedly, this was a much smaller theater of war, but the Prussian chief of the general staff, Helmuth von Moltke, achieved a local superiority with a field army totaling 254,000 men; the Austrian *Feldzugmeister*, Ludwig Benedek, deployed 245,000. In July 1866, 500,000

men were crowded onto the battlefield of Konnigrätz. For all the absolute numbers raised over four years, the American system could not sustain individual
armies of this size.[41]

It was not just a matter of replacing battle casualties. One half of the casualties during the Civil War, some three hundred thousand men, died of disease.
A system based on a combination of volunteering and the draft, but still permitted an individual a fair measure of choice as to whether he served or not,
could not cope with such high levels of wastage. As a result, armies of a quarter
of a million or more were out of the question.

Union armies might have been harnessed imperfectly but it is important to
emphasize that the majority of troops not only consented to serve enthusiastically, but supported an expansion of the destructive methods believed necessary
to destroy the Confederacy. A measure of this opinion was indicated by the proportions of three-year volunteers who decided to reenlist in March 1864. The
danger to the Union army was mortal: 455 out of a total of 956 infantry regiments, and 81 of the 158 volunteer batteries had every right to dissolve themselves. A number of incentives were offered if men reenlisted (a four-hundred-
dollar bounty, plus bonuses paid by local communities, a thirty-day furlough,
and the distinction of being called a "veteran volunteer"). More than 136,000
veterans reenlisted, partly because they found the inducements attractive, but
mainly because they wished to see the Confederacy defeated. Only 50 percent of
those whose time had expired agreed to reenlist for service in the Army of the
Potomac, some 26,000 men; but even these figures were thought hopeful. A
large slice of the army had made it clear that the troops would stick with the
cause and not abandon it.[42]

Some Northern politicians had been convinced since the beginning of the
Civil War that the men were more bellicose and determined than their commanders, that they were more resolute in the search for victory; the strength of
these 1864 reenlistments seem to bear these opinions out. The main reason for
the mighty escalation of war in thought and deed in 1863–64 is to be found in
the survival of the Confederacy after more than two years of war. The failure of
Union generals to bring about a rapid dissolution of the Confederacy allowed
the voices of those calling for more "vigorous" or "earnest" methods of warmaking to become more strident. Calls for "conciliation" became less influential
—and indeed less persuasive.[43]

Northern supporters of the war effort did not doubt that they were servants
of a just cause. Lawyers of the Roman Catholic Church's canon law had, since
medieval times, distinguished between a *jus ad bellum* (justified resort to war)

and *jus in bello* (just conduct of the war itself). A just cause would include response to flagrant, predatory aggression (an act of self-defense), but the protection of rights by offensive action was also sanctioned. Both sides in the Civil War sought to gain a moral advantage by claiming that they were acting defensively. The difficulty for both sides lay in Clausewitz's reminder that the conqueror always wishes to gain his objective without resistance. If both sides wished to enhance their strategic position and secure their objectives, some kind of offensive was required either to resist Southern insurgency or remove Northern troops from Southern soil.[44]

The just war tradition demanded, however, that the means must be proportionate to meet the desired end. As the first major war of the Industrial Revolution, one that unleashed immense destructive power and social dislocation, the Civil War signified an important step forward in the evolution of views about the nature of a just war in a democracy. The latter feature was significant because the Civil War was "a people's war" of opposing values. It involved mass participation. The war could not be waged, let alone won, unless it engaged widespread support and embraced the aspirations of a majority. Extensive literacy, universal white male suffrage, political awareness, as well as participation in the fighting itself, were important catalysts working on the expanding scope of warmaking, both in the North and the South.[45]

The frustrations of 1862–63 began a transformation in Northern attitudes to the war's conduct. Prior to the winter the war had often been justified as a just, defensive conflict waged reluctantly to preserve the legacy of the Founding Fathers. By 1863 the series of defeats and disappointments led many to argue that the war presented a God-given chance to regenerate, purify, and reorder the republic; wartime politicians, and the Republican voice rose most stridently here, could atone for the failures of Democrats before 1861. The view that the indecisiveness of the Civil War offered a chance to move the Union effort in an entirely new direction was put most frankly by Republican Senator Charles Sumner. "I fear more from our victories than from our defeats," he admitted in July 1862 to John Bright. "If the Rebellion should suddenly collapse," he predicted to Bright a year later, "democrats, copperheads, and Seward would insist upon amnesty and the Union, and 'no question asked about slavery.' God save us from any such calamity."[46]

The human suffering and cost of the war failed to agitate the imagination of the self-absorbed Sumner. Nevertheless, some kind of future radical change or improvement to the social order seemed to be sanctioned by the widespread need to justify the enormous loss in life. A justification could only be convincing if the limited objectives that had gained sway during the summer of 1862 were rejected, not least the insistence that the war should be waged to preserve the Union. The rising levels of destructiveness were tolerated in order to demonstrate that the great sacrifice had not been made in vain. The war would thus transcend self-imposed restraints, for the escalation could be justified by great ends. If the war was pursued solely for limited ends, while the Union stumbled and then gave up on failing to attain them, then the sacrifice would indeed have been made in vain. The greater effort needed to attain more ambitious goals of social reconstruction could be used to validate the huge human and material loss.[47]

In justifying a conflict that was transformed into a crusade against slavery, Protestant language and imagery grew in importance; 1862 was the crucial year in the transformation. The Congressional Crittenden-Johnson Resolutions of July 22 envisaged a strictly limited conflict based on a controlled use of military force. A fear of incipient anarchy urged many influential voices to endorse this view. A. L. Peabody, professor of Christian morals at Harvard University, defended the view that the war should take the form of "a grand police movement for the suppression of multitudinous crime" justified by criminal acts. It would resemble any action requiring the "apprehending [of] burglars or murderers, at the risk of their lives if they make violent resistance."[48]

Until the summer of 1862 the federal War Department pursued a policy of protecting Southern private property and individual constitutional rights. The autumn signaled a change of emphasis, especially in the west. During operations in Kentucky, Braxton Bragg's troops lived off the country. The Confederates were able to move rapidly while Don Carlos Buell's Union columns plodded along slowly masking their long wagon trains. Union forces later attempted to imitate the Confederate example, contrary to the usual image that presents the South as the innocent victim of Unionist ravaging.[49]

Southern hotheadedness and belligerence helped contribute to a combustible atmosphere that eventually ignited a chain of events that justified greater destructiveness. A notion had always lurked behind the emphasis on rational and limited objectives that claimed a righteous war carried forward God's work: the war was an instrument of divine progress. Arguments could be heard that claimed that the surgery made possible by the war would only have a permanent effect on a healthy national body; tumors that had previously afflicted national health should be cut away. Therefore the defense of American freedom and the destruction of all the vestiges of the "slave power" were providential tasks. Evangelical Protestantism influenced the shape and language of such thought. In the redemption of the Union, civil and religious liberty became indistinguishable.

Christian leaders in the North acquiesced, as Peter J. Parish has observed, "with a surprising degree of equanimity in the relentless march" of Northern armies toward victory gained by ferocious, ruthless methods. These were based first on "military necessity," the destruction of civilian property which denied Southern armies the sustenance needed to keep them in the field; second, psychological warfare that eroded morale; and third, the South bore the collective responsibility for starting the war and should be punished for it—the Confederacy deserved its suffering. These methods occasionally provoked criticism, but this grew out of politico-military calculation rather than from genuine ethical doubts. Northern clerics and intellectuals were altogether more robust than McClellan and his acolytes in their attitude toward the use of punitive methods.[50]

Explanations of earlier Union defeats stressed that they were God's punishment for American sins: luxury, idleness, self-indulgence, intemperance, apostasy, but above all else indifference in the face of the spread of slavery in a freedom-loving country. The setbacks were designed to prod the doubters to free the slaves and raise regiments of black troops. Eventually skeptics came to accept the force of this argument because it extended the principle of the just war. When a measure of consensus among Northern opinion came to the conclusion that a just reordering of the Union—without slavery—required the military subjugation of the South and the dismantling of its social system, then a more brutal form of war was not only fitting, but just; for the writ of the Constitution could not be restored without such drastic action.[51]

Such a perspective could be supported by technical military authorities. James Kent's *Commentaries on American Law* (1826), a work devoured by William T. Sherman, argued that retaliation could be sanctioned as a means of restraining a belligerent enemy and enforce obedience to the law. Sherman held unswervingly that obedience to the law provided the only way to mitigate the horrors of war. Dennis Hart Mahan, a leading military writer (if a thinker of limited range and vision) held in the 1830s that the only way to defeat the Seminoles in Florida was by the destruction of their food supplies.

By 1863 such an idea had been developed by those, like Sherman, who argued that Northern casualties could be reduced if the Union attack was switched away from Confederate armies to Southern warmaking resources, and if necessary, private property. Attacks on foodstuffs and property are not by themselves, of course, a specifically American stratagem; but they do have an identifiable American source—the frontier experience, especially the Indian wars. European precedents are far less important in fertilizing the resort to this expedient than western expansion.[52] Any initial reluctance to attack private property can be explained by an unwillingness to punish fellow citizens. The ferocity of civil war sometimes takes time to build up and overwhelm long-felt amity. Sherman expressed this view lucidly when he wrote with some satisfaction to Secretary Chase,

> Most unfortunately, the war in which we are now Engaged, has been complicated on the one hand that all on the other were *not* Enemies.
>
> It would have been better if at the outset this mistake had not been made, and it is wrong longer to be misled by it. The Government . . . may now proceed on the proper Rule that all in the South are enemies of all in the North.[53]

In 1863, General Order No. 100, "Instructions for the Government of Armies of the United States in the Field," popularly known after its author, Francis Lieber, as Lieber's Code, stressed that "the rules of regular war" as applied to wars between states should be applied to civil conflicts on the grounds of "humanity." Lieber had also stipulated "that the unarmed citizen is to be spared in person, property, and honor, as much as the exigencies of war will permit." Nonetheless, toward the end of the code, Lieber modifies this view considerably in accordance with the qualifying last clause. "The Commander will throw the burden of the war, as much as lies within his power, on the disloyal citizens of the revolted position or province, subjecting them to a stricter police than the non-combatant enemies have to suffer in regular war"; "he could demand they swear an oath of allegiance," but if their recalcitrance continues, "he may expel, transfer, imprison or fine the revolted citizens who refuse to pledge themselves anew as citizens obedient to the law and loyal to the government."[54]

The military "ratchet effect," to use Peter Parish's apt term, sustained a political and moral transformation of view. The Confiscation Acts of 1862 were passed as responses to the disappointments of 1861–62. The Confederacy replied with General Order No. 54 that promised "just measures of retribution and retaliation." For the North, rising overall casualties and costs demanded more far-reaching methods to attain the paramount objective—victory—meaning both reunion and the end of slavery. And as the portents of victory became clearer to the North after September 1864, the desire to discover some great meaning in the struggle became more urgent. The most favored interpretation was that the United States had endured an ordeal out of which emerged a stronger, more durable, and finer experiment in democracy.[55]

NOTES AND REFERENCES

1. A. J. P. Taylor, *English History, 1914–1945* (Oxford: Clarendon Press, 1965), pp. vi, 298.

2. Peter J. Parish, "The Will to Fight and the Will to Write: Some Recent Books on the American Civil War," *Journal of American Studies* 32 (1998): 305.

3. Russell F. Weigley, *History of the United States Army* (London: Batsford, 1968), pp. 104–105, 115; Ricardo A. Herrera, "Self-Governance and the American Citizen as Soldier, 1775–1865," *Journal of Military History* 65 (January 2001): 21–52; Jerry M. Cooper, *The Rise of the National Guard: The Evolution of the American Militia* (Lincoln: University of Nebraska Press, 1997), pp. 1–22.

4. Glyndon Van Deusen, *William Henry Seward* (New York: Oxford University Press, 1967), pp. 288, 324–35.

5. Brian Holden Reid, "A Survey of the Militia in Eighteenth-Century America," *Army Quarterly* 110 (1980): 217–20.

6. Marcus Cunliffe, *Soldiers and Civilians: The Martial Spirit in America, 1775–1865*, 3rd ed. (1968; Aldershot: Gregg Revivals, 1993), pp. 217–20.

7. Weigley, *United States Army*, pp. 8–9, 183.

8. Brian Holden Reid, *The Origins of the American Civil War* (London: Longman, 1996), pp. 283–84; Louis Fisher, *Presidential War Power* (Lawrence: University Press of Kansas, 1995), pp. 38–39.

9. Peter J. Parish, *The American Civil War* (London: Eyre Methuen, 1975), pp. 134–36; in addition to the war powers, the president had an obligation to see the laws faithfully executed, see Quincy Wright, "The American Civil War, 1861–1865," in *The International Law of Civil War*, ed. Richard A. Falk (Baltimore: Johns Hopkins University Press, 1971), p. 44.

10. James W. Geary, *We Need Men: The Union Draft in the Civil War* (DeKalb: Northern Illinois University Press, 1991), pp. 12–13; S. P. MacKenzie, *Revolutionary Armies in the Modern Era* (London: Routledge, 1997), p. 25.

11. Fred A. Shannon, *The Organisation and Administration of the Union Army, 1861–1865* (1928; Gloucester, MA: Peter Smith, 1965), vol. 1, pp. 259–60, 263–64; Herman Hattaway and Archer Jones, *How the North Won: A Military History of the Civil War* (Urbana: University of Illinois Press, 1982), p. 437; Benjamin P. Thomas and Harold M. Hyman, *Stanton: The Life and Times of Lincoln's Secretary of War* (New York: Alfred A. Knopf, 1962), pp. 201–202; William B. Hesseltine, *Lincoln and the War Governors* (New York: Alfred A. Knopf, 1948), pp. 194–200.

12. Geary, *We Need Men*, pp. 12, 16.

13. Ibid., pp. 22, 23–26, 27, 30.

14. Ibid., pp. 31, 34–35; Shannon, *Organisation and Administration*, vol. 1, pp. 290–91.

15. Hattaway and Jones, *How the North Won*, pp. 113–14; Clement Eaton, *A History of the Southern Confederacy* (New York: Collier, 1954), p. 89.

16. Quote from Eaton, *Confederacy*, p. 90.

17. Emory M. Thomas, *The Confederate Nation, 1861–1865* (1979; New York: Monticello, 1993), pp. 209–10.

18. Eaton, *Confederacy*, p. 93 overstates the importance of the draft; Hattaway and Jones, *How the North Won*, p. 116; for an able, brief discussion, see T. Harry Williams, *The History of American Wars from 1745 to 1918* (New York: Alfred A. Knopf, 1981), pp. 220–25.

19. George C. Rable, *The Confederate Republic* (Chapel Hill: University of North Carolina Press, 1994), pp. 138–43, 147; Richard E. Beringer, Herman Hattaway, Archer Jones, and Willian N. Still Jr., *Why the South Lost the Civil War* (Athens: University of Georgia Press, 1986), pp. 453–55.

20. Geary, *We Need Men*, pp. 28, 65.

21. Hattaway and Jones, *How the North Won*, p. 438; Parish, *American Civil War*, pp. 141–42; James M. McPherson, *The Battle Cry of Freedom: The Civil War Era* (New York: Oxford University Press, 1988), pp. 600–601.

22. Geary, *We Need Men*, p. 66. Geary is more critical of Fry (cf. pp. 70–71) for overzealousness than impatience; see also Hattaway and Jones, *How the North Won*, pp. 437–38, for the difficulties facing the bureau.

23. Geary, *We Need Men*, pp. 13, 51.

24. Hattaway and Jones, *How the North Won*, pp. 438–39; Shannon, *Organisation and Administration*, vol. 2, pp. 116–17.

25. Geary, *We Need Men*, pp. 38–39, 40.

26. Ibid., pp. 38–39, 40.

27. Iver Bernstein, *The New York City Draft Riots: Their Significance for American Society and Politics in the Age of the Civil War* (New York: Oxford University Press, 1990), pp. 5–6.

28. Leonard L. Richards, *"Gentlemen of Property and Standing": Anti-Abolition Mobs in Jacksonian America* (New York: Oxford University Press, 1970), p. 62; David Grimsted, *American Mobbing, 1828–1861: Toward Civil War* (New York: Oxford University Press, 1998), p. 136; Bernstein, *Draft Riots*, pp. 6–7.

29. Bernstein, *Draft Riots*, p. 8; Geary, *We Need Men*, p. 44. These fears are discussed in more detail in my successor book on 1864–65.

30. Bernstein, *Draft Riots*, pp. 10–11.

31. Ibid., 11–14.

32. Ibid., pp. 17–21, 27–31, 34–36, 38–40.

33. Ibid., pp. 22, 37.

34. Ibid., pp. 40–41; for the prosperous, skilled laborers who made up the bulk of anti-abolition mobs before 1840, see Richards, *"Gentlemen of Property and Standing,"* pp. 151–52.

35. Bernstein, *Draft Riots*, pp. 70–71, 259 (quotation p. 71).

36. Parish, "The Will to Fight and the Will to Write," p. 304; Bernstein, *New York Riots*, p. 70; Geary, *We Need Men*, pp. 51–52.

37. Geary, *We Need Men*, p. 66; McPherson, *Battle Cry of Freedom*, pp. 605, 758; Allan Nevins, *The War for the Union: The Organized War, 1863–1864* (New York: Scribner's, 1971), p. 8.

38. Geary, *We Need Men*, pp. 81–84, 89; *Under the Southern Cross: Soldier Life with Gordon Bradwell and the Army of Northern Virginia*, ed. P. Deloach Johnson (Macon, GA: Mercer University Press, 1999), pp. 40, 131; Bernstein, *Draft Riots*, p. 42.

39. Bruce Catton, *Grant Takes Command* (Boston: Little, Brown, 1968), pp. 369–73; Geary, *We Need Men*, pp. 101, 117.

40. Quotation from Grimsted, *American Mobbing*, p. 271; one member of this sizeable minority was Theodore Roosevelt Sr., the father of the future president. See Edward J. Renehan Jr., *The Lion's Pride: Theodore Roosevelt and His Family in Peace and War* (New York: Oxford University Press, 1998), p. 24.

41. Brian Holden Reid, *The American Civil War and the Wars of the Industrial Revolution* (London: Cassell, 1999), pp. 182–83, 186.

42. Bruce Catton, *This Hallowed Ground* (London: Victor Gollancz, 1957), pp. 317–19.

43. For an example of the lack of faith in generals, see above, p. 168 for the reaction in 1862 of the secretary of the treasury, Salmon P. Chase, to General George W. Cullum's despairing remark on the fighting qualities of Union soldiers. *Inside Lincoln's Cabinet: The Civil War Diaries of Salmon P. Chase*, ed. David Donald (New York: Longmans Green, 1954), p. 139.

44. Geoffrey Best, *Humanity in Warfare* (London: Weidenfeld and Nicolson, 1980), pp. 6–12; Carl von Clausewitz, *On War*, eds. Michael Howard and Peter Paret (Princeton, NJ: Princeton University Press, 1976), bk. 6, ch. 5, p. 370: "The aggressor is always peace loving (as Bonaparte always claimed to be); he would prefer to take over our country unopposed."

45. Peter J. Parish, "The War for the Union as a Just War," in *Aspects of War in American History*, eds. David K. Adams and Cornelius A. van Minnen, 81–82, 91 (Keele, UK: Keele University Press, 1997). For an analysis of Republican ideology see Michael S. Green, *Freedom, Union and Power: Lincoln and His Party During the Civil War* (New York: Fordham University Press, 2004), especially pp. 68–70, on Democratic failures.

46. Quoted in David Donald, *Charles Sumner and the Rights of Man* (New York: Alfred A. Knopf, 1970), pp. 118–19.

47. Parish, "War for the Union as a Just War," pp. 83–84.

48. Ibid., p. 86; for the Crittenden-Johnson Resolutions see idem., *American Civil War*, p. 206.

49. John W. Brinsfield, "The Military Ethics of General William T. Sherman: A

Reassessment," in *The Parameters of War*, ed. Lloyd J. Matthews and D. E. Brown, 93–94 (Washington, DC: Pergamon-Brassey's, 1987); on Confederate indiscipline in Maryland, see Terry L. Jones, *Lee's Tigers: The Louisiana Infantry in the Army of Northern Virginia* (Baton Rouge: Louisiana State University Press, 1987), p. 127.

50. Parish, "War for the Union as a Just War," pp. 90–93; Lance Janda, "Shutting the Gates of Mercy: The American Origins of Total War," *Journal of Military History* 59 (January 1995): 16–17.

51. Parish, "War for the Union as a Just War," pp. 94–95, 97.

52. Brinsfield, "The Military Ethics of Sherman," pp. 89, 91; Russell F. Weigley, *A Great Civil War* (Bloomington: Indiana University Press, 2000), pp. xv–xvi; on the Indian wars see John Ogden, *Tecumseh* (New York: Henry Holt, 1997), pp. 47, 62; Janda, "Shutting the Gates of Mercy," pp. 23–24.

53. Sherman to Salmon P. Chase, Aug. 11, 1862, in *Sherman's Civil War: Selected Correspondence of William T. Sherman, 1860–1865*, eds. Brooks Simpson and Jean V. Berlin (Chapel Hill: University of North Carolina Press, 1999), p. 269.

54. Quoted in Wright, "American Civil War," pp. 46–47, 55, 57–58; Mark Grimsley, *The Hard Hand of War: Union Military Policy toward Southern Civilians, 1861–1865* (Cambridge, MA: Cambridge University Press, 1995), p. 150.

55. *The Ordeal of the Union* is the collective title for Allan Nevins's eight-volume history of the Civil War period (New York: Scribner's, 1947–71).

Chapter Twelve

THE EXPERIENCE OF WAR

T he transformation of the aims of the Civil War had a more general significance that perhaps transcends the American context. The Civil War was the first major conflict characterized by a great effort to justify its conduct to a mass public. Public opinion on both sides, but especially in the North, was a driving force in the transformation; it was not an inert mass that needed shifting. The armies of the Civil War, both North and South, maintained a distinct, civilian character throughout the conflict. Nowhere was this process of hardening resolve to fight it out until complete victory be gained—either for reunion or independence—more important than among the ordinary soldiers in the ranks.

The experience of soldiers in battle had a profound political and social meaning. Its appearance notwithstanding, battle has rarely been futile, blood-drenched chaos. Participants often associate political values with the fighting in which they are engaged. In a democracy the feelings soldiers exhibit, especially the degree of enthusiasm shown for a cause, may have a major impact both on the shape of the war aims, and on the manner of its conduct. The "sharp end" of battle and the political and social context of the war can be intimately connected. These factors interact upon one another, forming a seamless Bayeux tapestry. Combat is not pointless, particularly if it engages great causes, although it is undoubtedly messy, bloody, and unpleasant for many. The experience of war lies at the very heart of the wartime political process.[1]

American Civil War soldiers were not "victims." Their sacrifice was not pointless. The great majority did adapt psychologically to the peculiar demands of soldiering. Civil War soldiers were a heterogeneous group, and they were sometimes conscious of ethnic and social differences.[2] There were four prime reasons why soldiers fought with varying degrees of enthusiasm. The first was love of country (variously interpreted, of course), its institutions, and what soldiers believed these represented to the rest of the world. On both sides, for example, soldiers believed they were fighting for a principle—freedom. Historians sometimes employ the term "ideology" to describe such impulses, although they often seem more reflective of a commitment to certain ideals rather than ideological fervor in the broadest sense. The oaths sworn by officers after 1865 stressed loyalty to the Constitution rather than to any particular form of political system.[3]

Soldiers mentioned idealistic issues rather more frequently in their correspondence than other aspects, such as excitement and adventure. Their opinions were sometimes expressed in commonplace, pious, even self-righteous terms. These views were also suffused with nineteenth-century romanticism and quite unrealistic expectations of what war was like. A lot of soldiers seemed to envisage battle as a development of childhood games; "glory" would replace fun—a deadly sport played by older, or "real," men. It is possible that the more elevated language conveyed in soldiers' letters is a device designed to conceal more mundane motives. There appears little evidence to support such a suggestion, otherwise morale would have been brittle indeed. If soldiers on both sides were insincere, it becomes difficult to explain why they sustained such heavy casualties over long periods or why they revealed a willingness to die for the causes they fought for.[4]

Second, a soldier's community exercised great influence over his behavior at the front. This was not just "peer group pressure"—although certainly the great majority of soldiers in a given company, until at least 1864, would have known one another. Moreover, the abandonment of small-town morality featured as an important element in a soldier's rite of passage to "real" manhood. Nonetheless, the sway of a community continued unbroken. Soldiers might play cards and drink, but that did not imply that they had abandoned the serious issues that their communities had sent them to defend, or that they did not cherish the high opinion of "the folks back home." Soldiers' letters were meant to be read not just by their immediate family and friends; some were written for publication in the local newspaper. They frequently expressed opinions on their officers, noncommissioned officers (NCOs), and fellow soldiers, most of whom would be known as neighbors or workmates. Reputations were both at a premium and vulnerable. Variations in political opinion would have an important effect over time.[5]

The way that these groups of unruly and opinionated soldiers were raised led to a shifting balance between informal "civilian" methods and the exigencies of war; the latter forged a consensus that upheld military discipline enforced by far more formal, coercive methods. As soldiers grew in experience, so they grasped the value of discipline and acquiesced more readily in it. Military success was the product of cohesion en masse rather than individual, feckless, histrionic gestures. Soldiers prized opportunities to "drill," that is, train for combat. Nonetheless, it is important to stress that no Civil War commander, at any level, could thrive without achieving a broad measure of consensus. Hostility toward "martinets"—those who enforced a rigid discipline and were noted for a mindless, disproportionate obsession with trivia—was widespread in both Union and Confederate armies. It was expressed not just by the lazy and the careless, but by the very best volunteer officers and men.[6]

Individual behavior was constrained by certain conventions. Probably the most important was that each fighting soldier carried the responsibility for his own actions—not the social forces that helped shape him. The attribute prized most highly by men of the nineteenth century was "character": an ability to overcome fear. All the energy and will required to overcome the obstacles to soldierly efficiency had to be generated by the inner resources of the individual. All soldiers were regarded as the exemplifications of the communities from whence they came. If a soldier dropped the standard of his community's ideals, then it was his fault, not the community's.[7]

The third factor concerns what military analysts term "primary group cohesion." The disciplined bond to fight and win together was strengthened by the mutual friendship, respect, and admiration of groups of young veteran soldiers fighting together over protracted periods. Civil War armies *were* young (with an average age of about twenty-four, much younger in the fighting echelons)—although not as young as the conscripted armies of the first half of the twentieth century.[8]

Finally, religious fervor played a major part in inspiring soldiers for battle. From 1863 onward, religious revivals spread through the armies of both sides.

416 AMERICA'S CIVIL WAR

Modern research has tended to focus on the Confederate army. Religious fervor in the Confederate army is not greatly different to that experienced in the Union army, though the former was more homogeneous because of the South's attachment to evangelical Protestantism. The immediacy of death patently stimulated an interest in the hereafter. Lieutenant Randolph McKin, a chaplain in the Army of Northern Virginia, averred that in "over forty-five years of ministerial life . . . I have never found men so open to the frank discussion of the subject of personal religion as the officers and men of Lee's army." The tone was set by the commanding general, who gave a high priority to his devotions—an interest shared by his staff. Lee's assistant adjutant general, Lieutenant Colonel Walter H. Taylor, read the lesson in church every Sunday and tried not to work on that day.[9]

There were numerous links between Christian worship in the field, the communities that sponsored the units, and the soldiers' comrades. Chaplains often came from the county of the soldiers they administered to. Common, outdoor worship (often attended by or even, in the case of Bishop Leonidas Polk, conducted by senior officers) permitted soldiers to identify with a wider cause, affirming national and cultural identity, and adding to esprit de corps by arousing regimental and individual pride; the soldiers had further reason to trust and respect one another. Religious ceremony reinforced or even replaced primary group cohesion if casualties wore away its bands. Religious convictions offered consolation in the face of terrible danger. William Dorsey Pender, a divisional commander in the Army of Northern Virginia who did not lack religious doubt, wrote in 1863, "I do not fear to die. I can confidently resign my soul to God, trusting in the atonement of Jesus Christ." There can be no coincidence that religious revivals tended to follow arduous campaigns and ferocious battles—after Antietam, Fredericksburg, and Gettysburg.[10]

Religious belief permeated all levels of the experience of the Civil War and reinforced social and political motivation. Reverend A. D. McVoy believed that "religion is infusing a spirit of fortitude, endurance and determination into the hearts of the soldiers that no hardship, no suffering, can undermine or break down." Not all soldiers, needless to say, accepted the consolations of religion. One colonel was the despair of the chaplains, who frankly claimed "that he did not believe that there was any such thing as genuine religion." Whatever its sources, however, the fighting spirit of armies, Northern and Southern, contributed to their remarkable resilience. The soldiers fought on no matter how wrongheadedly they were commanded. Such doggedness, perhaps most noticeable on the Northern side, had much to do with the value invested in the cause soldiers fought for. They were, after all, mostly volunteers who chose to go to war and had consented to learn the soldier's trade. As a soldier of the 12th Connecticut Infantry wrote of an action in Louisiana in October 1863, "all through the battle we labored to keep a straight line with a single-mindedness which greatly supported our courage."[11]

By the autumn of 1862 soldiers understood that the essence of effective disciplined action required the submerging of the self into the corporate. It also led to the unmasking of poseurs, bluffers, and braggarts. The Roman Emperor Commodus's gladiators had not proved very good soldiers. American soldiers soon discovered that those who impress in peacetime are often cruelly exposed by the pitiless reality of war. Bullies were the first to run. William M. Moore remembered a professional boxer who had served in the 3rd New York Light Battery. On joining he boasted that he would thrash any soldiers of his battery. The moment Confederate artillery opened fire, however, "he went into convulsions through fear." Despite his initial swagger, other soldiers felt sorry for him, and he was permitted to take up the post of company cook.[12]

In 1861–62 the great majority of soldiers were curious, if not eager, "to see the elephant," the phrase that meant to experience front-line action. The dense woods that covered so many Civil War battlefields prevented the troops from seeing very much. Innumerable trees and thickets obscured the view not only of the commanders, but of the men in the ranks, too, making copious demands on their morale and initiative—especially in the attack. Conscious of the dangers of firing too soon or too high, and when firing a volley determined to find a clear field of fire, Civil War soldiers tended to open fire later than was necessary.[13] The sheer volume of firepower thrown at either side forced a reappraisal of the desirability of entrenchment.

At the war's beginning soldiers were scornful of entrenchment and loathed the work it involved. However, by 1863–64 such casual arrogance had been replaced by pleasure that bullets and shells could be avoided: "I can stand two months of siege work; no more charging to be required of your humble sergeant-major," recorded one. But prolonged trench warfare could have a deleterious effect on the troops. Robert Stiles, an artilleryman in the Army of Northern Virginia, complained of conditions at Cold Harbor in June 1864:

> Thousands of men cramped up in a narrow trench, unable to go out, or to get up, or to stretch or to stand without danger to life and limb. Unable to lie down, or to sleep, for lack of room and pressure of peril; night alarms, day attacks, hunger, thirst, supreme weariness, squalor, vermin, filth, disgusting odors everywhere; the weary night succeeded by the yet more weary day; the

first glance over the way, at day dawn, bringing the sharpshooter's bullet singing past your ear or smashing through your skull, a man's life often exacted at the price of a cup of water from the spring.

The grinding pressure of continuous battle—already felt by the spring of 1863—with no relief ("so incessant and so indecisive") wore down even the most enthusiastic soldier. Sniping under siege conditions tended to exert "a strange fascination for men of a sporting turn of mind," James Harrison Wilson (then a lieutenant colonel) observed during the siege of Vicksburg. Exposure to cease-less skirmishing eroded the ardor for offensive action. Captain John De Forest, of the 12th Connecticut Infantry, wrote during the siege of Port Hudson in the summer of 1863 of the effects of six unbroken weeks in the trenches, that "lazy, monotonous, sickening, murderous, unnatural, uncivilized mode of being."[14]

That soldiers found the harrowing experience of protracted exposure to battle stressful and mentally exhausting is beyond dispute. Some modern studies have located cases of post-traumatic stress disorder (PTSD)—a psycho-logical syndrome that produces anxiety, depression, and various social patholo-gies; but it would be unwise to apply an excess of modern attitudes to the dis-section of their difficulties. Some enjoyed battle. Lieutenant William Wheeler of the 13th New York Battery thought "the danger was so great and so constant that it took away the sense of danger"; he only felt "joyous exaltation, a perfect indifference to circumstances"; he believed the three days at Gettysburg the most enjoyable of his life.[15]

In 1862–63 there was an undeniable tendency for some officers and men to try to gain a transfer to the Commissary or Quartermaster's branches. Those that were successful encountered scorn, even if previous wounds had rendered them unfit for battlefield service. A Confederate senator, Thomas J. Semmes, lam-basted Edgeworth Bird, who had been wounded at Second Manassas in August 1862. Bird confided to his wife that Semmes had claimed Bird "disgraced [him-self] and renounced glory by becoming a Quarter Master."[16]

The full range of battlefield experience cannot be conveyed here because the main focus should be on the way that soldiers' frustrations, as well as successes, shaped political activity. Significantly, men of both sides believed they were cus-todians of the legacy of 1776. Stereotypes of each section were traded in both private correspondence and in the public print. "[T]he scum of the North *cannot* face the chivalric spirit of the South," wrote one Confederate soldier in 1862. Views on the exact nature of the "legacy" of 1776 diverged, a divergence that grew as the war wore on.[17]

Nowhere was this clearer than in the diverse interpretations given to the influence of slavery on the war. The issue of slavery could not be said to have been controversial among Southern soldiers: they were unanimous in not wishing to see a change in Southern social institutions and race relations. Only those who hailed from slaveholding families wrote about slavery at any length. These were middle-ranking officers who proved themselves in their admiration for Robert E. Lee, faith in slavery, and the justice of the Southern cause, a vital and self-confident focus for Confederate nationalism. The latter might have been poorly formed and articulated in the Civil War years, but there are few grounds for assuming it was fragile, especially given the resilience of Confederate armies until the early months of 1865.[18]

Southerners carried into war a pre-1861 habit that stressed the importance of abstractions underlying their notion of "liberty"; this was coupled with spine-chilling, graphic depictions of what was in store for the South should it be defeated; these fears, too, projected prewar alarms and anticipated denunciations of the "horrors" of Reconstruction and the lurid, exaggerated accounts of the depredations of Sherman's marches. Most white Southerners never came to terms with the grisly reality of human bondage. They succeeded in their conscious efforts to push it to the margins of the Southern imagination. The paradox that Confederate soldiers fought to resist "slavery" (meaning political dominance by the North) while attempting to defend (if not extend) human bondage, escaped the majority of Southerners. What counted for them lay in the sense of superiority that sprang from the white skin that marked out the dominant race.[19]

The racial attitudes of the great majority of Northern soldiers hardly differed from their Southern counterparts. Southerners who enlisted in the federal army to preserve the Union (like many West Virginians) had views on the question of slavery and race relations that could hardly be distinguished from those of Confederates. Eventually such Southern Unionists accepted emancipation. So, too, did the great majority of Union soldiers. As the war continued, they recognized that the Union could not be restored without the destruction of slavery. For instance, in the early months of 1863 Private Chauncey Welton of the 103rd Ohio Infantry wrote a series of letters castigating the Emancipation Proclamation.

> I enlisted to fight for and vindicate the supremacy of the Constitution, we did not enlist to fight for the [N]egro and I can tell you that *we never shall* . . . sacrafise [*sic*] [our] lives for the liberty of a miserable race of beings. . . . Abolitionism is traitorism in its darkest color.

By June 1863 even Welton agreed that the extirpation of slavery would represent "a means of hastening the speedy Restoration of the Union and the termination of the war." In 1864 he became an ardent Republican, and by the spring of 1865 he rejoiced at the prospect of a country "*free free free* yes free from that blighting curse *Slavery* the cause of four years of Bloody Warfare."[20]

Union soldiers quickly grasped that any damage inflicted on the "peculiar institution" weakened the Confederate capacity to wage war. A trooper in the 18th Pennsylvania Cavalry also opposed the Emancipation Proclamation until he realized that "it was just the thing that was needed [*sic*] to weaken the strength of the rebels"; another soldier in the 86th Indiana Infantry wrote enthusiastically that "We use all kinds of rebel property and they see no reason why we should not use [N]egroes. Every [N]egro we get strengthens us and weakens the rebels." An increasingly violent tone should not be construed as evidence that every soldier enjoyed the act of killing. Ambivalence about killing remained, despite the widespread resort to sniping and sharpshooters. At the battle of Resaca, Georgia, in May 1864, a young abolitionist named Chauncey Cooke wrote that "I saw men often drop after shooting, but didn't know that it was my bullet that did the work and really hope it was not. But you know that I am a good shot."[21]

The pervasive tougher attitude and growing impatience to "clean out" the rebels had as its source the increasingly bellicose opinions of the Northern soldiers themselves. They wished to punish the South hard for its treason and rash foolhardiness in provoking war. In tracing the prevalence of "hard war" attitudes Civil War literature has perhaps given too much emphasis to the opinions of field commanders. Much more significant was the tenacious adherence of volunteer soldiers to the idea of complete victory; after 1862–63 they continued to behave as politically conscious (and alert) free men who happened to be wearing uniforms. Whether it is valid to claim, as James McPherson does, that the best soldiers were those most ideologically committed, is open to debate. There can be no doubt though that a determination to finish the job and secure reunion whatever it cost the South enthused Northern soldiers by 1864. A quiet confidence also permeated the ranks of the Army of Northern Virginia, a force that was surprisingly unaffected by its recent, costly setback at Gettysburg. Such a combination could only result in a savage war of attrition ending with the complete defeat of the weaker side.[22]

As understanding of the stakes at issue in the 1864 campaign were communicated by a number of vociferous Northern politicians, not just senators and congressmen, but also the war governors. All these spokesmen, even when not seeking reelection, sent copies of their speeches to their constituents in the ranks. One of the few regular officers with sufficient political sensitivity to understand the developing nature of the conflict was Major General Henry W. Halleck. The North, he predicted as early as 1861, "will become ultra anti-slavery, and I fear . . . will declare for emancipation and thus will add the horrors of a servile to that of a civil war."[23]

Ideas about emancipation and punitive strategies received their initial formulation in the east because of the proximity of the political pulse, Washington, DC. They then spread westward, and *not* vice versa as it is frequently suggested, thanks to the efforts of political leaders in Congress. After the presidential signature had been placed on the two Confiscation Acts in 1862, Senator Benjamin F. Wade delivered a number of impassioned speeches directed to Southerners declaring that "You cannot escape from this war without the emancipation of your [N]egroes." Major General John Pope's controversial general orders reflected this changing political climate. Halleck wrote to McClellan after they were issued, "I am fully agreed with you [as] to the manner in which the war should be conducted, and I believe that the present policy of the President to be conservative." He added, "I think some of General Pope's orders very injudicious and have so advised him." But thereafter sensing the direction that the political winds were turning, Halleck's military policy tacked to accommodate it. Hereafter he was the most articulate military spokesman for severe, punitive action; many of his field commanders were reluctant to follow his lead. Halleck accepted the logic of Lincoln's letter of July 31, 1862, to August Belmont, the leading Democratic Party boss previously referred to. Lincoln claimed that Southerners could not experiment for a decade attempting to destroy the government and then, after admitting failure, still return to the Union unscathed. This transformation of political and military opinion rested on shifts in public opinion after the summer of 1862. Harsher views did not follow dramatic or destructive military moves. They made them possible.[24]

The field commanders took time to catch up with these tides of opinion as they veered toward a more punitive and unforgiving stance. Ulysses S. Grant, for example, issued orders in January 1862 requiring that "severe punishment be inflicted upon any soldier who is guilty of taking or destroying private property." In July 1862, the date when Halleck underwent a radical change of mind, Grant complained of the "demoralizing effect" the Confiscation Acts would have. He reluctantly gave his subordinates, like Lew Wallace, permission to forage from the countryside "provided you think men can be got who will not disgrace our cause by acts of vandalism, such as are too frequent." Grant, however, would be impelled to change his mind; in any case, there was little that he could do to stop plundering.[25]

Grant's troops were opinionated, self-reliant, and ingenious. As he said himself of the men under his command, "there is nothing which men are called upon to do, mechanical or professional, that accomplished adepts [skilled men] cannot be found for the duty required in almost every regiment." A sizeable slice of them had previously served in the Army of the West. This force had been employed in the fratricidal conflict in Missouri and demonstrated zeal in attacking rebel property. Men of both the Army of the Tennessee and the Ohio were prevailed upon, especially by Senator Wade of Ohio and Senator Zachariah Chandler of Michigan, to think and act for themselves. A host of other politicians quarried *The Report of the Joint Committee on the Conduct of the War* (3 vols.) that appeared in April 1863, to make ever more severe denunciations of the South and those who sought reconciliation with its slave-owning elite. Wade's speeches were widely reported in the newspapers imploring that it was "Better to deluge the whole land in blood than that free men should be trampled underfoot as cowards." Politicians like Wade and Chandler both led and reflected opinion in their states. A spokesman for an Ohio regiment put their case: "This thing of guarding rebel property when the owner is in the field fighting us is played out. That is the sentiment of every private soldier in this army."[26]

Grant took many months to catch up with the views of his soldiers. From November 1862, during the first Vicksburg campaign, Grant spent months fulminating against "gross acts of vandalism." He published orders threatening the death penalty for looting; he deducted $1,200 from the pay of the 20th Illinois Infantry to cover the damage they had inflicted on a Tennessee store. Nevertheless, as one veteran remarked, "such orders got to be a joke with the men, they in a quiet way giving the commanding officers to understand that they did not go down South to protect Southern property." In December 1862 Grant was still of the opinion that the "country does not afford supplies for troops but a limited supply of forage." Within months Grant had changed his mind; yet he had little choice: all the military authority he could mobilize could not intimidate the majority of his soldiers out of the view they had reached independently concerning the conduct of the war, namely that the rebels should be punished and their property should suffer.[27]

From the spring of 1863 until the end of the Civil War, Northern opinion —especially in the ranks of the Union army—became more resolute in the search for vengeance for the wrongs inflicted by the South on the Union. A broad measure of consent was offered to the proposition that the war be conducted "in earnest." The only mitigating tendency differentiated sharply between arrogant, swaggering "aristocrats" who manipulated the "slave power" in their own overweening interest, and the hapless soldiers (and their families) who had been duped by those who had led them to disaster. After three years at the front, a Minnesota captain was determined that the war should end with nothing less than the "utter submission" of "these traitors to the government . . . when they have submitted I would propose to hang the leaders and let the poor *dupes* of soldiers go."[28]

A desire to fight the war to the finish on both sides may well have gained a broad measure of consent, but the simultaneous withdrawal of that consent also secured a wide level of support. This withdrawal of consent is best estimated by an analysis of the problem of desertion. Desertion is a subject that has not drawn enough interest, and those works that have appeared focus on the Confederacy.[29] The scale of the problem was huge. On February 1, 1865, Union reports show that absentees totaled 338,536 as against 630,924 present for duty. Confederate figures, though less exact, indicate 160,198 officers and men at their posts while 194,494 were absent.

A deserter is a soldier who leaves the ranks without permission and with no intention of returning. The motive, and not the act itself, determined what constituted as desertion in the American Civil War.[30]

The disciplinary structure of the Union and Confederate armies clearly had a strong bearing on the extent of the problem. Historian Fred A. Shannon puts it down to slack discipline. Contemporaries alluded frequently, and historian James W. Geary confirms, that the bounty system encouraged desertion.[31] There was a correlation between levels of desertion and payday—even those not eligible for bounties succumbed to the temptation to spend their money (especially if due a backlog of pay) content in the knowledge that they were safe from enemy bullets. Discipline in both Union and Confederate armies was eroded further by their inability to develop a large corps of experienced, hardy, noncommissioned officers (NCOs) who could overawe the troops under their command rather than identify with them. In American armies junior officers took on tasks such as drilling, which were the prime task of NCOs in European armies. Not only the election of officers and NCOs, but their identification with the men and their community corroded discipline if a consensus developed that they wished to return home.[32]

Indiscipline was obviously important but it cannot provide the sole explanation, as the motives for desertion were complex and variegated. In both armies the refusal to acknowledge that soldiers had lost their rights as civilians produced the reverse side of the coin to enthusiasm for more warlike measures. Many (though not the majority) decided that their part in the conflict was over.

Widespread literacy stimulated dissatisfaction. General Halleck admitted to the *New York Times* after the defeat at Fredericksburg, "They [the troops] feel that things are at loose ends, in fact they know it, for ours is one [an army] that reads and thinks." As the federal troops in the east were "stupefied by continual reverses," so levels of desertion rose there. The longer the war went on, the higher the numbers of deserters. Less well known and poorly understood is the estimate that 154,833 desertions occurred in the Union army between April 1863 and April 1865, when things mostly went well.[33]

In the Confederacy, facing imminent defeat, desertion rates were even higher. The entreaties of wives and families to come home were often blamed. In October 1864 Jefferson Davis admitted that two-thirds of the Confederate army were absent from the ranks. This enormous level of absenteeism had gone in tandem with a change in attitude toward deserters. Whereas in May 1863 one general claimed confidently that "The great majority of my brigade would shoot a deserter as quickly as they would a snake," by March 1865 it was tolerated. "So common is the crime," wrote the assistant secretary of war, John Campbell, "it has in popular estimation lost the stigma which justly pertains to it, and therefore the criminals are everywhere shielded by their families and by the sympathy of many communities."

A dangerous development that undermined the stability of the Confederacy was the creation of deserter strongholds in the mountains of Georgia, Alabama, and the Carolinas where the writ of the Confederate government failed to run and instead, anarchy prevailed. Morale was also undermined by North Carolina Unionists who, General D. H. Hill complained, "induced [soldiers] to believe that this is an unjust war on the part of the South." Military failure, disaffection with the Confederate cause, and desertion were closely related.[34]

Deserters found aid in the great expanse of the North American continent. They could slip away and escape detection. The provost marshals were empowered to arrest deserters, but this process was costly and ate up a large chunk of the commutation fees paid by those who had decided not to serve; a provost marshal was paid thirty dollars for each deserter arrested. For the Confederacy the cost could be even greater, as troops withdrawn to hunt for deserters might take the opportunity to desert themselves. "I have only resorted to them," Lee explained, "when in despair of otherwise mitigating the evil."[35]

In both Union and Confederate armies increasingly draconian punishments were introduced, including relying on the death penalty. Officers bent over backward to find a way of avoiding executions. President Lincoln himself set an example by commuting the death sentence on numerous occasions. The sheer number of deserters caused a major difficulty. "You cannot order men shot by dozens or twenties. People won't stand it and they ought not to stand it." Executions, in any case, did not guarantee a deterrent against desertion. Sylvanus Cadwallader, a correspondent of the *Chicago Times* who attached himself to Grant's staff, recorded an instance in the west when seven soldiers were paraded before their comrades and shot; but even more desertions followed that very night.[36]

Discontent with the pettiness and boredom of army life, as well as cowardice or strain, stimulated desertion. Those aroused by the excitement or dangers of battle "became morbidly discontented and homesick," as Cadwallader observed, "commencing perhaps with laziness, sulkiness, and ending in desertion." Warfare might be a fundamental element in American patriotism, but most Americans were hostile to outside authority. Neither was desertion something indulged in by private soldiers while officers selflessly attempted to prevent it. In a few instances entire units deserted "with their officers." Officer desertion in the Confederacy reflected a general rise after the summer of 1863. In the summer of 1864, of the 100,000 deserters listed on the muster rolls, 1,082 were officers.[37]

The frequency with which soldiers North and South deserted indicates how ideological commitment and more self-interested motives can exist side by side in the soldiery. In 1863 a New York volunteer, Charles A. Benson, revealed that "whoever announced that he enlisted because he loved his country is sure to become the target for shafts of ridicule." The decline in the quality of the Union army is usually dated from the summer of 1863 thanks to the draft, the bounty system, and desertion. The commander of the Fifth Corps, Gouverneur K. Warren, complained to his wife in February 1865 that "we are now getting to have an army of such poor soldiers that we have to lead them everywhere and even then they run away from us." But it would be wrong to draw a false line between the troops who served before July 1863 and those afterward. In August 1861 some regiments of three-year volunteers mutinied, resentful that the three-month volunteers could go home but they could not. Whatever their faults, the Union troops of 1864–65 were better disciplined than their forebears of 1861–62.[38]

Nonetheless they were more cynical and mercenary. "We no longer look on it as a war for country," admitted Samuel Budd, a New York volunteer to his brother in October 1863, "but as a great speculation in which each one is trying to make as much as he can." An Englishman, James Horrocks, serving in the Army of the James (which saw little fighting), was shocked by the mercenary attitude of his fellow American soldiers. "What I would consider myself as a disgraceful action is here regarded universally as a *smart thing* and the person who does it a *dem'd smart fellow.*"[39]

The true significance of desertion from both sides lies in the measure of Americans' unpreparedness to meet the challenges of war in the industrial age. It also reflects upon attitudes toward authority in a conflict of unexpected intensity and duration. Attempts by both sides to encourage desertion from the enemy were ineffective, mainly because desertion was an act of defiance to central authority. Finally, desertion illuminates the paradoxical element in the American military tradition, because before 1861 it did not embrace the full implications of mass involvement despite the principle of universal obligation to undertake military service enshrined in the pre-1861 militia system.

One reservoir of manpower could be tapped, but even the suggestion of doing so stirred fury and ridicule in 1861—the black population of the United States. Blacks had served during the American Revolution (indeed they represented a worthwhile fraction of the men who passed through George Washington's Continental Army, five thousand out of two hundred thousand). Antebellum state militias (especially in the South) had prohibited black attendance, but at the battle of New Orleans in 1815, Andrew Jackson had appealed to free blacks to fill his ranks with a rallying cry to America's "adoptive citizens." His cry anticipated the vital connection between military service and citizenship that would inspire black leaders during the Civil War.[40]

Such a correlation had frequently been denied. The Federal Militia Act of 1792 prevented blacks from serving and they were not permitted to enter the regular army (though they could and did enlist in the antebellum navy). The Supreme Court's 1857 Dred Scott decision ruled that blacks were not American citizens, though a percentage of the peacetime US Army had been comprised of noncitizens. In the 1840s and 1850s perhaps 20 percent of US Army soldiers were Irish and were not yet US citizens. In 1859 the Massachusetts legislature repealed the ban on blacks serving in the state's militia, but the move was vetoed by the governor, Nathaniel P. Banks, on the grounds that it contravened the 1792 Militia Act. Lincoln's first secretary of war, Simon Cameron, shared Banks's lack of enthusiasm for blacks taking any part in the war for the Union. When three hundred blacks offered to organize themselves to help guard Washington, DC, he replied disdainfully that "this Department has no intention at present to call into the service of the Government any colored soldiers." Frederick Douglass and other black leaders believed that the luster accorded by military service would establish for blacks an irrefutable claim to American citizenship. A willingness to shoulder its obligations would allow blacks as well as whites an equal share in constitutional rights and the opportunities such an access could provide. The cool reaction of the Lincoln administration to their enthusiasm to serve roused disappointment and frustration. "Colored men were good enough to fight under Washington, but they were not good enough to fight under McClellan," snarled Douglass.[41]

Over the next six months Cameron changed his mind about the value of black soldiers. In December 1861 a statement was inserted in his annual report that suggested that all escaped slaves entering Union camps should be armed. Lincoln instructed Cameron to delete this portion, but he had taken the precaution of leaking it to the press. Some commanders followed Cameron's advice on their own initiative. Major General Benjamin F. Butler at Fortress Monroe, Virginia, treated such slaves as "contrabands," but he hoped to use them as laborers rather than soldiers. In May 1862, Major General David Hunter, commanding the Department of the South, based in the South Carolina Sea Islands, tried to raise a regiment of black troops from liberated slaves. His zeal outran his discretion, let alone good sense. He damaged his own cause by attempting to force former slaves to join the colors. The freedmen hid from Hunter's agents. In any case, the new secretary of war, Cameron's successor, Edwin M. Stanton, refused to sustain Hunter's efforts by denying him arms, uniforms, and pay. Hunter was forced to disband his black regiment except for one company.[42]

Despite the caution shown by the executive branch, greater sympathy for the cause of black troops welled up in Congress. It passed two pieces of legislation that permitted the raising of black troops. First, the Confiscation Act of July 17, 1862, allowed the president to "employ as many persons of African descent as he may deem necessary and proper for the suppression of this rebellion." Second, the 1792 Militia Act was repealed, removing a powerful obstacle to black military service. Nonetheless, Lincoln remained cautious in his response. When on August 4, the Governor of Indiana, Oliver P. Morton, offered to raise two black regiments, the president declined to accept them on the grounds that his action would antagonize the border states. The solace of large numbers of black volunteers appeared insufficient to outweigh the possible loss of "50,000 bayonets from the loyal Border States against us that were for us." Lincoln offered to use the freedmen as laborers. Perhaps an unstated doubt about the fighting qualities of black troops lay behind this lack of enthusiasm.[43]

The work started by Hunter continued under Rufus Sexton in the South Carolina Sea Islands. By November 1862 he had created a volunteer regiment around the sole company raised by Hunter, the 1st South Carolina Volunteers, to fight for the Union. An abolitionist intellectual of drive and decision, Thomas

Wentworth Higginson was asked to command it. Higginson did not underestimate his task or the importance of his own role. "The first man who organizes and commands a successful black regiment," he wrote with himself in mind, "will perform the most important service in the history of the war." Indeed the tactical drill of his troops persuaded the skeptical *New York Times* that blacks could make an effective contribution to the war effort. Yet even Higginson indulged that air of condescending paternalism that all too frequently tinged the dealings of white, middle-class intellectuals with blacks, especially in large groups. He referred to his troops as "perpetual children, docile and gay and loveable"; by February 1864 he considered that their childish ways were being replaced by a more serious mien: "they are growing more like white men, less naïve—less grotesque."[44]

Lincoln's issue of the Emancipation Proclamation led to the raising of black troops on a large scale. The adjutant general, Major General Lorenzo Thomas, was sent on an important mission to the Mississippi valley to organize formations of fighting troops from "that class of population known as contrabands" and consider the ways that these units could be provided with effective white officers without reducing the efficiency of other regiments. Thomas' mission represents an important preliminary stage in developing the use of black troops under federal rather than state aegis. By the end of 1863 Thomas had organized twenty regiments.[45] In January 1863, the governor of Massachusetts gained approval to raise a black regiment; but he went too far in asking permission to commission blacks as officers, a proposal that received a blank refusal. Black abolitionists, like Douglass, offered their services as recruiting agents, and their efforts resulted in enough recruits to fill two regiments, 54th and 55th. On May 22, 1863, Stanton formed the Bureau of Colored Troops, headed by Major George L. Stearns, which created a national system for the recruitment of black troops that had been conspicuous in its absence in the raising of white regiments; candidates seeking commissions were interviewed and tested. Stearns was appointed assistant adjutant general, empowered to recruit blacks for the federal government; his tact and diplomatic skill tempered hostile attitudes toward black troops. "I know of no prominent loyal Tennessean," wrote one of Stearns's supporters, "who does not believe in, advocate, and encourage the raising of black troops." This favor might be explained by the willingness of blacks to fill Tennessee's quotas. At any rate, it is significant (and reflective of the wartime enlargement of federal power) that most black troops were raised directly by the federal government and used the designation "United States Colored Troops" rather than any state designation.[46]

Federal agents were most successful in raising black troops in the occupied Confederate states. Tensions between black and white Unionists remained inflammable. A captain of Florida troops reported that "it is almost impossible to get along with the colored troops. I am fully satisfied that each should be separate to accomplish anything." At the end of the war, the provisional governor of Tennessee observed of three regiments about to be mustered out, that "there is a bad state of feeling between them and the *colored troops*."[47]

Black soldiers were organized separately (save those of Connecticut and the 54th and 55th Massachusetts regiments) as United States Colored Troops (USCT), representing the branches of the service, US Colored Infantry, Cavalry, and Heavy Artillery. By the end of 1863, 50,000 black troops had entered the Union army; by 1865 their numbers totaled just over 186,000 (of these 134,111 had been recruited from the slave states). They comprised 10 percent of Union manpower. In all, 120 regiments of infantry were raised, plus 12 of heavy and 1 of light artillery, and 7 of cavalry. Over three thousand died on the battlefield and a large number from disease. They took part in 39 battles, 449 engagements, and 21 black soldiers were decorated with the Congressional Medal of Honor. Henry S. Harman of 3rd USCI (United States Colored Infantry) claimed at the end of 1863, "you can say of the colored man, we too have borne our share of the burden."[48]

By the summer of 1863 black troops had been engaged in action at Port Hudson, Milliken's Bend, and the heroic assault on Fort Wagner in Charleston Harbor, an action that raised the self-regard of black troops as well as their reputation among whites. The *Anti-Slavery Standard* proclaimed it as "a holy sepulcher to the black race, comparable to the Battle of Bunker Hill." Yet black soldiers still encountered prejudice and belittlement. Inequalities in pay between black and white troops provided the most vexed issue. The Militia Act of 1862 stipulated that blacks be paid $10 per month ($3 of this was deducted for clothing). By contrast, white soldiers were paid $13 *plus* $4.50 clothing allowance. This differential could be justified only on the grounds that blacks would be employed solely as laborers. Black leaders lobbied to remove this unjust discrimination. Frederick Douglass visited the president on August 10, 1863. Lincoln was sympathetic but, true to his pragmatic nature, claimed that prejudice against black troops remained so powerful that poor pay formed "a necessary concession to smooth the way to their employment at all as soldiers." Still, he promised Douglass that black soldiers eventually would be rewarded with equal pay.

Historian Susan-Mary Grant rightly observes that the controversy transcended racial prejudice. "It represented the crux of the problem for those African-American regiments who fought in the Civil War, and threw into sharp focus many of the inconsistencies and contradictions that lay at the heart of Union war aims."[49] The emancipation of slaves and equality for free blacks were not synonymous issues, but they obviously enjoyed a close relationship. Moreover, both were intertwined with the controversy over the place of slavery in the conflict; the Lincoln administration only permitted black troops to be raised after the issue on January 1, 1863, of the Emancipation Proclamation signaled that the Union could not be restored until the social system of the slave states had been destroyed.

Most Democrats denounced this course and believed that war aims should not embrace slavery at all; they sought to exploit racial prejudice in discrediting Lincoln's policy. The Democratic *New York World* held that equal pay for black soldiers would result in the humiliation of whites. "It is unjust in every way to the white soldier to put him on a level with the black."[50]

As Governor Andrew had elicited a promise that his black regiments would be treated on an equal footing with white ones, the 54th Massachusetts Infantry refused to accept any pay at all and broke into a state of near mutiny. Edward N. Hallowell, who succeeded Robert Gould Shaw as commanding officer of the regiment, conceded, "I believe them to be entirely right, morally, and yet military necessity has compelled me to shoot two of them." Congress was willing to consider only equality of *future* pay, not compensation for unequal back pay. Some conservative Republicans, like William Pitt Fessenden, opposed the principle of equal pay on grounds of cost—estimated at $1.5 million.

Congress did not concede the point until June 15, 1864. It legislated that all black soldiers would receive back pay only from January 1, 1864; it restricted payment of back pay to those free on April 19, 1861. Such a provision discriminated against freedmen, and obviously sacrificed morale in order to save expense. Colonel Hallowell devised the so-called "Quaker Oath." This required black soldiers to swear that they "owed no man unrequited labor," but this was of no help to regiments raised entirely in the South. The issue of back pay rumbled on until March 3, 1865, when Congress allowed the payment of full back pay to all regiments that had been promised equal treatment.[51]

Another issue of discrimination revolved around the refusal to commission blacks. Curiously, a regiment raised during the Civil War did commission blacks—but it was found in the Confederacy: the Louisiana Native Guards. Such an anomaly requires explanation. In April 1861 many free blacks in Louisiana joined this regiment of the state militia out of fear for the future safety of their

lives and property. After 1865 Arnold Bentannon tried to explain their surprising action by emphasizing "the condition [that is, defenseless] and position
of our people were extremely perilous." The Louisiana Native Guards were
raised from the free blacks of New Orleans who enjoyed privileges denied
Southern free blacks elsewhere. Consequently, its recruits were men of property,
intelligence, and exceptional skills (including some black slaveowners). They
owned two million dollars' worth of property.

They were hardly typical of American blacks of the period. The recruits of
the Louisiana Native Guards were motivated by a large measure of economic and
financial self-interest, and a frantic desire for social acceptance in a hostile,
unforgiving society. It was estimated that about 80 percent of New Orleans free
blacks had some white blood; they identified more closely with white Southerners than other blacks; they had no sympathy with the North or for aboli-
tionism. It should come as no surprise, for all that, to discover that this eager
show of loyalty to the South and its institutions failed to be reciprocated by
Confederate military authorities.[52]

After the occupation of New Orleans by Benjamin F. Butler on May 1, 1862,
he decided to bring the Native Guards into federal service; but, as at Fortress
Monroe, he thought black troops should be laborers not warriors. A shortage of
reinforcements persuaded Butler otherwise and he appealed to blacks to rejoin
the Native Guards with the added incentive that they would be commanded by
their own officers. Half the men recruited were former slaves. More black troops
rallied to the Union cause in Louisiana than in any other state. By August 1863
ten thousand were serving in the Department of the Gulf alone. Obviously, in the
three regiments fielded of Louisiana Native Guards, the Confederate character of
the Native Guards had been purged and three white colonels were appointed to
command them, although most of the original black officers remained. When a
black captain presented himself as the officer of the day at Fort Strong, New
Orleans, white soldiers refused to acknowledge his authority "by any virtue of the
shoulder straps he might wear, they would not."[53]

Butler's replacement as commander of the Department of the Gulf,
Nathaniel P. Banks, responded to this captain's complaints by assembling all
black officers under his command. He told them bluntly that they should all
resign their commissions as it was not government policy to commission blacks.
He also introduced measures that would facilitate their rapid removal: boards to
test their proficiency were set up and an order issued to pay white officers in
black regiments but not black officers. Even Banks came away from the action
at Port Hudson on May 27, 1863, impressed by the impetuous charges made by

black troops. "They require only good officers," he reported, "and careful discipline to make them excellent soldiers." His idea of speeding up such improvements required the removal of all black officers and their replacement with whites; a number of the former, though not all, were excellent. He also purged Butler's three colonels on the pretext of "frivolous charges," perhaps because they tended to the view that "It matters little what color a man has to his skin if his brains are right, mind stamps the man, not race."[54]

Some of the aspersions cast on black troops had a self-fulfilling ring about them. As in many white units, initial training of black soldiers was often not good. The commanding officer of the 39th US Colored Infantry admitted that his men did not know how to use their firearms. Lack of training and preparation before troops were committed to battle (reminiscent of many actions in 1861–62) allowed black soldiers to get overly excited and impulsive. Colonel Higginson of 1st US Colored Infantry recalled that many of his men "got so excited and earnest that they would stand right up on the rifle pits regardless of exposure." Incorporating battle experience into procedures and sensible minor tactics depended on the trust that should grow between officers and men. In spite of the tension caused by the equal pay dispute, such trust soon developed and subsequently, black regiments demonstrated "the steadiness and deliberation of veterans."[55]

Commanders were still inclined to consider black regiments as lacking tactical sophistication. Black units were fine as "storm troopers" but their poor training supposedly ill equipped them to undertake other tasks. The *New York Times* expressed a consensus of opinion: "The most unbiased opinion seems to be that they are best for a sudden *dash*, but they are not good in a great disaster—not having the moral stamina to see long and horrible effects on the human body which shell or round shot produce." These views were the outgrowth of a long-standing prejudice. White racist attitudes were contradictory. Blacks were simultaneously savage, audacious, *and* childlike and cowardly. Their savage nature saw them through a break-in assault before childlike timidity swamped their martial spirit and the advance halted.[56]

No matter what unpleasant prejudices might be aired, commanders hardly ever sacrificed black soldiers on the strength of a whim (Fort Wagner was a conspicuous exception). Although often illiterate, black soldiers demonstrated a quick grasp of the issues at stake in the Civil War and were ready to sacrifice themselves. After one action Colonel Higginson asked a badly wounded black soldier whether he regretted enlisting. "Dat's just what I went for," he replied sharply.[57]

White officers were copious in their admiration for individual acts, but when dealing with black regiments as a whole they often exhibited a form of displaced racial prejudice. The indiscipline and rowdiness of black regiments characterized all Civil War volunteers; even black officers encountered hostility to those who exercised authority. The complaint that a black soldier "was no slave to be driven" could be frequently heard. But the indulgence of freedom of speech and opinion common in white regiments would not be found in black. Desertion was negligible, but infringements of discipline were punished harshly —especially any hint of mutiny. White officers were fearful lest they lose control of their men and "savagery" suddenly erupt.[58]

Nor were tensions between blacks wholly absent. Free blacks were more than capable of showing the same condescension toward the former slaves that whites had directed at them. Skilled and cultured free blacks, such as the abolitionist journalist George E. Stephens, who served as a sergeant in the 54th Massachusetts, were scornful of Southern black religion and culture. He thought slave religion "grotesque" and "the bulk of the slaves . . . are infidels."[59]

Black regiments faced ceaseless sniping and harassment from Confederates; the fraternization often found between whites was wholly absent. If wounded, black soldiers faced the unpleasant handicap of separate and unequal medical facilities. Their hospitals were crudely equipped, shabby, and dirty. Incompetent surgeons assisted by "hospital stewards of low order of qualifications" administered to them. Complaints were soon voiced concerning the "inhumanity of subjecting the colored soldiers to medical treatment and surgical operations to such men." Death rates soared in black hospitals. At Vicksburg the black hospital had treated 646 patients; 197 of these died, a mortality rate of 30.5 percent. During the same period, the white hospital experienced 415 deaths out of 2,963 patients—a mortality rate of 14 percent. The disparity threatened the Department of the Gulf with scandal. Nathaniel Banks managed to avert this threat by persuading the finest medical schools in Massachusetts to provide his black units with qualified medical staff. No similar arrangement was made for Nashville, Tennessee, where conditions for black soldiers remained lamentable.[60]

Despite all the difficulties placed in their path and the frustrations they experienced, it must be emphasized that employing federal black troops represents a truly revolutionary feature of the Civil War. Their use is emblematic of a broadening of Union war aims and the scope of social change generated by the conflict. The result of military action should have been the destruction of slavery along with the political power of the slave-owning class, although the latter proved temporary and brief. Northern opinion also assumed a hardly enthusiastic commitment to the acceptance of blacks as citizens who were owed fundamental constitutional rights. This shift in Northern attitudes over a period of about two years appears little short of astonishing when the depth of racial prejudice in mid-nineteenth-century America is understood.

Given such a commitment to fundamental change, one final subject needs to be considered. Were Union armies "revolutionary armies"? One historian, Joseph Alan Frank, likens American Civil War armies to people's armies, reminiscent of those of the English Civil War or the French Revolution. Politics was their "defining feature," and in the absence of keen regimental loyalties, dedication to the cause became magnified; zeal in furthering it led to a desire to destroy the enemy and give no quarter. The soldiers were more radical in outlook than civilians back home—even though previously they had represented the moral values of their communities, and the life of small towns tended to shape political horizons. American armies of the mid-nineteenth century were the products of democracy—mass participation—and industrialization. "The army," Frank stresses, "was the embodiment and spearhead of the democratic idea."[61]

There is much of value in Frank's interpretation, but Civil War armies (particularly Confederate) failed to be imbued with any centrally directed revolutionary ideology that welcomed the crushing of the *existing political system* in pursuit of its furtherance. As Frank himself points out, the American system stressed individualism, not the common good, and despite the harrying of Democrats and the abridgement of civil liberties these were not sacrificed for the good of the cause, but preserved enthusiastically. American soldiers, and Northerners especially as the war continued, were imbued by a determination for victory and a zeal for the end of the war. The destruction of the slavocracy and the South's peculiar institution was a means to that end; not (for the majority) an end in itself. Hence the rapidity with which this radical tide ebbed after the conclusion of the war, certainly after 1867.[62] Persecution of Democratic or conservative generals was hardly absent, but reached its height in 1862 and became less significant as the tide of punitive action became most popular. Its leader, General William Sherman, was a regular army officer and politically very conservative. So any depiction of radical Republicans as "Jacobins," purging and controlling revolutionary armies is ridiculously overstated. Besides, such points depend on comparisons with other revolutionary armies, such as the French, that, on closer inspection, are spurious. French Revolutionary armies were less revolutionary than they appeared.[63]

It would be quite misleading though to suggest that the use of such levels of military force were without political significance. The antebellum American political system, especially after 1857, was designed to give the slave states advantages like the right to count slaves as three-fifths of a white person in politics. It also appeared to foster the expansion of slavery into the western territories (seemingly legitimized by the Dred Scott decision of 1857). While the results of the Civil War were lacking in many respects for blacks' rights and status, as well as only short-term limitations on the power of the former Confederate leadership, the "system" of 1790–1860 was altered irreversibly.[64]

The long-term social impact of the experience of the Civil War is difficult to estimate. For about twenty years after its end there were few attempts to evoke it or probe its significance. The war did provide, as historian Anne C. Rose observes, "an occasion for personal testing, shared adventure, and the resolution of political goals." War gave common as well as individual purpose and demonstrated the significance of routine, procedures, the impersonal mass (although many had rejected this and reasserted individual choice), as well as mass production.[65]

A paradox lay at the heart of this experience. In search of methods suitable for the extermination of "vermin," even a commander as anti-Democratic as Sherman permitted plunder and the destruction of Confederate, particularly slave owners', property; a measure of anarchy was implicit in these methods. It was hoped that nonetheless the experience of war would produce better and more responsible citizens. Northern opinion would exhibit a more conservative hue than so much of the rhetoric concerning the radical forces underlying the war would lead one to expect.[66]

NOTES AND REFERENCES

1. Brian Holden Reid, "What Made Civil War Soldiers Fight?" *Journal of Strategic Studies* 22 (December 1999): 132.

2. For an interesting assessment of a sense of unity that grew out of difference, see Jordan Ross, "Uncommon Union: Diversity and Motivation among Civil War Soldiers," *American Nineteenth Century History* 3 (Spring 2002): 17–44.

3. Lloyd J. Matthews, "Military Ideals," in *The Oxford Companion to American Military History*, ed. John Whiteclay Chambers II, 323 (New York: Oxford University Press, 1999). The current oath dates from 1884.

4. James M. McPherson, *For Cause and Comrades* (New York: Oxford University Press, 1997), pp. 27–28, 100; idem., *What They Fought For* (Baton Rouge: Louisiana State University Press, 1989), pp. 12–13; Earl J. Hess, *The Union Soldier in Battle* (Lawrence: University Press of Kansas, 1997), pp. 2–3, 98.

5. Reid Mitchell, *The Vacant Chair: The Northern Soldier Leaves Home* (New York: Oxford University Press, 1993), pp. 5–8.

6. Ibid., p. 7; for an example of a "martinet" (invariably West Point graduates), see

T. Harry Williams, *Hayes of the Twenty-Third* (New York: Alfred A. Knopf, 1965), pp. 50, 53–54, who details Rutherford B. Hayes's frustrations serving as lieutenant colonel to Colonel Eliakim P. Scammon, the worst kind of tiresome, fussy pedant; Mark A. Weitz, "Drill, Training, and the Combat Performance of the Civil War Soldier," *Journal of Military History* 62 (April 1998): 286–88.

7. McPherson, *Cause and Comrades*, pp. 12–13, 61, 80.

8. A point made by Mitchell, *Vacant Chair*, p. 5. The average age of RAF Bomber Command aircrew, 1942–45, was nineteen; that of the USAAF, under twenty-two. Mark K. Wells, *Courage and Air Warfare* (London: Frank Cass, 1995), pp. 92–93, 109n19.

9. Samuel J. Watson, "Religion and Combat Motivation in the Confederate Armies," *Journal of Military History* 58 (January 1994): 30; Taylor to Bettie Saunders, Apr. 13, Dec. 18, 1864, *Lee's Adjutant: The Wartime Letters of Colonel Walter Herron Taylor, 1862–1865*, ed. R. Lockwood Tower (Columbia: University of South Carolina Press, 1995), pp. 147, 212.

10. Watson, "Confederate Religion and Combat Motivation," pp. 34–35, 37–38, 40 (quotation), 52–53; J. Tracey Power, *Lee's Miserables: Life in the Army of Northern Virginia from the Wilderness to Appomattox* (Chapel Hill: University of North Carolina Press, 1998), p. 126, notes an example of Lee's attendance at an outdoor service, an eyewitness reporting that he was "humbly kneeling on the ground among the sunburnt soldiers of his army."

11. Watson, "Confederate Religion and Combat Motivation," p. 42; Hess, *Union Soldier in Battle*, pp. 75–76, 115.

12. Hess, *Union Soldier in Battle*, pp. 75–76.

13. Topography might explain the tendency noted by Paddy Griffith, *Rally Once Again: Battle Tactics of the American Civil War* (Ramsbury, UK: Crowood, 1987), pp. 73–74, 88–90, 104, 118–19, to open fire within one hundred yards.

14. Gerald F. Linderman, *Embattled Courage: The Experience of Combat in the American Civil War* (New York: Free Press, 1987), pp. 146–47, 153.

15. Quoted in Brian Holden Reid, *The American Civil War and the Wars of the Industrial Revolution* (London: Cassell, 1999), p. 99; for PTSD, see Eric T. Dean, *Shook over Hell: Post Traumatic Stress, Vietnam and the Civil War* (Cambridge, MA: Harvard University Press, 1997), although his main target is the notion that the Vietnam War was uniquely traumatic, see pp. 21, 188–89, 211.

16. Edgeworth Bird to Sally Bird, Feb. 27, 1863, *The Granite Farm Letters: The Civil War Correspondence of Edgeworth and Sallie Bird*, ed. John Rozier (Athens: University of Georgia Press, 1988), p. 109.

17. Quoted in McPherson, *For Cause and Comrades*, p. 17.

18. Gary W. Gallagher, *Lee and His Army in Confederate History* (Chapel Hill: University of North Carolina Press, 2001), pp. 92–93, 123, 127–31, 269–70.

19. McPherson, *What They Fought For*, pp. 49, 50–51.

20. Richard N. Current, *Lincoln's Loyalists: Union Soldiers from the Confederacy* (Boston: Northeastern University Press, 1992), pp. 144–45; McPherson, *For Cause and Comrades*, pp. 124–25.

21. McPherson, *For Cause and Comrades*, pp. 119–22, 125–26, 129; Hess, *Union Soldier in Battle*, pp. 105, 108–109.

22. For excessive preoccupation with generals, see Mark Grimsley, *Hard Hand of War: Union Military Policy toward Southern Civilians 1861–1865* (Cambridge: Cambridge University Press, 1995), pp. 144–45, 154, 157, 160–61, 167–68; Lance Jarda, "Shutting the Gates of Mercy: The American Origins of Total War, 1860–1880," *Journal of Military History* 59 (January 1995): 7–26; McPherson, *For Cause and Comrades*, pp. 142, 172–75; Gallagher, *Lee and His Army*, pp. 91–93.

23. Stephen E. Ambrose, *Halleck: Lincoln's Chief of Staff* (Baton Rouge: Louisiana State University Press, 1962), p. 9; Halleck's initial responses to the problem were conservative, see his "exclusion order" of Nov. 20, 1861. John F. Marszalek, *Commander of All Lincoln's Armies: A Life of General Henry W. Halleck* (Cambridge, MA: Belknap Press of Harvard University Press, 2004), pp. 110–12.

24. Hans L. Trefousse, *Benjamin Franklin Wade: Radical Republican from Ohio* (New York: Twayne, 1963), p. 183; Ambrose, *Halleck*, pp. 88, 92; Lincoln to August Belmont, July 31, 1862, *The Collected Works of Abraham Lincoln,* ed. Roy P. Basler (New Brunswick, NJ: Rutgers University Press, 1953), vol. 5, p. 350. See above, p. 236.

25. Grant to Lew Wallace, Feb. 19, 1862, *The Papers of Ulysses S. Grant*, ed. John Y. Simon (Carbondale: University of Southern Illinois Press, 1967), vol. 4, pp. 45, 250, 233.

26. *War of the Rebellion: The Official Records of the Union and Confederate Armies*, 128 parts in 70 vols. (Washington, DC: Government Printing Office, 1880–1901), series 1, vol. 24, p. 47; Bruce Catton, *Grant Moves South* (Boston: Little, Brown, 1960), p. 419; *Report of the Joint Committee on the Conduct of the War* (Washington, DC: Government Printing Office, 1863), vol. 1, pp. 3–4.

27. Catton, *Grant Moves South*, pp. 292, 296, 336, 342.

28. McPherson, *For Cause and Comrades*, p. 154.

29. For example, Mark A. Weitz, *A Higher Duty: Desertion among Georgia Troops* (Lincoln: University of Nebraska Press, 2000), p. 9; idem., *More Damning Than Slaughter: Desertion in the Confederate Army* (Lincoln: University of Nebraska Press, 2005).

30. Figures from Brian Holden Reid and John White, "'A Mob of Stragglers and Cowards': Desertion from the Union and Confederate Armies, 1861–1865," *Journal of Strategic Studies* 8 (March 1985): 64–65. Fred A. Shannon, *The Organization and Administration of the Union Army, 1861–1865* (1928; Gloucester, MA: Peter Smith, 1965), vol. 1, pp. 178–79, gives a lower figure of 260,339 Northern desertions but adds 161,286 who failed to appear when drafted; he estimates that the number who returned to the

ranks at 25 percent, leaving 200,000 "actual and complete desertions." James W. Geary, *We Need Men: The Union Draft in the Civil War* (De Kalb: Northern Illinois University Press, 1991), p. 15, argues that the actual number of Northern deserters was 278,644.

31. Shannon, *Organization and Administration*, vol. 1, pp. 168–69, 176–77, 247; Geary, *We Need Men*, pp. 13–14.

32. Holden Reid and White, "Mob of Stragglers and Cowards," pp. 66–76, 69, emphasize the poor caliber of NCOs; also see Judith L. Hallock, "The Role of the Community in Civil War Desertion," *Civil War History* 29 (June 1983): 123–34.

33. Quoted in Holden Reid and White, "Mob of Stragglers and Cowards," p. 67; Geary, *We Need Men*, p. 15.

34. Quoted in Holden Reid and White, "Mob of Stragglers and Cowards," pp. 70, 74; Richard E. Beringer, Herman Hattaway, Archer Jones, and William N. Still Jr., *Why the South Lost the Civil War* (Athens: University of Georgia Press, 1986), pp. 434–35, 439; Weitz, *More Damning than Slaughter*, pp. 43, 50–51, 55–62, argues that this is an incremental process that begins in 1861.

35. Shannon, *Organization and Administration*, vol. 2, pp. 31, 84; Lee's views are in *O.R.*, series 1, vol. 33, p. 1063; Lee to Davis, Apr. 13, 1864, in *Lee's Dispatches*, eds. Douglas Southall Freeman and Grady McWhiney (New York: Putnam, 1957), pp. 154–58.

36. Lincoln, Proclamation Granting Amnesty to Soldiers Absent Without Leave, Mar. 10, 1863, *Collected Works*, vol. 6, pp. 132–33; for an example of Lincoln's sympathy, see Lincoln to George G. Meade, Nov. 3, 1863, ibid., vol. 6, p. 561; Sylvanus Cadwallader, *Three Years with Grant*, ed. Benjamin P. Thomas (New York: Alfred A. Knopf, 1956), p. 246.

37. Paragraph based on Holden Reid and White, "A Mob of Stragglers and Cowards," pp. 70–71.

38. Ibid., p. 66; David M. Jordan, *"Happiness Is Not My Companion": The Life of General G. K. Warren* (Bloomington: Indiana University Press, 2001), p. 207; Shannon, *Organization and Administration*, vol. 1, pp. 180–81.

39. Holden Reid and White, "Mob of Stragglers and Cowards," pp. 68, 69; Horrocks's views can be found in *My Dear Parents: An Englishman's Letters Home from the American Civil War* (London: Gollencz, 1982), p. 67; Ross, "Uncommon Union," p. 34, doubts that Horrocks's views can be "taken at face value." But what struck Horrocks was an important feature of American national character: "Everyone tries to be smart," which contrasts with the more conformist and diffident values he was used to.

40. Brian Holden Reid, "A Survey of the Militia in 18th Century America," *Army Quarterly* 110 (January 1980): 52. A Virginia law of 1723 permitted blacks to serve as "drummers and trumpeters . . . but not to bear arms." Susan-Mary Grant, "Fighting for Freedom: African-American Soldiers in the Civil War," in *The American Civil War: Explorations and Reconsiderations*, eds. idem. and Brian Holden Reid (London: Longman, 2000), p. 193.

41. James M. McPherson, *The Struggle for Equality: Abolitionists and the Negro in the Civil War and Reconstruction* (Princeton, NJ: Princeton University Press, 1964), pp. 192–93; William S. McFeely, *Frederick Douglass* (New York: Norton, 1991), pp. 217–18; Michael J. Bennett, *Union Jacks: Yankee Sailors in the Civil War* (Chapel Hill: University of North Carolina Press, 2004), pp. 156–58.

42. Edward A. Miller, *Lincoln's Abolitionist General: The Life of David Hunter* (Columbia: University of South Carolina Press, 1997), pp. 99–106; McPherson, *Struggle for Equality*, pp. 195–96.

43. Lincoln, Remarks to Deputation of Western Gentlemen, Aug. 4, 1862, *Collected Works*, vol. 5, pp. 356–57; but Morton's efforts were stymied by racial prejudice. It was not until Massachusetts recruiting agents began "poaching" Indiana blacks that a regiment was raised. See Kenneth M. Stampp, *Indiana Politics during the Civil War* (1949; Bloomington: Indiana University Press, 1978), p. 215.

44. McPherson, *Struggle for Equality*, pp. 197, 202.

45. Dudley T. Cornish, *The Sable Arm: Negro Troops in the Union Army, 1861–1865* (1956; Lawrence: University Press of Kansas, 1987), pp. 110–15, 118–22. Thomas's speeches received a lot of criticism. See ibid., pp. 123–26. McPherson, *Struggle for Equality*, pp. 212–14; McFeely, *Douglass*, pp. 228–30.

46. Ibid., pp. 197, 202; Shannon, *Organization and Administration*, pp. 159–60; Russell F. Weigley, *History of the United States Army* (London: Batsford, 1968), pp. 212–13.

47. Current, *Lincoln's Loyalists*, pp. 150–51.

48. Grant, "Fighting for Freedom," pp. 195, 201; Weigley, *United States Army*, p. 212.

49. Grant, "Fighting for Freedom," pp. 205–206; Allen C. Guelzo, *Lincoln's Emancipation Proclamation* (New York: Simon and Schuster, 2004), pp. 217–20.

50. John Hope Franklin, *The Emancipation Proclamation* (1963; Wheeling, IL: Harlan Davidson, 1995), pp. 94–96, 98, 101, 116, 119, 126; McPherson, *Struggle for Equality*, pp. 214–15.

51. Cornish, *Sable Arm*, pp. 183–87, 189–96; McPherson, *Struggle for Equality*, pp. 215–19.

52. James G. Hollandsworth Jr., *The Louisiana Native Guards: The Black Military Experience during the Civil War* (Baton Rouge: Louisiana State University Press, 1995), pp. 1–8.

53. Ibid., pp. 13–19, 27–28, 43.

54. Ibid., pp. 55–56, 62–65, 78–79; *Thank God My Regiment an African One: The Civil War Diary of Colonel Nathanial W. Daniels*, ed. C. P. Weaver (Baton Rouge: Louisiana State University Press, 2004), pp. 127–28 (entry for Aug. 22, 1863).

55. Joseph T. Glatthaar, *Forged in Battle: The Civil War Alliance of Black Soldiers and White Officers* (New York: Free Press, 1990), pp. 145–47.

56. Ibid., p. 149; Bruce Catton notes the contradiction in *A Stillness at Appomattox* (New York: Doubleday, 1955), pp. 227–29.

57. Quotation from Hollandsworth, *Louisiana Native Guards*, p. 29; Glatthaar, *Forged in Battle*, p. 153; Catton, *Stillness at Appomattox*, p. 231, cites an example of a wounded black soldier who insisted on carrying his musket to the hospital: "I don't want de fellows at de hospital to mistake me for a teamster."

58. Glatthaar, *Forged in Battle*, pp. 113–20.

59. *A Voice of Thunder: The Civil War Letters of George E. Stephens*, ed. Donald Yacovone (Urbana: University of Illinois Press, 1997), p. 106.

60. Glatthaar, *Forged in Battle*, pp. 193–94.

61. Joseph Allan Frank, *With Ballot and Bayonet: The Political Socialization of American Civil War Soldiers* (Athens: University of Georgia Press, 1998), pp. vii–ix, 1–2, 4 (quotation), 19, 30, 180–81.

62. Ibid., pp. 6–7, 66–67.

63. Ibid., pp. 123, 143–35, 146–49; S. P. Mackenzie, *Revolutionary Armies in the Modern Era* (London: Routledge, 1997), pp. 4, 49–50.

64. See Leonard L. Richards, *The Slave Power: The Free North and Southern Domination* (Baton Rouge: Louisiana State University Press, 2000).

65. Anne C. Rose, *Victorian America and the Civil War* (Cambridge, MA: Cambridge University Press, 1992), pp. 19, 100–102, 106, 252.

66. Frank, *With Ballot and Bayonet*, p. 145.

POSTSCRIPT

THE PROBLEM OF INDECISIVENESS

The Union victory at Chattanooga was a signal success. Yet it fitted a consistent pattern. A ruthless and tenacious pursuit did not follow the battle and although battered, the Confederacy's second field army survived to fight on and its spirits would be restored in short order. Chattanooga is also a bracing reminder that fighting a defensive battle was not a magic solution to the Confederacy's operational and strategic problems. Defense cannot provide a shield against military errors, and Braxton Bragg made several that compromised the safety of his army.

In reviewing the question of indecisiveness, a distinction must be drawn between indecisiveness in war and indecisiveness in battle because the two are not synonymous.

Nonetheless, after so many battles (especially in 1862) the first thirty-one months of the Civil War failed to produce a decision that lent victory to one side or the other. It is unlikely that the war could have been ended by one single battle but the destruction of an enemy army would have aided the process, that much is clear. This question is often presented as a narrowly military matter, and a tactical one at that. The talents, calculations, and miscalculations of commanders are often weighed in the balance; the capabilities of troops and the way these were expended in battle, it is assumed, lie at the heart of the matter. These are far from unimportant considerations but the question of indecisiveness in war is essentially a *strategic* one. This book has sought to relate military activities to the issues that gave rise to the war in the first place and then exerted pressure on those who sought to fight it. These issues do not need a lengthy review here, but the decision in 1861 to wage a war solely to preserve the Union lacked unanimous support. Some members of Lincoln's cabinet and of the legislative branch argued strenuously that the North's war aims should be widened to embrace the destruction of slavery as well as Southern armies.

Others, mainly (but not exclusively) war Democrats, believed that military operations should be conducted with a mind to secure reconciliation with the Confederate leadership that would result in the return of the seceded states to the Union with slavery intact. A significant group of war Democrats, including Edwin M. Stanton, Senator Andrew Johnson, and Major Generals Benjamin F. Butler, Daniel E. Sickles, and John A. Logan had by 1862 begun to express views that sympathized with the harsher view of war aims. Such political disagreements that cut across parties increased pressure on the strategic decision-making process. In short, a great expansion of the level of military force was inherent in the political debate of 1862–63.

Strategy has been defined by Colin S. Gray as "the bridge that relates military power to political purpose; it is neither military power per se nor political purpose. By strategy, I mean *the use that is made of force and threat of force for the ends of policy.*"[1] It follows that strategy cannot operate in a vacuum and flows from various sources—the progress or otherwise of the armed forces, the degree of safety experienced by the political organs of the state (or, in this case, one putative state), and finally, the state of public opinion on both sides. The last two are distorted in the American Civil War because of the close proximity of the respective capital cities. These elements are captured in Carl von Clausewitz's trinity: the commander and his army, the government, and the people.[2]

Such interdependence is also reflected in the levels of war. The strategic rests on the operational and tactical levels. Operations, it has been emphasized, requires the employment of armed force to achieve military and political ends in a distinctive geographical environment. Tactics is the art of fighting. In 1861 both politicians and military men found it difficult to conceive of campaigns beyond the fighting of a single battle. After its initial defeat at the first battle of Manassas in July 1861, the Union greatly improved its strategic performance and began to organize coherent campaigns—albeit on a small scale. Even so, strategic performance does not resemble a successful sports team on its best form because it does not need to rest on consistent success at all three levels. But in wars between regular armies a degree of tactical success underlies a strategic success. But it took until 1863 before the best commanders began to realize that "Tactical achievement has meaning only in terms of operational intention and strategic effect."[3]

The major factors shaping strategy for both sides was the sheer size of the theater of war and the influence of the sea—the Confederacy being lapped on two sides by the Atlantic Ocean and the Gulf of Mexico. The strategic importance for the Union of command of the sea lay in its reduction of the enormity of the Confederacy's advantage in space, and the power it granted to isolate the slave republic from the outside world. Seapower proved itself vital in 1862 because the federal navy's ability to penetrate the great river system of the Mississippi valley helped nullify certain Confederate operational advantages that had become manifest in the east. The exploitation of the blockade brought an economic bonus, but its effects were slow and cumulative. The most sophisticated appreciation of the incremental strategic view could be found in the Anaconda Plan. This was an attritional document, but also a statement of the conservative view of war aims because it sought to shelter the South from the full rigors of war.

The essential precepts of the Anaconda Plan were put into practice in the Mississippi valley after the fall of forts Henry and Donelson, and the city of New Orleans. A concerted effort to seize most of the Confederacy's remaining posts followed. These efforts were far less systematic than Scott's scheme had envisaged. Further, the demands of an impatient public opinion forced simultaneous Northern efforts to destroy the rebel field armies in battle. As a result, the federal government adopted strategies of annihilation and exhaustion (or attrition) at the same time. It attempted to destroy Confederate fighting power and wear down its warmaking capacity in a single bound.

Strategy is an exacting art because it attempts to fuse diverse sources and serves as the link between policy makers and men sitting on horseback or laboring in the engine room of a ship.[4] All forms of military strategy in great wars aim at the destruction of the enemy's capacity to resist, so a combination of annihilation and attrition would be complementary rather than contradictory —the hammer and the anvil. The Union advances in the west offer proof of their joint effectiveness; but the failure to defeat, let alone destroy, the Army of Northern Virginia in five great campaigns, March 1862 through June 1863, led to the gradual acceptance by the Lincoln administration of the more radical view of Union war aims and the abandonment of any form of reconciliation.

It is odd that a more punitive form of war resulted from efforts to bring the Civil War to a rapid conclusion. But wars "tend to become 'total' as the price of victory rises and the quest for decision remains unsatisfied."[5] Victories in the west had much less political effect—especially on the distant political nerve center in Washington, DC, and the struggle for international opinion abroad. Indeed the political import of Northern victories in the Mississippi valley tended to be canceled out by Confederate victories in the east from the Seven Days' onward.

Northern leaders had been buoyed up by the belief in their superior cause—the defense of the Union—and the splendor of the appearance and quality of the equipment of Union armies. How could American soldiers fail? This confidence led to extravagant claims. In April 1863 Hooker wrote of the Army of the Potomac that it "was in condition to inspire the highest expectations." When repeatedly these expectations were not realized, military failure forced some commentators to conclude that perhaps the United States was not exceptional after all. Perhaps the Union had forfeited divine favor. In short, the string of federal defeats in the east resulted in a profound and debilitating crisis of confidence.[6]

In retrospect this crisis appears exaggerated, as does Confederate self-confidence. Whatever its deficiencies and overly ambitious reach, at least the Union developed a strategy. Throughout 1861–63 the Confederacy failed to develop any kind of coherent strategic view. The general defensive tenor of Confederate strategic policy in 1861–62 did not strike a chord with Southern public opinion and accorded ill with misconceived attempts to force European powers to intervene on its behalf by a cotton embargo; the most effective way of demonstrating Confederate success was by offensive action. The defense of the great western spaces was conducted ineptly; consequently, great swaths of territory were given up, but Union commanders found it difficult to muster enough strength to inflict a devastating blow.

The Confederate failure to evolve a viable strategy is most evident in the autumn of 1862 during the Confederate counteroffensive. This resulted not from any overall strategic success, but the individual exploitation of Union errors. The Confederacy failed to make the most of this success. It lacked a single guiding hand; by combining the office of president and general-in-chief, Jefferson Davis tried to do too much.

Both sides revealed significant weaknesses in organizing the proper institutions for the higher conduct of the war. As the Confederacy replicated the pre-

1861 US military system, it inherited its weaknesses. The departmental system was *area* rather than formation based, and tended to diffuse manpower over great expanses in numerous small garrisons. Within this structure army command was elevated over all others; army commanders were reluctant to cooperate with one another and the role of the commanding general was often confused with the command of an army, an error that added to the lack of strategic coordination. Consequently, there were multiple offensive efforts on both sides, all too weak to produce decisive results.

It is now appropriate to explore the operational and tactical techniques that contributed to the stalemate. The operational dimension serves as a test for the viability of the goals produced by the political sources of strategy. The Union had the opportunity and the resources to win the war by the autumn of 1862. The Confederacy at the same time had a fleeting chance to try and win it rather than just avoid losing it. Both sides, however, failed to exploit these opportunities because of errors in the attack rather than because a successful attack was beyond their resources in the first place. The latter argument has a circular, self-fulfilling air to it.

Innumerable assaults were piecemeal. They squandered the resources of armies that, although large by American standards, were not so big by the standards of some of the great European powers who could deploy large standing armies. On the Union side, a congenital inability to land concentrated, offensive blows was evident during the Peninsular campaign, Antietam, and Fredericksburg. Even when a success was achieved, as at Iuka, the great spaces of the west rendered it easier for the defeated Confederates to escape. For their part, the Confederates revealed an impressive ability to exploit what the poet John Keats called "the magic hand of chance" and take their foes by surprise. Yet this advantage was frittered away at Shiloh, the Seven Days', Perryville, and Murfreesboro by clumsy, ill-coordinated, and amateurishly organized attacks. Battles can only be won, whatever qualities of generalship have been shown on their eve, by selecting the decisive point, getting that choice right, and then gaining it with overwhelming strength.[7]

There were three tactical reasons for the failure to win battles decisively even when the auspices were most favorable. First, poor intelligence seems endemic. One of the prime reasons for Lee's success against the odds at Chancellorsville lay in the superiority of his intelligence; failure at Gettysburg, and the earlier errors in September 1862 that put him on the backfoot at Antietam, were due to a marked deterioration in its quality. Second, reconnaissance was also faulty, accentuated by dreadful maps. The great Duke of Marlborough reputedly once observed that time spent in reconnaissance is rarely wasted. From First Manassas onward, Union and Confederate commanders spent too little time on reconnaissance. A combination of misleading intelligence and inadequate reconnaissance resulted in too many attacks made blind based on guesswork, as at Antietam and Fredericksburg. The last degenerated into an artless battle lacking coherent, offensive design.[8]

Even Lee committed similar errors. At Gettysburg, on ground that he did not know at all, he was misled by a flawed reconnaissance carried out by Captain Samuel R. Johnston. As armies tended to be unaware of the presence of the enemy, a marked increase in the frequency of meeting engagements can be discerned—Gettysburg being the most famous of all.[9]

The main significance of the numerous meeting engagements lies in the severe limitations they imposed on the commander's ability to plan for the pursuit. If Civil War commanders were uncertain how to engage their enemy they could not, for obvious reasons, move to the next step rapidly, namely to distribute their formations so as to be ready to wreak destruction on a fleeing foe.

The other factor inherent in all of the foregoing tactical discussion is the poor quality of operational staffwork. The levels of organizational and logistical staffwork appear excellent down to the most junior levels, especially if staff officers could draw on their prewar business experience. It is in the crucial area of operational staffwork, from brigade upward, where the American staff system, North as well as South, was plainly underdeveloped.[10]

The staff system developed to aid the commander in wars of mass involvement. A restricted staff role made the job of the commander more difficult. The role of technology more generally will be surveyed in a later work. The telegraph permitted an enhanced strategic coordination but had a reduced effect operationally. The quality of top commanders represents a strategic dimension that is capable of giving one side an edge over the other. The war's indecisiveness has been explained by attributing to Southern generalship such superior qualities that it could cancel out Northern material advantages. Claims to a moral victory are rooted in the literature of the Lost Cause. They no longer persuade. The Southern pool of command talent at the highest level is shallow: Leonidas Polk and Earl Van Dorn are perhaps more typical of the corps of senior officers than Robert E. Lee and Stonewall Jackson.[11]

It cannot be denied though that the ability to attain policy goals is dependent on military performance in the field. The challenge posed by battle cannot be postponed indefinitely; at some point the enemy must be engaged and defeated. Union commanders built up a much better record of success in campaigns in Mississippi, Tennessee, and Kentucky; but in the last two they still showed an excessive prudence and tendency toward overinsurance. In the east this appears as almost pusillanimous. Northern commanders believed themselves outnumbered even when they enjoyed a level of numerical superiority. They also reveal a marked lack of enterprise in tactical execution. These weaknesses allowed the Confederates to compensate for their strategic weaknesses, especially by granting them space in which to maneuver for operational advantage. Numerical weakness encouraged Confederate commanders to take risks, even though Braxton Bragg's execution in Kentucky was deeply flawed and showed levels of anxiety comparable with those of his Union opponent, Don Carlos Buell.

Northern operational failures are not the exclusive preserve of the east. Henry W. Halleck, who made his reputation in the west, displayed a marked defensive outlook, and so too did William S. Rosecrans. But the greatest failure surely must be McClellan's. He is the most disappointing figure to hold high command in the first eighteen months of the war. McClellan showed a want of resilience and an inability to make choices in the field. Generals on active service must be capable of comprehending what military force can achieve. In June 1862 McClellan failed to take into account the effects on public opinion of his withdrawal to Harrison's Landing. So many of his decisions were influenced by his obsession that he was outnumbered that he could not arrive at a rational judgment as to his capabilities.[12]

McClellan's uncertainties amounted to a lack of operational confidence. This book has sought to place command calculations at the forefront of any interpretation of the events of 1861–63. Nonetheless, Civil War military history should not be reduced to the simplistic equation that battlefield success consists of setting one team of generals against another as in a lethal sports match. It needs to be acknowledged that military "misfortunes," that is, failure on the battlefield, is more the product of deficiencies in the *system* of making war rather than just a reflection of the limitations of the man at the top.

Commanders though are representative of the organizations over which they preside. McClellan helped create a system to fight war as he understood it: orderly, businesslike, rational in a management sense, much dedicated to schedules and targets. This desire to control the conditions of war probably arose from the lack of a standing army before 1861 and the resultant doubts that surfaced as to the ability of an inexperienced officer corps to operate such an unprecedentedly large military structure.[13]

McClellan's system was just as much a reflection of his political values as his military outlook. He promoted his protégés, such as Fitz John Porter and William B. Franklin; they agreed with McClellan's view that reconciliation should be an urgent priority.[14] However, the system that McClellan bequeathed to Burnside, Hooker, and Meade, despite their contrasting aspirations (for Hooker was often critical of McClellan's tactics), revealed two significant handicaps. First, it encouraged docility; second, it displayed a fundamental lack of adaptability. If the commanders of the Army of the Potomac were presented with opportunities—and the Antietam campaign is the exception that proves the rule—they agonized over taking them; sometimes they preferred not to take them.[15]

It is too little understood that gaining victories in war, or staving off defeat, involves just as much the taking advantage of the enemy's errors as it does in putting into place ambitious, well wrought, and intricately thought-out schemes. It is because Lee and Jackson were skillful at doing this that their armies could move so nimbly and evade the heavy but lumbering blows of the Union columns. They did so, too, because of the psychological ascendancy they had achieved over an enemy half disposed to believe that they were already defeated before the campaign was fully developed. The true significance of Jackson's campaign in the Shenandoah Valley lies in the realm of psychological warfare.

Several caveats need to be advanced to qualify this praise of Confederate practice. First, the quantity of Union manpower and resources tends to be exaggerated mainly as a result of the influence of the Lost Cause school. The Confederate Conscription Act of April 1862 produced armies by that summer comparable in size to the federal ones. Confederate commanders managed to reduce their comparative inferiority by concentrating tactical superiority at formation level, especially in the large corps of the Army of Northern Virginia. Artillery firepower was concentrated, too, and its command centralized in battalions by 1863. Both lent Confederate forces, especially in the east, a measure of *operational* superiority. This might not always have been expended wisely given the tendency toward dispersal, but compensated for a more general numerical inferiority. However, the string of resulting Confederate victories served only to promote further cycles of war because of Lee's failure either to consummate his success or his fatal tendency to stumble at the pivotal moment.

Confederate operational failures were also due to logistical failures. In both Confederate invasions of the North, the methods of Grant and Sherman were anticipated by Lee and Bragg. Yet the dispersal inherent in foraging on the country led to both commanders fighting battles on Northern soil under far less advantageous circumstances than either hoped for. At Gettysburg the Army of Northern Virginia escaped calamity thanks to audacity in the retreat. A tougher-minded federal opponent than George Meade, intent on driving his men until they dropped, might have gained a much more clear-cut victory. But the McClellan system did not produce such men.

War is, of course, just as much in the province of passion and chance as reason—perhaps more so. The many battles before November 1863 could be fought because of high morale among soldiers and their willingness to fight. Even so, Civil War campaigns were not fought out in a clinical laboratory. Soldiers were subject to the exhaustion of the march, the discomforts of the camp, and were often at the mercy of the elements. The influence, in particular, of the weather might determine the course of a campaign. Historians should not ignore the cold at Murfreesboro, the summer heat at Gettysburg, or the autumnal humidity at Antietam. In January 1863 the weather conspired to thwart Burnside's attempt to recapture the initiative after Fredericksburg. A combination of unexpectedly heavy rain and glutinous clay plunged the Army of the Potomac into the "Mud March." Yet the weather could not be counted on. Some Confederate leaders expected the summer heat of Mississippi and consequent disease to stop Grant's drive on Vicksburg; but it did not do so.[16]

For all the discomfort and suffering, by November 1863 soldiers on both sides were keen to increase the levels of violence thrown at the enemy. Soldiers in the Army of Northern Virginia wanted to fight another battle after Gettysburg because they felt they had not done themselves justice in Pennsylvania.[17] Union soldiers in the west were enthusiastic supporters of a "vigorous" war on Southern property, that is, slavery. War weariness did exist, but discussions on why it "took the North so long" to defeat the South are shaped largely by the military experiences of the Second World War (1941–45 for Americans), and by a characteristic American impatience with the passage of time.

The thirty-one months covered in this book do not constitute a long period of time considering the issues that both sides contested. The fighting of the American Revolution lasted seven years. Since 1960 the length of wars has increased greatly, and the four years it took the United States to defeat the Confederacy seems very short. What *is* impressive is the degree of military force that the federal government had mustered to gain complete victory. Victory could be predicted but not presumed. Errors could still be made, and the Confederacy could turn them to good account. A further seventeen months of arduous conflict remained. The challenges of the next campaign brought their own dangers.

NOTES AND REFERENCES

1. Colin S. Gray, *Modern Strategy* (New York: Oxford University Press, 1999), p. 17.

2. Carl von Clausewitz, *On War*, eds. Michael Howard and Peter Paret (Princeton: Princeton University Press, 1976), vol. 1, p. 89.

3. Gray, *Modern Strategy*, pp. 20–25, 28.

4. See ibid., pp. 52, 361.

5. Ibid., p. 157.

6. Stephen W. Sears, *Chancellorsville* (New York: Houghton Mifflin, 1996), p. 107; the general point is alluded to in Gray, *Modern Strategy*, p. 7.

7. Gray, *Modern Strategy*, p. 257, agrees.

8. See the indictment in Edwin C. Fishel, *The Secret War for the Union* (New York: Houghton Mifflin, 1996), pp. 235–37.

9. Brian Holden Reid, *Robert E. Lee: Icon for a Nation* (2005; Amherst, NY: Prometheus Books, 2007), p. 183; Philip Howes, *The Catalytic Wars: A Study of the Development of Warfare, 1860–1870* (London: Minerva Press, 1998), pp. 26, 30.

10. For an important case study in logistical excellence, see Lenette Taylor, *"The Supply for Tomorrow Must Not Fail": The Civil War Career of Captain Simon Perkins Jr., A Union Quartermaster* (Kent, OH: Kent State University Press, 2004).

11. See Marcus Cunliffe's pioneering discussion in *Soldiers and Civilians: The Martial Spirit in America, 1775–1865*, 3rd ed. (1968; London: Gregg, 1993), pp. 370–72.

12. Ethan S. Rafuse, *McClellan's War* (Bloomington: Indiana University Press, 2005), p. 230.

13. See Brian Holden Reid, "Introduction," in "The Vistas of American Military History," eds. Brian Holden Reid and Joseph G. Dawson III, special issue of *American Nineteenth Century History* 7, no. 2 (June 2006): 148–49.

14. See Porter's letter to the *New York World* after Antietam, quoted in Rafuse, *McClellan's War*, p. 342.

15. A pivotal influence on my interpretation is Eliot A. Cohen and John Gooch, *Military Misfortunes: The Anatomy of Failure in War* (New York: Free Press, 1990), pp. 3, 7, 10, 57, 121, 161, 163, 221, 231–33.

16. A pioneering attempt is Harold A. Winters and others, *Battling the Elements: Weather and Terrain in the Conduct of War* (Baltimore, MD: Johns Hopkins University Press, 1998), pp. 34–39.

17. Gary W. Gallagher, *Lee and His Army in Confederate History* (Chapel Hill: University of North Carolina Press, 2001), pp. 996–97.

BIBLIOGRAPHY

PRIMARY SOURCES

Basler, Roy P., ed. *The Collected Works of Abraham Lincoln*, 9 vols. Rutgers, NJ: Rutgers University Press, 1953.

Buell, D. C. "East Tennessee and the Campaign of Perryville," in *Battles and Leaders of the Civil War*, vol. 3: *Retreat from Gettysburg Part Three*, ed. Robert V. Johnson and Clarence C. Buel. New York: Century, 1956 ed., pp. 31–51.

Butler, Benjamin F. *Butler's Book: A Review of His Legal, Political and Military Career.* Boston: Thayer, 1892.

Cadwallader, Sylvanus. *Three Years with Grant*, ed. Benjamin P. Thomas. New York: Alfred A. Knopf, 1956.

Daniels, Nathan W. *Thank God My Regiment an African One: The Civil War Diary of Colonel Nathan W. Daniels*, ed. C. P. Weaver. Baton Rouge: Louisiana State University Press, 2004.

Donald, David, ed. *Inside Lincoln's Cabinet: The Civil War Diaries of Salmon P. Chase.* New York: Alfred A. Knopf, 1954.

Dowdey, Clifford, and Louis H. Manarin, eds. *The Wartime Papers of R. E. Lee.* New York: Bramhall House, 1961.

Fremantle, A. J. L. *Three Months in the Southern States, April–June 1863.* 1864; Lincoln: University of Nebraska Press, 1991.

Grant, Ulysses S. *Personal Memoirs,* 2 vols. London: Sampson Low, 1886.

Horrocks, James. *My Dear Parents: An Englishman's Letters Home from the American Civil War.* London: Gollancz, 1982.

Johnson, P. Deloach, ed. *Under the Southern Cross: Soldier Life with Gordon Bradwell and the Army of Northern Virginia.* Macon, GA: Mercer University Press, 1999.

Joint Committee on the Conduct of the War. *Report of the Joint Committee on the Conduct of the War,* 3 vols. Washington, DC: Government Printing Office, 1863.

Julian, George W. *Political Recollections, 1840–1872.* Chicago: Jansen McClurg, 1884.

Lee, Fitzhugh. *General Lee.* 1894; New York: Da Capo reprint, 1994.

Lee, Robert E. *Lee's Dispatches: Unpublished Letters of General Robert E. Lee to Jefferson Davis,* ed. Douglas Southall Freeman and Grady McWhiney. New York: Putnam's, 1957.

Lincoln, Abraham. "By the President of the United States, A Proclamation," April 15, 1861, original draft. Robert Todd Lincoln Collection of the Papers of Abraham Lincoln. Washington, DC: Library of Congress.

Longstreet, James. *From Manassas to Appomattox.* 1895; New York: Da Capo reprint, 1992.

Marshall, Jessie Ames, ed. *Private and Official Correspondence of Benjamin F. Butler,* 5 vols. Norwood, MA: Privately printed, 1917.

McClellan, George B. *McClellan's Own Story.* New York: Webster, 1881.

McClellan, H. B. *I Rode with Jeb Stuart: The Life and Campaigns of Major General J. E. B. Stuart.* Secaucus, NJ: Blue and Grey Press reprint, 1993.

Nicholas, Nicholas Harris, ed. *The Dispatches and Letters of Vice Admiral Lord Viscount Nelson,* 5 vols. London: Colburn, 1845.

Porter, Horace. *Campaigning with Grant,* with an introduction by Joseph G. Dawson III. New York: Bantam Books abridged edition, 1991.

Robert Todd Lincoln Collection of the Papers of Abraham Lincoln. Washington, DC: Library of Congress.

Rozier, John, ed. *The Granite Farm Letters: The Civil War Correspondence of Edgeworth and Sallie Bird.* Athens: University of Georgia Press, 1988.

Russell, W. H. *My Diary North and South,* ed. Eugene H. Berwanger. New York: Alfred A. Knopf, 1988.

Sears, Stephen W., ed. *The Civil War Papers of George B. McClellan; Selected Correspondence, 1860–1865.* New York: Ticknor and Fields, 1989.

Simon, John Y., ed. *The Papers of Ulysses S. Grant,* 30 vols. Carbondale and Edwardsville: University of Southern Illinois University Press, 1967–.

Simpson, Brooks, and Jean V. Berlin, eds. *Sherman's Civil War: Selected Correspondence of William T. Sherman, 1860–1865.* Chapel Hill: University of North Carolina Press, 1999.

Smith, Theodore Clarke, ed. *The Life and Letters of James Abram Garfield*, 2 vols. New Haven, CT: Yale University Press, 1925.

Strong, George T. *The Diary of George Templeton Strong*, 4 vols., ed. Allan Nevins and Milton H. Thomas. New York: Macmillan, 1952.

Thorndyke, Rachel Sherman, ed. *The Sherman Letters*. 1894; New York: Da Capo, 1969.

Tower, R. Lockwood, ed. *Lee's Adjutant: The Wartime Letters of Colonel Walter Herron Taylor, 1862–1865*. Columbia: University of South Carolina Press, 1995.

United States Naval War Records Office. *The War of the Rebellion: The Official Records of the Union and Confederate Navies*, 30 vols. Washington, DC: Government Printing Office, 1894–1927.

United States War Department. *The War of the Rebellion: The Official Records of the Union and Confederate Armies*, 128 parts in 70 vols. Washington, DC: Government Printing Office, 1880–1901.

Welles, Gideon. *Diary of Gideon Welles*, 3 vols., ed. Howard K. Beale. New York: Norton, 1960.

Yacovone, Donald, ed. *A Voice of Thunder: The Civil War Letters of George E. Stephens*. Urbana: University of Illinois Press, 1997.

SECONDARY SOURCES

Adams, Michael C. C. *Fighting for Defeat: Union Military Failure in the East, 1861–1865*. 1978; Lincoln: University of Nebraska Press reprint, 1992.

Ambrose, Stephen E. *Duty, Honor, Country: A History of West Point*. Baltimore: Johns Hopkins Press, 1966.

———. *Halleck: Lincoln's Chief of Staff*. Baton Rouge: Louisiana State University Press, 1962.

Army Code 71451. Design for Military Operations: The British Military Doctrine, 1989.

ATP(A)NATO Land Force Tactical Doctrine, annex A, p. xxv.

Badeau, Adam. *Military History of Ulysses S. Grant*, 3 vols. New York: Appleton, 1881.

Ballard, Michael B. *Pemberton: A Biography*. Jackson: University Press of Mississippi, 1991.

———. *Vicksburg: The Campaign That Opened the Mississippi*. Chapel Hill: University of North Carolina Press, 2004.

Barrett, John G. *The Civil War in North Carolina*. Chapel Hill: University of North Carolina Press, 1963.

Bartlett, Irving H. *John C. Calhoun: A Biography*. New York: Norton, 1991.

Beach, Edward L. "David Glasgow Farragut: Deliberate Planner, Impetuous Fighter," in *The Great Admirals: Command at Sea, 1587–1945*, ed. Jack Sweetman. Annapolis, MD: Naval Institute Press, 1997, pp. 254–77.

Bennett, Michael J. *Union Jacks: Yankee Sailors in the Civil War.* Chapel Hill: University of North Carolina Press, 2004.

Beringer, Richard E., Herman Hattaway, Archer Jones, and William N. Still Jr. *Why the South Lost the Civil War.* Athens: University of Georgia Press, 1986.

Berkey, Jonathan M. "In the Very Midst of the War Track: The Valley's Civilians and the Shenandoah Campaign," in *The Shenandoah Valley Campaign of 1862,* ed. Gary W. Gallagher. Chapel Hill: University of North Carolina Press, 2003, pp. 86–114.

Bernstein, Iver. *The New York City Draft Riots: Their Significance for American Society and Politics in the Age of the Civil War.* New York: Oxford University Press, 1990.

Best, Geoffrey. *Humanity in Warfare.* London: Weidenfeld and Nicolson, 1980.

Blainey, Geoffrey. *The Causes of War,* 3rd ed. London: Macmillan, 1988.

Bogue, Allan G. *The Congressman's Civil War.* New York: Cambridge University Press, 1989.

Bohannon, Keith S. "Dirty, Ragged, and Ill-Provided For: Confederate Logistical Problems in the 1862 Maryland Campaign and Their Solution," in *The Antietam Campaign,* ed. Gary W. Gallagher. Chapel Hill: University of North Carolina Press, 1999, pp. 101–42.

Bond, Brian. *Liddell Hart.* London: Cassell, 1977.

———. *The Pursuit of Victory.* New York: Oxford University Press, 1996.

———. *The Unquiet Western Front.* Cambridge: Cambridge University Press, 2002.

———. *The Victorian Army and the Staff College, 1854–1914.* London: Eyre Methuen, 1972.

Boritt, Gabor S. "'Unfinished Work': Lincoln, Meade and Gettysburg," in *Lincoln's Generals,* ed. idem. New York: Oxford University Press, 1994, pp. 79–120.

Brinsfield, John W. "The Military Ethics of General William T. Sherman: A Reassessment," in *The Parameters of War: Military History from the Journal of the US Army War College,* ed. Lloyd J. Matthews and D. E. Brown. Washington, DC: Pergamon-Brassey's, 1987, pp. 87–103.

Brock, W. R. *Conflict and Transformation: The United States, 1844–1877.* Harmondsworth, UK: Penguin, 1973.

———. *Parties and Political Conscience: American Dilemmas, 1840–1850.* Millwood, NY: KTO Press, 1979.

Brown, Kent Masterson. *Retreat from Gettysburg: Lee, Logistics and the Pennsylvania Campaign.* Chapel Hill: University of North Carolina Press, 2005.

Bucholz, Andrea. *Moltke, Schlieffen and Prussian War Planning.* New York: Berg, 1991.

Buechler, John. "'Give 'em the Bayonet': A Note on Civil War Mythology." *Civil War History* 7 (1961): 128–32.

Burton, Brian K. *Extraordinary Circumstances: The Seven Days Battles.* Bloomington: Indiana University Press, 2001.

Caesar, Julius. *The Conquest of Gaul.* Harmondsworth, UK: Penguin, 1970.

Canney, Donald L. *The Old Steam Navy*, vol. 2: *The Ironclads, 1842–1885*. Annapolis, MD: US Naval Institute Press, 1993.

Carmichael, Peter S. "Lee's Search for the Battle of Annihilation," in *Audacity Personified: The Generalship of Robert E. Lee*, ed. idem. Baton Rouge: Louisiana State University Press, 2004, pp. 1–26.

Carter, Samuel, III. *The Final Fortress: The Campaign for Vicksburg, 1862–1863*. New York: St. Martin's Press, 1980.

Casdorph, Paul D. *Confederate General R. S. Ewell: Lee's Hesitant Commander*. Lexington: University Press of Kentucky, 2004.

Castel, Albert. *General Sterling Price and the Civil War in the West*. 1968; Baton Rouge: Louisiana State University Press reprint, 1993.

———. "The Historian and the General." *Civil War History* 16 (1970): 50–63.

Catton, Bruce. *Glory Road*. 1952; London: White Lion reprint, 1977.

———. *Grant Moves South*. Boston: Little, Brown, 1960.

———. *Grant Takes Command*. Boston: Little, Brown, 1968.

———. *A Stillness at Appomattox*. New York: Doubleday, 1955.

———. *This Hallowed Ground*. London: Victor Gollancz, 1957.

Chandler, David G. *The Campaigns of Napoleon*. London: Weidenfeld and Nicolson, 1966.

Cleaves, Freeman. *Meade of Gettysburg*. 1960; Norman: University of Oklahoma Press, 1991.

———. *Rock of Chickamauga: The Life of General George H. Thomas*. 1948; Norman: University of Oklahoma Press, 1996.

Coddington, Edwin B. *The Gettysburg Campaign: A Study in Command*. 1968; New York: Scribner's, 1979.

Cohen, Eliot A., and John Gooch. *Military Misfortunes: The Anatomy of Failure in War*. New York: Free Press, 1990.

Collins, Bruce. "American Federation and the Sectional Crisis, 1844–1860," in *The Federal Idea*, vol. 1: *The History of Federalism from the Enlightenment to 1945*, ed. Andrea Bosco. London: Lothian Foundation, 1991, pp. 54–64.

Conger, A. L. *The Rise of U. S. Grant*. 1931; New York: Da Capo, 1996.

Connell-Smith, Gordon. *The United States and Latin America*. London: Heinemann, 1974.

Connelly, Thomas L. *Army of the Heartland: The Army of Tennessee, 1861–1862*. 1967; Baton Rouge: Louisiana State University Press, 1986.

———. *The Autumn of Glory: The Army of Tennessee, 1862–1865*. 1969; Baton Rouge: Louisiana State University Press, 1971.

———. "The Image and the General," *Civil War History* 19 (1973): 50–64.

———. *The Marble Man: Robert E. Lee and His Image in American Society*. New York: Alfred A. Knopf, 1977.

———. "Robert E. Lee and the Western Confederacy." *Civil War History* 15: 116–32.

Connelly, Thomas L., and Archer Jones. *The Politics of Command: Factions and Ideas in Confederate Strategy*. Baton Rouge: Louisiana State University Press, 1973.

Cooling, Benjamin Franklin. *Forts Henry and Donelson: The Key to the Confederate Heartland*. Knoxville: University of Tennessee Press, 1987.

Cooper, Jerry M. *The Rise of the National Guard: The Evolution of the American Militia*. Lincoln: University of Nebraska Press, 1997.

Cornish, Dudley T. *The Sable Arm: Negro Troops in the Union Army, 1861–1865*. 1956; Lawrence: University Press of Kansas, 1987.

Cozzens, Peter. *The Darkest Days of the War: The Battles of Iuka and Corinth*. Chapel Hill: University of North Carolina Press, 1997.

———. *The Shipwreck of Their Hopes: The Battles for Chattanooga*. Urbana: University of Illinois Press, 1994.

———. *This Terrible Sound: The Battle of Chickamauga*. Urbana: University of Illinois Press, 1992.

Cunliffe, Marcus. *Soldiers and Civilians: The Martial Spirit in America, 1775–1865*, 3rd ed., with a new introduction by Brian Holden Reid. 1968; Aldershot: Gregg Revivals, 1993.

Current, Richard N. *Lincoln's Loyalists: Union Soldiers from the Confederacy*. Boston: Northeastern University Press, 1992.

Daniel, Larry J. *Days of Glory: The Army of the Cumberland, 1861–1865*. Baton Rouge: Louisiana State University Press, 2004.

Daniel, Larry J., and Lynn Bock. *Island No. 10: Struggle for the Mississippi Valley*. Tuscaloosa: University of Alabama Press, 1996.

Davis, William C. *Battle at Bull Run*. New York: Doubleday, 1977.

———. *Breckinridge: Statesman, Soldier, Symbol*. 1974; Baton Rouge: Louisiana State University Press, 1986.

———. *Jefferson Davis: The Man and His Hour*. New York: HarperCollins, 1991.

Dawson, Joseph G., III. *Doniphan's Epic March*. Lawrence: University Press of Kansas, 1999.

Dean, Eric T. *Shook over Hell: Post Traumatic Stress, Vietnam and the Civil War*. Cambridge, MA: Harvard University Press, 1997.

Detzer, David. *Donnybrook: The Battle of Bull Run, 1861*. Orlando, FL: Harcourt, 2004.

Donald, David. *Charles Sumner and the Coming of the Civil War*. New York: Alfred A. Knopf, 1965.

———. *Charles Sumner and the Rights of Man*. New York: Alfred A. Knopf, 1970.

———. *Lincoln*. London: Jonathan Cape, 1995.

Dowdey, Clifford. *Lee: A Biography*. London: Gollancz, 1970.

———. *The Seven Days*. 1964; Wilmington, NC: Broadfoot reprint, 1988.

Doyle, Elizabeth J. "The Conduct of the War, 1861," in *Congress Investigates: A Documented History*, 5 vols., ed. Arthur M. Schlesinger Jr. and Roger Bruns. New York: Chelsea House, 1975, vol. 2, pp. 1198–1211.

Dupuy, R. E., and T. N. Dupuy. *A Compact History of the United States Army*. New York: Hawthorn Books, 1956.

Eaton, Clement. *A History of the Southern Confederacy*. New York: Collier, 1954.

Eicher, David J. *The Longest Night: A Military History of the Civil War*. New York: Simon and Schuster, 2001.

Eisenschiml, Otto. *The Celebrated Case of Fitz John Porter*. Indianapolis: Bobbs-Merrill, 1957.

Engle, Stephen D. *Don Carlos Buell: Most Promising of All*. Chapel Hill: University of North Carolina Press, 1999.

Epstein, Robert M. "The Creation and Evolution of the Army Corps in the American Civil War." *Journal of Military History* 55 (January 1991): 21–46.

Falls, Cyril. *The Nature of Modern Warfare*. London: Methuen, 1941.

Fishel, Edwin C. *The Secret War for the Union*. New York: Houghton Mifflin, 1996.

Fisher, Louis. *Presidential War Power*. Lawrence: University Press of Kansas, 1995.

Frank, Joseph Allan. *With Ballot and Bayonet: The Political Socialization of American Civil War Soldiers*. Athens: University of Georgia Press, 1998

Franklin, John Hope. *The Emancipation Proclamation*. 1963; Wheeling, IL: Harlan Davidson, 1995.

Frazier, Donald J. *Blood and Treasure: Confederate Empire in the Southwest*. College Station: Texas A&M University Press, 1995.

Fredrickson, George M. *The Inner Civil War: Northern Intellectuals and the Crisis of the Union*. New York: Harper and Row, 1965.

Freehling, William W. *Prelude to Civil War: The Nullification Controversy in South Carolina, 1816–1836*. 1965; New York: Oxford University Press, 1992.

Freeman, Douglas Southall. *Lee's Lieutenants*, 3 vols. New York: Scribner's, 1943.

———. *R. E. Lee*, 4 vols. New York: Scribner's, 1933.

Fuller, J. F. C. *The Conduct of War, 1789–1961*. London: Eyre and Spottiswoode, 1961.

———. *The Generalship of Ulysses S. Grant*. 1929, 1952; New York: Da Capo, 1991.

———. *The Generalship of Ulysses S. Grant*, 2nd ed. Bloomington: Indiana University Press, 1957.

———. *Grant and Lee: A Study in Personality and Generalship*. London: Eyre and Spottiswoode, 1933; Stevenage: Spa Books reprint, 1992.

———. *The Second World War*. London: Eyre and Spottiswoode, 1947.

———. *War and Western Civilization, 1832–1932: A Study of War as a Political Instrument and the Expression of Mass Democracy*. London: Duckworth, 1932.

Gallagher, Gary W. "You Must Either Attack Richmond or Give Up the Job and Come to the Defence of Washington: Abraham Lincoln and the 1862 Shenandoah Valley Campaign," in *The Shenandoah Valley Campaign of 1862*, ed. idem. Chapel Hill: University of North Carolina Press, 2003.

———. "Confederate Corps Leadership on the First Day at Gettysburg," in *The First*

Day at Gettysburg: Essays on Union and Confederate Leadership, ed. idem. Kent, OH: Kent State University Press, 1992, pp. 30–56.

———. "East of Chancellorsville: Jubal A. Early at Second Fredericksburg and Salem Church," in *Chancellorsville: The Battle and Its Aftermath*, ed. idem. Durham: University of North Carolina Press, 1996, pp. 36–64.

———. "Introduction," in *The Shenandoah Valley Campaign of 1862*, ed. idem. Chapel Hill: University of North Carolina Press, 2003, p. ix.

———. *Lee and His Army in Confederate History*. Chapel Hill: University of North Carolina Press, 2001.

———. *Lee and His Generals in War and Memory*. Baton Rouge: Louisiana State University Press, 1998.

Geary, James W. *We Need Men: The Union Draft in the Civil War*. DeKalb: Northern Illinois University Press, 1991.

Gienapp, William E. *The Rise of the Republican Party, 1852–1856*. New York: Oxford University Press, 1987.

Glatthaar, Joseph T. *Forged in Battle: The Civil War Alliance of Black Soldiers and White Officers*. New York: Free Press, 1990.

Gordon, Lesley J. "All Who Went into That Battle Were Heroes: Remembering the 16th Regiment Connecticut Volunteers at Antietam," in *The Antietam Campaign*, ed. Gary W. Gallagher. Chapel Hill: University of North Carolina Press, 1999, pp. 169–91.

Grabau, Warren E. *Ninety-Eight Days: A Geographer's View of the Vicksburg Campaign*. Knoxville: University of Tennessee Press, 2000.

Grant, Susan-Mary. "Fighting for Freedom: African-American Soldiers in the Civil War," in *The American Civil War: Explorations and Reconsiderations*, ed. idem. and Brian Holden Reid. London: Longman, 2000, pp. 191–213.

Gray, Colin S. *Modern Strategy*. New York: Oxford University Press, 1999.

Green, Michael S. *Freedom, Union and Power: Lincoln and His Party during the Civil War*. New York: Fordham University Press, 2004.

Greene, A. Wilson. "Stoneman's Raid," in *Chancellorsville: The Battle and Its Aftermath*, ed. Gary W. Gallagher. Durham: University of North Carolina Press, 1996, pp. 65–106.

Griffith, Paddy. *Rally Once Again: Battle Tactics of the American Civil War*. Ramsbury, UK: Crowood Press, 1987.

Grimsley, Mark. "Conciliation and Its Failure, 1861–1862." *Civil War History* 39 (December 1993): 317–35.

———. *The Hard Hand of War: Union Military Policy toward Southern Civilians, 1861–1865*. Cambridge, MA: Cambridge University Press, 1995.

Grimsted, David. *American Mobbing, 1828–1861: Toward Civil War*. New York: Oxford University Press, 1998.

Guelzo, Allen C. *Lincoln's Emancipation Proclamation: The End of Slavery in America*. New York: Simon and Schuster, 2004.

Hagerman, Edward. *The American Civil War and the Origins of Modern Warfare*. Bloomington: Indiana University Press, 1988.

———. "From Jomini to Dennis Hart Mahan: The Evolution of Trench Warfare and the American Civil War." *Civil War History* 13 (1967): 197–220.

Hallock, Judith Lee. *Braxton Bragg and Confederate Defeat*, vol. 2. Tuscaloosa: University of Alabama Press, 1991.

———. "The Role of the Community in Civil War Desertion." *Civil War History* 29 (June 1983): 123–34.

Hamilton, Nigel. *Monty: Master of the Battlefield*. London: Hamish Hamilton, 1983.

Harsh, Joseph L. *Confederate Tide Rising: Robert E. Lee and the Making of Confederate Strategy*. Kent, OH: Kent State University Press, 1998.

———. *Taken at the Flood: Robert E. Lee and Confederate Strategy in the Maryland Campaign of 1862*. Kent, OH: Kent State University Press, 1999.

Hart, B. H. Liddell. *A Greater Than Napoleon: Scipio Africanus*. London: Greenhill reprint, 1992.

———. *Memoirs*, 2 vols. London: Cassell, 1965.

———. "Why Lee Lost Gettysburg." *Saturday Review of Literature* 11 (March 23, 1938): 561–63.

Hartwig, D. Scott. "Robert E. Lee and the Maryland Campaign," in *Lee: The Soldier*, ed. Gary W. Gallagher. Lincoln: University of Nebraska Press, 1996, pp. 331–56.

Hattaway, Herman, and Archer Jones. *How the North Won: A Military History of the Civil War*. Urbana: University of Illinois Press, 1983.

Hearn, Chester G. *The Capture of New Orleans, 1862*. Baton Rouge: Louisiana State University Press, 1995.

Hebert, Walter H. *Fighting Joe Hooker*. Indianapolis: Bobbs-Merrill, 1944.

Henderson, G. F. R. *The Campaign of Fredericksburg*. 1886; Fall's Church, VA: Old Dominion reprint, 1984.

———. *Stonewall Jackson*. 1898; London: Longman, 1911.

———. *Stonewall Jackson and the American Civil War*, 2 vols. London: Longmans, Green and Company, 1898.

Hennessy, John J. *Return to Bull Run: The Campaign and Battle of Second Manassas*. New York: Simon and Schuster, 1993.

———. "We Shall Make Richmond Howl: The Army of the Potomac on the Eve of Chancellorsville," in *Chancellorsville: The Battle and Its Aftermath*, ed. Gary W. Gallagher. Durham: University of North Carolina Press, 1996, pp. 1–35.

Herrera, Ricardo A. "Self-Governance and the American Citizen as Soldier, 1775–1861." *Journal of Military History* 65 (January 2001): 21–52.

Hess, Earl J. *Banners to the Breeze: The Kentucky Campaign, Corinth and Stones River*. Lincoln: University of Nebraska Press, 2000.

————. *The Union Soldier in Battle*. Lawrence: University Press of Kansas, 1997.

Hesseltine, William B. *Lincoln and the War Governors*. 1948; New York: Alfred A. Knopf, 1955.

Hitchcock, E. A. *Fifty Years in Camp and Field*, ed. W. A. Croffat. New York: Putnam's, 1909.

Holien, Kim B. *Battle at Ball's Bluff: Leesburg, Virginia, October 21, 1861*. Mechanicsville, VA: Rapidan Press, 1985.

Hollandsworth, James G., Jr. *The Louisiana Native Guards: The Black Military Experience during the Civil War*. Baton Rouge: Louisiana State University Press, 1995.

Holmes, Richard. *The Road to Sedan: The French Army, 1866–1870*. London: Royal Historical Society, 1984.

Holsti, K. J. *The State, War, and the State of War*. Cambridge: Cambridge University Press, 1996.

Howes, Philip. *The Catalytic Wars: A Study of the Development of Warfare, 1860–1870*. London: Minerva Press, 1998.

Huston, James A. "Logistical Support of Federal Armies in the Field." *Civil War History* 7 (1961): 36–47.

Irwin, A. S. H. *The Levels of War: Operational Art and Campaign Planning*. SCSI Occasional Paper No. 5, 1993.

Irwin, Richard B. "Ball's Bluff and the Arrest of General Stone," in *Battles and Leaders of the Civil War*, 4 vols., ed. Robert U. Johnson and Clarence C. Buel. New York: Century, 1884–88, vol. 2, pp. 123–34.

Jamieson, Perry D. *Crossing the Deadly Ground: United States Army Tactics, 1865–1899*. Tuscaloosa: University of Alabama Press, 1994.

Janda, Lance. "Shutting the Gates of Mercy: The American Origins of Total War." *Journal of Military History* 59 (January 1995): 7–26.

Johnson, Ludwell H. "Civil War Military History: A Few Revisions in Need of Revising." *Civil War History* 17 (1971): 115–30.

Johnson, Michael P. *Toward a Patriarchal Republic: The Secession of Georgia*. Baton Rouge: Louisiana State University Press, 1977.

Johnston, R. M. *Bull Run: Its Strategy and Tactics*. 1913; Carlisle, PA: Kallmann, 1996.

Jomini, Baron Antoine-Henri. *The Art of War*. 1862; London: Greenhill, 1992.

Jones, Archer. *Confederate Strategy: From Shiloh to Vicksburg*. Baton Rouge: Louisiana State University Press, 1961.

————. "Military Means, Political Ends: Strategy," in *Why the Confederacy Lost*, ed. Gabor S. Boritt. New York: Oxford University Press, 1992, pp. 43–78.

Jones, Terry L. *Lee's Tigers: The Louisiana Infantry in the Army of Northern Virginia*. Baton Rouge: Louisiana State University Press, 1987.

Jordan, David M. *"Happiness Is Not My Companion": The Life of General G. K. Warren*. Bloomington: Indiana University Press, 2001.

Jordan, Winthrop D. *Tumult and Silence at Second Creek*. Baton Rouge: Louisiana State University Press, 1993.

Keegan, John. *The Mask of Command*. London: Jonathan Cape, 1987.

Kerby, Robert L. *Kirby Smith's Confederacy: The Trans-Mississippi South, 1863–1865*. 1972; Tuscaloosa: University of Alabama Press, 1991.

Kiper, Richard L. *Major General John Alexander McClernand: Politician in Uniform*. Kent, OH: Kent State University Press, 1999.

Kiszely, J. P. "The British Army and Approaches to War Since 1945," in *Military Power: Land Warfare in Theory and Practice*, ed. Brian Holden Reid. London: Frank Cass, 1997, pp. 179–206.

Koeniger, A. Cash. "Prejudices and Partialities: The Garnett Controversy Revisited," in *The Shenandoah Valley Campaign of 1862*, ed. Gary W. Gallagher. Chapel Hill: University of North Carolina Press, 2003, pp. 219–36.

Kolchin, Peter. *American Slavery, 1619–1877*. 1993; Harmondsworth, UK: Penguin, 1995.

Krick, Robert E. L. "Defending Lee's Flank: J. E. B. Stuart, John Pelham, and Confederate Artillery on Nicodemus Heights," in *The Antietam Campaign*, ed. Gary W. Gallagher. Chapel Hill: University of North Carolina Press, 1999, pp. 192–222.

———. "Maryland's Ablest Confederate: General Charles W. Winder and the Stonewall Brigade," in *The Shenandoah Valley Campaign of 1862*, ed. Gary W. Gallagher. Chapel Hill: University of North Carolina Press, 2003, pp. 178–218.

Krick, Robert K. "It Appeared as Though Mutual Extermination Would Put a Stop to the Awful Carnage: Confederates in Sharpsburg's Bloody Lane," in *The Antietam Campaign*, ed. Gary W. Gallagher. Chapel Hill: University of North Carolina Press, 1999, pp. 223–58.

———. "The Metamorphosis in Stonewall Jackson's Public Image," in *The Shenandoah Valley Campaign of 1862*, ed. Gary W. Gallagher. Chapel Hill: University of North Carolina Press, 2003, pp. 24–42.

———. "The Smoothbore Volley That Doomed the Confederacy," in *Chancellorsville: The Battle and Its Aftermath*, ed. Gary W. Gallagher. Durham: University of North Carolina Press, 1996, pp. 107–42.

Lee, Fitzhugh. *General Lee*. 1894; New York: Da Capo reprint, 1994.

Levine, Bruce. *Half Slave and Half Free: The Roots of Civil War*. New York: Hill and Wang, 1992.

Lewis, Lloyd. *Sherman: Fighting Prophet*. 1928; New York: Harcourt Brace, 1958.

Linderman, Gerald F. *Embattled Courage: The Experience of Combat in the American Civil War*. New York: Free Press, 1987.

Livermore, Thomas L. *Numbers and Losses in the Civil War in America, 1861–1865*, 2nd ed. Boston: Houghton Mifflin, 1901.

Longacre, Edward G. *The Cavalry at Gettysburg*. 1986; Lincoln: University of Nebraska Press reprint, 1993.

Luard, Evan. *The Broken Sword*. London: I. B. Tauris, 1988.

Luraghi, Raimondo. *A History of the Confederate Navy*. Annapolis, MD: Naval Institute Press, 1996.

Luvaas, Jay. "Lee at Gettysburg: A General without Intelligence," in *Intelligence and Military Operations*, ed. Michael I. Handel. London: Frank Cass, 1990, pp. 116–39.

MacKenzie, S. P. *Revolutionary Armies in the Modern Era*. London: Routledge, 1997.

Malone, Dumas. *Jefferson the President: Second Term, 1805–1809*. Boston: Little, Brown, 1974.

Marshall-Cornwall, James. *Napoleon as Military Commander*. London: Batsford, 1967.

Marszalek, John F. *Commander of All Lincoln's Armies: A Life of General Henry W. Halleck*. Cambridge, MA: Belknap Press of Harvard University Press, 2004.

———. *Sherman: A Soldier's Passion for Order*. New York: Free Press, 1993.

Martin, David G. *Gettysburg, July 1*. Conshohocken, PA: Combined Books, 1995.

Marvel, William. *Burnside*. Chapel Hill: University of North Carolina Press, 1991.

Maslowski, Peter. *Treason Must Be Made Odious: Military Occupation and Wartime Reconstruction in Nashville, Tennessee, 1862–65*. Millwood, NY: KTO Press, 1978.

Mathes, J. H. *General Forrest*. New York: Appleton, 1902.

Matthews, Lloyd J. "Military Ideals," in *The Oxford Companion to American Military History*, ed. John Whiteclay Chambers II. New York: Oxford University Press, 1999, p. 323.

Maurice, Sir Frederick. *British Strategy: A Study of the Application of the Principles of War*. London: Constable, 1929.

McCaslin, Richard B. *Tainted Breeze: The Great Hanging at Gainseville, Texas 1862*. Baton Rouge: Louisiana State University Press, 1994.

McDonough, James Lee. *Chattanooga: A Death Grip on the Confederacy*. Knoxville: University of Tennessee Press, 1984.

———. *Shiloh: In Hell before Night*. Knoxville: University of Tennessee Press, 1977.

McFeely, William S. *Frederick Douglass*. New York: Norton, 1991.

———. *Grant: A Biography*. New York: Norton, 1981.

McKitrick, Eric L. "Party Politics and the Union and Confederate War Efforts," in *The American Party Systems*, ed. William N. Chambers and Walter Dean Burnham. New York: Oxford University Press, 1967, pp. 117–51.

McMurry, Richard M. *John Bell Hood and the War for Southern Independence*. 1982; Lincoln: University of Nebraska Press paperback reprint, 1992.

———. *Two Great Rebel Armies*. Chapel Hill: University of North Carolina Press, 1989.

McPherson, James M. *Abraham Lincoln and the Second American Revolution*. New York: Oxford University Press, 1991.

———. "Antebellum Southern Exceptionalism: A New Look at an Old Question." *Civil War History* 29 (1983): 230–44.

———. *The Battle Cry of Freedom: The Civil War Era*. New York: Oxford University Press, 1988.

————. *Crossroads of Freedom: Antietam*. New York: Oxford University Press, 2002.

————. *For Cause and Comrades: Why Men Fought in the Civil War*. New York: Oxford University Press, 1997.

————. *The Struggle for Equality: Abolitionists and the Negro in the Civil War and Reconstruction*. Princeton, NJ: Princeton University Press, 1964.

————. "Ulysses S. Grant's Greatest Victory," in *Experience of War: An Anthology of Articles from MHQ: The Quarterly Journal of Military History*, ed. Robert Cowley. New York: Norton, 1992, pp. 221–31.

————. *What They Fought For, 1861–1865*. Baton Rouge: Louisiana State University Press, 1994.

McWhiney, Grady. *Braxton Bragg and Confederate Defeat*, vol. 1: *Field Command*. 1969; Tuscaloosa: University of Alabama Press, 1991.

————. *Cracker Culture*. Tuscaloosa: University of Alabama Press, 1988.

McWhiney, Grady, and Perry D. Jamieson. *Attack and Die: Civil War Military Tactics and the Southern Heritage*. Tuscaloosa: University of Alabama Press, 1982.

Meigs, Montgomery C. "General M. C. Meigs on the Conduct of the Civil War." *American Historical Review* 26 (1921): 285–303.

Miller, Edward A. *Lincoln's Abolitionist General: The Life of David Hunter*. Columbia: University of South Carolina Press, 1997.

Miller, William L. "'The Siege of Richmond Was Raised': Lee's Intentions in the Seven Days Battles," in *Audacity Personified: The Generalship of Robert E. Lee*, ed. Peter S. Carmichael. Baton Rouge: Louisiana State University Press, 2004, pp. 27–56.

————. "Such Men as Shields, Banks, and Frémont: Federal Command in Western Virginia, March–June 1862," in *The Shenandoah Valley Campaign of 1862*, ed. Gary W. Gallagher. Chapel Hill: University of North Carolina Press, 2003, pp. 43–85.

Mitchell, Reid. *The Vacant Chair: The Northern Soldier Leaves Home*. New York: Oxford University Press, 1993.

Morrison, James L., Jr. *"The Best School in the World": West Point, the Pre-Civil War Years, 1833–66*. Kent, OH: Kent State University Press, 1986.

Neely, Mark E., Jr. *The Union Divided: Party Conflict in the Civil War North*. Cambridge, MA: Harvard University Press, 2002.

Nevins, Allan. *Frémont: Pathmarker of the West*, new ed. 1933; New York: Longmans, Green and Company, 1955.

————. *The War for the Union*, 5 vols., part of *The Ordeal of the Union*, 8 vols. New York: Scribner's, 1947–71.

————. *The War for the Union*, vol. 3: *The Organized War, 1863–1864*. New York: Scribner's, 1971.

Newton, Steven H. *Joseph E. Johnston and the Defense of Richmond*. Lawrence: University Press of Kansas, 1998.

Noe, Kenneth W. *Perryville*. Lexington: University Press of Kentucky, 2001.

Nolan, Alan T. *Lee Considered*. Chapel Hill: University of North Carolina Press, 1991.

————. "R. E. Lee and July 1 at Gettysburg," in *The First Day at Gettysburg: Essays on Union and Confederate Leadership*, ed. Gary W. Gallagher. Kent, OH: Kent State University Press, 1992, pp. 1–29.

Ogden, John. *Tecumseh*. New York: Henry Holt, 1997.

Owsley, Frank L. *King Cotton Diplomacy*, 2nd ed. Chicago: Chicago University Press, 1959.

Paludan, Philip S. *The Presidency of Abraham Lincoln*. Lawrence: University Press of Kansas, 1994.

Parish, Peter J. *The American Civil War*. London: Eyre Methuen, 1975.

————. "The Instruments of Providence: Slavery, Civil War, and the American Churches," in *The Church and War*, ed. W. J. Sheils. Oxford: Basil Blackwell, 1984, pp. 291–320.

————. "The War for the Union as a Just War," in *Aspects of War in American History*, ed. David K. Adams and Cornelius A. van Minnen. Keele, UK: Keele University Press, 1997, pp. 81–103.

————. "The Will to Fight and the Will to Write: Some Recent Books on the American Civil War." *Journal of American Studies* 32 (1998): 295–305.

Phillips, Christopher. *Damned Yankee: The Life of General Nathaniel Lyon*. Columbia: University of Missouri, 1980.

Piston, William Garrett, and Richard W. Hatcher III. *Wilson's Creek*. Chapel Hill: University of North Carolina Press, 2000.

Pohl, James W. "The Influence of Antoine Henri de Jomini on Winfield Scott's Campaign in the Mexican War." *Southwestern Historical Quarterly* 77 (July 1973): 85–110.

Potter, David. *The Impending Crisis, 1848–1861*. New York: Harper and Row, 1976.

Power, J. Tracey. *Lee's Miserables: Life in the Army of Northern Virginia from the Wilderness to Appomattox*. Chapel Hill: University of North Carolina Press, 1998.

Rable, George C. *The Confederate Republic*. Chapel Hill: University of North Carolina Press, 1994.

————. *Fredericksburg! Fredericksburg!* Chapel Hill: University of North Carolina Press, 2002.

Rafuse, Ethan S. *McClellan's War*. Bloomington: Indiana University Press, 2005.

Ramage, James A. *Rebel Raider: The Life of General John Hunt Morgan*. Lexington: University Press of Kentucky, 1986.

Randall, James G. *Lincoln the President*, 4 vols. London: Eyre and Spottiswoode, 1945–55.

Reardon, Carol. "'I Think the Union Army Had Something to Do with It': The Pickett's Charge Nobody Knows," in *The Gettysburg Nobody Knows*, ed. Gabor S. Boritt. New York: Oxford University Press, 1997, pp. 122–43.

————. *Pickett's Charge in History and Memory*. Chapel Hill: University of North Carolina Press, 1997.

Reed, Rowena. *Combined Operations in the Civil War*. 1978; Lincoln: University of Nebraska Press paperback edition, 1993.

Reid, Brian Holden. "America and War," in *A New Introduction to American Studies*, ed. Howard Temperley and Christopher Bigsby. London: Pearson/Longman, 2005, pp. 302–25.

———. *The American Civil War and the Wars of the Industrial Revolution*. London: Cassell, 1999.

———. "British Military Intellectuals and the American Civil War," in *Warfare, Diplomacy and Politics; Essays in Honour of A. J. P. Taylor*, ed. C. Wrigley. London: Hamish Hamilton, 1986, pp. 42–57.

———. "The Commander and His Chief of Staff: Ulysses S. Grant and John A. Rawlins," in *Command and Leadership*, ed. G. D. Sheffield. London: Brassey's, 1996, pp. 17–36.

———. "The Crisis at Fort Sumter in 1861 Reconsidered." *History* 77 (February 1992): 3–32.

———. "Enduring Patterns in Modern Warfare," in *The Nature of Future Conflict: Implications for Force Development*. Strategic and Combat Studies Institute Occasional Paper No. 36, ed. Brian Bond and Mungo Melvin. Camberley: Strategic and Combat Studies Institute, 1998, pp. 15–30.

———. "First Blood to the South: Bull Run, 1861." *History Today* 42 (March 1992): 20–26.

———. "General McClellan and the Politicians." *Parameters* 17 (September 1987): 101–12.

———. "The Grip of the Anaconda Plan." *British-American* 5 (Winter 1993): 13–18.

———. "Historians and the Joint Committee on the Conduct of the War." *Civil War History* 38 (December 1992): 319–41.

———. "The Influence of the Vietnam Syndrome on the Writing of Civil War History." Inaugural Lecture, King's College London, November 26, 2001.

———. "The Influence of the Vietnam Syndrome on the Writing of Civil War History." *RUSI Journal* 147 (February 2002): 44–52.

———. "Introduction," in "The Vistas of American Military History," ed. idem. and Joseph G. Dawson III. Special issue of *American Nineteenth Century History* 7, no. 2 (June 1996): 139–51.

———. *J. F. C. Fuller: Military Thinker*. 1987; London: Macmillan, 1990.

———. *The Origins of the American Civil War*. London: Longman, 1996.

———. "Rationality and Irrationality in Union Strategy, April 1861–March 1862." *War in History* 1 (March 1994): 19–38.

———. *Robert E. Lee: Icon for a Nation*. 2005; Amherst, NY: Prometheus Books, 2007.

———. "'A Signpost That Was Missed?' Reconsidering British Lessons from the American Civil War." *Journal of Military History* 70 (April 2006): 385–414.

————. *Studies in British Military Thought: Debates with Fuller and Liddell Hart*. Lincoln: University of Nebraska Press, 1998.

————. "A Survey of the Militia in Eighteenth Century America." *Army Quarterly* 110 (1980): 48–55.

————. "What Made Civil War Soldiers Fight?" *Journal of Strategic Studies* 22 (December 1999): 131–38.

Reid, Brian Holden, and John White. "'A Mob of Stragglers and Cowards': Desertion from the Union and Confederate Armies, 1861–1865." *Journal of Strategic Studies* 8 (March 1985): 64–77.

Renehan, Edward J., Jr. *The Lion's Pride: Theodore Roosevelt and His Family in Peace and War*. New York: Oxford University Press, 1998.

Richards, Leonard L. *"Gentlemen of Property and Standing": Anti-Abolition Mobs in Jacksonian America*. New York: Oxford University Press, 1970.

————. *The Slave Power: The Free North and Southern Domination*. Baton Rouge: Louisiana State University Press, 2000.

Roberts, William H. *Now for the Contest: Coastal and Oceanic Naval Operations in the Civil War*. Lincoln: University of Nebraska Press, 2004.

Robertson, James I., Jr. *Stonewall Jackson: The Man, the Soldier, the Legend*. New York: Macmillan, 1997.

Roland, Charles P. *Albert Sidney Johnston: Soldier of Three Republics*. Austin: University of Texas Press, 1964, pp. 31–71.

————. "The Generalship of Robert E. Lee," in *Grant, Lee, Lincoln and the Radicals: Essays on Civil War Leadership*, ed. Grady McWhiney. Evanston, IL: Northwestern University Press, 1964.

Roman, Alfred. *The Military Operations of General Beauregard*, 2 vols. New York: Harper, 1884.

Rose, Anne C. *Victorian America and the Civil War*. Cambridge, MA: Cambridge University Press, 1992.

Ross, Jordan. "Uncommon Union: Diversity and Motivation among Civil War Soldiers." *American Nineteenth Century History* 3 (Spring 2002): 17–44.

Rowland, Thomas J. *George B. McClellan and Civil War History*. Kent, OH: Kent State University Press, 1998.

————. "In the Shadows of Grant and Sherman: George B. McClellan Revisited." *Civil War History* 40 (September 1994): 202–25.

Royster, Charles. *The Destructive War*. New York: Alfred A. Knopf, 1991.

Schutz, Wallace J., and Walter N. Trenerry. *Abandoned by Lincoln: A Military Biography of General John Pope*. Urbana: University of Illinois Press, 1990.

Sears, Stephen W. *Chancellorsville*. New York: Houghton Mifflin, 1996.

————. *George B. McClellan: The Young Napoleon*. New York: Ticknor and Fields, 1988.

————. *Gettysburg*. New York: Houghton Mifflin, 2003.

————. *Landscape Turned Red: The Battle of Antietam*. New York: Ticknor and Fields, 1983.

————. *To the Gates of Richmond: The Peninsula Campaign*. New York: Ticknor and Fields, 1991.

Selby, John. *Stonewall Jackson as Military Commander*. London: Batsford, 1968.

Shea, William J., and Earl J. Hess. *Pea Ridge: Civil War Campaign in the West*. Chapel Hill: University of North Carolina Press, 1992.

Shannon, Fred A. *The Organization and Administration of the Union Army, 1861–1865*, 2 vols. 1928; Gloucester, MA: Peter Smith, 1965.

Sheffield, G. D. "Introduction: Command, Leadership and the Anglo-American Military Experience," in *Leadership and Command: The Anglo-American Experience since 1861*, ed. idem. 1997; London: Brassey's, 2002, pp. 1–16.

Simpson, Brooks D. *Let Us Have Peace: Ulysses S. Grant and the Politics of War and Reconstruction*. Chapel Hill: University of North Carolina Press, 1991.

————. *Ulysses S. Grant: Triumph over Adversity, 1822–1865*. New York: Houghton Mifflin, 2000.

Smith, T. M. Melia. "David Dixon Porter: Fighting Sailor," in *Quarterdeck and Bridge: Two Centuries of American Naval Leaders*, ed. James C. Bradford. Annapolis, MD: Naval Institute Press, 1997, pp. 183–202.

Spiller, Roger. *An Instinct for War: Scenes from the Battlefields of History*. Cambridge, MA: Belknap Press of Harvard University Press, 2005.

Stagg, J. C. A. *Mr. Madison's War: Politics, Diplomacy, and the Early American Republic, 1783–1830*. Princeton, NJ: Princeton University Press, 1983.

Stampp, Kenneth M. *And the War Came: The North and the Secession Crisis, 1860–1861*. Baton Rouge: Louisiana State University Press, 1950.

————. *Indiana Politics during the Civil War*. 1949; Bloomington: Indiana University Press, 1978.

Starr, Stephen Z. *The Union Cavalry in the Civil War*, 3 vols. Baton Rouge: Louisiana State University Press, 1979–85.

Still, William N., Jr. "David Glasgow Farragut: The Union's Nelson," in *Quarterdeck and Bridge: Two Centuries of American Naval Leaders*, ed. James C. Bradford. Annapolis, MD: Naval Institute Press, 1997, pp. 125–50.

Strachan, Hew. *From Waterloo to Balaclava*. Cambridge: Cambridge University Press, 1985.

Suganami, Hidemi. *On the Causes of War*. Oxford: Clarendon Press, 1996.

Sutherland, Daniel E. *Fredericksburg and Chancellorsville: The Dare Mark Campaign*. Lincoln: University of Nebraska Press, 1998.

Swanberg, W. A. *Sickles the Incredible*. New York: Scribner's, 1956.

Symonds, Craig L. *Joseph E. Johnston*. New York: Norton, 1992.

————. *Stonewall of the West: Patrick Cleburne and the Civil War*. Lawrence: University Press of Kansas, 1997.

Tanner, Robert G. *Stonewall in the Valley*, 2nd ed. Mechanicsburg, PA: Stackpole Books, 1996.

Tap, Bruce. *Over Lincoln's Shoulder: The Committee on the Conduct of the War*. Lawrence: University Press of Kansas, 1998.

Taylor, A. J. P. *English History, 1914–1945*. Oxford: Clarendon Press, 1965.

Taylor, Lenette. *"The Supply for Tomorrow Must Not Fail": The Civil War Career of Captain Simon Perkins Jr., A Union Quartermaster*. Kent, OH: Kent State University Press, 2004.

Terraine, John. *Impacts of War*. 1970; London: Leo Cooper, 1993.

Thomas, Benjamin P. *Abraham Lincoln*. London: Eyre and Spottiswoode, 1952.

Thomas, Benjamin P., and Harold M. Hyman. *Stanton: The Life and Times of Lincoln's Secretary of War*. New York: Alfred A. Knopf, 1962.

Thomas, Emory M. *Bold Dragoon: The Life of J. E. B. Stuart*. New York: Harper and Row, 1986.

———. *The Confederacy as a Revolutionary Experience*. 1971; Columbia: University of South Carolina Press reprint, 1991.

———. *The Confederate Nation, 1861–1865*. 1979; New York: Monticello Edition reprint, 1993.

Thompson, Jerry. *Confederate General of the West: Henry Hopkins Sibley*. 1987; College Station: Texas A&M University Press, 1996.

Tolstoy, Leo. *War and Peace*. London: Macmillan, Oxford University Press, 1943.

Trefousse, Hans L. *Andrew Johnson: A Biography*. New York: Norton, 1989.

———. *Ben Butler: The South Called Him Beast*. New York: Twayne, 1957.

———. *Benjamin Franklin Wade: Radical Republican from Ohio*. New York: Twayne, 1963.

———. *"The Joint Committee on the Conduct of the War: A Reassessment." Civil War History* 10 (March 1964): 5–19.

———. *The Radical Republicans: Lincoln's Vanguard for Racial Justice*. New York: Alfred A. Knopf, 1969.

Trudeau, Noah Andre. *Gettysburg: A Testing of Courage*. New York: HarperCollins, 2002.

USMA. *Jomini, Clausewitz, and Schlieffen*. West Point, NY: USMA, 1948.

van Creveld, Martin. *Air Power and Maneuver Warfare*. Maxwell, AL: Air University Press, 1994.

———. *The Transformation of War*. New York: Free Press, 1990.

Van Deusen, Glyndon G. *Horace Greeley: Nineteenth Century Crusader*. Philadelphia: Pennsylvania University Press, 1953.

———. *William Henry Seward*. New York: Oxford University Press, 1967.

Vandiver, Frank E. *Mighty Stonewall*. 1957; College Station: Texas A&M University Press, 1995.

———. *Mighty Stonewall*. New York: McGraw-Hill, 1957.

———. *Ploughshares into Swords: Josiah Gorgas and Confederate Ordnance.* College Station: Texas A&M University Press edition, 1994.

von Clausewitz, Carl. *On War,* ed. Michael Howard and Peter Paret. Princeton, NJ: Princeton University Press, 1976.

Warner, Ezra J. *Generals in Blue.* 1964; Baton Rouge: Louisiana State University Press, 1989.

———. *Generals in Gray.* 1959; Baton Rouge: Louisiana State University Press, 1991.

Watson, Samuel J. "Religion and Combat Motivation in the Confederate Armies." *Journal of Military History* 58 (January 1994): 29–55.

Weigley, Russell F. *The American Way of War.* 1973; Bloomington: Indiana University Press reprint, 1977.

———. *A Great Civil War: A Military and Political History.* Bloomington: Indiana University Press, 2000.

———. *History of the United States Army.* London: Batsford, 1968.

Weitz, Mark A. "Drill, Training, and the Combat Performance of the Civil War Soldier." *Journal of Military History* 62 (April 1998): 263–89.

———. *A Higher Duty: Desertion among Georgia Troops.* Lincoln: University of Nebraska Press, 2000.

———. *More Damning Than Slaughter: Desertion in the Confederate Army.* Lincoln: University of Nebraska Press, 2005.

Wells, Mark K. *Courage and Air Warfare.* London: Frank Cass, 1995.

Wert, Jeffry D. *General James Longstreet.* New York: Simon and Schuster, 1993.

West, Richard J. *Lincoln's Scapegoat General: A Life of Benjamin F. Butler.* Boston: Houghton Mifflin, 1965.

Williams, Kenneth P. *Lincoln Finds a General: A Military Study of the Civil War,* 5 vols. New York: Macmillan, 1949–59.

Williams, T. Harry. *Hayes of the Twenty-Third.* New York: Alfred A. Knopf, 1965.

———. *The History of American Wars from 1745 to 1918.* New York: Alfred A. Knopf, 1981.

———. "Introduction," in *Rebel Brass: The Confederate Command System.* Baton Rouge: Louisiana State University Press, 1956, pp. xiii–xviii.

———. "Investigation: 1862." *American Heritage* 6, no. 6 (December 1954): 16–21.

———. *Lincoln and His Generals.* New York: Alfred A. Knopf, 1952.

———. *Lincoln and the Radicals.* 1941; Madison: University of Wisconsin Press paperback edition, 1965.

———. *McClellan, Sherman, and Grant.* New Brunswick, NJ: Rutgers University Press, 1962.

———. "The Military Leadership of North and South," in *Why the North Won the Civil War,* ed. David Donald. New York: Collier paperback, 1962, pp. 38–57.

———. *P. G. T. Beauregard: Napoleon in Gray.* 1955; Baton Rouge: Louisiana State University Press, 1989.

Williamson, Edwin. *The Penguin History of Latin America*. Harmondsworth, UK: Penguin, 1992.

Wiltse, Charles M. *The New Nation, 1800–1845*. New York: Macmillan, 1965.

Winters, Harold A., Gerald E. Galloway Jr., William J. Reynolds, and David W. Rhyne. *Battling the Elements: Weather and Terrain in the Conduct of War*. Baltimore, MD: Johns Hopkins University Press, 1998.

Wise, Jennings Cropper. *The Long Arm of Lee*, 2 vols. 1915; Lincoln: University of Nebraska Press, 1991.

Woodworth, Stephen E. *Beneath a Northern Sky: A Short History of the Gettysburg Campaign*. Wilmington, DE: S. R. Books, 2003.

———. *Davis and Lee at War*. Lawrence: University Press of Kansas, 1995.

———. "'The Indeterminate Quantities': Jefferson Davis, Leonidas Polk, and the End of Kentucky Neutrality." *Civil War History* 38 (December 1992): 289–97.

———. *Jefferson Davis and His Generals: The Failure of Confederate Command in the West*. Lawrence: University Press of Kansas, 1990.

———. *Six Armies in Tennessee: The Chickamauga and Chattanooga Campaigns*. Lincoln: University of Nebraska Press, 1988.

———. *Six Armies in Tennessee*. 1988; Lincoln: University of Nebraska Press, 1993.

Wright, Quincy. "The American Civil War, 1861–1865," in *The International Law of Civil War*, ed. Richard A. Falk. Baltimore: Johns Hopkins University Press, 1971, pp. 30–109.

INDEX

Maps are indicated by italic numbers.